2008
FUNK & WAGNALLS
NEW ENCYCLOPEDIA
YEARBOOK

A REVIEW OF THE EVENTS OF 2007

FUNK & WAGNALLS
Publishers Since 1876

An Imprint of Weekly Reader Publishing Group

Published 2008 by Weekly Reader Publishing Group.

Funk & Wagnalls and F&W are registered trademarks of Weekly Reader Corporation.

This annual is also published under the title *The 2008 World Book Year Book*
© 2008 World Book, Inc.

Library of Congress Control Number: 62-4818
ISBN-13: 978-0-8343-0375-1
ISBN-10: 0-8343-0375-2

Printed in the United States of America.

STAFF

EXECUTIVE COMMITTEE

President
Paul A. Gazzolo

Vice President and Chief Marketing Officer
Patricia Ginnis

Vice President and Chief Financial Officer
Donald D. Keller

Vice President and Editor in Chief
Paul A. Kobasa

Director, Human Resources
Bev Ecker

Chief Technology Officer
Tim Hardy

Managing Director, International
Benjamin Hinton

EDITORIAL

Editor in Chief
Paul A. Kobasa

Associate Director, Supplementary Publications
Scott Thomas

Managing Editor, Supplementary Publications
Barbara A. Mayes

Senior Editor, Supplementary Publications
Kristina A. Vaicikonis

Manager, Research, Supplementary Publications
Cheryl Graham

Administrative Assistant
Ethel Matthews

Editors
Shawn Brennan
Jeff De La Rosa
Drew Huening
Daniel Kenis
Nicholas Kilzer
Dawn Krajcik
Pete Kulak
Mike Lewis
S. Thomas Richardson
Kenneth J. Shenkman
Christine Sullivan
Daniel O. Zeff
Marty Zwikel

Contributing Editors
Robert Knight
Alfred J. Smuskiewicz

Statistics Editor
William M. Harrod

GRAPHICS AND DESIGN

Associate Director
Sandra M. Dyrlund

Associate Manager, Design
Brenda B. Tropinski

Senior Designers
Don Di Sante
Isaiah W. Sheppard, Jr.

Associate Manager, Photography
Tom Evans

Photographs Editor
Kathryn Creech

Manager, Cartographic Services
Wayne K. Pichler

Senior Cartographer
John M. Rejba

Graphics and Design Coordinator
Matthew Carrington

EDITORIAL ADMINISTRATION

Director, Systems and Projects
Tony Tills

Senior Manager, Publishing Operations
Timothy Falk

Manager, Editorial Operations
Loranne K. Shields

Indexing Services Manager
David Pofelski

Associate Manager, Indexing
Aamir Burki

Information Services Coordinator
Stephanie N. Kitchen

PRODUCTION

Director, Manufacturing and Pre-Press
Carma Fazio

Manufacturing Manager
Barbara Podczerwinski

Production/Technology Manager
Anne Fritzinger

Proofreading
Emilie Schrage

MARKETING

Chief Marketing Officer
Patricia Ginnis

Director, Direct Marketing
Mark R. Willy

Associate Director, School and Library Marketing
Jennifer Parello

Marketing Analyst
Zofia Kulik

CONTRIBUTORS

Contributors not listed on these pages are members of the editorial staff.

ANDREWS, PETER J., B.A., M.S.; free-lance writer. **[Chemistry]**

BARNHART, BILL, B.A., M.S.T., M.B.A.; financial markets columnist, *Chicago Tribune.* **[Stocks and bonds]**

BECK, STEFAN, B.A.; Associate editor, *The New Criterion* magazine. **[Literature]**

BERGER, ERIC R., B.A, M.A.; science writer, *Houston Chronicle.* **[Houston]**

BOYD, JOHN D., B.S.; Economics writer. **[Economics, U.S.; Economics, World; International trade]**

BRADSHER, HENRY S., A.B., B.J.; foreign affairs analyst. **[Asia and Asian country articles]**

BRETT, CARLTON E., B.A., M.S., Ph.D.; Professor of Geology, University of Cincinnati. **[Paleontology]**

CASEY, MIKE, B.S., M.A.; Assistant editor, *Kansas City Star.* **[Automobile]**

CITRIN, ADRIENNE, B.A.; Manager of Public Relations, Toy Industry Association, Incorporated. **[Toys and games]**

DEEB, MARIUS K., B.A., Ph.D.; Professor, School of Advanced International Studies, Johns Hopkins University. **[Middle East and Middle Eastern country articles; North African country articles]**

DEEB, MARY-JANE, B.A., Ph.D.; Chief of the African and Middle Eastern Division, Library of Congress. **[Middle East and Middle Eastern country articles; North African country articles]**

DeFRANK, THOMAS M., B.A., M.A.; Washington Bureau Chief, *New York Daily News.* **[Armed forces]**

DILLON, DAVID, B.A., M.A., Ph.D.; architecture and design editor, *The Dallas Morning News.* **[Architecture]**

ELLIS, GAVIN, former Editor in Chief, *The New Zealand Herald & Weekend Herald.* **[New Zealand]**

ESTERHUYSEN, PIETER, B.A.; political analyst, Africa Institute of South Africa, Pretoria. **[Africa and African country articles]**

FISHER, ROBERT W., B.A., M.A.; free-lance writer. **[Labor and employment]**

FRIEDMAN, EMILY, B.A.; health policy and ethics analyst. **[Health care issues]**

GADOMSKI, FRED, B.S., M.S.; Meteorologist, Pennsylvania State University. **[Global warming; Weather]**

GOLDBERG, BEVERLY, B.A.; Senior editor, American Library Association. **[Library]**

GOLDEN, JONATHAN J., B.A., M.J.Ed.; Chair, History Department at the Gann Academy, New Jewish High School of Greater Boston. **[Judaism]**

GOLDNER, NANCY, B.A.; free-lance dance critic. **[Dance]**

HARAKAS, STANLEY SAMUEL, B.A., B.Th., Th.D.; Archbishop Iakovos Professor (Emeritus) of Orthodox Theology, Holy Cross Greek Orthodox School of Theology. **[Eastern Orthodox Churches]**

HAVERSTOCK, NATHAN A., A.B.; affiliate scholar, Oberlin College. **[Latin America and Latin American country articles]**

HENDERSON, HAROLD, B.A.; staff writer, *Chicago Reader.* **[Chicago]**

JOHANSON, DONALD C., B.S., M.A., Ph.D.; Director and Professor, Institute of Human Origins, Arizona State University. **[Anthropology]**

JOHNSON, CHRISTINA S., B.A., M.S.; free-lance science writer. **[Ocean]**

JOHNSON, JULIET, A.B., M.A., Ph.D.; Associate Professor of Political Science, McGill University. **[Russia and other former Soviet republic articles]**

KATES, MICHAEL, B.S.J.; Associate sports editor, *Chicago Tribune.* **[Sports articles]**

KENNEDY, BRIAN, M.A.; free-lance writer. **[Australia; Australia, Prime Minister of; Australian rules football]**

KILGORE, MARGARET, B.A., M.B.A.; free-lance writer, Kilgore and Associates. **[Los Angeles]**

KING, MIKE, reporter, *The (Montreal) Gazette.* **[Montreal]**

KLINTBERG, PATRICIA PEAK, B.A.; Director of Constituent Affairs, Office of Communications, U.S. Department of Agriculture. **[Agriculture]**

KNIGHT, ROBERT N., B.A., M.M.; free-lance writer. **[Art Special Report: Ancient Art's Long Way Home; Bank; People in the news]**

KOPSTEIN, JEFFREY, B.A., M.A., Ph.D; Professor of Political Science and Director, Centre for European, Russian, and Eurasian Studies, University of Toronto. **[Europe and Western European country articles]**

LAWRENCE, ALBERT, B.A., M.A., M.Ed.; Executive Director, World Chess Hall of Fame. **[Chess]**

MANZO, KATHLEEN KENNEDY, B.A., M.Ed; Associate editor, *Education Week.* **[Education]**

MARCH, ROBERT H., A.B., M.S., Ph.D.; Professor Emeritus of Physics and Liberal Studies, University of Wisconsin at Madison. **[Physics]**

MARSCHALL, LAURENCE A., B.S., Ph.D.; W.K.T. Sahm Professor of Physics, Gettysburg College. **[Astronomy]**

MARTY, MARTIN E., Ph.D.; Fairfax M. Cone Distinguished Service Professor Emeritus, University of Chicago. **[Protestantism]**

McDONALD, ELAINE STUART, B.A.; free-lance public policy writer and editor. **[State government]**

McWILLIAM, ROHAN, B.A., M.A., D.Phil; Senior Lecturer in History, Anglia Polytechnic University, Cambridge, U.K. **[Ireland; Northern Ireland; United Kingdom; United Kingdom, Prime Minister of]**

MINER, TODD J., B.S., M.S.; Meteorologist, Pennsylvania State University. **[Weather]**

MORITZ, OWEN, B.A.; urban affairs editor, *New York Daily News.* **[New York City]**

MORRING, FRANK, Jr., B.A.; Senior Space Technology editor, *Aviation Week & Space Technology* magazine. **[Space exploration]**

MORRIS, BERNADINE, B.A., M.A.; free-lance fashion writer. **[Fashion]**

MULLINS, HENRY T., B.S., M.S., Ph.D.; Professor of Geology, Syracuse University. **[Geology]**

NGUYEN, J. TUYET, M.A.; United Nations correspondent, Deutsche Presse-Agentur. **[Population; United Nations]**

OGAN, EUGENE, B.A., Ph.D.; Professor Emeritus of Anthropology, University of Minnesota. **[Pacific Islands]**

REINHART, A. KEVIN, B.A., M.A., Ph.D.; Associate Professor of Religious Studies, Dartmouth College. **[Islam]**

4

RICCIUTI, EDWARD, B.A.; free-lance writer. [Biology Special Report: **A New Perspective on Primates; Biology; Conservation; Zoos**]

ROBERTS, THOMAS W., Editor, *The National Catholic Reporter*. [**Roman Catholic Church**]

ROSE, MARK J., B.A., M.A., Ph.D.; Executive editor, *Archaeology* magazine. [**Archaeology**]

RUBENSTEIN, RICHARD E., B.A., M.A., J.D.; Professor of Conflict Resolution and Public Affairs, George Mason University. [**Terrorism**]

RUBENSTONE, JEFFREY, B.A.; Editor, *Engineering News-Record* magazine. [**Building and construction**]

RUSSELL, MARY HARRIS, B.A., M.A, Ph.D.; Professor of English, Indiana University. [**Literature for children**]

SARNA, JONATHAN D., Ph.D.; Joseph H. & Belle R. Braun Professor of American Jewish History, Brandeis University. [**Judaism**]

SHAPIRO, HOWARD, B.S.; staff writer and travel columnist, *The Philadelphia Inquirer*. [**Philadelphia; Washington, D.C.**]

SMUSKIEWICZ, ALFRED J., B.S., M.S.; free-lance writer. [**AIDS; City; Crime; Drug abuse; Drugs; Medicine; Mental health; Prison; Public health; Safety**]

STEIN, DAVID LEWIS, B.A., M.S.; former urban affairs columnist, *The Toronto Star*. [**Toronto**]

STOS, WILLIAM, B.A., M.A.; free-lance writer. [**Canada; Canada, Prime Minister of; Canadian provinces; Canadian territories**]

TANNER, JAMES C., B.J.; former news editor—energy, *The Wall Street Journal*. [**Energy supply**]

TATUM, HENRY K., B.A.; retired Associate editor, *The Dallas Morning News*. [**Dallas**]

TURAM, BERNA, B.A., M.A., Ph.D.; Professor of Sociology and Middle East Studies, *Hampshire College*. [**Turkey Special Report: Modern Turkey: A Delicate Balance**]

VAN, JON, B.A., M.A.; technology writer, *Chicago Tribune*. [**Telecommunications**]

von RHEIN, JOHN, B.A.; classical music critic, *Chicago Tribune*. [**Classical music**]

WILLIAMS, BRIAN, B.A.; free-lance writer. [**Cricket; Soccer**]

WOLCHIK, SHARON L., B.A., M.A., Ph.D.; Professor of Political Science and International Affairs, George Washington University. [**Eastern European country articles**]

WUNTCH, PHILIP, B.A.; former film critic, *The Dallas Morning News*. [**Motion pictures**]

YEZZI, DAVID, B.F.A., M.F.A.; Executive editor, *The New Criterion* magazine. [**Poetry; Theater**]

CONTENTS

SPECIAL REPORTS

FOCUS ON

PORTRAITS

2007

From the troop surge in Iraq to a breakthrough in stem cell research, 2007 was a year of extraordinary events. On these three pages are stories that the editors picked as some of the most important of the year, along with details on where to find more information about them in this volume.

The Editors

POWER STRUGGLE IN PAKISTAN

In November, President General Pervez Musharraf dismisses the Supreme Court of Pakistan and declares a state of emergency. The move sparks massive public demonstrations and crackdowns on dissidents, particularly lawyers. Musharraf retains the presidency but, in a major loss of power, is forced to resign as commander of the army. On December 27, opposition leader and former Pakistani Prime Minister Benazir Bhutto was assassinated. See **Asia,** page 80; **Pakistan,** page 307.

IRAQ WAR

A "surge" involving the deployment of an additional 30,000 U.S. troops in Iraq in early 2007 reduces violence. Although the casualty rate of American forces in May reaches its highest monthly level since the war began in 2003, fatalities drop in late 2007. The U.S. commander in Iraq, David Petraeus, testifies before the U.S. Congress that greater security in Baghdad and Al Anbar province should allow the troop surge to end by mid-2008. Lacking a large-enough majority in the Senate, Democrats unsuccessfully try throughout the year to impose a timetable for the withdrawal of troops. President George W. Bush announces that he expects some American forces to be stationed in Iraq for decades to come. Various foreign leaders who participated in the U.S.-led coalition in Iraq are forced from office. See **Armed forces,** page 65; **Australia,** page 87; **Australia, Prime Minister of,** page 96; **Congress of the United States,** page 162; **Iraq,** page 249; **Poland,** page 323; **United Kingdom,** page 394; **United Kingdom, Prime Minister of,** page 399; **United States, Government of the,** page 400; **United States, President of the** page 405.

MYANMAR PROTESTS

Thousands of Buddhist monks, joined by civilians, take to the streets in Myanmar in September to protest the military government's decision to raise fuel prices. After monks characterize the government as "the enemy of the people," the junta responds with violence. Some 3,000 monks are jailed, and at least 31 people are killed. See **Asia,** page 80; **Myanmar,** page 292.

THE SUBPRIME MORTGAGE CRISIS

Widespread defaults on subprime home mortgages trigger a worldwide credit crunch. (Subprime mortgages are loans with adjustable interest rates offered to borrowers with below-standard credit histories.) Banks and other financial institutions discover in 2007 that many of their mortgage-backed investments are worthless and are forced to "write down" billions of dollars in losses. Stock markets reel in response, and the Federal Reserve (the Fed) drops various interest rates to keep credit from drying up. The Fed and other central banks around the world lend billions of dollars to banks to stabilize financial systems. See **Bank,** page 102; **Economics, U.S.,** page 199; **Economics, World,** page 201; **International trade,** page 245; **Labor and employment,** page 262; **Stocks and bonds,** page 354.

RECALL OF CHINESE IMPORTS

The safety of the U.S. food supply is questioned in 2007 after food products, toothpaste, and pet food from China are found to contain potentially harmful substances. An estimated 25 million Chinese-made toys containing lead or loose magnets are recalled, starting in June, intensifying the debate over globalization and outsourcing. See **China,** page 149; **Food,** page 220; **Public health,** page 329; **Toys and games,** page 374.

BREAKTHROUGH IN STEM CELL RESEARCH

Japanese and U.S. scientists announce in November that they have reprogrammed human skin cells to behave like embryonic stem cells. The breakthrough allows researchers to conduct stem cell research without destroying embryos, thus removing the ethical objection to the research. See **Biology,** page 110; **Medicine,** page 278.

WILDFIRES

Hundreds of thousands of acres of woodland and farmland burn in Greece as the worst wildfires in more than a century rage across the country in summer 2007. Wildfires in southern California in October and November destroy millions of dollars in property. See **Focus on Europe,** page 216; **Greece,** page 233; **Weather,** page 409.

GLOBAL WARMING

The European Space Agency announces in September that record summer melting of Arctic ice has led to the opening of the fabled Northwest Passage, the most direct shipping lane between Europe and Asia. In November, the Intergovernmental Panel on Climate Change releases a key report concluding that reductions in greenhouse gas emissions must begin immediately to avoid a climate disaster. The United Nations climate conference, meeting in Bali, Indonesia, in December, agrees on an agenda for the negotiation of a new climate treaty to reduce carbon emissions. See **Canada,** page 132; **Denmark,** page 193; **Global warming,** page 230; **Nobel Prizes,** page 302; **Russia,** page 333.

PRESIDENTIAL ELECTION CAMPAIGN

The 2008 presidential race gets underway in one of the most wide-open races in decades. See **Democratic Party,** page 192; **Elections,** page 206; **Republican Party,** page 331.

SPORTS SCANDALS

Scandals permeate professional sports in 2007, including criminal behavior by National Football League (NFL) players; gambling allegations against a National Basketball League (NBA) official; and doping violations that knock out the Tour de France leader and stain a past champion. In baseball, the Mitchell report, issued in December, alleges that at least 87 major league players have used performance-enhancing steroids or human growth hormone. See **Baseball,** page 103; **Football,** page 222; **Sports,** page 348.

2007

YEAR IN BRIEF

A month-by-month listing of the most significant world events that occurred during 2007.

A pickup truck passes under hanging power lines in McAlester, Oklahoma. The entire town was without power after a major ice storm in mid-January 2007. The storm spread from Texas to New England and left hundreds of thousands of households without power.

2 Former United States President Gerald R. Ford, who died on Dec. 26, 2006, is honored with a state funeral at the Washington (D.C.) National Cathedral.

4 The 110th United States Congress opens with Democrats in control of both houses for the first time in 12 years. Nancy Pelosi (D., California) becomes the first-ever woman speaker of the House of Representatives.

7 A U.S. helicopter gunship carries out air strikes in southern Somalia against suspected members of the terrorist network al-Qa`ida. The air strikes are the first acknowledged U.S. military action in Somalia since 1994.

8 According to the Iraqi Health Ministry, about 23,000 Iraqi civilians and police officers died violently in 2006, a ministry official discloses. This estimate is higher than the 13,896 deaths reported on Jan. 1, 2007, by Iraq's defense, health, and interior ministries.

10 In a televised speech to the nation, U.S. President George W. Bush announces plans to send more than 20,000 extra U.S. troops to Iraq in an attempt to regain control of Baghdad and suppress the insurgency in Al Anbar province. The troop "surge" comes in response to what Bush calls an unacceptable situation in Iraq.

11 Bangladeshi President Iajuddin Ahmed declares a state of emergency, resigns as temporary head of the country's caretaker government, and postpones parliamentary elections. Political protests and related violence in Bangladesh have resulted in dozens of deaths since October 2006.

15 Hundreds of thousands of U.S. households remain without electric power in the wake of a major ice storm. On January 12, 13, and 14, three waves of freezing rain left parts of Texas and much of Oklahoma and Missouri under a dangerous layer of ice that brought down trees and power lines. The storm continued to wreak havoc as it spread northeast from Texas through the Midwest and into New York and New England.

16 Violence in Baghdad leaves more than 100 people dead in a single day. Bombings at Mustansiriya University kill about 70 people. Elsewhere around the Iraqi capital, about 40 other people are killed in various bombings and shootings. The attacks are made as the United Nations reports that more than 34,000 Iraqi civilians were killed in violence in 2006.

17 The administration of U.S. President George W. Bush announces that it will seek the approval of the Foreign Intelligence Surveillance Court before conducting certain kinds of electronic spying. Previously, the administration had resisted such oversight, arguing that the National Security Agency could monitor phone and e-mail communications between the United States and overseas for antiterrorism purposes without first getting a warrant.

18 The U.S. Senate votes 96-2 to make expansive changes to congressional ethics and lobbying rules. The bill, which awaits consideration by the House of Representatives, would bar legislators from accepting gifts, meals, or trips from lobbyists. The bill also would mandate more transparency in the earmarking of public funds for individual lawmakers' favored projects. Legislators would have to attach their names to such funding proposals.

20 Twenty-five U.S. soldiers are killed in one of the deadliest days for U.S. forces in the Iraq War. Twelve of the soldiers die when their Black Hawk helicopter is shot down north of Baghdad. Another five troops are killed in the Shi`ah holy city of Karbala when gunmen dressed in U.S. military uniforms storm an office where U.S. and Iraqi officials are meeting.

20 Senator Hillary Rodham Clinton of New York announces that she will run for the 2008 Democratic nomination for president of the United States.

22 In Iraq, two car bombs explode in a Baghdad second-hand clothing market, killing at least 88 people and injuring about 160

others. Another 12 people die in a bomb and mortar attack in Al Khalis. The attacks take place as the first 3,200 U.S. troops of a deployment of more than 20,000 arrive in Baghdad.

23 A new rule goes into effect requiring all people entering the United States by air—including U.S. citizens returning from Canada, Mexico, or the Caribbean—to show a passport.

24 The U.S. Senate Foreign Relations Committee votes 12-9 in favor of a nonbinding resolution declaring that President George W. Bush's plan to send thousands of additional troops to Iraq is "not in the national interest of the United States."

25 Ford Motor Company of Dearborn, Michigan, reports the largest annual loss in its 103-year history—$12.7 billion for 2006. By comparison, Ford made a profit of $1.4 billion in 2005. In the process of restructuring, the company plans to eliminate some 45,000 jobs and close 16 factories in the United States and Canada.

27 Tens of thousands of demonstrators gather on the National Mall in Washington, D.C., to rally against the war in Iraq.

28 Fighting between insurgents and Iraqi army units backed by U.S. forces near Najaf leaves more than 200 militants dead. Two U.S. soldiers die when their helicopter is shot down, and a number of Iraqi policemen and soldiers are also killed. According to Iraqi officials, the insurgents were part of a messianic cult— the Soldiers of Heaven—made up of Shi`ah and Sunni Muslims from Iraq and elsewhere. The governor of An Najaf province claims that the militants had planned to assassinate Shi`ah clerics during the holy festival of Ashura and seize control of the Imam Ali Mosque in Najaf.

30 A report from Stuart Bowen, Jr., the U.S. special inspector general for Iraq reconstruction, reveals that millions of dollars in U.S. aid have gone to waste, including $43.8 million for a police training support camp that has never been used. The report is released as President George W. Bush is asking Congress for another $1.2 billion for Iraq reconstruction. About $37 billion has already been appropriated.

1 About 70 people are killed by two suicide bombers in Al Hillah, Iraq.

1 ExxonMobil, based in Irving, Texas, reveals that it posted a $39.5-billion profit for 2006, the largest profit in the history of U.S. capitalism.

2 Three tornadoes cut a swath through central Florida, leaving a trail of destruction and killing 21 people.

3 About 135 people are killed and more than 300 others are injured by a suicide truck bomber in a crowded market of a largely Shi`ah area in central Baghdad, Iraq.

4 The Indianapolis Colts defeat the Chicago Bears 29-17 to win the National Football League (NFL) championship in Super Bowl XLI. Coaches Tony Dungy of the Colts and Lovie Smith of the Bears make NFL history as the first African American head coaches to reach the Super Bowl.

5 United States President George W. Bush submits a $2.9-trillion budget to Congress for fiscal year 2008 that includes significant increases in military spending and a major reduction in the Medicare growth rate over five years. The plan would make permanent the tax cuts passed during President Bush's first term. The president says his plan would eliminate the budget deficit by 2012.

5 Former New York City Mayor Rudolph Giuliani enters the race for the 2008 Republican nomination for president of the United States.

7 A U.S. Sea Knight helicopter is shot down by insurgents near Fallujah, Iraq, killing all seven Marines aboard. It is the fifth U.S. helicopter to be lost in Iraq in 19 days.

10 Senator Barack Obama of Illinois announces that he will seek the 2008 Democratic nomination for president of the United States.

12 Multiple car bombs explode in two market areas of central Baghdad, Iraq, leaving about 90 people dead.

13 The Kansas State Board of Education repeals science standards, instituted by a previous board, that questioned evolution and included intelligent design theory in science curriculums. Advocates of intelligent design hold that life is too complex not to have been created by a higher power.

13 Former Massachusetts Governor Mitt Romney announces that he will be a candidate for the 2008 Republican nomination for U.S. president.

16 An Italian judge orders 26 U.S. citizens to stand trial on charges of kidnapping an Egyptian Muslim cleric in Milan, Italy, in 2003. Most of the Americans are agents of the Central Intelligence Agency. Five Italians are also indicted. The cleric, Hassan Mustafa Osama Nasr, alleges that he was seized in Milan and taken to Egypt, where he claims to have been tortured. Political experts believe it is unlikely that the U.S. government will extradite the Americans.

16 The U.S. House of Representatives votes 246-182 for a nonbinding resolution opposing President George W. Bush's troop "surge" in Iraq. The surge involves sending more than 20,000 additional U.S. troops to Iraq in an attempt to pacify Baghdad and Al Anbar province. On February 17, Democrats in the U.S. Senate fail to muster the 60 votes needed to end a Republican filibuster blocking a vote on a similar resolution.

18 More than 60 people die when two car bombs explode in a crowded market of a mainly Shi`ah area of Baghdad, Iraq.

18 Two terrorist bombs explode aboard a train en route from Delhi, India, to Lahore, Pakistan, killing 68 people. Most of the dead were Pakistanis.

21 The United Kingdom will pull 1,600 of its 7,100 troops out of Iraq within the next few months, announces British Prime Minister Tony Blair. Another 500 U.K. troops may be withdrawn by the end of the summer, he says. Meanwhile, the prime minister

A U.S. Sea Knight helicopter hovers over Baghdad, Iraq, on Feb. 7, 2007, just hours after another Sea Knight was shot down by insurgents near Fallujah. It was the fifth U.S. helicopter to be lost in Iraq in 19 days.

of Denmark, Anders Fogh Rasmussen, announces that his country's 460 troops in Iraq will come home by August. They are to be replaced by a unit of about 50 soldiers in four observational helicopters.

21 A truck bomb that combines explosives with poisonous chlorine gas blows up in southern Baghdad, Iraq, killing at least five people. The incident occurs on the heels of a similar attack a day earlier, when a tanker filled with chlorine gas exploded north of Baghdad, killing nine people. The U.S. military characterizes the use of chlorine as a new insurgent tactic. Chlorine burns the skin and can be fatal after only a few intakes of breath.

21 More than 50 people are killed when a truck bomb explodes near a Sunni mosque in Habbaniyah, Iraq.

26 The International Court of Justice rules that Serbia was not directly responsible for genocide during the war in Bosnia-Herzegovina (1992-1995). However, the United Nations court also rules that Serbia violated international law by failing to prevent the massacre of Bosnian Muslims at Srebrenica in 1995 and by failing to punish the perpetrators of the massacre. The case, brought against Serbia by Bosnia, marked the first time a nation had been tried for genocide.

27 United States Secretary of State Condoleezza Rice confirms that she and other senior officials plan to participate in talks between Iraq and its neighbors, including Iran and Syria. Foreign affairs experts note that the willingness to engage in high-level talks with Iran and Syria constitutes a significant policy shift for the administration of President George W. Bush.

27 A steep decline in Chinese stocks sets off a stock-selling frenzy in the United States, causing the Dow Jones Industrial Average to fall 416 points, its largest one-day point drop since 2001.

28 Senator John McCain of Arizona announces his intent to seek the 2008 Republican nomination for U.S. president.

In Baghdad, U.S. soldiers examine a window of their Humvee after an explosive device damaged the vehicle on March 19, 2007, the fourth anniversary of the launch of the Iraq War. Coalition soldiers faced almost daily insurgent attacks as the war entered its fifth year.

1 Twenty people are killed in Alabama, Georgia, and Missouri as storms and tornadoes sweep through the central and southeastern United States.

2 United States Army Secretary Francis J. Harvey is forced to resign by U.S. Secretary of Defense Robert Gates following reports of neglect at Walter Reed Army Medical Center in Washington, D.C. According to *The Washington Post,* some wounded soldiers are being housed in unclean conditions and are receiving slow and substandard treatment at the hospital. The former commander of the hospital, Major General George W. Weightman, was fired on March 1.

4 A suicide bomber attacks a U.S. Marine convoy of vehicles near Jalalabad, Afghanistan, prompting the Marines to open fire. Nineteen Afghan civilians are killed by the Marines. In response, hundreds of local people take to the streets, accusing the soldiers of deliberately killing civilians.

6 A double suicide bombing in Al Hillah, Iraq, kills about 120 Shi`ah pilgrims who were on their way to Karbala for a religious ceremony.

6 A federal jury convicts I. Lewis "Scooter" Libby of making false statements, perjury, and obstruction of justice. Libby, who was U.S. Vice President Dick Cheney's former chief of staff, is found guilty of lying to federal law enforcement agents and to a grand jury during an investigation into the 2003 leak of an undercover intelligence officer's identity. The officer, Valerie Plame, and her husband, former Ambassador Joseph C. Wilson IV, claim that her identity was leaked to the press by the administration of President George W. Bush as a retaliatory move against Wilson, who had publicly accused Cheney and Bush of justifying their plans for war in Iraq by exaggerating Iraq's military capability.

8 Leaders of the European Union (EU) countries agree to a 20-percent cut in carbon dioxide emissions from 1990 levels by 2020. On March 9, 2007, they agree that by 2020, renewable energy, such as wind and solar power, will make up 20 percent of all energy consumed by EU countries.

10 United States President George W. Bush announces plans to send an extra 8,200 U.S. troops to Iraq and Afghanistan in addition to the more than 20,000 troops for Iraq ordered in January.

11 President Jacques Chirac of France announces that he will not seek a third term and will retire from politics in May.

15 After months of negotiations, the rival Palestinian groups Hamas and Fatah reach agreement on a national unity government. On March 17, the Palestinian Authority parliament approves the new unity government. On March 18, Israel's Cabinet officially rejects the Palestinian government because it includes Hamas, an Islamist group that opposes a permanent peace settlement with Israel.

16 China's legislature adopts a historic and controversial law that provides some protections for private property rights.

21 A U.S. House Judiciary subcommittee authorizes subpoenas for five current and former officials of the administration of President George W. Bush. On March 22, the Senate Judiciary Committee follows suit, authorizing three subpoenas. The committees are investigating whether the 2006 dismissals of several federal attorneys by the U.S. Department of Justice were politically motivated. Among the officials targeted are Karl Rove, the deputy White House chief of staff, and Harriet Miers, the former White House counsel. Political experts expect President Bush to invoke executive privilege to keep the officials from testifying publicly under oath.

23 The U.S. House of Representatives votes 218-212 to approve a war-spending bill that would impose an Aug. 31, 2008, deadline for the withdrawal of U.S. combat troops from Iraq.

23 A British Royal Navy crew is seized in the Persian Gulf by Iranian naval forces. Iran claims that the 15 British sailors and marines were trespassing in Iranian waters. The British government responds that they were in Iraqi waters after having inspected a merchant vessel.

26 Northern Ireland's largest unionist and republican parties—the Democratic Unionist Party (DUP) and Sinn Féin, respectively—agree to share power in a move that will end the British government's suspension of the Northern Ireland Assembly. The agreement is reached at a historic gathering in which DUP leader Ian Paisley and Sinn Féin leader Gerry Adams meet face to face for the first time.

27 A truck bomb kills about 150 people in a Shi`ah market area of Tall Afar, Iraq. Hours later, as many as 70 people are killed in a Sunni neighborhood of Tall Afar in what authorities describe as reprisal attacks.

29 The U.S. Senate votes 51-47 for a war-spending bill that would force President George W. Bush to begin withdrawing troops from Iraq and would set a nonbinding goal of March 31, 2008, for the withdrawal of all combat troops. The Senate bill must be reconciled with a House bill passed on March 23, 2007. Bush has promised to veto the legislation.

29 Two suicide bombers blow themselves up in a crowded market of a Shi`ah neighborhood in Baghdad, Iraq, killing 82 people. Meanwhile, about 50 people are killed by three car bombs in Al Khalis.

2 The U.S. Supreme Court, in a 5-4 decision, rules that the federal Clean Air Act gives the Environmental Protection Agency (EPA) the authority to regulate carbon dioxide and other greenhouse gases emitted by new cars. According to the ruling, the EPA failed to justify its refusal to regulate such emissions in 2003.

4 Iranian President Mahmoud Ahmadinejad releases the 15 British sailors and marines whom Iran captured in the Persian Gulf on March 23. He calls their release a "gift to the British people."

6 Scientists attending a meeting of the Intergovernmental Panel on Climate Change in Brussels, Belgium, issue a report that offers a grim forecast for the effects of global warming. According to the report, climate change is likely to put hundreds of millions of people at greater risk of food and water shortages, malnutrition, and disease, with poorer populations facing the greatest risk. Major storms, heat waves, floods, and droughts are expected to be more frequent and extreme, and many species are likely to face a greater risk of extinction.

9 Iran is producing nuclear fuel on an industrial scale, announces Iranian President Mahmoud Ahmadinejad. Iranian officials claim that uranium is being enriched with 3,000 centrifuges, which would be a major expansion of Iran's nuclear program. An April 18 document from the International Atomic Energy Agency says that only about 1,300 centrifuges are enriching uranium. Iran claims its nuclear program is for energy purposes, but many experts believe Iran intends to make nuclear weapons.

9 Tens of thousands of Shi`ites demonstrate in Najaf against the presence of U.S. troops in Iraq. The demonstration was called by influential Shi`ah cleric Muqtada al-Sadr.

11 Suicide bombings at two sites in the Algerian capital, Algiers, kill 33 people. One bombing occurs outside the prime minister's headquarters. The North African branch of the terrorist group al-Qa`ida claims responsibility.

12 A suicide bombing occurs inside Iraq's parliament building, killing one member of parliament. The building is in Baghdad's highly fortified Green Zone, the site of most of Iraq's government buildings as well as the U.S. and British embassies. Elsewhere in Baghdad, a truck bomb destroys a major bridge over the Tigris River, killing at least 10 people.

16 Six Iraqi Cabinet ministers loyal to the Shi`ah cleric Muqtada al-Sadr resign upon Sadr's instruction. According to Sadr's spokesman, the cleric is trying to force Prime Minister Nouri al-Maliki to set a timetable for the withdrawal of U.S. troops from Iraq.

16 A senior at Virginia Polytechnic Institute and State University, armed with handguns, kills 32 students and faculty members on the Virginia Tech campus in Blacksburg. Two hours after killing 2 students in a dormitory, the gunman, a permanent U.S. resident from South Korea, enters an engineering building and kills 30 people in four classrooms and a hallway. He then kills himself. It is the deadliest shooting rampage in U.S. history.

18 A string of bombings and other attacks in Baghdad leave nearly 200 people dead. In the most lethal attack, some 140 people are killed by a car bomb in a food market of a mainly Shi`ah neighborhood.

18 The U.S. Supreme Court, in a 5-4 vote, rules that the Partial-Birth Abortion Ban Act, passed by Congress in 2003, does not violate a woman's right to an abortion. The act bans a specific late-term abortion procedure. Such a ban is acceptable, according to the ruling, because other abortion procedures will remain available.

19 The drought in Australia has become an "unprecedentedly dangerous" situation, announces Prime Minister John Howard. Unless substantial rain falls before mid-May, he says, no water will be allocated for irrigation

Thousands of people attend a candlelight vigil on April 17, 2007, on the campus of Virginia Polytechnic Institute and State University in Blacksburg. The vigil was held in memory of 32 Virginia Tech students and faculty members killed by a lone gunman on April 16 in the deadliest shooting rampage in U.S. history.

in Australia's prime agricultural region, the Murray-Darling River basin, in the coming year.

22 In the first round of France's presidential election, voters choose the center-right candidate Nicolas Sarkozy and the Socialist candidate Ségolène Royal. They will face each other in a May 6 runoff election.

23 Several suicide bombings in Iraq leave more than 50 people dead. One attack, on a U.S. patrol base in Diyala province, kills 9 U.S. soldiers. A roadside bomb kills a 10th U.S. soldier in the same region.

23 Boris Yeltsin, who was instrumental in bringing down the Soviet Union and who served as Russia's first democratically elected president, dies at age 76.

24 The Japanese carmaker Toyota has overtaken the Detroit-based General Motors (GM) as the world's leader in car and truck sales, Toyota announces. Toyota sold 2.35 million vehicles in the first quar-

ter of 2007, compared with GM's 2.26 million vehicles during the same period.

25 The Dow Jones Industrial Average closes above 13,000 for the first time in history.

26 Russian President Vladimir Putin declares a "moratorium" on Russia's compliance with the Conventional Armed Forces in Europe Treaty, citing U.S. plans to build an antimissile system in Poland and the Czech Republic. The treaty limits deployment of tanks, artillery, and other conventional arms on both sides of the old Iron Curtain between Eastern and Western Europe.

30 Seven of eight U.S.-funded reconstruction projects in Iraq previously labeled as successes by the U.S. government are not operating properly under Iraqi management, according to a report from Stuart Bowen, Jr., the special inspector general for Iraq reconstruction. The operational problems include faulty plumbing and wiring, lack of proper maintenance, and expensive equipment lying idle.

MAY

2007

Residents of Greensburg, Kansas, survey the devastation on May 7, 2007, three days after a massive tornado leveled most of the town. The tornado, which killed 11 people in Greensburg, struck with powerful winds in excess of 200 miles (320 kilometers) per hour.

1 United States President George W. Bush vetoes a $124-billion war-spending bill because it would have set timetables for troop withdrawals from Iraq. The president asserts that "setting a deadline for withdrawal is setting a date for failure."

3 United States Secretary of State Condoleezza Rice meets with Syria's foreign minister, Walid al-Muallem, in Egypt. It is the first ministerial-level diplomatic meeting between the United States and Syria in two years.

4 A massive tornado with winds in excess of 200 miles (320 kilometers) per hour levels most of Greensburg, Kansas, a town of 1,500 people. Eleven people are killed. The tornado is the most powerful to hit the United States since 1999.

6 Nicolas Sarkozy, running against Socialist candidate Ségolène Royal, takes 53 percent of the vote to win the French presidency. Sarkozy, who represents a center-right party, assumes office on May 16.

8 Northern Ireland's two major political parties, the Democratic Unionist Party (DUP) and Sinn Féin, officially form a power-sharing government, ending more than 4 ½ years of direct rule by the United Kingdom. DUP leader Ian Paisley takes office as first minister of Northern Ireland, and Martin McGuinness of Sinn Féin takes office as deputy first minister.

10 Tony Blair, prime minister of the United Kingdom, announces that he will leave office on June 27. Gordon Brown, chancellor of the exchequer, is widely expected to replace Blair as Labour Party leader and prime minister.

12 Four U.S. troops and their Iraqi interpreter are killed and three U.S. troops are kidnapped when their patrol is ambushed outside the Iraqi town of Al Mahmudiyah, a known stronghold of al-Qa`ida. On May 23, Iraqi police find the body of one of the kidnapped soldiers in the Euphrates River near Al Musayyib. The other two soldiers remain missing.

12 Politically motivated gun battles erupt in the streets of Karachi, Pakistan. The violence, which continues through May 13, pits supporters of President Pervez Musharraf against supporters of Iftikhar Muhammad Chaudhry, the suspended chief justice of Pakistan's Supreme Court. About 40 people are killed. Musharraf suspended Chaudhry on March 9, touching off protests. The president cited "misuse of authority" as the reason for the suspension, but Musharraf's opponents claim that the president was trying to undermine the independence of the judiciary.

14 The German automaker DaimlerChrysler announces that it will sell controlling interest of its U.S.-based Chrysler unit to a private equity firm, Cerberus Capital Management of New York City. Cerberus will pay $7.4 billion, most of which will be put into Chrysler. Daimler, which paid $36 billion for Chrysler in 1998, will receive only $1.35 billion from Cerberus.

14 The deputy U.S. attorney general, Paul J. McNulty, announces that he will resign. He is the fourth and most senior official to leave the Department of Justice since an uproar began earlier in 2007 over the controversial dismissal of nine U.S. attorneys in 2006.

17 Paul Wolfowitz announces that he will resign as World Bank president on June 30. The announcement follows weeks of controversy surrounding the promotion of his companion, Shaha Riza, a World Bank employee. An internal panel at the bank concluded on May 14 that Wolfowitz broke staff rules and the bank's code of conduct in setting the terms of Riza's work assignment and pay package in 2005. Wolfowitz, a former U.S. deputy secretary of defense, was a controversial

appointee to the World Bank post in 2005 because he had been a key architect of the U.S. invasion of Iraq in 2003.

20 Fighting erupts between Lebanese troops and Islamist militants in northern Lebanon. The militants are based in Nahr al-Bared, a large Palestinian refugee camp near Tripoli, and they belong to a radical group called Fatah al-Islam. Dozens of people are killed in initial clashes in May, and thousands of people flee the camp.

20 The average price of regular unleaded gasoline in the United States hits $3.18 per gallon, an all-time high even when compared with past prices adjusted for inflation, according to the Lundberg Survey, a market research service. The previous record was $1.35 in March 1981, which is equivalent to $3.15 in current dollars.

25 United States President George W. Bush signs a $120-billion war-funding bill that lacks the timetable that Democrats had wanted for the withdrawal of U.S. forces from Iraq. The bill sets 18 benchmarks for Iraq's government to achieve as a condition for receiving certain U.S. reconstruction aid. The bill also funds several non-war initiatives, including Gulf Coast hurricane recovery efforts, and it raises the federal minimum wage from $5.15 to $7.25 an hour over the next two years.

28 In Baghdad, Iraq, diplomats from the United States and Iran engage in the first formal bilateral talks between the two countries in nearly 30 years. The U.S. ambassador calls on Iran to stop arming insurgents in Iraq, an allegation that the Iranian ambassador denies.

29 The U.S. Supreme Court, in a 5-4 vote, rules that, under current federal law, workers who wish to sue their employers for pay discrimination may do so only if the worker has filed a formal complaint with the Equal Employment Opportunity Commission within 180 days after the alleged discriminatory act.

30 United States President George W. Bush nominates Robert Zoellick to head the World Bank. Zoellick, a former U.S. deputy secretary of state, will replace Paul Wolfowitz, who announced his resignation on May 17 amid an ethics controversy.

JUNE

2007

2 United States prosecutors charge four men with plotting to blow up fuel tanks and a fuel pipeline at John F. Kennedy International Airport in New York City. The men are alleged to have links to Islamist radical groups.

5 I. Lewis "Scooter" Libby, former chief of staff for U.S. Vice President Dick Cheney, is sentenced to 30 months in prison and fined $250,000. Libby was convicted on March 6 of lying to federal law enforcement agents and to a grand jury during their investigation into the 2003 leak of the identity of Valerie Plame, an undercover officer of the Central Intelligence Agency.

13 Insurgents, believed to be members of al-Qa`ida in Iraq, attack and destroy the twin minarets of al-Askari Mosque in Samarra. It is the second bombing of the mosque—one of the most sacred sites of Shi`ah Islam—in 16 months. A February 2006 attack destroyed the dome of the mosque and sparked an escalation of sectarian violence in Iraq. In the days after the June 2007 bombing, several Sunni mosques in Iraq are damaged or destroyed in retaliatory attacks.

13 The U.S. Department of Defense releases a report that details the initial effects of the 2007 "surge" of tens of thousands of U.S. troops into Iraq. According to the report, overall levels of violence in Iraq remain unchanged, though attacks have shifted away from Baghdad and Al Anbar province, where U.S. and Iraqi forces are most concentrated. The authors of the report note that Iraqi politicians are making little progress toward enacting reforms that could help reconcile competing factions.

14 A violent power struggle in the Gaza Strip between the two main Palestinian factions, Hamas and Fatah, reaches a climax. Hamas seizes control of much of the strip, including the Fatah-run Preventive Security headquarters in Gaza City. Palestinian Authority (PA) President Mahmoud Abbas, a Fatah leader, fires the prime minister, Ismail Haniyeh of Hamas; ends the Hamas-Fatah unity government; and

declares a state of emergency. The violence has left dozens of Palestinians dead since June 11. On June 15, Abbas appoints a political independent, Salam Fayyad, as prime minister of the PA, and the Gaza violence subsides as Hamas secures complete control of the Gaza Strip. Abbas's government remains in control of the West Bank.

19 A truck bomb explodes outside a Shi`ah mosque in Baghdad, Iraq, killing about 85 people and injuring more than 200 others. The incident is the latest in a string of attacks and counterattacks on Shi`ah and Sunni mosques since the June 13 bombing of al-Askari Mosque in Samarra.

20 United States President George W. Bush vetoes a bill that would have loosened restrictions on federal funding for embryonic stem cell research. The president vetoed a similar bill in July 2006.

21 The U.S. Senate votes 65-27 for an energy bill that would raise fuel mileage requirements for new passenger cars and light trucks to an average of 35 miles per gallon (mpg) by 2020. The current requirements are 27.5 mpg for cars and 22.2 mpg for light trucks. If the bill becomes law, the increase in fuel economy standards would be the first in more than 20 years.

25 The U.S. Supreme Court, in a 5-4 decision, weakens a restriction in the McCain-Feingold campaign finance law. The 2002 law prohibits organizations from broadcasting ads that mention federal candidates by name in the period right before an election. The court rules that such ads can be banned only if they explicitly promote a candidate's election or defeat. A total ban on naming candidates is an unconstitutional violation of free speech rights, the court rules.

27 Gordon Brown officially replaces Tony Blair as prime minister of the United Kingdom. Brown was elected to succeed Blair as leader of the Labour Party on June 24.

A member of the Palestinian Islamist group Hamas holds a copy of the Qur'an, Islam's holy book, inside the Preventive Security headquarters in Gaza City on June 14, 2007, shortly after Hamas seized control of the facility from Fatah, a rival Palestinian faction. Hamas secured complete control of the Gaza Strip on June 15.

28 In a 5-4 decision, the U.S. Supreme Court strikes down two public school district programs that used race as a factor in determining where students would attend school. The placement programs in Seattle and in Louisville, Kentucky, were designed to achieve student body diversity. Both districts were sued by parents of students who had been denied admission to their chosen schools on the basis of race. The court rules in favor of the parents, saying that the placement programs were a violation of the constitutional guarantee of equal protection.

28 A bipartisan coalition of 53 U.S. senators blocks a vote on a bipartisan bill that would have overhauled U.S. immigration laws. The procedural move effectively ends consideration in 2007 of an issue that is a priority for President George W. Bush. The bill would have tightened bor-

der security, created a guest worker program, and offered a path for many of the country's 12 million illegal immigrants to gain legal status and eventual citizenship.

29 British police defuse bombs hidden in two parked cars in London's busy theater and nightclub district. If detonated, the bombs would likely have killed or injured hundreds of people, according to the police.

30 Terrorists crash a Jeep Cherokee loaded with propane gas cylinders into the doors of the main terminal at Glasgow International Airport in Scotland. The vehicle bursts into flames without igniting the propane, and no bystanders are killed. One of the two attackers is badly burned and eventually dies on August 2. Police believe that the Glasgow attack is linked to the failed car bomb attacks in London one day earlier, on June 29.

23

People dressed as characters from the Harry Potter book series line up at a London bookshop on July 21, 2007, to buy the seventh and final book of the series, *Harry Potter and the Deathly Hallows.* Within hours of the book's release, millions of copies were sold worldwide.

2 United States President George W. Bush keeps I. Lewis "Scooter" Libby out of prison by commuting his 30-month sentence. Libby, the former chief of staff for Vice President Dick Cheney, was convicted on March 6 of lying to federal investigators and to a grand jury about a 2003 Bush administration leak of an undercover Central Intelligence Agency officer's identity. On July 3, 2007, the president tells reporters that he has not ruled out granting a full pardon to Libby.

7 About 160 people are killed by a truck bomb explosion in Amirli, a town in Iraq's Salah ad Din province.

10 Pakistani soldiers storm the Red Mosque in Islamabad, Pakistan's capital, to flush out Islamist militants barricaded inside. The troops finally take control of the mosque on July 11, ending a siege that began on July 3. The nine-day death toll includes more than 100 militants, civilians, and soldiers. For months leading up to the siege, leaders of the mosque and students at its *madrasahs* (religious schools) campaigned for the adoption of Shari`ah (Islamic law) in Pakistan, kidnapped police officers and other people, and engaged in other acts of defiance.

12 United States President George W. Bush submits a report to Congress that details how Iraq's government is progressing in meeting 18 benchmarks set by Congress in May. The report claims satisfactory progress on 8 benchmarks, unsatisfactory progress on 6, and mixed progress on 2, and says that conditions are not present for the final 2 benchmarks to be achieved.

14 North Korea announces that its nuclear reactor at Yongbyon has been shut down. On July 16, the International Atomic Energy Agency confirms the shutdown. North Korea agreed in February to shut down the reactor and take other steps toward dismantling its nuclear weapons program in exchange for fuel and other aid.

14 In a sign of worsening relations between Russia and the West, Russia formally suspends its participation in the Conventional Armed Forces in Europe Treaty, which limits deployment of tanks, artillery, and other conventional arms on both sides of the old Iron Curtain between Eastern and Western Europe. It is Russia's first official rejection of an arms control treaty signed by the former Soviet Union.

14 The Roman Catholic Archdiocese of Los Angeles agrees to a settlement in which more than 500 people who claim to have been sexually abused by priests will receive $660 million in compensation. The payout is the largest by the U.S. Catholic Church since its child sex abuse scandal began receiving mass publicity in 2002.

16 Three car bombs explode in Kirkuk, Iraq, killing about 85 people. In the most lethal attack, a suicide bomber crashes an explosive-laden truck into a crowded market near the offices of the Patriotic Union of Kurdistan, a Kurdish political party.

17 United States intelligence officials release a National Intelligence Estimate (NIE) predicting that the country "will face a persistent and evolving terrorist threat over the next three years," especially from al-Qa`ida's international network. Although increased counterterrorism efforts have made it harder for al-Qa`ida to attack the U.S. homeland, al-Qa`ida has reestablished much of its operational capacity since 2005, mainly because it has been able to create a safe haven in northwestern Pakistan, according to the NIE.

17 A TAM Airlines plane crashes upon landing in São Paolo, Brazil, killing all 187 people on board and 12 people on the ground. The plane skids off the runway during a rainstorm, slams into a TAM building near a gas station, and explodes. It is Brazil's worst-ever air disaster.

19 The Dow Jones Industrial Average closes above 14,000 for the first time in history.

20 Pakistan's Supreme Court reinstates Chief Justice Iftikhar Muhammad Chaudhry, whom President Pervez Musharraf suspended on March 9 for alleged misconduct. The court rules that Musharraf exceeded his constitutional powers when he suspended Chaudhry. The suspension sparked mass protests in Pakistan.

21 *Harry Potter and the Deathly Hallows*— the seventh and final book in the Harry Potter series by British children's author J. K. Rowling—goes on sale. In its first 24 hours, the book sells 8.3 million copies in the United States and 2.7 million copies in the United Kingdom, setting all-time first-day sales records in both countries.

22 In Turkey, the ruling Justice and Development Party, a moderate pro-Islamic party, wins 341 of 550 seats and 47 percent of the vote in parliamentary elections.

29 In elections for the upper house of Japan's legislature, the Liberal Democratic Party (LDP) loses control of the body for the first time since 1955. The elections leave the LDP and its coalition partners with 105 seats in the House of Councillors, compared with 137 for a coalition led by the Democratic Party of Japan. Despite his party's defeat, Prime Minister Shinzo Abe says he will not step down.

30 A report from Stuart Bowen, Jr., the U.S. special inspector general for Iraq reconstruction, indicates that the Iraqi government has failed to take over a single U.S.-built infrastructure project since July 2006. As a result, many projects are being maintained with continued U.S. funding or are being transferred to local entities that are unable to adequately maintain them.

31 The U.S. House of Representatives votes 411-8 for an ethics bill that would require greater disclosure of earmarks for individual lawmakers' favored projects and greater disclosure of campaign contributions raised by lobbyists. The bill awaits consideration by the Senate.

1 Bombs and political upheaval shake Baghdad, Iraq's capital. Fifty people die when a suicide bomber blows up a fuel tanker, and about 30 people are killed in other attacks. Meanwhile, Iraq's largest Sunni bloc, the Iraqi Accordance Front, withdraws its six ministers from Iraq's Cabinet, leaving only two Sunnis in Prime Minister Nouri al-Maliki's government.

1 The Interstate 35W bridge across the Mississippi River in Minneapolis collapses during the evening rush hour. The center spans of the bridge, along with dozens of vehicles, fall into the river or onto its banks, killing 13 people and injuring about 100 others.

2 The U.S. Senate votes 83-14 to approve ethics legislation passed by the House of Representatives on July 31. The measure would require greater disclosure of earmarks for individual lawmakers' favored projects and greater disclosure of campaign contributions raised by lobbyists.

4 The U.S. House of Representatives votes 241-172 for an energy bill that would require private utilities to produce 15 percent of their electric power from solar, wind, or other renewable energy sources. The bill also would require more energy efficiency in buildings and appliances. In addition, the House votes 221-189 for a separate bill to repeal $16 billion in tax breaks for oil companies. The House legislation must be reconciled with a Senate bill passed on June 21.

5 United States President George W. Bush signs a bill that gives U.S. intelligence agencies the power to eavesdrop on U.S. residents' international phone calls and e-mails without first getting a warrant. The law will expire in 180 days unless Congress renews it.

7 Barry Bonds, left fielder for the San Francisco Giants, hits the 756th home run of his career, breaking a Major League Baseball record that Hank Aaron had held since 1974.

9 The death toll from summer monsoon flooding in South Asia has surpassed 2,000, and millions of people have been displaced, according to national and local government officials. Over the past several weeks, heavy rains in northern India, Bangladesh, and Nepal have caused some of the worst flooding in years.

13 White House senior adviser Karl Rove announces that he will resign at the end of August. Rove was the "architect" of U.S. President George W. Bush's two presidential campaigns.

14 In the deadliest coordinated terrorist assault of the Iraq War, four suicide car bombs kill about 500 people in two Yazidi villages near Mosul. The Yazidi are a Kurdish religious minority. The U.S. military blames the bombings on al-Qa`ida.

14 The toy company Mattel, based in El Segundo, California, recalls more than 18 million toys for safety reasons. Most of the toys contain small but powerful magnets that can be harmful if swallowed. In other cases, a Chinese subcontractor used lead-based paint on the toys. Earlier, on August 2, the Mattel subsidiary Fisher-Price recalled about 1 million toys with lead-based paint.

15 An 8.0-magnitude earthquake hits the central coast of Peru, leaving more than 500 people dead.

17 In an effort to calm the turmoil in financial markets, the U.S. Federal Reserve cuts the discount rate—the rate at which it lends money to banks—from 6.25 percent to 5.75 percent. In response, U.S. and European markets rebound sharply.

21 Hurricane Dean slams into Mexico's Yucatán Peninsula with pounding rain and winds gusting as high as 165 miles (265 kilometers) per hour. The hurricane weakens as it moves across the peninsula, then regains some strength over the Gulf of Mexico. It makes a second landfall on the coast of Veracruz state on August 22 before mostly disintegrating over central Mexico. The hurricane's westward path through the Caribbean

In August 2007, two long-time associates of U.S. President George W. Bush—White House senior adviser Karl Rove (above, left) and Attorney General Alberto Gonzales—announced their resignations.

began on August 17. Weather experts note that despite Dean's intensity, it has caused less death and destruction than expected. About 40 deaths are reported.

22 Fourteen U.S. soldiers die in northern Iraq when their Black Hawk helicopter crashes, apparently from mechanical failure.

27 United States Attorney General Alberto Gonzales announces that he will resign on September 17. Gonzales endured months of criticism over the controversial firings of nine U.S. attorneys in 2006 as well as other matters. His critics accused him of politicizing the Department of Justice and giving misleading testimony to Congress.

28 Turkey's parliament elects Foreign Minister Abdullah Gül as the country's president. Gül, a devout Muslim, was originally nominated for president in April, but strong opposition by secularist parties prevented his election at that time.

28 Street battles between two rival Shi`ah militias leave more than 50 people dead during a large religious festival in Karbala, Iraq. The clashes pit members of the Mahdi Army, the militia of cleric Muqtada al-Sadr, against Iraqi police who are mostly members of the Badr Organization.

30 The Iraqi government has met only 3 of the 18 legislative, security, and economic benchmarks outlined by the U.S. Congress in May, according to a draft version of a U.S. Government Accountability Office (GAO) report leaked to the press. The draft report indicates that 2 other benchmarks have been partially met; the final report, issued on September 4, raises the number of partially met benchmarks to 4. The GAO report contrasts with a more positive report issued by the administration of President George W. Bush on July 12. That report indicated that Iraq had made satisfactory progress on 8 benchmarks and mixed progress on 2 others.

Traders work in the Eurodollar Options pit on the floor of the Chicago Mercantile Exchange on Sept. 18, 2007, shortly after the Federal Reserve cut a key interest rate by a larger-than-expected half percentage point. The rate cut prompted a rally in financial markets.

2 Lebanon's army takes control of Nahr al-Bared, a large Palestinian refugee camp near Tripoli, ending a 105-day siege that left about 400 people dead. The army was battling Islamist militants stationed inside the camp.

4 Hurricane Felix hits Nicaragua's northeastern coast with winds of up to 160 miles (260 kilometers) per hour. The hurricane leaves more than 100 people dead and destroys thousands of houses. It is the second Category 5 Atlantic hurricane of 2007; Hurricane Dean was the first.

5 Fred Thompson, an actor and former U.S. senator from Tennessee, enters the race for the 2008 Republican nomination for U.S. president.

6 The Israeli Air Force carries out an air strike on a site in Syria. Israeli and U.S. intelligence officials believe that a nuclear facility was under construction at the site.

6 The performance of the Iraqi military and police is improving, but they will still need U.S. help in the near term, according to an independent commission led by retired U.S. Marine General James Jones. He tells a U.S. Senate committee that Iraq's National Police force is so sectarian it should be disbanded and reorganized.

10 Army General David Petraeus, the top U.S. commander in Iraq, gives highly anticipated testimony to Congress on September 10 and 11. He tells lawmakers that the "surge"—a strategy that involved deploying thousands of extra U.S. soldiers to Iraq in 2007—is improving security and that U.S. forces can be reduced to presurge levels by mid-2008. But he warns that a larger and more rapid withdrawal would likely have devastating consequences. Petraeus is joined by the U.S. ambassador to Iraq, Ryan Crocker, who tells Congress that political and economic progress is being made in Iraq, albeit slowly and unevenly.

12 Prime Minister Shinzo Abe of Japan announces that he will resign. Abe's Liberal Democratic Party was defeated in upper-house legislative elections on July 29.

13 In a televised address to the nation, U.S. President George W. Bush announces a limited troop withdrawal from Iraq. The president says he is accepting the recommendations of Army General David Petraeus, the top U.S. commander in Iraq, who told Congress earlier in the week that security gains in Iraq make a limited force reduction feasible.

14 United States President George W. Bush signs an ethics and lobbying reform bill. The new law will require legislators to disclose more about their efforts to fund their favored projects through earmarks. The law will also require more disclosure of fund-raising by lobbyists on behalf of federal candidates. Lawmakers will be prohibited from accepting gifts from lobbyists or their clients, and politicians will have to wait one or two years to become lobbyists after they leave office.

16 Seventeen Iraqis are shot and killed in Baghdad by security guards employed by Blackwater USA, a private security contractor based in North Carolina. The guards were escorting a convoy of vehicles carrying U.S. State Department officials. Blackwater claims that the guards fired in self-defense after being attacked, but several Iraqi eyewitnesses dispute that account. The Iraqi government contends that the guards opened fire on civilians without provocation.

17 United States President George W. Bush nominates Michael Mukasey, a retired U.S. district judge, to replace Alberto Gonzales as U.S. attorney general.

18 In an aggressive move to calm financial markets and stave off damage to the economy, the U.S. Federal Reserve cuts the federal funds rate from 5.25 percent to 4.75 percent. This key interest rate is what a bank pays to borrow money from another bank overnight. The Fed also cuts the discount rate—the rate charged to a bank for borrowing money directly from the Fed—from 5.75 percent to 5.25 percent. The rate cuts prompt stock markets to rally. The Dow Jones Industrial Average ends the day up 336 points, or 2.5 percent, and the S&P 500 rises by 2.9 percent.

20 Thousands of people attend a rally in Jena, Louisiana, to protest what they believe to be unjust treatment of six black students charged with beating a white student at Jena High School. The beating incident occurred on Dec. 4, 2006, about three months after three white students hung nooses from a tree at the school. The white students were suspended from school. In the wake of the noose incident, tensions between blacks and whites in Jena led to fights and eventually to the beating incident. The black students were originally charged with attempted second-degree murder, but the charges were later reduced to aggravated second-degree battery. Protesters claim that the charges against the black teens were excessive and that the actions taken against white teens were too mild.

23 Japan's ruling Liberal Democratic Party elects Yasuo Fukuda as party president. Two days later, Japan's legislature formally installs Fukuda as prime minister.

24 The 73,000 General Motors (GM) employees belonging to the United Auto Workers (UAW) union go on strike. The action is the first nationwide strike against Detroit-based GM since 1970. On September 26, the strike ends when the UAW and GM agree on an employment contract.

26 Myanmar's military rulers crack down on Buddhist monks who have been staging antigovernment marches in Yangon and other cities for more than a week. Security forces fire shots at crowds, spray tear gas, strike people with rifle butts, raid monasteries, and detain hundreds of monks. The protests were sparked by a government increase of fuel prices on August 15—a move that created hardship for much of the population. Initial protests were small, but later protests included tens of thousands of monks and other people.

3 United States President George W. Bush vetoes a bill that would have expanded the State Children's Health Insurance Program. The joint federal-state program targets children whose families earn too much to qualify for Medicaid but not enough to afford private health insurance.

5 The Topps Meat Company of Elizabeth, New Jersey, ceases operations and lays off most workers. In September, Topps, a large U.S. manufacturer of frozen hamburgers, recalled 21.7 million pounds (9.8 million kilograms) of ground beef that may have been contaminated with a deadly strain of *E. coli* bacteria. It was the second-largest beef recall in U.S. history.

6 Pakistan's national and provincial assemblies elect President Pervez Musharraf to a new term. Opposition parties boycott the vote, calling it a farce. Pakistan's Supreme Court is considering whether Musharraf's status as army chief made him constitutionally ineligible to run in the first place.

7 Heavy fighting breaks out in the Waziristan region of northwestern Pakistan between Pakistani troops and militants associated with the Taliban and al-Qa`ida. By October 10, the fighting kills more than 250 militants, soldiers, and civilians. The clashes are the most intense in Waziristan since Pakistan joined the U.S.-led "war on terrorism" in 2001.

8 British Prime Minister Gordon Brown announces that the number of British troops in Iraq will be cut from 5,500 to 2,500 by mid-2008.

10 Most of the 45,000 Chrysler employees belonging to the United Auto Workers (UAW) union go on strike. The walkout ends after only six hours when the UAW and Chrysler agree on an employment contract.

12 Former U.S. Vice President Al Gore and the Intergovernmental Panel on Climate Change win the Nobel Peace Prize for their work in assessing and raising awareness of the risks of human-caused climate change.

15 At the urging of the U.S. Treasury Department, the three largest U.S. financial services firms—Citigroup, Bank of America, and JPMorgan Chase—announce that they will create a fund of up to $100 billion to buy highly rated mortgage-backed securities that have become harder to sell because of the recent global credit squeeze. The fund's purpose is to increase liquidity and confidence in credit markets, which have taken a hit from an ongoing subprime-mortgage financial crisis, in which many high-credit-risk borrowers have been unable to make mortgage payments.

17 Turkey's parliament votes to authorize military incursions into northern Iraq to pursue Kurdish rebels. The rebels belong to the Kurdistan Workers Party (PKK), which seeks to establish a Kurdish state that would include much of southeastern Turkey. PKK militants have been attacking Turkish troops and civilians from strongholds in Iraq. An October 7 PKK attack killed 13 Turkish soldiers.

18 Huge crowds greet former Prime Minister Benazir Bhutto upon her return to Pakistan after eight years of self-imposed exile. Her return follows an agreement by President Pervez Musharraf to grant her amnesty from corruption charges. Bhutto and Musharraf are engaged in power-sharing negotiations that could lead to her becoming prime minister again. On her way from the Karachi airport to a homecoming rally, two explosions near her motorcade leave about 140 people dead. Bhutto survives the assassination attempt.

21 Iraq-based members of the Kurdistan Workers Party (PKK) kill 12 Turkish soldiers in a cross-border raid. The Turkish army kills more than 30 rebels in response. In the following days, Turkey builds up its military presence along the Iraq border and sends jets to bomb PKK targets in Iraq. The PKK seeks to establish a Kurdish state that would include much of southeastern Turkey. Iraqi and U.S. diplomats are working to prevent a large-scale Turkish incursion into northern Iraq.

A fire truck races down Sierra Highway in Santa Clarita, California, toward a Los Angeles County wildfire on Oct. 21, 2007. Wildfires raged across southern California in late October, destroying more than 2,000 structures and forcing the evacuation of as many as 1 million people.

21 Numerous wildfires, driven by strong Santa Ana winds, begin to rage across seven southern California counties. The fires eventually spread over more than 500,000 acres (200,000 hectares), destroying more than 2,000 structures, killing at least 14 people, and forcing the evacuation of as many as 1 million others.

28 The Boston Red Sox complete a four-game sweep of the Colorado Rockies to win Major League Baseball's World Series.

28 In Argentina, Cristina Fernández de Kirchner wins the presidential election with 45 percent of the vote. Her nearest rival, Elisa Carrió, wins 23 percent. Kirchner is a senator and the wife of outgoing President Néstor Kirchner.

29 Tropical Storm Noel hits the island of Hispaniola, triggering floods and mudslides that leave more than 100 people dead in Haiti and the Dominican Republic.

30 A report from Stuart Bowen, Jr., the U.S. special inspector general for Iraq reconstruction, indicates that the total investment in Iraq reconstruction from all sources—the United States, Iraq, and other donors—has passed the $100-billion mark. The report notes that electric power production in Iraq has reached its highest levels since early 2003. However, public corruption remains a major problem.

31 In a continuing effort to prevent housing market troubles from causing a broad economic slump, the U.S. Federal Reserve cuts the federal funds rate from 4.75 percent to 4.5 percent. This key interest rate is what a bank pays to borrow money from another bank overnight. The Fed also lowers the discount rate—the rate that a bank pays to borrow money directly from the Fed—from 5.25 percent to 5 percent. The cut in the federal funds rate is the second in two months; the discount-rate cut is the third in three months.

With police surrounding them, lawyers chant slogans opposing Pakistani President Pervez Musharraf during a protest in Lahore on Nov. 29, 2007. Musharraf took the oath of office that day for a new five-year term as president. He put Pakistan under emergency rule on November 3.

3 Pakistan's president, Pervez Musharraf, declares a state of emergency, suspends the Constitution, and fires several Supreme Court judges, including the chief justice. Musharraf claims the actions are necessary because of rising extremist activity and because the judiciary is undermining the government's ability to fight terrorism. But many observers believe he is mainly trying to preempt a Supreme Court decision that would disqualify him from serving another term. In the following days, the government blocks independent TV news broadcasts and arrests thousands of political activists and lawyers. On November 5, thousands of lawyers demonstrate against Musharraf's actions. Many of the protests turn violent when police respond with tear gas and batons.

4 Citigroup, the world's largest financial services firm, announces the resignation of its chairman and CEO, Charles Prince, and reveals it is facing up to $11 billion in subprime-mortgage-related losses in the fourth quarter, on top of $6.5 billion lost in the third quarter. The losses stem from an ongoing subprime-mortgage crisis, in which many high-risk borrowers have been unable to make mortgage payments. Citigroup, based in New York City, has been an active marketer of securities backed by subprime mortgages. Prince's departure follows the October 30 resignation of Stanley O'Neal, the head of Merrill Lynch, another New York City-based financial giant. Merrill Lynch posted a third-quarter subprime-mortgage-related write-down of $8.4 billion.

5 Six U.S. soldiers are killed in Iraq. Their deaths bring to 852 the number of U.S. troops killed in Iraq this year, making 2007 the deadliest year for U.S. forces in Iraq.

6 A suicide bombing outside a recently renovated sugar factory in Baghlan, Afghanistan, kills about 75 people, including 59 schoolchildren and 6 visiting members of parliament. Suicide attacks are on the rise in Afghanistan, where fighting between coalition troops and a resurgent Taliban has escalated in 2007.

8 The U.S. Congress enacts a $23-billion water projects bill over President George W. Bush's veto. The veto override is the first of the Bush presidency. It takes effect with a 79-14 vote in the Senate. Two days earlier, the House of Representatives voted 361-54 for the override.

8 The U.S. Senate votes 53-40 to confirm Michael Mukasey, a retired U.S. district judge, as U.S. attorney general.

13 Public transport workers in France begin a strike in protest of President Nicolas Sarkozy's attempt to reform special pension plans that allow some of them to retire early. The strike severely disrupts most public transportation, including the national rail network and the Paris rapid transit and bus systems, and results in traffic jams as private vehicles pour into the streets. On November 23, most trains, buses, and subways return to service, but pension negotiations continue between unions and the government.

15 Cyclone Sidr smashes into the coast of Bangladesh with winds of up to 155 miles (250 kilometers) per hour. Although hundreds of thousands of people were evacuated before the storm, at least 3,300 people are killed as the storm levels villages, uproots trees, and damages crops.

15 The International Atomic Energy Agency issues a report confirming that Iran now has 3,000 centrifuges in operation for uranium enrichment—a major expansion of the country's nuclear program and a continuation of Iran's defiance of international demands to stop enriching uranium. Iran claims its program is for energy purposes only, but many experts believe Iran intends to make nuclear weapons.

17 The Intergovernmental Panel on Climate Change releases a key report at a press conference in Valencia, Spain. Scientists on the panel have concluded that reductions in greenhouse gas emissions must begin immediately to avoid a climate disaster that could leave island states under water, reduce crop yields in Africa by 50 percent, and cut the global gross domestic product by 5 percent.

19 Pakistan's Supreme Court—now packed with allies of President Pervez Musharraf—dismisses most of the legal challenges to Musharraf's reelection. Musharraf removed several judges from the court on November 3, shortly after he decreed a state of emergency in Pakistan.

24 In Australian parliamentary elections, the Labor Party defeats the coalition of the Liberal and National parties that has governed for 11 years. Prime Minister John Howard loses his seat, which he held for 33 years. Labor wins 83 of the 150 seats in the House of Representatives, a 23-seat gain. Labor leader Kevin Rudd will become prime minister on December 3. On November 30, Rudd announces his intention to withdraw Australia's 550 combat troops from Iraq by mid-2008.

25 Former Prime Minister Nawaz Sharif returns to Pakistan after seven years in exile. Sharif was overthrown in a 1999 coup led by General Pervez Musharraf.

27 The United States hosts a Middle East peace conference in Annapolis, Maryland. In attendance are Palestinian President Mahmoud Abbas, Israeli Prime Minister Ehud Olmert, U.S. President George W. Bush, and representatives of many other countries and international organizations. Abbas and Olmert sign a statement expressing their intent to negotiate an end to the Israeli-Palestinian conflict, with the goal of establishing an independent Palestinian state, by the end of 2008.

28 President Pervez Musharraf of Pakistan steps down as chief of the army. Tremendous domestic and international pressure was brought to bear on Musharraf to give up the command so that he would be sworn in for a new presidential term as a civilian. On November 29, Musharraf takes the oath of office as president.

3 United States intelligence officials release a National Intelligence Estimate (NIE) concluding that Iran halted its nuclear weapons program in 2003. The NIE is a reversal of previous intelligence reports, which judged that Iran was actively working to build such weapons. On December 4, U.S. President George W. Bush asserts that Iran continues to pose a danger to international security.

6 *The New York Times* reports that the Central Intelligence Agency (CIA) in 2005 destroyed videotapes of terrorism suspects being interrogated in 2002. The CIA claims that the tapes no longer had intelligence value and were destroyed simply to safeguard the identities of CIA agents. Human rights advocates allege that the tapes contained evidence of torture and were destroyed to keep agents from being indicted.

10 Russian President Vladimir Putin endorses First Deputy Prime Minister Dmitry Medvedev as his successor, and the pro-Putin United Russia party—which won legislative elections on December 2—indicates that it will nominate Medvedev for president. Medvedev, chairman of the state-owned natural gas company Gazprom, is now essentially guaranteed to win the March 2008 election. Later in December 2007, Medvedev announces that he wants Putin to become prime minister, and Putin indicates he would accept the post.

11 Two suicide bombings in Algiers, the capital of Algeria, kill about 40 people, including 17 United Nations workers. The North African affiliate of the terrorist group al-Qa`ida claims responsibility.

11 In a continuing effort to prevent housing market troubles from causing a broad economic slump, the U.S. Federal Reserve (Fed) cuts the federal funds rate from 4.5 percent to 4.25 percent. This key interest rate is what a bank pays to borrow money from another bank overnight. The Fed also lowers the discount rate—the rate that a bank pays to borrow money directly from the Fed—from 5 percent to 4.75 percent. The cut in the federal funds rate is the third since September; the discount-rate cut is the fourth since August.

15 Pakistani President Pervez Musharraf lifts the state of emergency he imposed on November 3 and restores the Constitution, shortly after issuing several constitutional amendments and decrees designed to forestall court challenges to his recent actions.

15 At the end of the United Nations Climate Change Conference in Bali, Indonesia, delegates from more than 180 countries adopt a "roadmap" for negotiations aimed at producing a new climate change agreement to replace the Kyoto Protocol, which expires in 2012. The roadmap states that deep cuts in greenhouse gas emissions will be needed to avoid dangerous climate change, but it contains no binding commitments. European nations tried to include explicit language in the roadmap calling on developed countries to cut emissions by 25 to 40 percent, but the United States successfully resisted the inclusion of this language.

16 Turkey carries out air raids on more than 200 Kurdish rebel targets in northern Iraq near the Turkish border. The next day, hundreds of Turkish troops cross the border to attack rebel positions. The rebels belong to the Kurdistan Workers Party (PKK), which seeks to establish a Kurdish state that would include much of southeastern Turkey. PKK militants have staged a number of cross-border attacks on Turkish troops in recent months. Turkish warplanes continue to bomb PKK targets in Iraq throughout the rest of December.

19 In South Korea, Lee Myung-bak of the conservative Grand National Party wins the presidential election with nearly 50 percent of the vote.

19 United States President George W. Bush signs an energy bill that raises fuel mileage requirements for cars and light trucks and mandates a

Mortgage defaults and home foreclosures rose dramatically in 2007. Many defaults were on subprime-mortgage loans that had been granted to high-credit-risk home buyers. In late 2007, the value of mortgage-backed securities held by banking and investment firms dropped sharply, forcing the firms to write off billions of dollars in losses.

large boost in the production of ethanol and other biofuels. Under the bill, new passenger vehicle fleets must average 35 miles per gallon (mpg) by 2020, up from the current requirements of 27.5 mpg for cars and 22.2 mpg for light trucks. To avoid a Bush veto, Democrats in Congress had to drop provisions from the bill that would have reduced tax breaks for oil and gas companies and extended tax breaks for alternative energy projects.

19 Morgan Stanley, a New York City-based investment banking giant, reports the first quarterly loss in its 72-year history. The firm is taking a $9.4-billion write-down on its mortgage-related assets in the fourth quarter. The write-down stems from an ongoing subprime-mortgage crisis, in which many high-credit-risk borrowers have been unable to make mortgage payments. Wall Street financial services firms

have so far announced more than $40 billion in write-downs as a result of the subprime-mortgage crisis. Foreign firms are also taking hits. On December 10, the Swiss firm UBS AG announced a fourth-quarter subprime-mortgage-related write-down of about $10 billion.

21 A suicide attack on a mosque in a remote town near Peshawar in northwestern Pakistan leaves about 50 people dead.

27 Former Pakistani Prime Minister Benazir Bhutto is assassinated in a shooting and bomb attack after speaking at a political rally in Rawalpindi. The suicide bombing also leaves at least 20 other people dead. Bhutto returned to Pakistan in October after eight years of exile and was leading the Pakistan People's Party in its campaign for parliamentary elections scheduled for January 2008.

2007 UPDATE

The major events of 2007 are covered in more than 250 alphabetically arranged articles, from "Afghanistan" to "Zoos." Included are Special Reports that offer an in-depth look at such subjects as archaeology at Jamestown and Australia's drought. Special Reports are found on the following pages.

Afghanistan. Savage warfare ravaged Afghanistan throughout 2007, killing civilians in suicide attacks and crossfire incidents, as well as in aerial bombings by allies of the troubled government. With the government lacking control over much of the country, the illegal production of opium flourished.

The United Nations (UN) Department of Safety and Security noted in August that Afghanistan was suffering its most violent year since American-led forces drove the Islamic militant Taliban movement from power in 2001. The report said violence rose almost 25 percent from 2006 to late 2007. Journalists counted more than 5,100 Taliban-related deaths in the first nine months of 2007.

In a television interview that aired on August 4, Afghan President Hamid Karzai said that Afghanistan's "security situation ... over the past two years has definitely deteriorated." His government, whose weak police and armed forces were getting Western training, was backed by approximately 41,000 troops in a 37-nation International Security Assistance Force (ISAF) led by European members of the North Atlantic Treaty Organization (NATO). The ISAF included many of the 23,500 American troops in Afghanistan.

The ISAF fought increasing guerrilla activity by the Taliban. Based in the Pashtun ethnic areas of eastern and southern Afghanistan, the Taliban dominated a third of Afghanistan's provinces in a bloody stalemate with Western and Afghan forces. The Taliban opposed foreign influence and any changes in Pashtun traditions, many of which were pre-Islamic village customs, including inequality for women.

The Taliban drew support from Pashtuns and others living across the rugged border with Pakistan. Some Taliban leaders had retreated in 2001 to frontier areas of Pakistan outside the control of its government, where they recruited and trained new fighters. After long denying this, Pakistani President Pervez Musharraf admitted on Aug. 12, 2007, "There is no doubt Afghan militants are supported from Pakistan soil."

United States officials said the Taliban were using Iranian-made weapons, some of them similar to the roadside bombs used against U.S. forces in Iraq. On a visit to the Afghan capital, Kabul, on August 14, Iranian President Mahmoud Ahmadinejad denied that his government was supplying weapons to the Taliban.

Fighting. Taliban attacks on ISAF forces in the south were often answered by artillery fire or air raids that killed civilians. Observers criticized Western forces for what they said was the indiscriminate and excessive use of force.

After more than 90 civilian deaths were reported in a single week in June, Karzai rebuked ISAF forces. "Innocent people are becoming victims of careless operations," he said. He warned that the fight against the Taliban could not succeed unless ISAF troops showed more restraint. The ISAF acknowledged that it must be more careful in using its firepower.

Suicide attacks, which were rare in Afghanistan before 2006, increased by 69 percent in the first eight months of 2007. Although Karzai claimed on June 18 that the increased suicide attacks showed the Taliban were frustrated with insurgent efforts to control areas, the guerrillas remained strong in many areas.

On September 29, Karzai expressed a willingness to meet with Taliban leader Mohammad Omar and urged negotiations. A Taliban spokesman said they would not negotiate so long as foreign troops remained in Afghanistan.

Kidnappings. A number of foreigners were seized and held by hostile groups in 2007. In some cases, the Taliban kidnapped aid workers and journalists in an effort to force their nations to withdraw troops from Afghanistan and to pay money so the Taliban could finance their operations. In one highly publicized instance, Taliban militants kidnapped 23 Christian volunteers from South Korea on July 19. Two of the hostages were executed, but the remaining 21 were released in August amid rumors that the South Korean government had paid the Taliban a $20-million ransom.

Agriculture. Opium poppy cultivation in Afghanistan set another record in 2007, up 17 percent from the previous year, according to the UN Office on Drugs and Crime. In a report issued on August 27, the office noted that output of the narcotic was down in northern Afghanistan but up in the south.

Some 53 percent of the crop came from Helmand province, where American aid in the 1950's had helped Afghan farmers develop the land for wheat, citrus, and other foods. In recent years, the United States had spent $600 million to try to curtail poppy growth. The Taliban encouraged the crop to raise money for its fighting, however, and farmers earned more from opium than available alternative crops.

Despite expanded poppy cultivation, Afghan grain production more than doubled from 2001 to 2007, the UN Food and Agriculture Organization reported on August 6. Good weather and development aid had brought Afghanistan close to food self-sufficiency.

Muhammad Zahir Shah, who was king of Afghanistan from 1933 until he was ousted and forced into exile in 1973, died on July 23, 2007. He had returned to Afghanistan in 2002.

■ Henry S. Bradsher

See also **Armed forces; Asia; Korea, South; Pakistan; Terrorism.**

AFRICA

In early 2007, the chief executive of the United Nations (UN)-affiliated International Monetary Fund (IMF), Rodrigo de Rato, advised African governments to seize the opportunity provided by the global economic upswing to further develop their own economies.

The growing demand for raw materials over the last three years affected Africa positively and brought new hope for the continent's economic revival. Despite chronic political instability in a handful of African countries, the continent's economic growth averaged 5 to 6 percent in 2005 and 2006. Analysts predicted economic growth of between 6 and 7 percent in 2007.

Foreign direct investment into Africa increased substantially in 2007 as well, though its distribution was uneven, with 10 out of the 33 countries receiving 90 percent of the $39 billion in total investments. These investments were also concentrated in the continent's export commodities, especially oil, natural gas, and minerals.

Civil strife occurred across the continent in such countries as Congo (Kinshasa), Côte d'Ivoire, Somalia, Sudan, and Zimbabwe. Peacekeeping forces deployed in these countries struggled to create conditions for peace. In some cases, the forces had to be expanded. In Somalia, the response by African governments to send more troops was too slow to stabilize the country.

On a positive note, a record number of democratic polls were held in Africa in 2007—more than 20 elections in at least 18 countries. Unfortunately, some of these elections were badly administered, leading to political disputes and even violence. In most countries, the ruling parties retained control of the government. Only Mauritania and Sierra Leone changed governments as a result of elections.

African Union (AU). The annual summit of the AU's heads of state and government took place in Ghana in July 2007, the 50th anniversary of Ghana's independence. Despite Africa's many urgent problems, the meeting focused on the creation of a "United States of Africa," the ideal of Kwame Nkrumah, Ghana's first president.

Only a small minority of member nations supported Libyan President Mu'ammar Muhammad al-Qadhafi's proposal that the political integration of Africa be implemented at once. The majority of countries followed the lead provided by South Africa, Nigeria, and various East African countries that argued that Africa should first accomplish economic integration before attempting political union.

Central Africa. Despite the successful elections carried out in Congo (Kinshasa) in 2006, the eastern parts of this enormous country remained unstable with remnant rebel forces still active. The violence threatened the rare mountain gorillas inhabiting the Virunga National Park on the border with Uganda.

Much of the fighting was instigated by a strong Tutsi rebel group, led by General Laurent Nkunda, who defied attempts by the UN peacekeeping force (MONUC) to disarm his group. Newly elected President Joseph Kabila expressed his determination to enforce a military solution on the conflict zones. In December 2007, the Congolese government and MONUC launched an offensive against the rebels in the eastern region of the country. However, the rebels managed to regain some of their lost territories.

Throughout 2007, security in the Central African Republic and Chad was threatened by various rebel groups linked to rebels in Congo (Kinshasa) and in Sudan's Darfur region. In Congo (Brazzaville), the chaotic conduct of the June legislative elections led to the dismissal of the top electoral official. There was, however, improvement during the second round of the polls in August, when President Denis Sassou-Nguesso's Congolese Labor Party retained its large parliamentary majority.

In Cameroon, the ruling party Cameroon People's Democratic Movement (CPDM) remained the country's strongest party after the National Assembly elections in July. The Social Democratic Front (SDF), supported by the English-speaking minority in the bilingual country, retained its position as Cameroon's largest opposition party. In May, a Kenyan passenger plane crashed into a swamp near Douala, Cameroon's largest city, killing all 114 people on board.

East Africa and the Horn. In July 2007, the nations of Burundi and Rwanda joined the East African Community (EAC), a regional organization promoting economic cooperation between its member nations. Burundi and Rwanda, two landlocked, poor countries heavily reliant on transport routes in the rest of the region, stood to benefit from their membership in the EAC. The other members of this

group included Kenya, Tanzania, and Uganda.

The war in Somalia and the lingering border dispute between Ethiopia and Eritrea caused tensions and divisions in the region during 2007. In late 2006, Ethiopian forces had assisted the transitional Somalian government in fighting off the Islamists that had held control of much of the country since June. The Ethiopian government was concerned that the Islamist operations along the country's eastern border might spill over into its Somali-speaking Ogaden region. By January 2007, the Islamist militias were defeated, giving the transitional government of President Abdullahi Yusuf Ahmed the opportunity to establish itself in the Somali capital, Mogadishu.

Appeals by the AU to its member nations to send peacekeeping troops to Somalia resulted in only about 1,500 Ugandan soldiers arriving by the end of 2007. Internal divisions precluded the transitional government from holding peace talks

with clan leaders opposed to its rule. In November, a new prime minister was appointed.

While Kenya was preparing for its national elections in December, two island nations off the coast of eastern Africa went to the polls. In Seychelles, the elections were peaceful, resulting in no change of government. By contrast, the polls on Anjouan, one of the three islands that make up the country of Comoros, erupted into unrest.

In 2001, Comoros introduced a complex electoral system, which provided greater *autonomy* (independence) for each of its three main islands. Each island elects its own president and government, and the country's presidency rotates among the three islands. In 2006, Ahmed Abdallah Mohamed Sambi, from Anjouan, had been elected president of Comoros for a four-year term. In 2007, the islands elected their local presidents, who each were to serve only one five-year term. While the presidents on the other islands were

An enormous sandstorm with strong winds, known as a *haboob* in Arabic, threatens Khartoum, the capital of Sudan, on April 29, 2007. These storms, which can tower 3,000 feet (914 meters) above the horizon, occur as often as 24 times a year in the region, but usually last for only three hours.

FACTS IN BRIEF ON AFRICAN COUNTRIES

Country	Population	Government	Monetary unit*	Foreign trade (million U.S.$)	
				Exports†	Imports†
Algeria	34,355,000	President Abdelaziz Bouteflika; Prime Minister Abdelaziz Belkhadem	dinar (67.43 = $1)	55,600	27,600
Angola	17,313,000	President José Eduardo dos Santos	kwanza (74.99 = $1)	35,530	10,210
Benin	8,067,000	President Thomas Yayi Boni	CFA franc (463.72 = $1)	563	927
Botswana	1,758,000	President Festus Mogae	pula (6.08 = $1)	4,836	3,034
Burkina Faso	14,425,000	President Blaise Compaoré	CFA franc (463.72 = $1)	544	1,016
Burundi	8,349,000	President Pierre Nkurunziza	franc (1,112.91 = $1)	56	207
Cameroon	18,002,000	President Paul Biya	CFA franc (463.72 = $1)	4,318	3,083
Cape Verde	523,000	President Pedro Pires; Prime Minister José Maria Pereira Neves	escudo (77.68 = $1)	97	495
Central African Republic	4,157,000	President François Bozizé	CFA franc (463.72 = $1)	131	203
Chad	10,591,000	President Idriss Déby	CFA franc (463.72 = $1)	4,342	823
Comoros	712,000	President Ahmed Abdallah Mohamed Sambi	franc (347.79 = $1)	34	115
Congo (Brazzaville)	3,921,000	President Denis Sassou-Nguesso	CFA franc (463.72 = $1)	5,996	1,964
Congo (Kinshasa)	64,827,000	President Joseph Kabila	franc (560.00 = $1)	1,108	1,319
Côte d'Ivoire (Ivory Coast)	20,092,000	President Laurent Gbagbo; Prime Minister Guillaume Soro	CFA franc (463.72 = $1)	7,832	5,548
Djibouti	838,000	President Ismail Omar Guelleh; Prime Minister Dileita Mohamed Dileita	franc (177.72 = $1)	250	987
Egypt	77,243,000	President Hosni Mubarak; Prime Minister Ahmed Nazif	pound (5.58 = $1)	24,220	35,860
Equatorial Guinea	538,000	President Obiang Nguema; Prime Minister Ricardo Mangue Obama Nfubea	CFA franc (463.72 = $1)	8,961	2,543
Eritrea	4,886,000	President Issaias Afewerki	nafka (15.00 = $1)	18	702
Ethiopia	78,326,000	President Girma Woldegiorgis; Prime Minister Meles Zenawi	birr (9.08 = $1)	1,085	4,105
Gabon	1,457,000	President El Hadj Omar Bongo; Prime Minister Jean Eyeghe Ndong	CFA franc (463.72 = $1)	6,677	1,607
Gambia	1,582,000	President Yahya A. J. J. Jammeh	dalasi (19.25 = $1)	131	212
Ghana	23,542,000	President John Agyekum Kufuor	new cedi (0.94 = $1)	3,286	5,666
Guinea	10,044,000	President Lansana Conté; Prime Minister Lansana Kouyaté	franc (4,169.44 = $1)	615	730
Guinea-Bissau	1,454,000	President João Bernardo Vieira	CFA franc (463.72 = $1)	116	176--
Kenya	37,190,000	President Mwai Kibaki	shilling (66.73 = $1)	3,614	6,602
Lesotho	2,248,000	King Letsie III; Prime Minister Pakalitha Mosisili	loti (6.93 = $1)	779	1,401

*Exchange rates as of Oct. 4, 2007.　　　　†Latest available data.

Country	Population	Government	Monetary unit*	Exports[†]	Imports[†]
				Foreign trade (million U.S.$)	
Liberia	3,556,000	President Ellen Johnson-Sirleaf	dollar (61.50 = $1)	910	4,839
Libya	6,266,000	Leader Mu'ammar Muhammad al-Qadhafi; General People's Committee Secretary (Prime Minister) al-Baghdadi Ali al-Mahmudi	dinar (1.25 = $1)	37,020	14,470
Madagascar	18,774,000	President Marc Ravalomanana	ariary (1,835.00 = $1)	994	1,544
Malawi	13,630,000	President Bingu wa Mutharika	kwacha (139.79 = $1)	513	768
Mali	14,724,000	President Amadou Toumani Touré; Prime Minister Mobido Sidibé	CFA franc (463.72 = $1)	323	1,858
Mauritania	3,342,000	President Sidi Ould Cheikh Abdallahi; Prime Minister Zeine Ould Zeidane	ouguiya (259.37 = $1)	784	1,124
Mauritius	1,276,000	President Sir Anerood Jugnauth; Prime Minister Navinchandra Ramgoolam	rupee (30.20 = $1)	2,318	3,391
Morocco	31,851,000	King Mohammed VI; Prime Minister Abbas El Fassi	dirham (8.01 = $1)	11,720	21,220
Mozambique	20,854,000	President Armando Guebuza	new metical (25.84 = $1)	2,429	2,815
Namibia	2,091,000	President Hifikepunye Pohamba	dollar (6.93 = $1)	2,321	2,456
Niger	15,367,000	President Mamadou Tandja	CFA franc (463.72 = $1)	222	588
Nigeria	140,923,000	President Umaru Yar'Adua	naira (125.20 = $1)	59,010	25,100
Rwanda	9,548,000	President Paul Kagame	franc (546.65 = $1)	135	390
São Tomé and Príncipe	169,000	President Fradique de Menezes	dobra (13,743.54 = $1)	10	49
Senegal	12,507,000	President Abdoulaye Wade; Prime Minister Cheikh Hadjibou Soumaré	CFA franc (463.72 = $1)	1,478	2,980
Seychelles	86,000	President James Michel	rupee (7.38 = $1)	365	571
Sierra Leone	5,915,000	President Ernest Bai Koroma	leone (2,980.51 = $1)	185	531
Somalia	9,007,000	President Abdullahi Yusuf Ahmed; Prime Minister Nur Hassan Hussein	shilling (1,358.40 = $1)	241	576
South Africa	47,114,000	President Thabo Mvuyelwa Mbeki	rand (6.93 = $1)	59,150	61,530
Sudan	39,076,000	President Umar Hassan Ahmad al-Bashir	pound (2.05 = $1)	7,505	8,693
Swaziland	1,102,000	King Mswati III; Prime Minister Absalom Themba Dlamini	lilangeni (6.93 = $1)	2,201	2,274
Tanzania	40,675,000	President Jakaya Kikwete	shilling (1,245.50 = $1)	1,831	3,180
Togo	6,637,000	President Faure Gnassingbé	CFA franc (463.72 = $1)	868	1,208
Tunisia	10,352,000	President Zine El-Abidine Ben Ali; Prime Minister Mohamed Ghannouchi	dinar (1.26 = $1)	11,610	13,890
Uganda	30,730,000	President Yoweri Kaguta Museveni	shilling (1,752.00 = $1)	962	1,945
Zambia	12,255,000	President Levy Mwanawasa	kwacha (3,885.00 = $1)	3,928	3,092
Zimbabwe	13,242,000	President Robert Gabriel Mugabe	dollar (30,000.00 = $1)	1,766	2,055

successfully elected, the incumbent on Anjouan, Mohammed Bacar, who had already served his term, refused to step down, causing a constitutional crisis.

Bacar ignored a court ruling that his election to the Anjouan presidency was invalid. To make matters worse, a task force sent by President Sambi from the Union capital on Grande Comore Island failed to take control of Anjouan. The AU started talks to end the situation, but Bacar was inaugurated as president of Anjouan on June 14.

Southern Africa. In 2007, the political climate in southern Africa was heavily influenced by the deteriorating conditions in Zimbabwe and their effect on neighboring countries. It was estimated that millions of Zimbabweans had left their country, which was experiencing record levels of inflation and unemployment, for South Africa and other neighboring countries over the past few years. In March, the Southern African Development Community (SADC) appointed South Africa's president, Thabo Mbeki, to mediate between Zimbabwe's main political players to resolve the crisis.

Among the southern African countries, only Lesotho and Madagascar, the large island off the southeastern coast of Africa's mainland, held elections in 2007, both for their national assemblies. In Lesotho, the governing Lesotho Congress for Democracy (LCD) party retained an overall majority in parliament, and the All Basotho Convention (ABC), led by former Finance Minister Tom Thabane, emerged as the strongest opposition party. Contrasting with previous elections, the polling went smoothly and was declared free and fair by independent observers.

In Madagascar, the party supporting President Marc Ravalomanana won the National Assembly elections held in September. However, voter turnout was low compared with previous elections.

Angola's elections were further delayed to leave enough time for the preparation of a new voters' roll because the existing roll had become obsolete since the last elections in 1992. Angola was scheduled to hold National Assembly polls in 2008 and presidential polls in 2009. Meanwhile, Angola's oil production reached record levels. Producing almost 2 million barrels per day, the country became the second leading oil producer in sub-Saharan Africa after Nigeria.

West Africa. In March 2007, an agreement mediated by Burkina Faso's President Blaise Compaoré raised hopes for a resolution to the conflict in neighboring Côte d'Ivoire. The country had been destabilized by civil war since 2002.

Ivorian President Laurent Gbagbo and Guillaume Soro, leader of the New Forces rebels, agreed to cooperate to reunite Côte d'Ivoire and to hold national elections. Shortly after this accord, Soro was appointed prime minister, a move that was expected to lead to the integration of Soro's New Forces rebels with the national Ivorian Army and to the restoration of Gbagbo's administration in the north of the country, the area held by the rebels. The presidential and legislative elections, postponed since 2005, were scheduled for 2008, to take place after the government had issued voters national identification cards.

However, disgruntled elements within the New Forces attempted to disrupt the peace process. At the end of June 2007, rebels fired rockets at Soro's aircraft after it landed in the rebel-held town of Bouake. Soro escaped unhurt. Afterward, he and Gbagbo said that the incident strengthened their resolve to proceed with the peace process.

In 2007, eight West African countries held elections, but Mauritania and Sierra Leone were the only regional countries that changed governments. The military government in Mauritania held elections in March to transfer power to a civilian government. The presidential polls were won by Sidi Ould Cheikh Abdallahi. The parties supporting Abdallahi also gained a parliamentary majority.

In Sierra Leone, the northern-based All People's Congress (APC) defeated the ruling Sierra Leone People's Party (SLPP) at the legislative elections in August. Presidential polls were held at the same time, though no candidate won a majority of votes. A runoff election was held in September, and APC leader Ernest Bai Koroma won the majority of votes and became the country's new president, succeeding Ahmed Kabbah, who had been in power since 1996.

In Nigeria, President Olusegun Obasanjo, in office since 1999, stepped down after his second term and was succeeded by the ruling party's presidential candidate, Umaru Yar'Adua, who was elected in the April 2007 presidential polls.

At the elections in Burkina Faso, Gambia, Mali, Senegal, and Togo, the governing parties either retained or increased their majorities in parliament. Senegal's president, Abdoulaye Wade, and Mali's president, Amadou Toumani Touré, were both reelected for another term.

Africom. The United States government announced plans for an African Command (Africom) to coordinate U.S. military deployments in Africa. Concerns that terrorist groups hostile to the United States would gain footholds in Africa's sparsely populated areas prompted the U.S. government to expand its antiterrorism operations on the continent. Africom was scheduled to provide small teams of American security specialists to train African soldiers to increase governmental control of remote areas.

An ethanol boom in 2007 driven by record-high oil prices pushed the construction of at least 30 new ethanol plants across the Midwest. An estimated 24 percent of the U.S. corn crop was used to produce 9 billion gallons (34 million liters) of ethanol in 2007.

Many of Africa's governments and organizations became apprehensive in 2007 about the increasing U.S. military presence on the continent. Senior American officials tried to allay African concerns by explaining that Africom would not entail a significant increase in U.S. military personnel in Africa. They said that it would be primarily involved in training activities and would operate only where it had been invited.

Africom temporarily established its headquarters at European Command in Stuttgart, Germany. Many European governments supported the U.S. initiative because terrorist bases in Africa were also threats to Europe. For example, the perpetrators of the 2004 train bombings in Madrid had entered the country from Morocco.

Africom was scheduled to begin operating in Africa in 2008. Both Liberia, a country with a long-standing relationship with the United States, and Djibouti, home to the only U.S. base on the continent, offered to host the command.

In early 2007, the United States launched air attacks on suspected Qa`ida terrorists in Somalia from its military base in Djibouti; U.S. forces had battled al-Qa`ida since it bombed the American embassies in Kenya and Tanzania in 1998, killing more than 200 people.   ■ Pieter Esterhuysen

See also **AIDS; International trade; Middle East; United Nations;** various African country articles.

Agriculture. In 2007, investment in renewable fuels and tighter supplies of grain caused farm prices and food prices to rise. Globally, wheat stocks were at the lowest levels in nearly 60 years due to increased demand and the continuing drought in Australia, where rainfall hit a 17-year low. Record prices for oil accelerated interest in renewable fuels. A decline in the dollar increased United States exports. Both factors helped push world commodity prices higher, prompting the United Nations Food and Agriculture Organization to predict higher food prices into 2008.

World crop production. World wheat production of 600 million metric tons in 2007 was up slightly from 2006, according to a report from the U.S. Department of Agriculture (USDA) released in November 2007. Global supplies tightened, however, because of weather-related declines in production in Australia, Europe, and elsewhere. Although U.S. wheat production increased by 14 percent—yielding 56 million metric tons (2 billion bushels)—global demand caused world stocks to fall from 124 million metric tons in 2006 to 110 million metric tons in 2007, the lowest level in 30 years.

World production of coarse grains set a new record of 1,055 million metric tons in 2007. (Coarse grains include corn, barley, sorghum,

Bent Skovmand
Packing Noah's Ark

The largest seed bank in the world—a massive depository for some 4 million seeds built into a mountainside—was scheduled to open in 2008. But one of the people responsible for creating it, plant scientist Bent Skovmand, would not be there to see it. Skovmand died on Feb. 6, 2007, at the age of 62.

Bent Skovmand was born in Frederiksberg, Denmark, in 1945. He attended the University of Minnesota, where he earned a bachelor's degree in agriculture and master's and doctoral degrees in plant pathology. He spent some time in Mexico, studying and preserving rare old varieties of wheat in the hope that they might be used to breed stronger, more disease-resistant strains. He also traveled throughout the world, identifying more than 150,000 varieties of wheat seed, as well as more than 20,000 types of corn. In 2003, Queen Margrethe II of Denmark knighted Skovmand for his scientific achievements. That same year, he was appointed director of the Nordic Gene Bank, a center that collects, studies, and preserves the seeds of Denmark, Finland, Iceland, Norway, and Sweden.

Skovmand and other botanists became concerned as early as the 1980's that such factors as political instability, natural disasters, plant diseases, and contamination by genetically modified plants could result in the loss of thousands of varieties of seeds, limiting plant diversity and perhaps even threatening the world's food supply. Out of that concern was born the project that came to be called a "Noah's Ark for plants," a "Fort Knox for seeds," and a "doomsday vault"—the Svalbard Global Seed Vault.

The Norwegian government in 2005 offered to fund the project, and planners chose a site for the facility on Spitsbergen, an island in the Svalbard archipelago of the Arctic Ocean, about 300 miles (483 kilometers) north of the Norwegian mainland. The island's remote location—along with the ferocious local polar bear population—would help to keep the facility secure. In addition, the cold climate and *permafrost* (ground that remains nearly permanently frozen) would help to preserve the seeds, even if cooling systems failed.

The seed vault is constructed as a cavern in the side of a mountain. A tunnel 330 feet (100 meters) long leads to three underground chambers, each of which holds about 1.5 million seeds. The seeds, which were to be contributed by at least 100 nations (which would continue to own them), would be kept at a constant temperature of -0.4 °F (-18 °C). Should disaster strike and eliminate a country's own seeds—such as a typhoon in the Philippines or the wars in Iraq and Afghanistan—the seeds at Svalbard would replace them. For Skovmand, who fervently believed that plant research could help save the world from hunger, the Svalbard vault was indeed a Noah's Ark. ■ Kristina Vaicikonis

and oats, with corn making up two-thirds of this category.) Nearly all of the increase was due to a record-breaking U.S. corn harvest of 336 million metric tons (13.2 billion bushels). In 2007, U.S. farmers planted 93.6 million acres (37.9 million hectares) of corn, nearly 20 percent more than in 2006 and the largest acreage planted to corn since 1933. In U.S. markets, the season average price for corn hit a new record at $3.50 per bushel, reflecting demand for biofuels.

World oilseed production—soybeans, sunflower seeds, cottonseed, and rapeseed—was expected to total 390 million metric tons in 2007. Soybean production, the largest component of oilseeds, was down 19 percent in the United States at 70 million metric tons (2.6 billion bushels). United States producers planted fewer acres to soybeans in order to plant more corn. Globally, total supply was nearly equal to the 2006 oilseed crop due to larger harvests of sunflower seeds and cottonseed. In addition, Brazil increased soybean plantings in response to prices that were 40 percent higher in 2007 than in 2006. In U.S. markets, prices for soybeans hit a new record in 2007, with a season average price of $9.00 per bushel.

The 2007 global rice harvest of 420 million metric tons nearly matched the 2006 harvest of 417 million metric tons. China, the world's top rice grower, harvested about 130 million metric tons. India with 92 million metric tons, Indonesia with 34 million metric tons, and Vietnam with 23 million metric tons experienced trouble-free harvests in 2007. The U.S. rice harvest came in at 6.3 million metric tons (138.9 hundredweight), up slightly from 2006 but still short of the 2005 harvest.

World cotton production at 120 million bales was up slightly in 2007 due to production increases for China and Brazil, which offset reductions for drought-plagued Australia. (One bale is equivalent to 480 pounds [217 kilograms] of cotton.) China produced 35.5 million bales, nearly double the U.S. crop of 19 million bales. Severe drought in the southeastern United States reduced the U.S. cotton crop by 16 percent.

Food prices. In 2007, the cost of food in the United States increased by about 4 percent, a higher rate than the historical average annual increase of 2.5 percent. Usually two-thirds of food costs can be attributed to higher costs for energy, labor, and advertising, but in 2007, higher commodity prices also played a role. Analysts cited the rush to produce renewable fuels from corn as a major factor in rising food prices. In 2007, 30 new ethanol plants were constructed in the United States, and 24 percent of the corn crop was used to produce 9 billion gallons (34 million liters) of ethanol. Soybean prices also rose because of increased demand for soybean oil to make biodiesel fuel.

GM crops. Farmers in the United States planted more land in genetically modified (GM) crops than those in any other country in 2007. GM crops (also called biotech crops) are genetically modified to resist herbicides or insects or both. Such crops made new inroads in India and other major agricultural nations where they had previously been shunned.

In 2007, biotech cotton, which is resistant to boll worms, accounted for 35 percent of India's cotton acreage. According to the East India Cotton Association, cotton yields in 2007 rose by 500 kilograms per hectare (2,724 pounds per acre), and experts predicted that Indian farmers would in 2008 plant 80 percent of cotton acreage in biotech varieties. The 2007 cotton crop in India was estimated at 24 million bales.

The International Service for the Acquisition of Agri-biotech Applications (ISAAA), an organization that promotes the use of biotechnology in developing nations, reported that global biotech crop acreage reached 252 million acres (102 million hectares) in 22 countries in 2006, a 13-percent increase from 2005. In the United States, acreage planted to biotech crops increased for the 11th year in a row: corn acreage was 73 percent biotech; soybean acreage, 91 percent; and cotton acreage, 87 percent.

Organic crops. In late 2005, crop and pasture land totaling 77 million acres (31 million hectares) worldwide was certified organic, according to a report issued by the Research Institute of Organic Agriculture in Frick, Switzerland. This figure represented less than 1 percent of total land worldwide devoted to farming. Australia, Argentina, and China led the world in organic land use. In the United States, farmers in 2005 dedicated over 4 million acres (1.6 million hectares) of farmland to organic production systems.

Farm bill. On Jan. 31, 2007, the administration of U.S. President George W. Bush released its farm bill proposals, which called for an end to payments to farmers with an adjusted gross income of at least $200,000 a year; increased direct payments for all other eligible producers; expanded conservation, renewable fuels, research, and beginning farmer and rancher programs; and larger purchases of fruits and vegetables for the USDA's School Lunch and other feeding programs. The House and Senate passed bills in July and December, respectively, that included some administration proposals. These bills were expected to be reconciled by a House-Senate conference committee in early 2008. Bush administration officials said both bills were flawed in their current form because they would increase taxes on certain U.S. businesses and continue to provide unnecessary farm subsidies to wealthy Americans.

Trade. On May 22, the Paris-based World

Organization for Animal Health (OIE) formally classified the United States as a controlled-risk country for bovine spongiform encephalopathy (BSE), also known as "mad cow disease." The classification signified that U.S. beef from cattle of all ages could be safely traded. United States officials used the new classification to prod Japan to reopen its market to U.S. beef. Since 2003, Japan had enforced a policy of importing beef only from cattle less than 20 months old. Critics of the Japanese policy pointed out that the United States had reported only two cases of BSE since 2003, while Japan had reported 33 cases since 2001.

Avian flu continued to spread in 2007, killing hundreds of thousands of domestic and wild birds and about 200 human beings. Outbreaks were most common in Vietnam, Indonesia, and other East Asian countries. The United States helped fund the United Nations Food and Agriculture Organization in efforts to assist more than 100 countries to prevent and control the dangerous viral disease.

Change at top. On Oct. 31, 2007, President Bush nominated former North Dakota Governor Ed Schafer to replace Secretary of Agriculture Mike Johanns. Johanns resigned in September to run for the U.S. Senate. ■ Patricia Peak Klintberg

See also **Africa; Australia; Energy supply; Food; International trade.**

AIDS. In 2007, the first members of two new classes of drugs designed to fight HIV (the virus that causes AIDS) won sales and marketing approval from the United States Food and Drug Administration (FDA). In August, the FDA granted conditional approval to maraviroc, which belongs to a class of drugs that bind to CCR5, a protein on the surface of body cells through which certain types of HIV enter and infect cells. Maraviroc, manufactured by Pfizer Inc. of New York City, is intended for HIV-infected patients who have developed some resistance to other medications.

In licensing the drug, the FDA required Pfizer to include a so-called black-box warning, the strongest form of advisory, on the drug's label. The warning cautions users that maraviroc may increase the risk of heart attack. The agency also required Pfizer to conduct additional research on the drug's long-term side effects.

In October, the FDA approved the use of the first integrase inhibitor, Isentress. Integrase inhibitors prevent HIV from inserting itself into the genetic material inside cells to reproduce. Made by Merck & Co. of Whitehouse Station, New Jersey, Isentress is intended for HIV-infected adults who are resistant to anti-HIV drugs or are infected with drug-resistant strains of the virus.

AIDS totals. The United Nations (UN) in 2007 cut its estimate of the number of people world-wide infected with HIV from 40 million to 33 million. According to UN demographics, there were fewer HIV infections in India than previously believed. However, there were still 6,800 new cases and 5,700 deaths due to AIDS per day. Although Africa had the largest number of infections, parts of Asia had the fastest-growing rates of infections.

AIDS and African Americans. The spread of HIV and AIDS in the black community must be recognized as a public health emergency by the federal government, declared dozens of African American clergy, medical professionals, political officials, and others at an October conference in New York City. Blacks, who made up only 13.5 percent of the U.S. population in 2007, accounted for almost half of new diagnoses of HIV. The clergy called for new legislation to combat the problem and pledged to work to increase AIDS awareness and promote testing in their congregations.

Benefits of routine HIV screening. Two reports published in June by researchers at the U.S. Centers for Disease Control and Prevention in Atlanta indicated that routine screening in emergency rooms and at gay pride events would help the public health community to increase the identification rate of people with HIV. Approximately one-quarter of the estmated 1 million people in the United States who are HIV positive are believed to be unaware that they are infected. Routine screening, said the researchers, would also improve medical care for more HIV-positive patients.

Male circumcision. In February, the U.S. National Institutes of Health reported that clinical trials in Kenya, Uganda, and South Africa strongly suggested that circumcision reduced a man's risk of contracting HIV from heterosexual intercourse by up to 65 percent. In Africa, HIV is spread primarily through heterosexual intercourse. These results were so convincing that the investigators stopped the trials, so that circumcision could be offered to those patients who had not had the procedure.

Theory challenged. The most common theory explaining how HIV depletes the body's supply of immune system cells known as helper T cells is incorrect, according to a study published in May. Scientists had long proposed that HIV causes helper T cells to produce more HIV, which, in turn, leads to the activation of more T cells, which are then infected and destroyed. However, a mathematical model created by American and British researchers indicated that this proposed process would deplete T-cell numbers in a matter of months. In reality, it takes several years for T cells to become depleted. ■ Alfred J. Smuskiewicz

See also **Africa; Drugs; Medicine; Public health.**

Air pollution. See Environmental pollution.

Albania. Politics in Albania continued to be highly polarized in 2007 between the center-right governing coalition led by Prime Minister Sali Berisha of the Democratic Party and the opposition Socialists, led by Edi Rama, mayor of Tirane, the capital. In June, Socialist leaders in parliament attempted to block the election of a new president, a mainly ceremonial position, by boycotting the vote. However, seven Socialist deputies broke with party leaders, which enabled parliament to elect Bamir Topi, a Berisha ally, in July.

Albania held nationwide local elections in February, closely monitored by international observers. Key European observers reported that the elections had not met international standards, and Oli Rehn, the European Union (EU) enlargement commissioner, cited Albanian political feuding as the chief reason for the failure to achieve satisfactory electoral reforms. EU officials and Albanian leaders entered negotiations in June 2006 on the country's prospective admission to the association of European nations.

Economists projected that Albania's economy would expand by 5 percent in 2007. The World Bank, a United Nations affiliate, reported that about 20 percent of Albanians were living on less than $2 per day in 2007.   ■ Sharon L. Wolchik

See also **Europe.**

Alberta. See **Canadian provinces.**

Algeria suffered through a wave of terrorist attacks in 2007 for which Islamist militants called al-Qa`ida in the Islamic Maghreb claimed responsibility. On April 11, three suicide bombings near Algiers, the capital, killed 33 people. On September 8, approximately 30 people died when a van packed with explosives blew up at a coast guard barracks east of Algiers. Two days earlier, a suicide bomber detonated explosives at al-Atik mosque in Batna, killing at least 20 people. On December 11, two bombings in Algiers killed about 40 people, including 17 United Nations employees.

The All Africa Games were held in Algiers from July 11 through July 23. The opening ceremony included a parade of all 52 African delegations participating in the multisport event.

In May, President Nicolas Sarkozy of France visited Algerian President Abdelaziz Bouteflika to discuss the French proposal for a Mediterranean Union, a regional association of countries cooperating in trade, security, and other matters. The presidents also discussed the creation of an Algerian-French university in Algeria. Algerian officials signed agreements in 2007 with the United States and Russia regarding development of civilian nuclear technology.   ■ Mary-Jane Deeb

See also **Africa; France; Terrorism.**

Andorra. See **Europe.**
Angola. See **Africa.**

Anthropology. The first human ancestors to migrate from Africa may have been more primitive than scientists had believed, according to a study reported by an international team of scientists in the Sept. 20, 2007, issue of *Nature.* The fossils, found by the team at Dmanisi, a site in the country of Georgia, display a surprising combination of modern and primitive features. The fossils are dated to about 1.8 million years ago, making them the oldest known *hominid* (human ancestor) fossils found outside Africa. The fossils consist of the partial skeleton, including the skull, of an adolescent and the *postcranial* (bones other than the skull) remains of three adults.

The fossils have humanlike spines as well as long legs and feet with well-developed arches, features that would have enabled them to walk long distances. However, these hominids also had relatively small brains and more apelike hands and shoulders, similar to those of *Homo habilis,* an early hominid species that lived in Africa from about 2 million to about 1.4 million years ago.

Famous fossil on exhibit. The fossil remains of a prehuman ancestor nicknamed "Lucy" began a six-year tour of museums in the United States in August 2007. The female specimen was the star of the exhibit titled *Lucy's Legacy: The Hidden Treasures of Ethiopia,* which opened at the Houston Museum of Natural Science and was to travel to 10 other cities. Unearthed in 1974 at Hadar, Ethiopia, Lucy is assigned to the early hominid species *Australopithecus afarensis.* Dating from 3.2 million years ago, she is the most complete fossil of an early prehuman ancestor known.

For decades, Lucy had been stored at the National Museum of Ethiopia in Addis Ababa. Ethiopian officials, who arranged the tour to raise much-needed funds for the museum and encourage tourism, deemed the fossil travel worthy. However, the decision to display such a rare and fragile fossil generated controversy. Many scientists worried that this important fossil might be lost or damaged during the tour. Others maintained that it was important for people to see the actual fossil rather than the replicas that are often displayed in museums. They argued that the Lucy exhibit would help inspire a new generation of scientists.

Fossil gorillalike ape found. Nine fossil teeth found in the Afar region of Ethiopia may represent the beginnings of an evolutionary lineage that led to modern gorillas. The 10-million-year-old fossil teeth were assigned to a new species, *Chororapithecus abyssinicus,* by Gen Suwa of the University of Tokyo Museum in Japan and colleagues in an announcement in the Aug. 23, 2007, issue of *Nature.* The gorilla-sized molars have distinct ridges, or *shearing crests,* to accommodate a fibrous vegetarian diet, much like that of modern gorillas but with thicker dental enamel. Scientists are not certain that *C. abyssinicus* gave rise to modern gorillas. But the fossils support the widely held view that the lineage leading to today's gorillas had already branched off from more ancient apes well over 10 million years ago.

Wrist bones point to new species. Analysis of three fossil wrist bones published in September in the journal *Science* by a team led by Matt Tocheri of the Smithsonian Institution, Washington, D.C., confirmed the assertion that the diminutive fossil hominid found in Flores, Indonesia, in 2004 is a distinct species of human. The *Homo floresiensis* skeletal remains, nicknamed "the hobbit," dating to 18,000 years ago, were considered by some to be a modern human being suffering from a pathology or growth defect.

The wrist bones, however, are more like those of gorillas and chimpanzees and differ distinctively from those of Neandertals and modern human beings. The implication is that the Flores hominids evolved from ancestors prior to the appearance of the modern human wrist. Scholars have suggested that the ancestor to this species became isolated on Flores and underwent a process called island dwarfing.   ■ Donald C. Johanson

Antigua and Barbuda. See **Latin America; West Indies.**

Archaeology. The government of Spain was at loggerheads throughout much of 2007 with Odyssey Marine Exploration over ownership of 17 tons (15.5 metric tons) of silver and gold coins and other artifacts recovered from a shipwreck somewhere in the Atlantic Ocean. Odyssey, a private deep-ocean shipwreck exploration firm based in Tampa, Florida, claimed that the treasure, worth over $500 million, was recovered legally in May from a shipwreck in international waters. However, Odyssey's owners refused to say precisely where the wreck was located or what evidence they had concerning the ship's identity to protect the artifacts that remained with the wreck. Spanish officials, suspecting that the wreck might be of a colonial-era Spanish vessel, claimed that if the vessel was Spanish, any treasure recovered belonged to Spain. Spanish officials boarded and searched two Odyssey-owned ships in July and October, but the company had already sent the treasure to the United States. Spain then filed claims in a U.S. federal court over the treasure.

Archaeologists and private salvage companies have often been at odds. Archaeologists prefer to excavate remains slowly, conserve and study any finds, and publish results of their work—a long and costly process—in addition to the expense of housing the artifacts in a museum. By contrast, companies that salvage shipwrecks usually try to make

money by selling whatever valuable artifacts they find. Such firms typically get to keep any treasure recovered from wrecks in international waters. Ships owned by countries, such as naval vessels, are an exception. These remain property of their respective governments, which explains Spain's interest in the Odyssey case.

Ancient observatory. Archaeologists identified a row of 13 ancient stone towers along the crest of a hill at Chankillo, north of Lima, Peru, as the earliest solar observatory in the Americas. Archaeologists Iván Ghezzi of the Pontifical Catholic University in Lima and Clive Ruggles of the University of Leicester in the United Kingdom described the observatory in the March 2, 2007, issue of the journal *Science*. The towers, from 6 to 20 feet (2 to 6 meters) tall, were built about 2,300 years ago. From observation points to the east and west, viewers could mark the progression of the sun over the year through gaps between the towers. The researchers concluded that the towers were designed to help fix the time of sunrise and sunset. The sun appeared in gaps at either end of the row on the winter and summer solstices.

Chankillo was built as part of a major religious complex by Andean peoples hundreds of years before the rise of the Inca civilization in the 1300's. Archaeologists noted that the structure proves that the people had a detailed knowledge of astronomy long before the development of more complex societies.

Polynesian travelers. A study of genetic material from modern and ancient hogs published in March 2007 challenged established ideas about the first people to colonize Pacific islands and the migration routes they used. According to one pop-

The discovery of the remains of what may have been a village for the workers who erected Stonehenge (left) beginning around 2600 B.C. on the Salisbury Plain in southwestern England was announced in February 2007. At Durrington Walls, about 2 miles (3 kilometers) from the stone monoliths, archaeologists found the outlines of at least eight small houses (below). Each house had a hard clay floor and a sunken central fireplace. Tools, jewelry, pottery, and human and animal bones were also found. Archaeologists believe the houses were part of a larger settlement for hundreds of workers.

ular theory, people originally from Taiwan moved down the Southeast Asia mainland more than 3,500 years ago, then sailed to New Guinea and later to the islands of Polynesia. Geneticist Greger Larson of Durham University, United Kingdom, and his colleagues examined DNA obtained from nearly 800 modern and ancient hog specimens from various locations across the Pacific and reached a different conclusion. Their results suggest that people came from southern China to Taiwan, the Philippines, and western Pacific Islands, taking domestic hogs with them. Another type of hog, however, spread along a more southern route, out of Vietnam, at an earlier date and is now found primarily in the eastern Pacific. The researchers concluded that the colonization of the Pacific Islands was more complex than scholars had thought.

Another DNA study, published in June, presented evidence that ancient Polynesians reached South America long before European explorers. When Spaniards first arrived in Peru in the early 1500's, they observed that the local Inca people had domestic chickens. How these Old World birds were introduced to South America before Spanish contact has been a mystery to historians. Alice Storey of the University of Auckland, New Zealand, compared DNA from chicken bones found at a Peruvian site dated to about A.D.1424 with DNA of ancient and modern chickens in Poly-

nesia. The ancient Peruvian DNA matched that from prehistoric sites and modern chickens in Tonga and Samoa, indicating Polynesian travelers landed in South America before the Spanish.

Earliest chocolate. Excavations at Puerto Escondido, a village in northern Honduras, by archaeologists John Henderson of Cornell University in Ithaca, New York, and Rosemary Joyce of the University of California at Berkeley recovered pottery fragments that resembled vessels used much later in Mesoamerica to serve beverages made with chocolate. Chemical analysis of residues in several of the pots revealed traces of *theobromine,* a substance found in cacao pods, the source of chocolate. The discovery pushed the earliest date of chocolate consumption in the Americas to at least 1100 B.C., about 500 years earlier than archaeologists had previously thought. ■ Mark Rose

See also **Anthropology.**

Replicas of the ships that carried the first English colonists to Virginia in 1607 sail in celebration of the 400th commemoration of the founding of Jamestown, the first permanent English settlement in North America.

Queen Elizabeth II of the United Kingdom (inset above), whose ancestor James I authorized the expedition to the New World, mingles with Chief Stephen R. Adkins of the native Virginian Chickahominy Tribe during anniversary celebrations. His ancestors provided crucial aid to the English settlers.

A nearly 500-year-old token commemorating Queen Elizabeth I (left) is one of more than 1 million artifacts found during archaeological excavations at Jamestown.

Rediscovering Jamestown on its 400th Anniversary

By Barbara A. Mayes

The commemoration and celebrations marking the 400th anniversary of the founding of Jamestown, the first permanent English settlement in North America, wound through much of 2007. A replica of one of the ships that carried the settlers to their new world retraced their historic voyage up the James River. An international conference on the future of democracy honored the 1619 establishment, in Jamestown, of the first representative legislative body in the American Colonies. A Native American festival focused on the culture of native people before and after Europeans began claiming Indian territory in Virginia. Scholars and community leaders discussed the African American imprint on America in the years since a group of Africans captured from a slaving ship were sold or traded for supplies in Jamestown in 1619. Special concerts were presented as well as magnificent fireworks and an opera about Pocahontas commissioned for the 400th anniversary.

Celebrations honoring the establishment of Jamestown have been held regularly in Virginia since 1807. The 2007 commemoration, however, offered visitors to the settlement a more personal way of connecting with its first residents. On the northwestern end of the island, in a new facility called the Archaearium, visitors examined thousands of artifacts recovered from James Fort, built on the site where the settlers disembarked on May 14, 1607 (May 24 on the modern calendar). For more than 200 years, archaeologists believed that James Fort had fallen into the James River in

A 1612 map by Captain John Smith shows the area of eastern Virginia controlled by the powerful Indian chief Wahunsonacock, commonly known then and now as Powhatan. Depicted in the upper left corner of the map, Powhatan led a confederation of more than 30 tribes with a total population of about 15,000 people in a region the Indians called *Tsenacomacah*.

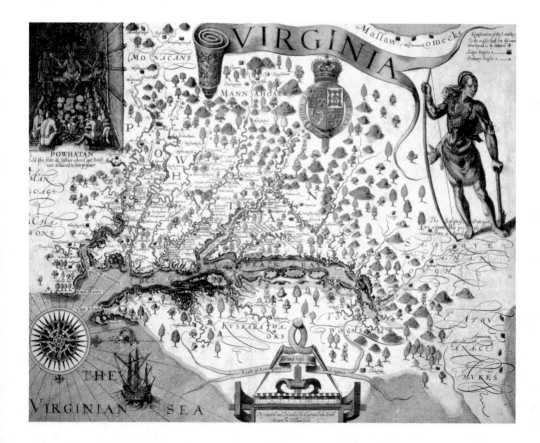

the 1700's, as the land on which it sat was washed away by fast-moving currents. The discovery of the fort's remains has been called one of the most significant archaeological discoveries of the second half of the 1900's.

The settlers finished building James Fort on June 15, 1607 (June 5), only 19 days after an estimated 200 Indian warriors attacked their camp. The fort walls, which formed a triangle, consisted of *palisades* (logs set upright side by side), which were probably 11 to 15 feet (3.4 to 4.6 meters) tall and weighed about 800 pounds (363 kilograms) each. In early 1608, fire severely damaged or destroyed the fort, which was replaced by what was probably a five-sided fortification. The second fort quickly fell into decay, however, and by 1624, when King James I made Virginia a royal colony, most, if not all, traces of it had disappeared above ground.

Although archaeologists have been digging at Jamestown since the late 1880's, excavations had offered only vague hints that any remains of the original fort still existed. In 1994, archaeologist William M. Kelso, who had become intrigued with James Fort 30 years earlier, volunteered to head up a search for the fort sponsored by the Association for the Preservation of Virginia Antiquities. The project involved digging on the northwestern edge of Jamestown Island on land that the nonprofit organization had purchased in 1893. Almost immediately, Kelso and his team found artifacts dating from the early 1600's. Within weeks, they found the remains of a palisade wall. In fall 1996, they found the remains of what appeared to be a corner watchtower. By 2005, Kelso had found the last piece of evidence he needed to establish the precise location and dimensions of the fort.

Kelso's excavations of James Fort also uncovered the remains of a number of buildings—as well as those of about 100 settlers—and more than 1 million artifacts. The findings offer a stunningly personal view of the settlement where, Kelso has said, "the American dream began in earnest." In his 2006 book, *Jamestown, the Buried Truth*, Kelso writes, "Perhaps even more than the documentary, architectural, and skeletal evidence the colonists left behind, these artifacts enable us to trace a process that began the transformation of Englishmen into Americans."

Captain John Smith, an English soldier and early leader of Jamestown, helped ensure the colony's survival by ordering settlers to "work or starve." Pocahontas, the favorite daughter of Chief Powhatan, strove to maintain friendly relations between her people and the settlers. A friend of Smith's, Pocahontas married John Rolfe, a prominent Jamestown colonist, and traveled to England, where she died.

The author:
Barbara A. Mayes is the Managing Editor of *The World Book Year Book.*

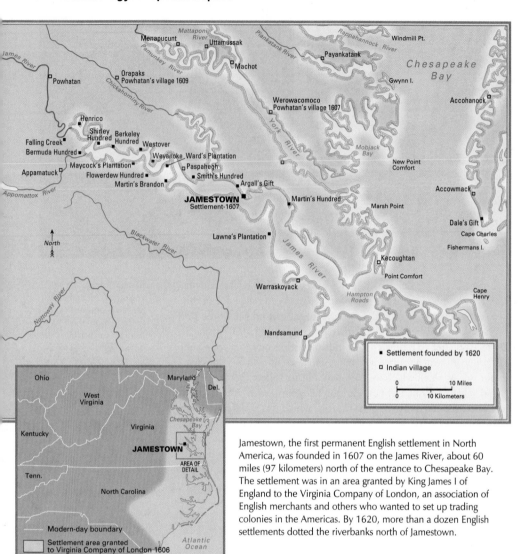

Jamestown, the first permanent English settlement in North America, was founded in 1607 on the James River, about 60 miles (97 kilometers) north of the entrance to Chesapeake Bay. The settlement was in an area granted by King James I of England to the Virginia Company of London, an association of English merchants and others who wanted to set up trading colonies in the Americas. By 1620, more than a dozen English settlements dotted the riverbanks north of Jamestown.

JAMESTOWN TIME CAPSULE

Some of the artifacts recovered from a well at James Fort appear in a three-dimensional representation (opposite) at the Archaearium, a new exhibition facility at Historic Jamestowne. The artifacts, which were preserved by the water-logged deposits in which they lay, are positioned at the level where archaeologists found them.

The style of the objects and the layers in which they were found helped archaeologists to date the construction of the well to about 1610. They also determined that the well had been abandoned as a water source and used as a trash dump in the early 1620's, as the fort fell into permanent decay. Objects found in the well

included coins, tools, drinking vessels, pitchers, and pipes. Some of these objects apparently fell into the well as people were drawing water.

The most surprising discovery was a nearly complete suit of armor, including a breastplate and helmet. Archaeologists speculated that the armor may have been discarded in favor of protection that was more comfortable in Virginia's warm climate. The armor might also have been thrown away during an eight-year period of peace shattered in 1622, when Indian attacks on settlements along the James River killed about one-fourth of the European colonists.

REDISCOVERING JAMES FORT

A reconstruction of the second James Fort (above)—which was built in 1608 after fire destroyed the original fort—is superimposed on a photograph of the settlement's site on Jamestown Island. Excavations have revealed the remains of the 1607 triangular *palisade* (log) wall that protected the fort as well as the foundations of several buildings, including possible rowhouses (left side of triangle), a barracks (right corner of triangle), and a building now known as "the factory" (along wall, far right). (Ghosted images, including riverside buildings, represent structures described in historical documents but not yet confirmed by excavations.) Circular *bulwarks* (guard towers) fortified with cannons sat at the corners of the palisade wall. The 1996 discovery of a curved trench (below) that outlined part of a bulwark helped confirm that James Fort had not been washed away by the James River.

An archaeologist (left) uncovers the remains of a line of palisades that protected James Fort. As the wooden palisades decayed, they left stains in the soil that retained the shape of the logs. A pipe, bead, and other artifacts found in the clay packed around the base of the palisades for support helped archaeologists date the posts to the time of Jamestown's founding.

Holes (above) mark the location of palisades used to attach the walls of "the factory" to the fort's fence. Probably used as a trading post and for storage, the building had three rooms, including a cellar (foreground) that may have served as a prison. Two archaeologists (rear in photo) stand near one of the brick hearths found in the "workshop," possibly a room for working metal.

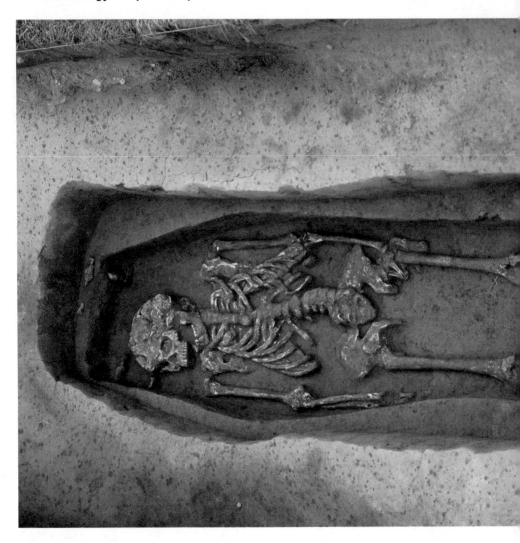

DEATH IN JAMESTOWN

A fairly well-preserved skeleton found in 1996 during excavations of the fort's palisade walls are the remains of one of the first colonists to die in Jamestown. The bones belonged to a European man who stood about 5 feet 9 inches (175 centimeters) tall and who died while in his late teens or early 20's. Artifacts dating from around 1607 found in soil covering the grave were among the clues that led archaeologists to conclude that the man had died only months after his arrival in Jamestown.

The stained soil around the skeleton marks the decayed remains of a coffin. The man's burial in a coffin and evidence from his bones of only moderate muscle development suggest that he was one of the "gentlemen" in the expedition who did not intend to work.

The discovery of a lead musket ball and pieces of lead shot just below the man's right knee testified to his violent end. The bullets shattered the lower bones of his leg, probably severing an artery and causing him to quickly bleed to death.

The events surrounding the man's death remain a mystery. The bullets suggest that he was probably shot by another colonist, as the Indians initially had only limited access to guns. He may have been killed accidentally during a skirmish or during one of the colonists' regular military drills. He may also have been a victim of the tensions that roiled the colony during the summer and fall of 1607, as disease, periodic Indian attacks, bad drinking water, and poor diet killed off nearly two-thirds of the colonists. Because the grave had no tombstone or other marker, the man's identity is uncertain.

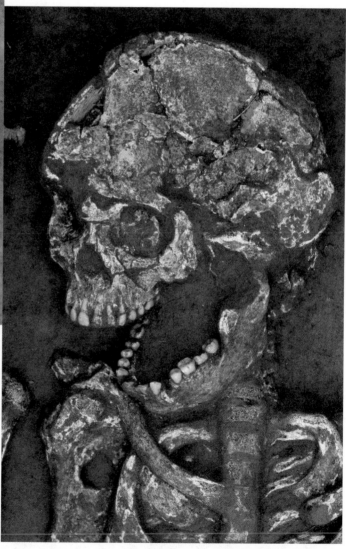

Artifacts recovered from colonial Jamestown include numerous pieces of European-made pottery. The most common type of this pottery found in deposits dating from the Fort James period are drug jars. They contained medicine and salves for use by the *apothecaries* (pharmacists), physicians, and *chirurgeons* (surgeons) sent by the Virginia Company to treat the colonists' illnesses and wounds.

Clay pipe bowls and pieces of pipestems are among the most common artifacts excavated in Jamestown. A pipemaker joined the colony in 1608, and clay pipes became one of the colony's first commercial products. At first, pipe bowls were small because tobacco was scarce, expensive, and strong. Over time, however, the sizes and style of the pipe bowls changed, giving modern archaeologists a way to date the pipes.

An Indian clay pot, digitally reconstructed from fragments found in deposits dating from 1607 to 1611, symbolizes the close relationship between the Jamestown settlers and the Native Americans during the settlement's early years. Fragments of Indian pottery make up about half of the artifacts found from this period. Although the two groups fought frequently, corn, meat, and other foods traded by the Indians for metal tools and pots often made the difference between survival and starvation for the colonists.

Architecture. The scientific community, the Swedish Academy, and the oil industry gave green architecture a big boost in 2007. The Intergovernmental Panel on Climate Change, a United Nations committee, issued a final report firmly connecting carbon emissions with global warming and warning of rising seas, poisonous air, and the widespread destruction of plant and animal life. The panel shared the 2007 Nobel Peace Prize with former United States Vice President Al Gore, whose Academy Award-winning documentary *An Inconvenient Truth* dramatically raised public awareness of the consequences of global warming. As though on cue, crude oil prices raced toward $100 a barrel, making energy conservation an economic necessity rather than just a hot topic.

Renzo Piano's *New York Times* headquarters was the most publicized "green building" opening in 2007. The facade of this tailored, 52-story skyscraper is wrapped in a sunscreen of ceramic rods that reduces heat absorption while allowing sunlight to penetrate the interior's core. A sophisticated underfloor air system gives employees temperature control at their workstations as they enjoy spectacular views of the city. The lobby, open to the public, features a manicured garden of grass and birch trees—a vision of pastoral calm in the heart of New York City.

Another significant office building opened in 2007 just south of the *Times* headquarters, in the city's Chelsea neighborhood. In Frank Gehry's headquarters for Barry Diller's InterActiveCorporation (IAC), glass curves and flows like a melting iceberg, with corners eroding and facades appearing to slump toward the sidewalk. Unlike the *Times* tower, the IAC building makes few concessions to the street and neighborhood. Its interior spaces are as blandly matter-of-fact as those of almost any 1960's office building. However, from

from above by five rectangular glass "lenses" that tumble across the landscape like a string of magic lanterns. The addition actually enhances the original, a rarity in architecture.

CoopHimmelb(l)au arranged a different marriage between classical and contemporary forms at the Akron (Ohio) Museum of Art. To a Renaissance-revival box, the Viennese architects attached floating and slashing planes of aluminum and glass to create a dramatic lobby. A grand staircase leads to galleries on the second floor. The effect is that of a dour maiden aunt succumbing to an extreme makeover. Although the bland second-level galleries somewhat undercut this effect, the renovation nevertheless puts Akron on the cultural map.

The new building at the Spertus Institute of Jewish Studies, by Krueck & Sexton Architects, is a laser-cut diamond in the middle of Chicago's historic and largely masonry South Michigan Avenue. The facade is a 10-story faceted curtain wall assembled, like a gigantic mosaic, from more than 700 pieces of glass. Behind it are an auditorium, exhibition space, library, theater, and one of the city's best views of Grant Park.

Awards. The American Institute of Architects awarded its 2007 Gold Medal posthumously to Edward Larrabee Barnes, a leading modernist known for refined, understated houses and museums. He made his name with the Haystack Mountain School of Crafts on Deer Isle, Maine, a village of simple shingled studios that stairstep down a granite ledge to the sea. He designed major museums, including the Walker Art Center in Minneapolis and the Dallas Museum of Art. Barnes also designed such high-profile corporate towers as Manhattan's IBM and Equitable headquarters, which many critics dismissed as stiff and heavy-handed compared with his earlier work.

The 2007 Pritzker Prize, the profession's most prestigious honor, went to British architect Richard Rogers, who in the 1970's collaborated with Renzo Piano on the freewheeling, inside-out Centre Pompidou in Paris. A museum, town square, and cultural playground rolled into one, the Pompidou launched Rogers as a master of high-tech and energy-efficient architectural machines. These included the Lloyd's of London headquarters and the European Court of Human Rights in Strasbourg, France.

The Aga Khan Awards, given every three years to projects in the Islamic world, were announced in September 2007. In keeping with the program's goal of preserving and celebrating traditional Islamic design, a majority of the awards went to restoration and community projects, including the rehabilitation of the Yemen city of Shibam, a market in Burkina Faso, and a rural school in Bangladesh.   ■ David Dillon

certain angles and at certain times of day, they become hypnotic pieces of architectural sculpture.

The National Portrait Gallery in Washington, D.C., reopened in 2007 with a stunning glass-roofed courtyard by London-based Foster and Partners, headed by renowned architect Norman Foster. Similar in concept, but subtler in execution than his celebrated Great Court at the British Museum, the canopy floats like a cloud on slender aluminum columns, never touching the building. In addition to creating a sparkling indoor space, the courtyard transforms a rather neglected institution into a cultural destination.

The Midwest. Intriguing buildings were completed in 2007 in the Midwest, most notably Steven Holl's masterful expansion of the Nelson-Atkins Museum of Art in Kansas City, Missouri. Instead of an aboveground addition that would have obscured much of the original Beaux-Arts building, Holl designed a series of subterranean galleries to house contemporary and African art and photography. These rooms are illuminated

Two residents of Buenos Aires, who are called *porteños* (port dwellers), use their cell phone camera to record a rare snowstorm on July 9, 2007. Much of Argentina suffered under a record-breaking temperature of –8 °F (–22 °C).

Argentina. On Dec. 10, 2007, Cristina Fernández de Kirchner, 54, of the incumbent Justicialist (Peronist) Party, was sworn in for a four-year term as president. Following a landslide victory, she succeeded her husband, Néstor Carlos Kirchner, who became Argentina's first "first gentleman." An experienced politician in her own right, Fernández de Kirchner had served as a senator for the province of Buenos Aires since 2005 and, before that, as a senator and federal deputy for the province of Santa Cruz.

During her campaign, Fernández de Kirchner promised to continue the unorthodox policies of her husband, who was credited with having engineered an amazing economic recovery following the worst recession in Argentine history. In doing so, Kirchner had managed to refinance Argentina's foreign debts without help from the International Monetary Fund (IMF), whose conditions for assistance, he argued, would have prolonged the economic crisis. The IMF is a United Nations agency that provides short-term credit to member nations.

Contrary to conventional wisdom, Néstor Kirchner also had embarked on public-works projects aimed at reducing record unemployment and imposed price controls on such necessities as food and energy. By the end of June 2007, Argentina's unemployment rate had fallen to 8.5 percent, its lowest level in more than a decade.

"The change is only beginning," Cristina Fernández de Kirchner promised during her campaign, in a year during which Argentines appeared well satisfied with the Kirchners' leadership. The unofficial husband-and-wife team was affectionately known as "the penguins" because of their origins in southern Patagonia. Approaching her inauguration, Fernández de Kirchner stressed the importance of maintaining the "social pact" whereby government, business, and trade unions had worked together to tame inflation, maintain a trade surplus, and achieve a budget surplus. She called upon private businesses to accept smaller profit margins and upon unions to cap their wage demands as means to encourage investment in Argentina.

Venezuelan investment. In early August, Venezuelan President Hugo Chávez made an official visit to Buenos Aires and announced that his government would buy an additional $1 billion of Argentine bonds. This purchase would bring to nearly $5 billion Venezuela's investment in refinancing Argentina's total foreign debt during Néstor Kirchner's presidential term. To help alleviate Argentina's worsening energy shortage, President Chávez also agreed to help finance a new $400-million liquid natural gas conversion plant in Argentina. When completed, the plant would convert liquid natural gas supplied by Venezuela into a usable form of fuel.

Economy minister resigns. On July 17, Argentine economy minister Felisa Josefina Miceli resigned after more than $60,000 in cash was discovered in her private office bathroom during a routine check by fire inspectors. Following allegations that she had accepted bribes in connection with public-works projects, Miceli stepped down to save the government embarrassment. She claimed that she was innocent and said the money was a loan from her brother to purchase a house.

Ex-president arrested. In January, Argentine courts ordered the arrest of former President María Estela "Isabel" de Perón, who governed the country from 1974 to 1976. Perón was charged with involvement in the murders of hundreds of political dissidents by right-wing death squads during her time in office. Police officials in Spain, where Perón was living in exile, detained the former president at Argentina's request. The Argentine government wanted Perón and several members of her former administration *extradited* (handed over) to stand trial for human rights abuses committed while they were in office.

■ Nathan A. Haverstock

See also **Latin America; Venezuela.**

Armed forces.
The Iraq War continued to dominate United States political and military affairs in 2007, when it surpassed in length U.S. participation in World War II (1939-1945). Public frustration with the inability of Iraq's leaders to quell sectarian violence and create political stability fueled widespread opposition to continuing the war at current levels. As President George W. Bush argued that U.S. national interests required an indefinite American military presence in Iraq, the Democratic-controlled Congress attempted but failed to legislate withdrawal deadlines.

Troop surge. On Jan. 10, 2007, President Bush announced that he was sending five more combat brigades to Iraq in hopes of stabilizing a deteriorating security situation. In a televised address to the nation, President Bush conceded his Iraq strategy had been flawed but argued that U.S. homeland security dictated a more robust combat presence. "For the safety of our people, America must succeed in Iraq," he said.

The so-called "troop surge" was expanded from 21,500 to 30,000 in March. Most of the new combat forces were deployed around the capital, Baghdad. President Bush appealed to Congress to give the new commander, U.S. Army General David H. Petraeus, time to implement the strategy.

President Bush pledged that Petraeus and Ryan Crocker, U.S. ambassador to Iraq, would report to Congress in September on the status of the war. On September 10, General Petraeus told legislators that the surge had made enough progress that, barring a reversal, about 30,000 U.S. troops could be withdrawn from Iraq by summer 2008. The reduction would essentially remove the "surge" forces.

Analysts credited the surge with a decline in the rate of U.S. troop fatalities in late 2007. On Dec. 1, 2007, 169,000 U.S. troops were stationed in Iraq, and approximately 3,900 had died since the 2003 invasion.

Roadside attacks. By Dec. 1, 2007, more than 28,500 American troops had been wounded in Iraq, most by roadside bombs known as improvised explosive devices (IED's). In 2007, U.S. war planners rushed to get 15,000 heavily armored vehicles—Mine Resistant Ambush Protected Vehicles (MRAP's)—into the field. Secretary of Defense Robert Gates called deploying the MRAP's his highest priority.

Private security controversy. On September 16, private security contractors working for the Moyock, North Carolina-based Blackwater USA fired on Iraqi civilians on a busy Baghdad thoroughfare, killing 17 and wounding more than 20 others. Officials with Blackwater, which had a contract to protect U.S. Department of State officials in Iraq, claimed that their security agents were responding to an insurgent attack. Nearby witnesses, however, claimed that no shots had been fired from the street. In response to the incident, high-ranking officials in the Iraqi government demanded the expulsion of Blackwater, which had been awarded more than $1 billion in U.S. government contracts for security work in Iraq.

Days after the incident, Secretary Gates dispatched U.S. Department of Defense (DOD) investigators to Iraq to examine oversight of security contractors. According to DOD sources, some 7,300 private contractors provided security to U.S. officials in Iraq in 2007, though some press sources publicized much higher estimates. Representative Henry Waxman (D., California) called on Erik Prince, chairman of Blackwater, to testify before the House Oversight and Government Reform Committee. At the October 2 hearing, Prince stated that he believed, based on facts known to him at that time, that the Blackwater team had "acted appropriately."

In October, a Philadelphia-based law firm filed suit against Blackwater officials in the U.S. District Court in Washington, D.C., on behalf of the estates of several Iraqis killed in the incident and of one Iraqi who sustained serious injuries. The lawsuit requested $136 million in punitive and compensatory damages.

War costs. According to the Congressional Research Service (CRS), the combined costs of the Iraq and Afghanistan wars reached an estimated

$610 billion by May 2007. Based on projected troop levels, the CRS predicted that total spending on the wars could approach $1 trillion by 2009. In September 2007, a Congressional Budget Office report estimated that a long-range U.S. peace-keeping role in Iraq, similar to the U.S. presence in South Korea, would cost between $10 billion and $25 billion annually.

Afghanistan war. In 2007, military operations continued in Afghanistan, primarily under a NATO command structure, though the majority of forces deployed were U.S. troops. (NATO is a military alliance between the United States, the United Kingdom, Canada, and more than 20 other countries.) Early in the year, coalition offensive operations thwarted a planned spring offensive by militants supporting the fundamentalist Islamic Taliban, whose government was ousted in the initial 2001 U.S.-led invasion. The insurgents subsequently changed tactics, launching more suicide attacks against civilians. As casualties rose during 2007, Afghan President Hamid Karzai warned President Bush that support among Afghans for the international coalition could diminish.

In late 2007, about 26,000 U.S. troops were serving in Afghanistan under NATO command. By December 1, at least 465 U.S. soldiers had been killed in Afghanistan and nearly 1,800 had been wounded since the war began in 2001.

Walter Reed scandal. In February 2007, a series of articles in *The Washington Post* detailing the substandard care of seriously wounded soldiers at the Army's Walter Reed Medical Center in Washington, D.C., led to shakeups in the Army's civilian command chain. The investigative report described roach- and rat-infested living quarters at an annex used to house outpatients. It also revealed how injured veterans were kept in limbo for months awaiting clarification of their classification status.

On March 2, Secretary of the Army Francis J. Harvey resigned under pressure from Secretary Gates. The resignation followed Harvey's own dismissal the day before of Major General George Weightman, the commander of Walter Reed.

Secretary Gates appointed a DOD panel to investigate conditions at Walter Reed, and President Bush appointed a bipartisan civilian commission, headed by former Senator Bob Dole and Donna E. Shalala, former secretary of the U.S. Department of Health and Human Services, to recommend changes to the military's health care system for veterans. On April 11, the DOD panel issued a stinging indictment of the Walter Reed command. In July, the Dole/Shalala commission called for major reforms in the armed services' treatment of injured and disabled veterans.

Personnel strains. The intensity of operations in Iraq and Afghanistan produced serious strains

Mary McHugh mourns at the grave of her fiancé, Sergeant James Regan, in Arlington National Cemetery on Memorial Day, May 27, 2007. Regan, 26, was killed by a roadside bomb while on patrol in northern Iraq on February 9.

on soldiers and their families trying to cope with extended combat deployments. An Army report issued on August 16 disclosed that 99 active duty soldiers committed suicide in 2006. The report found a "significant relationship" between suicide attempts and number of days deployed in combat.

To help ease the load on active troops in Iraq, the DOD announced in October 2007 that an additional 18,000 members of the Army National Guard would be deployed in Iraq in summer 2008. Two of the Guard combat brigades would replace active Army units being rotated home. In late 2007, approximately 91,000 reserve and National Guard soldiers were on active duty, including many in Iraq and Afghanistan.

The Army began offering cash bonuses in September to encourage junior officers to remain in the service. With thousands of officers serving unprecedented third and fourth combat tours, the Army projected a shortfall of 3,000 through 2013. By October 2007, 6,000 captains had accepted a bonus and agreed to remain in the service.

During 2007, President Bush and Secretary Gates endorsed a five-year plan to expand active forces in the Army by 65,000 and in the Marine Corps by 27,000. The cost of the expansion was estimated at $10 billion per year through 2012, contingent upon congressional funding.

Defense budget. On Feb. 5, 2007, the DOD submitted its budget for fiscal year 2008, which began on Oct. 1, 2007. The request totaled $481.4 billion, an 11.3-percent increase over appropriations for fiscal 2007. The budget included a 20-percent increase in spending on weapons systems, to $101.7 billion. In November, Congress passed a $459.3-billion defense spending bill. The proposed level of defense spending was the largest since the military build-up begun by President Ronald Reagan in the early 1980's. An additional $195 billion was sought for global war on terror operations, primarily for the wars in Iraq and Afghanistan.

Weapons systems. In 2007, the DOD continued to develop a variety of weapons systems, including a joint strike fighter, new classes of nuclear aircraft carriers and destroyers, a new generation of armored fighting vehicles, a strategic bomber, and the littoral combat ship (LCS), a small, shallow-draft vessel capable of close-in warfare at high speed along enemy coastlines.

The LCS development program ran into trouble in 2007 as cost overruns approached 100 percent. In April, Secretary of the Navy Donald Winter canceled the construction of one of the four contracted ships when the defense contractor, Lockheed Martin Corporation of Bethesda, Maryland, refused to absorb the cost of the overruns.

On January 16, Navy officials announced that the next nuclear aircraft carrier, CVN-78, would be named for former President Gerald R. Ford, who had served as an officer on an aircraft carrier during World War II. Ford died on Dec. 26, 2006.

Nuclear glitch. Air Force officials announced on Oct. 19, 2007, that 70 personnel had been disciplined due to an incident in August in which a B-52 bomber flew from its base in North Dakota to Louisiana with six nuclear-tipped cruise missiles aboard. The nuclear warheads were beyond normal security procedures for 36 hours.

Command changes. Former Representative Pete Geren (D., Texas) succeeded Francis Harvey as secretary of the Army in March 2007 in the wake of the Walter Reed scandal. The Senate confirmed Geren on July 13. On October 1, Admiral Michael Mullen, who had been serving as chief of naval operations, became chairman of the Joint Chiefs of Staff, replacing Marine General Peter Pace. Admiral Gary Roughead became chief of naval operations on October 11. Admiral Edmund P. Giambastiani, Jr., retired as vice chairman of the Joint Chiefs and was replaced in October by Marine General James E. Cartwright, chief of the U.S. Strategic Command. General Peter J. Schoomaker retired as Army chief of staff and was succeeded by General George W. Casey, Jr.

■ Thomas M. DeFrank

See also **Afghanistan; Iraq; People in the news** (Robert Gates; David Petraeus); **United States, Government of the.**

Armenia. Prime Minister Serzh Sargsyan's ruling Republican Party of Armenia (HHK) retained power in May 12, 2007, parliamentary elections. President Robert Kocharian had appointed Sargsyan prime minister on April 4, after the death of former Prime Minister Andranik Margarian. The HHK won 64 of the 131 seats in the National Assembly. Its coalition partners, Prosperous Armenia and the Armenian Revolutionary Federation-Dashnaktsutiun, came in second and third, winning 25 and 16 seats, respectively. The three parties agreed on June 6 to form a new government. Opposition parties fared poorly in the election.

Although international observers from the Organization for Security and Co-operation in Europe (OSCE) criticized certain aspects of the polling, they found that the elections "were conducted largely in accordance with international standards." This represented a step forward for Armenian democracy, as OSCE observers had condemned previous elections as neither free nor fair.

Nagorno-Karabakh, a territory claimed by both Armenia and Azerbaijan, held presidential elections on July 19. Former National Security Service head Bako Sahakyan won with 85 percent of the vote. International organizations did not monitor the elections. ■ Juliet Johnson

See also **Asia.**

ANCIENT ART'S LONG WAY HOME

By Robert N. Knight

**MAJOR MUSEUMS THROUGHOUT THE WORLD ARE
RETHINKING THEIR ACQUISITION POLICIES AS
NATIONS RECLAIM THEIR CULTURAL HERITAGE.**

Antiquities that had languished in storerooms for decades grace the new Greek and Roman galleries at New York City's Metropolitan Museum of Art (above). The galleries, which opened to the public in April 2007, were the result of a 15-year, $220-million renovation of the museum's south wing. One of the treasures on display is a terra cotta bowl known as the Euphronios Krater (left), which the Italian government contends was stolen and then sold to the museum. The museum has agreed to return the bowl to Italy in January 2008.

In April 2007, New York City's Metropolitan Museum of Art (the Met) opened its renovated Greek and Roman galleries to critical and public acclaim—the culmination of a 15-year, $220-million restoration effort. The project transformed the heart of the museum's south wing, which had been converted to restaurant space in the 1950's, into an atrium evoking the Pantheon, Rome's greatest surviving temple from ancient times. Designed by the architectural firm Kevin Roche John Dinkeloo and Associates LLP, the new gallery space provides a fitting repository for the Met's 5,300-piece collection of classical art, much of which had languished for decades in the museum's basements.

Among the most spectacular of the Met antiquities is the Euphronios Krater—a decorated terra cotta ceremonial bowl for mixing wine and water, meticulously painted about 515 B.C. by the Greek artist Euphronios. Also highly prized is a 16-piece collection known as the Hellenistic silver or the Morgantina silver, for the ancient Greek settlement of Morgantina in eastern Sicily in which it was discovered.

These treasures, however, no longer belong to the Met. In February 2006, Met director Philippe de Montebello agreed to return the Euphronios Krater and the Hellenistic silver, along with several other

Italian Deputy Premier and Culture Minister Francesco Rutelli (right) greets Malcolm Rogers, director of Boston's Museum of Fine Arts (MFA), in Rome in September 2006. The MFA had just returned the second-century statue of Sabina, wife of the Roman Emperor Hadrian, in response to Italian claims that it had been looted from Hadrian's Villa near Tivoli and illegally sold to the museum. The MFA voluntarily returned 12 other disputed antiquities as well.

The author:
Robert N. Knight is a free-lance writer.

selected antiquities, to the Italian government. (Although Greek in origin, these antiquities had been unearthed at sites in Italy.) The Krater was to be returned in January 2008, after making its debut in the new Met galleries, and the Hellenistic silver was scheduled to return to Italy in 2010. The agreement included provisions for future loans to the Met on a regular basis.

A number of art museums in the United States have contended with ownership claims made by countries rich in archaeological treasures. Among such countries, Italy has led the way in efforts to identify allegedly looted art and artifacts and secure their repatriation, or return to the home country. Since mid-2006, Francesco Rutelli, Italy's minister of culture, has aggressively pursued this initiative.

In September 2006, Boston's Museum of Fine Arts (MFA) settled claims with Rutelli and returned 13 antiquities. Among them was a highly regarded statue of Sabina, wife of the Roman emperor Hadrian, who reigned from A.D. 117 to 138. Italian detective work indicated that the statue had been stolen sometime in the 1970's from Hadrian's Villa, the ruins of the emperor's summer retreat near Tivoli.

Visitors at the National Archaeology Museum in Athens in March 2007 view a rare Macedonian funerary wreath from the 300's B.C. The wreath, which Greek officials claim was illegally excavated and smuggled out of the country, had been purchased by the J. Paul Getty Museum in Los Angeles in 1993 for $1.1 million. After lengthy negotiations, the Getty returned the piece, as well as several others.

Collecting art in the 21st century

These developments underscored fundamental changes in the modern art world. The holdings of world-class art museums, such as Boston's MFA or New York City's Metropolitan, were built up through a gradual and often haphazard acquisition of art treasures donated by wealthy individuals or purchased by museum officials called curators. Before very recent times, art works were usually gratefully accepted into collections,

Mythological beasts called griffins attack a doe in an elaborate marble table support made in Italy during the 300's B.C. The artifact was one of 40 objects that the Getty Villa in Malibu, California, agreed to return to Italy in 2007.

no questions asked. Their *provenance* (record of ownership) was typically of little interest either to sellers or buyers. Provenance includes where an artwork originated—or was dug up—and the history of its transmittal to the present possessor.

In many world-class museums, significant holdings are essentially the fruits of *imperialism* (the policy of extending the rule of one country or empire over other nations). From the 1700's to the 1900's, agents of such powers as the British and French empires removed thousands of art treasures from various countries, including Greece and Egypt.

Such historical conditions have resulted in globally distributed world-class art collections with pedigrees that, by and large, do not bear scrutiny. Today's cultural and political sensitivities, magnified by the reach of the global media, pose tremendous challenges to the professionals who seek to acquire—or retain—artworks for their respective institutions.

The legal landscape

In 1970, the United Nations Educational, Scientific and Cultural Organization (UNESCO), an agency of the United Nations, crafted a *convention* (agreement) on the permissible transfer and sale of such cultural property as valuable artworks or artifacts. Fundamental to this convention is the idea that governments must approve any removal of antiquities or other cultural property from their countries. Most nations have joined the convention, some—including the United Kingdom and Switzerland—as recently as the early 2000's.

Rules established in the 1970 UNESCO convention and later treaties have led, in effect, to a 1970 dividing line in consideration of art and antiquities ownership. Items removed from a country of origin before 1970 are subjected to different ownership criteria than those removed in the post-1970 era. For these reasons, scrupulous collectors try to show clear and legal provenance of their acquisitions at least as far back as 1970.

In the United States, one of the largest collections of classical Greek and Roman antiquities is housed in the Getty Villa in Malibu, California, in a renovated and expanded facility that was reopened to the public in January 2006. The collection was begun in the 1930's by oil billionaire J. Paul Getty (1892–1976). It is currently maintained by the J. Paul Getty Trust, headquartered in Los Angeles. The Getty collection is at the forefront of international controversy over provenance and ownership of antiquities.

The 7 ½-foot (2.3-meter) statue of a Greek goddess usually considered to be Aphrodite will remain at the Getty Villa in Malibu until 2010, as part of an agreement between the Italian government and Getty officials. Italian authorities believe the statue was unearthed at Morgantina, in eastern Sicily, smuggled out of the country, and then sold to the Getty for $18 million in 1988.

At the forefront of the controversy

Since the early 2000's, controversies surrounding Getty acquisition of antiquities have embroiled the museum's officials, trustees, and donors in quarrels and legal entanglements with Greek and Italian authorities. In May 2005, Marion True, then curator of antiquities at the Getty Museum, was indicted in Rome on charges of criminal conspiracy to receive stolen goods. Italian prosecutors contended that True had knowingly purchased antiquities looted by illegal antiquities trafficking operations. True's indictment sent chills through the art world, as experts predicted that museum officials would refrain from expending scarce resources on items whose ownership might be questioned.

At issue in True's trial were some 40 artifacts allegedly stolen and smuggled out of Italy. One of the most valuable items is a rare, well-preserved 7 ½-foot (2.3-meter) statue of what is believed to be a Greek cult goddess, which was acquired by the Getty in 1988 at a cost of $18 million. Some experts believe the statue, usually identified as "perhaps the goddess Aphrodite," was unearthed in Sicily—possibly at Morgantina—and spirited out of the country by art smugglers.

As the True trial wore on in Rome, Getty officials entered into negotiations with Italian officials over disputed Getty holdings. In November 2006, Getty officials agreed to return 26 pieces to Italy but

A conservator at the British Museum in London examines the Rosetta Stone, a granite slab discovered in 1799 that enabled researchers to decode ancient Egyptian writings known as hieroglyphics. The head of Egypt's Supreme Council of Antiquities has demanded the return of the stone, as well as other iconic Egyptian artifacts.

at the same time declared the negotiations at an impasse. Not included in the group of 26 were the Aphrodite statue and other items specifically demanded by Italian Cultural Minister Rutelli. One such item was a Greek bronze statue of a young athlete dating to the 300's B.C. that the Getty contends was discovered in a shipwreck off the coast of Italy in international waters.

An additional agreement was signed in September 2007. Getty officials agreed to return 40 objects to Italy, including the 26 objects discussed in November 2006, as well as the Aphrodite. In return, Italy would allow the goddess to be displayed at the Getty Villa until 2010. Other important Italian cultural artifacts would also be made available to the Getty for loans and joint exhibitions. Italy agreed to drop its demand that the bronze youth be returned immediately, pending the result of an inquiry by an Italian court on how the statue was found and how it was taken out of Italy.

The Getty also had to contend with ownership claims by the government of Greece. Negotiations between Greek and Getty officials resulted in the return to Greece in March 2007 of an extremely rare gold *funerary wreath* (a crown of leaves and flowers that was believed to have been buried with its owner) and several items of lesser value.

Beyond the legalities

For decades, museum curators and others involved in art acquisition have acknowledged the legal strictures imposed by the UNESCO convention and other treaties on art ownership—even if such rules have occasionally been side-stepped or ignored. In the 21st century, however, world public opinion seems to be shifting toward more rigorous standards of art ownership.

Some of the world's most spectacular collections of classical antiquities repose in the great museums of Europe and North America. In recent years, Italy, Greece, and Egypt—all successor states to empires of the ancient world—have increasingly claimed ownership of precious antiquities taken from their soil before 1970. Many of these claims target the world's most prestigious museums, including the British Museum in London, the Louvre in Paris, and the Altes Museum (Old Museum) in Berlin. Ultimately, the issue of ownership rights comes

A bust of Egyptian Queen Nefertiti—which some critics consider one of the greatest works of art of the ancient world—remains on display at the Altes Museum in Berlin, despite calls by Zahi Hawass, secretary-general of Egypt's Supreme Council of Antiquities, for its return. The bust was discovered in 1912 and donated to the museum in 1920.

The Parthenon (top)—the most famous temple of ancient Greece—crowns the Acropolis, a hill overlooking Athens. In the early 1800's, Lord Elgin (above), the British ambassador to the Ottoman Empire, which ruled Greece at the time, removed statues and other decorative carvings from the Parthenon and sent them to England.

down to a single question: who has the right to possess items that, through twists and turns of history, have ended up where they are today?

Perhaps the greatest surviving material legacy of any ancient culture is that of Egypt. Since 2002, the interests of the modern Republic of Egypt in the repatriation of antiquities have been represented by Zahi Hawass, an archaeologist and the secretary-general of the government's Supreme Council of Antiquities. Most notably, at a meeting held at UNESCO in Paris in 2005, Hawass demanded repatriation of a spectacular group of some of the most famous and iconic of Egyptian antiquities. Among these are the bust of the ancient Egyptian Queen Nefertiti, held by the Altes Museum in Berlin; the Rosetta stone (which enabled researchers to decode ancient Egyptian writings known as hieroglyphics), held by the British Museum in London; and the Dendera Zodiac (a painted map of the heavens taken from the ceiling of an Egyptian temple by a French archaeologist in 1821), held by the Louvre in Paris. The removal of each of these three great treasures from Egypt considerably predates the 1970 UNESCO convention.

The case of the Parthenon treasures

Similarly, the Greek government has long demanded the return of the Parthenon sculptures—a group of statues and *friezes* (statuary carved into walls) also known as the Parthenon marbles. Bits and pieces of sculptures from the Parthenon can be found in nine museums in eight countries. However, a large portion of the sculptures—and the collection most actively pursued by the Greek government—is located in the British Museum, where it is known as the Elgin *(EHL gihn)* marbles.

The Elgin marbles were removed from the Acropolis—a hill in Athens that contained both ancient temples and military installations—between 1802 and 1804. At that time, Greece was under the control of the Ottoman Empire, the predecessor to modern Turkey. Lord Elgin, the British ambassador to the Ottoman Empire, claimed to have obtained permission from the Ottoman government to remove pieces of the Parthenon and other temples and ship them to England. He sold the sculptures to the British government in 1816. The government then presented them to the British Museum.

Lord Elgin's removal of the marbles may have been legal (the question remains in dispute). However, the Ottoman Empire was an occupying power, and in 1832, Greece became an internationally recognized independent nation. Subsequent Greek governments have insisted that they would never have agreed to part with the Parthenon treasures.

The case for repatriation of the Parthenon marbles to Greece has been highlighted by the construction of a new museum, scheduled to open to the public in early 2008. The Acropolis Museum features an

The British Museum in London displays a grouping of statues removed by Lord Elgin from the east pediment of the Parthenon. The figures are part of the collection known as the Elgin marbles. British officials continue to reject Greek demands that they be returned.

High school students in Athens encircle the Acropolis during a protest in January 2007. The students, as well as others in both Greece and the United Kingdom, demanded the return to Greece of the Elgin marbles, statues that once graced the Parthenon.

immense glass gallery designed to hold the entire array of Parthenon sculptures. The display will pointedly include gaps in places where the British Museum's Elgin marbles would be placed should they be returned to Greece.

Despite public support expressed in recent polls in both Greece and the United Kingdom for return of the sculptures, officials of the British Museum have rejected the idea of repatriation of the treasures. Meanwhile, officials of the British Museum and Greek authorities continue negotiations to find a middle ground that could involve mutual loans of some of the Parthenon artworks.

Moving toward consensus

The question of where the Parthenon treasures belong is, in fact, ethically complex. The pieces removed to the British Museum in the early 1800's are in far better condition than those left in place on the Acropolis. Vandalism, wear by the steady flow of sightseers, and atmospheric conditions have all taken their toll. Supporters of Greece's ownership rights counter that the new Acropolis Museum will provide state-of-the-art environmental conditions designed to preserve the treasures. In addition, the location of the museum at the base of the Acropolis will allow visitors to see the sculptures in the context for which they were created.

Another concern that arose in the summer of 2007 was the vulnerability of a collection that is concentrated in one place. The fires that swept across southern Greece in July and August reached as far as Athens and the ancient ruins of Olympia before they were contained. Some art experts contend that if the treasures of the

Parthenon remain scattered throughout the world as they are now, they will be in less danger of disappearing in a single tragic accident.

As professionals representing the world's great museums continue to negotiate with countries over possession of valuable art and cultural artifacts, one clear consensus has emerged: items that find their way into the legitimate art market through shadowy means should not be acquired. Museums across the world are implementing stricter guidelines for art acquisitions, requiring dealers to prove unambiguous provenance back to at least 1970. Accordingly, art and antiquities traders are taking greater responsibility for providing research on provenance. Karol Wight, who became curator of antiquities at the Getty in July 2007, has noted that auction houses now even publish extensive research data about provenance of items in their catalogs.

However, the larger question—that is, who has the right to possess objects representing or embodying a particular cultural heritage—will likely remain unanswered for some time to come. Agreement on this issue is greatly complicated by real-world considerations. In 1992, Islamic guerrillas and fundamentalist Islamic forces took control of Afghanistan's capital, Kabul. The fundamentalists sacked Afghanistan's national museum, one of the richest cultural repositories in the world with antiquities dating from the country's Alexandrian, Greek, Buddhist, Zoroastrian, and Muslim periods. What was not stolen was destroyed, and the museum was burned.

In similar fashion, looters ransacked the National Museum of Iraq in Baghdad after the fall of Saddam Hussein's regime in April 2003. Thieves made off with about 12,000 items, including 32 ancient objects that archaeologists described as "of extreme importance."

In early 2001, people around the world looked on, horrified and helpless, as agents of the Taliban, the radical Islamic movement that then ruled much of Afghanistan, blasted apart two colossal Buddha figures that the group considered to be "false idols." The figures had been hewn out of solid rock at least 1,500 years before.

Opponents of wholesale repatriation pointedly observed that Taliban-ruled Afghanistan was the successor state to the ancient kingdom that commissioned the sculpting of the Buddhas. The incident raised the question of whether a successor state has the right to destroy as well as possess its cultural heritage.

With no easy resolution to ownership conflicts, curators and other players in the world of art trade looked closely at the settlements that the New York Met and the Getty made with Italy in 2006 and 2007, respectively. In returning the Euphronios Krater and the Hellenistic silver, Met officials tacitly acknowledged curators' responsibility for ensuring that acquisitions be aboveboard, while obtaining special consideration for future sharing of the objects through generous loans. Getty officials reached a similar agreement with regard to the Aphrodite. Such a strategy, some experts judged, could be the key to resolving disputes over art ownership rights in the future.

ASIA

While most Asian nations quietly concentrated on expanding their economies in 2007, warfare worsened in Afghanistan and Sri Lanka, terrorist violence spread in Pakistan, and the military rulers of Myanmar put down demonstrations for democracy. Food shortages plagued Myanmar and North Korea; environmental problems worsened in a number of countries, including China; earthquakes shook Indonesia; and typhoons battered areas facing the Pacific Ocean.

Fighting intensified in Afghanistan between the Islamic radical Taliban and soldiers from the North Atlantic Treaty Organization supporting the Afghan government. Weapons similar to those used in Iraq and an increase in suicide bombings took a toll on the foreign forces while hindering reconstruction of the war-battered nation. Taliban and Qa`ida terrorist units organized attacks into Afghanistan from bases in Pakistan along the Afghan frontier that were beyond the Pakistani government's control. Pakistan's stability was increasingly threatened by terrorists based along its frontier.

The civil war in Sri Lanka built in intensity. In Myanmar, the generals who had ruined the nation's economy tightened their grip by killing and imprisoning those who challenged their rule.

Overall, however, Asia had a fairly peaceful year. Elections were held in a number of nations. The Communist dictatorships in China, North Korea, and Vietnam went through the motions of running parliamentary governments.

Natural disasters in Asia in 2007 included heavier-than-normal monsoon rains. The rains caused floods that were responsible for the deaths of more than 2,000 people in Bangladesh, India, and Nepal in July and August. The monsoon rains also caused flooding in China that left more than 700 people dead. The World Meteorological Organization, a United Nations (UN) affiliate, noted on August 7 that "monsoon extremes and incessant rains" in South Asia had destroyed "vast areas of croplands, livestock, and property." In addition, an estimated 30 million people were displaced.

A Category 4 cyclone called Sidr smashed into the southern coast of Bangladesh on November 15 with winds as high as 150 miles (240 kilometers) per hour. Despite mass evacuations, at least 3,100 people were killed as the storm leveled whole villages, displacing some 280,000 people and damaging recently harvested crops.

Regional organization. Many Asian nations worked in 2007 on economic and political cooperation. The oldest regional organization in Asia, the Association of Southeast Asian Nations (ASEAN), marked its 40th birthday on August 8. Its members are Brunei, Cambodia, Indonesia, Laos, Malaysia, Myanmar, the Philippines, Singapore, Thailand, and Vietnam.

Meeting in January, ASEAN agreed to establish a free-trade zone by 2015. Trade within ASEAN had grown 129 percent from 2000 through 2006, but member nations still conducted 75 percent of their trade with nonmembers. ASEAN representatives also met in January 2007 with Prime Minister Wen Jiabao of China. He agreed to allow members easier business access to such Chinese sectors as banking, engineering, transport, and construction.

The 21-nation Asia-Pacific Economic Cooperation group met in September and pledged to improve energy efficiency. They also adopted nonbinding targets to slow the growth of heat-trapping greenhouse-gas emissions.

Meeting in April, the South Asian Association for Regional Cooperation (SAARC), an eight-nation organization established in 1985, focused on an urgent need to move discussion to action. SAARC members had talked about improving ties in trade, infrastructure, technology, and other areas but had achieved little. Several SAARC members were wary of domination by India, which is larger than all the other nations combined.

Silk Road. Representatives from eight Asian nations agreed in September 2007 to establish rail and road links to revive the famed "Silk Road." From the 100's B.C. to the A.D. 1500's, trade between China and the Mediterranean passed along the Silk Road's camel, donkey, and mule routes. Afghanistan, Azerbaijan, China, Kazakhstan, Kyrgyzstan, Mongolia, Tajikistan, and Uzbekistan agreed to develop six trade corridors by 2018. Many international financial institutions, including the World Bank and the Asian Development Bank (ADB), both UN affiliates, backed the plan.

Rapid economic growth was on track to cut poverty by half in most Asian countries by 2015, according to a report issued by the ADB and UN agencies in September 2007. The report said goals of universal education and of educational equality for boys and girls were also achievable by 2015. However, the report noted slow progress on reducing child deaths, improving child nutrition and mothers' health, and providing safe drinking water and sanitation. Half of the 641 million people in Asia who live on less than $1 a day are in disaster-prone areas—many subject to flooding—or live in urban slums, the report said.

Another ADB study, issued in August 2007, reported that in most Asian nations, the gap be-

Pakistani tribesmen survey the remains of a 13-truck fuel convoy destroyed by pro-Taliban militants on June 28. The fuel was intended for NATO forces in Afghanistan. Security officials in 2007 warned that Taliban militants were expanding into Afghanistan from the border region with Pakistan.

tween rich and poor continued to widen. The greatest gap increases were in Bangladesh, Cambodia, China, Nepal, and Sri Lanka. In Indonesia, Malaysia, and Thailand, economic growth was more equally distributed.

Other studies showed that migrant labor from Asia's poorer, more stagnant nations was a key to economic growth in some richer, more productive countries. Some 2.6 million foreign workers helped power Malaysia's growth. Experts estimated that other Asian nations, including Japan, South Korea, Taiwan, and Thailand, hosted from several hundred thousand to several million migrant workers each.

Health. An epidemic of dengue that rivaled the worst outbreak on record, which hit in 1998, ravaged Southeast Asia in mid-2007. The mosquito-borne disease causes severe headaches plus muscle and joint pain that gives it the name "breakbone fever." One of the worst-hit nations was Indonesia with more than 123,000 cases and some 1,250 deaths. In Cambodia, some 38,500 people became sick, and nearly 400 people, mostly children, died. Malaysia, Thailand, and Vietnam also reported numerous cases.

Avian influenza (bird flu) made a deadly comeback among chickens and other fowl across East Asia from South Korea to Indonesia in early 2007, four years after it had first become a threat in the region. Margaret Chan, the head of the World Health Organization, a UN affiliate, noted on January 22 that it would take years to bring the disease under control. Since 2003, millions of birds had died, while millions more were killed in an effort to contain the disease. As of late 2007, at least 206 people in Asia had died from bird flu.

East Timor, also known as Timor-Leste, held two elections in 2007 that resulted in its president and prime minister swapping jobs. In the first, on April 9, Prime Minister José Ramos-Horta became president. Ramos-Horta was one recipient of the Nobel Peace Prize in 1996 for his role in the independence movement during Indonesia's occupation of the impoverished tropical island north of Australia from 1975 to 1999.

President Xanana Gusmão, the hero of guerrilla resistance to Indonesian rule, took the more powerful position of prime minister after elections on June 30, 2007, for the

FACTS IN BRIEF ON ASIAN COUNTRIES

Country	Population	Government	Monetary unit[†]	Foreign trade (million U.S.$)	
				Exports[††]	Imports[††]
Afghanistan	32,253,000	President Hamid Karzai	afghani (49.73 = $1)	471	3,870
Armenia	2,994,000	President Robert Kocharian; Prime Minister Serzh Sargsyan	dram (333.50 = $1)	1,056	1,684
Azerbaijan	8,607,000	President Ilham Aliyev; Prime Minister Artur Rasizade	manat new spot (0.85 = $1)	12,510	5,176
Bangladesh	150,060,000	Chief Adviser Fakhruddin Ahmed	taka (68.74 = $1)	11,170	13,770
Bhutan	718,000	King Jigme Khesar Namgyel Wangchuck; Prime Minister Lyonpo Kinzang Dorji	ngultrum (39.57 = $1)	186	410
Brunei	379,000	Sultan and Prime Minister Haji Hassanal Bolkiah	dollar (1.48 = $1)	6,247	1,481
Cambodia (Kampuchea)	14,656,000	King Norodom Sihamoni; Prime Minister Hun Sen	riel (4,052.50 = $1)	3,380	4,446
China	1,346,606,000	President Hu Jintao; Premier Wen Jiabao	yuan (7.50 = $1)	1,585,600	1,107,700 (includes Hong Kong)
East Timor	995,000	President José Ramos-Horta; Prime Minister Xanana Gusmão	U.S. dollar (1.00 = $1)	10	202
Georgia	4,421,000	President Nino Burdzhanadze (acting); Prime Minister Lado Gurgenidze	lari (1.65 = $1)	1,761	3,320
India	1,144,734,000	President Pratibha Patil; Prime Minister Manmohan Singh	rupee (39.48 = $1)	112,000	187,900
Indonesia	232,269,000	President Susilo Bambang Yudhoyono	rupiah (9,082.50 = $1)	102,300	77,730
Iran	72,048,000	Supreme Leader Ayatollah Ali Khamenei; President Mahmoud Ahmadinejad	rial (9,310.00 = $1)	63,180	45,480
Japan	127,994,000	Emperor Akihito; Prime Minister Yasuo Fukuda	yen (116.50 = $1)	590,300	524,100
Kazakhstan	15,367,000	President Nursultan A. Nazarbayev; Prime Minister Karim Masimov	tenge (121.00 = $1)	35,550	22,000
Korea, North	23,059,000	Chairman of National Defense Commission Kim Jong-il	won (2.20 = $1)	1,340	2,720
Korea, South	48,877,000	President Lee Myung-bak*; Prime Minister Han Duck-soo	won (916.55 = $1)	326,000	309,300
Kyrgyzstan	5,336,000	President Kurmanbek Bakiev Prime Minister Igor Chudinov	som (35.75 = $1)	702	1,177

*Due to take office on Feb. 25, 2008   [†]Exchange rates as of Oct. 4, 2007.   [††]Latest available data.

65-seat parliament. His personal political party won only 23 percent of the vote, while the left-wing Fretilin party won 29 percent. Other parties refused to cooperate with Fretilin, which had controlled the outgoing parliament. They accused Fretilin leaders of incompetence and corruption that had created chaos instead of promised stability and economic prosperity. When Gusmão formed a coalition government and was named prime minister by Ramos-Horta, Fretilin charged that the move was illegal. Its supporters rioted in Dili, the capital.

Voters in the Maldives on Aug. 18, 2007, agreed to establish a presidential form of government, according to official returns. Opponents of President Maumoon Abdul Gayoom, who had ruled since 1978, accused him of rigging the vote. They favored a British-style parliamentary system.

Bhutan held practice elections on April 21, 2007. The nation's 718,000 people were asked to choose among four dummy political parties to familiarize themselves with the voting process in preparation for real elections scheduled for June 2008, when Bhutan will become a multiparty par-

Country	Population	Government	Monetary unit[†]	Foreign trade (million U.S.$)	
				Exports[††]	Imports[††]
Laos	6,361,000	President Choummaly Sayasone; Prime Minister Bouasone Bouphavanh	kip (9,618.00 = $1)	982	1,376
Malaysia	27,526,000	Paramount Ruler Mizan Zainal Abidin, the Sultan of Terengganu; Prime Minister Abdullah bin Ahmad Badawi	ringgit (3.41 = $1)	158,700	127,300
Maldives	313,000	President Maumoon Abdul Gayoom	rufiyaa (12.80 = $1)	214	832
Mongolia	2,670,000	President Nambaryn Enkhbayar; Prime Minister Sanjaa Bayar	tugrik (1,181.70 = $1)	1,064	1,184
Myanmar (Burma)	51,988,000	Chairman of the State Peace and Development Council Than Shwe; Prime Minister Thein Sein	kyat (6.42 = $1)	3,560	1,980
Nepal	27,416,000	Prime Minister Girija Prasad Koirala	rupee (63.33 = $1)	822	2,000
Pakistan	167,947,000	President Pervez Musharraf; Interim Prime Minister Mohammedmian Soomro	rupee (60.74 = $1)	19,240	26,790
Philippines	89,681,000	President Gloria Macapagal-Arroyo	peso (44.73 = $1)	47,200	51,600
Russia	141,358,000	President Vladimir Putin; Prime Minister Viktor Zubkov	ruble (25.02 = $1)	317,600	171,500
Singapore	4,467,000	President Sellapan Rama Nathan; Prime Minister Lee Hsien Loong	dollar (1.48 = $1)	283,600	246,100
Sri Lanka	20,140,000	President Mahinda Rajapakse	rupee (113.45 = $1)	7,076	9,655
Taiwan	23,111,000	President Chen Shui-bian; Premier (President of the Executive Yuan) Chang Chun-hsiung	dollar (32.60 = $1)	215,000	205,300
Tajikistan	7,292,000	President Emomali Rahmon; Prime Minister Oqil Oqilov	somoni (3.44 = $1)	1,160	1,513
Thailand	65,591,000	King Bhumibol Adulyadej (Rama IX); Interim Prime Minister Surayud Chulanont	baht (31.63 = $1)	123,500	119,300
Turkmenistan	5,232,000	President Gurbanguly Berdimuhammedov	manat (5,200.00 = $1)	5,421	3,936
Uzbekistan	27,890,000	President Islam A. Karimov; Prime Minister Shavkat Mirziyayev	som (1,275.98 = $1)	5,510	3,990
Vietnam	87,009,000	Communist Party Secretary-General Nong Duc Manh; President Nguyen Minh Triet; Prime Minister Nguyen Tan Dung	dong (16,082.50 = $1)	39,920	39,160

liamentary democracy. Another practice election was held on May 28, 2007.

Laos. In May, the American embassy in Laos warned of fighting near the capital, Vientiane. Sporadic fighting had been reported since the Communists came to power at the end of the Vietnam War (1957-1975). Some of the conflict was reportedly continuing guerrilla resistance by the Hmong ethnic minority. Many anti-Communist Hmong had fought for the Americans during the war under the leadership of Vang Pao.

On June 4, 2007, Vang Pao and eight other Hmong were arrested in California and accused of plotting to overthrow the Laotian government. They were held on federal charges of conspiracy and violation of a law forbidding Americans from taking military action against a country with which the United States is at peace. The arrests came after a six-month undercover operation exposed the group's alleged efforts to buy $10 million worth of weapons. Vang was freed on bail on July 14.   ■ Henry S. Bradsher

See also **Disasters; Public health; Terrorism;** various Asian country articles.

Thousands of residents of South and East Asia died in 2007 in one of the most severe monsoon seasons on record.

A man attempts to climb a floodgate in southern China on June 9, 2007. Weeks of monsoon rains caused flash floods and landslides that led to more than 700 deaths in China alone.

Flooding along coastal areas of Pakistan leaves a mosque nearly submerged in June 2007 after a cyclone and torrential rain drenched the region. Some 800,000 Pakistanis were stranded by the flooding, which left at least 235 people dead.

Residents of Mumbai, India's financial capital, wade through city streets flooded by unusually heavy monsoon rains on Aug. 3, 2007.

Astronomy. Astronomers in 2007 discovered surprising information about Mercury and analyzed striking features on Saturn's moons. They also observed unusual planets outside the solar system and recorded a previously unknown phenomenon in the distant universe.

Mercury's molten core. Mercury, the closest planet to the sun, is not completely solid, as had long been thought. Instead, it has a *molten* (partially melted) core, like that of Earth. That was the conclusion announced in May by a team of scientists led by astronomer Jean-Luc Margot of Cornell University in Ithaca, New York. The researchers used two giant radio telescopes—the Robert C. Byrd Green Bank Telescope in West Virginia and the Arecibo Observatory in Puerto Rico—and radar antennas in California to bounce radio waves off Mercury's surface and record the returning "echoes." Analysis of the echo patterns allowed the team to identify miniscule wobbles in Mercury's rotation that could be explained only by the effects of a liquid core spinning at a different rate than that of the planet's solid shell.

The astronomers noted that the new finding offered an explanation for Mercury's magnetic field. They proposed that electric currents flowing inside the molten core are likely responsible for generating the weak magnetic field.

Secrets of Saturn's moons. Images from the Cassini spacecraft revealed details of two of Saturn's strange moons in 2007—Hyperion and Iapetus. Cassini, which has orbited Saturn since 2004, is a cooperative project of the National Aeronautics and Space Administration (NASA), the European Space Agency, and the Italian Space Agency.

The Cassini team reported in July 2007 that the bizarre spongelike appearance of Hyperion results from the low density of the moon, which is more like a pile of loose rubble than a solid body. Photographs taken by Cassini's cameras show that craters on Hyperion's surface are deep and steep-sided. When *meteoroids* (small rocky bodies from space) strike the surface, they form the deep craters by compressing the rubbly material, rather than blasting the material out and forming shallow craters (as happens on such denser bodies as Earth's moon).

Cassini's close-up photographs of Iapetus revealed why this moon has one white side and one black side. The Cassini team reported in September that the appearance of black spots in the transition region between the two sides suggests that the black material fell from space onto the surface of the moon—mostly on the leading side of the moon, the side facing the direction that Iapetus moves in its orbit around Saturn. The scientists speculated that Iapetus "scooped up" the black material, which may have come from another Saturnian moon that broke apart.

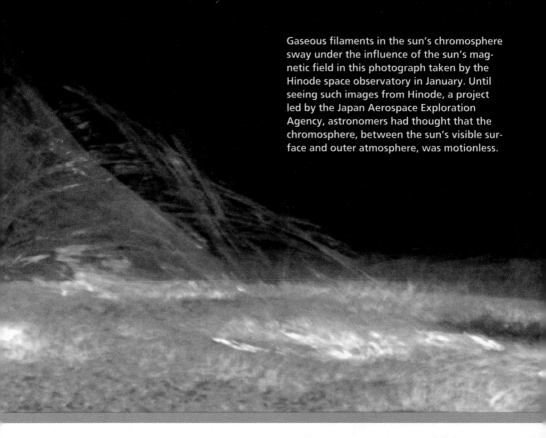

Gaseous filaments in the sun's chromosphere sway under the influence of the sun's magnetic field in this photograph taken by the Hinode space observatory in January. Until seeing such images from Hinode, a project led by the Japan Aerospace Exploration Agency, astronomers had thought that the chromosphere, between the sun's visible surface and outer atmosphere, was motionless.

Exciting extrasolar planets. Discoveries of the hottest, largest, most massive, and most Earth-like extrasolar planets (planets outside our solar system) were announced in 2007. To study extrasolar planets, astronomers use a variety of telescope-based techniques, including analyzing changes in a star's visible light and infrared light (heat) and measuring tiny wobbles in the star's motion as a planet moves around the star.

Astronomer Joseph Harrington of the University of Central Florida in Orlando reported finding the hottest extrasolar planet in May. He estimated that this planet, orbiting the star HD149026, has a surface temperature of approximately 3700 °F (2038 °C). In order to absorb that much heat from its host star, Harrington said, the planet must be blacker than charcoal.

The discovery of the largest known extrasolar planet was reported in August by an international team of astronomers led by Georgi Mandushev of Lowell Observatory in Flagstaff, Arizona. The scientists found that this planet, named TrES-4, consists of a large amount of gas, like Jupiter, but it is 1.7 times as great in size as Jupiter. In May, astronomers at the Harvard-Smithsonian Center for Astrophysics in Cambridge, Massachusetts, announced the discovery of the most massive known planet. This planet, named HAT-P-2b, is only slightly larger than Jupiter, but the investigators determined that it contains about eight times as much mass.

In April, a team of Swiss, French, and Portuguese astronomers reported discovering a planet that has the most Earthlike properties of any known extrasolar world. The researchers estimated that the planet is approximately 1.5 times as large as Earth and is cool enough to have liquid water (and thus, perhaps, life) on its surface. It orbits a red dwarf star, Gliese 581, that is only 20.5 light-years from our sun. A light-year, the distance light travels in one year, equals 5.88 trillion miles (9.46 trillion kilometers).

A new astronomical phenomenon was described in September by astronomers using the Parkes Observatory radio telescope in Australia. The scientists, led by Duncan Lorimer of West Virginia University in Morgantown, recorded a powerful burst of radio energy that lasted only 5 *milliseconds* (5/1,000 of a second) coming from an unknown source at least 3 billion light-years away. The researchers speculated that the energy may have been produced by the collision of two neutron stars (the smallest and densest type of star) or the disappearance of a black hole (a concentration of mass so dense that not even light can escape its gravity). ■ Laurence A. Marschall

See also **Space exploration.**

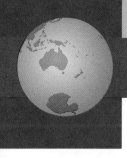

AUSTRALIA

Australians went to the polls on Nov. 24, 2007, and resoundingly rejected Prime Minister John Howard's conservative coalition of the National and Liberal parties, which had been in power since 1996. In its place, voters elected the Australian Labor Party (ALP), led by Kevin Rudd.

Campaign. Few issues divided the two parties. Early in the election campaign, the coalition announced a plan to cut taxes. Labor countered with a tax scheme that was almost identical. During the previous election, in 2004, Labor's stand against logging in Tasmania had cost it vital seats. In the 2007 election, both parties supported plans for a controversial pulp mill in Tasmania, which was bitterly opposed by Bob Brown, leader of the Australian Greens party.

The largest issue separating the two main parties was the coalition's industrial relations policy. It had proved unpopular with many voters because it introduced individual workplace contracts at the expense of general agreements negotiated by the trade unions. Apart from public servants, comparatively few Australians in 2007 belonged to trade unions. The coalition's advertising campaign emphasized the proportion of former trade union members among Labor's shadow Cabinet.

Election. The ALP won a substantial majority in the 150-seat House of Representatives. However, the party failed to gain control of Australia's upper house, the Senate, which is largely a house of review.

The election results came as no surprise, as public opinion polls throughout the year had shown the ALP leading the coalition and Rudd outpacing Howard. Most commentators put the result down to the feeling, particularly among younger voters, that it was time for a change of government after 11 years of Howard's coalition.

John Howard's long political career came to an end when he lost his seat in Parliament to ALP candidate Maxine McKew, a former Australian Broadcasting Corporation presenter. On November 25, Howard's deputy, Peter Costello, announced that he would not run for the leadership of the Liberal Party. On November 29, former Minister of Defense Brendan Nelson narrowly defeated former Environment Minister Malcolm Turnbull for the top Liberal position. Former Education Minister Julie Bishop became the Liberal Party's first female deputy leader.

Also on November 29, Rudd announced his Cabinet, which included seven women. His deputy, Julia Gillard, became the first woman to serve as deputy prime minister of Australia.

Economy. The coalition's loss came at a time when most Australians were enjoying a period of record prosperity, as China continued to buy iron ore, coal, and other mined goods from the country. The price of stock in Australia's mining giant BHP Billiton continued to rise in 2007 as a result of the demand for minerals. Its value was further enhanced by the announcement in September that its Olympic Dam site in South Australia might prove to be the world's largest gold mine. Unemployment dropped to a 33-year low of 4.2 percent of the work force in September.

The Coles Group, Australia's troubled second largest retail chain, attracted interest from several overseas investors in 2007. Eventually, Perth-based conglomerate Wesfarmers made a successful $20-billion takeover bid. (All amounts in Australian dollars.) Coles shareholders approved the takeover on November 7, and Wesfarmers officially took control of Coles on November 23.

Prices on the Australian Stock Exchange reached new heights during 2007. In February, the All Ordinaries Index, which represents the country's 500 leading companies, passed the 6,000 mark for the first time. On October 15, the Australian dollar passed the 90-U.S.-cents mark for the first time since 1984. On Oct. 29, 2007, the Australian dollar set a new high, at more than 92 U.S. cents.

The main negative economic figures stemmed mainly from Australia's continuing problems with its balance of trade as it imported more than it exported. Observers also expressed concern about inflation, which threatened to rise above 3 percent and trigger further rises in interest rates.

State and federal politics. On March 24, voters in New South Wales reelected the Labor government led by Premier Morris Iemma. On July 27, the Labor premier of Victoria, Steve Bracks, resigned, as did his deputy, John Thwaite. Bracks was replaced on July 30 by former Treasurer John Brumby. On September 10, Peter Beattie, Queensland's long-serving Labor premier, announced his retirement. His successor was his deputy, Anna Bligh, who was sworn in on September 13 and became the first woman to serve as premier of Queensland. Clare Martin, chief minister of the Northern Territory, resigned on November 26. She was replaced by former Education Minister Paul Henderson. Indigenous Minister Marion Scrymgour was elected as his deputy and became the first Aborigine to occupy such a high political post.

Federal-state relations were frequently

strained during 2007, with all state and territory governments in the hands of the ALP and the federal government controlled by the Liberal-National party coalition for most of the year. State and territory leaders met with Prime Minister Howard at the 19th Council of Australian Governments (COAG) meeting in Canberra, the national capital, on April 13. Despite political differences, the leaders were able to reach some agreement on a number of issues, including health, transport, and energy. The states took up the federal offer of funding for the treatment of diabetes on a national scale as well as a system of national regulation for doctors and other health professionals. In addition, they decided to overhaul prices for the use of road and rail freight.

However, at a similar meeting held on the same day in Darwin, in the Northern Territory, the state ministers rebuffed a proposal by federal Minister for Education Julie Bishop to introduce performance pay for teachers. Bishop's proposal called for better-performing teachers to receive higher pay. Opponents of the plan said that it would result in pay cuts for many teachers. The ministers at the Darwin meeting also rejected a plan to establish a national curriculum for key subjects but agreed to work for national standards of skills for teachers, headmasters, and students.

Climate change. Rudd's first act after being sworn in as prime minister on December 3 was to sign the Kyoto Protocol on climate change, an international agreement that Howard had resisted signing. The agreement is designed to decrease the rate at which greenhouse gases are released into the atmosphere. These gases trap heat near Earth's surface, contributing to global warming.

On March 31, more than 2 million Sydney

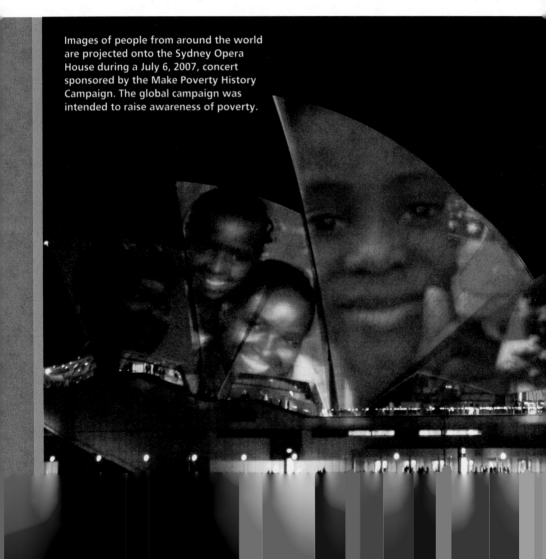

Images of people from around the world are projected onto the Sydney Opera House during a July 6, 2007, concert sponsored by the Make Poverty History Campaign. The global campaign was intended to raise awareness of poverty.

residents turned off their lights from 7:30 p.m. to 8:30 p.m. The event, known as Earth Hour, was designed to raise awareness about climate change and highlight ways of conserving energy to reduce emissions of greenhouse gases.

At the April 13 COAG meeting, the states welcomed the federal government's offer to establish an Australian Centre for Climate Change. The body, funded by a $126-million grant, was intended to research ways to lessen the impact of global warming. The states agreed to the development of plans to encourage hydrogen, geothermal, solar, and coal gasification technologies that would produce fewer greenhouse gases. The COAG representatives also welcomed a plan to establish a reporting system to track the volume of greenhouse gases being emitted into Australia's atmosphere.

On October 5, Epuron, an Australian subsidiary of the Hamburg, Germany-based renewable energy company Conergy AG, announced plans to build a $2-billion wind farm in western New South Wales. The wind farm was scheduled to begin construction in 2009, and was expected to take several years to complete. Officials hoped the wind farm would contribute up to 4.5 percent of the state's electrical power when it became operational.

Water. On Jan. 25, 2007, Prime Minister Howard made a $10-billion offer to take over the management of the Murray Darling Basin, which contains Australia's largest river system. However, Howard accused one of the states most affected, Victoria, of not cooperating, and the proposal failed.

The offer came at a time when the Murray River was badly affected by the drought that had afflicted southeastern Australia since 2001. This period of sustained low rainfall was the longest since the 1930's. During 2007, most of the dwindling flow of water entering the Murray was needed for household use, leaving little water for the irrigation of one of the country's most important fruit-producing areas.

Not all parts of Australia were equally affected by the drought. Melbourne in Victoria and Perth in Western Australia had enough rainfall during the year to fill the main dams serving these two state capital cities to about 40 percent of capacity.

Inland areas of Queensland experienced floods in January. Nevertheless, the state capital, Brisbane, was forced to continue imposing severe restrictions on household water use as the levels of the reservoirs serving the city fell below 20 percent of capacity.

In January, Queensland Premier Peter Beattie dropped plans to hold a referendum on whether to recycle wastewater for drinking water, saying the problem had become too severe to be an issue of choice. He said that Queensland residents would be forced to drink recycled wastewater as early as 2008.

Heavy rains on June 8, 2007, caused severe flooding in the Hunter Valley, north of Sydney. Rain also fell in the catchment area around Sydney's main dams, filling them to nearly 60 percent of capacity. Nevertheless, the New South Wales state government decided in June to go ahead with the construction of a desalination plant to produce fresh water from seawater off the coast south of Sydney. The $1.76-billion, wind-powered plant was scheduled for completion in 2010.

Adelaide, the capital city of South Australia, depends heavily for its water supplies on the drought-affected Murray River. The city's water authorities in 2007 also decided to proceed with plans for a water desalination plant.

Arts. In February, Australian filmmaker George Miller's *Happy Feet,* an animated tale of dancing penguins, won the Academy Award for best animated feature. In March, Sydney-based artist John Beard won the Archibald Prize, Australia's most prestigious award for painting. His prizewinning

FACTS IN BRIEF ON AUSTRALIA

Population	20,979,000
Government	Governor General Michael Jeffery; Prime Minister Kevin Rudd
Monetary unit*	dollar (1.13 = $1 U.S.)
Foreign trade (million U.S.$)	
Exports[†]	117,000
Imports[†]	127,700

*Exchange rate as of Oct. 4, 2007.
[†]Latest available data.

THE CABINET OF AUSTRALIA*

Kevin Rudd—prime minister
Julia Gillard—minister for education, employment, and workplace relations; deputy prime minister
Anthony Albanese—minister for infrastructure, transport, regional development, and local government
Wayne Swan—treasurer
Simon Crean—minister for trade
Joel Fitzgibbon—minister for defence
Stephen Conroy—minister for broadband, communications, and digital economy
Stephen Smith—minister for foreign affairs
Chris Evans—minister for immigration and citizenship
Peter Garrett—minister for the environment, heritage, and the arts
Robert McClelland—attorney general
Lindsay Tanner—minister for finance
Tony Burke—minister for agriculture, fisheries, and forestry
Jenny Macklin—minister for families, community services, and indigenous affairs
Joseph Ludwig—minister for human services
John Faulkner—special minister of state; cabinet secretary
Penny Wong—minister for climate change and water
Kim Carr—minister for innovation, industry, science, and research
Nicola Roxon—minister for health and ageing
Martin Ferguson—minister for resources, energy, and tourism

*As of December 7, 2007.

PREMIERS OF AUSTRALIAN STATES

State	Premier
New South Wales	Morris Iemma
Queensland	Anna Bligh
South Australia	Mike Rann
Tasmania	Paul Lennon
Victoria	John Brumby
Western Australia	Alan Carpenter

CHIEF MINISTERS OF AUSTRALIAN MAINLAND TERRITORIES

Australian Capital Territory	Jon Stanhope
Northern Territory	Paul Henderson

Aborigines. In June, Prime Minister Howard told the Australian Parliament that excessive consumption of alcohol in Aboriginal communities had reached a crisis point and had led to widespread child abuse. He announced plans to intervene by banning alcohol and pornography on Aboriginal land in the Northern Territory. Australian Greens leader Bob Brown labeled the bans "selective, cynical, and racist."

The federal intervention received a mixed reaction from Aboriginal leaders. One of the most outspoken critics of the federal policy was Marion Scrymgour, the first Aboriginal woman to be elected to the Northern Territory Assembly. In an October 24 speech at Sydney University, she described the federal actions as "a circus." She criticized the plan for ignoring other factors, such as poor housing, health, and education conditions, which had existed for decades. She noted that it was unlikely that survey teams sent by the federal government would uncover anything that was not already well known.

During his 11 years as prime minister, John Howard had consistently refused calls from both sides of the political spectrum to make a symbolic formal apology to Australia's Aboriginal community for past injustices. However, in October, just before he called the federal elections, Howard surprised many people by proposing to hold a referendum that would enable the government to add a preamble to the Australian Constitution recognizing the role of Australia's first inhabitants. The announcement was met with skepticism and was seen by critics as merely a campaign move. Soon after his election victory, Kevin Rudd announced that the Australian government would issue an apology for the mistreatment of Aborigines throughout the country's history.

Defense and security. In 2007, members of Australia's defense forces continued to serve in Afghanistan and Iraq. They also helped to maintain law and order in East Timor and the Solomon Islands. In April, Prime Minister Howard announced that 375 more service personnel would be sent to Afghanistan to join a North Atlantic Treaty Organization-led offensive against a resurgent Taliban.

David Hicks, an Australian convert to Islam who was arrested in Afghanistan in 2001, was finally released from prison in Guantánamo Bay, Cuba, in May 2007. Hicks pleaded guilty to a charge of providing material support for terrorism but denied any prior knowledge of the Sept. 11, 2001, terrorist attacks on the United States. Hicks was sentenced to seven years imprisonment, all but nine months of which was suspended, and was allowed to return to South Australia to serve the remaining months of his term in an Adelaide jail.

■ Brian Kennedy

See also **Australia, Prime Minister of.**

work depicted installation artist Janet Laurence in stark black and white. The annual award is given for achievement in portraiture of a distinguished Australian.

In June, Aboriginal writer Alexis Wright won the Miles Franklin Literary Award for her novel *Carpentaria,* which depicts a family's fight against mine owners. The award, Australia's most prestigious literary prize, is bestowed annually for a work portraying Australian life.

MEMBERS OF THE AUSTRALIAN HOUSE OF REPRESENTATIVES

The House of Representatives of the 42nd Parliament was scheduled to first meet Feb. 12, 2008. The House of Representatives was to consist of the following members: 83 Australian Labor Party, 55 Liberal Party of Australia, 10 National Party of Australia, and 2 Independents. This table shows each legislator and party affiliation. An asterisk (*) denotes those who served in the 41st Parliament.

Australian Capital Territory
Annette Ellis, A.L.P.*
Bob McMullan, A.L.P.*

New South Wales
Tony Abbott, L.P.*
Anthony Albanese, A.L.P.*
Bob Baldwin, L.P.*
Sharon Bird, A.L.P.*
Bronwyn Bishop, L.P.*
Chris Bowen, A.L.P.*
David Bradbury, A.L.P.
Tony Burke, A.L.P.*
Jason Clare, A.L.P.
John Cobb, N.P.*
Greg Combet, A.L.P.
Mark Coulton, N.P.*
Bob Debus, A.L.P.
Justine Elliot, A.L.P.*
Pat Farmer, L.P.*
Laurie Ferguson, A.L.P.*
Joel Fitzgibbon, A.L.P.*
Peter Garrett, A.L.P.*
Joanna Gash, L.P.*
Jennie George, A.L.P.*
Sharon Grierson, A.L.P.*
Jill Hall, A.L.P.*
Luke Hartsuyker, N.P.*
Alex Hawke, L.P.
Chris Hayes, A.L.P.
Joe Hockey, L.P.*
Kay Hull, N.P.*
Julia Irwin, A.L.P.*
Mike Kelly, A.L.P.
Sussan Ley, L.P.*
Louise Markus, L.P.*
Robert McClelland, A.L.P.*
Maxine McKew, A.L.P.
Daryl Melham, A.L.P.*
Scott Morrison, L.P.
John Murphy, A.L.P.*
Belinda Neal, A.L.P.
Brendan Nelson, L.P.*
Julie Owens, A.L.P.*
Tanya Plibersek, A.L.P.*
Roger Price, A.L.P.*
Philip Ruddock, L.P.*
Janelle Saffin, A.L.P.
Alby Schultz, L.P.*
Craig Thomson, A.L.P.
Malcolm Turnbull, L.P.*
Mark Vaile, N.P.*
Danna Vale, L.P.*
Tony Windsor, Ind.*

Northern Territory
Damian Hale, A.L.P.
Warren Snowdon, A.L.P.*

Queensland
Arch Bevis, A.L.P.*
James Bidgood, A.L.P.
Steven Ciobo, L.P.*
Yvette D'Ath, A.L.P.
Peter Dutton, L.P.*
Craig Emerson, A.L.P.*
Michael Johnson, L.P.*
Robert Katter, Ind.*
Andrew Laming, L.P.*
Peter Lindsay, L.P.*
Kirsten Livermore, A.L.P.*
Ian Macfarlane, L.P.*
Margaret May, L.P.*
Shayne Neumann, A.L.P.
Paul Neville, N.P.*
Graham Perrett, A.L.P.
Brett Raguse, A.L.P.
Kerry Rea, A.L.P.
Bernie Ripoll, A.L.P.*
Stuart Robert, L.P.
Kevin Rudd, A.L.P.*
Bruce Scott, N.P.*
Peter Slipper, L.P.*
Alexander Somlyay, L.P.*
Jon Sullivan, A.L.P.
Wayne Swan, A.L.P.*
Warren Truss, N.P.*
Jim Turnour, A.L.P.

South Australia
Mark Butler, A.L.P.
Nick Champion, A.L.P.
Alexander Downer, L.P.*
Kate Ellis, A.L.P.*
Steve Georganas, A.L.P.*
Christopher Pyne, L.P.*
Rowan Ramsey, L.P.
Amanda Rishworth, A.L.P.
Patrick Secker, L.P.*
Andrew Southcott, L.P.*
Tony Zappia, A.L.P.

Tasmania
Dick Adams, A.L.P.*
Jodie Campbell, A.L.P.
Julie Collins, A.L.P.
Duncan Kerr, A.L.P.*
Sid Sidebottom, A.L.P.

Victoria
Kevin Andrews, L.P.*
Fran Bailey, L.P.*
Bruce Billson, L.P.*
Russell Broadbent, L.P.*
Anna Burke, A.L.P.*
Anthony Byrne, A.L.P.*
Darren Cheeseman, A.L.P.
Peter Costello, L.P.*
Simon Crean, A.L.P.*
Michael Danby, A.L.P.*
Marc Dreyfus, A.L.P.
Martin Ferguson, A.L.P.*
John Forrest, N.P.*
Petro Georgiou, L.P.*
Steve Gibbons, A.L.P.*
Julia Gillard, A.L.P.*
Alan Griffin, A.L.P.*
David Hawker, L.P.*
Greg Hunt, L.P.*
Harry Jenkins, A.L.P.*
Catherine King, A.L.P.*
Jenny Macklin, A.L.P.*
Richard Marles, A.L.P.
Peter McGauran, N.P.*
Sophie Mirabella, L.P.*
Brendan O'Connor, A.L.P.*
Chris Pearce, L.P.*
Andrew Robb, L.P.*
Nicola Roxon, A.L.P.*
Bill Shorten, A.L.P.
Tony Smith, L.P.*
Sharman Stone, L.P.*
Mike Symon, A.L.P.
Lindsay Tanner, A.L.P.*
Kelvin Thomson, A.L.P.*
Maria Vamvakinou, A.L.P.*
Jason Wood, L.P.*

Western Australia
Julie Bishop, L.P.*
Gary Gray, A.L.P.
Barry Haase, L.P.*
Steve Irons, L.P.
Sharryn Jackson, A.L.P.
Dennis Jensen, L.P.*
Michael Keenan, L.P.*
Nola Marino, L.P.
Judi Moylan, L.P.*
Melissa Parke, A.L.P.
Don Randall, L.P.*
Luke Simpkins, L.P.
Stephen Smith, A.L.P.*
Wilson Tuckey, L.P.*
Mal Washer, L.P.*

The Great Drought Down Under

Australia suffers its worst drought in 500 years.

A drought described as "grim" and "unprecedentedly dangerous" by Prime Minister John Howard continued to plague much of Australia through 2007. The states of South Australia and New South Wales were especially hard hit, recording their lowest rainfall totals in 500 years. The "big dry" fueled out-of-control wildfires that raged through four states, claiming lives and damaging homes, businesses, and farms. One of the fires, in January, knocked down utility lines in Victoria, throwing the transportation system in Melbourne into chaos and leaving hundreds of thousands of people without electric power as summer temperatures soared. Snakes invaded Australian towns and cities to find water. Thirst-crazed *feral* (wild) camels rampaged through settlements and farms in the Northern Territory to reach water troughs and died by the thousands.

City reservoirs remained well below capacity despite some rainfall and even flooding in May and September that helped farmers meet predicted winter crop targets. Perth and Sydney began relying on desalination plants to supplement water supplies. Queensland's premier announced that, in 2008, purified recycled wastewater would be added to that state's water supply.

A girl wades in shallow water (left) as a helicopter refills its water tank to fight wildfires on the hills beyond the lake. During 2007, wildfires threatened four states in Australia.

A "Keep off grass" sign offers a sad reminder of the once-lush surface of this now-parched golf course.

KEEP OFF GRASS

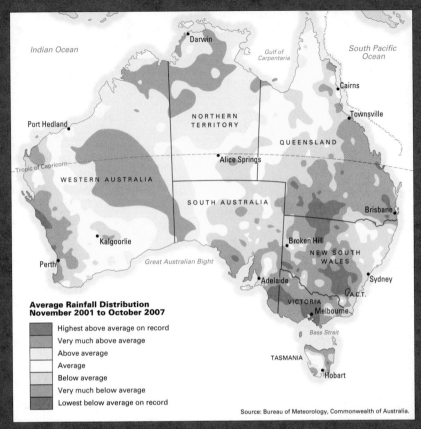

Average Rainfall Distribution
November 2001 to October 2007

- Highest above average on record
- Very much above average
- Above average
- Average
- Below average
- Very much below average
- Lowest below average on record

Source: Bureau of Meteorology, Commonwealth of Australia.

From 2001 to 2007, sections of far western, eastern, and southeastern Australia experienced their lowest rainfall totals in that continent's recorded history. In some areas, the accumulated total of yearly rainfall shortages since 1996 is greater than a full year's normal rainfall.

An Australian farmer near Wimmera, northwest of Melbourne, inspects wheat stunted by the extended drought.

Low water levels in a reservoir in Victoria offer workers unexpected aid in their efforts to clear European carp, a pest species, from the state's waterways. The fish, introduced into Australia for fishing and aquariums, has spread widely throughout southeastern Australia. Omnivorous eaters, the carp have destroyed aquatic plants, damaged aquatic habitats, and caused a serious decline in many native species of fish and water birds.

A man and his dog view the dry lake bed of Lake Marma in Murtoa, a town in Victoria. Before the drought, the lake was a popular fishing and boating destination.

Australia, Prime Minister of.

Kevin Rudd was sworn in as Australia's 26th prime minister in December 2007. He replaced John Howard. Howard's conservative coalition of the National and Liberal parties—which had governed Australia for 11 years—was decisively defeated in national elections by Rudd's Australian Labor Party (ALP). Howard also lost his seat in Parliament.

Howard saw his popularity wane in 2007, frequently trailing Rudd in opinion polls. In October, Howard agreed that, if reelected, he would stand aside at some point during his next term of office and hand over the post of prime minister to his long-serving treasurer, Peter Costello.

Rudd, a former diplomat, was first elected to Parliament in 1998, serving in the House of Representatives. He was reelected in 2001 and 2004. In 2006, he became head of the ALP and opposition leader. Upon winning the election, Rudd announced that the Australian government would issue an apology for the mistreatment of Australian Aborigines, a measure that Howard had resisted for years. On Nov. 30, 2007, Rudd announced that he would withraw all Australian troops from Iraq by mid-2008. On Dec. 3, 2007, Rudd was sworn in and almost immediately signed the Kyoto Protocol on global warming, which Howard had also resisted.   ■ Brian Kennedy

See also **Australia.**

Australian rules football.

The Geelong Cats defeated Port Adelaide 24 goals 19 behinds (163 points) to 6 goals 8 behinds (44 points) to win the Australian Football League (AFL) premiership in Melbourne on Sept. 29, 2007. The 119-point win was the largest in grand final history. Geelong half-forward Steve Johnson was awarded the Norm Smith Medal for best on the ground in the grand final.

Despite a run of grand final appearances, Geelong had not won a title for 44 years. However, 2007 proved to be the year of the Cats. They achieved a 19-win, 1-loss record to secure the minor premiership, and one of their players, Jimmy Bartel, won the Brownlow Medal for the best and fairest player during the season.

Geelong also had a victory at regional level when the Cats defeated the Coburg Tigers 17.24 (126) to 7.10 (52) to win the Victorian Football League premiership on September 23. On the same day, Subiaco beat Claremont 15.13 (103) to 9.8 (62) in the West Australian Football League grand final. In the AFL Queensland grand final, which was held on October 7, Mount Gravatt beat Southport 16.12 (108) to 10.10 (70). Central District defeated North Adelaide 16.11 (107) to 5.12 (42) to win the 2007 South Australian National Football League premiership.

■ Brian Kennedy

Austria.

A so-called "grand coalition" of Austria's two largest parties—the liberal Social Democratic Party and the conservative People's Party—was sworn into office on Jan. 11, 2007. The new government was formed three months after an extremely close national election, in which the Social Democrats won 35.3 percent of the vote and the previous People's Party government won 34.3 percent. Alfred Gusenbauer, leader of the Social Democrats, became chancellor.

The parties agreed to continue many of the probusiness programs of the previous conservative government. However, they also added new initiatives in social programs, set a minimum wage for the first time in Austria's history, and began various education reforms to please the Social Democrats. The new government expanded spending, especially on infrastructure and research and development, using higher-than-expected government revenues that ensured that the budget deficit would remain low.

Austria's economy continued its strong growth in 2007, exceeding the 2.6 percent average growth rate for countries in the *euro zone* (the group of European Union [EU] countries that use the common currency, the euro). EU economists projected that Austria's economy would grow by 3.3 percent in 2007, the same growth rate the country experienced in 2006. Unemployment remained low at 4.3 percent.

New election law. Austria's parliament enacted several major reforms to the country's election rules on June 5, 2007. The nation became the first in the EU to allow 16-year-olds to vote in national elections. (Several provinces already allowed the practice in local elections.) The minimum age at which Austrians can become candidates for all offices except that of president was also lowered, from 19 to 18. Presidential candidates must still be at least 35 years of age. Finally, the new legislation permitted absentee ballots and extended the term of the legislative session from four years to five. Austria's next national election is expected to take place in 2010.

Deaths. Kurt Waldheim, a former president of Austria and secretary-general of the United Nations (UN), died on June 14, 2007. Waldheim was known for his quiet diplomacy during his term at the UN from 1972 to 1982. After stepping down from that post, however, he fell into disgrace after falsifying his memoirs regarding his service as an intelligence officer in a German Army unit during World War II (1939-1945). The unit had deported the Jews of northern Greece to death camps. Waldheim ran for president of Austria and served from 1986 to 1992 but was banned from a state visit to the United States during his term in office.   ■ Jeffrey Kopstein

See also **Europe.**

Automobile. High gasoline prices and low consumer confidence drove down light-vehicle sales in the United States by 3 percent to 12.3 million units through September 2007, compared with the same period in 2006. Analysts had predicted sales of slightly over 16 million for 2007.

Individual sales at the traditional Big Three automakers—General Motors (GM) Corporation of Detroit; Ford Motor Company of Dearborn, Michigan; and Chrysler of Auburn Hills, Michigan—all declined in 2007, and their combined market share fell by nearly 3 percent to 51.2 percent.

The year was far different for Toyota. The Japanese-based automaker's sales surpassed Ford's, making it the second-largest seller in the United States. Toyota, Honda, Nissan, and other Japanese automakers boosted their combined market share to 37 percent through September, up from 34.6 percent for the same period in 2006. European automakers' market share rose slightly, to 7 percent, and Korean manufacturers had a small market share gain to 4.8 percent.

The Big Three lost sales even though they offered customers more generous discounts than the leading Japanese automakers. For the first nine months of 2007, the average per-vehicle incentive totaled $3,926 for Chrysler; $3,095 for Ford; and $2,937 for GM. Nissan's average incentive per vehicle was $2,035; Honda's was $1,164; and Toyota's was $841.

Hybrids continued to be popular in 2007, with sales growing 34 percent to 258,358 units through September. The Ford F-series pickup was the most popular light truck, with 537,211 units sold. Toyota's Camry was the number-one car for the period, with 365,140 units sold.

Big Three. DaimlerChrysler AG announced in May that it was selling its money-losing American unit. In early August, the German company finalized the sale of 80.1 percent of its interest in Chrysler to Cerberus Capital Management LP, a New York City private equity firm, in a $7.4-billion deal. Former Home Depot chairman Bob Nardelli became chairman and chief executive officer (CEO) of the renamed Chrysler Holdings LLC. Chrysler's former CEO, Thomas W. LaSorda, became president. In September, James E. Press, formerly Toyota's highest-ranking American executive, was named co-president.

Chrysler's total sales fell slightly, to 1.58 million units during the first nine months of the year, compared with 1.63 million during the same period in 2006. Its market share held at 12.8 percent. However, the automaker had too many unsold vehicles, and in November 2007, Chrysler announced plans to eliminate up to 12,000 jobs and entire shifts at five assembly plants. It also planned to eliminate four models through 2008.

The company was counting on its new minivans to help in the coming year.

At GM, sales fell to 2.9 million units, compared with 3.1 million for the nine-month period a year earlier. Its market share dropped nearly a full percentage point to 23.8 percent. For the third quarter of 2007, the nation's number-one automaker announced a record $39-billion loss—the second-largest quarterly loss in U.S. corporate history. The vast majority of the loss was from a noncash accounting charge-off involving deferred tax credits in the United States, Canada, and Germany. For the first nine months, GM had a net loss of $38 billion, compared with a net loss of $3 billion for the same period in 2006. The loss prompted some analysts to question the success of GM's turnaround plan. In September 2007, the automaker sold Allison Transmission, based in Indianapolis, in a private equity deal for $5.6 billion. GM hoped to improve its midsize car sales with the new Chevrolet Malibu.

Ford continued its turnaround plans through 2007 after a record loss of nearly $13 billion a year earlier. The automaker's sales slid to 2 million units through September, compared with 2.3 million through the same period a year ago, and its market share dropped nearly 2 percentage points to 16 percent. Ford reported a net income of $88 million through September, compared with a net loss of $7 billion through the same period a year earlier. In March, Ford completed the sale of its Aston Martin sports car line to a business group for $930 million in cash and preferred stock. In December, Ford announced it was in talks to sell its Jaguar and Land Rover business. A final signed deal was expected to be announced in early 2008. Ford was counting on its new Taurus—which replaced the slow-selling Five Hundred sedan—for better sales in 2008.

Asian manufacturers. Even in a down market, Toyota was a winner in 2007. Toyota's U.S. sales improved to 2 million units through September, compared with 1.9 million for the same period one year ago. The company's market share rose a full point to 16.2 percent, barely edging out Ford. On the world stage, Toyota and GM were in a close race for the title of number-one automaker. Toyota's success in the United States was helped by its new full-size pickup, the Tundra, which recorded sales of 144,480 units. In February, the company announced it would build its eighth North American assembly plant in Tupelo, Mississippi. The plant, which was expected to employ 2,000 workers, was scheduled to open in 2010 and have the annual capacity to build 150,000 Highlanders, a sport utility vehicle (SUV).

Honda also had a good year, with its sales growing slightly to 1.2 million units, but improv-

1957 Chevrolet Bel Air coupe

The year 2007 marked the 50th anniversary of a turning point in American automobile design.

1957 Ford Thunderbird

1957 Lincoln Premier four-door sedan

1957 Chrysler 300 two-door hardtop

Form triumphed over function in American automobile design in 1957—the year of the tailfin and the first American retractable hardtop convertible. Ford, General Motors, and Chrysler all came out with classic models with exuberant designs that embodied the confidence and optimism of the Eisenhower era. By the end of the 1957 model year, foreign car sales in the United States topped the 1-million mark for the first time, and the United States went into a recession, which depressed car sales. By the end of the decade, American cars were smaller and duller, if more functional.

Motors, Ford, and Chrysler made it a point to address this issue in their 2007 negotiations with the United Automobile Workers (UAW) in the fall. Negotiations between the UAW and GM and between the UAW and Chrysler were contentious, with short strikes against both companies. The union reached an agreement with Ford without a walkout. The agreements called for the three automakers to contribute billions of dollars to retiree health care funds that will be managed by the union. The union won promises from the automakers to invest in new vehicles in U.S. plants. General Motors and Chrysler UAW members ratified their contracts in October; Ford workers ratified their contract in November.

■ Mike Casey

See also **Labor and employment; Transportation.**

Automobile racing.
The United Kingdom's Lewis Hamilton, Formula One's first black driver in its 57-year history, enjoyed a rookie season for the ages in 2007. Hamilton became the first black driver to win a major auto race, capturing the Canadian Grand Prix and the United States Grand Prix in back-to-back weeks. Hamilton eventually finished second to Finland's Kimi Räikkönen for the Formula One championship.

In a highly publicized divorce in NASCAR, Dale Earnhardt, Jr., broke from the racing team started by his father and run by his stepmother. Earnhardt declared his intention on June 13 to drive after the 2007 season for Hendrick Motorsports, already a powerhouse with Jeff Gordon and Jimmie Johnson. Together, the two have won six NASCAR championships.

Indianapolis 500. Dario Franchitti captured a rain-shortened Indy 500 on May 27, taking the checkered flag in the pouring rain after completing just 166 of the scheduled 200 laps. The race was frequently interrupted by rain and cautions, with 55 laps run under a yellow flag. Scotsman Franchitti took the lead when the previous leaders made a final pit stop. He had opted to stay on the track and risk running out of fuel if the rain did not arrive. It did, and he

ing its market share to 9.7 percent, compared with 9.1 percent for the first nine months of 2006. The Japanese-based car company introduced its new Accord, the company's most popular vehicle in the United States. Meanwhile, Nissan's sales grew by 4.7 percent to 813,049 units through September 2007, and its market share increased half a percentage point to 6.6 percent.

Labor developments. For years, the Big Three automakers said that health care expenses for retired workers put them at a cost disadvantage compared with Asian automakers, which had not operated manufacturing plants in the United States long enough to have a great number of retirees. General

pocketed a record $1.65 million for the victory. Franchitti, in capturing his first Indy 500, led for 34 laps. Scott Dixon finished second. Danica Patrick, one of three women in the field, finished eighth.

Formula One. With seven-time champion Michael Schumacher retired, Hamilton and teammate Fernando Alonso battled for control of the points standings. Alonso closed the gap to two points with a win in Nürburg, Germany, on July 22. However, Kimi Räikkönen captured the title by winning the Brazilian Grand Prix on October 21.

NASCAR. Jimmie Johnson captured his second consecutive Nextel Cup championship on November 18, finishing with 6,723 points, 77 points more than his teammate Jeff Gordon. Johnson won 4 of the final 10 races of the "Chase for the Championship." After a fast start, struggles in the middle of the season left Johnson in jeopardy of not making the final 10-race Chase, while Earnhardt and Gordon also were on the cusp. NASCAR had tinkered with the Chase format in 2007, expanding the field of those who qualify by 2 to the top 12 drivers in the points standings and seeding the field by race victories instead of overall points.

Champ Car. Three-time defending points champion Sébastien Bourdais of France took a big step in securing an unprecedented fourth straight title with his win on July 22 in Edmonton, Canada, to take the lead at the midpoint in the 16-race series. Bourdais eventually won the title with 364 points, 83 more points than Justin Wilson of the United Kingdom.

IRL. Franchitti held a narrow lead over Dixon in the point standings in the 17-race series entering the final stretch. Franchitti, with 16 Top Ten finishes and 4 wins, took the title with 637 points, 13 more than Dixon, who also had 16 Top Ten finishes and 4 wins.

Endurance. Audi won its seventh Le Mans 24-hour endurance race, as Frank Biela and Marco Werner of Germany and Emanuele Pirro of Italy repeated as champions on June 17. The team, driving car No. 1, completed 369 laps, 10 more than the Peugeot No. 8 car. Juan Pablo Montoya, who raced in his first full season of NASCAR in 2007, captured the Rolex 24 at Daytona, Florida, on January 28. Montoya and teammates Salvador Durán and Scott Pruett finished 668 laps and covered 2,378 miles (3,827 kilometers).

Dragsters. Tony Schumacher won the 2007 National Hot Rod Association (NHRA) top fuel division championship, his fifth championship and fourth in a row. Tony Pedregon won the funny car division, his second title, and Jeg Coughlin, Jr., won the pro stock division, his third title. ■ Michael Kates

Aviation. Several factors in 2007 caused air travelers in the United States to face increased delays and inconvenience. Security measures continued to cause lengthy waiting times for passengers before boarding. Further, a steady increase in air traffic was overtaxing the U.S. air-traffic control system—a system already hampered by aging technology and a decrease in the number of seasoned controllers. Breakdowns in this aging system caused lengthy delays.

Experts believed a second factor in delays stemmed from airline policies adopted to increase profitability, such as booking flights to near-capacity. Domestic flights in the United States were between 85 and 90 percent full, meaning that on popular routes every seat was taken. Additionally, some aircraft had been reassigned from domestic to more lucrative international routes. Therefore, there were no other flights on which to book stranded passengers.

The number of on-time domestic flights in the United States fell to less than 70 percent for certain periods of 2007, an all-time low. This statistic, however, did not fully tell the story. Because of the methods used by the U.S. Department of Transportation to tabulate delays, flights that taxi to the tarmac, sit for hours, and then taxi back to the gate are not counted. During an ice storm on Feb. 14, 2007, U.S. carrier JetBlue held nine planes on the tarmac of a New York City airport within view of the terminal for hours—some for more than 10 hours. Eventually, the carrier canceled the flights. Often, airlines are reluctant to cancel; they do not want outgoing planes to lose their place in line for a runway, and they may not have enough gates to accommodate the canceled flights. This "strandings" of passengers on tarmacs became more frequent in 2007.

Two rival strategies. Industry analysts predicted a growing demand for air travel that would continue to strain airport gates, runways, and air-traffic control systems. Two rival aircraft manufacturers, Airbus and Boeing, developed different strategies for helping airlines reduce congestion.

Airbus's A380 is a huge airliner capable of carrying more than 800 passengers. With the A380, the strategy was to enable airlines to fly fewer flights per day to and from major airports, while still serving the same number of passengers. Because three A380's can fly about the same number of passengers as four Boeing 747's, an airline could run three flights a day to a major airport instead of four. This strategy, however, still depended on the hub-and-spoke model of air travel, wherein airlines fly passengers from *spokes* (smaller cities) on smaller planes to a *hub* (large city), where passengers then board a larger plane. A large number of smaller planes were still flying from already congested airports under this system.

Workers assemble a 787 Dreamliner at the Boeing plant in Everett, Washington. The plane is made of lightweight, composite materials for greater fuel efficiency. Delivery of the first Dreamliner, originally scheduled for 2007, was delayed because of production problems.

With the 787, known as the Dreamliner, Boeing promoted a different idea. Although the 787, which was due out in 2008, held fewer passengers than the A380, the aim was still to reduce airport congestion by flying fewer flights to the busiest airports. Because the 787 is constructed with *composite materials* (carbon-reinforced plastics) that are lighter than conventional metal, the 787 is more fuel efficient. This gives the airplane a longer range, permitting airlines to offer longer direct flights between spokes along so-called point-to-point routes instead of flying passengers to a congested hub to board a larger plane.

After nearly a two-year delay, the first A380 was delivered in autumn 2007 to Singapore Airlines. Both Airbus and Boeing had large numbers of orders for their planes as of 2007. It was too soon to know if either strategy would prevail.

Congested airports. At major urban airports, runways were at as much of a premium as gates. At some urban airports, shorter runways had originally been intended for smaller planes flying domestic routes. By 2007, domestic routes were often served by the same large jets used for international flights. The short runways were more difficult for larger jets, but there was little possibility of building more

runways in these already overbuilt and densely populated locations.

An Airbus A320, operated by Brazil's TAM Airlines, went off the runway on July 17 after landing at Congonhas airport in central São Paulo, Brazil. The plane skidded, tried to take off again and then crashed into a building and a fuel depot and burst into flames. The short runway at Congonhas had been likened to the deck of an aircraft carrier, and pilots who landed too close to the runway's end were advised to retry the landing. All 187 people aboard the TAM plane and about 12 others on the ground were killed.

These accidents, known as *runway overruns,* accounted for nearly 30 percent of the serious airline accidents worldwide. In the United States, the Federal Aviation Administration asked airports to add safety zones (empty areas) of 1,000 feet (300 meters) at the end of runways. Some urban airports with no room for safety zones were instead installing crushable concrete barriers to slow jets at the end of runways.

Pilots. In December, the U.S. Congress passed legislation extending the mandatory retirement age of commercial airline pilots from to 60 to 65.

■ Christine Sullivan

See also **Disasters; Transportation.**

Azerbaijan. See Asia.

Bahrain. See Middle East.

Ballet. See Dancing.

Baltic States. See Estonia; Europe; Latvia.

Bangladesh. The armed forces effectively took control of Bangladesh on Jan. 11, 2007, postponed parliamentary elections scheduled for January 22, and charged dozens of politicians and business people with corruption. The nation had long been notorious for corruption.

Trouble brews. Prime Minister Khaleda Zia had resigned in October 2006 under laws requiring that the 2007 election be supervised by a neutral caretaker government. President Iajuddin Ahmed named himself as head of the caretaker government.

Zia's main opponent, former Prime Minister Sheikh Hasina Wajed, argued that Zia had packed election boards, voter rolls, and the judiciary to rig the election. Demanding reforms, Wajed's supporters staged weeks of violent protests. In addition, they said they would boycott the January 22 elections.

Emergency. After the United Nations warned that incomplete elections could jeopardize Bangladesh's profitable role of providing international peacekeeping troops, Ahmed declared a state of emergency on January 11, postponed elections, and resigned as caretaker. A former central bank governor, Fakhruddin Ahmed, became the head of an army-backed caretaker government led by nonpolitical administrators. In April, a new election commissioner said it would take at least 18 months to prepare new voter lists.

The new regime began bringing corruption and other felony charges against many followers of Zia and Wajed, whose bitter feuding had distorted Bangladeshi politics since the early 1990's. Zia's eldest son, Tarique Rahman, was arrested on March 8, 2007, and another of Zia's sons was arrested on April 16. In April, a local human rights group reported that 50 people had died in police custody since January 12.

By August, more than 170 prominent politicians, business people, and bureaucrats had been jailed amid sensational press accounts of corruption and abuse of power. Some were quickly convicted by special fast-track courts. Media reports claimed that 15,000 less prominent people were also jailed. Efforts to restart the long-dormant National Security Council further demonstrated the army's role in national politics.

After being charged on April 11 with responsibility for four deaths in an October 2006 protest, Wajed was jailed on July 16, 2007, on charges of corruption and extortion. On September 3, Zia and a third son were arrested on similar charges.

Cyclone Sidr struck Bangladesh on November 15, bringing winds as high as 155 miles (250 kilometers) per hour. Nearly 3,300 people were killed in the storm, and nearly 900 others were still missing by late 2007. ■ Henry S. Bradsher

See also **Asia; Disasters.**

Bank. In 2007, a crisis in subprime mortgage-related securities resulted in enormous losses for the United States banking industry and chilled credit on financial markets worldwide. Subprime mortgages are loans made to home buyers whose credit histories do not qualify them for conventional mortgages. In recent years, banks and other financial institutions have offered subprime mortgage products to consumers with marginal credit ratings at higher fees and interest rates to compensate for the higher risk. Overinvestment in such loans exposed financial institutions to huge losses when the U.S. housing bubble burst.

The Wall Street investment firm Merrill Lynch disclosed third-quarter losses due to writedowns of $8.4 billion. A writedown is a quantity of commercial and consumer debt that banks write off as uncollectible. Merrill Lynch chairman E. Stanley O'Neal, who had led the company into heavy investments in the mortgage market, resigned in the wake of the report.

Citigroup Inc. of New York City, parent company of the largest U.S. bank, Citibank, reported that its third-quarter profits were off by 57 percent, spooking U.S. stock exchanges into a sharp dip. Third-quarter writedowns of $6.5 billion had dragged down Citibank's earnings, and in early November, Citigroup officials announced further writedowns of up to $11 billion.

Bank of America of Charlotte, North Carolina, reported third-quarter earnings off by 32 percent. Wachovia Bank, also of Charlotte, reported a third-quarter earnings decline of 10 percent, due to $1.3 billion in writedowns. Wachovia later reported additional writedowns of $1.1 billion. Among the top five U.S. banks, only Chase of Chicago and Wells Fargo of San Francisco posted positive earnings in the third quarter, though both banks reported large writedowns as well.

In December, the Wall Street investment bank Bear Stearns announced a fourth-quarter loss of about $854 million, after writing down $1.9 billion in mortgage-based securities. Another New York City investment bank, Morgan Stanley, reported the first fourth-quarter loss in that company's 72-year history, after writing down a total of $10.8 billion. In total, U.S. investment companies and banks disclosed losses of at least $40 billion in mortgage-related securities in 2007.

The subprime mortgage crisis began in the United States in 2006 and had roots in historically low interest rates set by the Federal Reserve (the Fed), the nation's central bank. Fed policies led banks to offer fixed-rate consumer mortgages at or even slightly under 5 percent in 2004. Banks invested heavily in the mortgage market, and millions of consumers applied for mortgages, fueling a housing and construction boom.

The housing and mortgage boom occurred in

a climate of deregulation in financial markets as a result of banking laws passed by the U.S. Congress in the 1990's. Financial institutions had greater latitude in the marketing and *monetizing* (selling off) of mortgages than they had had since before the Great Depression of the 1930's.

Banks and other financial institutions repackaged mortgages in complex bonds known as collateralized debt obligations (CDO's) and sold these around the world. The worldwide dispersal of U.S. mortgage debt ensured that a high rate of defaults would impact the global economy.

In the superheated mortgage market of 2004-2005, lenders offered a wide range of consumer mortgages, including subprime. Many had adjustable rates—that is, rates that change, usually going up, after a predefined period. Depending upon interest rates, consumer payments on adjustable mortgages can double over time. During the housing boom, many consumers and lenders downplayed the dangers of such mortgages, reasoning that homeowners pinched by rising mortgage payments could profitably resell their properties. In December 2007, the Fed proposes new regulations, to go into effect in 2008, that would protect prospective homeowners from such unscrupulous mortgage practices.

The U.S. real estate market slowed dramatically in late 2006 and 2007, knocking out the resale prop from marginal mortgage holders in the subprime market. As adjustable rates kicked in, many homeowners found themselves with untenable expenses. During the third quarter, mortgage lenders foreclosed on more than 600,000 properties in the United States, involving about 0.05 percent of all U.S. households. In October, Congress's Joint Economic Committee forecast that 2 million borrowers would lose their homes through foreclosure by the end of 2009.

Bank superfund. In October 2007, the three largest U.S. banks—Citibank, Bank of America, and Chase—announced the creation of a "bank superfund" to selectively buy up CDO's believed to be inherently sound but whose negotiability had been harmed by subprime fallout. The move, analysts said, aimed to boost global investor confidence in U.S. mortgage-backed securities and halt further damage to world credit markets. Secretary of the U.S. Treasury Henry Paulson facilitated the creation of the fund and applauded the banks' concerted action. Analysts estimated the value of the superfund at around $80 billion.

Global reach. In 2007, the U.S. subprime crisis also took a toll on financial institutions in Europe. The stock value of London-based Barclays, the United Kingdom's third-largest bank, declined by 26 percent in the first 10 months of 2007. During the same period, Edinburgh, Scotland-based Royal Bank stock lost 28 percent of its

value. In November, analysts estimated that Barclays was holding $25-billion worth of securities tied to the U.S. subprime market.

Credit Suisse Group and UBS AG, both based in Switzerland, reported writedowns of $4.6 billion and $1.9 billion respectively. Germany's largest bank, Frankfurt-based Deutsche Bank AG, reported $3.17 billion in writedowns.

Central banks and interest rates. Central banks of major world economies took decisive steps to counteract the crisis. The Fed, the European Central Bank—which manages the euro—and the central banks of Japan, Canada, and Australia injected U.S. dollars into their banking systems to prime the credit pump and prop up the sinking U.S. dollar. On December 12, various central banks, including the Fed, announced that they would provide billions in loans to banks to ease the availability of credit.

In August, September, October, and December, the Fed cut the discount rate, which is charged to banks for temporary loans, and the federal funds rate, which directly affects consumer mortgage and credit card rates. The cumulative effect of these cuts was a decline in the discount rate from 6.25 percent to 4.75 percent; and in the federal funds rate, from 5.25 percent to 4.25 percent. ■ Robert N. Knight

See also **Economics, U.S.; Economics, World.**

Baseball. The Boston Red Sox won their second World Series title in four years, completing a four-game sweep of the Colorado Rockies on Oct. 28, 2007. Whereas the 2004 World Series victory had ended the Red Sox's torturous 86-year championship drought, the 2007 win helped cement their reputation as a dominant team. The Red Sox outscored their play-off opponents 99 to 46, including a record 29-to-10 World Series margin over the Rockies. Boston trailed just 3 out of 63 innings in its final seven games, all wins.

The upstart Rockies made one of the most exciting runs in sports history to reach the series. Colorado won 13 of its last 14 regular season games to tie the San Diego Padres in the National League (NL) wild-card race. After winning a tie-breaker game with San Diego, Colorado swept both the division and league championship series, becoming the first team ever to do so.

Bonds breaks Aaron's record. San Francisco Giants slugger Barry Bonds broke the career home run record, held by Hank Aaron, on August 7. Bonds hit his 756th homer off Washington Nationals pitcher Mike Bacsik. Commentators noted that celebration of the feat seemed subdued, with fans' lingering doubts about steroid use in baseball continuing to cast uncertainty on the achievements of Bonds and other sluggers.

Bonds, 43, finished the season with 762 career

home runs, but his future as a player appeared uncertain after the Giants declined to ask him back. In November, a federal grand jury indicted Bonds for perjury and obstruction of justice. The charges stemmed from his 2003 testimony during a government investigation into steroid distribution by the Bay Area Laboratory Co-operative (BALCO). The 2007 indictment accused Bonds of making several false statements, including lying when he testified that he had never used steroids.

World Series. Balanced hitting and spectacular pitching helped the Red Sox shut down the streaking Rockies, who seemed to cool in their eight-day break before the series. Play began in Boston on October 24, with a stunning 13-1 Red Sox victory behind ace Josh Beckett, who climbed to 4-0 in the 2007 postseason. Boston won Game 2 the next night, 2-1, with pitcher Curt Schilling improving to an 11-2 lifetime postseason record. The Red Sox

pulled away late for a 10-5 victory on October 27 in Denver and completed the sweep with a 4-3 win the next night. Boston outhit Colorado .333 to .218 in the series, batting a phenomenal .419 with runners in scoring position. The series Most Valuable Player (MVP), third-baseman Mike Lowell, hit .400 with a homer, 4 RBI's, and 6 runs.

Play-offs. The Rockies earned their first World Series trip with a four-game sweep of the National League Championship Series (NLCS), outscoring the league-leading Arizona Diamondbacks 18 to 8. Colorado finished off Arizona on October 15 with a 6-4 win in Denver. The Rockies reached the NLCS with a three-game National League Division Series (NLDS) sweep of the Philadelphia Phillies. Arizona swept the Chicago Cubs in the NLDS.

Boston rallied from a three-games-to-one deficit in the American League Championship Series (ALCS) to eliminate the Cleveland Indians on October 21, with an 11-2 victory in Boston. The Red Sox swept the Los Angeles Angels three games to none in the American League Division Series (ALDS), while the Indians ousted the New York Yankees three games to one.

The regular season featured many close races, with no team clinching a division title until the final week. The Red Sox, however, became the first team to lock up a play-off spot, securing at least a wild-card berth on September 22.

The Red Sox won the American League (AL) East title, ending the Yankees' nine-year stranglehold on that crown. The Yankees closed a 14 ½-game gap on May 29 to just 1 ½ games the final week but had to settle for the wild-card. Boston and Cleveland tied with a 96-66 record, best in the majors. The surprising Indians took the AL Central lead on August 15 and went 27-9 to grab their first division title since 2001. The Angels (94-68) won the AL West.

The New York Mets suffered an unprecedented collapse in the NL East, blowing a 7-game lead in the last 17 games. The Mets ended a game behind the Phillies, who finished 89-73. The Rockies, essentially counted out with two weeks to go, surged to tie the Padres in the NL wild-card race, each team a game behind NL West champ Arizona (90-72). The Rockies beat the Padres in a tie-breaker on October 1 in Denver, scoring three runs in the bottom of the 13th inning off all-time saves leader Trevor Hoffman. The Cubs made the play-offs for the second time in a 5-year span—a first for the franchise since the 1930's—taking the NL Central title with an 85-77 record.

Pitching milestones. The Mets' Tom

San Francisco Giants slugger Barry Bonds cracks his 756th homer on Aug. 7, 2007, in San Francisco, breaking major league baseball's career home run record. The record, perhaps the sport's most celebrated mark, had been held by Hank Aaron for more than 30 years.

FINAL STANDINGS IN MAJOR LEAGUE BASEBALL

AMERICAN LEAGUE

American League champions—
Boston Red Sox
(defeated Cleveland Indians, 4 games to 3)
World Series champions—
Boston Red Sox (defeated Colorado Rockies, 4 games to 0)

Eastern Division	W.	L.	Pct.	G.B.
Boston Red Sox	96	66	.593	—
New York Yankees*	94	68	.580	2
Toronto Blue Jays	83	79	.512	13
Baltimore Orioles	69	93	.426	27
Tampa Bay Rays	66	96	.407	30

Central Division				
Cleveland Indians	96	66	.593	—
Detroit Tigers	88	74	.543	8
Minnesota Twins	79	83	.488	17
Chicago White Sox	72	90	.444	24
Kansas City Royals	69	93	.426	27

Western Division				
Los Angeles Angels	94	68	.580	—
Seattle Mariners	88	74	.543	6
Oakland Athletics	76	86	.469	18
Texas Rangers	75	87	.463	19

Offensive leaders

Batting average	Magglio Ordonez, Detroit	.363
Runs scored	Alex Rodriguez, New York	143
Home runs	Alex Rodriguez, New York	54
Runs batted in	Alex Rodriguez, New York	156
Hits	Ichiro Suzuki, Seattle	238
Stolen bases	Carl Crawford, Tampa Bay	50
	Brian Roberts, Baltimore	50
Slugging percentage	Alex Rodriguez, New York	.645

Leading pitchers

Games won	Josh Beckett, Boston	20
Earned run average		
(162 or more innings)	John Lackey, Los Angeles	3.01
Strikeouts	Scott Kazmir, Tampa Bay	239
Saves	Joe Borowski, Cleveland	45
Shut-outs	Paul Byrd, Cleveland	2
	José Contreras, Chicago	2
	John Lackey, Los Angeles	2
	Jeff Weaver, Seattle	2
Complete games	Roy Halladay, Toronto	7

Awards†

Most Valuable Player	Alex Rodriguez, New York
Cy Young	C. C. Sabathia, Cleveland
Rookie of the Year	Dustin Pedroia, Boston
Manager of the Year	Eric Wedge, Cleveland

NATIONAL LEAGUE

National League champions—
Colorado Rockies
(defeated Arizona Diamondbacks, 4 games to 0)

Eastern Division	W.	L.	Pct.	G.B.
Philadelphia Phillies	89	73	.549	—
New York Mets	88	74	.543	1
Atlanta Braves	84	78	.519	5
Washington Nationals	73	89	.451	16
Florida Marlins	71	91	.438	18

Central Division				
Chicago Cubs	85	77	.525	—
Milwaukee Brewers	83	79	.512	2
St. Louis Cardinals	78	84	.481	7
Houston Astros	73	89	.451	12
Cincinnati Reds	72	90	.444	13
Pittsburg Pirates	68	94	.420	17

Western Division				
Arizona Diamondbacks	90	72	.556	—
Colorado Rockies*	90	73	.552	0.5
San Diego Padres	89	74	.546	1.5
Los Angeles Dodgers	82	80	.506	8
San Francisco Giants	71	91	.438	19

Offensive leaders

Batting average	Matt Holliday, Colorado	.340
Runs scored	Jimmy Rollins, Philadelphia	139
Home runs	Prince Fielder, Milwaukee	50
Runs batted in	Matt Holliday, Colorado	137
Hits	Matt Holliday, Colorado	216
Stolen bases	José Reyes, New York	78
Slugging percentage	Prince Fielder, Milwaukee	.618

Leading pitchers

Games won	Jake Peavy, San Diego	19
Earned run average		
(162 or more innings)	Jake Peavy, San Diego	2.54
Strikeouts	Jake Peavy, San Diego	240
Saves	José Valverde, Arizona	47
Shut-outs	Brandon Webb, Arizona	3
Complete games	Brandon Webb, Arizona	4

Awards†

Most Valuable Player	Jimmy Rollins, Philadelphia
Cy Young	Jake Peavy, San Diego
Rookie of the Year	Ryan Braun, Milwaukee
Manager of the Year	Bob Melvin, Arizona

*Qualified for wild-card play-off spot.
†Selected by the Baseball Writers Association of America.

Glavine became just the 23rd pitcher in major league history to reach 300 wins. Glavine got his 300th victory against the Cubs on Aug. 5, 2007, in Chicago.

Three pitchers tossed their first no-hitters in 2007. Mark Buehrle of the Chicago White Sox faced the minimum 27 batters—picking off the lone hitter who reached on a walk—to no-hit the Texas Rangers on April 18 in Chicago. Justin Verlander tossed the Detroit Tigers' first no-hitter since 1984 on June 12, 2007, dazzling the visiting Milwaukee Brewers with nasty curve balls and 100-mile-per-hour fast balls. Boston rookie Clay Buchholz pitched a no-hitter against the Baltimore Orioles on September 1 in his second career start. The 23-year-old became just the third pitcher to toss a no-hitter in his first or second start since 1900.

Other achievements. Texas Ranger Sammy Sosa became just the fifth hitter to reach 600 home runs with a June 20, 2007, blast against his former team, the Cubs. Three players joined the 500-homer club in 2007: Toronto Blue Jay Frank Thomas on June 28, Yankee Alex Rodriguez on August 4, and Jim Thome of the White Sox on September 16. Rodriguez became the youngest player to reach the mark, at 32 years and 8 days.

Craig Biggio of the Houston Astros became the 27th player to reach 3,000 hits on June 28. Jimmy Rollins of the Phillies and Detroit's Curtis Granderson joined Willie Mays and Frank Schulte as the only players to have 20 homers, 20 triples, 20 doubles, and 20 stolen bases in a season.

The Mitchell Report. In December, former U.S. Senator George Mitchell reported on an investigation commissioned by Major League Baseball into the use of performance-enhancing drugs by players. He concluded that such use had been widespread for more than a decade and named dozens of players implicated during the investigation, including some of baseball's biggest stars.

College. With a 9-3 win on June 24, Oregon State University took the National Collegiate Athletic Association World Series title, its second straight over the University of North Carolina.

Youth. On August 26, Warner Robins, Georgia, beat a team from Tokyo, 3-2, to win the Little League World Series.

Deaths. Bowie Kuhn, 80, baseball commissioner from 1969 to 1984, died on March 15, 2007. Joe Nuxhall, 79, pitcher and later broadcaster for the Cincinnati Reds, died on November 15. Phil Rizzuto, 89, Hall of Fame shortstop with the Yankees and later a sportscaster, died on August 14. Hank Bauer, 84, veteran of nine Yankees World Series teams, died on February 9. St. Louis Cardinals' reliever Josh Hancock, 29, died on April 29 in St. Louis in a car accident.   ■ Michael Kates

See also **Sports.**

Basketball. The San Antonio Spurs won their third National Basketball Association (NBA) title in five years and their fourth in nine seasons, sweeping the Cleveland Cavaliers with an 83-82 victory on June 14, 2007, in Cleveland. The Spurs also won in 1999, 2003, and 2005 and became the fourth franchise in NBA history to win four titles.

In men's college basketball in 2007, the University of Florida (Gainesville) became the first school to take the National Collegiate Athletic Association (NCAA) men's championship for two years in a row since Duke in 1991-1992, toppling Ohio State. The Gators became the first team to win two straight titles with the same five players starting both games. In women's college basketball, the University of Tennessee (Knoxville) captured its seventh championship, throttling first-time finalist Rutgers University.

After leading the Gators to their back-to-back titles, Coach Billy Donovan agreed to a five-year, $27.5-million offer from the NBA's Orlando Magic. However, Donovan had second thoughts and managed to get out of the contract only days after signing it. The Magic agreed to release him from the deal, on one condition—that he not coach in the NBA for five seasons. Donovan returned to Florida with a six-year contract.

Professional men. San Antonio captured the title in four straight games. Riding the play of guard Tony Parker, who averaged nearly 25 points and hit 57 percent of his shots, the Spurs easily won the first two games at home. The Spurs won

Tony Parker of the San Antonio Spurs (left) drives to the basket as Anderson Varejao (center) and LeBron James of the Cleveland Cavaliers look on during the fourth game of the NBA finals on June 14, 2007, in Cleveland.

Game 3 on June 12, 2007, in Cleveland 75-72, the second lowest total points in a Finals game in history. The sweep was the eighth since the Finals began in 1947. French-born Parker became the first European-born Most Valuable Player of a Finals.

Cleveland advanced to its first-ever Finals by toppling the Detroit Pistons 4 games to 2. In Game 5, which allowed the Cavs to take control, LeBron James scored 48 points, including 29 of his team's final 30, in a double-overtime win on May 31, 2007, in Detroit. The Cavaliers had swept the Washington Wizards in the first round and ousted the New Jersey Nets 4 games to 2 in the second round. In the Western Conference, the Spurs beat the Denver Nuggets in five games in the first round and then the Phoenix Suns 4 games to 2. The Spurs beat the Utah Jazz 4 games to 1 to gain the Finals.

The Dallas Mavericks, the top seed in the Western Conference, became the first No. 1 seed to lose to a No. 8 seed since the NBA went to best-of-seven series in the first round in 2003, falling to the surprising Golden State Warriors 4 games to 2. Denver in 1994 and the New York Knicks in 1999 also accomplished the feat, but those series were best-

of-five. Regular season Most Valuable Player Dirk Nowitzki of Germany, the first European player to win the award, struggled through a horrible Game 6. Chicago captured its first postseason series since 1998, when Michael Jordan played for the Bulls, sweeping the defending champion Miami Heat 4 games to 0.

In the regular season, Dallas rolled to the best record, 67-15, in winning the Southwest Division in the Western Conference. Phoenix had the second-best mark, 61-21, to win the Pacific by 19 games over the Los Angeles Lakers, and Utah won the Northwest with a 51-31 mark. In the Eastern Conference, Detroit posted the best record, 53-29, to win the Central Division, the Toronto Raptors won the Atlantic with a 47-35 mark, and Miami won the Southeast with a record of 44-38.

With his 50 points on March 23, 2007, in New Orleans, the Lakers' Kobe Bryant became just the second player in NBA history to score 50 points in four consecutive games, joining Wilt Chamberlain, who topped the 50-point plateau seven straight times during the 1961-1962 season. Bryant had scored 65, 50, and 60 in the previous three games.

NATIONAL BASKETBALL ASSOCIATION STANDINGS

EASTERN CONFERENCE

Atlantic Division	W.	L.	Pct.	G.B.
Toronto Raptors*	47	35	.573	—
New Jersey Nets*	41	41	.500	6
Philadelphia 76ers	35	47	.427	12
New York Knicks	33	49	.402	26
Boston Celtics	24	58	.293	23
Central Division				
Detroit Pistons*	53	29	.646	—
Cleveland Cavaliers*	50	32	.610	3
Chicago Bulls*	49	33	.598	4
Indiana Pacers	35	47	.427	18
Milwaukee Bucks	28	54	.341	25
Southeast Division				
Miami Heat*	44	38	.537	—
Washington Wizards*	41	41	.500	3
Orlando Magic*	40	42	.488	4
Charlotte Bobcats	33	49	.402	11
Atlanta Hawks	30	52	.366	14

WESTERN CONFERENCE

Northwest Division	W.	L.	Pct.	G.B.
Utah Jazz*	51	31	.622	—
Denver Nuggets*	45	37	.549	6
Minnesota T'wolves	32	50	.390	19
Portland Trail Blazers	32	50	.390	19
Seattle SuperSonics	31	51	.378	20
Pacific Division				
Phoenix Suns*	61	21	.744	—
Golden State Warriors*	42	40	.512	19
Los Angeles Lakers*	42	40	.512	19
Los Angeles Clippers	40	42	.488	21
Sacramento Kings	33	38	.402	28
Southwest Division				
Dallas Mavericks*	67	15	.817	—
San Antonio Spurs*	58	24	.707	9
Houston Rockets*	52	30	.634	15
New Orleans Hornets	39	43	.476	28
Memphis Grizzlies	22	60	.268	45

INDIVIDUAL LEADERS

Scoring	G.	F.G.M.	F.T.M.	Pts.	Avg.
Kobe Bryant, Los Angeles	77	813	667	2,430	31.6
Carmelo Anthony, Denver	65	691	459	1,881	28.9
Gilbert Arenas, Washington	74	647	606	2,105	28.4
Dwyane Wade, Miami	51	472	432	1,397	27.4
LeBron James, Cleveland	78	772	489	2,132	27.3
Michael Redd, Milwaukee	53	477	345	1,416	26.7
Ray Allen, Seattle	55	505	279	1,454	26.4
Allen Iverson, Denver	65	581	485	1,709	26.3
Vince Carter, New Jersey	82	726	462	2,070	25.2
Yao Ming, Houston	48	423	356	1,202	25.0
Joe Johnson, Atlanta	57	536	235	1,426	25.0

Rebounding	G.	Off.	Def.	Tot.	Avg.
Kevin Garnett, Minnesota	76	183	792	975	12.8
Tyson Chandler, N. Orleans	73	320	584	904	12.4
Dwight Howard, Orlando	82	283	725	1,008	12.3
Carlos Boozer, Utah	74	235	632	867	11.7
Marcus Camby, Denver	70	164	652	816	11.7
Emeka Okafor, Charlotte	67	258	499	757	11.3
Al Jefferson, Boston	69	237	519	756	11.0
Chris Bosh, Toronto	69	186	555	741	10.7
Ben Wallace, Chicago	77	303	518	821	10.7
Tim Duncan, San Antonio	80	213	632	845	10.6
David Lee, New York	58	196	406	602	10.4

NBA champions—San Antonio Spurs
(defeated Cleveland Cavaliers, 4 games to 0)

*Made play-offs.

THE 2006-2007 COLLEGE BASKETBALL SEASON

COLLEGE TOURNAMENT CHAMPIONS

NCAA (Men)
	Division I:	Florida
	Division II:	Barton
	Division III:	Amherst

(Women)
	Division I:	Tennessee
	Division II:	Southern Connecticut State
	Division III:	DePauw

NAIA (Men)
	Division I:	Oklahoma City
	Division II:	MidAmerica Nazarene

(Women)
	Division I:	Lambuth
	Division II:	Indiana Wesleyan

NIT (Men) West Virginia
(Women) Wyoming

MEN'S COLLEGE CHAMPIONS

CONFERENCE	SCHOOL
America East	Vermont
	Albany (tournament)
Atlantic 10	Massachusetts–Xavier (tie)
	George Washington (tournament)
Atlantic Coast	North Carolina*–Virginia (tie)
Atlantic Sun	East Tennessee State
	Belmont (tournament)
Big 12	Kansas*
Big East	Georgetown*
Big Sky	Weber State*–Northern Arizona (tie)
Big South	Winthrop*
Big Ten	Ohio State*
Big West	Long Beach State*
Colonial	Virginia Commonwealth*
Conference USA	Memphis*
Horizon League	Butler–Wright State* (tie)
Ivy League	Pennsylvania*
Metro Atlantic	Marist
	Niagara (tournament)
Mid-American	Miami of Ohio (tournament)
East Division	Akron
West Division	Toledo
Mid-Continent	Oral Roberts*
Mid-Eastern	Delaware State
	Florida A & M (tournament)
Missouri Valley	Southern Illinois
	Creighton (tournament)
Mountain West	Brigham Young
	Nevada (Las Vegas) (tournament)
Northeast	Central Connecticut State*
Ohio Valley	Austin Peay
	Eastern Kentucky (tournament)
Pacific 10	UCLA
	Oregon (tournament)
Patriot League	Bucknell–Holy Cross* (tie)
Southeastern	
East Division	Florida*
West Division	Mississippi State
Southern	
North Division	Appalachian State
South Division	Davidson*
Southland	
East Division	Northwestern State
West Division	Texas A & M (Corpus Christi)*
Southwestern	Mississippi Valley State
	Jackson State (tournament)
Sun Belt	North Texas (tournament)
East Division	South Alabama
West Division	Arkansas State–Louisiana (Monroe) (tie)
West Coast	Gonzaga*
Western Athletic	Nevada
	New Mexico State (tournament)

Nicky Anosike (number 55) of the Tennessee Lady Volunteers reaches for a rebound against Rutgers during the 2007 NCAA Women's Basketball Championship game in Cleveland on April 3. Tennessee won the game, 59-46.

WOMEN'S COLLEGE CHAMPIONS

CONFERENCE	SCHOOL
America East	Hartford
	UMBC (tournament)
Atlantic 10	George Washington
	Xavier (tournament)
Atlantic Coast	Duke
	North Carolina (tournament)
Atlantic Sun	Belmont*
Big 12	Texas A&M–Oklahoma* (tie)
Big East	Connecticut
	Rutgers (tournament)
Big Sky	Montana
	Idaho State (tournament)
Big South	High Point
	Asheville (tournament)
Big Ten	Ohio State
	Purdue (tournament)
Big West	UC-Riverside*
Colonial	Old Dominion*
Conference USA	Tulane
	East Carolina (tournament)
Horizon League	UW-Green Bay*
Ivy League	Harvard*
Metro Atlantic	Marist*
Mid-American	
East Division	Bowling Green*
West Division	Ball State
Mid-Continent	Oakland
	Oral Roberts (tournament)
Mid-Eastern	Coppin State*
Missouri Valley	Southern Illinois
	Drake (tournament)
Mountain West	Brigham Young
	New Mexico (tournament)
Northeast	Robert Morris*–Long Island (tie)
Ohio Valley	Southeast Missouri State*
Pacific 10	Stanford*
Patriot League	Bucknell
	Holy Cross (tournament)
Southeastern	Tennessee
	Vanderbilt (tournament)
Southern	
North Division	Western Carolina
South Division	Chattanooga*
Southland	
East Division	Southeastern Louisiana
West Division	Texas-Arlington*
Southwestern	Jackson State–Prairie View A&M* (tie)
Sun Belt	
East Division	Middle Tennessee*
West Division	Louisiana-Lafayette
West Coast	Gonzaga*
Western Athletic	Boise State–Louisiana Tech* (tie)

*Regular season and conference tournament champion.

Sources: National Collegiate Athletic Association (NCAA); National Association of Intercollegiate Athletics (NAIA); National Invitation Tournament (NIT); Conference Web sites.

Dennis Johnson dies. The five-time NBA All-Star guard, who played on three championship teams (Seattle in 1979, Boston in 1984 and 1986), died Feb. 22, 2007, in Austin, Texas. Johnson suffered a heart attack while leaving a practice for the Austin Toros of the NBA Developmental League, where he was the coach.

Professional women. The Phoenix Mercury won their first WNBA championship, defeating the defending champion Detroit Shock 108-92 in the fifth and deciding game on September 16 in Detroit. Cappie Pondexter of the Mercury was named the Most Valuable Player of the Finals.

College men. The Florida Gators opened up a double-digit lead in the first half and were never threatened by the Ohio State Buckeyes and their talented freshmen, Greg Oden and Mike Conley, Jr., rolling to an 84-75 victory on April 2, 2007, in Atlanta. Al Horford had 18 points and 12 rebounds, Taurean Green added 16 points, and Corey Brewer, the Final Four Most Outstanding Player, netted 13 points, helping offset a 25-point, 12-rebound performance by Oden, the first pick in the June 2007 NBA draft. The Gators hit 10 of 18 three-pointers in the title game.

Florida (35-5), the top seed in the Midwest Regional, reached the title game on March 31 by beating UCLA (30-6), the No. 2 seed in the West, 76-66 in a rematch of the 2006 title game. Brewer, arguably the team's best defender, led the way with 19 points. Ohio State (35-4), the top seed in the South Regional, slipped past Georgetown (30-7), seeded second in the East, 67-60 in its national semifinal. The Buckeyes needed huge rallies just to escape their region, tying ninth-seeded Xavier with a three-pointer only two seconds before the buzzer in the second round and coming back from a double-digit deficit in the second half to beat Tennessee and advance to the Elite Eight.

The only major shocker in the tournament was 11th-seeded Virginia Commonwealth's first-round triumph over sixth-seeded Duke. The Blue Devils lost in the first round for the first time since 1996 and missed the Sweet 16 for the first time since 1998.

College women. The Tennessee Lady Vols (34-3), seeded No. 1 in the Dayton Regional, rode the stellar play of the Final Four Most Outstanding Player and national Player of the Year Candace Parker to a 59-46 win over Rutgers (27-9) on April 3, 2007, in Cleveland. Parker scored 17 points in the title game. Rutgers, the No. 4 seed in the Greensboro Regional, had earned its spot in the title game with a 59-35 win over Louisiana State University (Baton Rouge) on April 1. LSU (30-8) was seeded third in the Fresno Regional. Tennessee rallied from a 12-point deficit in the final 8:18 to beat North Carolina (34-4), the No. 1 seed in the Dallas Regional, in its national semifinal on April 1. ■ Michael Kates

See also **Sports.**

Belarus. See Europe.

Belgium experienced a tumultuous year in 2007, as the ruling Liberal-Socialist coalition government lost power in a general election in June. Liberal Party leader Guy Verhofstadt, who had served as prime minister for eight years, submitted his resignation to King Albert II. Yves Leterme, whose Flemish Christian Democratic Party made large gains in the election and who was expected to become prime minister of a center-right coalition, began attempts to form a government.

However, coalition negotiations remained bogged down over the question of increased autonomy for Belgium's main regions—Flanders and Wallonia—in a country that is already the most decentralized in Europe. Leterme, who had caused controversy by characterizing Belgium as "an accident of history," favored increased autonomy for the regions. Surveys showed that a majority of Flemish Belgians supported more autonomy, but French-speaking Walloons—who experience unemployment at twice the rate that the Flemish do—remained in favor of the federation. Political analysts feared that the divide between the 60-percent majority Dutch-speaking Flemish in the north and the 40-percent minority French-speaking Walloons in the south may lead to the breakup of Belgium.

On Dec. 1, 2007, Leterme conceded to King Albert that he was unable to form a government and resigned his mandate. King Albert asked outgoing Prime Minister Verhofstadt to form an interim government. The interim government was to "take care of urgent matters and start negotiations leading to institutional reform."

Immigration. The one issue that united Belgians in 2007 was a desire to restrict immigration, particularly among asylum seekers and economic migrants from non-European Union (EU) nations. In October, the country's 11 political parties agreed that non-EU citizens may only be hired in Belgium for positions that cannot be filled by migrants from the EU; that family members may join immigrants in Belgium only if they show proof of sufficient income; and that immigrants may attain Belgian citizenship only after five years of residence and after demonstrating proficiency in one of Belgium's three official languages—Dutch, French, or German. The agreement was to go into effect when a new government was formed.

Economy. According to EU economists, Belgium's economic growth rate fell slightly in 2007 to 2.7 percent, from 2.8 percent in 2006. The unemployment rate also fell, from 8.2 percent in 2006 to 7.5 percent in 2007, fueled by strong economic growth.   ■ Jeffrey Kopstein

See also Europe.

Belize. See Latin America.
Benin. See Africa.
Bhutan. See Asia.

Biology. Honey bees mysteriously disappeared from their hives in 2007, and in September scientists revealed that a virus may be linked to the problem. The honey bee die-offs, called *colony collapse disorder* (CCD), occurred coast-to-coast in the United States. Seemingly healthy worker bees vanished from their hives, leaving the queen and the young behind to die. Many beekeepers lost almost all of their colonies. Beekeepers in Asia, Europe, and South America also reported cases of CCD.

The honey bee die-offs had the potential to greatly disrupt the food supply. Bees pollinate many fruit and vegetable crops, which provide about a third of the human diet. In the United States, bees pollinate more than 130 crops, with a yearly value of $15 billion. These crops include apples, nuts, soybeans, and squash.

In July, the U.S. Department of Agriculture announced a Research Action Plan in response to CCD. The plan identified possible causes of the disorder, including diseases, parasites, pesticides, and stress from environmental and nutritional factors.

In September, a group of bee researchers announced that a virus called *Israel acute paralysis virus* (IAPV) was possibly associated with CCD. Scientists at Columbia University in New York City discovered that the virus was found in most hives afflicted with CCD, but in almost no healthy hives. IAPV may have come to the United States with bees imported from Australia. However, the virus had not caused problems in Australia or in Israel, where it had also been found.

Scientists in Israel discovered that many bees there had developed genetic resistance to IAPV. If the virus was a cause of CCD, scientists hoped to breed resistant bee stocks from those found in Israel. However, the bees afflicted by CCD might have become susceptible to the virus because of some other unknown factor.

Sudan surprise. In June, the Wildlife Conservation Society in New York announced a wildlife spectacle in the war-torn region of southern Sudan: a herd of migrating antelopes 50 miles (80 kilometers) long and 30 miles (48 kilometers) across. Numbering about 1.3 million, the animals consisted chiefly of Mongalla gazelles, tiang, and white-eared kob.

The aerial survey, which revealed the antelope migration, was the first performed in southern Sudan since a civil war began there in 1982. The migration rivaled the vast migrating herds on the Serengeti Plain, an African region that stretches from Tanzania into southern Kenya.

Primate genomes. In April 2007, scientists announced that they had sequenced the *genome* (total amount of hereditary information) of the rhesus macaque monkey. The monkey was the third primate genome sequenced since 2000, along with chimpanzee and human genomes. Researchers at the Baylor College of Medicine in Houston led the project.

Genomes consist of genes, which are codes in the form of DNA (deoxyribonucleic acid). Genes determine an organism's various physical traits. In sequencing, the genome is mapped in the order of its coded parts, a process that helps scientists to study which codes correspond to which traits. By comparing the rhesus monkey's genome with those of chimpanzees and humans, scientists hoped to trace the development of primates from older ancestors that lived millions of years ago.

"Junk" DNA not so junky. The first *marsupial* genome—that of the South American short-tailed opossum—was sequenced in May 2007. Marsupials are mammals that give birth to extremely undeveloped young and carry them in pouches. The project was led by researchers from the Massachusetts Institute of Technology and Harvard University, both in Cambridge.

Data from the opossum genome helped scientists understand how so-called *junk DNA* affects the evolution of species. Junk DNA is the portion of an organism's genome that exists outside of genes. Much of the DNA in an organism's genome can be junk DNA, which was once thought to play a small role in evolution.

Marsupials and *placentals* (mammals that give birth to fully developed young) have many of the same genes. However, some of these genes are active in one group and inactive in the other, which helps to explain their differing traits. When researchers examined the junk DNA of marsupials and placentals, they found that parts of the junk DNA actually control which of the animals' genes are activated.

These findings showed that junk DNA can play a vital role in evolution. Species evolve through natural selection, in which the organisms with physical characteristics best suited to their environment survive more often. Those physical characteristics are determined by genes. But if certain genes are activated by controls in junk DNA, this means that changes in junk DNA can indirectly affect the evolution of a species.

Height gene identified. In September, scientists announced that they found a gene that influences a person's height. Researchers from the Peninsula Medical School and University of Oxford, both in the United Kingdom (U.K.), and the Massachusetts Institute of Technology and Harvard University studied DNA samples of 5,000 people. The gene, called HGMA2, was the first such "height gene" discovered.

Each person inherits two copies of every gene, one from each parent. Each copy, in turn, can be one of two variants, called *alleles*. In HGMA2, the two alleles seem to correspond to either tallness or shortness. People with two "tall" alleles of HGMA2 were, on average, about ⅖ inch (1 centimeter) taller than people with two "short" alleles. HGMA2 is thought to be one of several genes that contribute to height.

The study may have additional implications for fighting disease. For example, tall people suffer from certain kinds of cancer more frequently than short people. Researchers speculated that HGMA2 may relate to height by controlling cell production and thus may be related to cancer, a disease in which cells multiply wildly.

Super strong silk. Researchers from the University of California, Riverside, announced in June that they had discovered the genetic code for the dragline silk of the black widow spider. The discovery could pave the way for making the extremely strong and light silk synthetically, using *genetic engineering* (techniques that alter organisms' genes). The material could be used in athletic gear, body armor, and medical devices.

Black widows use dragline silk to anchor their webs and support their bodies. It has more elasticity and strength than most other spiders' silk.

Bird brains. In January, scientists from several European countries reported that birds with larger brains, relative to their weight, have better odds of survival in the wild. Researchers from the University of Bath in the United Kingdom and the Center for Ecological Research and Forestry Applications in Spain compared the brain size, body mass, and mortality rate of hundreds of bird species.

Large-brained birds, such as parrots and crows, can more easily learn to adapt to new situations and changing conditions. Scientists believed they may, therefore, be more likely to survive major environmental shifts and climate change.

Deadly droppings. Engineers announced in August that a build-up of pigeon droppings may have contributed to the Minneapolis bridge collapse on August 1, which killed 13 people. Bridges are a favorite nesting site of pigeons, whose wild ancestors roosted on cliffs. Bird droppings contain ammonia and acids, which can trigger electrochemical reactions that cause steel to rust.

A million species. By 2007, scientists had identified an estimated 1.75 million living species. In April, researchers from the Smithsonian National Museum of Natural History in Washington, D.C., and the University of Reading in the U.K. announced that they had cataloged over 1 million of them. About 3,000 biologists from around the world collaborated on the project, which began in 2001. They hoped to catalog all known living species by 2011.   ■ Edward Ricciuti

See also **Biology: A Special Report; Conservation; Global warming; Ocean; Zoos.**

IN 2007, SCIENTISTS
CAME CLOSER TO
ANSWERING THE QUESTION
"WHAT MAKES HUMAN
BEINGS HUMAN?"

A New Perspective on
PRIMATES

By Ed Ricciuti

Throughout the 2000's, scientists have reported exciting break-throughs in the knowledge of how human beings and other primates evolved. So, too, genetic and anthropological research have given us a greater understanding of the similarities we share with other primates and the differences that distinguish us. The announcement in April 2007 that scientists had *sequenced* (mapped the order of) the rhesus macaque *genome* was the third involving a primate since 2000. (A genome is a complete set of all of the hereditary information for a particular organism.) The first primate genome to be mapped was that of human beings; the second, in 2005, was that of chimpanzees. By comparing these genomes, researchers have confirmed that chimpanzees are human beings' closest primate relative. The studies have also shed light on how the two species developed their own branches on the primate family tree.

Studies of apes in the wild are aiding scientists seeking to trace the evolutionary roots of human behavior. For example, scientists had thought that only human beings could use the same gesture to mean different things, depending on the situation. Now it appears that the great apes—bonobos, chimpanzees, gorillas, and orangutans—can communicate this way as well.

Moreover, researchers' findings in primate studies are complementing and supporting conclusions drawn in genetic studies. For example, in 2004, genetic researchers reported that they had discovered a miniscule difference in one of the genes shared by people and primates. The form of the gene in human beings makes human bite muscles smaller than those of monkeys and apes. The change allowed for the growth of a larger brain in human beings. About that same time, fossil records show, humanlike creatures began to make tools of stone.

A chimpanzee at Monkey World, an ape rescue center in Wareham, Dorset, in the United Kingdom, appears to study the raindrops striking its hand. Throughout the 2000's, scientists uncovered more details about the physical, mental, and genetic similarities and differences between chimpanzees and human beings.

A bonobo at a sanctuary in Congo (Kinshasa) prepares to use a "hammer" to crack a nut that it has placed on an "anvil." Scientists have found that bonobos, just like the chimpanzees to which they are closely related, have a much longer history of tool use than previously thought.

Apes and their tool kits

Until the 1960's, scientists believed that toolmaking was an ability that only human beings possessed. That view changed when British zoologist Jane Goodall observed a chimpanzee in Tanzania using grass stems to "fish" termites out of their mounds. Goodall watched as the ape inserted the stem, waited for termites to bite into it, then withdrew it and feasted on the insects. She also observed chimpanzees stripping leaves from twigs to create "fishing poles."

An interesting variation in the termite fishing behavior of the Tanzanian chimpanzees was reported in 2005 by researchers at the Yerkes National Primate Research Center at Emory University in Atlanta. Although most human beings are right-handed, 12 of 17 chimpanzees observed by the researchers "fished" with their left hand. This observation may help further scientists' understanding of how the primate brain evolved. Each hand is controlled by the opposite side of the brain, an aspect of what is known as brain *lateralization* (the division of brain function into right and left sides). Chimpanzee brains do not show the degree of lateralization seen in human beings, but the Yerkes researchers contend that their finding indicates that brain lateralization may have begun in the ancestors of chimpanzees and human beings at least 5 million years ago, before the two species went their separate ways.

Since Goodall's discovery, researchers have observed chimpanzees in many parts of Africa using a variety of tools. Some chimpanzees crack nuts with a stone hammer on a stone anvil. Others use logs as a pestle to pound tree bark until they reach its soft, edible pulp. In 2004, researchers from the New York City-based Wildlife Conservation Society and Washington University in St. Louis offered videotaped

The author:
Edward Ricciuti is a free-lance writer.

evidence that chimpanzees not only use tools but also have their own version of tool kits. The tape showed chimpanzees in Congo (Brazzaville) using short sticks to poke open termite mounds that stand aboveground, then switching to slender, longer stems to fish out the insects. The chimps even stripped the ends of stems through their teeth to create a paintbrushlike tool that improved their chances of catching termites. To puncture underground nests, the chimpanzees used heavy sticks, which they pushed into the ground with their feet, as if using a spade.

Like human children, chimpanzee youngsters learn by watching their elders. Mothers seem to teach their young the proper use of tools—and correct them when they do something the "wrong" way. Many scientists believe that passing on traditional knowledge from one generation to the next in this way indicates that chimpanzees have a culture. The fact that chimpanzees that live in areas filled with termite mounds "invented" the use of sticks to catch insects while those in places with an abundance of nuts learned to crack them with stones suggests that different chimpanzee cultures developed in response to the availability of different kinds of food.

Chimpanzees began using tools far in the past, according to research reported in 2007 by Julio Mercader of the University of Calgary in Canada. In Africa's Côte d'Ivoire, at the only prehistoric chimpanzee site known to science, Mercader found stones somewhat larger than softballs. The stones had marks similar to those found on stone tools used by modern chimpanzees and prehistoric human ancestors to crush nuts. The "hammers" are more than 4,000 years old. This finding indicates that tool use by chimpanzees is not a recent development but has existed for perhaps thousands of years.

Primatologist Christophe Boesch of the Max Planck Institute for Evolutionary Anthropology in Leipzig, Germany, uncovers a stone "hammer" at a site in Africa's Côte d'Ivoire. Scientists determined that such tools were used by chimpanzees more than 4,000 years ago to crack nuts.

On the hunt

Tool use is connected to another surprising behavior among chimpanzees—hunting. A group of chimpanzees in West Africa has been observed manipulating sticks to extract nutritious marrow from the cracked bones of monkeys they have caught and killed, much as ancient human hunters did with the bones of their prey.

In early 2007, scientists at Iowa State University in Ames reported seeing chimpanzees in West Africa habitually hunting with a method previously known only to human beings. The apes were wielding "spears"—specifically, sticks that the chimps modified with their teeth. In most cases, the chimps using the sticks were either juveniles or adult females. They preyed mostly on bush babies, big-eyed little primates that sleep by day in tree hollows. The chimpanzees used the sticks to stab at the bush babies while they slept. They flushed them out, caught, and ate them.

Chimpanzees in Uganda "fish" for termites with "fishing poles" that they have specifically chosen for that purpose. Scientists learned in 2004 that the apes use short sticks to poke holes in the tough termite mounds, then switch to slender, longer stems to fish out the insects.

The reason that female and young male chimps are more likely to use spears may be related to the way that bands share meat acquired through hunting. Adult male chimpanzees in certain areas—particularly the rain forest—cooperate extensively when they hunt. Certain members of the group chase the prey as "drivers," while others act as "blockers" to prevent the prey from escaping. In this way, members of a band who hunt together are much more successful than individual chimps in catching such fast-moving prey as colobus monkeys and small antelope.

Most of the meat from a hunt among rain forest chimps goes to adult males who have participated in the hunt. Juveniles and females often get no share. It may be that females and young males began using "spears" to compete for prey with the strong, well-organized males.

Chimpanzees who live in the savannah handle the distribution of meat from a hunt a little differently. An older male with status in the group may receive a share of meat even if he does not hunt. Scientists have been particularly interested in studying the close cooperation by chimpanzees during hunts because they believe it may reflect the way prehuman ancestors learned to work together.

Learning to share?

However, the cooperation shown by chimpanzees on a hunt does not necessarily carry over into sharing in other ways, according to a report in 2007 by German and American researchers. When they presented a pair of captive chimpanzees with two dishes of food accessible only by a joint effort on their part, the chimps worked well together, as they do while hunting in the wild. But if only one dish was available, cooperation dwindled, and one of the two chimpanzees tended to monopolize the meal. According to the researchers, the tendency in chimpanzee societies to compete for food and other resources won out over the tendency to cooperate while hunting when the resource—in this case the dish of food—was limited.

The scientists tried the same experiment with another type of ape called a bonobo. Bonobos are found in only one area, south of the Congo River in Congo (Kinshasa). These apes were once thought to be a pygmy version of the common variety of chimpanzee but are now recognized as a separate slender, slightly smaller species. Unlike the common chimpanzee, from which they diverged some 2 million to 3 million years ago, bonobos are good-natured and not aggressive. They

A gorilla nicknamed Leah in Nouabal-Ndoki National Park in Congo (Brazzaville) uses a stick to test the depth of a pool. Scientists observing the gorilla in 2004 saw her enter the pool, find herself waist-deep in water, and return to shore to break a dead branch off a tree to use as a testing stick. Previously, researchers had thought that gorillas and other great apes use tools only to obtain food.

seldom fight, even against members of other bands, and often use sexual activity to diffuse conflicts rather than resort to aggression.

The tolerant lifestyle of the bonobo seems to encourage even more cooperation than that exhibited by hunting chimpanzees. Bonobos willingly worked together to obtain food presented by scientists even when it was in a single dish. The meal, moreover, was shared affably. Scientists are focusing on this behavior because they believe that tolerance of others is a trait that can lead to the development of social problem-solving skills and thus provide an advantage for one group over another.

Walking the walk

Bipedalism (BYE peh duh liz uhm—walking on two legs with an upright posture) and the ability to speak were critical to the development of the Hominidae—the family of human beings and their ancestors. To increase our understanding of how these traits developed, scientists have long looked for their roots in other primates. Developments in 2007 showed progress in this area, though not in the directions researchers had expected.

The most familiar theory explaining how human beings came to walk upright begins with tree-dwelling primates about 25 million years ago. As forests began to thin, open savannah grassland areas developed between the trees. According to this scenario, primates were forced to travel across the ground to move between forest patches. Perhaps by 10 million years ago, they began to walk on their feet and knuckles as chimpanzees, bonobos, and gorillas do today. At some point, prehumans began to use their hands for such tasks as carrying fruit, and developed an upright posture.

Some researchers, however, contend that bipedalism may have developed much earlier than 25 million years ago, when human ancestors still lived in the forest. The orangutan, the only great ape native to Asia, lives in the forest canopy, seldom coming to the ground. Researchers from the University of Birmingham in the United Kingdom spent a year observing these creatures in a national park in Sumatra in Indonesia. They watched orangutans walk on two legs as they ventured out onto thin branches to pick fruit. The apes steadied themselves by grasping the branches above them with their hands, which they also used to gather fruit. The scientists noted that the posture of tree-walking orangutans is upright, rather than bent over like that of other great apes traveling on the ground.

These new observations raise the possibility that human ancestors began walking upright in the trees and retained the ability after moving to the ground millions of years later. The theory is bolstered by the fact that the knee joint of the orangutan is more like that of human beings than that of any other ape. The structure of the joint allows the orangutan to extend its leg, as required for walking upright. Some ancient fossils of creatures that may be the common ancestors of human beings and apes have a joint structure that suggests upright walking, a trait that human beings retained while chimps, gorillas, and bonobos developed a four-legged knuckle walk instead. Until now, scientists have not understood how the fossils fit into the puzzle of modern primate evolution. The orangutan observations may provide the key.

An orangutan at Gunung Leuser National Park in Indonesia walks along a tree branch in an upright posture, using its arms to help it balance. In 2007, British researchers studying orangutans proposed that *bipedalism* (BYE peh duh liz uhm—walking upright on two legs) may have begun much earlier than previously thought, at a time when human ancestors still lived in the treetops.

Another benefit of bipedalism was suggested by unusual research reported in 2007. Scientists at the University of Arizona in Tucson, Washington University in St. Louis, and the University of California-Davis taught chimpanzees to walk on a treadmill. Some of the chimps used their knuckles to walk on all fours while others walked upright. All of the apes were fitted with masks to measure oxygen use in each position. Walking upright seems to require less energy than knuckle walking, which would improve the ability to forage for food. (The researchers also found that when the chimps became bored with walking on the treadmill, they quickly figured out how to push the button to make it stop.)

Spreading the word

Primate research is also challenging a popular theory about the development of human language. Scientists have long speculated that speech evolved from *vocalizations* (sounds such as grunts) accompanied by facial expressions made by prehuman ancestors. However, some scientists now question that idea, based on studies of bonobos and chimpanzees at the Yerkes National Primate Research Center. The researchers studied 31 different gestures and 18 vocalizations/facial expressions used by the apes. Vocalizations, the researchers discovered, always mean the same thing when used by the chimpanzees and bonobos. The "bared-teeth scream," for example, indicates fear.

A single chimpanzee or bonobo gesture, however, may have several meanings, depending on its context. A hand stretched out with palm extended may be a way of begging for food or help. It may also signal a desire for reconciliation after a fight. In nonhuman primates, the researchers discovered, gestures are a much more versatile way of communicating than vocalizations and facial expressions, which are often involuntary and based on emotional reactions. The use of gestures, therefore, may have played an important role in the development of language.

Some scientists now speculate that as human ancestors began to increasingly use their hands for tasks, the body structures involved in speech—lips, mouth, and *larynx* ("voice box")—became more involved in communication. Genetic evidence backs this idea. In 2001, researchers at Oxford University in the United Kingdom identified the first gene in human beings that is directly related to language. The gene, FOXP2, allows human beings to control their lips, tongue, and mouth to a much greater degree than other primates can. It also plays a role in brain development, particularly in the human ability to string sounds in the proper order to form words and sentences. FOXP2 differs from a similar gene in chimpanzees in a small but perhaps monumentally important way—2 of 715 *amino acids*. (Amino acids make up the proteins in all living things.) The difference may allow for the fine-tuning of muscle control that enables human beings to speak.

TALK TO THE ANIMALS

One of the most obvious differences between human beings and other primates is the human capacity for spoken language. However, some studies have shown that apes do have some language ability. One of the first major studies began in 1967 with a young chimpanzee named Washoe. Psychologists Beatrice and Allen Gardner of the University of Nevada in Las Vegas taught Washoe about 130 words over a period of three years. Because Washoe lacked the anatomical structure that people possess to produce spoken words, the Gardners taught Washoe American Sign Language (ASL). In 1980, Washoe joined the Chimpanzee and Human Communication Institute (CHCI) at Central Washington University in Ellensburg. There, she taught three other chimps, including her adopted son, Loulis, to use as many as 47 different ASL signs. Washoe died in 2007, but several studies continue to explore the language capability of great apes. A bonobo named Kanzi has learned to sign up to 256 words and can understand about 500 spoken word commands.

A chimpanzee reaches its hand out in a gesture. In 2007, researchers at the Yerkes National Primate Research Center in Atlanta reported that chimpanzee gestures are much more flexible in meaning than are facial expressions or *vocalizations* (sounds such as grunts). The meaning of a chimp's gesture depends on the context in which it is made. This finding suggests to some scientists that gestures may have played an important role in the development of language.

Breaking the genetic code

Along with behavioral studies and data from fossils, research into the genetic basis of primate evolution has resulted in several major breakthroughs for scientists probing human origins. In 2000, scientists in the United States and several other countries reported that they had sequenced the human genome. The mapping of the chimpanzee genome, announced in 2005, allowed scientists to compare the two, making information uncovered in the human genome even more meaningful.

The code of hereditary information stored in a genome consists of chemical building blocks called nucleotides that make up DNA (deoxyribonucleic acid). DNA is a thin, chainlike molecule that is found on threadlike structures called chromosomes in the *nucleus* (center) of every living cell on Earth. Each nucleotide contains a molecule of sugar, a compound called a phosphate, and a compound called a base. The sugar and phosphate are the same in all DNA nucleotides, but nucleotides may carry any of four different bases: adenine, guanine, cytosine, and thymine. These bases are described as the "letters" of the genetic code. The sequence in which bases are positioned in a genome determines the traits of a species, just like the order of letters in the alphabet spells out a particular word.

Both the human genome and the chimpanzee genome have about 3 billion base pairs. The two genomes are between about 95 percent and 98 percent similar. The remaining small percentage is critical because it accounts for the differences between the two species. In effect, the genetic letters form different words in human beings than they do in chimpanzees. The problem for scientists was that they had no way to determine which words represent evolutionary change in either human beings or chimpanzees and which represent characteristics inherited from primate ancestors.

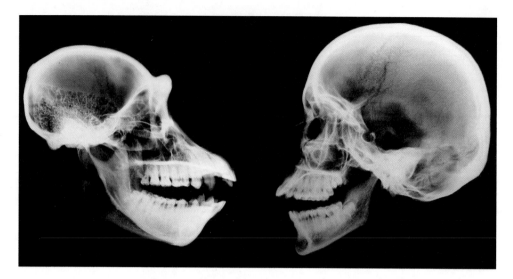

The skull of a chimpanzee (above left) displays a large bony ridge above the eyes, a large lower jawbone, and a much smaller braincase than the skull of a human being (above right). In 2004, researchers determined that a *mutation* (change) in a gene that regulates the muscle protein myosin about 2.4 million years ago caused human jaw muscles to become smaller and weaker. The muscles no longer constrained the growth of the braincase, allowing a larger brain to develop.

What we learned from the macaque

The sequencing of the rhesus macaque genome offers a way to solve the problem. The rhesus is an Old World monkey, a member of a group that diverged from the line leading to apes and human beings about 25 million years ago. Its genome is 93-percent similar to the genomes of human beings and chimpanzees. By using the macaque genome as a baseline model, scientists hope to determine how the genomes of human beings and chimpanzees have diverged over time. What they specifically want to learn is, if the position of a base in a human gene differs from that in a chimpanzee, which is the older form and which was a step in the development of human beings? So far, scientists have identified about 200 genes that seem to have changed in either the rhesus or human/chimpanzee lines. These include genes regulating a hair-forming protein and the immune system.

One thing leads to another

Genome sequencing can confirm or expand upon anthropological findings. For example, primates have large jaw muscles that are supported by bony ridges on their skulls. However, fossils show that the skull of human ancestors lacked such a ridge. Humanlike creatures apparently lost this feature about 2.4 million years ago. In 2004, researchers at the University of Pennsylvania in Philadelphia reported that 2 particular base pairs in 1 of the 10 genes that regulate the muscle protein myosin in other primates are missing from human genes. A mutation must have occurred in the gene that caused human jaw muscles to become smaller and weaker. Although such a loss sounds like a disadvantage, it may have had the opposite result in human beings, at least as far as brain size is concerned, researchers speculated. Without such big muscles, the skull of a human infant can continue growing for three months after birth, allowing room for the development of a larger brain.

In 2007, scientists at the Chinese Academy of Sciences in Kunming discovered another key genetic difference among primates. They found that a certain form of a protein called neuropsin is present in the central nervous system of human beings but not in those of apes or Old World monkeys. The human gene differs from its counterpart in other primates by only one genetic "letter." Neuropsin stimulates memory and learning, so a tiny genetic change may have given a huge push to the evolution of intelligence in the ancestors of modern human beings.

Interestingly, the human genome has undergone fewer *adaptive* changes than the chimp genome has over time. (An adaptive change is one that increases an organism's chances of surviving and reproducing.) In 2007, scientists at the University of Michigan in Ann Arbor compared the sequences of DNA in nearly 14,000 human and chimpanzee genes that control proteins, using rhesus macaque genes as a baseline for comparison. They discovered that since the time that chimpanzees and human beings diverged, 233 chimpanzee genes have mutated. The score for human beings was 154. The scientists speculated that though human proteins have experienced less mutation than have chimp proteins, perhaps those mutated proteins had more significant effects in human beings than the changes in chimp proteins did.

Moving on

Now that the genomes of human beings, chimpanzees, and rhesus macaques have been sequenced, scientists have undertaken those of other primates. Next in line are the orangutan and the marmoset monkey. Researchers hope that as genomes of other primates are mapped, the roots of primate evolution may be traced further into the past. At the same time, the genomes already sequenced hold great promise for learning about diseases, especially those with genetic origins. For example, mutated genes associated with a condition called phenylketonuria, which leads to mental retardation in human beings, are present in their "normal" form in the macaque. Therefore, they probably were normal in the ancestors of human beings. Understanding what caused the mutations and how they are associated with retardation may help researchers treat this condition.

Years of research lie ahead. Yet each discovery brings human understanding closer to an answer to the question: What makes human beings human?

■ FOR ADDITIONAL INFORMATION

Periodicals

"The Chimpanzee Genome." *Science,* Sept. 1, 2005, pp. 47-108+.
"The Rhesus Macaque Genome." Special Section in *Science,* April 13, 2007, pp. 215-246.

Web sites

Great Ape Trust of Iowa—http://www.greatapetrust.org/
National Human Genome Research Institute—http://www.genome.gov/11006943
Primate Info Net—http://pin.primate.wisc.edu/
Primates: The Taxonomy and General Characteristics of Prosimians, Monkeys, Apes, and Humans—http://anthro.palomar.edu/primate/default.htm

Boating. The Swiss yacht *Alinghi* defended its America's Cup title in 2007, topping *Emirates Team New Zealand* in a rematch of the final meet held four years earlier. The 5-2 victory in the best-of-nine series off the coast of Valencia, Spain, was the closest in 24 years. It was the first America's Cup held in Europe.

In the International Sailing Federation (ISAF) world championships held during the first two weeks of July off the coast of Cascais, Portugal, the United Kingdom finished on top of the medal standings with two gold medals and four bronzes.

America's Cup. *Emirates Team New Zealand* earned its spot in the America's Cup final by sweeping past Italian entry *Luna Rossa* in five straight races on June 6, in the Louis Vuitton Cup final. It was the first time a boat went undefeated in a best-of-nine series since the event began in 1983. *Luna Rossa* had defeated the entry from the United States, *BMW ORACLE Racing*, in the semifinals of the Louis Vuitton Cup. The American team switched helmsman in an attempt to change its fortunes but still lost.

In the America's Cup final, *Alinghi* sailed to a 30-second victory in race 4 on June 27, 2007, to even the series. Three more consecutive victories turned around its initial 2-1 deficit. The Swiss team closed out the title with a photo finish one-second triumph on July 3, letting a huge lead slip

The Swiss yacht *Alinghi* (left) sails ahead of *Emirates Team New Zealand* during the seventh race of the 32nd America's Cup competition off the coast of Valencia, Spain, on July 3, 2007. *Alinghi*, the defending champion, won the Cup, 5-2, in the best-of-nine series.

away on the final leg but crossing just ahead of the New Zealand boat.

World championships. On July 9, Spain's Fernando Echavarri (helm) and Anton Paz (crew) won the gold medal in the Tornado class. Australian Tom Slingsby took the Laser title while Tatiana Drozdovskaya of Belarus took the Laser Radial title. Brazilians Robert Scheidt (helm) and Bruno Prada (crew) won the Star gold without a final race on July 10 because of high winds.

Spain earned its second and final gold when Rafael Trujillo captured the Finn division on July 11. That same day, the United Kingdom's Sarah Ayton (helm) and Sarah Webb and Pippa Wilson (crew) won the Yngling title. The next day, in RS:X Racing, Ricardo Santos of Brazil took the men's gold while Poland's Zofia Klepacka won the women's title.

On July 13, the final day of racing, Stevie Morrison and Ben Rhodes of the United Kingdom won the 49er gold. Australia's Nathan Wilmot and Malcolm Page captured the men's 470, and Marcelien de Koning and Lobke Berkhout of the Netherlands won their third straight women's 470.

Powerboats. Dave Villwock captured his sixth APBA Gold Cup in Detroit on July 15, averaging 147.687 miles (237.679 kilometers) per hour in his U-16 *Miss Elam Plus.*   ■ Michael Kates

Bolivia. In 2007, President Juan Evo Morales Ayma encountered stiffening resistance to his plan to have Bolivia's Constitution rewritten by a constituent assembly elected in 2006 for that purpose. Morales hoped that by ensuring poor Bolivians, especially those of the indigenous majority, like himself, a greater voice in their own governance, he could end decades of bitter social and regional divisions that had mired Bolivia in political gridlock.

Because of political infighting, the assembly had not approved even one article for the constitution after meeting for more than a year in Sucre. In 2007, the assembly's work was sidetracked by a proposal to move Bolivia's administrative capital from La Paz, in the western highlands—a region strongly supportive of the incumbent president—to Sucre, the country's official capital and the seat of the Supreme Court. In July, 1 million people took to the streets of La Paz to protest the proposed move. In August and September, counterdemonstrations in Sucre were sufficiently violent to delay the proceedings of the assembly for a month.

Bolivians in the prosperous eastern lowlands continued in 2007 to demand greater regional autonomy and a larger share of public revenues from gas, oil, and agricultural production in their area. President Morales characterized such

demands as part of a battle between the rich and the poor. His fiery rhetoric did little to bridge the social and economic divisions that had led to the ousting of several presidents before him.

Aid from Venezuela, Bolivia's close ally, totaled approximately $800 million during the first eight months of 2007. Roughly two-thirds of this amount was intended to help modernize Bolivia's energy sector, which Morales had nationalized in 2006. It included $240 million for oil and gas exploration, $170 million to build two liquid natural gas extraction plants, and $58 million to build diesel electricity and thermoelectric power plants.

Venezuelan President Hugo Chávez supplied Venezuelan personnel to oversee these and other projects, such as the construction of a $150-million asphalt plant and 15 fuel distribution stations. As 2007 progressed, some Bolivians became leery of Venezuela's increased involvement in their country's affairs. Of particular concern to some people was the presence in Bolivia of Venezuelan military personnel, whom President Morales had welcomed as advisers to the poorly trained and equipped Bolivian army.

■ Nathan A. Haverstock
See also **Latin America; Venezuela.**

Books. See Literature; Literature for children; Poetry.

Bosnia-Herzegovina. A political crisis in late 2007 threatened to unravel the governing structure established in Bosnia-Herzegovina (generally called Bosnia) by the Dayton Accords, the peace pact that ended the Bosnian War (1992-1995). Bosnia is an ethnic patchwork of Bosnian Muslims, called Bosniaks; Bosnian Serbs; and Croats. Under the Dayton provisions, Bosnia consists of two ministates: the Serb enclave, called the Republika Srpska (RS); and the Muslim-Croat Federation, populated mainly by Bosniaks and Croats. These ministates are loosely linked under a national government, headed by a tripartite presidency of one Croat, one Bosniak, and one Bosnian Serb representative. The Dayton Accords also provided for an International High Representative (IHR), a United Nations-appointed official empowered to intervene in Bosnia's political institutions to enforce the Dayton Accords.

The crisis began on Oct. 19, 2007, when IHR Miroslav Lajcak demanded changes in Bosnia's parliamentary rules. Under existing rules, the national parliament required the presence of members of all three major Bosnian ethnic groups to constitute a *quorum* (minimum number required to conduct business). Lajcak demanded that the quorum be redefined as a simple majority of all members of parliament (MP's). According to political analysts, ethnic Serb MP's in the national parliament had used the quorum power to block an internationally sponsored reform that would integrate the country's police forces—controlled separately by the two ministates—into a single national force.

In response to IHR Lajcak's ultimatum, Milorad Dodik, prime minister of the RS, warned that members of his Union of Independent Social Democrats (SNSD), the dominant political party of ethnic Serbs, would resign en masse from the national government unless Lajcak backed down. Vojislav Kostunica, prime minister of neighboring Serbia, issued a statement in support of Dodik.

Bosnia's political crisis came to a head on November 1, when the national prime minister, Nikola Spiric, a Bosnian Serb, resigned. "The international community has cooked this soup and now it is time for them to take the spoon," he challenged.

On November 30, Bosnia's Serb, Muslin, and Croat leaders finally agreed to accept IHR Lajcak's reforms of parliamentary voting rules, thus ending the political crisis. On December 4, the European Union (EU) initialed a pre-membership agreement with Bosnia. The EU required Bosnia's police forces to be integrated before the EU membership process could begin. On December 10, the SNSD nominated Spiric as prime minister.   ■ Sharon L. Wolchik

See also **Europe**.

Botswana. See Africa.

Bowling. Doug Kent of Newark, New York, captured Player of the Year honors in 2007 for his performances during the Professional Bowlers Association (PBA) 2006-2007 season. Kent captured two titles—both majors. He won the first major of the season, the United States Bowling Congress (USBC) Masters, on Oct. 29, 2006, in West Allis, Wisconsin, beating Jack Jurek 277-230 in the title match. He captured his second PBA World Championship on March 25, 2007, in Grand Rapids, Michigan, topping Chris Barnes 237-216 for the title.

Pete Weber defeated Wes Malott 210-204 on March 4 to win his fourth U.S. Open, in North Brunswick, New Jersey. In the other major, Tommy Jones, the 2006 Player of the Year, captured his 10th career title, winning the PBA Tournament of Champions on April 1, 2007, in Uncasville, Connecticut. Jones defeated Tony Reyes 257-222 to break the tour record for quickest time between a 1st and 10th title. Jones did it in two years, six months, and seven days, four days quicker than the legendary Dick Weber did it 45 years earlier.

In the first major of the 2007-2008 season, Sean Rash from Wichita, Kansas, won the 2007 USBC Masters on October 28 in Milwaukee, beating Steve Jaros 269-245 in the final.

Women's bowling. The PBA announced in late July that it would hold a four-event mini-series for women, the first tour for women since the Professional Women's Bowling Association folded in 2003. Liz Johnson of Cheektowaga, New York, captured the USBC U.S. Women's Open in Reno, Nevada, on Oct. 14, 2007, defeating Shannon O'Keefe of Rochester, New York, 248-215.

Women still competed on the men's circuit. On October 25, Carolyn Dorin-Ballard of Fort Worth, Texas, rolled the first 300 game by a woman in the history of the USBC Masters, the first major of the PBA's 2007-2008 tour. Dorin-Ballard lost that three-game match to Chris Barnes.

Seniors. Tom Baker of King, North Carolina, won an unprecedented third straight Player of the Year award, buoyed by a season-ending victory over his main competitor, David Ozio, in the PBA Senior Dick Weber Invitational on Aug. 21, 2007. Baker beat Ozio 256-213 for his third title of the season, bringing his career total to eight PBA Senior Tour titles in his three seasons.

Baker's 658-625 victory over Shannon Starnes at the USBC Senior Masters on July 13 in Reno was his fourth major title on the Senior Tour. Rick Minier of Houston captured the tour's other major, beating Ozio 240-223 in the Senior U.S. Open on June 23 in Las Vegas.
      ■ Michael Kates

Boxing. Evander Holyfield in 2007 failed to capture his fifth heavyweight title, losing a unanimous decision for the World Boxing Organization (WBO) belt to the reigning champ, Russian Sultan Ibragimov on October 13 in Moscow. Holyfield, just shy of his 45th birthday at the time of the fight, was attempting to become the second-oldest heavyweight champion, but Ibragimov (22-0-1) used an effective counter-punching strategy to deny the American.

Marquee match-up. In a bout billed as "the" fight to save boxing from the growing popularity of ultimate fighting, Floyd Mayweather, Jr., remained unbeaten with a split decision over Oscar De La Hoya on May 5 in Las Vegas. Mayweather took the World Boxing Council (WBC) title from De La Hoya, who won the fight 115-113 on one judge's card but lost 116-112 and 115-113 on the other two judges' cards.

The contest set a record for most television subscriptions for a fight, with 2.15 million households shelling out $54.95 for the pay-per-view event. De La Hoya reportedly received $45 million for the fight; Mayweather, $20 million.

Fighters in trouble. On September 24, former heavyweight champion Mike Tyson pleaded guilty to charges of cocaine possession and driving under the influence in December 2006 and was sentenced to one day in jail, which he served on Nov. 19, 2007.

Light heavyweight Bernard Hopkins was fined $200,000 by Nevada boxing regulators for starting a melee during the weigh-in for his July 20 fight with Winky Wright. Hopkins won the fight and the $3-million prize.

Shane Mosley was accused of using steroids he obtained from the scandal-plagued Bay Area Laboratory Co-operative (BALCO) as part of a doping regimen before a 2003 light middle-weight title fight against De La Hoya. According to news reports, Mosley began using two steroids that were undetectable at the time as well as the blood-doping drug erythropoietin (EPO) several weeks before he won the title in a unanimous decision. Mosley said he was misled and did not know what he was taking.

Other notable title fights. Wladimir Klitschko of Ukraine retained his International Boxing Federation (IBF) and International Boxing Organization (IBO) heavyweight titles in Cologne, Germany, on July 7, 2007, pummeling U.S. fighter Lamon Brewster for a technical knockout (TKO) after the sixth round. Brewster had beaten Klitschko for the WBO title in 2004. On Oct. 13, 2007, in Hoffman Estates, Illinois, World Boxing Association (WBA) and WBO lightweight champ Juan Diaz beat Julio Diaz by a TKO to take the IBF title.   ■ Michael Kates

WORLD CHAMPION BOXERS

WORLD BOXING ASSOCIATION

Division	Champion	Country	Date won
Heavyweight	Ruslan Chagaev	Uzbekistan	4/07
Light heavyweight	Stipe Drews	Croatia	4/07
Middleweight	Felix Sturm	Germany	4/07
Welterweight	Miguel Cotto	Puerto Rico	12/06
Lightweight	Juan Diaz	United States	7/04
Featherweight	Chris John	Indonesia	9/03
Bantamweight	Wladimir Sidorenko	Ukraine	2/05
Flyweight	Takefumi Sakata	Japan	3/07

WORLD BOXING COUNCIL

Division	Champion	Country	Date won
Heavyweight	Oleg Maskaev	Kazakhstan	8/06
Light heavyweight	Chad Dawson	United States	2/07
Middleweight	Kelly Pavlik	United States	9/07
Welterweight	Floyd Mayweather	United States	11/06
Lightweight	David Diaz	United States	8/06
Featherweight	Jorge Linares	Venezuela	7/07
Bantamweight	Hozumi Hasegawa	Japan	4/05
Flyweight	Daisuke Naito	Japan	7/07

Brazil. Luiz Inácio Lula da Silva, 62, of the Workers' Party, was sworn in as president for a second four-year term on Jan. 1, 2007. Shortly after the inauguration, Lula unveiled a plan to raise Brazil's annual economic production by 5 percent for the next four years, beginning in 2008. The plan called for $235 billion in public and private investment. Most of the money was intended for a large-scale upgrade of Brazil's infrastructure, including the construction of high-ways, hydroelectric dams, and railroads.

Corruption plagued Lula's administration during 2007. In May, Minister of Mines and Energy Silas Rondeau resigned after being accused of accepting a $50,000 bribe from a construction company to which he had awarded a lucrative contract. In August, José Dirceu de Oliveira e Silva, the president's former chief-of-staff, and Delúbio Soares de Castro, a former Workers' Party trea-surer, were ordered by Brazil's Supreme Federal Court to stand trial in connection with a vote-buying scheme revealed in 2005. About 40 others, also implicated in the scheme to bribe legislators for their votes, faced similar charges of embezzle-ment, fraud, money laundering, and racketeering.

A hydroelectric project that would use water from the Madeira River increasingly con-cerned environmentalists during 2007. Some peo-ple feared that the proposed $11-billion project, which involved the construction of two dams, would lead to deforestation as new settlers cleared huge areas of rain forest to cultivate soy-beans. Opponents also worried about the dams' impact on thousands of indigenous people living in the state of Rondônia and on hundreds of fish species in the Madeira, an important tributary of the Amazon River.

Also in Rondônia, the indigenous Surui people employed computer technology to protect their 618,000-acre (250,000-hectare) reservation from illegal logging and mining. The Surui used com-puters provided by the nonprofit Amazon Con-servation Team to map their land and Google Earth software to monitor it via satellite imagery.

Rancher convicted in nun's murder. In May, a Brazilian court found rancher Vitalmiro Bastos de Moura guilty of masterminding the 2005 murder of Dorothy Stang, a 73-year-old nun from the United States who had worked to pro-tect the rain forest. Bastos de Moura received the maximum sentence of 30 years in prison.

First Brazilian saint. On May 11, 2007, Pope Benedict XVI canonized Antônio de Sant'Anna Galvão, a Franciscan monk who lived from 1739 to 1822. Galvão became the first Roman Catholic saint born in Brazil, which has the world's largest Catholic population. He was credited with mirac-ulously curing the sick with pills that he made of rice paper and inscribed with prayers. The canonization ceremony, attended by about 1 million people, took place in São Paulo.

Aviation tragedy. On July 17, 2007, an Airbus A320 passenger plane operated by Brazil's TAM Airlines crashed while landing in rainy weather at São Paulo's Congonhas airport, killing about 200 people. Congonhas was South America's busiest airport, despite its short runways and close proximity to residential high-rise buildings. The crash, the worst in Brazilian aviation history, set off strong criticism of the country's air travel system, which is controlled by the Brazilian Air Force. In late July, President Lula appointed a new defense minister to oversee air safety. The government also promised to build a new airport for São Paulo's sprawling metropolitan area.

Musical treasure. In 2007, the government of São Paulo issued a set of six compact discs titled *Traditional Music of the North and Northeast 1938*. A four-member team recorded the collection in 1938 in isolated regions of Brazil. The music in the collection, which combines African, Amerindian, and European traditions, influenced many important styles of contemporary Brazilian music.   ■ Nathan A. Haverstock

See also **Aviation; Latin America.**

British Columbia. See Canadian provinces.

Brunei. See Asia.

Building and construction. On
Aug. 1, 2007, the Interstate 35W bridge over the Mississippi River in Minneapolis collapsed due to massive structural failure. Thirteen people were killed and more than 100 others were injured when the 456-foot (139-meter) main span of the bridge gave way during a busy rush hour traffic jam.

The 1,907-foot (581-meter) bridge was constructed with a *truss* design. Truss bridges are supported by frameworks of supports arranged in triangles. The Minneapolis Interstate 35W bridge had steel trusses that supported concrete road slabs above.

Safety investigators looking for the causes of the collapse focused on the bridge's steel *gusset plates* (flat brackets that reinforce a structure's joints). Although the bridge was inspected regularly, investigators believed that small, nearly invisible stress fractures in the gusset plates might have gone unnoticed. These cracks could have contributed to the bridge collapse.

The bridge was completed in 1967 and was expected to last for 50 years with proper maintenance before a total replacement would be needed. The news of the collapse triggered a nationwide effort to inspect aging bridges and other infrastructure to prevent similar failures.

New addition to famous skyline. In New

The Penobscot Narrows Bridge (right), spanning Maine's Penobscot River, opens to the public on May 21, 2007, complete with a pier-top observatory offering 360-degree views. Replacing the old Waldo-Hancock Bridge (left), the new Narrows Bridge incorporates a number of engineering innovations that make it more durable and easier to maintain.

York City, The New York Times Building was opened for business in October 2007 after four years of construction. Designed by Italian architect Renzo Piano, the 52-story, 1,046-foot (319-meter) skyscraper became the third tallest building in New York City, after the Empire State and the Chrysler buildings. The steel frame structure is encased in glass walls that give the building a more open design than traditional skyscrapers. The building's outer walls are cov-

ered in screens made of thousands of ceramic tubes. These tubes are intended to cool the building and allow daylight to enter without creating excessive glare. The ceramic tube screens extend vertically past the building's rooftop, creating a unique profile on the crowded New York skyline.

Chunnel high-speed railway. On November 14, the first high-speed railway system linking London and Paris opened for general use. Called High Speed 1, it took over nine years to construct. The first segment, connecting the coast of France to Paris, was completed in 1994. A year later, the underwater tunnel used by High Speed 1 was completed. Called the Chunnel, this tunnel was dug underneath the English Channel, which separates the United Kingdom (U.K.) from mainland Europe. By moving at speeds up to 199 miles (320 kilometers) per hour, High Speed 1 travels between the two capitals in only 123 minutes.

The European Union defines a high-speed train as one that travels faster than 200 kilometers (124 miles) per hour. High Speed 1 is the U.K.'s only high-speed rail line. While the construction of high speed rail lines has been common throughout continental Europe, the United Kingdom has been slower to embrace the technology.

New life for an iconic train station. After years of renovation, the St. Pancras International Train Station of London reopened on Nov. 7, 2007, in conjunction with the new High Speed 1 rail line. Known to some as "the cathedral of railways," the St. Pancras station was built in 1868. The main train shed was an engineering marvel of its time, featuring the largest single-span structure to date. The station's massive front structure was built in the high Victorian Gothic style and originally housed a hotel.

St. Pancras fell into decline after World War I (1914-1918). Railway reorganizations led to reduced use of the station, and the hotel was closed in 1935. The main train shed was damaged by bombing in World War II (1939-1945) and then only partially rebuilt after the war ended. In the 1960's, a proposal to demolish the hotel was defeated by citizens who wanted to preserve the building's distinct architecture. Along with the connection to High Speed 1, the renovated St. Pancras includes restaurants, shops, and plans for a five-star hotel.

Race to the top. The Burj Dubai, a new skyscraper under construction in Dubai, United Arab Emirates, surpassed in 2007 the Taipei 101 tower in Taipei, Taiwan, as the tallest skyscraper in the world. On July 21, the Burj Dubai reached 1,711 feet (521.5 meters), or about 141 stories, breaking the previous record.

Construction of the Burj Dubai began in February 2005, and the tower was currently expected to be finished by mid-2009. Although the final height was a secret, experts expected that it would top out at more than 2,625 feet (800 meters).

At this height, the Burj Dubai would be the world's tallest constructed structure. The current record holder is the KVLY-TV radio mast in North Dakota, which is 2,063 feet (629 meters). Previously, the tallest constructed structure was the 2,120-foot (646-meter) Warsaw Radio Mast, which collapsed in 1991.

Burj means *tower* in Arabic, and the building was to be the centerpiece of a massive development effort currently underway in the small Persian Gulf country. Plans for the area around the tower included the world's largest shopping mall. ∎ Jeffrey Rubenstone

See also **Architecture; Transportation; United Kingdom.**

Bulgaria. On Jan. 1, 2007, Bulgaria, along with neighboring Romania, joined the European Union (EU). Unlike the other post-Communist states admitted in 2004, Bulgaria's and Romania's membership statuses would be subjected to postaccession review to ensure they met benchmarks conforming to EU standards. The arrangement allowed the European Commission, the organization's executive, to impose penalties restricting the benefits of EU membership if specified criteria were not met. Benchmarks for Bulgaria concerned judicial reform, combating corruption, and proper use of EU funds.

Bulgaria's economy grew by 5.8 percent during 2007, compared with 6.1 percent in 2006. Inflation, which averaged 7.4 percent in 2006, declined to 4.3 percent in the first quarter of 2007, and economists predicted that it would decline further through the year. Unemployment hovered around 8 percent, down slightly from the 2006 average. ∎ Sharon L. Wolchik

See also **Europe.**

Burkina Faso. See Africa.

Burma. See Myanmar.

Burundi. See Africa.

Bush, George W. See United States, President of the.

Business. See Bank; Economics, U.S.; Economics, World; International trade.

Cabinet, U.S. Three Cabinet officials left the Republican administration of United States President George W. Bush in 2007.

Attorney General Alberto Gonzales, after enduring months of criticism over the firing of federal prosecutors as well as other matters, stepped down on September 17. Numerous congressional Democrats and some Republicans had called for his resignation. They accused Gonzales of politicizing the Department of Justice, giving misleading or false testimony to Congress, and lacking the competence to run the department.

Much of the criticism stemmed from Gonzales's role in the dismissals of nine U.S. attorneys in 2006 and his testimony about the dismissals during a congressional inquiry in 2007. Gonzales testified that the firings had been routine and based on performance, but later testimony and documents showed that some attorneys had been targeted for political reasons, such as a perceived lack of loyalty to the Bush administration. Gonzales frustrated lawmakers by repeatedly testifying that he could not recall key details related to the firings.

Gonzales also was criticized for his testimony during congressional inquiries into other matters. He testified in 2006 and 2007 that there had been no serious disagreement within the Bush administration about the legality of a National Security Agency antiterrorism program involving domestic surveillance without warrants. But other testimony and documents indicated that a number of senior Justice Department officials had concluded that the program was illegal and required changes.

On September 17, President Bush nominated Michael Mukasey to replace Gonzales. Mukasey served as a judge of the U.S. District Court for the Southern District of New York from 1988 to 2006. On Nov. 8, 2007, the Senate voted 53-40 to confirm Mukasey. Many Democrats voted against Mukasey because during his confirmation hearings, he claimed not to know enough about an interrogation technique called waterboarding to classify it as torture.

Agriculture and veterans affairs. The secretary of the Department of Agriculture, Mike Johanns, resigned on September 20. On October 31, President Bush nominated former North Dakota Governor Edward Schafer to replace Johanns. The secretary of the Department of Veterans Affairs, Jim Nicholson, resigned on October 1. On October 30, President Bush nominated retired Army Lieutenant General James Peake to replace Nicholson. The Senate unanimously confirmed Peake on December 14. Schafer remained unconfirmed at the end of 2007.　■ Mike Lewis

See also **People in the news** (Robert Gates; Michael Mukasey); **United States, Government of the; United States, President of the.**

Cambodia. In elections for local communes on April 1, 2007, the Cambodian People's Party (CPP) won control of 1,592 of the country's 1,621 communes. Although election abuses were reported by foreign observers, the voting was more peaceful than in past years.

The results confirmed domination of Cambodia by CPP boss Hun Sen, who is the prime minister. The only significant opposition group left after years of CPP violence against opponents, the Sam Rainsy Party, won control of only 27 communes. A royalist party that Hun Sen had suppressed in 1997 lost many of its dwindling footholds in local governments.

In 2006, a tribunal backed by the United Nations began legal proceedings against leaders of the Khmer Rouge (KR), the Communist regime responsible for the deaths of some 1.5 million Cambodians during its rule from 1975 to 1979. In 2007, the court charged five former KR leaders with crimes against humanity: prison boss Kaing Khek Iev; Nuon Chea, second-in-command to deceased KR boss Pol Pot; former KR president Khieu Samphan; former Foreign Minister Ieng Sary; and Sary's wife, Ieng Thirith, who was a member of the KR central committee. Trials were expected to begin in 2008.　■ Henry S. Bradsher

See also **Asia.**

Cameroon. See Africa.

A protester indicates her opinion of Attorney General Alberto Gonzales as he begins to testify before the U.S. Senate Judiciary Committee on April 19, 2007, about the controversial dismissal of nine U.S. attorneys in 2006. After months of criticism that the firings were politically motivated, Gonzales resigned on Sept. 17, 2007.

CANADA

Canada entered its third consecutive year of minority government rule in Parliament in 2007. The second parliamentary session under the center-right Conservative Party began on October 16. Observers had speculated that Canada's three opposition parties would trigger a general election by voting down the Conservatives' Speech from the Throne, which set out their agenda for the new session. The opposition consisted of the center-left Liberal Party; the left-wing New Democratic Party (NDP); and the Bloc Québécois, which seeks a *sovereign* (independent) Quebec. Although the NDP and the Bloc voted against the throne speech, the Liberals, not wanting an election, abstained in the confidence vote, allowing the speech to pass.

Quebec. Several dramatic political shifts in the largely French-speaking province of Quebec in 2007 showed potential to transform national politics. Quebec's political scene, long polarized between the Parti Québécois—the provincial separatist party—and the federalist Liberals, was shattered in March by a third party, the right-wing Action Démocratique du Québec (ADQ), which calls for a more *autonomous* (self-determining) Quebec within Canada. The ADQ displaced the Parti Québécois as the Official Opposition in Quebec's legislature and forced the Liberals into minority rule.

Many political observers saw the election results as a call from voters in Canada's second largest province to shift the political focus from separation. Quebec had narrowly voted to remain in Canada in a 1995 provincial referendum. The issue again grew in prominence in 2004 when a scandal in Quebec involving Canada's previous Liberal government became public, reviving the flagging fortunes of the separatist forces in Quebec and contributing to voters' weariness with the Liberals throughout Canada. However, in the 2006 general election, the Conservative Party, headed by soon-to-be Prime Minister Stephen Harper, emerged as a second serious federalist challenger to the Bloc Québécois in some areas of Quebec that were traditionally outside the Liberals' reach.

New constitutional talks proposed. After his party's dramatic election gains, ADQ leader

The editors would like to express their heartfelt appreciation to David Farr, who retired in 2007 after contributing the Canadian articles to *The World Book Year Book* since 1960.

Mario Dumont said in April 2007 that he was interested in reopening talks with the federal government about Quebec signing Canada's Constitution. The issue had been tied to the separatist question since the province refused to sign on to a revised Constitution that had been brought home to Canada from the United Kingdom in 1982. In exchange for greater freedom in how Quebec spends money it receives from the federal government, Dumont said that he was amenable to gradually negotiating Quebec's acceptance of the document. The failure of past attempts to make the Constitution more acceptable to Quebec—the Meech Lake Accord of 1990 and the Charlottetown Accord of 1992—had caused rising separatist sympathy in the province.

Quebec by-elections. The political climate in the province appeared even more tumultuous in federal by-elections on Sept. 17, 2007, when the Liberals and the Bloc Québécois both lost long-held *ridings* (districts). The Conservatives won Roberval-Lac-Saint-Jean from the Bloc, a

Canadian soldiers flank the Canadian National Vimy Memorial in France in April 2007 to commemorate the 90th anniversary of the World War I Battle of Vimy Ridge, a hard-won fight by Canadian troops that some historians have described as solidifying Canada's identity as a nation. Thousands of Canadians traveled to the site to witness the rededication of the restored monument.

constituency that the separatist party had held since 1993, and the Liberals came in a distant third. The Conservatives also finished a close second to the Bloc in Saint-Hyacinthe-Bagot, where the Liberals came in fourth place.

More troubling for the Liberals was their loss of the Outremont riding to the NDP. The Liberals had won the riding in every election but one since 1935. The victory marked only the second time that the NDP had represented a Quebec riding, and the party used the victory to position itself as a left-wing alternative to the Liberals and the Bloc. Following these by-election losses, the national Liberal leader, Stéphane Dion, faced severe public criticism from some members of his party.

Afghanistan. Canada's participation in a mission in Afghanistan led by the North Atlantic Treaty Organization (NATO) continued to dominate foreign policy in 2007. Of the 74 Canadian deaths during the mission, 65 occurred after the Canadian Forces entered frontline duties in the province of Kandahar in 2006, including 29 deaths

in 2007, as of December 26. Public support for continuing the mission declined as casualties mounted. However, the Conservative government, in its throne speech, called for extending the mission until at least 2011.

In April 2007, a scandal erupted over the treatment of prisoners, detained by Canadian troops, who had been transferred to the custody of the Afghan security forces. With the Canadian media reporting prisoner claims of torture and starvation, the federal government scrambled to explain its monitoring policy. Defence Minister Gordon O'Connor had earlier told Parliament that the International Committee of the Red Cross would keep track of prisoner conditions in Afghan jails and would report any problems to Canadian officials. In March, he was forced to apologize to the House of Commons for providing inaccurate information when the Red Cross said that it was not obliged to report to the Canadian government. *The Globe and Mail* newspaper, based in Toronto, obtained some uncensored por-

MEMBERS OF THE CANADIAN HOUSE OF COMMONS

The House of Commons of the second session of the 39th Parliament convened on October 16, 2007. As of Dec. 20, 2007, the House of Commons consisted of the following members: 125 Conservative Party of Canada, 96 Liberal Party, 49 Bloc Québécois, 30 New Democratic Party, and 4 Independent. This table shows each legislator and party affiliation. An asterisk (*) denotes those who served in the 38th Parliament.

Alberta
Diane Ablonczy, C.P.C.*
Rona Ambrose, C.P.C.*
Rob Anders, C.P.C.*
Leon E. Benoit, C.P.C.*
Blaine Calkins, C.P.C.
Rick Casson, C.P.C.*
Ken Epp, C.P.C.*
Peter Goldring, C.P.C.*
Art Hanger, C.P.C.*
Stephen Harper, C.P.C.*
Laurie Hawn, C.P.C.
Rahim Jaffer, C.P.C.*
Brian Jean, C.P.C.*
Jason Kenney, C.P.C.*
Mike Lake, C.P.C.
Ted Menzies, C.P.C.*
Rob Merrifield, C.P.C.*
Bob Mills, C.P.C.*
Deepak Obhrai, C.P.C.*
Jim Prentice, C.P.C.*
James Rajotte, C.P.C.*
Lee Richardson, C.P.C.*
Monte Solberg, C.P.C.*
Kevin Sorenson, C.P.C.*
Brian Storseth, C.P.C.
Myron Thompson, C.P.C.*
Chris Warkentin, C.P.C.
John Williams, C.P.C.*

British Columbia
Jim Abbott, C.P.C.*
Alex Atamanenko, N.D.P.
Catherine Bell, N.D.P.
Don H. Bell, Lib.*
Dawn Black, N.D.P.
Ron Cannan, C.P.C.
Raymond Chan, Lib.*
Jean Crowder, N.D.P.*
Nathan Cullen, N.D.P.*
John Cummins, C.P.C.*
Libby Davies, N.D.P.*
Stockwell Day, C.P.C.*
Sukh Dhaliwal, Lib.
Ujjal Dosanjh, Lib.*
David Emerson, C.P.C.*
Ed Fast, C.P.C.
Hedy Fry, Lib.*
Nina Grewal, C.P.C.*
Richard Harris, C.P.C.*
Russ Hiebert, C.P.C.*
Jay Hill, C.P.C.*
Betty Hinton, C.P.C.*
Peter Julian, N.D.P.*
Randy Kamp, C.P.C.*
Gary Lunn, C.P.C.*
James Lunney, C.P.C.*
Keith Martin, Lib.*
Colin Mayes, C.P.C.*
James Moore, C.P.C.*
Penny Priddy, N.D.P.
Denise Savoie, N.D.P.
Bill Siksay, N.D.P.
Chuck Strahl, C.P.C.*
Mark Warawa, C.P.C.*
Blair Wilson, Lib.

Manitoba
James Bezan, C.P.C.*
Bill Blaikie, N.D.P.*
Rod Bruinooge, C.P.C.
Steven Fletcher, C.P.C.*
Tina Keeper, Lib.
Inky Mark, C.P.C.*
Pat Martin, N.D.P.*
Anita Neville, Lib.*
Brian Pallister, C.P.C.*
Raymond Simard, Lib.*
Joy Smith, C.P.C.*
Vic Toews, C.P.C.*
Mervin Tweed, C.P.C.*
Judy Wasylycia-Leis, N.D.P.*

New Brunswick
Mike Allen, C.P.C.
Jean-Claude D'Amours, Lib.*
Yvon Godin, N.D.P.*
Charles Hubbard, Lib.*
Dominic LeBlanc, Lib.*
Rob Moore, C.P.C.*
Brian Murphy, Lib.
Andy Scott, Lib.*
Greg Thompson, C.P.C.*
Paul Zed, Lib.*

Newfoundland and Labrador
Gerry Byrne, Lib.*
Norman Doyle, C.P.C.*
Loyola Hearn, C.P.C.*
Fabian Manning, C.P.C.
Bill Matthews, Lib.*
Todd Russell, Lib.*
Scott Simms, Lib.*

Northwest Territories
Dennis Bevington, N.D.P.

Nova Scotia
Scott Brison, Lib.*
Bill Casey, Ind.*
Rodger Cuzner, Lib.*
Mark Eyking, Lib.*
Gerald Keddy, C.P.C.*
Peter MacKay, C.P.C.*
Alexa McDonough, N.D.P.*
Geoff Regan, Lib.*
Michael Savage, Lib.*
Peter Stoffer, N.D.P.*
Robert Thibault, Lib.*

Nunavut
Nancy Karetak-Lindell, Lib.*

Ontario
Harold Albrecht, C.P.C.
Omar Alghabra, Lib.
Dean Allison, C.P.C.*
Charlie Angus, N.D.P.*
Navdeep Bains, Lib.*
John Baird, C.P.C.
Sue Barnes, Lib.*
Colleen Beaumier, Lib.*
Mauril Bélanger, Lib.*
Carolyn Bennett, Lib.*
Maurizio Bevilacqua, Lib.*
Raymond Bonin, Lib.*
Ken Boshcoff, Lib.*
Bonnie Brown, Lib.*
Gord Brown, C.P.C.*
Patrick Brown, C.P.C.
John Cannis, Lib.*
Colin Carrie, C.P.C.*
Brenda Chamberlain, Lib.*
Chris Charlton, N.D.P.
Michael Chong, C.P.C.*
Olivia Chow, N.D.P.
David Christopherson, N.D.P.*
Tony Clement, C.P.C.
Joe Comartin, N.D.P.*
Joe Comuzzi, Lib.*
Roy Cullen, Lib.*
Patricia Davidson, C.P.C.
Dean Del Mastro, C.P.C.
Barry Devolin, C.P.C.*
Paul Dewar, N.D.P.
Ruby Dhalla, Lib.*
Ken Dryden, Lib.*
Rick Dykstra, C.P.C.
Diane Finley, C.P.C.*
Jim Flaherty, C.P.C.
Royal Galipeau, C.P.C.
Cheryl Gallant, C.P.C.*
John Godfrey, Lib.*
Gary Goodyear, C.P.C.*
Albina Guarnieri, Lib.*
Helena Guergis, C.P.C.*
Mark Holland, Lib.*
Michael Ignatieff, Lib.
Susan Kadis, Lib.*
Jim Karygiannis, Lib.*
Wajid Khan, Ind.*
Daryl Kramp, C.P.C.*
Guy Lauzon, C.P.C.*
Jack Layton, N.D.P.*
Derek Lee, Lib.*
Pierre Lemieux, C.P.C.
Dave Mackenzie, C.P.C.*
Gurbax Malhi, Lib.*
John Maloney, Lib.*
Diane Marleau, Lib.*
Wayne Marston, N.D.P.
Tony Martin, N.D.P.*
Brian Masse, N.D.P.*
Irene Mathyssen, N.D.P.
John McCallum, Lib.*
David McGuinty, Lib.*
John McKay, Lib.*
Dan McTeague, Lib.*
Larry Miller, C.P.C.*
Peter Milliken, Lib.*
Maria Minna, Lib.*
Peggy Nash, N.D.P.
Rob Nicholson, C.P.C.
Rick Norlock, C.P.C.
Gordon O'Connor, C.P.C.*
Bev Oda, C.P.C.*
Glen Pearson, Lib.
Pierre Poilievre, C.P.C.*
Joe Preston, C.P.C.*
Yasmin Ratansi, Lib.*
Karen Redman, Lib.*
Scott Reid, C.P.C.*
Anthony Rota, Lib.*
Gary Schellenberger, C.P.C.*
Judy Sgro, Lib.*
Bev Shipley, C.P.C.
Mario Silva, Lib.*
Lloyd St. Amand, Lib.*
Brent St. Denis, Lib.*
Bruce Stanton, C.P.C.
Paul Steckle, Lib.*
Belinda Stronach, Lib.*
David Sweet, C.P.C.
Paul Szabo, Lib.*
Andrew Telegdi, Lib.*
Lui Temelkovski, Lib.*
David Tilson, C.P.C.*
Alan Tonks, Lib.*
Garth Turner, Ind.
Roger Valley, Lib.*
Dave Van Kesteren, C.P.C.
Peter Van Loan, C.P.C.*
Joseph Volpe, Lib.*
Mike Wallace, C.P.C.
Tom Wappel, Lib.*
Jeff Watson, C.P.C.*
Bryon Wilfert, Lib.*
Borys Wrzesnewskyj, Lib.*

Prince Edward Island
Wayne Easter, Lib.*
Lawrence MacAulay, Lib.*
Joe McGuire, Lib.*
Shawn Murphy, Lib.*

Quebec
Guy André, B.Q.*
Arthur André, Ind.
Gérard Asselin, B.Q.*
Claude Bachand, B.Q.*
Vivian Barbot, B.Q.
André Bellavance, B.Q.*
Maxime Bernier, C.P.C.
Bernard Bigras, B.Q.*
Jean-Pierre Blackburn, C.P.C.
Raynald Blais, B.Q.*
Steven Blaney, C.P.C.
France Bonsant, B.Q.*
Robert Bouchard, B.Q.*
Sylvie Boucher, C.P.C.
Diane Bourgeois, B.Q.*
Paule Brunelle, B.Q.*
Lawrence Cannon, C.P.C.
Serge Cardin, B.Q.*
Robert Carrier, B.Q.*
Denis Coderre, Lib.*
Irwin Cotler, Lib.*
Paul Crête, B.Q.*
Claude DeBellefeuille, B.Q.
Nicole Demers, B.Q.*
Johanne Deschamps, B.Q.*
Stéphane Dion, Lib.*

THE MINISTRY OF CANADA*

Stephen Harper—prime minister

Marjory LeBreton—leader of the government in the Senate

Peter Van Loan—leader of the government in the House of Commons and minister for democratic reform

James Flaherty—minister of finance

Rona Ambrose—president of the Queen's Privy Council for Canada, minister of intergovernmental affairs, and minister of Western economic diversification

Maxime Bernier—minister of foreign affairs

David Emerson—minister of international trade

Chuck Strahl—minister of Indian affairs and Northern development and federal interlocutor for Métis and non-status Indians

Gerry Ritz—minister of agriculture and agri-food and minister for the Canadian Wheat Board

Gregory Thompson—minister of veterans affairs

Michael Fortier—minister of public works and government services

Peter MacKay—minister of national defence and minister of the Atlantic Canada Opportunities Agency

Diane Finley—minister of citizenship and immigration

Monte Solberg—minister of human resources and social development

Jean-Pierre Blackburn—minister of labour and minister of the Economic Development Agency of Canada for the Regions of Quebec

Gordon O'Connor—minister of national revenue

Tony Clement—minister of health and minister for the Federal Economic Development Initiative for Northern Ontario

Vic Toews—president of the Treasury Board

Loyola Hearn—minister of fisheries and oceans

Lawrence Cannon—minister of transport, infrastructure, and communities

Douglas Nicholson—minister of justice and attorney general of Canada

Josée Verner—minister of Canadian heritage, status of women, and official languages

Gary Lunn—minister of natural resources

John Baird—minister of the environment

Jim Prentice—minister of industry

Stockwell Day—minister of public safety

Beverley Oda—minister of international cooperation

*As of Dec. 20, 2007

PREMIERS OF CANADIAN PROVINCES

Alberta ....Ed Stelmach
British Columbia ....Gordon Campbell
Manitoba...................................Gary Doer
New Brunswick ....Shawn Graham
Newfoundland and Labrador ......Danny Williams
Nova Scotia...............................Rodney MacDonald
Ontario......................................Dalton McGuinty
Prince Edward Island ....Robert W. J. Ghiz
Quebec......................................Jean Charest
Saskatchewan ....Brad Wall

GOVERNMENT LEADERS OF TERRITORIES

Northwest Territories ....Floyd Roland
Nunavut ....Paul Okalik
Yukon..Dennis Fentie

tions of a document written by Canadian diplomats in Afghanistan that revealed that the government had been warned about the potential for inhumane treatment in Afghan facilities. In late April, O'Connor announced that Canada had come to an agreement with Afghan officials that would permit Canadian officials to visit the prisoners.

Cabinet shuffle. O'Connor's miscommunication regarding Afghanistan was widely deemed to be the reason for his demotion in an August Cabinet shuffle. Prime Minister Harper selected Foreign Affairs Minister Peter MacKay of Nova Scotia to replace O'Connor in defence. O'Connor was demoted to minister of revenue, replacing Carol Skelton of Saskatchewan, who had announced that she would not run for office again. Maxime Bernier, a promising Quebec Cabinet minister, was promoted from industry to foreign affairs. Albertan Jim Prentice moved from the Indian affairs department to the industry portfolio. Chuck Strahl of British Columbia moved to

Indian affairs from agriculture. He, in turn, was replaced by Gerry Ritz of Saskatchewan, the secretary of state for tourism.

Ontarian Beverley Oda, another minister who was criticized by political commentators—for her performance as heritage minister—traded places with Minister of International Cooperation Josée Verner of Quebec. Albertan Diane Ablonczy was a new addition to the Cabinet, assuming Ritz's place as secretary of state for tourism. Ablonczy, an effective government critic while in opposition, had been omitted from Harper's first Cabinet, a move that was considered a surprise in media circles. However, the Conservatives' dominance in Alberta, and the prime minister's need to provide a regional balance in the Cabinet, initially prevented Ablonczy and other strong parliamentary performers from winning a place in the Cabinet.

Harper made the changes to his Cabinet partly in response to claims from members of Parliament and the public that his government had lost direc-

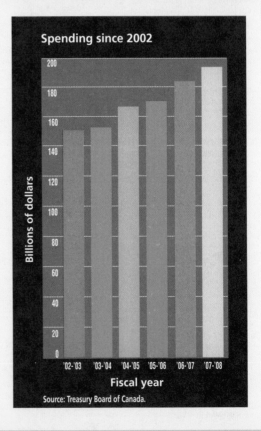

FEDERAL SPENDING IN CANADA
Estimated budget for fiscal 2007-2008*

Department or agency	Millions of dollars†
Agriculture and agri-food	3,060
Atlantic Canada opportunities agency	375
Canada revenue agency	3,380
Canadian heritage	3,291
Citizenship and immigration	1,301
Economic development agency of Canada for the regions of Quebec	395
Environment	1,463
Finance	75,948
Fisheries and oceans	1,539
Foreign affairs and international trade	5,191
Governor general	19
Health	4,585
Human resources and skills development	41,610
Indian affairs and northern development	6,841
Industry	4,097
Justice	1,235
National defence	16,891
Natural resources	2,451
Parliament	540
Privy Council	290
Public safety and emergency preparedness	6,506
Public works and government services	2,534
Transport	3,921
Treasury board	3,159
Veterans affairs	3,376
Western economic diversification	253
Total	**194,252**

*April 1, 2007, to March 31, 2008.
†Rounded in Canadian dollars; $1 = U.S. $1 as of Oct. 4, 2007.

Spending since 2002

Billions of dollars

Fiscal year

Source: Treasury Board of Canada.

tion. After a busy first year of legislative work based on Harper's five-point campaign promise, the Conservatives had difficulty developing a new agenda for a minority government that had held power for longer than many had first expected.

The economy continued to boom in 2007, fueled by world demand for Canada's oil, minerals, and other commodities and maintained by careful financial practices. The Canadian dollar, which had surged 62 percent since 2002, reached parity with the United States dollar on Sept. 20, 2007. The last time the two currencies were level was in November 1976. The Canadian dollar hit US $1.10 on Nov. 7, 2007. Observers suggested that the rising price of oil, a slumping U.S. housing market, and a large cut to U.S. interest rates contributed to the Canadian dollar's rise.

In September, Canada's unemployment rate fell to 5.9 percent, its lowest level since November 1974. The economy unexpectedly added 51,000 jobs in September 2007, most of them full-time. Most jobs created in 2007 were among the self-employed or in the public sector.

Following a series of high-profile foreign take-overs of Canadian businesses in recent years, on October 9 Industry Minister Jim Prentice announced that the government was considering enacting new rules to regulate such foreign investment. In the first eight months of 2007, foreign companies bought more than $90 billion worth of Canadian corporate assets, and Canadians bought more than $61 billion worth of corporate assets outside the country (all amounts in Canadian dollars). The loss of several major Canadian company icons, such as Inco Ltd. of Toronto; Montreal-based Alcan Inc.; and Dofasco Inc. of Hamilton, Ontario, prompted consideration of a new screening process to ensure that future sales pass a national security test.

Budget. On March 19, Finance Minister Jim Flaherty presented a balanced budget for fiscal year 2007 (April 1-March 31, 2008) that cut taxes, invested in key social programs, and reduced the federal debt. The biggest new item in the budget, a pledge to spend $39 billion over seven years to restore the "fiscal balance" in the country, was designed to quell unrest among some provinces that had complained that they were not receiving a fair share of federal payments.

Flaherty also announced a "tax-back guarantee" that would return money the government saves on federal debt interest payments to individual Canadians through income-tax reductions. The budget projected that $2.4 billion would be returned to Canadians over the next two years.

Other notable items included a new $2,000 child-tax credit; $500 million each year, starting in fiscal year 2008, for job training; $1.5 billion for the Canada ecoTrust for Clean Air and Climate

2007 CANADIAN POPULATION ESTIMATES

PROVINCE AND TERRITORY POPULATIONS

Alberta	3,477,100
British Columbia	4,362,200
Manitoba	1,181,300
New Brunswick	747,000
Newfoundland and Labrador	505,600
Northwest Territories	41,100
Nova Scotia	932,500
Nunavut	31,600
Ontario	12,813,900
Prince Edward Island	138,800
Quebec	7,705,100
Saskatchewan	980,500
Yukon	31,300
Canada	32,948,000

CITY AND METROPOLITAN AREA POPULATIONS

	Metropolitan area	City
Toronto, Ont.	5,207,200	2,507,700
Montreal, Que.	3,674,100	1,628,300
Vancouver, B.C.	2,144,100	584,900
Ottawa-Gatineau	1,144,100	
Ottawa, Ont.		820,100
Gatineau, Que.		245,400
Calgary, Alta.	1,108,200	1,012,700
Edmonton, Alta.	1,056,500	744,500
Quebec, Que.	721,500	494,200
Hamilton, Ont.	699,300	507,500
Winnipeg, Man.	698,400	636,300
London, Ont.	462,400	355,700
Kitchener, Ont.	459,300	207,700
St. Catharines-Niagara	393,000	
St. Catharines, Ont.		132,600
Niagara Falls, Ont.		82,900
Halifax, N.S.	375,700	375,500
Oshawa, Ont.	338,300	142,100
Victoria, B.C.	333,900	78,900
Windsor, Ont.	326,600	218,000
Saskatoon, Sask.	235,600	203,500
Regina, Sask.	195,400	179,500
Sherbrooke, Que.	188,900	149,000
Barrie, Ont.	183,900	134,600
St. John's, Nfld. Lab.	182,800	100,900
Kelowna, B.C.	165,500	109,000
Abbotsford, B.C.	161,500	125,700
Greater Sudbury/Grand		
Sudbury, Ont.	158,800	158,400
Kingston, Ont.	153,500	117,800
Saguenay, Que.	151,000	143,000
Trois-Rivieres, Que.	142,300	127,100
Guelph, Ont.	129,100	116,800
Moncton, N.B.	128,100	64,800
Brantford, Ont.	126,000	91,000
Thunder Bay, Ont.	123,100	109,200
Saint John, N.B.	122,300	67,700
Petersborough, Ont.	117,800	75,600

Source: World Book estimates based on data from Statistics Canada.

Canadian Forces gather on Ellesmere Island, Nunavut, in March 2007 during a mission in Canada's Arctic territory. Three teams on a "sovereignty patrol" trekked thousands of miles by snowmobile.

Canada and other nations in 2007 took steps to stake their claim on a rapidly melting Arctic.

The world's northern powers scrambled in 2007 to stake and defend claims in an Arctic that was undergoing rapid thawing due to global warming. As Arctic sea ice hit record seasonal lows, numerous countries sought sovereignty over newly navigable waters as well as the fuel and mineral riches buried under the seafloor below.

In March and April, patrol teams made up of Canadian soldiers and Canadian Rangers—part-time personnel who conduct surveillance in isolated areas—carried out a "sovereignty patrol" of Canada's Far North. Three eight-member teams traveled by snowmobile across some 5,000 miles (8,000 kilometers) of frigid terrain to establish a military presence and to look for evidence of foreign polar bear hunters.

Canadian Prime Minister Stephen Harper announced plans in July to construct six to eight patrol ships to monitor Canada's Arctic coastal waters. Also during the summer, Harper said that Canada would build a new army training facility and refurbish a deepwater port in the northern territory of Nunavut.

In August, Russian explorers in minisubmarines planted the Russian flag on the seabed 13,100 feet (4,000 meters) below the North Pole in a move to claim the submerged land and its resources. However, nations such as Canada, Denmark, Norway, and the United States had rival claims in the region. The territorial jousting became even more urgent in September when the European Space Agency announced that Arctic sea ice had shrunk to its lowest level since record keeping began in 1978. The melting had completely opened the Northwest Passage, a long-fabled shipping route between Asia and Europe, for the first time in recorded history.

Canadian Prime Minister Stephen Harper surveys the shore in Nanisivik, Nunavut, during an August 2007 trip to assert Canada's Arctic sovereignty. Harper announced that Canada would refurbish a deepwater port in Nanisivik and construct a new army training center in nearby Resolute Bay, which lies close to an entrance to the Northwest Passage.

A Russian explorer uses the robotic arm of a minisubmarine to plant a Russian flag in the seabed under the North Pole in August 2007. Russia sought to claim much of the seafloor for its oil, gas, and mineral resources.

The disappearance of record amounts of ice from the Arctic Ocean in summer 2007 opened the vaunted Northwest Passage, a direct water route from Europe to Asia across North America long sought by explorers, for the first time in history. Although not yet suitable for commercial shipping, such a "shortcut" was expected to eventually be a boon for international trade.

Change; $400 million for an electronic health record system; $612 million to reduce wait times for certain priority medical procedures; $300 million for a vaccination program to prevent cervical cancer; and $1 billion for farm-income initiatives.

Flaherty projected a modest budget surplus of $300 million for fiscal year 2007 and no surplus for the following year. However, the government planned to use $3 billion in each of the two years to pay down the debt. The budget also forecast a surplus of $9.2 billion for fiscal year 2006, which would also go toward debt reduction. However, on Sept. 27, 2007, the budget's projections were shattered when the government announced that fiscal year 2006 ended with a $13.8-billion surplus. The rise was due mainly to a jump in corporate income tax revenues.

Federal-provincial relations. The 2007 budget also included revisions to Canada's equalization program, changes that angered the governments of Newfoundland and Labrador, Nova Scotia, and Saskatchewan. The program redistributes tax dollars among the provinces through transfer payments to ensure that each province has a similar per-capita financial capacity to deliver social programs. Agreements with Newfoundland and Labrador and Nova Scotia allowed them to continue to receive royalties from their nonrenewable natural resource developments in recent years without having their equalization payments reduced as the price of oil rises. Saskatchewan had no such deal. However, all three governments believed that any new equalization formula should exclude non-renewable resource revenues, a view that Prime Minister Harper had expressed support for earlier.

The governments of Newfoundland and Labrador and Nova Scotia reacted with outrage as the federal government created an enriched equalization program that they could access only if they gave up their special exemptions. Newfoundland and Labrador Premier Danny Williams urged his province's voters not to support Harper's Conservatives in the next federal election. Nova Scotia Premier Rodney MacDonald initially campaigned against the changes, but on October 10, he accepted a compromise that would allow the province to choose either the new or the old system every year, depending on which was richer. Saskatchewan Premier Lorne Calvert said that his government would fight the federal plans in court.

Arctic. The effects of global warming continued in 2007 to become particularly apparent in the north polar region. Environment Canada officials were shocked to see that summer ice melting in the Arctic reached levels in 2007 that climatologists had not expected to record until 2030. Officials also raised the specter that 2007 may have been the "tipping point" when winter freezing no longer restores ice lost to the spring and summer melting.

In September, the European Space Agency announced that satellite images had revealed that the fabled Northwest Passage—the most direct shipping route between Europe and Asia—was free of ice for the first time on record. Canada had argued that the passage is under its jurisdiction, but the European Union and the United States countered that it is part of international waters.

Prime Minister Harper, anticipating challenges to Canada's territorial claims, announced plans on July 9 to build six to eight patrol ships at a cost of $7 billion over 25 years to guard coastal waters, including the Northwest Passage. He also announced plans to build a new deepwater port in the Far North for commercial and military use.

Security and intelligence agencies in Canada were rocked by scandals in 2007 that further damaged their already shaky public standing. On July 16, William Elliott assumed control of the Royal Canadian Mounted Police (RCMP), becoming the first civilian ever to be appointed RCMP commissioner. One of Elliott's duties was to bring greater accountability and transparency to the force.

The previous RCMP commissioner, Giuliano Zaccardelli, resigned in late 2006 after admitting that he gave incorrect testimony about the handling of the Maher Arar case. Arar, a Syrian-born Canadian, was arrested in the United States by U.S. officials after being accused of terrorist links. He was imprisoned in Syria and tortured for months. A commission led by Justice Dennis O'Connor found that the RCMP had supplied U.S. officials with misleading and false information that likely led to Arar's deportation.

The RCMP's leaders came under fire in March and April 2007 as a parliamentary committee investigated alleged corruption surrounding the federal police force's insurance and pension plan. Whistleblowers who notified top RCMP officials, including Zaccardelli, of irregularities and inappropriate actions told the committee that they were either disciplined or ignored. Zaccardelli called the allegations baseless.

The Canadian Security Intelligence Service (CSIS) came under attack in 2007 for its own role in the Arar affair. On August 9, newly declassified information from O'Connor's report revealed that CSIS officials were aware of the U.S. practice of sending terrorist suspects to be harshly interrogated in other countries.

In September, the CSIS was criticized at a public inquiry about the 1985 Air India bombing, in which 329 people, including 280 Canadians, died when their plane exploded off the coast of Ireland. James Jardine, a former prosecutor, accused the agency of incompetence for erasing tapes of wiretapped conversations that could have been critical to the prosecution of a main suspect. Retired CSIS Deputy Director James Warren told the inquiry that erasing the tapes was an innocent mistake. However, an RCMP official had earlier described intense interagency rivalry related to CSIS and RCMP reluctance to share information about the case with each other.

CN Tower no longer tallest building. In September 2007, the Canadian National (CN) Tower, also known as Canada's National Tower—which stands 1,814 feet (553 meters) tall in Toronto—lost its title as the world's tallest free-standing structure. A Dubai office building and residence called the Burj Dubai, at 1,820 feet (555 meters) and still under construction, captured the record that the CN Tower had held for 30 years.

Mulroney controversy. On November 13, Prime Minister Harper bowed to opposition and public pressure and promised a full inquiry into some of the business dealings of former Prime Minister Brian Mulroney. The inquiry was to examine allegations that Mulroney, while still prime minister, discussed a private business arrangement with German-Canadian businessman Karlheinz Schreiber. A parliamentary ethics committee held its own investigation in late 2007 into $300,000 in cash that Schreiber gave Mulroney shortly after he left office.   ■ William Stos

See also **Afghanistan; Canada, Prime Minister of; Canadian provinces; Canadian territories; Environmental pollution; Montreal; Toronto.**

Canada, Prime Minister of. Stephen

Harper began his second year as head of a minority government in 2007. Observers noted that Harper had made progress on his Conservative Party's election platform, which focused on select goals in anticipation of a quick return to the polls.

New agenda. Nearly six months into Harper's second year in office, however, political commentators accused his government of being adrift. Conservative Party members met in August to discuss a new agenda. Harper then ended the current session of Parliament in September. A new session began on October 16 with a forceful Speech from the Throne that pledged tougher crime legislation and a vote to extend Canada's Afghan mission and announced that Canada would not meet its Kyoto Protocol commitments. Harper's throne speech passed with the consent of the Opposition Liberal Party, led by Stéphane Dion, which was eager to avoid a snap election.

Senate reform. Harper promoted his goal of transforming Canada's Senate, whose members are chosen by the prime minister, into an elected body by appointing Bert Brown of Alberta on July 10. The province had elected Brown in a 2004 vote that the federal government was not required to recognize.   ■ William Stos

See also **Afghanistan; Canada; Canadian provinces; Canadian territories.**

Canadian provinces. General elections

took place in 6 out of 10 Canadian provinces in 2007. Some provincial governments returned to office with large majorities, while others were soundly defeated or reprimanded with only a minority victory. Provinces with booming natural resource developments labored to manage their unprecedented economic growth, while others worked to maintain struggling economies.

Alberta. A booming oil and gas sector continued to drive economic growth in 2007, but Alberta struggled to cope with inflation, a shortage of workers, and stressed infrastructure. The right-of-center Progressive Conservative government announced a balanced budget on April 19 that projected a moderate $2.2-billion surplus on $35.3 billion in revenue for fiscal year 2007 (April 1-March 31, 2008). (All amounts are in Canadian dollars.) The only debt-free province in Canada in 2007, Alberta derived almost one-third of its revenue from oil and gas royalties. Finance Minister Lyle Oberg announced that, to meet the province's immediate needs, the government would raise spending by 12 percent from 2006. Oberg warned, however, of Alberta's potential to run a deficit in future years if the province continued to steeply increase spending.

Alberta was forced to increase its education, health, and infrastructure spending in 2007 in the face of unprecedented economic growth of 7 percent in 2006. In that year, nearly 60,000 new residents moved to Alberta, many to look for work, though the unemployment rate held steady at around 3 percent. Due to an acute housing shortage and a strained health care system, the government pledged $18.2 billion in capital spending over three years, up 37 percent from the previous budget. The government attributed about 25 percent of the increase, or $1.3 billion, to inflation, which observers linked mainly to high housing prices. In an August 2007 economic update, the province reported that it expected an additional $830 million in the forecast surplus due to projected increases in natural resources revenues, income from investments, and income taxes.

British Columbia. Premier Gordon Campbell's centrist Liberal government delivered a Speech from the Throne on February 13 that outlined an ambitious environmental program to fight climate change. The province planned by 2020 to cut greenhouse gas emissions to 33 percent below 2007 levels, a target equal to 10 percent below 1990 levels. Canada's national target under the international Kyoto Protocol climate agreement was to reduce emissions to 6 percent below 1990 levels by 2012. The speech called for the establishment of a climate team that would identify ways to make the province's government operations *carbon-neutral*—that is, to compensate for all of its emissions of the greenhouse gas carbon dioxide—by 2010. The plan also proposed that all electric power produced in the province be emission-free by 2016.

Finance Minister Carole Taylor introduced a provincial budget on Feb. 20, 2007, that projected a $3.2-billion surplus. The budget included a 10-percent cut in personal income taxes for people earning up to $108,000. Homelessness and housing stood out as the key theme of Taylor's 2007 financial plan. The province pledged to create 900 new shelter beds, to increase the housing allowance for people using income assistance programs by $50 a month, and to exempt first-time home buyers from paying a property transfer tax when they purchase a residence valued at up to $375,000.

On April 3, Premier Campbell and Rich Coleman, the minister responsible for housing, announced the single largest purchase of social housing in the province's history. British Columbia earmarked $80 million to purchase 15 buildings, totaling nearly 1,000 units, in Vancouver, Victoria, and Burnaby to combat homelessness.

On December 9, Robert Pickton of British Columbia was found guilty of six counts of second-degree murder of women who disappeared from Vancouver from 1997 through 2001. Relatives of the victims expressed gratitude for the verdict but were also disappointed that he was not convicted of first-degree murder.

Manitoba. Premier Gary Doer led his left-of-center New Democratic Party (NDP) to a third consecutive majority government in a general election on May 22, 2007. The party won 36 seats in the provincial legislature. The Progressive Conservatives retained their status as Official Opposition with 19 seats, and the Liberals held the same 2 seats. Doer promised to shorten wait times for public health care by hiring more providers and staff. During the campaign, Doer pledged to create an additional 4,000 apprenticeship positions in post-secondary schools.

Doer had often stressed his desire to turn the province's vast hydroelectric energy sources into an economic powerhouse for Manitoba, the way oil led to a boom in Alberta. Earlier in the year, Manitoba's plan to develop an east-west power grid to sell hydroelectric power to Ontario received help from the federal government. On March 6, Prime Minister Stephen Harper announced that Ontario would use some of its $586-million portion of the $1.5-billion national Canada ecoTrust fund to begin work on transmission lines.

New Brunswick. Premier Shawn Graham's Liberal government, elected in 2006, introduced its first budget on March 13, 2007. The budget reversed a long-standing policy of reducing taxes that was established to make the province attractive to prospective workers and industry. Finance Minister Victor Boudreau modestly raised personal income taxes and the small business tax rate. He also added $356 million to the provincial debt in order to pay for high-quality social programs that the Liberals hoped would attract new immigrants and keep current residents from moving elsewhere. The $6.6-billion budget projected a $37-million surplus for fiscal year 2007.

The Liberals, who defeated the Progressive Conservatives in 2006, gained new members in the legislature in April 2007, when married couple Wally Stiles and Joan MacAlpine-Stiles left the Conservatives for the Liberal government. MacAlpine-Stiles expressed dissatisfaction with the recent "negative tone" of her former party.

Newfoundland and Labrador. Premier Danny Williams and his Progressive Conservative party won reelection on October 9. The party increased its presence in the legislature by winning 44 seats, leaving the Liberals with just 3 seats and the NDP with only 1 seat.

Williams had become exceptionally popular among the province's residents as he had engaged in pitched battles with the federal government and with industry over oil and gas royalties from offshore developments. He fought the federal government in 2006 over how much of a province's nonrenewable resource revenues should be included when calculating equalization transfers. Such transfers are designed to ensure that all provinces have a relatively equal capacity to provide services to residents.

Williams had also negotiated hard with a group of oil and gas companies that included ExxonMobil Canada Ltd. of Halifax, Nova Scotia; Chevron Canada Ltd. of Vancouver, British Columbia; and Petro-Canada of Calgary, Alberta, over the terms of the $6-billion Hebron offshore project. In August 2007, the province came to an agreement with the companies. Williams announced that Newfoundland and Labrador would pay $110 million for a 4.9-percent share in the project. The province would also receive a "super-royalty" payment if oil prices reach or exceed a monthly average of $65 per barrel.

Nova Scotia. After more than 20 years of study and debate, the federal and provincial governments in January announced a decision to bury the toxic tar ponds and Sydney Steel coke ovens site on Cape Breton Island. The $400-million project involved solidifying and then burying the 770,000 tons (700,000 metric tons) of toxic sludge in the 250-acre (100-hectare) region, one of Canada's most polluted areas. It could take up to seven years to finish work on a site that nearby residents blamed for unexplained illnesses and heightened cancer rates.

On March 23, Progressive Conservative Finance Minister Michael Baker introduced the province's sixth consecutive balanced budget. The province reluctantly signed on to the federal government's revised equalization program in preparing the budget. In exchange for larger payments from the federal government in the short term, Nova Scotia risked losing future royalties from offshore developments that it had negotiated under the 2005 Atlantic Accord. That agreement, which was scheduled to expire in fiscal year 2011 but could be extended to fiscal year 2019, excluded natural resource revenues from the province's equalization formula. The budget forecast a $118.4-million surplus. It also increased health care spending, froze university tuition, and pledged $50 million over 10 years to construct and upgrade recreational facilities.

Ontario. In a preelection budget introduced on March 22, 2007, Ontario's Liberal government moved leftward in response to several by-election wins by the NDP. The government vowed to phase in an increase in the minimum wage from $8 in 2007 to $10.25 in 2010. It also pledged to fight child poverty with a five-year, $2.1-billion Ontario Child Benefit to aid more than 1 million children in low-income families. Finance Minister Greg Sorbara announced a $350-million surplus for fiscal year 2007 and projected that the province's robust economy would produce surpluses through fiscal year 2009. The government also accelerated the elimination of the capital gains tax and promised to make changes to the province's controversial property tax assessment system.

The Ipperwash Inquiry, an investigation into the 1995 shooting death of an unarmed Native Canadian protester by police during a native occupation of a provincial park, issued its final report on May 31, 2007. After nearly four years of collecting evidence, the inquiry found that then-Premier Mike Harris had uttered a racial slur to officials during a tense meeting on the day of the stand-off, but that he did not order the Ontario Provincial Police into the park to remove the protesters. The head of the inquiry, Justice Sidney Linden, found that the racism and cultural insensitivity of some officers prevented them from finding a peaceful solution to the stand-off.

Ontarians went to the polls on October 10 in the province's first fixed-date election. The governing Liberal Party returned to office with another majority government of 71 of 107 seats. The Progressive Conservatives won 26 seats, and the NDP won 10 seats. A controversial and unpopular Conservative policy to extend public funding to faith-based schools and accusations of broken promises by Liberal Premier Dalton McGuinty characterized the election.

Prince Edward Island. Progressive Conservative Treasurer Mitch Murphy introduced a budget on April 10, in advance of a provincial election, that promised tax cuts and increased spending on health and education. The budget yielded a small $2.1-million surplus but added $18.1 million to the small province's debt. Key budget items included personal income tax cuts, a cap on the provincial gasoline tax, and $2.1 million to roll back university tuition by 10 percent.

On May 28, the Liberal Party and its 33-year-old leader Robert Ghiz defeated the Conservatives, who had governed under Premier Pat Binns for 11 years. The Liberals won 23 out of the province's 27 seats yet collected just 53 percent of the popular vote. The remaining 4 seats went to the Conservatives, who garnered 41 percent of the vote. Ghiz's father, Joe, served as premier from 1986 to 1993. When Robert Ghiz was sworn in on June 12, 2007, it marked the second time in the province's history that a father and son had each occupied the premier's office.

Quebec. Canada's predominantly French-speaking province, which had long claimed a distinctive culture and liberal political attitudes, engaged in an explosive debate in 2007 over reasonable accommodation for new immigrants and ethnic and religious minorities. The issue made national headlines in January, when the town council in small, rural Herouxville adopted a code of "norms" for prospective immigrants. Among other rules, the code stressed that it was not acceptable to stone women or to cover a person's face except on Halloween—which were seen as references to Islam—or to bring such weapons as the ceremonial Sikh *kirpan* (dagger) to school. Religious and minority rights groups condemned the code as perpetuating negative stereotypes. Some towns in the area indicated support for the code, while others denounced it and stressed that the region welcomed newcomers.

The debate over reasonable accommodation grew during the year as several other incidents attracted media attention. In February, a Muslim girl was asked by a soccer referee to remove her *hijab* (headscarf) during a tournament. She refused, and her team and others pulled out of the tournament in support. On April 15, a tae kwon do team consisting of mostly Muslim girls withdrew from a tournament near Montreal after its Muslim members were barred from competing while wearing hijabs, which were deemed safety risks. The debate became so explosive that Liberal Premier Jean Charest announced a commission to investigate the issue in hopes of diffusing tension. Hearings began on September 10.

Quebec's political scene underwent a dramatic change following an election on March 26. The province elected its first minority government in more than 100 years as the governing Liberal Party lost 26 seats, returning to office with only 48 of 125 seats. Quebec, long polarized between the federalist Liberals and the separatist Parti Québécois, saw the right-wing Action Démocratique du Québec form the Official Opposition with 41 seats. That party supports autonomy from the federal government but not independence from Canada. The Parti Québécois's third-place finish, with only 36 seats, amounted to its worst election result since 1973. Party leader André Boisclair resigned in May 2007 and was replaced in June by former party Finance Minister Pauline Marois.

Saskatchewan. Finance Minister Andrew Thompson presented a budget on March 22 that highlighted education initiatives, including a $10,000 tax exemption for the first five years after a post-secondary student graduates, a university tuition freeze until 2008, and $107 million in education property tax relief. The NDP government also cut business taxes and invested $534.8 million in the largest capital infrastructure budget, including several highway projects, in the province's history. The NDP went down in defeat on Nov. 7, 2007, after 16 years in office. The center-right Saskatchewan Party, under Brad Wall, won a majority government with 38 of 58 seats.   ■ William Stos

See also **Canada; Canada, Prime Minister of; Canadian territories.**

Canadian territories.
Governments in Canada's three northern territories continued in 2007 to benefit from demand for their natural resources. They sought to work with the federal government and private companies to improve infrastructure and establish social programs needed to support their industrial growth.

Northwest Territories. Minister of Finance Floyd K. Roland presented a budget on February 8 that attempted to prepare for an expected boom in natural resource revenue. The government forecast a surplus of $44 million on $1.23 billion in estimated revenues for fiscal year 2007 (April 1-March 31, 2008). (All amounts are in Canadian dollars.) The budget included a spending increase of 8.3 percent, or $89 million, over fiscal year 2006. Much of it went toward education, social services, and health care, including nearly $1 million to implement a full-day kindergarten program and $3.9 million to lower student-to-teacher ratios.

In March 2007, the federal government signed an agreement to establish the Sahoyue-Edacho National Historic Site to protect two large peninsulas that run into Great Bear Lake, in the territory's north-central region. The site, totaling about 2,200 square miles (5,800 square kilometers), is a habitat for grizzly bears, wolverines, caribou, and peregrine falcons. The government established the site, which is representative of the northern ecosystem,

to conserve such areas before they are affected by industrialization. The agreement called for $5 million over five years to begin development and $700,000 each year for operations.

A multibillion-dollar natural gas pipeline in the Mackenzie Valley looked to be in jeopardy in May. The chief executive officer of Exxon Mobil Corporation of Irving, Texas, warned that escalating construction costs would make the pipeline impossible without federal assistance. The project had been long delayed as aboriginal groups resolved unsettled land claims and as gas prices fluctuated.

Northwest Territories Premier Joe Handley and Nunavut Premier Paul Okalik pressed the federal government to *devolve* (pass on) more provincelike powers to their territories at an annual meeting of territorial leaders on May 26. Although Yukon achieved devolution of some powers in 2003, the Northwest Territories and Nunavut continued to rely on the federal government to manage their natural resource developments and to collect and distribute royalties.

On Aug. 15, 2007, Premier Joe Handley announced his intention to resign as premier following the October election. Handley was first elected to the territory's legislative assembly in 1999 and became premier in 2003. The Northwest Territories' nonpartisan, consensus-style government chose Floyd K. Roland as the new premier.

Nunavut. Minister of Finance David Simailak introduced a restrained budget on March 7, 2007, which projected a small, $6.6-million deficit. No significant new spending was announced, and tax rates were expected to remain unchanged. However, Nunavut's economy stayed strong: The value of building permits tripled from 2005 to 2006; mineral exploration and development rose for three consecutive years, from 2004 to 2006; and unemployment in the territory's largest communities declined each year during the same period.

Inuit hunters from Nunavut went to The Hague, the seat of the government of the Netherlands, on March 15, 2007, to participate in a counterprotest to an International Day of Action Against the Canadian Seal Hunt organized by activists in 36 cities around the world. The Inuit maintained that the hunt is a cultural tradition and an essential economic activity. The hunters hoped to combat antisealing initiatives in Europe that could eliminate key seal product markets.

An extensive health survey of the Inuit in Nunavut, part of International Polar Year research and funded by the federal government, began in August. The $10.6-million survey was titled Qanuippitali, or "How about us, how are we?" Medical staff planned to visit many Inuit communities and conduct health tests aboard a Canadian Coast Guard icebreaker over two summers.

Yukon. On February 23, Yukon welcomed

thousands of athletes and spectators to its capital, Whitehorse, for the first Canada Winter Games held north of the 60th parallel. The event was hailed as a great success despite temperatures that hovered around −22 °F (−30 °C). Some Canadians viewed the two-week-long games as a lead-up to the 2010 Winter Olympics to be held in Vancouver/Whistler, British Columbia.

Premier Dennis Fentie, who also acted as Yukon's finance minister, presented a $862-million budget on April 19, 2007, the biggest projected budget in the territory's history. With a modest $2.6-million projected deficit, the government left personal income tax rates unchanged. The budget included $32.5 million for affordable housing for Native Canadian communities, $10 million for improvements to the Alaska Highway, and $9.2 million for expanding the Whitehorse airport.

On October 9, Minister of Economic Development Jim Kenyon called for the federal government to expand a pilot project that would make it easier for foreign workers to move to Yukon. The project, which operated in neighboring British Columbia and in Alberta, was designed to combat an acute labor shortage in the booming Western provinces. Kenyon argued that Yukon suffered from a similar labor crunch.   ■ William Stos

See also **Canada; Canadian provinces.**

Cape Verde. See Africa.

Census. According to data released by the United States Census Bureau in 2007, the percentages of older workers, homeowners, and non-English speakers in the United States all increased from 2000 to 2006. In addition, from 2005 to 2006, the country's minority population surpassed 100 million, the median income rose, the poverty rate declined, and the percentage of people without health insurance increased.

Older workers. Nearly one-fourth (23.2 percent) of all U.S. residents between 65 and 74 were either working or looking for work in 2006, up from 19.6 percent in 2000, according to data released on Sept. 12, 2007. South Dakota and Nebraska had the highest rates of older workers in the labor force in 2006. West Virginia, Michigan, and Arizona had the lowest rates.

Homeowners. More than two-thirds (67.3 percent) of all occupied U.S. residences in 2006 were owned by the occupant, compared with 66.2 percent in 2000, the bureau reported on Sept. 12, 2007. Minnesota had the highest rate of homeownership, and New York had the lowest. Owner-occupied homes in California and Hawaii had a higher median value (more than $500,000) than those in any other state. In California, more than half of homeowners with a mortgage spent 30 percent or more of their income on mortgage payments and other owner costs.

Languages. In 2006, 19.7 percent of U.S. residents age 5 and older spoke a language other than English at home, compared with 17.9 percent in 2000, according to data released on Sept. 12, 2007. California led all states in this category, followed by New Mexico and Texas. Among Hispanics age 5 and older, 84.4 percent of Cubans, 79.1 percent of Mexicans, and 69 percent of Puerto Ricans spoke Spanish at home in 2006.

Minorities. The country's minority population—that is, people other than non-Hispanic, single-race whites—reached 100.7 million in 2006, up from 98.3 million in 2005, the bureau reported on May 17, 2007. The 2006 minority figure was 34 percent of the total U.S. population of 299.4 million. The country's 44.3 million Hispanics made up the largest minority group. Hispanics may be of any race. African Americans were the largest racial minority group in 2006. The black population, including Hispanics and non-Hispanics, was 40.2 million.

Income and poverty. A census report released on Aug. 28, 2007, revealed that the country's real median household income grew by 0.7 percent from 2005 to 2006, reaching $48,201. The proportion of U.S. residents in poverty declined from 12.6 percent (37 million people) in 2005 to 12.3 percent (36.5 million) in 2006. The proportion of U.S. residents without health insurance coverage rose from 15.3 percent (44.8 million) in 2005 to 15.8 percent (47 million) in 2006.

Growth and decline. In late 2006 and in 2007, the bureau announced which U.S. areas had the fastest population growth rates from 2005 to 2006. The West was the fastest-growing region, with a growth rate of 1.5 percent. The South was a close second (1.4 percent). The Midwest and Northeast grew by only 0.4 percent and 0.1 percent, respectively. Arizona was the fastest-growing state (3.6 percent), and Nevada was a close second (3.5 percent). The St. George, Utah, metropolitan area grew by 6 percent, the fastest rate among metropolitan areas. Among counties with populations of 10,000 or more, the fastest-growing was Georgia's Chattahoochee County (13.2 percent). Among cities with populations of 100,000 or more, North Las Vegas, Nevada, grew the fastest (11.9 percent).

During the same period, New Orleans underwent a 50.6-percent drop in population, which was by far the largest percentage drop of any city with a population of 100,000 or more. Hialeah, Florida, was in second place with a loss of 1.6 percent. New Orleans's monumental population loss was mainly a result of Hurricane Katrina in August 2005.   ■ Mike Lewis

See also **City; Population; State government.**

Central African Republic. See Africa.
Chad. See Africa.

Chemistry. The development of thin, lightweight, flexible batteries that can be cut into any shape—like paper—was reported in August 2007 by a team of materials scientists at Rensselaer Polytechnic Institute (RPI) in Troy, New York. Robert J. Linhardt, a professor of biocatalysis and metabolic engineering at RPI, described how his team discovered the material while attempting to create a sturdier membrane for kidney dialysis machines.

The scientists' goal was to coat a base material of cellulose—the primary constituent of paper—with vertically aligned *nanotubes* (carbon molecules with atoms arrayed like tiny rolls of chicken wire). After first aligning the nanotubes on a silicon wafer, the researchers added a solution of cellulose dissolved in an *ionic liquid* (a liquid salt), which could conduct electric current. They next peeled off the cellulose-nanotube paper, which they found could act like a *supercapacitor,* a device that can hold electric charges and release the charges in powerful bursts.

The researchers then coated one side of the paper with lithium oxide, which served as a positive terminal, while the nanotube side of the paper served as a negative electrode. With the cellulose between the two layers holding the charges apart, the device could act as a battery.

The paper battery developed by Linhardt's team could store as much energy as traditional commercial batteries. Furthermore, because the ionic solution used in the device did not contain water, supercapacitors and batteries based on the device could work over a wide range of temperatures, from −100 to 300 °F (−73 to 149 °C). In addition, the paper device does not contain toxic substances, as do traditional batteries.

The researchers noted that the paper supercapacitor/battery might make an efficient energy-storage device for *hybrid vehicles* (vehicles that are powered by both a gasoline engine and an electric motor). The researchers also observed that blood and sweat can serve as ionic liquids for conducting a current. Thus, these body liquids might help power implanted medical devices (such as pacemakers) based on the cellulose-nanotube device.

Passport to the brain. A new method for selectively ferrying medications to the central nervous system (CNS) was revealed in June by a team led by physician Manjunath N. Swamy of the Center for Blood Research Institute for Biomedical Research and Harvard Medical School, both in Boston. (The central nervous system consists of the brain and spinal cord.) The method might eventually lead to new treatments for patients with neurological disorders.

Most chemicals cannot pass through the walls of the capillaries that regulate the flow of substances to the brain. This so-called blood-brain barrier limits the delivery of medications that can fight neurological infections and diseases.

The scientists bypassed this barrier, delivering small interfering ribonucleic acid (siRNA), a compound in certain experimental drugs that have shown promise in fighting Alzheimer's disease, Huntington's disease, and other neurological illnesses. To the siRNA, the researchers attached a short protein derived from the rabies virus. In ways still not understood, this protein opens a passageway through the capillary wall for the rabies virus. In the same way, the protein carried the siRNA across the barrier.

The researchers then delivered siRNA to the brains of one of two groups of mice infected with *encephalitis* (a viral inflammation of the brain). Mice treated with this technique had an 80-percent survival rate, while all of the untreated mice died. The researchers cautioned that the safety and effectiveness of this approach to delivering medications to the human CNS had yet to be established.

Testing communities for drug use. A reliable, inexpensive 30-minute test of municipal wastewater can help public health and law enforcement authorities better understand patterns of drug use in communities. In August, environmental chemist Jennifer A. Field of Oregon State University in Corvallis and graduate student Aurea Chiaia demonstrated the ability to detect trace amounts of 14 commonly abused or illegal drugs, including cocaine, lysergic acid diethylamide (LSD), and methamphetamine.

Field told a meeting of the American Chemical Society in Boston that she used a slightly modified version of high-performance liquid chromatography (HPLC) to analyze chemicals in water samples from the sewage-treatment intakes of 10 cities in the United States. HPLC is commonly used to detect illegal substances in the urine of professional athletes. Drugs and drug-breakdown products were measured in quantities as low as 1 *nanogram* (billionth of a gram). The test results were sensitive enough, reported Field, to show differences in drug use among cities—and even surges in the use of certain drugs during weekends.

User surveys have long been the main source of information about drug use. However, some researchers have expressed doubts over such survey information, noting that survey participants may not always be truthful when asked to admit to breaking drug laws. The community chemical-analysis technique described by Field raised questions about community privacy. Nevertheless, supporters of the technique noted that patterns of drug use discovered through community testing could be used to help public officials focus local responses to drug use.   ■ Peter Andrews

Chess. In 2007, Viswanathan Anand of India became the undisputed world champion of chess by outscoring seven of the world's other top players in Mexico City. Vladimir Kramnik of Russia, who entered the tournament as defending world champion, had the right to challenge Anand to a one-on-one match for the world champion's title in 2008.

United States tournaments. In May 2007, Alexander Shabalov of Pittsburgh won the U.S. Chess Championship. It was the fourth time Shabalov had won or shared the title since 1993. In July 2007, Irina Krush of New York City won the U.S. Women's Chess Championship for the second time. Both tournaments were held in Oklahoma.

The U.S. Open Chess Championship in Cherry Hill, New Jersey, ended in a seven-way tie in August. Boris Gulko of Fair Lawn, New Jersey, won the tournament trophy on a tie-breaker. More than 400 players competed.

Young champions. Only 14 years of age, Marc Arnold of New York won the U.S. Junior Invitational Chess Championship, held for players under age 21, in Tampa in June. In an event held simultaneously in Tampa, Evan D. Ju of New Jersey and Warren Harper of Texas tied for first place in the 2007 U.S. Cadet Invitational Championship, held for players under age 16.

Also in Tampa, later in June, Brian Goldstein of Florida and Edward J. Lu of Virginia tied for first place in the 2007 U.S. Junior Open Championship, held for players under age 21.

School championships. Warren Harper of Texas took first place at the Denker Tournament of High School Champions, winning a full, four-year scholarship to Texas Tech University in Lubbock. The event, held in late July and early August in New Jersey in conjunction with the U.S. Open, brought together the U.S. high school champion from each state and Washington, D.C.

The National High School Championship held in Kansas City, Missouri, in April attracted a record-breaking number of competitors—more than 1,400. Catalina Foothills High School of Tucson, Arizona, won top team honors on tie-breakers over Edward R. Murrow High School of Brooklyn, New York. This varsity chess team from Murrow High School was the subject of New York sportswriter Michael Weinreb's *The Kings of New York: A Year Among the Geeks, Oddballs and Geniuses Who Make Up America's Top High-School Chess Team* (2007). The book chronicles the Brooklyn team's 2004-2005 season.

The Hunter College Campus Schools of New York City won the team award at the National Junior High Championships, which was contested by more than 1,000 players in late March through early April 2007 in California.   ■ Al Lawrence

Chicago. Mayor Richard M. Daley equaled the record of his father, the late Richard J. Daley, by winning a sixth consecutive term in municipal elections on Feb. 27, 2007. His overwhelming win did not carry all of his City Council allies to victory, but he remained in control and on track to become the longest-serving mayor in Chicago history.

Corruption. Daley's landslide did not bury the ongoing hiring scandals in his administration. On March 21, the city agreed to pay millions of dollars in damages to past jobseekers who were not hired because of a lack of political connections. On March 22, former top Daley aide Al Sanchez was indicted on federal charges of running a scheme to favor campaign workers for the Hispanic Democratic Organization with jobs, promotions, and raises.

Activism. Julian High School students walked out of school May 14 to protest ongoing gang violence. On May 10, a gunman killed Blair Holt and wounded four other Julian students on a city bus.

Recycling activists, who had long criticized the city's "Blue Bag" program for mixing recyclables with garbage, were vindicated in August. Records published by the *Chicago Tribune* showed that wards using the curbside "Blue Carts" system almost tripled their recycling rates over Blue Bags.

Elvira Arellano, an illegal immigrant from Mexico who spent a year in sanctuary at a Northwest Side church, left Chicago and was arrested in California on August 19. Arellano, who inspired a number of proimmigration rallies, had been resisting a deportation order so she could remain in the United States with her U.S.-born son, Saul.

Sports. In their first appearance in the professional football championship since 1986, the Chicago Bears lost the Super Bowl to the Indianapolis Colts 29-17 on Feb. 4, 2007. On October 7, record high temperatures led organizers of the LaSalle Bank Chicago Marathon to cut short the race about 3 ½ hours after its 8 a.m. start. Water shortages along the race course, along with numerous reports of runners collapsing, led to the decision to close the race course early.

Chicago continued its quest to host the 2016 Olympics. Chicago 2016 Chairman Patrick Ryan predicted on March 9, 2007, that the city would make money on the games. However, the International Olympic Committee required the city to put up a $500-million guarantee, funded by taxpayers, in case the games lost money.

Media. On April 2, Chicago real estate developer Sam Zell arranged to buy the Tribune Company, parent company of the *Chicago Tribune*. The deal closed on December 20. On July 24, the city's alternative weekly, the *Chicago Reader*, was sold to Creative Loafing in Atlanta. On December 10, Canadian-born press magnate Conrad Black was sentenced to 6 ½ years in prison for various illegal

In July 2007, the Chicago Board of Trade (CBOT) merged with the Chicago Mercantile Exchange, which was scheduled to move into the CBOT's venerable headquarters (above) at the foot of LaSalle Street in 2008. The merger, which created the world's largest trading exchange, forestalled a take-over of the CBOT by IntercontinentalExchange, Inc., of Atlanta.

manipulations involving his media empire, which included the *Chicago Sun-Times*.

Transportation. Over the opposition of air carriers, the Federal Aviation Administration allowed Chicago to spend nearly $1.3 billion in passenger ticket taxes on expanding O'Hare Airport rather than on upgrading the existing facilities.

Chicago-area mass transit labored much of the year under the threat of major service cutbacks due to inadequate funding. In a devastating March 15 report, the Illinois auditor general said that money would not solve all the Regional Transportation Authority's problems, which included high salaries and benefits, high absenteeism rates, underfunded pensions, and a lack of regional planning.

Milestones. Charles R. Walgreen, Jr., who had led the Walgreens drugstore chain, died on February 10 at age 100. Chicago author-activist Studs Terkel observed his 95th birthday on May 16. Florence Scala, the Italian-American activist who led the fight against the demolition of her neighborhood to build the campus of the University of Illinois at Chicago in the early 1960's, and who often appeared in Terkel's books, died on Aug. 28, 2007, at the age of 88.   ■ Harold Henderson

See also **Baseball; City; Newspapers.**

Children's books. See Literature for children.

Chile. Discontent with the economic policies of Chilean President Verónica Michelle Bachelet Jeria sparked labor protests in 2007. Many Chileans thought the president was not doing enough to invest windfall profits from Chilean copper mines to improve the lives of ordinary people. Demonstrators also protested the growing economic disparity between rich and poor Chileans. According to the United Nations Development Programme, just 10 percent of the population controlled 47 percent of the nation's wealth.

In August, Chile's Central Workers Union led demonstrations in several cities against the president's perceived mishandling of the economy. In Santiago, the capital, hundreds of demonstrators were arrested and dozens of people were hurt in clashes between protesters and the police. Socialist Senator Alejandro Navarro and Raúl Zurita, a prominent poet, were among the injured.

Labor strikes also affected a number of large Chilean companies in 2007. In May, thousands of nonunion employees of Bosques Arauco, a large forestry company, went on strike against salaries of less than $100 per month. During the strike, police shot dead a worker named Rodrigo Cisternas. In June and July, some 28,000 workers at mining operations of the National Copper Corporation (CODELCO) went on strike for 36 days, costing the state-run company about $90 million in lost production and damaged property. The workers, hired by a private subcontractor, earned far less than employees hired directly by CODELCO. As a result of the strike, each worker received a bonus of about $860, plus assurances of better health benefits and working conditions in the future.

Anniversary violence. The 2007 commemoration of the bloody military overthrow of President Salvador Allende on Sept. 11, 1973, prompted violence in several working-class neighborhoods of Santiago. More than 200 people were arrested, about 40 were wounded, and a police officer was killed. At a memorial honoring Allende, President Bachelet urged Chileans to remember the hardships suffered during the military dictatorship of Augusto Pinochet that followed the coup. Bachelet herself had been a victim of torture during Pinochet's regime.

Pinochet family arrested. In October 2007, a judge ordered the arrests of the widow and five children of the late Chilean dictator General Augusto Pinochet. The family was charged with misusing public funds when Pinochet controlled the country, from 1973 to 1990. Authorities also arrested 17 of Pinochet's closest military and civilian advisers on similar charges, as well as on charges of complicity in human rights abuses.

■ Nathan A. Haverstock

See also **Latin America.**

China. The ruling Chinese Communist Party (CCP) held its 17th National Congress, a meeting of some 2,200 delegates representing its 73.4 million members, from Oct. 15 to 21, 2007. The congress, held every five years, promoted officials in line for future national leadership positions.

National politics. Hu Jintao, the CCP general secretary and the nation's president, opened the meeting in Beijing, the capital, with a speech that used the word "democracy" 61 times. He stressed the need for "solidarity and unity," however. "All party members must firmly uphold the centralized and unified leadership of the party," he said. Delegates then unquestioningly approved the decisions made by party leaders.

Four men were elevated to the CCP's key group, the Standing Committee of the Politburo (Political Bureau). Observers saw two of the men, Shanghai party boss Xi Jinping and Li Keqiang, party boss of Liaoning province, as potential successors to Hu.

The choice of these two men suggested to observers that Jiang Zemin, Hu's predecessor as CCP boss and president, had won a backroom struggle over the party's future. Li was widely believed to be Hu's choice as his successor after the next congress, to be held in 2012. However, Jiang was believed to back Xi, who appeared to be in line for the top job, with Li likely to succeed

Prime Minister Wen Jiabao. The significance of this line-up for future policies remained unclear.

At the congress, Hu emphasized that rapid economic growth was the party's top priority. Economic growth for 2007 was running well over 11 percent, and inflation was more than 6 percent. He added that the party also needed to pay more attention to the environment and social welfare.

In March, the National People's Congress, China's CCP-controlled legislature, approved a law to protect private property. This followed a year of opposition from old-line Marxists, who argued that Communism meant common ownership. The law was intended to reassure the rapidly increasing middle class that their houses, cars, and other goods were safe, and thus stimulate further economic growth. Critics said the law protected ill-gotten gains of corrupt officials and dishonest businessmen.

A United States think tank, the Carnegie Endowment for International Peace, estimated in an October report that corruption cost China as much as 3 percent of its *gross domestic product* (GDP)—the total value of all goods and services produced in a country in a year. The author of the report noted that "even a relatively low-level official can amass an illicit fortune."

Wan Gang, a German-trained scientist, was appointed on April 27 as minister for science and technology. Wan was the first Chinese official since 1958 to hold ministerial rank without being a CCP member. A French-trained scientist who did not belong to the party was named minister of health on June 29, 2007. However, observers questioned how much power the two men would have.

Tainted products. The explosion of industrialization in China in 1978 turned the country into "the workshop of the world." In 2007, however, problems with the quality of a variety of Chinese products became a worldwide concern.

Shoddy manufacturing with cheap components had long plagued China's virtually unregulated industries. Dozens of Chinese infants died in 2004 from contaminated baby formula. In 2005, the government reported that it had banned 114,000 unlicensed drug makers. By 2007, deaths had been reported from tainted injections, a flawed antibiotic, a fake blood protein used in hospitals, and other similar problems. In September, government officials announced that food poisoning had killed 96 people in the first half of the year. In July, the government said it had found 23,000 food safety violations and closed 180 food factories. On July 10, the former head of the State Food and Drug Administration was executed for taking bribes to approve fake medicines, which had killed several people.

New skyscrapers dominate Chongqing, one of China's leading industrial centers, in 2007. In one of the greatest economic booms in history, investments in real estate in China grew to $94.9 million in 2007, a 27.5-percent increase in a single 12-month period.

Officials from China's standards watchdog agency said in July that 20 percent of the domestic products they tested had failed safety standards. That same month, a U.S. senator reported that some 60 percent of the goods recalled by the main U.S. safety regulator came from China.

Safety problems first gained attention abroad in March 2007 when pet food from China caused animal deaths in the United States. Then it became known that some 100 people had died in Panama in 2006 from a Chinese cold medicine that contained a toxic industrial chemical. In 2007, Chinese-made toothpaste and food containing poisonous chemicals were found in many countries.

China's toy industry, the world's largest, also became a source of alarm in 2007, after many Chinese toys were discovered to contain lead-based paint, posing a danger to children who might put the toys in their mouths. Experts noted that using lead to make bright paint colors was cheaper than using other, safer materials. Millions of Chinese-made toys were recalled in 2007 for fear of contamination by lead and other chemicals. By June, Chinese authorities had begun tightening inspections of food and many products.

China's economy was not significantly damaged by these problems. Exports for the first nine months of 2007 were 27 percent higher than the record set in that same period in 2006. In late

2007, exports of more than $1 trillion a year had created a trade surplus of at least $187 billion. Economists attributed the surplus to China's cheap land, labor, and energy.

Inflation hit an 11-year high of 6.5 percent in August. Rising production costs, linked to higher global oil prices, contributed to the increase. A highly infectious swine virus caused a shortage of pork, a basic Chinese food, which touched off further inflation worries. Foreign health experts accused the government of suppressing information about the disease.

China's rapid economic growth meant that many of its people were becoming affluent, but prosperity was unequally distributed. People in cities, especially those along the coast, prospered, while rural residents saw few benefits. According to a report issued in August by the Asian Development Bank, a United Nations (UN) affiliate, the gap between rich and poor in China was one of the widest in Asia.

More than 160 people were arrested in June for abducting hundreds of people, including children, and forcing them to work as virtual slaves to make bricks. A law passed on June 29 required written contracts for laborers, limited the use of temporary laborers, and enhanced long-term job security. By August, more than 1,300 people had been freed nationwide from illegal brickmakers.

An emphasis on production regardless of environmental effects created major problems of air, water, and soil pollution. In July, the deputy head of the State Environmental Protection Administration, Pan Yue, said 26 percent of the water in China's seven largest river systems was so polluted that contact with it was dangerous. A study by the World Bank, a UN affiliate, found that more than 750,000 Chinese died prematurely every year because of pollution. The Chinese government complained the finding could cause "social unrest" and had the bank censor its number.

Gambling. The world's largest casino opened on August 28 in Macao. The $2.4-billion Venetian Macao, owned by the U.S.-based Las Vegas Sands casino chain, featured 870 tables and 3,400 slot machines, as well as 350 shops and a 15,000-seat arena. Macao had rapidly become an international gambling destination since a local monopoly was broken up in 2002.

Dalai Lama. In October 2007, China reacted angrily to a decision by the U.S. Congress to award the country's highest civilian honor, the Congressional Gold Medal, to the Dalai Lama, the exiled leader of Tibet's chief Buddhist sect. The Dalai Lama advocated a return to the internal self-rule that Tibet held before Chinese forces entered the country in 1950.

Military. In January 2007, a Chinese ballistic missile destroyed an old Chinese weather satellite in orbit around Earth. This demonstration of a new capability alarmed Western nations that depend upon satellite communications. On October 24, China launched its first lunar orbiter.

On September 2, China promised to submit to the United Nations data on its military budget and weapons imports and exports. China had been criticized by nations increasingly nervous over its rapid and secretive military modernization program. Australian officials noted on July 5 that the arms build-up could create "misunderstanding and instability" in the Asia-Pacific area. In September, officials from the U.S. Department of Defense (DOD) accused the Chinese military of hacking into DOD computer systems. British and German officials made similar allegations, but Chinese officials denied making such attacks.

Religion. In a June 30 letter to the Chinese people, Pope Benedict XVI urged the millions of Roman Catholics in both the Chinese state-run church and an underground church loyal to the Vatican to overcome animosity and distrust. On September 21, Chinese Catholics witnessed the consecration of the first bishop of Beijing in more than 50 years to take office with the tacit approval of the Vatican. ■ Henry S. Bradsher

See also **Asia; Disasters; Food; Japan; Public health; Toys and games.**

City. Mayors from around the United States gathered in Los Angeles from June 22 to June 26, 2007, for the 75th annual meeting of the United States Conference of Mayors (USCM). The Washington, D.C.-based USCM is a *nonpartisan* (politically unaffiliated) organization made up of mayors of cities with populations of at least 30,000. Among the topics addressed by the mayors were poverty, immigration reform, climate change, and the conflicts in Iraq and Sudan.

Poverty. One resolution passed at the USCM meeting urged the federal government to reform programs to help low-income families receive the full spectrum of benefits for which they are eligible. The resolution called for antipoverty programs to be broad enough to include middle-class families who are at risk of slipping into poverty. In a separate resolution, the mayors reiterated their call for doubling the funding for Community Development Block Grants, funds for assisting low-income families provided by the U.S. Department of Housing and Urban Development.

Immigration reform. The mayors at the USCM meeting adopted a wide-ranging resolution on immigration reform addressing the economic, educational, political, security, and social aspects of the immigration debate. The resolution supported promoting investment and economic opportunities in Mexico and developing a tempo-

50 LARGEST URBAN CENTERS IN THE WORLD

Rank	Urban center*	Population
1.	Tokyo, Japan	35,303,000
2.	Mexico City, Mexico	19,907,000
3.	New York City, U.S.	18,981,000
4.	Mumbai, India	18,905,000
5.	São Paulo, Brazil	18,820,000
6.	Delhi, India	15,785,000
7.	Shanghai, China	15,000,000
8.	Kolkata, India	14,769,000
9.	Jakarta, Indonesia	13,968,000
10.	Dhaka, Bangladesh	13,251,000
11.	Buenos Aires, Argentina	12,754,000
12.	Los Angeles, U.S.	12,471,000
13.	Karachi, Pakistan	12,231,000
14.	Lagos, Nigeria	11,915,000
15.	Rio de Janeiro, Brazil	11,744,000
16.	Cairo, Egypt	11,482,000
17.	Osaka, Japan	11,284,000
18.	Manila, Philippines	11,113,000
19.	Beijing, China	11,113,000
20.	Moscow, Russia	10,778,000
21.	Istanbul, Turkey	10,035,000
22.	Paris, France	9,834,000
23.	Seoul, South Korea	9,608,000
24.	Chicago, U.S.	8,961,000
25.	Guangzhou, China	8,815,000
26.	London, U.K.	8,546,000
27.	Bogotá, Colombia	8,006,000
28.	Shenzhen, China	7,570,000
29.	Tehran, Iran	7,505,000
30.	Lima, Peru	7,345,000
31.	Wuhan, China	7,269,000
32.	Tianjin, China	7,207,000
33.	Hong Kong, China	7,188,000
34.	Chennai, India	7,159,000
35.	Taipei, Taiwan	6,803,000
36.	Bengaluru, India	6,751,000
37.	Bangkok, Thailand	6,738,000
38.	Lahore, Pakistan	6,634,000
39.	Kinshasa, Congo	6,589,000
40.	Chongqing, China	6,491,000
41.	Hyderabad, India	6,358,000
42.	Baghdad, Iraq	6,167,000
43.	Santiago, Chile	5,800,000
44.	Madrid, Spain	5,752,000
45.	Miami, U.S.	5,553,000
46.	Belo Horizonte, Brazil	5,548,000
47.	Philadelphia, U.S.	5,480,000
48.	Toronto, Canada	5,477,000
49.	Ahmadabad, India	5,348,000
50.	St. Petersburg, Russia	5,333,000

Source: 2007 estimates based on data from the United Nations and other official government sources.

*The United Nations defines an urban center as a city surrounded by a continuous built-up area having a high population density.

rary worker program in the United States to allow undocumented immigrants to earn permanent residence status through employment and education. The resolution opposed the building of a wall along the U.S-Mexico border and condemned all acts that violate the human rights of documented and undocumented immigrants.

Climate change. The mayors at the Los Angeles meeting endorsed the U.S. Mayors' Federal Climate Policy Framework, a list of steps to guide federal policy on reducing the threat posed by global warming. The steps included an 80-percent reduction in emissions of carbon dioxide and other greenhouse gases, compared with 1990 levels, by 2050. Most scientists believe that greenhouse gases, which are released in the burning of fossil fuels, are responsible for global warming. A new survey released at the meeting highlighted the efforts of more than 130 cities to address climate change, such as incorporating vehicles that operate on alternative fuels into city fleets.

Iraq and Sudan. In another resolution passed at the June 2007 USCM meeting, the mayors called on the administration of U.S. President George W. Bush to begin immediate planning for the swift redeployment of U.S. troops out of Iraq. The mayors also called for an international conference to develop strategies for achieving peace and stability in Iraq. More than 3,500 U.S. troops had been killed in Iraq since the U.S. invasion of that country in 2003.

In regard to Sudan, where hundreds of thousands of people had been killed in the western region of Darfur since fighting between government forces and rebel groups began there in 2003, the mayors proposed a number of steps in 2007 to establish peace and reduce human rights violations. A resolution urged the Bush administration and the U.S. Congress to work more closely with the United Nations, the North Atlantic Treaty Organization (NATO), and other international bodies to achieve those steps.

Ten-point plan. The mayors at the USCM meeting reaffirmed their commitment to the USCM's legislative agenda, titled 10-Point Plan: Strong Cities, Strong Families, for a Strong America. The plan, which the USCM leadership had approved in January 2007, included the following proposals: (1) a national grant program to fund cities' development of energy and environmental initiatives; (2) a federal trust fund to improve resources for local law enforcement; (3) doubling of federal funding for Community Development Block Grants; (4) a new fund to support affordable housing; (5) restoration of all operating subsidies for public housing; (6) a program of tax incentives and other measures to support local efforts to improve transportation and other

50 LARGEST CITIES IN THE UNITED STATES

Rank	City	Population*
1.	New York, NY	8,215,013
2.	Los Angeles, CA	3,851,698
3.	Chicago, IL	2,823,920
4.	Houston, TX	2,171,378
5.	Phoenix, AZ	1,557,447
6.	Philadelphia, PA	1,440,481
7.	San Antonio, TX	1,330,632
8.	San Diego, CA	1,256,574
9.	Dallas, TX	1,249,845
10.	San Jose, CA	944,426
11.	Detroit, MI	858,949
12.	Jacksonville, FL	806,236
13.	Indianapolis, IN	788,332
14.	San Francisco, CA	747,069
15.	Columbus, OH	736,674
16.	Austin, TX	729,025
17.	Fort Worth, TX	684,985
18.	Memphis, TN	671,942
19.	Charlotte, NC	645,218
20.	Baltimore, MD	626,394
21.	El Paso, TX	620,799
22.	Seattle, WA	589,099
23.	Boston, MA	584,946
24.	Washington, DC	581,011
25.	Denver, CO	575,409
26.	Milwaukee, WI	570,395
27.	Las Vegas, NV	560,225
28.	Nashville, TN	555,981
29.	Louisville, KY	553,097
30.	Oklahoma City, OK	544,562
31.	Portland, OR	540,719
32.	Tucson, AZ	522,324
33.	Albuquerque, NM	515,643
34.	Atlanta, GA	496,546
35.	Fresno, CA	472,034
36.	Long Beach, CA	470,688
37.	Sacramento, CA	455,828
38.	Mesa, AZ	452,761
39.	Kansas City, MO	450,318
40.	Cleveland, OH	438,153
41.	Virginia Beach, VA	434,221
42.	Omaha, NE	424,706
43.	Miami, FL	422,263
44.	Oakland, CA	398,274
45.	Tulsa, OK	384,270
46.	Honolulu, HI	377,836
47.	Colorado Springs, CO	375,747
48.	Minneapolis, MN	372,992
49.	Arlington, TX	371,924
50.	Raleigh, NC	370,362

*2007 World Book estimates based on data from the U.S. Census Bureau.

50 LARGEST METROPOLITAN AREAS IN THE UNITED STATES

Rank	Metropolitan area*	Population†
1.	New York–Northern New Jersey–Long Island, NY-NJ	18,858,631
2.	Los Angeles, Long Beach–Santa Ana, CA	12,992,577
3.	Chicago–Naperville–Joliet, IL-IN-WI	9,564,926
4.	Dallas–Fort Worth–Arlington, TX	6,153,824
5.	Philadelphia–Camden–Wilmington, PA-NJ-DE-MD	5,848,344
6.	Houston–Sugar Land–Baytown, TX	5,692,693
7.	Miami–Fort Lauderdale–Miami Beach, FL	5,528,894
8.	Washington–Arlington–Alexandria, DC-VA-MD-WV	5,355,484
9.	Atlanta–Sandy Springs–Marietta, GA	5,303,034
10.	Detroit–Warren–Livonia, MI	4,465,049
11.	Boston–Cambridge–Quincy, MA-NH	4,456,240
12.	Phoenix–Mesa–Scottsdale, AZ	4,204,027
13.	San Francisco–Oakland–Fremont, CA	4,187,511
14.	Riverside–San Bernardino–Ontario, CA	4,167,216
15.	Seattle–Tacoma–Bellevue, WA	3,305,105
16.	Minneapolis–St. Paul–Bloomington, MN-WI	3,206,997
17.	San Diego–Carlsbad–San Marcos, CA	2,948,046
18.	St. Louis, MO–IL	2,812,045
19.	Tampa–St. Petersburg–Clearwater, FL	2,758,177
20.	Baltimore–Towson, MD	2,669,510
21.	Denver–Aurora, CO	2,446,758
22.	Pittsburgh, PA	2,359,305
23.	Portland–Vancouver–Beaverton, OR-WA	2,171,488
24.	Cincinnati–Middletown, OH-KY-IN	2,119,511
25.	Cleveland–Elyria–Mentor, OH	2,105,817
26.	Sacramento–Arden-Arcade–Roseville, CA	2,099,527
27.	Orlando–Kissimmee, FL	2,052,614
28.	Kansas City, MO-KS	1,988,279
29.	San Antonio, TX	1,988,103
30.	Las Vegas–Paradise, NV	1,853,806
31.	San Jose–Sunnyvale–Santa Clara, CA	1,804,830
32.	Columbus, OH	1,743,457
33.	Indianapolis–Carmel, IN	1,689,167
34.	Virginia Beach–Norfolk–Newport News, VA-NC	1,658,920
35.	Charlotte–Gastonia–Concord, NC–SC	1,636,408
36.	Providence–New Bedford–Fall River, RI-MA	1,610,321
37.	Austin-Round Rock, TX	1,564,001
38.	Milwaukee–Waukesha–West Allis, WI	1,509,747
39.	Nashville–Davidson–Murfreesboro, TN	1,485,207
40.	Jacksonville, FL	1,307,666
41.	Memphis, TN-MS-AR	1,288,384
42.	Louisville–Jefferson County, KY–IN	1,233,149
43.	Richmond, VA	1,213,200
44.	Hartford–West Hartford–East Hartford, CT	1,192,476
45.	Oklahoma City, OK	1,186,655
46.	Buffalo–Niagara Falls, NY	1,131,192
47.	Birmingham–Hoover, AL	1,109,505
48.	New Orleans–Metairie–Kenner, LA	1,100,000
49.	Salt Lake City, UT	1,089,306
50.	Raleigh–Cary, NC	1,034,377

*The U.S. Census Bureau defines a metropolitan area as a large population nucleus with adjacent communities having a high degree of economic and social integration.

†2007 World Book estimates based on data from the U.S. Census Bureau and other sources.

infrastructure; (7) full funding of programs to sustain development of local work forces; (8) increased funding for various children's programs; (9) plans to improve communication and transit security in the event of terrorist attacks or natural disasters; and (10) restricting the ability of Congress to impose *unfunded mandates* (statutes that require local governments to carry out certain actions but do not appropriate funds for those actions).

City livability awards. Mayors Manuel A. Diaz of Miami; Edwin G. Winborn of Davenport, Iowa; and Mark W. Schwiebert of Rock Island, Illinois, were awarded first-place honors in the 2007 City Livability Awards Program in June. The awards, sponsored by the USCM and Waste Management, Inc., of Houston recognize outstanding mayoral leadership in implementing programs that improve quality of life in cities.

Mayor Diaz was honored for the program "ELEVATE Miami," which coordinated city resources with those of the federal, state, business, and nonprofit sectors to reduce long-term poverty in Miami. Mayors Winborn and Schwiebert were both recognized for the "RiverVision" program, a wide-ranging waterfront development plan along the Mississippi River in Davenport and Rock Island.

Climate protection awards. Also in June, mayors Martin Chavez of Albuquerque, New Mexico, and Dan Coody of Fayetteville, Arkansas, were awarded first-place honors in the 2007 Mayors' Climate Protection Awards Program. This program, sponsored by the USCM and Wal-Mart Stores, Inc., of Bentonville, Arkansas, recognizes mayors for innovative practices that increase energy efficiency and curb global warming.

Mayor Chavez was recognized for the "AlbuquerqueGreen" program, which promoted the use of bicycles and alternative fuels, as well as investment in environmentally friendly companies. Mayor Coody was honored for Fayetteville's "Alternative Transportation and Trail Master Plan," a program to encourage alternative modes of transportation through the development of new trails for bicycles and pedestrians.

Fastest-growing cities. Many of the fastest-growing cities in the United States from July 2005 to July 2006 were suburbs, according to data released by the U.S. Census Bureau in June 2007. Among cities with a population of at least 100,000, the highest growth rate—11.9 percent—occurred in North Las Vegas, Nevada, a suburb of Las Vegas. Three of the other top 10 fastest-growing cities were suburbs of Dallas: McKinney (ranking second), Grand Prairie (ranking sixth), and Denton (ranking ninth). Two cities in Florida (Port St. Lucie [third], Cape Coral [fourth]) and two in Arizona (Gilbert [fifth], Peo-

ria [seventh]) were also in the top 10. Rounding out the top 10 were Cary, North Carolina (eighth), and Lancaster, California (tenth).

The largest population loss among cities from 2005 to 2006 occurred in New Orleans, which lost more than half its population as a result of Hurricane Katrina in August 2005. Other cities with large population losses from 2005 to 2006 included, in order, Detroit; Cleveland; Pittsburgh; and Buffalo, New York.

2016 Summer Olympic Games. In April 2007, the U.S. Olympic Committee board of directors selected Chicago over Los Angeles as the U.S. candidate to host the 2016 Summer Olympic Games. The selection enabled Chicago to compete against several other cities, including Madrid, Spain; Rio de Janeiro, Brazil; and Tokyo, to host the 2016 Games. The International Olympic Committee was scheduled to announce the winning host city in October 2009.

Chicago won the U.S. bid by promising to build a $1.1-billion Olympic Village, a $366-million Olympic Stadium, and an $80-million aquatics center. In addition, a group of Chicago-area colleges and universities agreed to provide scholarships for athletes competing in the 2016 Games.

■ Alfred J. Smuskiewicz

See also **Chicago; Dallas; Houston; Los Angeles; New York City; Philadelphia; Washington, D.C.**

Civil rights. A racial controversy in the tiny town of Jena, Louisiana, made national headlines in 2007 in the United States. In addition, the U.S. government's detention and treatment of terrorism suspects continued to raise civil rights concerns.

The "Jena Six." On September 20, thousands of people from all over the country attended a rally in Jena to protest what they considered to be unfair treatment of six black students charged with beating a white student at Jena High School. The beating incident had occurred on Dec. 4, 2006, about three months after three white students hung nooses from a tree at the school.

News coverage and school, law enforcement, and court records provided varying accounts of the events that led up to the beating. On Aug. 31, 2006, at an assembly to discuss school policies, a black student, who was perhaps joking, asked the assistant principal whether black students were permitted to sit under a large tree in the center of campus. The assistant principal told the student that he could sit wherever he wanted. According to some reports, white students usually gathered at the tree, with black students gathering in another area of campus, but other reports indicated that students of all races sat under the tree. After school, the black student who asked the question and a few friends sat under the tree.

The next morning, two or three nooses were

In 1957, nine teens made history when they became the first black students at Little Rock Central High School. The Arkansas governor, in defiance of a U.S. Supreme Court desegregation order, had sent the state National Guard to bar the students from the school. President Dwight Eisenhower responded by sending U.S. Army troops to escort them in. In 2007, a U.S. judge ruled that the Little Rock School District no longer required court supervision of its desegregation efforts.

The 50th anniversary of a milestone civil rights event, the integration of Little Rock (Arkansas) Central High School, was observed in 2007.

found hanging from the tree. School officials quickly removed them. The school principal recommended that the three white students responsible for the nooses be expelled. But an expulsion committee decided that it would be more appropriate to suspend the students rather than expel them. It concluded that the incident was a prank and that the white students were unaware of the racist symbolism of nooses, which were used to lynch thousands of African Americans in the 1800's and 1900's.

Many black students and parents reacted with anger and disbelief to the noose incident, the school's decision to suspend rather than expel,

and the rationale for that decision. On Sept. 6, 2006, two fights between black and white students occurred at the school. About 12 weeks later, on December 1 and 2, two off-campus fights erupted between black and white students.

Finally, on December 4, a white student, Justin Barker, was jumped from behind, knocked unconscious, and kicked repeatedly by black students. Barker, who was not involved in the noose incident or, apparently, in any of the previous fights, was taken to the hospital and released the same day. Either six or seven black students were arrested, and LaSalle Parish District Attorney J. Reed

Walters charged them with attempted second-degree murder and conspiracy to commit murder. Five of them were charged as adults, including Mychal Bell, who was 16 at the time of the incident. The district attorney cited Bell's criminal record in deciding to charge him as an adult. The others were charged as juveniles.

On June 28, 2007, an all-white jury convicted Bell of the reduced charges of aggravated second-degree battery and conspiracy to commit battery. On September 14, an appeals court overturned Bell's conviction on the grounds that he should have been tried as a juvenile. On December 3, under a plea deal, Bell pleaded guilty to a juvenile second-degree battery charge in exchange for an 18-month sentence and the dropping of the conspiracy charge. No other trials for the accused black students took place in 2007. However, their attempted murder charges were downgraded to charges of aggravated second-degree battery.

The events in Jena drew a storm of nationwide criticism from African American leaders and others. A number of smaller protests took place in Jena prior to the massive protest of September 20. The protesters claimed that the criminal charges against the black teens were excessive, that the actions taken against the white teens involved in the previous incidents were too mild, and that the Jena case was representative of the treatment received by black people accused of crimes nationwide. "Jena is not just Jena," the civil rights leader Jesse Jackson said. "There is a Jena everywhere."

Terrorism detainees. The detention, interrogation, and treatment of suspects in the U.S. government's "war on terror" continued to draw international criticism in 2007. Human rights groups issued reports and statements claiming that many suspects were being detained indefinitely without proper judicial due process and that abusive tactics were being used during interrogations. More than 300 foreign detainees remained in the controversial U.S. military prison at Guantánamo Bay, Cuba. In March, legal proceedings began against Guantánamo detainees under a new military commissions law enacted by Congress in 2006. But by the end of 2007, most Guantánamo detainees were still being held without charge or without a scheduled date of release.

On February 20, the U.S. Court of Appeals for the District of Columbia Circuit upheld a provision in the 2006 military commissions law that denied Guantánamo detainees the right to have a federal civilian court consider whether their detention was justified. The U.S. Supreme Court agreed on June 29, 2007, to hear an appeal of this ruling. A decision was expected in 2008.   ■ Mike Lewis

See also **Canada; Courts; Crime; Immigration; Prisons; State government; Supreme Court of the United States; United States, Government of the.**

Classical music. Training in music may be more important than learning phonics for enhancing children's communication skills, according to a study published in April 2007 by the Auditory Neuroscience Laboratory at Northwestern University in Evanston, Illinois. Researchers led by neuroscientist Nina Kraus analyzed electrical activity in the brains of 20 adults as the subjects were played sounds of different pitches and shown a movie. Only some of the volunteers had musical training as children. The investigators found that the brains of the adults who had musical training as children could better distinguish the different pitches of the sounds even as their attention was focused on the movie.

The researchers explained that the ability to distinguish the different pitches was indicative of brain activity that would also improve communication skills for listening, speaking, and reading in the musically trained individuals. This finding, in turn, suggested that music aids the development of the brain in a growing child.

U.S. conductors in the news. Marin Alsop conducted her first concerts as music director of the Baltimore Symphony Orchestra in September. Alsop was the first woman to hold the music director's post at a major symphony orchestra in the United States. In October, Leonard Slatkin, one of the most prominent conductors in the United States, was named music director of the Detroit Symphony Orchestra. Slatkin had previously been director of the National Symphony Orchestra in Washington, D.C., for 12 years.

New operas. The San Francisco Opera performed the premiere of Minimalist composer Philip Glass's *Appomattox,* set to a libretto by Christopher Hampton, in October. The opera uses a pivotal moment in history—the surrender of Confederate General Robert E. Lee to his Union counterpart, Ulysses S. Grant, in the final days of the American Civil War (1861-1865)—as the basis for a larger meditation on racial issues and violence in modern times.

Also in October 2007, the Detroit-based Michigan Opera Theatre presented the first performances of *Cyrano,* by David Di Chiera, the company's founder and general director. Bernard Uzan's text for the opera is based on *Cyrano de Bergerac,* the famous play by French playwright Edmond Rostand (1868-1918) about the triumph of spiritual values over physical appearances.

The Minnesota Opera, of Minneapolis-St. Paul, premiered *The Grapes of Wrath,* with music by Ricky Ian Gordon and libretto by Michael Korie, in February 2007. Based on the classic novel by John Steinbeck (1902-1968), the opera traces the Joad family's journey in the 1930's Dust Bowl-era from the ruins of their Oklahoma farm to the false promise of a better life in California.

Beverly Sills
America's down-to-earth diva

Beverly Sills, whose radiant voice and engaging personality made her one of the most popular American opera singers of her generation, died on July 2, 2007. After she retired from singing, she remained an influential presence in the cultural world through her roles as administrator, fund-raiser, and passionate advocate for the arts. She was, wrote John von Rhein in the *Chicago Tribune*, "among the handful of solidly trained operatic stars of her era, along with Luciano Pavarotti and Placido Domingo, who could bridge the gap between popular culture and high art through their outsized talent and the charismatic force of their personalities."

Sills was affectionately regarded for her warm and outgoing nature. She appeared on late-night television talk shows and co-starred with comedian-singer Carol Burnett in a television special that won an Emmy nomination in 1977, while remaining one of the most in-demand divas in the world's greatest opera houses.

Sills was a coloratura soprano who excelled in the style of singing called *bel canto*. Originating in Italy during the 1600's, this style requires a full, rich, broad, and flexible tone. Sills's voice was particularly suited to the operas of such Italian composers as Vincenzo Bellini, Gaetano Donizetti, and Gioacchino Rossini. She was also one of the finest operatic actresses of her time. Perhaps her most acclaimed performance came in the title role of *Manon* by the French composer Jules Massenet.

Beverly Sills was born Belle Miriam Silverman to Jewish Eastern European immigrant parents on May 25, 1929, in the Brooklyn section of New York City. Despite the family's modest resources, Sills's mother believed her daughter, whom she nicknamed "Bubbles," was destined for stardom. Sills was a child prodigy who began singing and acting on radio shows when she was only 3. Sills began taking vocal lessons when she was 7 and made her operatic debut in 1947 with the Philadelphia Civic Grand Opera Company while still a teen-ager. She spent the next several years singing with touring opera companies and the San Francisco Opera and performing recitals of *lieder* (German art songs).

In 1955, after seven previously unsuccessful auditions, Sills was accepted into the New York City Opera. She did not become a star with the company until 1966, when her performance as Cleopatra in Georg Frideric Handel's *Julius Caesar* created a sensation. Sills began performing outside the United States in 1967, making guest appearances at the Vienna State Opera and the Colón Theater in Buenos Aires, Argentina. She appeared at La Scala in Milan, Italy, in 1969, and at the German Opera in Berlin and the Royal Opera House at Covent Garden in London in 1970. She made her debut at the Metropolitan Opera in New York City in 1975 in Rossini's *The Siege of Corinth*.

Sills retired as a singer in 1980 and immediately became the general director of the New York City Opera, serving in that position until 1989. From 1994 to 2002, she was chairperson of Lincoln Center in New York City. Sills then served as board chairperson of the Metropolitan Opera from 2002 to 2005. ■ Dan Zeff

In April 2007, David Carlson's *Anna Karenina* had its premiere by the Florida Grand Opera in Miami. The romantic tragedy, with a libretto by Colin Graham, is based on the novel by Russian author Leo Tolstoy (1828-1910) about a love triangle involving the unhappily married Anna.

In July 2007, the Central City Opera, of Denver, presented the premiere of *Poet Li Bai,* by Chinese composer Guo Wenjing, set to a libretto by Diana Liao and Xu Ying. The opera, drawing on both Eastern and Western musical influences, tells of the life and dreams of the renowned Chinese poet Li Bai (701-763).

New orchestral and chamber works. In February 2007, Finnish composer and conductor Esa-Pekka Salonen led the New York Philharmonic in the first performances of his *Piano Concerto.* Yefim Bronfman was the soloist. In November, Alan Pierson conducted the ensemble Alarm Will Sound in the world premiere of *Son of Chamber Symphony,* by John Adams, at Stanford University in California.

The world premiere of Elliott Carter's *Horn Concerto* was presented by the Boston Symphony Orchestra under conductor James Levine in November. James Sommerville, the orchestra's principal horn, was the soloist. The Chicago Symphony Orchestra in October performed the world premiere of *Chicago Remains,* an homage to the "Second City" and inspired by its skyline, by British composer Mark-Anthony Turnage. Bernard Haitink conducted the orchestra.

Composer Christopher Rouse had two world premieres of his works in March. The Los Angeles

Master Chorale under conductor Grant Gershon debuted Rouse's *Requiem,* for double chorus, children's chorus, orchestra and baritone solo, in Los Angeles. The University of Miami's Frost Wind Ensemble, under Gary Green's direction, presented the first performance of Rouse's *Wolf Rounds* at Carnegie Hall in New York City.

David Del Tredici's song cycle *Love Addiction,* with text by poet John Kelly, had its premiere in May at a New York City concert by the Riverside Opera Ensemble honoring the composer's 70th birthday. Chris Pedro Trakas was the baritone soloist, with Del Tredici at the piano. In October, the Orion String Quartet and clarinetist David Krakauer debuted Del Tredici's *Magyar Madness* at the University of Iowa in Iowa City.

Michael Daugherty's *Deus ex Machina* (Latin

Soprano Andrea Gruber sings the title role in Giacomo Puccini's *Turandot,* performed at the Metropolitan Opera in New York City in March 2007. Lavishly produced by Italian film, theater, and opera director Franco Zeffirelli, the opera featured tenor Richard Margison as Calaf and South Korean-born soprano Hei-Kyung Hong as Liu.

for "God from the machine"), a tribute to railways in the United States, had its premiere in March by the Charlotte (North Carolina) Symphony. Pianist Terrence Wilson was the soloist. In April, pianist Ian Hobson and the Tampa Bay-based Florida Orchestra presented the premiere of *Piano Concerto No. 3* by Benjamin Lees. *Orphic Memories,* a concerto grosso by

Ingram Marshall, received its world premiere by the Orpheus Chamber Orchestra in April at Carnegie Hall in New York City.

Deaths. Beverly Sills, the celebrated Brooklyn- (New York City) born coloratura soprano, who also did much to popularize opera and the fine arts, died in July at age 78. Luciano Pavarotti, whose spectacular tenor voice and magnetic personality attracted millions of people to opera, died at age 71 in September.

Gian Carlo Menotti, the prolific Italian-born composer who was for many years the most-performed opera composer in the United States, died at age 95 in February. Russian cellist and conductor Mstislav Rostropovich, whose passionate performances on the cello made him one of the foremost exponents of the instrument, died in April at age 80.

Régine Crespin, the acclaimed French operatic soprano (and later mezzo-soprano) whose lustrous singing voice thrilled opera and concert audiences around the world, died in July at age 80. Also passing away in July, at age 55, was tenor Jerry Hadley, who rose from a humble upbringing on an Illinois farm to become one of the world's leading opera singers.   ■ John von Rhein

See also **Popular music.**

Clothing. See Fashion.
Coal. See Energy supply.

Colombia. An investigation of collusion between leading politicians and military officers with right-wing paramilitary groups responsible for assassinations, kidnappings, electoral fraud, and protecting drug traffickers cast a pall over the administration of President Álvaro Uribe Vélez in 2007. In February, Colombian Foreign Minister María Consuelo Araújo resigned following the arrest of her brother, a senator, in connection with the investigation. The inquiry also targeted Araújo's father, a former state governor.

Also in February, the indictment of Jorge Noguera, Uribe's former intelligence chief, added fuel to the "parapolitica" scandal. Noguera was charged with murder for supplying a hit list of Colombian political dissidents to paramilitary death squads. In October, public protests broke out, amid daily revelations of other political and military leaders' complicity with the paramilitaries. Increasingly credible allegations of the Uribe administration's involvement in human rights atrocities jeopardized the passage by the United States Congress of a free-trade deal with Colombia, as well as continued large-scale U.S. military assistance in combating illegal drugs.

War on drugs. Critics of U.S. aid to Colombia noted that in 2007 Colombia was the source of 90 percent of the cocaine consumed in the United States. Colombian Vice President Francisco Santos

Calderón blamed this fact on the failure of a U.S.-backed campaign to spray coca plants with herbicide from low-flying planes. He said this method of eradication was less effective than uprooting the plants by hand, a more time-consuming practice.

In a rare victory in the war on illegal drugs, elite Colombian commandos captured Diego Montoya, head of the Norte del Valle drug cartel, in southwestern Colombia in September. Montoya was handed over to authorities in the United States, where he was on the Federal Bureau of Investigation's "Ten Most Wanted Fugitives" list.

By 2007, the Pacific port of Buenaventura had become Colombia's deadliest city. Despite the deployment of 2,000 soldiers and police officers to Buenaventura, more than 200 homicides occurred from January through April. Authorities attributed the violence to a turf war between rival drug cartels, leftist guerrillas, and right-wing paramilitaries involved in the cocaine trade. The destitution of the city's neglected, overwhelmingly Afro-Colombian population added to the violence.

■ Nathan A. Haverstock

See also **Latin America.**

Commonwealth of Independent States. See Armenia; Georgia; Kazakhstan; Kyrgyzstan; Russia; Ukraine; Uzbekistan.
Comoros. See Africa.

Computer. Many of the most substantial computing developments of 2007 came from Microsoft Corporation of Redmond, Washington, and Apple Inc. of Cupertino, California, companies that continued to maintain high profiles in hardware and software markets. The competitive but amicable relationship between the two companies was demonstrated in May at a public discussion by their founders, Microsoft's Bill Gates and Apple's Steve Jobs. The two men chatted about their shared pasts and visions for the future. They also discussed new operating systems and multitouch devices. Both companies released one of each in 2007.

Microsoft began 2007 with the release of its long-anticipated Windows Vista operating system. More than five years in the making, Vista was developed with a focus on security and stability. Other new features in Vista included improved file searching, more advanced visualizations, and built-in management of multimedia content. Vista was also released in many different versions.

In late May, Microsoft unveiled a new computer called Surface. Surface is a tablelike device topped with a large horizontal multitouch screen. Whereas most computers are controlled with a mouse and keyboard, Surface is controlled by directly touching the screen. Unlike older touch-screen technologies, multitouch technology recognizes motion and direction in addition to multiple simultaneous fin-

A Microsoft employee demonstrates the new 2007 Surface computer. In addition to detecting his hand, the Surface also recognizes credit cards placed at opposite corners. Relying on wireless signals, visual cues, and built-in barcode-like devices, the designers of Surface sought to reduce the number of cords and peripheral devices.

gers. Many people can work together on one multitouch device such as Surface. Additionally, Surface recognizes objects and wirelessly communicates with electronic devices placed on it. For example, placing a compatible digital camera on Surface will automatically download and display the camera's pictures.

Apple generated an unprecedented media frenzy when Steve Jobs announced the iPhone in January. Like other advanced mobile phones, the iPhone acts as a cell phone, a device to connect to the Internet, and a portable media player. Unlike previous mobile devices, the iPhone is physically sleek and controlled almost entirely with a large multitouch display.

In October, Apple released Leopard, the newest version of its operating system. Leopard's new features focused on improving efficiency and ease of use with tools that promote multitasking and document visualization.

Checkers. Computer scientists at the University of Alberta in Edmonton completed a computer program that cannot lose at the game of checkers. Previous programs often beat human champions, but this program was mathematically guaranteed to tie or win.　　■ Drew Huening

See also **Electronics; Internet; Telecommunications.**

Congo (Brazzaville). See Africa.

Congo (Kinshasa). In 2007, the Democratic Republic of the Congo (DRC) completed its first free, multiparty democratic elections since 1965. The polling began in 2006, during which Joseph Kabila was elected president. Kabila's electoral alliance also won majorities in seven provincial assemblies; Jean-Pierre Bemba's alliance obtained majorities in the other four provinces. Bemba was Kabila's main opponent in the presidential polls.

In January 2007, the provincial assemblies elected their own governors and the Senate's 108 members. Neither Kabila's nor Bemba's alliance won majorities in the Senate, though Bemba was elected senator of the Kinshasa urban province. Bemba's alliance won only the governorship of Equateur, his home province.

After the elections. The completion of elections gave the DRC new government structures as prescribed by the new Constitution. However, democratization did not immediately bring the stability needed for economic and social development. Violence erupted soon after the election.

One reason for the instability had been the slow progress made integrating the various rebel forces into the new army. Especially in the eastern DRC, remnants of rebel forces continued to fight against government forces, hoping to secure advantages for themselves. International mediation, notably through MONUC (the United Nations peacekeeping force in the DRC), resulted in peace deals with most rebel groups. The peace remained fragile, however, with thousands of Congolese fleeing to such neighboring countries as Burundi, Rwanda, and Uganda.

In addition, people in Matadi, the main port, and Kinshasa, the capital, protested violently against election outcomes. Having previously clashed with Kabila's private guard, Bemba's private army was defeated by the DRC army in two days of open warfare in March. Bemba sought refuge in the South African embassy and then visited Portugal for medical reasons.

In December 2006, Kabila had appointed Antoine Gizenga, leader of the strongest opposition party that supported him, as prime minister. In February 2007, Gizenga assembled a Cabinet, which consisted mostly of members of Kabila's Alliance of the Presidential Majority (AMP). The AMP controlled the majority of National Assembly seats. The Cabinet, containing 60 ministers and deputy ministers, was criticized for being too large in view of the government's heavy financial commitments. However, Kabila regarded as more important the participation of a wide array of political leaders in his government, which the new Cabinet reflected.   ■ Pieter Esterhuysen

See also **Africa; Disasters; South Africa.**

Congress of the United States.

Democrats assumed control of both houses of Congress in 2007 for the first time in 12 years. Nancy Pelosi (D., California) made history by becoming the first woman speaker of the House of Representatives. Throughout 2007, congressional Democrats battled extensively with Republican President George W. Bush and congressional Republicans over Iraq War policy. Democrats also clashed with Republicans over several spending measures. But the two sides cooperated on legislation to raise fuel efficiency standards for passenger vehicles, reform congressional ethics and lobbying rules, and increase the minimum wage.

Public opinion of Congress in 2007 was low— often even lower than public opinion of President Bush. Most polls early in the year indicated that between 30 percent and 40 percent of Americans approved of Congress's job performance. However, from June onward, congressional approval ratings dipped below 30 percent.

Iraq. In early 2007, President Bush announced that about 30,000 additional U.S. troops would be sent to Iraq to try to reduce violence in Baghdad and Al Anbar province. This troop "surge" met with considerable opposition from congressional Democrats, most of whom objected to the president's Iraq policies and instead sought partial or complete withdrawal of U.S. troops. On

February 16, the House voted 246-182 for a nonbinding resolution disapproving of the surge. But the Senate failed on two occasions in February to pass a similar resolution. Because Democrats controlled the Senate by only a slim 51-49 margin, Republicans were able to prevent them on both occasions from getting the 60 votes needed to move forward on consideration of the measure.

On several occasions in 2007, congressional Democrats tried to pass legislation establishing a timetable for the withdrawal of U.S. troops from Iraq. The most notable attempt was in March and April, when Congress attached troop withdrawal requirements to a war-spending bill for fiscal year (FY) 2007 (Oct. 1, 2006-Sept. 30, 2007). Under the bill, withdrawal of troops would have begun no later than October 1, with a goal of completing the withdrawal within six months. The bill passed on narrow, mostly party-line votes in both the House and Senate. President Bush vetoed the bill on May 1. He asserted that "setting a deadline for withdrawal is setting a date for failure."

Later in May, Congress passed a revised FY 2007 war-spending bill, this time with no troop withdrawal timetable. President Bush signed the bill on May 25. It provided about $100 billion for the U.S. wars in Iraq and Afghanistan. It established 18 benchmarks for Iraq's government to achieve as a condition for receiving certain U.S. reconstruction aid. The bill also required the president and the Government Accountability Office to submit reports to Congress on Iraq's benchmark progress. Enactment of the bill brought the total amount appropriated since September 2001 for Iraq, Afghanistan, and counterterrorism operations to nearly $610 billion. This amount included funds for military operations, base security, reconstruction, foreign aid, embassy operations, and veterans' health care.

In 2007, the Bush administration requested another $195 billion for war-related activities for FY 2008 (Oct. 1, 2007-Sept. 30, 2008). By the end of the 2007 calendar year, Congress had appropriated about $87 billion of that amount. About $70 billion was included in an omnibus FY 2008 budget bill passed in December 2007, and about $17 billion was appropriated earlier for Mine Resistant Ambush Protected (MRAP) vehicles.

Energy. In December, Congress passed a bill to raise fuel mileage standards for new passenger cars and light trucks, mandate a large boost in the production of ethanol and other biofuels, and establish new efficiency standards for government buildings and home appliances. President Bush signed the bill on December 19. Under the bill, new vehicle fleets must average 35 miles per gallon (mpg) by 2020, up from the 2007 requirements of 27.5 mpg for cars and 22.2 mpg for light trucks. In addition, the nation's motor fuel supply

MEMBERS OF THE UNITED STATES SENATE

The Senate of the second session of the 110th Congress consisted of 49 Democrats, 49 Republicans, and 2 Independents when it convened on Jan. 15, 2008. The first date in each listing shows when the senator's term began. The second date in each listing shows when the senator's term expires.

STATE	TERM	STATE	TERM	STATE	TERM
Alabama		**Louisiana**		**Ohio**	
Richard C. Shelby, R.	1987-2011	Mary L. Landrieu, D.	1997-2009	Sherrod Brown, D.	2007-2013
Jeff Sessions, R.	1997-2009	David Vitter, R.	2005-2011	George V. Voinovich, R.	1999-2011
Alaska		**Maine**		**Oklahoma**	
Theodore F. Stevens, R.	1968-2009	Olympia Snowe, R.	1995-2013	James M. Inhofe, R.	1994-2009
Lisa Murkowski, R.	2002-2011	Susan M. Collins, R.	1997-2009	Tom Coburn, R.	2005-2011
Arizona		**Maryland**		**Oregon**	
John McCain III, R.	1987-2011	Benjamin L. Cardin, D.	2007-2013	Ron Wyden, D.	1996-2011
Jon Kyl, R.	1995-2013	Barbara A. Mikulski, D.	1987-2011	Gordon Smith, R.	1997-2009
Arkansas		**Massachusetts**		**Pennsylvania**	
Blanche Lambert Lincoln, D.	1999-2011	Edward M. Kennedy, D.	1962-2013	Arlen Specter, R.	1981-2011
Mark Pryor, D.	2003-2009	John F. Kerry, D.	1985-2009	Bob Casey, Jr., D.	2007-2013
California		**Michigan**		**Rhode Island**	
Dianne Feinstein, D.	1992-2013	Carl Levin, D.	1979-2009	Jack Reed, D.	1997-2009
Barbara Boxer, D.	1993-2011	Debbie Stabenow, D.	2001-2013	Sheldon Whitehouse, D.	2007-2013
Colorado		**Minnesota**		**South Carolina**	
Wayne Allard, R.	1997-2009	Amy Klobuchar, D.	2007-2013	Lindsey Graham, R.	2003-2009
Ken Salazar, D.	2005-2011	Norm Coleman, R.	2003-2009	Jim DeMint, R.	2005-2011
Connecticut		**Mississippi**		**South Dakota**	
Christopher J. Dodd, D.	1981-2011	Thad Cochran, R.	1978-2009	Tim Johnson, D.	1997-2009
Joseph I. Lieberman, I.	1989-2013	Roger Wicker, R.	2008	John Thune, R.	2005-2011
Delaware		**Missouri**		**Tennessee**	
Joseph R. Biden, Jr., D.	1973-2009	Christopher S. (Kit) Bond, R.	1987-2011	Bob Corker, R.	2007-2013
Thomas Carper, D.	2001-2013	Claire C. McCaskill, D.	2007-2013	Lamar Alexander, R.	2003-2009
Florida		**Montana**		**Texas**	
Bill Nelson, D.	2001-2013	Max Baucus, D.	1978-2009	Kay Bailey Hutchison, R.	1993-2013
Mel Martinez, R.	2005-2011	Jon Tester, D.	2007-2013	John Cornyn, R.	2003-2009
Georgia		**Nebraska**		**Utah**	
Saxby Chambliss, R.	2003-2009	Chuck Hagel, R.	1997-2009	Orrin G. Hatch, R.	1977-2013
Johnny Isakson, R.	2005-2011	Ben Nelson, D.	2001-2013	Robert F. Bennett, R.	1993-2011
Hawaii		**Nevada**		**Vermont**	
Daniel K. Inouye, D.	1963-2011	Harry M. Reid, D.	1987-2011	Patrick J. Leahy, D.	1975-2011
Daniel K. Akaka, D.	1990-2013	John Ensign, R.	2001-2013	Bernie Sanders, I.	2007-2013
Idaho		**New Hampshire**		**Virginia**	
Larry E. Craig, R.	1991-2009	Judd Gregg, R.	1993-2011	John W. Warner, R.	1979-2009
Mike Crapo, R.	1999-2011	John E. Sununu, R.	2003-2009	Jim Webb, D.	2007-2013
Illinois		**New Jersey**		**Washington**	
Richard J. Durbin, D.	1997-2009	Robert Menendez, D.	2006-2013	Patty Murray, D.	1993-2011
Barack Obama, D.	2005-2011	Frank R. Lautenberg, D.	2003-2009	Maria Cantwell, D.	2001-2013
Indiana		**New Mexico**		**West Virginia**	
Richard G. Lugar, R.	1977-2013	Pete V. Domenici, R.	1973-2009	Robert C. Byrd, D.	1959-2013
Evan Bayh, D.	1999-2011	Jeff Bingaman, D.	1983-2013	John D. Rockefeller IV, D.	1985-2009
Iowa		**New York**		**Wisconsin**	
Charles E. Grassley, R.	1981-2011	Charles E. Schumer, D.	1999-2011	Herbert Kohl, D.	1989-2013
Tom Harkin, D.	1985-2009	Hillary Rodham Clinton, D.	2001-2013	Russell D. Feingold, D.	1993-2011
Kansas		**North Carolina**		**Wyoming**	
Sam Brownback, R.	1996-2011	Elizabeth Dole, R.	2003-2009	John Barrasso, R.	2007-2009
Pat Roberts, R.	1997-2009	Richard Burr, R.	2005-2011	Mike Enzi, R.	1997-2009
Kentucky		**North Dakota**			
Mitch McConnell, R.	1985-2009	Kent Conrad, D.	1987-2013		
Jim Bunning, R.	1999-2011	Byron L. Dorgan, D.	1992-2011		

MEMBERS OF THE UNITED STATES HOUSE OF REPRESENTATIVES

The House of Representatives of the second session of the 110th Congress consisted of 232 Democrats, 199 Republicans (not including representatives from American Samoa, the District of Columbia, Guam, Puerto Rico, and the Virgin Islands), and 4 vacancies when it convened on Jan. 15, 2008. This table shows congressional district, legislator, and party affiliation. Asterisk (*) denotes those who served in the 109th Congress; dagger (†) denotes "at large."

Alabama
1. Jo Bonner, R.*
2. Terry Everett, R.*
3. Mike Rogers, R.*
4. Robert Aderholt, R.*
5. Bud Cramer, D.*
6. Spencer Bachus, R.*
7. Artur Davis, D.*

Alaska
†Donald E. Young, R.*

Arizona
1. Rick Renzi, R.*
2. Trent Franks, R.*
3. John Shadegg, R.*
4. Ed Pastor, D.*
5. Harry E. Mitchell, D.
6. Jeff Flake, R.*
7. Raúl Grijalva, D.*
8. Gabrielle Giffords, D.

Arkansas
1. Marion Berry, D.*
2. Vic Snyder, D.*
3. John Boozman, R.*
4. Mike Ross, D.*

California
1. Mike Thompson, D.*
2. Wally Herger, R.*
3. Dan Lungren, R.*
4. John Doolittle, R.*
5. Doris O. Matsui, D.*
6. Lynn Woolsey, D.*
7. George E. Miller, D.*
8. Nancy Pelosi, D.*
9. Barbara Lee, D.*
10. Ellen Tauscher, D.*
11. Jerry McNerney, D.
12. Tom Lantos, D.*
13. Pete Stark, D.*
14. Anna Eshoo, D.*
15. Mike Honda, D.*
16. Zoe Lofgren, D.*
17. Sam Farr, D.*
18. Dennis Cardoza, D.*
19. George Radanovich, R.*
20. Jim Costa, D.*
21. Devin Nunes, R.*
22. Kevin McCarthy, R.
23. Lois Capps, D.*
24. Elton Gallegly, R.*
25. Howard McKeon, R.*
26. David Dreier, R.*
27. Brad Sherman, D.*
28. Howard Berman, D.*
29. Adam Schiff, D.*
30. Henry Waxman, D.*
31. Xavier Becerra, D.*
32. Hilda Solis, D.*
33. Diane Watson, D.*
34. Lucille Roybal-Allard, D.*
35. Maxine Waters, D.*
36. Jane Harman, D.*
37. Laura Richardson, D.
38. Grace Napolitano, D.*
39. Linda Sánchez, D.*
40. Ed Royce, R.*
41. Jerry Lewis, R.*
42. Gary Miller, R.*
43. Joe Baca, D.*
44. Ken Calvert, R.*
45. Mary Bono, R.*
46. Dana Rohrabacher, R.*
47. Loretta Sanchez, D.*
48. John Campbell, R.*
49. Darrell Issa, R.*
50. Brian Bilbray, R.*
51. Bob Filner, D.*
52. Duncan Hunter, R.*
53. Susan Davis, D.*

Colorado
1. Diana DeGette, D.*
2. Mark Udall, D.*
3. John Salazar, D.*
4. Marilyn Musgrave, R.*
5. Doug Lamborn, R.
6. Tom Tancredo, R.*
7. Ed Perlmutter, D.

Connecticut
1. John Larson, D.*
2. Joe Courtney, D.
3. Rosa DeLauro, D.*
4. Christopher Shays, R.*
5. Christopher S. Murphy, D.

Delaware
†Michael Castle, R.*

Florida
1. Jeff Miller, R.*
2. Allen Boyd, D.*
3. Corrine Brown, D.*
4. Ander Crenshaw, R.*
5. Virginia Brown-Waite, R.*
6. Clifford B. Stearns, R.*
7. John Mica, R.*
8. Ric Keller, R.*
9. Gus Bilirakis, R.
10. C. W. Bill Young, R.*
11. Kathy Castor, D.
12. Adam Putnam, R.*
13. Vern Buchanan, R.
14. Connie Mack, R.*
15. Dave Weldon, R.*
16. Tim Mahoney, D.
17. Kendrick Meek, D.*
18. Ileana Ros-Lehtinen, R.*
19. Robert Wexler, D.*
20. Debbie Wasserman Schultz, D.*
21. Lincoln Diaz-Balart, R.*
22. Ron Klein, D.
23. Alcee Hastings, D.*
24. Tom Feeney, R.*
25. Mario Diaz-Balart, R.*

Georgia
1. Jack Kingston, R.*
2. Sanford Bishop, Jr., D.*
3. Lynn Westmoreland, R.*
4. Hank Johnson, D.
5. John Lewis, D.*
6. Tom Price, R.*
7. John Linder, R.*
8. Jim Marshall, D.*
9. Nathan Deal, R.*
10. Paul Broun, R.
11. Phil Gingrey, R.*
12. John Barrow, D.*
13. David Scott, D.*

Hawaii
1. Neil Abercrombie, D.*
2. Mazie K. Hirono, D.

Idaho
1. Bill Sali, R.
2. Mike Simpson, R.*

Illinois
1. Bobby Rush, D.*
2. Jesse L. Jackson, Jr., D.*
3. Daniel Lipinski, D.*
4. Luis Gutierrez, D.*
5. Rahm Emanuel, D.*
6. Peter J. Roskam, R.
7. Danny Davis, D.*
8. Melissa Bean, D.*
9. Janice Schakowsky, D.*
10. Mark Kirk, R.*
11. Gerald Weller, R.*
12. Jerry F. Costello, D.*
13. Judy Biggert, R.*
14. [vacant]
15. Timothy Johnson, R.*
16. Donald Manzullo, R.*
17. Phil Hare, D.
18. Ray LaHood, R.*
19. John Shimkus, R.*

Indiana
1. Peter J. Visclosky, D.*
2. Joe Donnelly, D.
3. Mark Souder, R.*
4. Steve Buyer, R.*
5. Dan Burton, R.*
6. Mike Pence, R.*
7. [vacant]
8. Brad Ellsworth, D.
9. Baron P. Hill, D.

Iowa
1. Bruce Braley, D.
2. David Loebsack, D.
3. Leonard Boswell, D.*
4. Thomas Latham, R.*
5. Steve King, R.*

Kansas
1. Jerry Moran, R.*
2. Nancy E. Boyda, D.

3. Dennis Moore, D.*
4. Todd Tiahrt, R.*

Kentucky
1. Edward Whitfield, R.*
2. Ron Lewis, R.*
3. John A. Yarmuth, D.
4. Geoff Davis, R.*
5. Harold (Hal) Rogers, R.*
6. Ben Chandler, D.*

Louisiana
1. [vacant]
2. William J. Jefferson, D.*
3. Charles Melancon, D.*
4. Jim McCrery, R.*
5. Rodney Alexander, R.*
6. Richard Hugh Baker, R.*
7. Charles Boustany, Jr., R.*

Maine
1. Thomas Allen, D.*
2. Michael Michaud, D.*

Maryland
1. Wayne T. Gilchrest, R.*
2. C. A. Ruppersberger, D.*
3. John P. Sarbanes, D.
4. Albert Wynn, D.*
5. Steny H. Hoyer, D.*
6. Roscoe Bartlett, R.*
7. Elijah Cummings, D.*
8. Chris Van Hollen, D.*

Massachusetts
1. John W. Olver, D.*
2. Richard E. Neal, D.*
3. James McGovern, D.*
4. Barney Frank, D.*
5. Niki Tsongas, D.
6. John Tierney, D.*
7. Edward J. Markey, D.*
8. Michael Capuano, D.*
9. Stephen F. Lynch, D.*
10. William Delahunt, D.*

Michigan
1. Bart Stupak, D.*
2. Peter Hoekstra, R.*
3. Vernon Ehlers, R.*
4. Dave Camp, R.*
5. Dale Kildee, D.*
6. Frederick S. Upton, R.*
7. Timothy Walberg, R.
8. Mike Rogers, R.*
9. Joseph Knollenberg, R.*
10. Candice Miller, R.*
11. Thaddeus McCotter, R.*
12. Sander M. Levin, D.*
13. Carolyn Kilpatrick, D.*
14. John Conyers, Jr., D.*
15. John Dingell, D.*

Minnesota
1. Timothy J. Walz, D.
2. John Kline, R.*

3. Jim Ramstad, R.*
4. Betty McCollum, D.*
5. Keith Ellison, D.
6. Michele Bachmann, R.
7. Collin C. Peterson, D.*
8. James L. Oberstar, D.*

Mississippi
1. [vacant]
2. Bennie Thompson, D.*
3. Charles Pickering, R.*
4. Gene Taylor, D.*

Missouri
1. William Clay, D.*
2. Todd Akin, R.*
3. Russ Carnahan, D.*
4. Ike Skelton, D.*
5. Emanuel Cleaver II, D.*
6. Samuel Graves, R.*
7. Roy Blunt, R.*
8. Jo Ann Emerson, R.*
9. Kenny Hulshof, R.*

Montana
†Dennis Rehberg, R.*

Nebraska
1. Jeff Fortenberry, R.*
2. Lee Terry, R.*
3. Adrian Smith, R.

Nevada
1. Shelley Berkley, D.*
2. Dean Heller, R.
3. Jon Porter, Sr., R.*

New Hampshire
1. Carol Shea-Porter, D.
2. Paul W. Hodes, D.

New Jersey
1. Robert E. Andrews, D.*
2. Frank LoBiondo, R.*
3. H. James Saxton, R.*
4. Christopher H. Smith, R.*
5. Scott Garrett, R.*
6. Frank Pallone, Jr., D.*
7. Mike Ferguson, R.*
8. William Pascrell, Jr., D.*
9. Steven Rothman, D.*
10. Donald M. Payne, D.*
11. Rodney Frelinghuysen, R.*
12. Rush Holt, D.*
13. Albio Sires, D.*

New Mexico
1. Heather Wilson, R.*
2. Steve Pearce, R.*
3. Thomas Udall, D.*

New York
1. Tim Bishop, D.*
2. Steve Israel, D.*
3. Peter King, R.*
4. Carolyn McCarthy, D.*
5. Gary L. Ackerman, D.*
6. Gregory Meeks, D.*
7. Joseph Crowley, D.*
8. Jerrold Nadler, D.*
9. Anthony Weiner, D.*
10. Edolphus Towns, D.*
11. Yvette D. Clarke, D.

12. Nydia Velázquez, D.*
13. Vito J. Fossella, R.*
14. Carolyn Maloney, D.*
15. Charles B. Rangel, D.*
16. José E. Serrano, D.*
17. Eliot L. Engel, D.*
18. Nita M. Lowey, D.*
19. John J. Hall, D.
20. Kirsten E. Gillibrand, D.
21. Michael R. McNulty, D.*
22. Maurice Hinchey, D.*
23. John McHugh, R.*
24. Michael Arcuri, D.
25. James Walsh, R.*
26. Thomas Reynolds, R.*
27. Brian Higgins, D.*
28. Louise M. Slaughter, D.*
29. Randy Kuhl, R.*

North Carolina
1. G. K. Butterfield, D.*
2. Bob Etheridge, D.*
3. Walter Jones, Jr., R.*
4. David Price, D.*
5. Virginia Foxx, R.*
6. Howard Coble, R.*
7. Mike McIntyre, D.*
8. Robin Hayes, R.*
9. Sue Myrick, R.*
10. Patrick McHenry, R.*
11. Heath Shuler, D.
12. Melvin Watt, D.*
13. Brad Miller, D.*

North Dakota
†Earl Pomeroy, D.*

Ohio
1. Steve Chabot, R.*
2. Jean Schmidt, R.*
3. Michael Turner, R.*
4. Jim Jordan, R.
5. Robert E. Latta, R.
6. Charles A. Wilson, D.
7. David L. Hobson, R.*
8. John A. Boehner, R.*
9. Marcy Kaptur, D.*
10. Dennis Kucinich, D.*
11. Stephanie Tubbs Jones, D.*
12. Pat Tiberi, R.*
13. Betty Sutton, D.
14. Steven LaTourette, R.*
15. Deborah Pryce, R.*
16. Ralph Regula, R.*
17. Timothy Ryan, D.*
18. Zachary T. Space, D.

Oklahoma
1. John Sullivan, R.*
2. Dan Boren, D.*
3. Frank Lucas, R.*
4. Tom Cole, R.*
5. Mary Fallin, R.

Oregon
1. David Wu, D.*
2. Greg Walden, R.*
3. Earl Blumenauer, D.*
4. Peter A. DeFazio, D.*
5. Darlene Hooley, D.*

Pennsylvania
1. Robert Brady, D.*
2. Chaka Fattah, D.*
3. Philip English, R.*
4. Jason Altmire, D.
5. John Peterson, R.*
6. Jim Gerlach, R.*
7. Joe Sestak, D.
8. Patrick J. Murphy, D.
9. Bill Shuster, R.*
10. Christopher P. Carney, D.
11. Paul E. Kanjorski, D.*
12. John P. Murtha, D.*
13. Allyson Schwartz, D.*
14. Michael Doyle, D.*
15. Charles Dent, R.*
16. Joseph Pitts, R.*
17. Tim Holden, D.*
18. Tim Murphy, R.*
19. Todd Platts, R.*

Rhode Island
1. Patrick Kennedy, D.*
2. James Langevin, D.*

South Carolina
1. Henry Brown, Jr., R.*
2. Joe Wilson, R.*
3. J. Gresham Barrett, R.*
4. Bob Inglis, R.*
5. John M. Spratt, Jr., D.*
6. James Clyburn, D.*

South Dakota
†Stephanie Herseth
   Sandlin, D.*

Tennessee
1. David Davis, R.
2. John J. Duncan, Jr., R.*
3. Zach Wamp, R.*
4. Lincoln Davis, D.*
5. Jim Cooper, D.*
6. Bart Gordon, D.*
7. Marsha Blackburn, R.*
8. John S. Tanner, D.*
9. Steve Cohen, D.

Texas
1. Louis Gohmert, R.*
2. Ted Poe, R.*
3. Sam Johnson, R.*
4. Ralph M. Hall, R.*
5. Jeb Hensarling, R.*
6. Joe Barton, R.*
7. John Culberson, R.*
8. Kevin Brady, R.*
9. Al Green, D.*
10. Michael McCaul, R.*
11. Mike Conaway, R.*
12. Kay Granger, R.*
13. Mac Thornberry, R.*
14. Ron Paul, R.*
15. Rubén Hinojosa, D.*
16. Silvestre Reyes, D.*
17. Chet Edwards, D.*
18. Sheila Jackson Lee, D.*
19. Randy Neugebauer, R.*
20. Charlie Gonzalez, D.*
21. Lamar S. Smith, R.*
22. Nick Lampson, D.

23. Ciro Rodriguez, D.
24. Kenny Marchant, R.*
25. Lloyd Doggett, D.*
26. Michael Burgess, R.*
27. Solomon P. Ortiz, D.*
28. Henry Cuellar, D.*
29. Gene Green, D.*
30. Eddie Bernice Johnson, D.*
31. John Carter, R.*
32. Pete Sessions, R.*

Utah
1. Rob Bishop, R.*
2. Jim Matheson, D.*
3. Christopher Cannon, R.*

Vermont
†Peter Welch, D.

Virginia
1. Robert J. Wittman, R.
2. Thelma Drake, R.*
3. Robert Scott, D.*
4. J. Randy Forbes, R.*
5. Virgil Goode, Jr., R.*
6. Robert Goodlatte, R.*
7. Eric Cantor, R.*
8. James P. Moran, Jr., D.*
9. Rick C. Boucher, D.*
10. Frank R. Wolf, R.*
11. Tom Davis, R.*

Washington
1. Jay Inslee, D.*
2. Rick Larsen, D.*
3. Brian Baird, D.*
4. Doc Hastings, R.*
5. Cathy McMorris Rodgers, R.*
6. Norman D. Dicks, D.*
7. Jim McDermott, D.*
8. Dave Reichert, R.*
9. Adam Smith, D.*

West Virginia
1. Alan B. Mollohan, D.*
2. Shelley Moore Capito, R.*
3. Nick J. Rahall II, D.*

Wisconsin
1. Paul Ryan, R.*
2. Tammy Baldwin, D.*
3. Ron Kind, D.*
4. Gwen Moore, D.*
5. James Sensenbrenner, Jr., R.*
6. Thomas E. Petri, R.*
7. David R. Obey, D.*
8. Steve Kagen, D.

Wyoming
†Barbara Cubin, R.*

Nonvoting representatives

American Samoa
Eni F. H. Faleomavaega, D.*

District of Columbia
Eleanor Holmes Norton, D.*

Guam
Madeleine Bordallo, D.*

Puerto Rico
Luis Fortuño, R.*

Virgin Islands
Donna Christian-Christensen, D.*

must include at least 36 billion gallons (136 billion liters) of biofuels per year by 2022. To secure passage of the bill, Democrats had to remove provisions that would have reduced tax breaks for oil and natural gas companies and extended tax breaks for alternative energy projects. The president had threatened to veto legislation with those provisions. Also omitted from the final bill was a proposed requirement, pushed by many Democrats, that utilities produce 15 percent of their electric power from renewable sources.

Child health insurance. Congress unsuccessfully tried in 2007 to expand the State Children's Health Insurance Program (SCHIP), which, like Medicaid, pays for medical care for lower-income Americans. SCHIP targets children whose families earn too much to qualify for Medicaid but not enough to afford private health insurance. Both Medicaid and SCHIP are funded jointly by federal and state dollars and are administered by the states. Congress passed two SCHIP expansion bills in 2007, but President Bush vetoed them on October 3 and December 12. They would have expanded SCHIP to cover about 10 million people, mainly children, up from 6.6 million covered in 2007. The bills would have raised SCHIP spending over the next five years from $25 billion to $60 billion and would have raised the federal cigarette tax from 39 cents to $1 a pack to fund the expansion. President Bush had proposed raising SCHIP spending by a smaller amount, from $25 billion to $30 billion. In December, Congress passed a bill to maintain SCHIP's current coverage level until 2009.

Budget. On Nov. 13, 2007, President Bush signed a $459.3-billion FY 2008 appropriations bill for the Department of Defense. On Dec. 26, 2007, he signed an omnibus bill that contained $473.5 billion in FY 2008 appropriations for the 14 other Cabinet departments and for other agencies; $70 billion in funds for the Iraq and Afghanistan wars; and $11.2 billion in emergency funds for other purposes, including veterans' programs and border security. Legislators had created the omnibus bill by combining the provisions of 11 appropriations bills. The signing of the omnibus bill brought an end to a contentious budget battle between Democrats and Republicans, in which the president vetoed an earlier appropriations bill and threatened to veto others because they exceeded the spending amounts he had proposed.

Minimum wage. On May 25, 2007, President Bush signed legislation to raise the federal minimum wage. Congress had incorporated this legislation into the FY 2007 war-spending bill. The hourly minimum wage rose from $5.15 to $5.85 on July 24, 2007. It was scheduled to rise to $6.55 in July 2008 and to $7.25 in July 2009. The legislation provided for $4.8 billion in tax breaks to ease the impact of the wage hike on small businesses.

Ethics and lobbying. President Bush signed a bill on Sept. 14, 2007, that overhauled congressional ethics and lobbying rules. The bill was a response to several instances of federal politicians and lobbyists being convicted or accused of corruption or other improper behavior. The bill established new rules requiring more disclosure of lawmakers' efforts to fund their pet projects through earmarks in spending legislation. The bill also required broader and more detailed disclosure of fund-raising by lobbyists on behalf of federal candidates. In addition, it banned lawmakers from accepting gifts from lobbyists or their clients, and it created waiting periods for politicians wishing to become lobbyists after leaving office.

9/11 Commission. On August 3, President Bush signed a bill to implement some of the homeland security recommendations of the National Commission on Terrorist Attacks upon the United States, also known as the 9/11 Commission. Congress had passed the final version of the bill in July. From 2002 to 2004, the 9/11 Commission investigated the Sept. 11, 2001, terrorist attacks and issued a report in 2004 that included recommendations to guard against future attacks. The 2007 bill shifted homeland security money to high-risk states and cities, expanded the screening of air and sea cargo, and funded a program designed to improve communication among security officials at all levels.

Surveillance. Congress and President Bush battled in 2007 over the Bush administration's efforts to conduct counterterrorism surveillance. The administration had come under fire after news reports revealed in 2005 that the National Security Agency had been secretly authorized to monitor phone calls and e-mails between the United States and overseas without a warrant. In January 2007, the administration agreed to seek approval from the Foreign Intelligence Surveillance Court before doing such monitoring. But later in 2007, the administration asked Congress for expanded spying authority, arguing that current law limited the intelligence community's ability to keep tabs on foreign terrorism suspects. Under pressure from Republicans, Congress in August passed a bill authorizing, until February 2008, warrantless surveillance of any communications involving at least one person outside the United States. President Bush signed the bill on Aug. 5, 2007. Negotiations then began on a more long-lasting revision of surveillance law, with Democrats hoping to ensure that the revision would not violate U.S. citizens' privacy rights. Democrats and Republicans failed to reach agreement before the end of 2007.

Water projects. In its first successful override of a Bush veto, Congress enacted a bill in November that authorized $23.2 billion for hundreds of flood control, navigation, and environmental restoration projects. The president had vetoed the bill on November 2, saying it lacked fiscal discipline. The House voted 361-54 to override the veto on November 6, and the Senate followed suit with a 79-14 vote on November 8.

Stem cells. Congress in 2007 tried, but failed, to expand federally funded embryonic stem cell research. The president imposed restrictions on such research in 2001 because of his opposition to the destruction of human embryos. On June 20, 2007, President Bush vetoed a bill that Congress passed to overturn his stem cell restrictions.

Immigration. A failed vote to end debate in the Senate on June 28 halted a bipartisan bill to overhaul U.S. immigration laws. The bill, which had President Bush's support, would have created a means by which many of the country's 12 million illegal immigrants could have gained legal status and eventual citizenship. The bill also would have set up a temporary guest worker program and allocated billions of dollars for border security. Many conservatives opposed the bill's immigrant legalization scheme, calling it amnesty for breaking the law. A number of liberals opposed provisions that would have made it harder for extended family members to join their relatives in the United States.

Retirements. A wave of Republican retirements soured the party's hopes of regaining control of either house of Congress in the 2008 elections. Five Senate Republicans—Wayne Allard of Colorado, Larry Craig of Idaho, Pete Domenici of New Mexico, Chuck Hagel of Nebraska, and John Warner of Virginia—announced in 2007 that they would not seek reelection in 2008. Former Majority Leader Trent Lott (R., Mississippi) resigned his Senate seat in late 2007. More than 15 House Republicans announced that they would not seek reelection in 2008, compared with only about 5 House Democrats. Former Speaker Dennis Hastert (R., Illinois) resigned his House seat in late 2007. Bobby Jindal (R., Louisiana) was set to resign in early 2008 to take over his state's governorship.

Craig's retirement decision came after news reports revealed in August 2007 that he had been arrested on June 11 after an airport rest room incident and had pleaded guilty on August 8 to disorderly conduct. An undercover police officer alleged that Craig sat in a stall next to him and used hand and foot signals to try to solicit sex. But Craig said that his actions had been misread and that his guilty plea had been a mistake. He asked to withdraw the guilty plea, but a judge denied Craig's request on October 4.   ■ Mike Lewis

See also **Agriculture; Armed forces; Cabinet, U.S.; Education; Health care issues; Immigration; Iraq; People in the news** (Nancy Pelosi); **Syria; Taxation; United States, Government of the; United States, President of the; Washington, D.C.**

Conservation. Three types of spectacular North American animals were *delisted* (removed) from the list of federally protected endangered species in the United States in 2007. Delisted animal populations generally become the responsibility of individual states in their native region, as opposed to a federal protection plan.

The animals, which included bald eagles, one group of grizzly bears, and two populations of gray wolves, were determined by the United States Department of the Interior (USDI) to no longer be in danger of extinction. However, conservationists strongly opposed some of the delisting decisions.

Bald eagles. In June, the USDI announced the delisting of the bald eagle. Since 1963, nesting pairs of bald eagles increased from 400 to about 10,000 in 2007. Conservationists supported the bald eagle delisting. Unlike other delisted animals, the bald eagle remained protected under federal law, as well as an international treaty.

Grizzly bears. The USDI announced its plan to delist grizzly bears in the Yellowstone region in March. The Yellowstone region includes parts of Idaho, Montana, and Wyoming. Many conservation and animal protection groups strongly opposed the USDI's decision. In June, a number of organizations—including the Humane Society of the United States, the Fund for Animals, the Sierra Club, and the National Resources Defense Council—filed lawsuits to reverse the grizzly bear delisting.

The conservation and protection groups worried that delisting grizzly bears would open the door for future trophy hunting. They also expressed concern that the grizzly bear population lacked sufficient protected habitat outside of Yellowstone National Park. Grizzly bears in the region numbered about 500 in 2007, four times as many as when they were first listed in 1975. Delisting opponents claimed the population still required federal protection because it was too small and fragmented and because state management plans were ineffective.

Gray wolves. In January 2007, the USDI announced its decision to delist gray wolves in the western Great Lakes region of Michigan, Minnesota, and Wisconsin. The wolf populations there had increased from hundreds in the 1970's to thousands in 2007. The delisting took effect in March, and conservationists generally supported the move.

However, conservation groups strongly opposed the USDI's proposal to delist another population of gray wolves in the Rocky Mountain region of Idaho, Montana, and Wyoming. As with the grizzly bear delisting in the same states, conservationists worried that state management

CITES meeting. In June, representatives from 171 nations gathered at the 14th meeting of the Convention on International Trade in Endangered Species (CITES) in the Netherlands.

As in previous years, the participants debated whether or not to continue the ban on elephant ivory exports. Botswana, Namibia, South Africa, and Zimbabwe, where elephants are thriving, argued that the sale of their ivory stockpiles would help impoverished local communities that live close to elephant populations. But several other African nations claimed the sale would encourage poaching. In the end, CITES agreed to allow the sale of existing, registered ivory stockpiles. Following the sale, the African countries agreed to a nine-year ban on ivory trade.

Red List. The annual Red List of threatened species, published in September by the World Conservation Union (IUCN), showed Earth's species were becoming extinct at an increasingly rapid rate. In 2007, a total of 188 species were added to the categories that the IUCN classified as critically endangered, endangered, or vulnerable. More than 16,000 species were classified as heading toward extinction.

Three types of corals from the Galapagos Islands were added, marking the first time corals appeared on the list. The list also recognized growing threats to such primates as western lowland gorillas and Sumatran orangutans.

In 2007, the United States Department of the Interior removed the bald eagle from its list of federally protected endangered species, citing the bald eagle population's successful recovery. The eagles remained protected under other federal and international laws.

plans were ineffective at ensuring that the Rocky Mountain wolf population remained stable.

Part of the controversy lay in the differing attitudes toward Rocky Mountain wolves at the local level. Many people in the region—such as ranchers who feared losing livestock—saw wolves as dangerous pests not worth protecting. There was also strong support for wolf hunting and wolf control in Wyoming and Idaho, both among the public and elected officials. Conservationists worried that the Rocky Mountain wolves might face extinction under state government protection plans.

River dolphin lives? A photograph taken in August in Tongling City, China, appeared to show a Yangtze River dolphin (also called a *baiji*), a species believed to be extinct. The grayish-white dolphin once inhabited the lower and middle Yangtze River. Dams, pollution, and run-ins with ships and fishing nets caused the dolphin's population to dwindle, and scientists declared it extinct in 2006. Scientists thought the creature in the photograph may have been one of the last surviving baiji. However, they cautioned that even with a few survivors, the species was still functionally extinct and unable to recover.

Jungle animals caught on film. Two extremely endangered jungle animals were caught on film in 2007 by camera traps set up by the World Wildlife Fund (WWF), headquartered in Washington, D.C. In April, a hidden camera on Sabah, the Malaysian part of Borneo, captured the first-ever video of a Borneo rhinoceros in the wild. Scientists believed only 25 to 50 of these animals survived in their native habitat.

In July, a WWF camera photographed a Sumatran tiger, found only on Indonesia's island of Sumatra. The tiger's front paw was missing, possibly cut off by a poacher's snare. Poaching remained a problem for Sumatran tigers, of which only about 400 remained in the wild.

Money for a mystery. In August, the U.S. Fish and Wildlife Service released a $27-million recovery plan for the ivory-billed woodpecker—a species long believed to be extinct. The plan called for studying and surveying possible habitats for the bird. Researchers from Cornell University, in Ithaca, New York, reported sighting and videotaping the supposedly extinct woodpecker in an Arkansas swamp in 2004. But some scientists disputed the sighting, saying the bird may have been another species.   ■ Edward Ricciuti

See also **Biology; Ocean; Zoos.**

Costa Rica. See Latin America.

Côte d'Ivoire. See Africa.

Courts in the United States issued several key rulings in 2007, including a conviction of a former top executive branch official and a pair of decisions striking down parts of the USA PATRIOT Act.

Plame CIA leak affair. On March 6, a U.S. district court jury convicted I. Lewis "Scooter" Libby, the former chief of staff for Vice President Dick Cheney, of making false statements, perjury, and obstruction of justice. Libby was found guilty of lying to federal law enforcement agents and to a grand jury during an investigation into the 2003 leak of the identity of a covert Central Intelligence Agency officer. The officer, Valerie Plame, and her husband, former Ambassador Joseph C. Wilson IV, had claimed that the administration of President George W. Bush leaked her name to the press as a retaliatory move against Wilson, who had publicly accused Cheney and Bush of justifying their plans for war in Iraq by exaggerating Iraq's military capability. Libby was the only person charged as a result of the leak investigation. No one was charged for the leak itself. On June 5, 2007, Libby was sentenced to 30 months in prison, followed by two years of supervised release, and fined $250,000. On July 2, President Bush commuted the prison sentence, calling it excessive. He left the probation and fine in place.

On July 19, a U.S. district judge dismissed a civil suit that Plame and Wilson had filed against Cheney, Libby, former White House adviser Karl Rove, and former Deputy Secretary of State Richard Armitage. The suit accused the officials of violating the couple's constitutional rights. But the judge ruled that Plame and Wilson were not legally entitled to damages.

PATRIOT Act. Two U.S. district judges issued separate rulings in September declaring parts of the USA PATRIOT Act unconstitutional. The act, passed shortly after the terrorist attacks of Sept. 11, 2001, expanded the powers of law enforcement to prevent and respond to terrorism.

On Sept. 6, 2007, a judge struck down provisions that allowed the Federal Bureau of Investigation (FBI) to send secret "national security letters" (NSL's) to private telecommunications companies demanding that the companies turn over phone call and e-mail data. The FBI could send the letters without first getting a warrant and could forbid the companies from disclosing that they had received the letters. The judge ruled that the NSL provisions violated free speech rights and the principle of separation of powers.

On September 26, another judge struck down sections of the act that made it easier for the U.S. government to obtain warrants for searches and surveillance. The judge ruled that the sections violated the constitutional requirement that probable cause be shown before a warrant is issued.

Terrorism trials. In 2007, the U.S. military began the process of trying terrorism suspects under a military commissions law enacted in 2006. The commissions were established to try foreigners being detained in a U.S. military prison at Guantánamo Bay, Cuba. David Hicks, an Australian citizen, was the first detainee to go on trial. On March 26, 2007, Hicks pleaded guilty to giving support to the international terrorist network al-Qa`ida. Under a plea deal, Hicks was sentenced to nine more months in prison. He had already been held for five years at Guantánamo Bay.

On August 16, a U.S. district court jury convicted José Padilla, a U.S. citizen, of conspiring to murder, kidnap, and maim people overseas and of providing material support to terrorists. Padilla had been transferred to civilian custody in January 2006 after being held for 3 ½ years in a military prison as an "enemy combatant." He had been arrested in May 2002. The Justice Department had accused him of plotting to set off a radioactive "dirty bomb" in the United States. But in November 2005, the government dropped his "enemy combatant" status and indicted him on criminal charges unrelated to the dirty bomb allegations.

Detainee rights. On Feb. 20, 2007, a three-judge panel of the U.S. Court of Appeals for the District of Columbia Circuit upheld a provision in the 2006 military commissions law that denied Guantánamo detainees the right to have a fed-

I. Lewis "Scooter" Libby, former chief of staff to U.S. Vice President Dick Cheney, leaves a Washington, D.C., courthouse on June 5, 2007, after being sentenced to 30 months in prison and fined $250,000 for making false statements, perjury, and obstruction of justice. On July 2, President George W. Bush commuted the prison sentence.

eral civilian court consider whether their detention was justified. The U.S. Supreme Court agreed on June 29, 2007, to hear an appeal of this ruling, and a decision was expected in 2008.

On June 11, 2007, a three-judge panel of the U.S. Court of Appeals for the Fourth Circuit ruled that the government could not indefinitely detain a legal U.S. resident as an "enemy combatant." The ruling came in the case of Ali Saleh Kahlah al-Marri, a Qatari national being held in a U.S. military prison in South Carolina. Marri had been arrested at his residence in Peoria, Illinois, in December 2001 and designated an "enemy combatant" in June 2003. The judges ordered that Marri be either charged as a civilian or released.

Teen sex case. On Oct. 26, 2007, the Georgia Supreme Court ordered the release of Genarlow Wilson, who had been given a 10-year prison sentence in 2005 for aggravated child molestation. He had engaged in consensual sexual activity with a 15-year-old girl in 2003, when he was 17. The age of consent in Georgia is 16. The court ruled that Wilson's sentence was cruel and unusual under the state and federal constitutions.   ■ Mike Lewis

See also **Chicago; Civil rights; Crime; Dallas; Democratic Party; Disability; Immigration; Indian, American; Los Angeles; Popular music; Republican Party; Sports; Supreme Court of the United States; United States, President of the; Washington, D.C.**

Cricket. Commercial demands in 2007 meant too many short tours and international matches, according to some critics of modern cricket. During its 2007 tour of England, West Indies played few games other than five-day tests and one-day internationals (ODI's) and so had little time to adjust to English conditions. From April to October, England played 7 test matches, 10 ODI's, and 2 Twenty20's. The team later played in the Twenty20 world championship in South Africa and toured Sri Lanka.

The World Cup was played under one-day rules (50 overs each team) in the Caribbean in March and April. Playing against the Netherlands, Herschelle Gibbs of South Africa struck six sixes in one over. The final at Bridgetown, Barbados, between Sri Lanka and Australia degenerated into near-farce, with rain and bad light reducing the playing time, and the result—a win for Australia—decided by mathematics.

Test matches. Australia topped the 2007 test rankings, followed by England, India, and Pakistan. England played dismally in Australia, to lose 5-0, and Australia triumphantly regained the Ashes. Australian spin-bowler Shane Warne captured his 708th wicket to end his international career, and fast bowler Glenn McGrath bowed out from test cricket. Australia's captain, Ricky Ponting, topped both the test and ODI batting rankings in 2007. Top-rated test bowler was Muttiah Muralitharan of Sri Lanka. During his team's successful three-match series with England, he passed Shane Warne's record of 708 test wickets.

By winning the home series 3-0 against West Indies, England test captain Michael Vaughan (2003-) passed Peter May (1955-1961) as England's most successful captain. England lost a second home series 0-1 to India. In other test series, Sri Lanka defeated Bangladesh 4-1 but lost 0-2 to Australia, and South Africa defeated Pakistan 2-1. India beat Pakistan 1-0 in an end-of-year series. During his team's earlier 2-0 defeat of West Indies, Pakistan batter Muhammad Yousuf broke a 30-year record (held by Viv Richards of West Indies) for the most test runs in a calendar year—1,788 runs in 11 matches.

ODI's. In the triangular Commonwealth Bank ODI series, England played New Zealand and host Australia, defeating Australia in the final 2-0— the first series win by England in Australia since 1987. West Indies beat England 2-1, but England fared better under new ODI captain Paul Collingwood, with a 4-3 win in a thrilling series against India. England went on to a first-ever series win in Sri Lanka by 3-2. Pakistan beat West Indies 3-1 but lost twice to South Africa, 1-3 away and 2-3 at home. The top-ranked ODI team, Australia, beat India 4-2 but lost 0-3 to New Zealand.

India beat Sri Lanka 2-1, West Indies 3-1, and Pakistan 3-2, but surprisingly lost to Bangladesh 0-3. Low-ranking Zimbabwe beat Bangladesh 3-1, and Bangladesh also lost to Sri Lanka 3-0.

Twenty20. The short version of cricket continued to pull in crowds. With only 20 six-ball overs for each side, the game is fast and furious. The first Twenty20 World Cup, held in South Africa in September 2007, drew 12 national teams. India hit 157 for 5 wickets to beat Pakistan (all out 152) in an exciting final at Johannesburg. In an earlier defeat of England, India's Yuvraj Singh hit six sixes in one over, emulating Gibbs in the World Cup. The 36-run feat had been achieved before only by West Indies' Garry Sobers and India's Ravi Shastri.

Coaches come and go. International coaches came and went in rapid succession. England's Duncan Fletcher was replaced by Peter Moores. West Indies dispensed with Bennett King and eventually appointed another Australian, John Dyson. Bangladesh replaced Dav Whatmore with Australian Jamie Siddons, while Gary Kirsten of South Africa took over as coach of India.

Administration. The Marylebone Cricket Club (MCC), cricket's lawmaking body, appointed an executive Guardian of the Laws to protect the integrity of the game, still played with a wooden bat and leather ball on a natural turf field. A new advisory body was the World Cricket Committee, of former international cricketers. The breakaway Indian Cricket League (ICL) indicated more fragmentation in the game, reflecting tensions not just in India but also in the world governing body, the International Cricket Council (ICC).

American cricket. The ICC expelled the United States in March 2007, apparently because of disagreements in the U.S. cricket administration about how to expand the game. There were more than 650 U.S. clubs, but most players came from immigrant communities with cricket traditions.

Deaths. ICC President Percy Sonn died in May 2007, a month after he had presented the World Cup to Australia's captain Ricky Ponting. The World Cup was overshadowed by the death on March 18 of Pakistani Coach Bob Woolmer, hours after his team unexpectedly lost to Ireland. Jamaican police launched a murder investigation amid lurid speculation of betting rings and Mafia-style criminality. However, police later stated that Woolmer had died of natural causes.

The death of Arthur Milton in April reminded British fans of a bygone era. Milton was the last of only 12 people to have played international soccer and cricket for England. Another notable loss was bowler Derek Shackleton, who took 2,857 first-class wickets from 1948 to 1969 and claimed 100 or more victims in 20 consecutive seasons, a unique feat in English cricket.

■ Brian Williams

Crime. The rate of violent crime in the United States increased in 2006 for the second consecutive year, while the rate of property crime decreased for the fourth year in a row, reported the Federal Bureau of Investigation (FBI) in September 2007. The FBI's annual "Crime in the United States" report includes data from more than 17,500 U.S. law enforcement agencies on the violent crimes of murder, nonnegligent manslaughter, forcible rape, robbery, and aggravated assault, as well as the property crimes of burglary, larceny-theft, motor vehicle theft, and arson.

According to the report, more than 1.4 million violent crimes occurred in the United States in 2006. The number of murders and nonnegligent manslaughters increased by 1.8 percent and the number of robberies increased by 7.2 percent, compared with 2005. The number of aggravated assaults and forcible rapes decreased in 2006.

The authors of the report noted that there were slightly fewer than 10 million property crimes in 2006. Of these crimes, burglary was the only one to increase, by 1.3 percent, compared with 2005. The FBI estimated that authorities made approximately 14.4 million arrests in 2006, excluding those for traffic offenses. This number compared with 14.1 million arrests in 2005.

Deaths in police custody. More than 2,000 criminal suspects died in police custody in the

United States from 2003 to 2005—55 percent as a result of homicide by police officers—according to a 2007 U.S. Department of Justice report. The report was the first to compile the reasons for arrest-related deaths in the nation. Thirteen percent of the deaths were caused by alcohol or drug intoxication, 12 percent by suicide, 7 percent by accidental injury, 6 percent by illness or other natural causes, and 7 percent by unknown causes. The number of deaths considered "justified" according to law enforcement standards was undetermined.

Virginia Tech massacre. In the deadliest massacre in modern U.S. history, a 23-year-old gunman named Cho Seung-Hui killed 5 faculty members and 27 students at Virginia Polytechnic Institute and State University (Virginia Tech) in Blacksburg on April 16, before committing suicide. Cho was a student at Virginia Tech.

Cho began his rampage at 7:15 a.m. in a student dormitory, where he shot and killed two people. Approximately two hours later, he continued the shootings in the campus engineering building. Moving from classroom to classroom, Cho murdered 30 additional individuals. He used two semi-automatic handguns, both of which he had purchased legally in Virginia earlier in the year.

Many Virginia Tech students criticized university leaders for not alerting students or locking down the campus immediately after reports of the first two shootings. An August report by an investigative panel appointed by Virginia Governor Timothy M. Kaine described failures by campus police, the university administration, and a mental health center where Cho had briefly been treated.

Duke lacrosse case. In a racially charged case that captured nationwide attention, a disciplinary committee of the North Carolina State Bar voted in June to disbar Durham County District Attorney Mike Nifong. The committee concluded that Nifong had lied to the court and withheld DNA (deoxyribonucleic acid) evidence revealing that three lacrosse players from Duke University in Durham did not rape a female exotic dancer who had accused them of the act in March 2006. A Superior Court judge immediately suspended Nifong from office. In August 2007, another Superior Court judge sentenced Nifong to 24 hours in jail for lying under oath.

The case was racially charged because the accused were white and the accuser was African American, and Nifong was running for reelection in a district with a sizable number of African American voters. State prosecutors dropped the rape charges against the students in late 2006 after the woman changed a key detail of her story. In April 2007, state prosecutors debunked the remaining charges and cleared the students.

"Fundamentalist" Mormon guilty. In September, a Utah jury found Warren Jeffs, leader of a sect of "fundamentalist" Mormons who practice *polygamy* (having more than one wife), guilty of being an accomplice to the rape of a 14-year-old girl. The jury concluded that the girl was married against her will to, and forced to engage in sex with, her cousin. Both individuals were members of Jeffs's sect. On November 20, Jeffs was sentenced to 10 years in prison. The trial highlighted the continuing practice of polygamy, which is a violation of the Utah Constitution and has been banned by the Mormon church since 1890. An estimated 30,000 people continued to practice polygamy in the western United States.

Sentencing. On Dec. 10, 2007, the U.S. Supreme Court issued two 7-to-2 rulings that gave federal judges more leeway in criminal sentencing. The court upheld a crack cocaine sentence that was more lenient than that prescribed by federal sentencing guidelines, which called for tougher sentences for crack than for powder cocaine. Critics have called the guidelines racially unfair, because crack is most often used by blacks, and powder cocaine is most often used by whites. The court also upheld a relatively light sentence involving the drug Ecstasy. In both cases, the court ruled that sentencing guidelines were advisory and judges could make reasonable deviations from them. ■ Alfred J. Smuskiewicz

See also **Courts; Prisons; Sports; Terrorism.**

Croatia. Prime Minister Ivo Sanader formed a new coalition government in Croatia in December 2007. In parliamentary elections in November, his ruling Croatian Democratic Union (HDZ) won a narrow victory over the opposition Social Democratic Party (SDP) but failed to attain a majority of parliamentary seats. Sanader, Croatia's prime minister since 2003, pledged to work for Croatia's integration into the NATO military alliance and the European Union (EU). Croatia, which began negotiations with EU officials in 2005, was tentatively scheduled to join the European association in 2010.

Financial scandal. A corruption scandal involving the Croatian Privatization Fund (HPF), the government-appointed body responsible for overseeing the privatization of enterprises in postcommunist Croatia, became public on June 16, 2007, when law enforcement officials announced the arrest of six high-ranking HPF officials. A Croatian court subsequently charged the officials with corruption, including bribery and real estate fraud. Since the early 1990's, the HPF had overseen the transfer of millions of dollars of state assets to the private sector.

On June 28, 2007, the opposition in parliament brought a no-confidence vote against Sanader's government, alleging that the prime minister and his Cabinet had failed to act to prevent corruption in the HPF. However, Sanader's coalition government garnered enough votes in parliament to defeat the no-confidence motion.

Croatia's economy continued to expand in 2007. Economists projected that the nation's *gross domestic product* (GDP)—the value of all goods and services produced in a country in a year—would grow by 5.7 percent in 2007, compared with 4.8 percent in 2006. Inflation remained low, declining from 3.2 percent in 2006 to 2.2 percent in 2007. The rate of unemployment declined from 16 percent in 2006 to 15.1 percent in the second quarter of 2007.

Foreign policy. Croatian leaders in 2007 continued to emphasize accession to the EU and admission to NATO as their chief foreign policy goals. In October, United States officials expressed firm support for Croatia's bid to join NATO in April 2008, along with Albania and Macedonia. In preparation for eventual NATO membership, the Croatian government modernized its armed forces in 2007 and abolished compulsory military service as a first step toward professionalizing its military. In October, Croatia hosted NATO forces from 12 member countries conducting a military training exercise involving 8,000 troops and numerous ships and aircraft along the country's Adriatic seacoast. ■ Sharon L. Wolchik

See also **Europe.**

Acting president of Cuba Raúl Castro delivers the annual Revolution Day speech on July 26, 2007, in the city of Camagüey. The day marks a 1953 rebel attack that sparked the Cuban revolution. Cuban President Fidel Castro, depicted in the stone relief, temporarily handed over power to his brother in late 2006 because of ill health.

Cuba. Raúl Modesto Castro Ruiz, Cuba's acting president, addressed several quality-of-life issues in 2007. Ordinary Cubans applauded Raúl's public criticism of bureaucratic managers and his blunt acknowledgment that many Cubans' salaries were insufficient to cover basic living expenses. To help Cubans cope with low incomes, the government began offering subsidized meals at schools, hospitals, workplace cafeterias, and community centers. In addition, it significantly raised the prices it paid farmers for such products as meat and milk.

Foreign investment. The Cuban economy continued to be buoyed by subsidized fuels from Venezuela; easy credit from China, including large investments to boost nickel production; and growing assistance from Iran. In September, Venezuela announced a $100-million loan to rehabilitate Cuba's aging railway system. As part of the overdue modernization, China was to provide 100 locomotives, and Iran planned to provide a similar number of railway freight cars.

During 2007, China also supplied Cuba with hundreds of buses, making urban and intercity travel easier for islanders. Daily bus ridership in Havana, the capital, was expected to double to 1 million by the end of the year.

Agriculture. Speaking in the province of Camagüey in late July, Raúl Castro recognized the need to increase output and lower consumer prices in the agricultural industry, which was dominated by the state. He also said that the government should provide better incentives to small-scale farmers, who owned a small percentage of Cuba's arable land but produced a major portion of the nation's food supply.

In recent years, highly invasive weeds rendered many cattle ranchers' pastures useless. Because Cubans could not afford costly seeds, fertilizers, pesticides, and farm equipment, these plants had taken over an estimated one-third of the island's fertile land, or about 3 million acres (1.2 million hectares), by 2007. To help small-scale farmers and farming cooperatives survive, the state paid off $23 million in debts that it owed them.

Fidel on the mend. Looking alert, Fidel Castro appeared on television in late September. He jokingly mocked the recurrent rumors of his death that had circulated within Miami's Cuban-exile community. While recovering throughout 2007, Fidel wrote dozens of newspaper columns and essays on familiar anti-imperialist themes.

Death of a revolutionary. Cubans mourned the loss of Vilma Espín, 77, wife of Raúl Castro, in June. Honored as a hero of the 1959 Cuban revolution, Vilma often had served as Cuba's unofficial first lady, appearing with Fidel, a divorcé, at government events.   ■ Nathan A. Haverstock

See also **Latin America; Venezuela.**

Czech Republic.
In January 2007, Mirek Topolánek of the Civic Democratic Party (CDP) succeeded in forming a right-of-center coalition government with the Christian Democratic-Peoples Party and the Green Party, ending seven months of political stalemate in the Czech Republic. In the June 2006 parliamentary elections, Topolánek's CDP and the opposing left-of-center Social Democratic Party (SDP), headed by then-Prime Minister Jiří Paroubek, achieved parity, with each expecting a likely coalition strength of 100 votes in the 200-member parliament. For much of the latter half of 2006, Topolánek headed an unstable caretaker government.

In early 2007, Topolánek pledged to enact tax reforms or else call new elections. The reforms were designed to reduce the Czech Republic's budget deficit and bring the country in line with European Union (EU) mandates that would make it eligible to adopt the euro currency. Economists projected that in 2007, the Czech budget deficit would mount to 4 percent of *gross domestic product* (GDP)—the total value of all goods and services produced in a country in a year, exceeding the EU target of 3 percent of GDP.

Economic reforms. In August, the Czech parliament approved Topolánek's economic reform package. The plan set flat rates that lowered both corporate and personal income taxes

and raised the VAT (a value-added sales tax). Economists predicted that the new tax structure would reduce the deficit from 4 percent of GDP in 2007 to 3.5 percent in 2008. With the reforms in place, analysts predicted that the Czech Republic would be ready to adopt the euro in 2012.

Economy. In 2007, the Czech GDP expanded at approximately 6 percent. Inflation for the first half of 2007 registered a low 2.3-percent rate, and unemployment dipped below 8 percent. Direct foreign investment continued to expand, particularly in tourism and the automotive industry.

Foreign policy. In January 2007, Prime Minister Topolánek endorsed a United States proposal to build a radar station in the Czech Republic as part of a proposed Eastern Europe-based missile defense system. The antimissile plan, which prompted strong objections from Russian President Vladimir Putin, prompted protesters to stage demonstrations in Prague, the Czech capital, in January and November. With polls showing a substantial majority of Czech citizens against the missile defense system, protest leaders demanded that the issue be put to a national referendum. Topolánek's government refused, however, to consider a public vote and instead hired a public relations firm to try to sell the plan to the public.   ■ Sharon L. Wolchik

See also **Europe; Russia.**

Dallas.
Voters decided on Nov. 6, 2007, to permit a tollway to be built along a levee as part of a multibillion-dollar revitalization of the Trinity River corridor near downtown Dallas. A proposal to limit the road to low-speed traffic was rejected by 53 percent of the voters. The special election was held after City Council member Angela Hunt led a petition drive to force a vote on the issue.

Opponents of the tollway said it detracted from plans to build a chain of lakes, athletic fields, an outdoor amphitheater, and an environmental center in the river corridor. Supporters argued that the toll road was necessary to relieve traffic congestion. In 1998, voters approved $246 million in bonds for Trinity River revitalization.

Former city officials indicted. On Oct. 1, 2007, a federal grand jury indicted two former City Council members and a state legislator following a two-year probe by the U.S. Federal Bureau of Investigation (FBI) into corruption at Dallas City Hall. Named in the indictments stemming from a bribery investigation were former Dallas Mayor Pro Tem Don Hill, state Representative Terri Hodge, and former City Plan Commission member D'Angelo Lee. The indictments were based on charges that developer Brian Potashnik, who also was indicted, bribed the public officials in an effort to receive tax credits for his company's low-income housing projects. In a case that was not related to the housing scandal, former City Council member James Fantroy was indicted in September on charges of embezzling funds from Paul Quinn College. Fantroy had stepped down in June because of term limits.

Leppert elected mayor. Former construction company executive Tom Leppert was elected Dallas mayor in a runoff election on June 16. Leppert defeated City Council member Ed Oakley in the runoff. Eleven candidates ran in the regular election in May to replace outgoing Mayor Laura Miller. Leppert, former chairman and chief executive officer of Turner Corporation, pledged to bring the business community and City Hall together to work on needed Dallas projects.

Super Bowl. The National Football League announced on May 22 that the new Dallas Cowboys Stadium in Arlington, Texas, would be the site of the 2011 Super Bowl. The stadium, under construction 15 miles (24 kilometers) west of downtown Dallas, was chosen over facilities in Arizona and Indiana.

Dallas schools top list. Two Dallas schools were listed as the top public high schools in the nation by *Newsweek* on May 28, 2007. For the second straight year, the School for the Talented and Gifted received the No. 1 spot in the magazine report. Dallas's School of Science and Engineering moved up from No. 8 to No. 2 on the list.

Downtown explosion. On July 25, fiery gas explosions at a downtown area warehouse prompted officials to shut down two interstate freeways and evacuate businesses within a half mile of the site. Gas canisters stored at Southwest Industrial Gases were hurled hundreds of feet from the warehouse by the explosions. Only three people were injured in the blaze.

Bank headquarters moves to Dallas. Comerica announced plans in March to move its national headquarters from Detroit to downtown Dallas. In August, the major banking and financial firm announced that it would move into the former Bank One Center, designed by famed architect Philip Johnson. The building became available when Bank One merged with JPMorgan Chase of New York City in 2004.

DNA testing. Dallas County District Attorney Craig Watkins agreed in February 2007 to let DNA testing determine whether there had been any wrongful convictions in more than 350 murder, rape, and serious felony cases since 1970. Watkins agreed to let the Innocence Project of Texas, an advocacy group for reviewing convictions, study serious felony convictions in Dallas County. The study was expected to determine which convictions might be overturned by DNA testing. Dallas County had had more DNA exonerations than any other county in Texas. ■ Henry Tatum

See also **City.**

Dance. A new ballet company was born in 2007—Morphoses/The Wheeldon Company. At age 34, Christopher Wheeldon was one of the most acclaimed and prolific choreographers of his generation. He had created dozens of ballets for the world's major troupes, including the New York City Ballet, where he was to remain as resident choreographer until 2008. Despite the risk of starting a new company in a financially difficult climate, Wheeldon began his own company in order to achieve complete control over all facets of a dance organization. Wheeldon also strove to bring dance to the notice of young audiences while maintaining the classical tradition in which he trained at the United Kingdom's Royal Ballet.

Morphoses, named for a ballet Wheeldon choreographed for the New York City Ballet, made its debut on Aug. 10, 2007, at the Vail International Dance Festival in Colorado. It was then performed for five days in September at London's Sadler's Wells and for five days in October at the New York City Center.

In Morphoses's first year, it was a pickup company with leading dancers borrowed from such groups as the City Ballet, the Royal Ballet, the Frankfurt Ballet, and the National Ballet of Canada. The company's long-term aim was for a permanent 20-dancer roster and a budget of $5 million. Although Wheeldon was the principal choreographer, he planned to invite others to contribute. At the City Center engagement, guest choreography was by William Forsythe, Liv Lorent, Michael Clarke, and Edwaard Liang.

Kirstein tribute. Lincoln Kirstein, a powerful force in the cultural life of the United States until his death in 1996, was honored by many institutions in 2007, the 100th anniversary of his birth. One of Kirstein's outstanding cultural contributions was inviting Russian-born choreographer George Balanchine to the United States in 1933 to begin a native ballet tradition. Eventually, in 1948, Kirstein and Balanchine founded the New York City Ballet. This company celebrated Kirstein's life in 2007 by performing many of the classics Balanchine choreographed under Kirstein's patronage. During the troupe's winter season at New York City's Lincoln Center for the Performing Arts, *Tribute* by Christopher d'Amboise was performed in Kirstein's honor.

In the Lincoln Center Plaza, the New York Public Library for the Performing Arts mounted an exhibition in October focusing on the many artists, designers, composers, and choreographers whom Kirstein commissioned for the various organizations he was involved with beyond the City Ballet.

The New York City Ballet premiered Peter Martins's *Romeo + Juliet* on May 1, a full-evening ballet to the familiar score by Sergei Prokofiev,

British prima ballerina Darcey Bussell takes a curtain call after her farewell performance at the Royal Ballet at London's Covent Garden on June 8, 2007. Bussell danced *Songs of the Earth*, created by Kenneth MacMillan, the choreographer who brought Bussell to the company as a young dancer.

performed during the company's spring run at Lincoln Center. Martins's chief innovation was to cast the roles of Romeo and Juliet with young dancers—some in their teens. Although critics could understand the rationale behind this decision, some believed it backfired, as the young dancers could not project the dramatic depth that mature stars give to the roles in other productions of *Romeo and Juliet*. Given that this ballet had been produced often, many felt that the conception and choreography of *Romeo + Juliet* were not sufficiently original to warrant another production.

Modern dance premieres. Three of the most distinguished modern dance choreographers in the United States presented significant new works

in 2007. On March 2, at the opening of the Paul Taylor Dance Company's annual spring season at the New York City Center, Taylor's powerful *Lines of Loss* debuted. A suite of nine dances, it sets individuals and groups against and within an anonymous crowd. Taylor's other new piece, *De Sueños* ("Of Dreams"), inspired by Mexican culture and music, premiered at the American Dance Festival in Durham, North Carolina, in July.

At age 88, Merce Cunningham remained a force in dance in 2007. *Xover* (pronounced "Crossover") premiered October 8 at Dartmouth College in Hanover, New Hampshire. The dance was titled for the many ways in which the dancers cross the stage. In between these crossovers are luminous quartets and duets, highlighted by one of the longest pas de deux Cunningham had created, more than seven minutes long. In this duet, Cunningham instills images of privacy and independence, even though the dancers move in close quarters and seamless flow. Like Cunningham's best work, *Xover* is marked by poetical ambiguity and extraordinary invention.

New work by a younger modern choreographer, Mark Morris, was performed in wildly different venues in 2007. His *Italian Concerto* was shown in January in Morris's own intimate studio space in Brooklyn, New York. Although Morris now rarely dances, he choreographed a strange, menacing solo for himself in the middle of this new work.

In May, Morris directed and choreographed a new production of Christoph Willibald Gluck's *Orfeo ed Euridice* (Orpheus and Eurydice) at the Metropolitan Opera House in New York City. Less than two weeks later, Morris and company danced at Boston's Institute of Contemporary Art, where the site informed the content of a new piece, *Looky*. Characterized by one critic as a nightmarish comedy, *Looky* parodies the way in which people look at art. The dancers perform in the piece as both sculptures and museum patrons.

Northwestern dance. Morris was born in Seattle, in the Pacific Northwest, as were many other famous American choreographers. The Pacific Northwest Ballet, located in Seattle, honored these artists in a festival in April. Four troupes, in addition to the host company, performed works by Morris, Cunningham, Trisha Brown, Robert Joffrey, and others. Joffrey was the least performed of these choreographers, and so his dance *Remembrances* was of special note.

Appointments and retirements. The Joffrey Ballet's artistic director, Gerald Arpino, retired during the summer of 2007 from the troupe he founded with Joffrey in 1956. Ashley Wheater, a former dancer with the Joffrey, was appointed the new chief in September 2007. At Chicago's Auditorium Theatre in October, the troupe produced a company premiere of *Giselle*, staged by Frederic Franklin, under Wheater's direction. The Joffrey's repertory had always been unusually eclectic, but this production was its first venture into classical ballet of the 1800's.

On June 8, 2007, in London, British ballerina Darcey Bussell, age 38, gave an emotional farewell performance from the Royal Ballet at Covent Garden, her company for nearly 20 years. Kyra Nichols, age 48, a leading ballerina with the New York City Ballet for 33 years, retired on June 22. A day later, Alessandra Ferri, 44, gave her last performance with the American Ballet Theatre. ■ Nancy Goldner

DEATHS

in 2007 included those listed below, who were Americans unless otherwise indicated.

Abbé Pierre (Henri Antoine Grouès) (1912-January 22), French priest whose campaign for the homeless in the 1950's marked the beginning of his "uprising of goodness" movement for social justice.

Adler, Robert (1913–February 15), Austrian-born physicist whose many inventions included the first remote control device for television.

Alexander, Lloyd (1924–May 17), prolific author of coming-of-age and fantasy and adventure novels who wrote the critically acclaimed *The Chronicles of Prydain* series.

Ando, Momofuku (1910–January 5), Japanese food-industry executive and inventor whose instant noodles (1958) and cup noodles (1971) became a global phenomenon.

Antonioni, Michelangelo (1912–July 30), Italian filmmaker whose carefully composed studies of alienation are credited with helping to establish cinema as a serious international art form.

Arfons, Art (1926–December 3), jet-car driver and drag racer who was inducted into the Motorsports Hall of Fame of America.

Arnold, Edmund C. (1913–February 2), journalist who designed or redesigned hundreds of newspapers, profoundly changing the look of U.S. journalism.

Astor, Brooke (1902–August 13), New York City socialite and philanthropist who personally oversaw the charitable distribution of some $200 million for the "amelioration of human misery."

Avis, Warren E. (1915–April 24), Detroit car dealer who founded Avis Airlines Rent-A-Car, the first company that rented automobiles at airports.

Backus, John W. (1924–March 17), computer pioneer who led the IBM team that developed Fortran, the first widely comprehensible and commonly used computer language.

Bakker (Messner), Tammy Faye (1942–July 20), mascara-eyed gospel singer who with husband Jim Bakker built a televangelist empire that collapsed in a whirl of sexual and legal scandals. She later reinvented herself as a campy TV guest.

Balon, Dave (1938–May 29), Canadian hockey player who helped the Montreal Canadiens win two Stanley Cups in the 1960's.

Bampton, Rose (1907–August 21), opera star whose ability to sing both mezzo-soprano and soprano roles led composer Arnold Schoenberg to describe her voice as "a miracle."

Baudrillard, Jean (1929–March 6), French Postmodernist philosopher and sociologist who in 2005 was chosen by *Prospect* and *Foreign Policy* magazines as one of the world's top 100 living public intellectuals.

Bauer, Hank (1922–February 9), outfielder who played with the Yankees during the team's run of nine pennants and seven World Series from 1949 to 1959. Bauer held a World Series record of hitting safely in 17 consecutive games.

Beck, Rod (1968–June 23), three-time All-Star pitcher who twice in his 13 major league seasons led the National League in saves.

Bennett, Bruce (Herman Brix) (1906–February 24), athlete who parlayed his 1928 Olympic silver medal for the shot put into a film career that included playing Joan Crawford's husband in *Mildred Pierce* (1945) and an ill-fated prospector in *The Treasure of the Sierra Madre* (1948).

Benzer, Seymour (1921–November 30), biologist whose work linking behavior and genes formed the foundation for modern neuroscience.

Bergman, Ingmar (1918–July 30), Swedish film-maker who is generally regarded as one of the greatest directors in motion picture history. See Portrait at Motion Pictures.

Bhutto, Benazir (1953–December 27), former Pakistan prime minister who was assassinated after returning to Pakistan after self-imposed exile.

Bishop, Joey (Joseph Abraham Gottlieb) (1918–October 17), deadpan nightclub, TV, and film comedian who was the last surviving member of Frank Sinatra's infamous Rat Pack.

Blair, Janet (Martha Janet Lafferty) (1921–February 19), singer and actress who most famously played the title role in *My Sister Eileen* (1942).

Boris, Ruthanna (1918–January 5), dancer and choreographer who in the 1940's became the first U.S. ballerina given star billing with the Ballet Russe de Monte Carlo.

Bracken, Peg (1918–October 20), humorist who wrote the 1960 best-seller *The I Hate to Cook Book* as well as other irreverent books on life as a housewife.

Brecker, Michael (1949–January 13), winner of 13 Grammy Awards who was often called the most influential jazz saxophonist since John Coltrane.

Brewer, Teresa (1931–October 17), "the little girl with the big voice" who became a pop star in the 1950's with such specialty hits as "Music, Music, Music," "Choo'n Gum," and "Ricochet."

Brown, Robert "Buck" (1936–July 2), *Playboy* magazine cartoonist who was best known for his salacious "Granny" character.

Browne, Roscoe Lee (1925–April 11), character actor who appeared in many Broadway productions and whose dignified bearing and deep, rich voice made him a standout on such TV series as "All in the Family" and "Soap."

Buchwald, Art (1925–January 17), Pulitzer Prize-winning columnist whose satirical "interviews" with the politically and socially powerful made him the most widely read humorist of his time.

Buckley, Pat (1926–April 15), Canadian-born socialite and wife of political theorist William F. Buckley, Jr. Pat Buckley raised millions of dollars for New York City institutions and charities.

Bulla, Clyde Robert (1914–May 23), author who wrote more than 60 children's books, many with historical settings or figures.

Carey, Ron (1935–January 16), comic TV and film actor who appeared in *High Anxiety* (1977) and "Barney Miller."

Claiborne, Liz (1929–June 26), Belgian-born fashion designer who in the 1970's anticipated a market for affordable business clothes for women. Liz Claiborne Inc. was the first company founded by a woman to be on the Fortune 500.

Clark, Bob (1939?–April 4), film director who was best known for the 1983 film *A Christmas Story*.

Cohen, Paul (1934–March 23), mathematician who won the 1966 Fields Medal—the "Nobel Prize" of mathematics—for his work in set theory.

Corbitt, Ted (1919–December 12), distance running pioneer who was one of the first inductees into the National Distance Running Hall of Fame.

Crespin, Régine (1927–July 5), French soprano and mezzo-soprano who mastered a wide repertory singing at European and U.S. opera houses.

Crick, Odile (1920–July 5), British artist whose most famous work was a graceful double helix based on a description by her husband, Francis Crick, who with James Watson discovered the molecular structure of DNA.

Crowe, William, Jr. (1925–October 18), U.S. Navy admiral who was described as the "most powerful peacetime military officer in American history." He served as chairman of the Joint Chiefs of Staff and ambassador to the United Kingdom.

Danby, Ken (1940–September 23), Canadian painter whose 1972 work *At the Crease*, depicting a masked hockey goaltender, became an iconic image and won praise from fellow Realist Andrew Wyeth as "terrifying and exciting."

Art Buchwald, columnist

Davidson, Sidney (1919–September 15), University of Chicago accounting scholar whose *Financial Accounting: An Introduction to Concepts, Methods, and Uses* transformed modern accounting.

Davis, Art (1934–July 29), renowned double bassist who played with John Coltrane and other jazz masters, earned a doctorate in clinical psychology, and established a practice while still performing.

Day, Laraine (Laraine Johnson) (1920–November 10), actress who most famously played Nurse Lamont opposite Lew Ayres in the Dr. Kildare films of the 1930's and 1940's.

Deaver, Michael (1938–August 18), media consultant and White House deputy chief of staff who was credited with "choreographing" the public images of President Ronald Reagan and First Lady Nancy Reagan.

De Carlo, Yvonne (Peggy Yvonne Middleton) (1922?–January 8), sultry, Canadian-born veteran of more than 100 films who is best remembered as Moses's wife in *The Ten Commandments* (1956) and as Lily Munster in "The Munsters."

DeDomenico, Vincent (1915–October 18), pasta industry icon who with his brothers created Rice-A-Roni, the "San Francisco treat." DeDomenico also launched the Napa Valley wine train.

de Gennes, Pierre-Gilles (1932–May 18), physicist who was awarded the Nobel Prize in 1991 for his groundbreaking study of the boundary between order and disorder in substances that have the properties of both solids and liquids.

Doherty, Denny (1940–January 19), Canadian lead singer of the folk-pop group the Mamas and the Papas.

Eagleton, Thomas (1929–March 4), Democratic politician who represented Missouri in the U.S. Senate for 18 years (1968-1987) and was dropped as George McGovern's running mate in the 1972 presidential election after it was disclosed that Eagleton had been treated for depression.

Ebsen, Vilma (1911–March 12), dancer who with her partner, brother Buddy Ebsen, appeared in vaudeville and on Broadway in Eddie Cantor's *Whoopee!* and the *Ziegfeld Follies*.

Edwards, Doris (1911?–June 10), last of the widows of the nine policemen killed by Bonnie and Clyde during their 1930's crime spree.

Ellis, Albert (1913–July 24), psychotherapist who developed a confrontational approach that he called rational emotive behavior therapy.

Ellison, Lillian (1923–November 2), professional wrestler known as the "Fabulous Moolah" who was the first woman inducted into the World Wrestling Entertainment Hall of Fame.

Evans, Bob (1918–June 21), restaurateur whose homemade sausage transformed a lunch counter into a retail food empire.

Evans, Ray (1915-February 15), songwriter who co-wrote "Que Sera, Sera," "Mona Lisa," and "Buttons and Bows," which won Academy Awards.

Falwell, Jerry (1933–May 15), evangelist who founded the Moral Majority and is credited with organizing the religious right into a powerful force in American politics.

Fields, Freddie (1923–December 11), legendary talent agent who cofounded Creative Management Associates and produced such films as *Crimes of the Heart* (1986) and *Glory* (1989).

Fischer, Ernst Otto (1918–July 23), German chemist who won the Nobel Prize in chemistry in 1973.

Flemming, Bill (1926–July 20), sports announcer who was part of the original "Wide World of Sports" team and who covered 11 Olympics.

Fogelberg, Dan (1951–December 16), singer-songwriter who reached the peak of his popularity with three big 1981 hits—"Leader of the Band," "Hard To Say," and "Same Old Lang Syne."

Fossett, Steve (1944–September ?), aviator, sailor, and adventurer who held multiple world records and who disappeared on a solo flight.

Franca, Celia (Celia Franks) (1921–February 19), British-born Canadian ballerina who founded the National Ballet of Canada.

France, Bill, Jr. (1933–June 4), former National Association for Stock Car Auto Racing president who promoted NASCAR from backwater tracks into the forefront of U.S. auto racing.

Gabler, Norma (1923–July 22), conservative who with her husband, Mel, gained national influence through their zealous examination of textbooks for errors and perceived left-wing bias.

Gallo, Ernest (1909–March 6), vintner who with his brother Julio founded the E&J Gallo Winery, the world's largest winemaking operation.

Gallo, Joseph (1919–February 17), Ernest and Julio Gallo's younger half brother who left winemaking to found a successful California ranch and dairy operation renowned for its cheeses.

Ghostley, Alice (1926–September 21), Tony Award-winning actress who was best known for portraying wacky TV characters on "Bewitched" and "Designing Women."

Gittings, Barbara (1932–February 18), pioneer gay-rights activist who successfully lobbied the American Psychiatric Association to rescind its definition of homosexuality as a mental disorder.

Goulet, Robert (1933–October 30), entertainer whose striking looks and rich baritone voice landed him the role of Lancelot in the 1960 musical *Camelot*, making him an instant star.

Graham, Ruth Bell (1920–June 14), wife of the evangelist Billy Graham, author of 14 books, and recipient of the Congressional Gold Medal.

Greer, Dabbs (1917–April 28), character actor who appeared in nearly 100 films and 600 television episodes but most famously played the minister on the "Little House on the Prairie" TV series.

Kitty Carlisle Hart, entertainer

Merv Griffin, entertainer

Griffin, Merv (1925–August 12), big-band singer, talk-show host, and entrepreneur who turned the profits from his TV game shows, "Jeopardy!" and "Wheel of Fortune," into a hotel and casino empire.

Griffith, Charles B. (1930–September 28), prolific screenwriter who wrote a number of quirky scripts for director Roger Corman, including the classic *The Little Shop of Horrors* (1960).

Grizzard, George (1928–October 2), actor who earned renown as Nick in the original 1962 production of *Who's Afraid of Virginia Woolf?* and a Tony Award for his performance in the 1996 revival of Edward Albee's *A Delicate Balance*.

Halberstam, David (1934–April 23), Pulitzer Prize-winning author who published more than 20 books, including the groundbreaking *The Best and the Brightest* (1972), an intensive investigation into U.S. policies in Vietnam.

Handelsman, J. B. (1922–June 20), cartoonist whose dry, witty work appeared in *The New Yorker* for nearly five decades.

Hardwick, Elizabeth (1916–December 2), novelist, essayist, and critic who cofounded *The New York Review of Books*.

Harris, Mark (Mark Harris Finkelstein) (1922–May 30), prolific author who was best known for his four baseball novels, including *Bang the Drum Slowly* (1956).

Hart, Johnny (1931–April 7), creator of the comic strip "B.C." and creator of "The Wizard of Id" in collaboration with Brant Parker, who died eight days after Hart.

Hart, Kitty Carlisle (Catherine Conn) (1910–April 17), singer, personality, and arts advocate who appeared on stage and in films; sang at the Metropolitan Opera and in nightclubs well into her 90's; and graced the panels of "To Tell the Truth" and other TV game shows for decades.

Hartack, Bill (1932–November 26), jockey who won the Kentucky Derby five times, the Preakness three times, and the Belmont Stakes once.

Helmsley, Leona (1920–August 20), real-estate broker who became president of a hotel chain upon marrying its owner. Helmsley acquired the title "queen of mean" after her relations with employees were revealed during her trial for tax evasion, for which she went to jail in 1992.

Herbert, Don (1917–June 12), former actor who became "Mr. Wizard," host of the Peabody Award-winning science TV program (1951-1965).

Herbert, Sir Wally (1934–June 12), English explorer who in 1969 became the first man to walk across the icebound Arctic and, according to authorities who dispute Admiral Robert Peary's claims, was the first man to reach the North Pole on foot.

Hill, Andrew (1931–April 20), jazz pianist known for his complex, intellectually challenging post-bop compositions.

Hill, Oliver (1907–August 5), lawyer who worked on a number of civil rights lawsuits, including *Brown v. Board of Education of Topeka*.

Hillier, James (1915–January 15), Canadian-born physicist and inventor who in 1938 helped develop a prototype for the first commercially successful electron microscope and worked to improve its magnification abilities and its applications for scientific and medical research.

Ho, Don (1930–April 14), musician whose string of albums and hit single "Tiny Bubbles" (1966) sustained a nightclub act that became a 40-year tourist institution on Hawaii's Waikiki Beach.

Hoffleit, E. Dorrit (1907–April 9), astronomer who edited *The Bright Star Catalog*, a standard reference in the study of the features of stars visible to the naked eye. At 100, she was believed to be the world's oldest working scientist in her field.

Hoisington, Elizabeth (1918–August 21), one of the U.S. Army's first female brigadier generals. Hoisington led the Women's Army Corps in the 1960's and 1970's.

Howell, F. Clark (1925–March 10), anthropologist who is credited with bringing a multidisciplinary approach to the study of human origins.

Humbard, Rex (1919–September 21), revival preacher who pioneered televangelism in 1953 with "The Cathedral of Tomorrow."

Molly Ivins, columnist

Deborah Kerr, actress

Hunt, E. Howard (1918–January 23), Central Intelligence Agency operative who became a secret Nixon administration agent who bungled a break-in of the Democratic National Party offices in Washington's Watergate complex.

Hutton, Betty (Elizabeth June Thornburg) (1921–March 11), singer and actress known as "the Incendiary Blond" for her high-energy performances in such films as Preston Sturges's *Miracle of Morgan Creek* (1944) and Cecil B. DeMille's *The Greatest Show on Earth* (1952).

Hyde, Henry (1924–November 29), former congressman from Illinois who prosecuted the 1998 impeachment of President Bill Clinton and lent his name to the 1976 Hyde Amendment, which forbids federal funding of abortions.

Inman, John (1935–March 8), English actor who was best known for playing Mr. Humphries, the campy haberdashery salesman, on the British TV series "Are You Being Served?"

Ivins, Molly (1944–January 31), political columnist who honed her considerable barbed wit to skewer the politically powerful, particularly the Texas legislature and George W. Bush, first as Texas governor and then as president.

Jamieson, Joseph (1906–May 20), Associated Press photographer who was best known for his coverage of the veterans' Bonus Marches of 1932, President Franklin Delano Roosevelt, and the great Mississippi River flood of 1937.

Jeni, Richard (Richard John Colangelo) (1957–March 10), stand-up comedian who was a regular guest on "The Tonight Show" and appeared in *The Mask* (1994) and the HBO special and UPN sitcom "Platypus Man."

Johnson, Dennis (1954–February 22), five-time National Basketball Association All-Star guard who helped lead the Seattle SuperSonics to the NBA championship in 1979 and the Boston Celtics to championships in 1984 and 1986.

Johnston, Bill (1922–May 24), Australian cricketer who was one of the great test bowlers during the period from 1946 to 1950, when Australia was the reigning world cricket champion.

Kapuscinski, Ryszard (1932–January 23), Polish journalist who covered revolution and conflict in developing countries and wrote a number of influential books on 20th-century politics.

Kennedy, Ken (1945–February 7), computer scientist whose work in software design helped lay the foundation for the broad use of supercomputers in science and engineering, particularly in simulations and weather and climate prediction.

Kerr, Deborah (1921–October 16), versatile British actress who was nominated for six Academy Awards for best actress, including *From Here to Eternity* (1953) and *The King and I* (1956), but who may best be remembered as the object of Cary Grant's affections in the classic "tear-jerker" *An Affair to Remember* (1957).

Kidd, Michael (1915–December 23), Tony- and Academy Award-winning choreographer of the Broadway musical *Guys and Dolls* (1950) and the 1953 film *The Band Wagon*.

King (Conkling), Donna (Donna Olivia Driggs) (1918–June 20), one of four King sisters who

Dennis Johnson, basketball star

sang with bands in the 1930's and 1940's and hosted "The King Family Show" in the 1960's.

King, Roger (1944–December 8), TV executive who with his brother Michael built King World Productions into a TV syndication powerhouse with such hits as "Wheel of Fortune," "Jeopardy!" and "The Oprah Winfrey Show."

King, Yolanda (1955–May 15), civil rights advocate who was the daughter of Martin Luther King, Jr.

Knievel, Evel (Robert Knievel) (1938–November 30), daredevil whose widely televised motorcycle jumps landed him in *The Guinness Book of World Records* on several accounts, including a record 40 broken bones.

Kollek, Teddy (1911–January 2), one of the founders of Israel and a five-term mayor of Jerusalem whose lead in building cultural institutions won him praise as "the greatest builder of Jerusalem since Herod the Great."

Kornberg, Arthur (1918–October 26), biochemist who in 1959 was awarded the Nobel Prize in physiology or medicine for discovering "the mechanisms in the biological synthesis of deoxyribonucleic acid (DNA)."

Koshland, Daniel, Jr. (1920–July 23), molecular biologist who revised the scientific understanding of enzymes, transformed *Science* into a "must read" journal, and used his fortune as a Levi Strauss heir to found a science museum and fund university programs.

Kovacs, George (1926–June 22), Austrian-born designer, manufacturer, and importer of innovative lighting fixtures, including the wobble and Dumbbell lamps and the halogen torchiere.

Kovács, László (1933–July 22), Hungarian-born cinematographer who changed the look of American cinema with such films as *Easy Rider* (1969), *Five Easy Pieces* (1970), *Paper Moon* (1973), and *New York, New York* (1977).

Kuhn, Bowie (1926–March 15), baseball commissioner (1969–1984) who presided over the sport's transformation from 20 to 26 teams in four divisions and from contract players earning an average annual salary of $19,000 to free agents with average annual salaries of $330,000.

Labouisse, Eve Curie (1904–October 22), French-born journalist who most famously wrote a critically acclaimed biography, *Madame Curie*, of her Nobel Prize-winning mother Marie Curie.

Ladd, Ernie (1938–March 10), athlete who switched from defensive tackle to professional wrestler and became the only man elected to both the American Football League Hall of Fame and the World Wrestling Entertainment Hall of Fame.

Laine, Frankie (Francesco Paolo LoVecchio) (1913–February 6), popular singer whose many hits sold millions of records in the pre-rock 'n' roll era.

Lane, Charles (1905–July 9), long-faced, bespectacled actor who played crotchety characters in hundreds of movies, including 10 Frank Capra films, and television episodes, particularly "I Love Lucy" and "Petticoat Junction."

Lauterbur, Paul C. (1929–March 27), chemist who shared the 2003 Nobel Prize in physiology or medicine for developing magnetic resonance imaging (MRI), which transformed diagnostics by allowing patients to avoid unnecessary surgery or exposure to X-ray radiation.

L'Engle, Madeleine (1918–September 6), prolific author whose enigmatic novel *A Wrinkle in Time* (1962) won the Newbery Medal for best children's book and established her as a major literary figure.

Lerner, Aaron (1920–February 3), Yale University dermatologist who led the team of scientists who discovered melatonin, the hormone that regulates human sleep-and-wake cycles.

LeTang, Henry (1915–April 26), Tony Award-winning master tap dancer who at age 17 toured with Sophie Tucker; choreographed such Broadway musicals as *Eubie!* (1987) and *Sophisticated Ladies* (1981); and taught tap dancing to Gregory Hines, Bette Midler, Chita Rivera, and Ben Vereen, among others.

Levin, Ira (1929–November 12), author of *Rosemary's Baby* (1967), *The Stepford Wives* (1972), and *The Boys from Brazil* (1976) and the Broadway hits *No Time for Sergeants* (1955) and *Deathtrap* (1978).

LeWitt, Sol (1928–April 8), artist of Conceptual and Minimal art whose sculpture and line drawings earned him an international reputation.

Lindberg, Charles (1920–June 24), World War II veteran who was part of the patrol that raised the first flag on Iwo Jima, as opposed to the patrol captured in the famous photograph.

Lundy, Lamar (1935–February 24), Los Angeles

Norman Mailer, writer

Rams defensive end who was part of the "Fearsome Foursome" defensive line of the 1960's.

MacCready, Paul B. (1925–August 28), inventor who created a solar-powered car and tiny robotic planes for military reconnaissance and realized Leonardo da Vinci's dream of crafting a human-powered flying machine.

MacDiarmid, Alan (1927–February 7), New Zealand-born chemist who shared the 2000 Nobel Prize in chemistry, with Alan Heeger and Hideki Shirakawa, for the discovery of plastics that conduct electricity.

Mailer, Norman (1923–November 10), one of the leading novelists and men of letters of the post–World War II generation. Mailer's more than 30 works include *The Naked and the Dead* (1948), *The Armies of the Night* (1968), *The Executioner's Song* (1979), and *Ancient Evenings* (1983). He also cofounded *The Village Voice*.

Maiman, Theodore (1927–May 5), physicist who in 1960 crafted the first working laser.

Manulis, Martin (1915–September 28), stage, film, and TV producer who created "Playhouse 90," a live, dramatic anthology series that was the centerpiece of TV's "golden age" in the 1950's.

Marceau, Marcel (Marcel Mangel) (1923–September 22), French master of mime who is credited with single-handedly reviving an art form that dates back to the theater of ancient Greece.

Marlette, Doug (1949–July 10), Pulitzer Prize–winning political cartoonist who created the popular syndicate strip "Kudzu," collaborated on a screenplay, and wrote two novels.

Maxwell, Lois (1927–September 29), Canadian actress who played Miss Moneypenny in 14 James Bond movies.

McGee, Max (1932–October 20), Green Bay Packers receiver who scored the first touchdown at the first Super Bowl, played in Los Angeles in January 1967.

McNair, Barbara (1934–February 4), nightclub singer who broke into film and television, hosting her own TV variety show from 1969 to 1971.

McRae, Colin (1968–September 15), Scottish rally racer who drove to 25 wins and 1 world title, in 1995, in his 17-year World Rally Championship career.

Medress, Hank (1938–June 18), founding member of the doo-wop group the Tokens, whose biggest hit, "The Lion Sleeps Tonight," hit No. 1 on the charts in 1961.

Melman, Larry "Bud" (Calvert DeForest) (1921–

Marcel Marceau, mime

Stanley Miller, scientist

March 19), actor whose naive delivery, childlike demeanor, and idiosyncratic impersonations on "Late Night with David Letterman" earned him a cult following.

Menotti, Gian Carlo (1911– February 1), Italian-born composer of instrumental works and operas, including *Amahl and the Night Visitors*. In 1958, Menotti founded the Spoleto Festival in Spoleto, Italy, and in 1977, the Spoleto Festival in Charleston, South Carolina.

Miller, Stanley (1930–May 20), scientist who in 1953 demonstrated experimentally how amino acids and other simple biochemical compounds considered necessary for the development of life could have formed from organic molecules that were presumably present on the primitive Earth.

Morley, Sheridan (1941–February 16), British broadcaster, actor, theater critic, and author of 18 biographies of actors—including Noël Coward, Sir John Gielgud, Robert Morley (his father), and Dame Gladys Cooper (his grandmother)—and a play, *Noël and Gertie*, which ran for nine years in London.

Nelson, Barry (Robert Haakon Nielsen) (1920–April 7), actor who appeared opposite Barbara Bel Geddes in *The Moon Is Blue* (1951), Lauren Bacall in *Cactus Flower* (1963), and Deborah Kerr in Edward Albee's *Seascape* (1973). Nelson also starred in the classic "Twilight Zone" episode *Stopover in a Quiet Town*.

Norton, Jim (1938–June 12), four-time American Football League All-Star safety who was an original member of the Houston Oilers team.

O'Brien, Parry (1932–April 21), shot putter who captured the Olympic gold medal twice and is in the U.S. Olympic Hall of Fame.

Oerter, Al (1936–October 1), discus thrower who took four Olympic gold medals and is listed in the U.S. Olympic Hall of Fame.

Orgel, Leslie (1927–October 27), British biochemist whose investigations into the earliest forms of life on Earth contributed to a widely accepted theory about the origin of DNA.

Parker, Brant (1920–April 15), co-creator of the comic strip "The Wizard of Id." Parker's collaborator, Johnny Hart, who also created the strip "B.C.," died on April 7.

Parks, Wally (1913–September 28), drag racing pioneer who was inducted into the International Motorsports Hall of Fame and the Motorsports Hall of Fame of America.

Parsons, Benny (1941–January 16), NASCAR auto racer who was inducted into the International Motorsports Hall of Fame and the Motorsports Hall of Fame of America and was named one of the 50 greatest NASCAR drivers of all time in 1998.

Pavarotti, Luciano (1935–September 6), Italian tenor whose pristine but rich and penetrating sound, keen understanding of the emotional power of lyrics and music, and wholly natural stage presence made him one of the great stars of opera in the 1900's as well as a pop culture powerhouse.

Peet, Alfred (1920–August 29), Dutch tea trader whose company—Peet's Coffee & Tea in Berkeley, California—started the gourmet coffee craze in the United States. Peet taught the founders of Starbucks the coffee trade.

Peterson, Oscar (1925–December 23), Canadian pianist and composer whose

Luciano Pavarotti, tenor

technical brilliance and mastery of the medium made him one of the great jazz figures of the 1900's.

Pickett, Bobby (1938–April 25), singer whose 1962 "Monster Mash," revived annually for Halloween, made him one of pop music's best-remembered "one-hit wonders."

Ponti, Carlo (1912–January 9), Italian producer of more than 150 films, including Academy Award winners *La Strada* (1954), *Doctor Zhivago* (1965), and *Two Women* (1960), which starred Sophia Loren, whom he "discovered" and later married.

Poston, Tom (1921–April 30), comic actor whose 50-year career, primarily on television, ranged from the slow-witted Everyman on "The Steve Allen Show" to regular appearances on "The Bob Newhart Show," "Mork & Mindy," "Newhart," and "Committed."

Reilly, Charles Nelson (1931–May 25), Tony Award-winning Broadway actor and director who made numerous appearances on "The Tonight Show," "The Hollywood Squares," and "Match Game."

Richardson, Ian (1934–February 9), British stage, screen, and television actor who gained international fame for his portrayal of Francis Urquhart, the suave but utterly immoral politician on the British miniseries "House of Cards."

Rizzuto, Phil (Fiero Francis Rizzuto) (1917– August 13), Hall of Fame shortstop who during his 13 years with the New York Yankees in the 1940's and 1950's won seven World Series titles and played in five All-Star games. He later enjoyed a second career as a sportscaster much given to regular exclamations of "Holy Cow!"

Roach, Max (1924–August 16), jazz drummer whose endless innovations helped spark several jazz movements, from 1940's bebop, to 1950's "cool jazz," and 1960's black nationalism.

Oscar Peterson, pianist

Phil Rizzuto, baseball player

Robinson, Eddie (1919–April 3), Grambling State University football coach who won 408 games during a 57-year career and who had more than 200 of his players drafted into the National Football League.

Roddick, Dame Anita (1942–September 10), British entrepreneur who founded the highly successful Body Shop International chain of retail outlets.

Wally Schirra, astronaut

Rorty, Richard (1931–June 8), intellectual whose long teaching career and such books as *Philosophy and the Mirror of Nature* and *Contingency, Irony, and Solidarity* brought him broad recognition as a leading pragmatist philosopher.

Rosenberg, Stuart (1927–March 15), director of dozens of television episodes—including classic "Alfred Hitchcock Presents" and "The Twilight Zone"—and four Paul Newman films, including *Cool Hand Luke* (1967).

Rostropovich, Mstislav (1927–April 27), Russian musician celebrated as one of the greatest cellists of all time and an outspoken advocate of human rights in his defense of Soviet dissidents.

de Rothschild, Baron Elie (1917–August 6), French banker and sportsman who restored the renowned vineyard Château Lafite Rothschild after World War II.

de Rothschild, Baron Guy (1909–June 12), French banker who was as well known for producing renowned wines and thoroughbred racehorses as he was for rebuilding his family's financial empire after World War II.

Saffir, Herbert (1917–November 21), structural engineer who invented the 5-category scale to rate the strength of a hurricane.

Sardi, Vincent, Jr. (1915–January 4), proprietor of Sardi's, the landmark Broadway restaurant that was once described as "the club, mess hall, lounge, post office, saloon, and marketplace of the people of the theater."

Schirra, Wally (1923–May 3), one of the original Mercury 7 astronauts who was the only astronaut who flew in all three of the early space programs—Mercury, Gemini, and Apollo.

Schlesinger, Arthur M., Jr. (1917–February 28), historian, special assistant to U.S. President John F. Kennedy, and author of *The Age of Jackson*, which was awarded the Pulitzer Prize in 1946; *The Age of Roosevelt* (1957, 1959, 1960); and *A Thousand Days: John F. Kennedy in the White House*, which won the Pulitzer and a National

Book Award in 1966.

Schmidt, Jean Kennedy (1918–March 3), one of the nurses dubbed the "angels of Bataan" for continuing to treat patients under extreme conditions on Corregidor while held as Japanese prisoners of war from 1942 to 1945 during World War II.

Selberg, Atle (1917–August 6), Norwegian-born mathematician whose proof of a challenging theory about the distribution of prime numbers earned him the Fields Medal, regarded as the "Nobel Prize" of mathematics.

Serrault, Michel (1928–July 29), French film actor who became an international star as the drag queen Zaza in *La Cage aux Folles* (1978).

Sheldon, Sidney (1917–January 30), best-selling author who abandoned a career as an award-winning screenwriter and Broadway lyricist to write steamy page-turners about decadence and intrigue among the beautiful and the privileged.

Shoulders, Jim (1928–June 20), city-born rodeo cowboy who was known as the "Babe Ruth of professional rodeo." Shoulders rode bucking broncos and bulls to a record 16 world championship titles.

Siegbahn, Kai (1918–July 20), Swedish physicist who won the 1981 Nobel Prize in physics for developing a technique using electrons to test the composition and purity of materials. His father, Karl M. G. Siegbahn, also won a Nobel Prize in physics, in 1924.

Siegel, Joel (1943–June 29), film critic who received an Emmy Award for his witty but generally gentle reviews on ABC's "Good Morning America."

Sills, Beverly (Belle Silverman) (1929–July 2), coloratura soprano who became the best known and most popular American opera star of her era. After retiring from the stage, she directed the New York City Opera, became chairwoman of the Lincoln Center for the Performing Arts, and then became chairwoman of the Metropolitan Opera. See Portrait at Classical Music.

Skovmand, Bent (1945–February 6), Danish botanist who searched the world to preserve and propagate the best strains of food plants and helped found the "doomsday vault," a repository of 4 million kinds of unique crop seeds. See Portrait at Agriculture.

Smith, Anna Nicole (Vickie Lynn Hogan Marshall) (1967–February 8), former *Playboy* centerfold, who was famous for being famous.

Smith, Ian (1919–November 20), former prime minister of Rhodesia (now Zimbabwe) whose white-minority government ruled over that nation's 5 million black citizens for 14 years.

Snyder, Tom (1936–July 29), mercurial, chain-smoking television broadcaster who pioneered late-late TV talk shows with "The Tomorrow Show," which followed "The Tonight Show Starring Johnny Carson" from 1973 to 1982.

Somers, Brett (Audrey Johnston) (1924–September 15), Canadian-born actress and comedian best known for quips on TV's 1970's "Match Game."

Stern, Daniel (1928–January 24), musician, movie executive, and university professor whose widely praised novels and short stories, including *Twice Told Tales: Stories* (1989), offer a wry but humane perspective on modern existence.

Stewart, Fred Mustard (1932–February 7), concert pianist who transformed himself into a best-selling novelist whose works included *The Mephisto Waltz* (1969), *Six Weeks* (1976), and *Ellis Island* (1983), all of which were filmed.

Stewart, Marjabelle Y. (1924–March 3), etiquette expert known as the "Queen of Couth" for her many books and network of etiquette classes for young people. Stewart's pupils included Lynda and Luci Johnson and Tricia and Julie Nixon.

Stockhausen, Karlheinz (1928–December 5), influential German composer who helped develop electronic music and other musical innovations.

Swearingen, John (1918–September 14), executive who in the 1960's and 1970's transformed Standard Oil of Indiana, later Amoco, from a regional energy company into an international conglomerate, which in 1980 was the world's sixth most valuable corporation.

Takamoto, Iwao (1925–January 8), animator best known for creating the canine cartoon detective Scooby-Doo and who helped produce "The Flintstones" and "The Jetsons."

Tanumafili II (1913–May 11), Malietoa (paramount chief) who was Samoa's head of state and the world's oldest national leader.

Tawney, Lenore (1907–September 24), artist whose monumental weavings contributed to the creation of the fiber art genre.

Taylor, Sean (1983–November 27), football star who played for the University of Miami and the Washington Redskins before his murder.

Taylor, Zola (1938–April 30), singer who was the only female member of the Platters from 1954 to 1962.

Thomas, Craig (1933–June 4), Wyoming Republican whose 23-year career spanned the Wyoming legislature, U.S. House of Representatives, and U.S. Senate.

Thompson, Hank (1925–November 6), honky-tonk singer who charted 79 hits between 1948 and 1983, including "The Wild Side of Life."

Tibbets, Paul W., Jr. (1915–November 1), Army colonel (later brigadier general) who piloted the *Enola Gay*, the B-29 from which the atomic bomb was dropped on Hiroshima, Japan, on Aug. 6, 1945.

Tillman, Emma Faust (1892–January 28), woman who lived independently until she was 100 years old and died four days after becoming the world's oldest living person.

Traisman, Edwin (1915–June 5), food scientist who invented Cheez Whiz for Kraft Foods and standardized the French fry for McDonald's.

Troyat, Henri (1911–March 2), Russian-born French author whose more than 100 novels and biographies lauded for their style and lucidity earned him a huge following in France.

Turner, Ike (1931–December 12), innovative rock musician who most famously performed "River Deep, Mountain High" and "Proud Mary" with his then-wife Tina Turner.

Tuttle, William (1912–July 27), MGM makeup artist who was the first in his profession to win an Academy Award, for *7 Faces of Dr. Lao* (1964).

Umeki, Miyoshi (1929–August 28), Japanese-born actress who won an Academy Award for her performance in *Sayonara* (1957) and a Tony Award nomination for her role as Mei Li in Rodgers and Hammerstein's *Flower Drum Song*.

Valenti, Jack (1921–April 26), aide and confidant of U.S. President Lyndon Johnson. Valenti led the Motion Picture Association of America for 38 years and created the film rating system.

van Breda Kolff, Butch (1922–August 22), fiery coach who from 1951 through 1994 coached more than 1,300 professional, college, and even high school basketball games.

Porter Wagoner, country singer

Willye B. White, Olympic athlete

Jane Wyman, actress

White, Willye B. (1939–February 6), track-and-field athlete who competed in every Olympics from 1956 through 1972, winning silver medals in 1956 for the long jump and in 1964 for the 4x100-meter relay.

Willis, Bill (1921–November 27), Cleveland Browns Hall of Fame guard who was a major figure in breaking the color barrier in pro football.

Wilson, Dick (Riccardo DiGuglielmo) (1916–November 19), English-born character actor who played Mr. Whipple, the Charmin-squeezing grocer, in some 500 commercials shown for more than 21 years.

Wilson, Robert Anton (1932–January 11), author of 35 books. Wilson and Robert J. Shea, a fellow editor at *Playboy* in the 1960's, wrote *The Illuminatus! Trilogy*, a work of science fiction that has become a cult classic.

Winters, Charlotte (1897–March 27), the last surviving woman to have served in the U.S. military in World War I and "one of the first enlisted women officially serving in uniform in the U.S. Navy," according to the U.S. Navy Museum.

Woodruff, John (1915–October 30), athlete who was the first African American runner to win a gold medal at the infamous 1936 Berlin Olympics hosted by German dictator Adolf Hitler.

Worsley, Gump (Lorne John Worsley) (1929–January 26), Canadian goaltender who helped the Montreal Canadiens win four National Hockey League championships. One of the last pro hockey players to play without a face mask, he was inducted into the Hockey Hall of Fame in 1980.

Wyler, Gretchen (Gretchen Patricia Wienecke) (1932–May 27), singer, dancer, and actress who appeared in such Broadway musicals as *Guys and Dolls* (1950), *Silk Stockings* (1955), and *Damn Yankees* (1955) before giving up show business to become an animal-rights advocate.

Wyman, Jane (Sarah Jane Fulks) (1917–September 10), Academy Award-winning actress and Ronald Reagan's first wife. Wyman's career in films—*The Yearling* (1946), *Johnny Belinda* (1948), *Magnificent Obsession* (1954)—and TV—"The Jane Wyman Show" (1955-1958), "Falcon Crest" (1981-1990)—spanned more than 50 years.

Yeltsin, Boris (1931–April 23), first freely elected leader of Russia who presided over the dissolution of the Soviet Union and its Communist Party. See Portrait at Russia.

Vonnegut, Kurt (1922–April 11), acclaimed writer who became a cult figure in the 1960's and 1970's with *Cat's Cradle* (1963) and *Slaughterhouse-Five* (1969). See Portrait at Literature.

von Trapp, Werner (1915–October 11), Austrian-born member of the Trapp Family Singers. Werner was depicted as the character Kurt in the musical and film *The Sound of Music.*

von Weizsäcker, Carl F. (1912–April 28), German physicist and philosopher whose discoveries advanced the study of nuclear astrophysics and whose work toward developing a nuclear bomb for Nazi Germany led him to become a leader of Germany's antinuclear movement in the 1950's.

Wagoner, Porter (1927–October 28), rhinestone-costumed country music legend who recorded more than 80 hits (including "Green, Green Grass of Home"), hosted television's longest-running country music variety show, and launched Dolly Parton's career.

Waldheim, Kurt (1918–June 14), Austrian leader and former United Nations secretary-general who was elected president of Austria in 1986 despite revelations that he had concealed youthful ties to Nazi organizations and may have been involved in war crime activities.

Walgreen, Charles R., Jr. (1906–February 10), former chairman and president of Walgreens drugstores who helped build his father's Chicago company into the world's biggest drugstore chain.

Walkabout, Billy (1949–March 7), U.S. Army sergeant who was awarded the Distinguished Service Cross, a Purple Heart, five Silver Stars, and five Bronze Stars, making him one of the most decorated soldiers of the Vietnam War.

Walsh, Bill (1931–July 30), football coach whose West Coast offense turned the San Francisco 49ers into a National Football League powerhouse that won three Super Bowls and six division titles during his 10-year tenure.

The former first lady maintained a gracious presence in the White House through the turbulent 1960's while championing the beautification of the nation.

Lady Bird Johnson

(1912–2007)

By Scott Thomas

The author:
Scott Thomas is the Associate Director of World Book's Supplementary Publications, which include the *Year Book*.

*L*yndon Johnson often said that he would never have been president were it not for his wife. He described Lady Bird Johnson as "the brains and money of this family." As her husband rose from teacher to bureaucrat, congressman, senator, vice president, and finally, president of the United States, Mrs. Johnson managed the household and his office, launched and operated businesses, served as a political aide, and raised a family. She also provided a steadying influence on her often mercurial husband, functioning as a calming mediator who softened his hard edges. Her press secretary, Liz Carpenter, noted, "If President Johnson was the long arm, Lady Bird Johnson was the gentle hand. . . . Mrs. Johnson was an implementer and translator of her husband and his purpose. . . ." The 94-year-old former first lady died on July 12, 2007, after an extraordinary life.

Early life

Claudia Alta Taylor was born on Dec. 22, 1912, in Karnack, an east Texas town of 100 people. Her father, Thomas Jefferson Taylor, was a prosperous merchant, but Lady Bird, like most rural Americans at the time, grew up in a house without electric power or indoor plumbing. Unlike most rural Americans, her mother, Minnie Patillo Taylor, championed a woman's right to vote and enjoyed the leisure time to be a voracious reader. She died when Lady Bird was only 5, and an unmarried aunt moved in to care for the child and her two older brothers. It was a nursemaid who dubbed young Claudia "Lady Bird" because she was as "purty as a lady bird."

After being married in Austin, Texas, in 1934, Lyndon and Lady Bird Johnson moved to Washington, D.C., where he had a job as an administrative assistant to a Texas congressman.

After graduating from high school, Lady Bird attended a junior college in Dallas and the University of Texas in Austin, where she met Lyndon Johnson in 1934. Describing her young suitor, Mrs. Johnson wrote, "He was the most outspoken, straightforward, determined person I'd ever encountered. I knew I'd met something remarkable, but I didn't know quite what." He proposed on their first date, and they were married two months later. Their first home was in Washington, D.C., where Johnson had a job as administrative assistant to Representative Richard M. Kleberg (D., Texas). They returned to Texas when Johnson was appointed administrator of the Texas National Youth Administration, a New Deal program. His skill as an administrator brought him to the attention of official Washington, including President Franklin D. Roosevelt, and in 1937 Lyndon was encouraged to run in a special election for the vacant Texas 10th Congressional District. Lady Bird financed the campaign, and Johnson won handily.

The young congressman befriended Sam Rayburn (D., Texas), who became speaker of the house in 1937 and held the post longer than any other speaker in history. The powerful Rayburn handed Johnson plum committee assignments and opened many doors. According to some Johnson biographers, Rayburn was actually closer to Lady Bird than to Lyndon. She provided a home away from home for the bachelor, who became a surrogate grandfather to the Johnson daughters—Lynda Bird, born in 1944, and Lucy Baines, born in 1947.

The shy Lady Bird became active in politics when Johnson went on active duty during World War II (1939-1945). In his absence, she managed his office. In 1942, she used an inheritance to buy a radio station, which eventually grew into a multimillion-dollar corporation.

Lady Bird continued to share Lyndon's public life after the war. According to biographers, she maintained a nationwide list of politicians on index cards from which she memorized names and details that she would whisper in Lyndon's ear in receiving lines. When he ran for vice president with John F. Kennedy in 1961, she campaigned endlessly, particularly in the South. During the 34 months of Kennedy's presidency, she made 47 domestic trips and traveled to 33 countries promoting administration goals. She often substituted for the first lady, Jacqueline Kennedy, whose newborn son died soon after the election and who was not fond of politics.

The White House years

The Johnsons' tumultuous five years in the White House began on Nov. 22, 1963. They were two cars behind the open limousine carrying President and Mrs. Kennedy in Dallas when an assassin shot the president. In one of the iconic images of the 20th century, Lady Bird and Jacqueline Kennedy flank Lyndon as he takes the oath of office.

The glamorous Jacqueline Kennedy was a very hard act to follow. Sensibly, Lady Bird did not try. When the Johnsons took up residence in the White House, she wrote that she felt "as if I am suddenly on stage for a part I never rehearsed." The Johnson state dinners were less elaborate than the Kennedys', and Lady Bird often entertained informally, hosting Texas barbecues on the South Lawn. They also

Flanked by Lady Bird Johnson and Jacqueline Kennedy, Lyndon Johnson (top) takes the oath of office as president of the United States aboard Air Force One in Dallas after the assassination of President John F. Kennedy on Nov. 22, 1963.

Lady Bird Johnson visits a Head Start classroom (above) in 1968. Head Start was part of President Johnson's War on Poverty initiative.

entertained official guests at the LBJ Ranch in Stonewall, Texas, where the president would give guests tours of the ranch, driving at breakneck speeds.

Very few political couples in U.S. history experienced the dizzying heights and crushing depths that the Johnsons lived between 1963 and 1969. In the wake of the Kennedy assassination, the country was remarkably united behind the federal government. Backed by majorities in both the House and the Senate, Johnson, who perhaps understood the workings of Congress better than any president in history, sent a raft of legislation for passage "on the Hill," legislation that profoundly changed the nation: the Civil Rights Act of 1964 and additional civil rights legislation in 1965 and 1968; a broad-ranging social initiative called "The Great Society"; and Medicare, a health insurance plan for the aged. He also established two new executive departments—Housing and Urban Development and Transportation. Lady Bird made countless trips to promote and explain his goals, touting the importance of such programs as Head Start, the Job Corps, and the War on Poverty.

Mrs. Johnson also championed her own cause, highway beautification. She worked tirelessly to banish billboards and plant trees. She raised hundreds of thousands of dollars to beautify Washington, D.C. In 1965, Lyndon pushed through Congress the $320-million Highway Beautification Bill, known as "The Lady Bird Bill," in her honor. After returning to Texas, she founded the National Wildflower Research Center (now the Lady Bird Johnson Wildlife Center) in Austin.

Johnson won the presidency in his own right in 1964, carrying 44 states. He took 486 electoral votes, compared with the 52 captured by his opponent, Senator Barry Goldwater (R., Arizona). The Johnson presidency essentially peaked with the 1964 landslide, however.

Johnson's nightmare

In 1965, Johnson ordered the first U.S. combat troops into South Vietnam to protect U.S. bases there and to stop the Communists from overrunning the country. Bombing attacks were stepped up against North Vietnam, and casualties mounted, triggering a bitter national debate that erupted into demonstrations and violence. Day after day, Lyndon and Lady Bird listened to demonstrators outside the White House chant "Hey! Hey! LBJ! How many kids have you killed today?" And, the cost of the war swamped The Great Society initiative. Knowing that he could not be reelected, Johnson announced on March 31, 1968, that he would not seek the nomination.

The worst was not over. Martin Luther King's assassination on April 4 triggered riots across the nation. The country, so united after the Kennedy assassination, was in flames less than five years later. Two months after King was murdered, Robert F. Kennedy, a leading opponent of the war, was also assassinated. Johnson's presidency had become a nightmare. Even before the assassinations and riots, Mrs. Johnson had written in her diary, "I do not know whether we can endure another four-year term in the presidency. I use the word 'endure' in Webster's own meaning, 'to last, remain, continue in the same state without perishing.'"

The Johnsons returned to Texas in January 1969 and largely disappeared from public life in the years before Lyndon's death on Jan. 22, 1973. Lady Bird later served on various boards and continued to champion beautification of the country. *Time* magazine reporter Bonnie Angelo, who had covered Mrs. Johnson in the White House, wrote of her stoicism, "She took a lot from him, but she always said, 'Lyndon is larger than life,' and she took him with equanimity. She was the eye of the hurricane, the calm center of the maelstrom that was Lyndon Johnson." Years after Lyndon's death, Lady Bird confided to Liz Carpenter that for all the highs and lows, her life had been wonderful. "I feel like a jug into which wine is poured until it overflows."

In a 1990 portrait, Lady Bird Johnson poses in a field of wildflowers near her home in the Texas Hill Country. As first lady, she championed the beautification of the nation, which included the widespread planting of wildflowers along U.S. highways.

Democratic Party. For the first time in 12 years, Democrats assumed control of both houses of the United States Congress in January 2007. Nancy Pelosi (D., California) made history by becoming the first woman speaker of the House of Representatives. The campaign for the 2008 U.S. presidential election got off to a vigorous start in 2007, with nine candidates seeking the Democratic Party nomination and hoping to take the presidency from the Republican Party. Democrats also picked up one governorship and lost another in elections in 2007, maintaining their 28-to-22 lead over Republicans in number of state governors.

Presidential race. Senator Hillary Rodham Clinton of New York was the leading candidate for the 2008 Democratic nomination. Clinton, a former U.S. first lady, held double-digit leads over her Democratic opponents in nearly all national polls throughout 2007. The other top contenders, based on polls and media coverage, were Senator Barack Obama of Illinois and former Senator John Edwards of North Carolina. Rounding out the field were Senator Joe Biden of Delaware, Senator Christopher Dodd of Connecticut, former Senator Mike Gravel of Alaska, Representative Dennis Kucinich of Ohio, Governor Bill Richardson of New Mexico, and former Governor Tom Vilsack of Iowa. Vilsack left the race in February.

The calendar for the 2008 presidential primaries and caucuses underwent significant upheaval in 2007, creating uncertainty about how the nominating process would play out. In almost all states, primaries or caucuses are the means by which voters select the delegates who in turn choose a party's presidential candidate at the party's national convention. Many states scheduled their delegate selection contests earlier than usual in an effort to gain greater influence on the presidential nomination. More than 20 states—including California, Georgia, Illinois, New Jersey, and New York—scheduled primaries or caucuses for Feb. 5, 2008.

Some states scheduled their contests for earlier than February 5, violating national party organization rules. On Aug. 25, 2007, the Democratic National Committee (DNC) voted to bar all Florida delegates from the national convention unless Florida reversed its decision to hold a January 2008 primary. On Dec. 1, 2007, the DNC imposed the same penalty on Michigan, which had also scheduled a January 2008 primary. DNC rules allowed only Iowa, Nevada, New Hampshire, and South Carolina to hold January primaries or caucuses. On Oct. 9, 2007, Biden, Edwards, Obama, and Richardson announced that they would pull their names from the Michigan primary ballot.

Governors. In Louisiana, Democratic Governor Kathleen Blanco announced on March 20, 2007, that she would not seek reelection to a second term. She had been widely criticized for the state's response to Hurricane Katrina in 2005. On Oct. 20, 2007, U.S. Representative Bobby Jindal, a Republican, was elected to succeed Blanco. He defeated 11 other candidates, including Democratic State Senator Walter Boasso, who came in second.

In Kentucky, the Democrat, former Lieutenant Governor Steve Beshear, unseated Republican Governor Ernie Fletcher in a November 6 election. Fletcher had been accused of political discrimination in a hiring scandal during his term. In the only other gubernatorial race of 2007, Mississippi Governor Haley Barbour, a Republican, easily won reelection on November 6. His Democratic opponent was John Arthur Eaves, Jr., a lawyer.

Fund-raising. During the first six months of 2007, Democratic Party committees—including the Democratic National Committee, the Democratic Congressional Campaign Committee, the Democratic Senatorial Campaign Committee, and state and local committees—raised $111.5 million and spent $67.7 million, according to the Federal Election Commission. Their Republican counterparts raised $108.8 million and spent $87.1 million during the same period. The Democrats' fund-raising total was 29 percent higher than their total for the first half of 2005 and 98 percent higher than their total for the first half of 2003.

In August and September 2007, a scandal emerged involving Norman Hsu, a businessman and major fund-raiser for Hillary Rodham Clinton and other Democrats. News reports revealed that Hsu was a fugitive from justice. In 1992, he had pleaded no contest in California to a charge of defrauding investors, but he failed to appear at his sentencing hearing, and a warrant was issued for his arrest. Starting in 2003, Hsu donated to several Democratic candidates and also gathered donations from other people to give to candidates. The donations totaled hundreds of thousands of dollars. After news organizations began publicizing his fugitive status in August 2007, Hsu surrendered to California authorities on August 31 and posted $2 million in bail, but then he fled the state again. Federal agents arrested Hsu in Colorado on September 6. In response to the Hsu scandal, many Democrats gave the money that Hsu had personally donated to them to charity. On September 10, Clinton's presidential campaign announced that it would return about $850,000 in donations that Hsu had solicited from other people. On December 4, a federal grand jury charged Hsu with defrauding investors and with illegally reimbursing donors for their campaign contributions.   ■ Mike Lewis

See also **Cabinet, U.S.; Congress of the United States; Elections; People in the news** (Al Gore; Nancy Pelosi); **Republican Party; State government; United States, Government of the; United States, President of the.**

Denmark. Anders Fogh Rasmussen narrowly won a third term as prime minister of Denmark in early elections in November 2007. Fogh Rasmussen's Liberal-Conservative coalition, which consisted of the prime minister's Liberal Party and the Conservative Party, had been in power since 2001. However, because the government did not control a majority of seats in the 179-seat parliament, it was forced to depend on the cooperation of the far-right, anti-immigrant Danish People's Party to pass legislation. In 2007, the coalition, together with the Danish People's Party, won a majority of 90 seats. Fogh Rasmussen sought support from the small, centrist New Alliance party to broaden the coalition's majority bloc. New Alliance, which won 5 seats in the assembly, favored immigration reform and cuts to the nation's high income taxes.

Economy. European Union economists projected that Denmark's economy would grow at a slower pace in 2007—by 1.9 percent, compared with 3.5 percent in 2006—because of a slowdown in private consumption. The unemployment rate was expected to fall from 3.9 percent in 2006 to 3 percent in 2007.

Youth house riots. In March 2007, nearly 700 people were arrested in Copenhagen after riots broke out over the city's eviction of squatters from the Ungdomshuset, or youth house, which had become a center of underground culture. Leftist youths had occupied the building since 1982 with the tolerance of municipal authorities. The squatters were evicted after a court order during a dawn raid by local police. City authorities were criticized for their handling of the matter after it came to light that the eviction followed the sale of the building to an ideologically conservative Christian organization. The group immediately demolished the structure upon taking possession.

Arctic sovereignty. Danish scientists explored the Arctic Ocean in August 2007, in an attempt to substantiate claims that the area surrounding the North Pole—which contains an estimated 25 percent of the world's oil and gas reserves—belongs to Denmark. Canada, Norway, Russia, and the United States had made similar claims. The conflict centered on the question of whether the Lomonosov Ridge, an underwater mountain range that passes through the North Pole, is an extension of any of the five nations' *continental shelf* (the submerged land at the edge of a continent). Until the mid-2000's, when the sea ice began to melt, the area was relatively inaccessible and thus of no particular concern to governments. Ultimately, a United Nations commission must decide the issue. In September 2007, Denmark invited the other claimant nations to meet in 2008 to discuss the claims. ■ Jeffrey Kopstein

See also **Canada; Europe.**

Dinosaur. See Paleontology.

Disability. A South African runner whose legs were amputated as an infant because of a birth defect sought in 2007 to compete in professional track events against able-bodied athletes. Oscar Pistorius, who had broken Paralympic records and sought to compete in the 2008 Summer Olympic Games, ran on a pair of J-shaped carbon-fiber blades. During 2007, the International Association of Athletics Federations (IAAF)—the governing body for track and field sports—debated whether Pistorius's prosthetics gave him an advantage over able-bodied sprinters. In July, Pistorius was allowed to compete against world and Olympic-class sprinters while the IAAF conducted a biomechanical analysis of the sprinter and his prosthetics. The IAAF planned to render its decision in early 2008.

Supreme Court education rulings. In May 2007, the United States Supreme Court ruled that parents may sue a school district over their child's special education plan without hiring a lawyer. Federal appeals courts had ruled that parents must hire an attorney to bring such a lawsuit, a position that caused hardship for those who could not afford a lawyer or find one willing to take the case.

According to the 1975 Individuals with Disabilities Act, school districts must provide "free appropriate education" to children with disabilities. School officials and parents work together to prepare an individualized education plan. In the case before the court, school officials determined that a particular family's autistic child should attend a public school. The family believed that a specialized private school—whose tuition the school district would pay—better suited their child's needs. The family's appeal was denied, and they were unable to hire a lawyer to sue the district. The justices ruled that because parents are allowed to appeal their child's special eduation plan, they also have the right to sue if the appeal is denied.

In October 2007, the Supreme Court upheld a lower court ruling that a school system must pay for the private school education of a child with disabilities even if that child had not tried to attend a public school first. In the case brought before the court, the child's parents had argued before the lower court that their school district had not provided an acceptable education plan. The lower court agreed with the parents.

Treaty on disability rights. On March 30, 81 member nations and the European Union signed the United Nations (UN) Convention on the Rights of Persons with Disabilities. The treaty was designed to protect the rights of about 650 million people worldwide with disabilities. According to the UN, only about one-third of its member countries guaranteed legal protection for disabled people. By the end of 2007, the convention had not yet been ratified. ■ Kristina Vaicikonis

See also **Track and field.**

Disasters. The deadliest disaster of 2007 was Cyclone Sidr, which struck Bangladesh on November 15, killing at least 3,300 people. Disasters that resulted in major loss of life include the following:

Aircraft crashes

January 1—Indonesia. An Adam Air Boeing 737-400 on a flight from Surabaya on Java Island to Manado on Sulawesi Island disappears during a storm. Ten days later, remnants of the plane wash up on the coast of Sulawesi Island; all 102 passengers and crew members are presumed dead.

May 5—Cameroon. All 114 passengers and crew members aboard a Kenya Airways flight from Douala, Cameroon's largest city, to Nairobi, capital of Kenya, are killed as the plane crashes into a swamp shortly after taking off in heavy rain.

July 17—Brazil. All 187 passengers and crew members aboard a TAM Airlines Airbus A320, as well as 12 people on the ground, are killed as the plane crashes into an airline building and explodes. The flight, from Porto Alegre, Brazil, attempted to land in São Paolo during a rainstorm.

September 16—Thailand. A Thai One-Two-GO jet crashes and burns as it attempts to land at Phuket International Airport in southern Thailand during a storm. The flight originated in Bangkok; 89 of the 130 passengers and crew are killed.

October 4—Congo (Kinshasa). A Russian Antonov 26 cargo plane crashes minutes after takeoff from Kinshasa International Airport. At least 39 people are killed, including passengers and crew members as well as people in several houses into which the plane crashes in a nearby suburb.

November 30—Turkey. A plane carrying 57 passengers and crew members from Istanbul to Isparta crashes near the town of Keciborlu in southwestern Turkey, leaving no survivors.

Earthquakes

March 6—Indonesia. Seventy people are killed when an earthquake of 6.3 magnitude strikes the island of Sumatra. The epicenter of the quake lies about 30 miles (50 kilometers) northeast of Padang, capital of West Sumatra.

April 2—Solomon Islands. Fifty-two people are killed when an undersea earthquake triggers a tsunami that strikes the west coast of the Solomon Islands. The 8.1-magnitude earthquake originated about 25 miles (40 kilometers) from Gizo, the second-largest town.

August 15—Peru. More than 500 people are killed when an 8.0-magnitude earthquake strikes Peru. The town of Pisco, 150 miles (240 kilometers) south of Lima, is hardest hit, with 308 deaths.

Explosions and fires

February 2—Philippines. At least 50 people are killed when a tanker truck carrying liquefied carbon dioxide careens down a highway in Tigbao in Zanboanga del Sur province after its brakes fail and the truck explodes. Dozens are injured.

March 20—Russia. At least 63 people are killed when a fire sweeps through a nursing home in the Azov Sea coast village of Kamyshevatskaya in southern Russia.

March 26—Nigeria. An overturned oil tanker bursts into flames, killing at least 89 people who had gathered to loot it. The accident occurs in the town of Katugal in northern Nigeria.

August 27—Greece. At least 60 people are killed as more than 170 forest fires rage across Greece. The fires began on August 24 and have been particularly devastating in the mountain villages of the Peloponnesus in the south.

Mine disasters

February 3—Colombia. A methane gas explosion causes a tunnel to collapse at a coal mine in Sardinata in northeast Colombia, killing 32 miners. Three days later, 8 workers are killed in an explosion in a coal mine in Gámeza, 110 miles (177 kilometers) north of Bogotá, the capital.

March 19—Russia. A methane gas explosion in a coal mine in Siberia leaves 110 people dead, including nearly the entire management of the mine. The explosion occurs at the Ulyanovskaya mine, near the town of Novokuznetsk, about 1,850 miles (3,000 kilometers) east of Moscow.

May 24—Russia. Methane gas explodes in the Yubileynaya coal mine near Novokuznetsk in southwestern Siberia. Thirty-nine of the 217 miners working at the time are killed.

August 17—China. Heavy rain triggers flash floods that pour down several mineshafts, trapping 181 coal miners in Xintai, 280 miles (450 kilometers) south of Beijing. Provincial officials halt efforts to drain the mine on August 23, stating that no hope for the miners' survival remains.

November 18—Ukraine. Methane gas explodes in the Zasyadko coal mine in Ukraine's eastern Donetsk region, killing 100 miners in the worst mining accident in the nation's history.

December 6—China. An explosion in a coal mine in China's northern Shanxi province kills 105 miners. Although the cause of the blast is not determined, the state media reported that the miners were working in an unauthorized area.

Shipwrecks

February 12—Yemen. At least 112 people are drowned when their boat capsizes in the Gulf of Aden during a late-night crossing. The passengers were migrants from Somalia and Ethiopia trying to reach Yemen.

May 4—Turks and Caicos Islands. A sailboat carrying some 160 migrants from Haiti capsizes

A bridge in Minneapolis lies in ruins after its collapse at the height of the evening rush hour on Aug. 1, 2007. Thirteen people were killed and more than 100 others were injured as the bridge—the city's busiest—fell into the Mississippi River. The collapse triggered concerns about the safety of bridges throughout the United States.

people in Belgium, the Czech Republic, France, Germany, the Netherlands, Poland, and the United Kingdom.

February 2—United States. Twenty-one people are killed as a swarm of thunderstorms and tornadoes strikes central and northeastern Florida. Lady Lake, a town about 30 miles (48 kilometers) northwest of Orlando, is hardest hit.

February 7—Angola. A government report confirms that 114 people were killed in torrential rains that began in mid-January and lasted about two weeks in 12 of the country's 18 provinces.

March 1—United States. At least 20 people are killed in Alabama, Georgia, and Missouri as deadly storms and tornadoes sweep through the central and southeastern United States. Eight of the victims are teen-agers killed when a tornado struck their Enterprise, Alabama, high school.

March 3—Indonesia. Forty-three people are killed and dozens of others are missing after three days of rain trigger landslides on Flores Island in eastern Indonesia.

April 14—Thailand. Holidaymakers celebrating the Thai New Year at picturesque waterfalls in southern Trang province are swept to their death by flash floods caused by unseasonably early rains. At least 37 people are killed and some 20 others are injured.

June 6—Oman. Nearly 50 people are killed and several dozen others are missing as Cyclone Gonu strikes Oman's eastern provinces. The storm, the worst disaster the country has experienced since record keeping began in 1945, causes at least $1 billion in damage.

June 11—Bangladesh. Heavy rain in the port of Chittagong triggers mudslides that kill at least 130 people. Hundreds more are missing in an area of shanty towns buried under a collapsed hill.

June 23—Pakistan. Torrential rains and gale-force winds leave at least 235 people dead in Karachi, Pakistan's largest city and chief port.

during a storm in the Atlantic Ocean off Providenciales Island in the West Indies. More than 60 people are drowned.

July 19—Canary Islands. An open wooden boat carrying some 100 migrants capsizes in the Atlantic Ocean south of the Canary Islands. At least 50 of the passengers, who were traveling from Africa to Europe, are missing and presumed dead.

Storms and floods

January 19—United States. A giant winter storm that began on January 12 and spread from Texas to Maine in three waves of freezing rain followed by snow is blamed for the deaths of at least 74 people in 9 states.

January 19—Eastern Europe. A storm carrying driving rain and gale-force winds sweeps through eastern Europe, causing the deaths of at least 43

Some 200 others are injured, and the city of 12 million loses electric power for several days.

June 26—South Asia. A cyclone slams into Pakistan's Baluchistan province with torrential rain. Flooding over several days leaves as many as 1 million people homeless and kills at least 600 people in Afghanistan, India, and Pakistan.

July 4—Mexico. A landslide triggered by heavy rain buries a bus carrying 40 to 60 passengers under as much as 23 feet (7 meters) of mud, fallen trees, and jagged boulders. The bus was traveling on a mountainous road in the San Miguel Eloxochitlán region of Mexico's Puebla state.

July 8—India. Government officials report that at least 660 people have died in devastating floods caused by monsoon rains. The state of Maharashtra is the hardest hit.

August 2—China. Government officials report that 114 people have died from lightning strikes in July and more than 700 others have been killed by flash floods and landslides caused by weeks of monsoon rains. About 119 million people have been displaced in the worst flooding to hit the country in decades.

August 9—South Asia. Government officials report that flooding from heavier-than-usual monsoon rains in July and August has displaced an estimated 19 million people in India and Bangladesh and caused the deaths of more than 2,000 people in India, Bangladesh, Nepal, and Indonesia.

August 25—North Korea. At least 454 people have died in the worst flooding North Korea has experienced in more than 10 years, announces the country's official news agency.

September 4—Nicaragua. More than 100 people are killed as Hurricane Felix strikes the impoverished Miskito Coast area of Nicaragua.

October 17—Africa. A United Nations report indicates that nearly 400 people died in July when half the countries of Africa were struck by the worst flooding to hit the continent in 30 years.

October 31—Hispaniola. Flooding and mudslides by Tropical Storm Noel—the deadliest storm of the 2007 Atlantic hurricane season—leave at least 48 people dead in Haiti and 82 people dead in the Dominican Republic. The two nations share the island of Hispaniola.

November 19—Papua New Guinea. At least 150 people are killed as heavy rain in the wake of Cyclone Guba triggers massive flooding.

December 26—Indonesia. A landslide triggered by flooding buries dozens of people in central Java, one of the islands making up Indonesia. At least 120 people are killed, and tens of thousands are left homeless.

Train wrecks

January 23—Montenegro. At least 45 people are killed and nearly 200 others are injured as a passenger train derails and plunges into a ravine near the capital, Podgorica.

August 1—Congo (Kinshasa). A freight train carrying both passengers and cargo between the cities of Ilebo and Kananga in West Kasai province derails, killing at least 100 people and injuring dozens of others in the worst rail accident in Congo's history. Several cars jumped the tracks as the train turned on the banks of the Luembe River.

Other disasters

July 24—Hungary. Health officials report that about 500 people have died as the result of a heat wave that lingered over the country from July 15 to July 22. On July 20, in the town of Kiskunhalas, the temperature reached 107 °F (41.9 °C), the hottest day in Hungary's recorded history.

July 25—Peru. Health officials reveal that at least 70 children have died over the past several weeks as a spell of unusually cold weather—with temperatures as low as -4 °F (-20 °C)—lingers in the Andes mountain regions of Peru.

October 3—Vietnam. At least 53 workers are killed when a bridge under construction over the river Hau in southern Vietnam collapses. Dozens of others are injured.   ■ Kristina Vaicikonis

See also **Asia; Greece; Weather.**

Drought. See Weather.

Drug abuse. An estimated 20.4 million Americans age 12 or older were current (within the previous month) users of illegal drugs, 125 million were current drinkers of alcohol, and 72.9 million were current users of tobacco in 2006, according to the National Survey on Drug Use and Health (NSDUH), released in September 2007. The NSDUH is an annual survey by the United States Substance Abuse and Mental Health Services Administration.

Illegal drugs. The 8.3-percent rate of illegal drug use reported for 2006 was similar to the 8.1-percent rate in 2005. User rates for most types of illegal drugs were also similar in 2005 and 2006. However, the rate of current marijuana use among Americans ages 12 to 17 fell from 8.2 percent in 2002 to 6.7 percent in 2006. Marijuana use among people ages 18 to 25 also fell.

The NSDUH found a substantial increase in the number of Americans currently using prescription pain relievers for nonmedical purposes, from 4.7 million in 2005 to 5.2 million in 2006. The current nonmedical use of prescription pain relievers among people ages 18 to 25 increased from 4.1 percent in 2002 to 4.9 percent in 2006.

The 2006 Monitoring the Future Survey, released by the National Institute on Drug Abuse in December 2006, reported increases in the rates of nonmedical uses of prescription pain relievers among students in the 8th, 10th, and 12th grades from 2005 to 2006. In addition, this survey revealed that 4.2 percent of 8th-graders, 5.3 percent of 10th-graders, and 6.9 percent of 12th-graders used cold or cough medicines containing dextromethorphan (DXM, a substance that can alter mood) during the past year to get high.

Alcohol. The 2006 NSDUH reported that 50.9 percent of Americans were current drinkers of alcohol, similar to the 51.8 percent reported for 2005. Twenty-three percent of Americans in 2006 participated in *binge drinking* (having five or more drinks on the same occasion on at least one day) during the previous month. The 2006 NSDUH found that the rates of current drinking (28.3 percent) and binge drinking (19 percent) among people ages 12 to 20 were essentially unchanged from 2002. The rate of driving under the influence of alcohol declined from 14.2 percent of Americans in 2002 to 12.4 percent in 2006.

Tobacco. According to the 2006 NSDUH, 29.6 percent of Americans used a tobacco product (cigarettes, smokeless tobacco, cigars, or pipe tobacco) within the previous month, similar to the 29.4 percent in 2005. Among Americans ages 12 to 17, the rate of current cigarette use decreased from 13 percent in 2002 to 10.4 percent in 2006. ■ Alfred J. Smuskiewicz

See also **Drugs.**

Drugs. Children under the age of 6 should not be given over-the-counter (OTC) cold and cough medicines because such medications are ineffective in such young children and may cause serious side effects and even death, according to an October 2007 resolution by an advisory panel of the United States Food and Drug Administration (FDA). The nonbinding resolution, which passed on a 13-9 vote, followed the voluntary withdrawal a week earlier of more than a dozen popular OTC multisymptom pediatric cold medications by drug manufacturers, who cited "rare patterns of misuse leading to overdosing." In September, an FDA review of side-effect records filed with the agency identified 54 child deaths linked to decongestants and antihistamines from 1969 to fall 2006. Most of the victims were under 2.

The FDA panel called for additional studies on the safety and effectiveness of multisymptom medications in very young children and called for the creation of standardized dosing devices for all liquid cold medicines to reduce the risk of overdosing. Panel members concluded that multisymptom cold products can be used by children ages 6 to 12.

Avandia warning. Following publication of a study linking the popular diabetes drug rosiglitazone (sold under the brand name Avandia) to an increased risk of heart attack, a medical advisory panel recommended in July 2007 that the FDA require a strict warning label about this risk on the drug's packaging. The panel did not vote to ban the drug as some researchers had urged, however.

In May, *The New England Journal of Medicine* had published a detailed analysis of 42 studies of rosiglitazone, manufactured by British-based GlaxoSmithKline. The analysis concluded that individuals using rosiglitazone had a 43-percent greater risk of heart attack than those using other diabetes medications.

Eliminating periods. The first drug designed to prevent pregnancy by suppressing a monthly menstrual cycle indefinitely won FDA approval in May. Manufactured by Wyeth Pharmaceuticals of Madison, New Jersey, the drug is sold under the brand name Lybrel. Taken daily, the pill releases the same hormones—progestin and estrogen—that standard birth control pills use to stop *ovulation* (the release of eggs during the menstrual cycle). Unlike standard birth control pills, which are typically taken for 21 days followed by 7 days without pills, daily use of Lybrel completely eliminates a woman's regular menstrual periods.

The FDA reported that, in tests with more than 2,400 women, Lybrel was just as effective at preventing pregnancy as were standard birth control pills. However, some medical researchers expressed concerns about Lybrel's safety, noting that the health consequences of the long-term

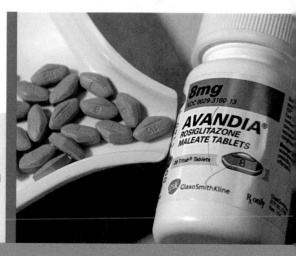

Avandia, a drug commonly used to manage diabetes mellitus, was shown to increase the risk of heart attack in patients in a large analysis published in May 2007. The study prompted the United States Food and Drug Administration to require that Avandia's label carry a warning noting that the drug may be associated with chest pain and heart attack.

suppression of menstrual periods were unknown.

Alzheimer's patch. The first skin patch to treat patients with mild to moderate dementia resulting from Alzheimer's disease or Parkinson disease received FDA approval in July. The Excelon Patch, manufactured by Swiss-based Novartis Pharmaceuticals, continuously releases rivastigmine, the same drug available for Alzheimer's and Parkinson patients in pill form, into the patient's bloodstream. The manufacturers noted that the patch would be easier for many patients to use than pills. In addition, clinical trials indicated that the patch produces fewer adverse effects than do pills.

Malaria drug for children in Africa. A new and affordable combination of antimalarial medications, with the potential for saving millions of lives, became available for children in Africa in 2007. The medication, known as ASAQ (a combination of artemisinin [also called artesunate] and amodiaquine), was made available at greatly reduced costs by a collaboration between Sanofi-aventis, a pharmaceutical giant based in France, and the Drugs for Neglected Diseases Initiative, a nonprofit organization in Geneva, Switzerland. The drug was not patented, so it could be manufactured by any company interested in doing so.

Malaria, which is transmitted in mosquito bites by parasites called plasmodia, kills more than 1 million people every year, primarily children under age 5 living in sub-Saharan Africa. Previously, the main drug used to fight malaria in most African countries was artemether-lumefantrine (sold under the brand name Coartem), which costs five times as much as ASAQ.

Dietary supplements. A study released in January raised concerns about the widespread use of herbal products and dietary supplements. These substances, such as echinacea, gingko, garlic, and vitamin tablets, were being used by millions of Americans for various health-related purposes.

In the report, published in *JAOA—The Journal of the American Osteopathic Association,* researchers at the Kansas City (Missouri) University of Medicine and Biosciences and the University of Missouri-Kansas City School of Medicine concluded that most older Americans using herbs and dietary supplements had many misunderstandings about these products. In surveying almost 300 Americans aged 60 years or older, the researchers found that most of the participants incorrectly believed that herbs and supplements were regulated and tested by the FDA to ensure their purity and safety. The researchers also noted that most participants knew little about the risks of adverse interactions between certain supplements and prescription drugs.   ■ Alfred J. Smuskiewicz

See also **AIDS; Drug abuse; Health care issues; Medicine; Mental health; Public health.**

East Timor. See also Asia.

Eastern Orthodox Churches. The Supreme Court of Appeals of Turkey sparked conflict with Orthodox Christians worldwide when it ruled in June 2007 that the Ecumenical Patriarch, who by tradition resides in Istanbul, is not the spiritual head of the world's Orthodox Christians, but only the head of the Greek Orthodox in Turkey. About 200 million Orthodox Christians recognized the patriarch as their spiritual leader. Although the ruling held no force outside of Turkey, it was seen as another case of the government of largely Muslim Turkey pressuring its Orthodox minority.

Cyprus. On August 6, during a church service at the Monastery of the Apostle Varnavas in Turkish-occupied northern Cyprus, the Turkish military expelled the abbot. The free Cypriot government in the south condemned the action. That same month, Turkey's government barred Archbishop Chrysostomos II of Cyprus from visiting Ecumenical Patriarch Bartholomew in Istanbul, a stance protested by the archbishop.

Romania. Patriarch Teoctist, whose surname was Arapasu, died on July 30 after a turbulent 20-year period of leadership of the Romanian Orthodox Church, which included surviving under Communist rule. The funeral, held in Bucharest on August 3, was led by Ecumenical Patriarch Bartholomew. After 40 days of mourning, Daniel, Metropolitan of Moldova and Bucovina, was elected on September 12 as the new patriarch.

United States. The Standing Conference of Canonical Orthodox Bishops in the Americas (SCOBA), an umbrella group, met in Spring Session on May 23 in Crestwood, New York, hosted by Metropolitan Herman of the Orthodox Church in America. SCOBA approved a "Statement on Global Climate Change," a theologically based call to care for the environment, during the session.

An important step toward resolution of the ongoing financial crisis in the Orthodox Church in America was made in 2007 with a verdict of the church's Spiritual Court regarding a former chancellor, Robert S. Kondratick. The court ruled that the priest was to be defrocked effective July 31.

Russia. The Russian Orthodox Church and the Russian Orthodox Church Outside Russia (ROCOR) established full communion at a ceremony in Moscow on May 17, ending a political conflict that began in 1927. ROCOR was to retain some independence, but the Russian Patriarchate would confirm the election of ROCOR's senior clergy.

The Russian Orthodox Church pulled out of a Roman Catholic-Orthodox theological conference held in Ravenna, Italy, in October 2007 due to a disagreement with the Estonian Apostolic Church. The Russian church believed that the Estonian Orthodox were in its jurisdiction instead of that of the Ecumenical Patriarchate. The move distressed other participants.   ■ Stanley S. Harakas

Economics, United States. Growth of commerce and output in the United States was steady for much of 2007, despite a slowing factory sector, a deteriorating housing market, soaring energy costs, and the steady decline of the dollar on foreign markets. In the second half of 2007, economic threats loomed, prompting some economists to predict weak growth or even a recession in 2008. The Federal Reserve—the Fed, the nation's central bank—tried to limit these risks with interest rate cuts, the first in four years.

Subprime credit crunch. The chief reason for alarm in late 2007 was a wrenching shock to credit markets that first surfaced in July. The credit crisis began with some banks and other financial firms unwilling to buy more high-risk U.S. mortgage debt—so-called subprime mortgages—as new home sales and existing home prices slid and more borrowers defaulted on mortgages with adjustable interest rates.

Subprime mortgages, which had been offered widely by banks during the overheated housing boom of the early 2000's, enabled borrowers to get loans with little or no money down and often with low interest rates. However, the interest was often programmed to reset after a predefined period at a much higher rate. When the inherent risk in such mortgages was coupled with deflat-

ing house prices as the housing bubble burst in 2006 and 2007, lenders were left with massive uncollectible debt. Lenders—top U.S. banks among them—began writing off such debt and took huge hits to their profits, driving down the value of companies' stocks. Credit tightened, creating a "crunch" that spread throughout global money markets, hindering normal finance that underwrites everyday business transactions.

A tired expansion. The U.S. economy was already showing strains well before credit issues dominated economic news, especially in the manufacturing sector and such services as transportation linked to the manufacturing of consumer goods. Analysts who track goods-hauling companies reported that a "freight recession" had taken hold in traffic volumes during 2007. Railroad traffic in lumber, wood products, crushed stone, and sand declined at double-digit volume levels throughout the year. Such commerce, economists emphasized, was closely tied to the sagging U.S. housing market.

After slow growth in the second half of 2006, the U.S. *gross domestic product* (GDP)—the total value of goods and services produced in a country in a year—managed a scant 0.8-percent growth rate in the first three months of 2007, reported the U.S. Department of Commerce. GDP

SELECTED KEY U.S. ECONOMIC INDICATORS

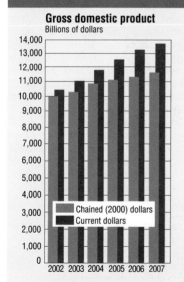

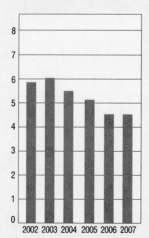

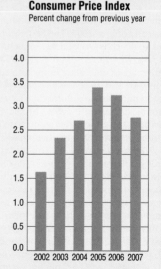

Sources: U.S. Department of Commerce and U.S. Department of Labor, except 2007 figures, which are estimates from The Conference Board.

The gross domestic product (GDP) measures the value in current prices of all goods and services produced within a country in a year. Many economists believe the GDP is an accurate measure of the nation's total economic performance. Chained dollars show the amount adjusted for inflation. The unemployment rate is the percentage of the total labor force that is unemployed and actively seeking work. The Consumer Price Index measures inflation by showing the change in prices of selected goods and services consumed by urban families and individuals.

improved to 3.8 percent in the second quarter and was even stronger in the third quarter, but economists warned of anticipated stresses.

One of the most worrisome economic developments—for consumers as well as for economists—was intense upward pressure on oil prices. The price of crude oil doubled between January and December, with prices reaching the psychologically significant $100-per-barrel threshold in November. Predictably, both gasoline and diesel costs climbed to record highs. A mild autumn delayed the domino effects on the price of home heating oil used in the Northeast, but analysts warned that winter could bring a new energy cost shock to many households.

Amid rising energy costs and falling home equity, major retailers voiced concern that consumer spending had cooled to the slowest pace in more than a year. In 2007, consumer spending accounted for more than two-thirds of U.S. GDP.

Stock markets went though extreme turbulence in 2007, with the Dow Jones Industrial Average and other closely watched indexes periodically setting new highs only to plunge again. The indexes hit record highs in July with the Dow topping 14,000 points but soon falling sharply as the drying up of credit threatened a range of business deals. Stocks recovered to again set new highs in October but fell again through November, in what was labeled a "correction."

The Fed cut its federal funds rate—the rate that most directly affects consumer mortgage and credit card rates—from 5.25 percent to 4.25 percent in three successive announcements in the second half of 2007. The Fed also cut its discount rate, which is charged to banks for temporary loans, four times. The first was in August and then again with each funds rate cut from 6.25 percent to 4.75 percent. In November, Fed Chairman Ben Bernanke forecast a slowdown in economic growth into 2008. The U.S. Department of Labor's consumer price index rose 2.8 percent from October 2006 to September 2007.

Trade balance. The United States, as it had for years, imported far more in 2007 than it exported. However, a declining dollar in 2007 boosted exports by making U.S. goods and services cheaper in foreign markets. With consumer spending down in 2007 and the dollar in decline on world markets, imports became more expensive, which helped narrow the trade deficit. The Department of Commerce reported a September trade deficit of $56.5 billion, down slightly from August, and somewhat reduced from the $64.2 billion deficit reported for September 2006.

Consumer confidence. The Conference Board, a New York City-based research group that measures consumer attitudes monthly, reported that its consumer confidence index for October

2007 dipped to 95.6, registering its third consecutive monthly drop. Only three months earlier, in July, the index had hit a seven-year high of 112.6. Analysts speculated that the subprime crisis had taken a toll on consumer attitudes.

Factory sector. Manufacturing in the United States appeared to stumble early in the year but regained its footing and peaked around midyear before weakening steadily into the third and fourth quarters. The Institute for Supply Management (ISM), a Tempe, Arizona-based professional organization of U.S. purchasing managers, reported that its index of factory activity for October slowed to a level of 50.9, near the 50 level that marks the boundary between factory sector expansion and contraction. The ISM gauge had risen as high as 56 in June before starting to slide again.

U.S. auto industry. U.S. automakers General Motors (GM) Corporation of Detroit; Ford Motor Company of Dearborn, Michigan; and Chrysler LLC of Auburn Hills, Michigan, all announced cutbacks in future output and employment in 2007. Labor unrest also impacted the automakers, with the United Auto Workers launching brief strikes against GM and Chrysler during the year. A historic shift also occurred in the first quarter of 2007, when Japanese rival Toyota outsold GM globally for the first time in history. Auto industry analysts predicted that the milestone would have significant psychological and marketing impacts.

Sales of heavy commercial vehicles to truck lines also slowed in 2007, as the fall-off in freight traffic reduced demand. Industry experts noted that trucking companies were delaying new purchases because of new-vehicle costs associated with government-mandated emissions controls.

Contradictory indicators. The Commerce Department announced on October 31 a 3.9-percent rate of growth in the July-through-September third quarter, a more vigorous measure than many economists had predicted, and later revised it up to 4.9 percent, though analysts said this rear view of growth did not mitigate coming threats. The report credited strong consumer spending and export trade, but spending remained a major risk factor.

The U.S. Department of Labor reported in October that payroll employment grew by 166,000 jobs in the third quarter. The job growth, more robust than most economists had predicted— along with the positive third-quarter GDP—suggested that the U.S. economy remained resilient in late 2007, in spite of the subprime credit crunch, high fuel prices, and the weak housing market.

■ John D. Boyd

See also **Automobile; Bank; Economics, World; Energy supply; International trade; Labor and employment; Transportation.**

Economics, World. Global output of goods and services slowed in late 2007, as a crisis in world credit markets emerged. The crisis stemmed from overinvestment in the United States mortgage market and the collapse of the U.S. housing boom. Although output continued very strong in major emerging economies, such as China and India, constricted credit markets weakened economies in some major industrial nations in the second half of 2007 and raised the threat of recession in 2008.

The subprime credit squeeze. During the third quarter of 2007, big commercial banks in the United States, Europe, and elsewhere revealed large exposures to high-risk or "subprime" loans. Such loans had been widely offered in the United States during 2004 and 2005, when historically low mortgage rates triggered a real estate boom. Earnings statements posted by a number of major financial institutions in October and November 2007 itemized huge "write-downs" of uncollectible mortgage debt. As a result, credit and stock markets entered a period of turmoil not seen since 1998.

In the second half of 2007, central banks in Europe and the United States—agencies that control the money supply in their regions or nations—injected large amounts of dollars and euros (the common currency of 13 nations of the European Union, or EU) into financial markets to provide short-term liquidity and boost credit reserves. The U.S. central bank, the Federal Reserve (the Fed), cut its key federal funds rate from 5.25 percent to 4.25 percent in three successive moves, joined in early December by quarter-point rate cuts by the central banks of Canada and England. The first two Fed actions appeared to calm fears temporarily, but global stock markets remained jittery, with occasional wide swings in indexes. The third cut of a quarter point was viewed as too mild and set off a sharp drop in disappointed stock markets.

Slower growth was evident in some world regions in 2007 well before the credit crunch took hold. In the United States, signs of a housing slowdown in late 2006 foreshadowed sharp declines in home values in 2007. Some transportation analysts also described a "freight recession" under way during 2007, as demand slumped for construction materials and cargoes linked to automobile manufacturing. Statistics on *gross domestic product* (GDP)—the total value of all goods and services produced in a country in a year—showed the U.S. economy growing at an anemic 0.8 percent in the first quarter of 2007 but accelerating to better than 3 percent in the second quarter and nearly 5 percent in the third quarter. However, economists predicted a slowdown for the fourth quarter, and weakness spread beyond the housing and automobile sectors.

In the EU, Germany—the region's largest economy—posted moderate 2.5-percent growth in 2007, but economists projected a slowdown to 2.1-percent growth in 2008. France's economy, sluggish in 2007, was projected to register 1.9-percent growth, down from 2006. By contrast, some smaller economies among newer eastern EU members boomed throughout 2007.

International trade slowed in 2007 even before the financial market turmoil of late summer, with some U.S. ports reporting declining imports for several months. This development was closely linked, economists said, to a steady decline in the value of the U.S. dollar against other major world currencies through most of 2007, which raised the cost of imports.

From a U.S. point of view, the low dollar was not all bad, since it spurred U.S. exports and thereby narrowed the longstanding U.S. trade deficit. However, a decline in U.S. imports had serious implications for other major world economies, because the consumer-driven U.S. economy had for so long served as an engine for global economic growth. According to forecasts by economists with the International Monetary Fund (IMF)—a United Nations-affiliated agency that provides short-term credit to member nations—the volume of global trading in goods and services was expected to expand only by 6.6 percent in 2007, down from a 9.2-percent expansion in 2006.

Oil and other raw materials. Soaring commodity prices presented a significant challenge to all sectors of industrial economies, but particularly to manufacturers. Heightened competition from rapidly industrializing economies, such as those of China and India, applied relentless upward pressure on a wide range of commodity prices. Such raw materials as metals and lumber also became substantially more expensive.

Surging crude oil costs in 2007 hit consumers and producers alike throughout the world's economies as oil prices hovered just below $100 per barrel in November—nearly double the $50 cost in January. Price pressures created by increased worldwide demand were intensified by rising tensions between the United States and major Mideast oil producer Iran, analysts noted.

World economic outlook. In October, the IMF estimated that global economic growth would slow during 2007 from 5.4 percent to 5.2 percent and then retreat to 4.8 percent in 2008. IMF projections showed the U.S. economy—the world's largest—braking to a weak 1.9-percent rate of growth in 2008. Mexico, a key U.S. trading partner, would also feel the pinch, IMF economists predicted, with growth slowing to 2.9 percent in 2007 from 4.8 percent in 2006. In the

Eurozone—the EU nations that use the euro currency—economic output showed signs of slowing in 2007 and was forecast to grow at a relatively modest rate of 2.1 percent in 2008. IMF economists predicted that China's economy would grow 11.5 percent in 2007, that India's economy would grow at 8.9 percent, and that both economies would remain strong into 2008.

The economics of climate change. In 2007, consumer awareness of a growing consensus among scientists that Earth's climate was warming due to human activity began to weigh on individual and collective economic decisions. Amid growing calls by consumers and governments for cleaner-burning fuels, the demand for biofuels spiked in many parts of the world, driving up prices of corn, soybeans, sugar cane, and other fuel-producing crops.

A small but growing number of consumers in the United States turned to hybrid cars and other vehicles for greater fuel economy. The popularity of the Prius, Japanese automaker Toyota's hybrid offering, helped Toyota outsell U.S. automaker General Motors Corporation of Detroit in the first quarter of 2007 for the first time ever.

■ John D. Boyd

See also **Automobile; Bank; China; Economics, United States; Energy supply; Europe; Global warming; India; International trade.**

Ecuador. Rafael Vicente Correa Delgado, 43, of the center-left Alianza País (Country Alliance) party, was sworn in for a four-year term as president on Jan. 15, 2007. Early in his term, Correa emphasized environmental issues. He made the preservation of Ecuador's Galapagos Islands a national priority. He imposed a one-year moratorium on the exploitation of oil reserves estimated at one billion barrels under Yasuní National Park. The park, home to rare and exotic species of plants and animals, lies between the Napo and Curaray rivers in the Amazon River basin. Correa hoped to persuade the international community to compensate Ecuador for the revenue it would lose by leaving the oil in the ground.

In August, Venezuelan President Hugo Chávez pledged financial assistance to build a $5-billion oil refinery capable of handling 300,000 barrels of oil a day near Ecuador's Pacific coast. The facility would save Ecuador, which exports oil, money spent to import refined petroleum products. Also in August, Correa served notice that his administration would not renew the lease with the United States government, due to expire in 2009, on an air base at Manta, Ecuador. The U.S. Air Force had been using the base to intercept shipments of illegal drugs to the United States.

■ Nathan A. Haverstock

See also **Latin America.**

Education. A record 55.6 million students were enrolled in United States prekindergarten, elementary, and secondary school programs in fall 2007, according to estimates issued by the Department of Education. A continuing increase in the number of Hispanic students fueled the growth.

An estimated 6.5 million students were enrolled in private schools in 2006 (the latest year for which data were available), or about 12 percent of all children in prekindergarten through grade 12. Roman Catholic schools enrolled 46 percent of private school students; 36 percent attended other religious schools; and 18 percent went to nonreligious private schools.

Nearly 1.1 million children were schooled at home in 2003 (latest available data), according to federal statistics. Forty-three percent of those students studied at the kindergarten through grade 5 level, and 29 percent studied at the high school level. The National Home Education Research Institute, an advocacy organization based in Salem, Oregon, that supports research on home education, claimed that federal statistics underreported the growth in home schooling. The institute estimated the figure to be closer to 2 million students.

An estimated 18 million students were enrolled in U.S. colleges and universities in 2007, continuing an upward trend that began in the late 1990's and was expected to continue through at least 2015, according to the Education Department. About 6 million of those students attended two-year institutions. Women made up nearly 60 percent of the college student body, and their numbers were expected to continue to rise. The number of men enrolled held steady.

The federal No Child Left Behind Act was hotly debated in 2007 as it came up for reauthorization. The law represented the nation's standards-based school improvement effort and set testing and accountability guidelines for public schooling in kindergarten through grade 12. Throughout the year, lawmakers in both the Senate and the House of Representatives worked on bills to revise the law's testing requirements and on ways for schools to measure whether students were making adequate yearly progress.

A federal study and independent reports highlighted wide variations in the ways states defined proficiency on reading and mathematics tests. Such tests were required under the law for students in grades 3 through 8 and during one of the high school years. Some states set rigorous test standards; others set a lower bar to ensure more students met grade-level benchmarks.

The No Child Left Behind law, enacted in 2002, was credited with bringing greater attention to the academic needs of struggling students. However, it also drew criticism for narrowing the curriculum by focusing on test results in math and reading. States were required to begin reporting results on science tests in 2008. By the end of 2007, legislators had failed to reauthorize the law.

Graduation rates. An estimated 3.2 million students earned a high school diploma in 2007, according to federal statistics. That number represented 74.4 percent of students who entered public schools as freshmen four years earlier. Policymakers, business leaders, educators, and foundations continued to debate ways to reform secondary education to better prepare students for the demands of college and the workplace.

Campus safety and student privacy laws came under intense scrutiny in 2007 in the wake of a shooting spree at Virginia Polytechnic Institute and State University in Blacksburg. A student, Cho Seung-Hui, killed 32 people and wounded several others before taking his own life. Cho had a history of mental illness prior to his April 16 rampage and had been referred to mental health professionals by a professor who was disturbed by his violent writings.

The tragedy brought to light weaknesses in campus emergency alert procedures and caused universities around the country to review their policies. It also highlighted confusion among school leaders over the Family Education Rights and Privacy Act (FERPA), which requires educational institutions to keep student records private. Cho's records of emotional problems had not been shared by his high school's administrators with the Virginia Tech administration, in part because officials believed FERPA prohibited it. In September, the National Association of Attorneys General recommended that lawmakers "remove barriers to effective information sharing."

College costs grew again for the 2007-2008 academic year, according to an annual survey by the College Board. In-state students at public four-year institutions paid an average $6,185 in tuition and fees, an increase of 6.6 percent over 2006-2007. Costs for nonresident students at those colleges and universities hit an average $16,640, a 5.5-percent increase over the preceding year. Private colleges and universities cost 6.3 percent more in 2007-2008, jumping to an average $23,712 in tuition and fees. Costs at the nation's two-year colleges rose 4.2 percent, to an average $2,361.

Student loans. The U.S. Congress passed the College Cost Reduction and Access Act in September 2007, providing $20.2 billion in federal aid to college students and overhauling a student loan system amid a scandal among private lenders. An investigation in 2007 found that private lending companies had offered college officials lavish gifts and vacations in exchange for promoting their loan programs. The new law would reduce interest rates on loans over time for low- and middle-income students and forgive loans for those who commit to certain public-sector jobs. Federal subsidies to private lenders would be cut significantly.

SAT's and ACT's. A record 1.5 million students took the SAT college-admission test in 2007, according to the College Board, which administers the test. The average composite score dropped slightly to 1511 on a 2400-point scale, with the average critical reading score declining 1 point to 502. Average scores declined 3 points on the math and writing portions of the test, to 515 and 494, respectively. In August, the College Board and NCS Pearson, the company that scans the SAT answer sheets, agreed to pay $2.85 million to some 4,400 students who took the test in October 2005 and whose tests were scored incorrectly.

On the ACT college-admission test, the average composite score among the test-takers graduating in 2007 was 21.2 on a 36-point scale, a 0.1-point increase over 2006. Scores rose on the English, math, reading, and science sections of the test. More students also met the ACT's college readiness benchmarks in those subjects. However, officials at ACT, Inc., which administers the test, warned that the results indicated the core curriculum taken by most high school students was not rigorous enough. ■ Kathleen Kennedy Manzo

See also **Crime.**

Egypt emerged in 2007 as a moderating force in the Middle East by supporting democratically elected Palestinian President Mahmoud Abbas and the democratically elected governments of Iraq and Lebanon. In June, Egyptian President Hosni Mubarak condemned the Palestinian militant organization Hamas after it seized control of the Gaza Strip from Abbas's government. Many Middle East experts believed that Syria and Iran had encouraged the seizure.

Crackdown to ensure succession. President Mubarak continued in 2007 to groom his son Gamal for succession to the presidency. The main threat to the Mubarak regime came from *secular* (characterized by separation of religion and state) opposition leaders, including Ayman Nour, the leader of the al-Ghad (Tomorrow) Party. Nour was imprisoned in December 2005 based on what many experts said were fabricated charges. Democracy activist and academician Saad Edin Ibrahim, who had spent three years in prison in Egypt for his political activities before fleeing the country, was threatened with arrest in 2007 should he return to Egypt.

In August, the Egyptian government began a crackdown against the Muslim Brotherhood, an Islamic-based opposition movement. Political analysts noted that the crackdown against the group was designed to cast it as the "bogeyman," high-

The magnificent mortuary temple built for Hatshepsut by the legendary architect Senemut approximately 3,500 years ago stands on the west bank of the Nile River at Deir el-Bahri in Egypt. A mummy discovered in 1903 in a rough-hewn tomb near this temple is the mummy identified in 2007 as that of Hatshepsut.

The broken head of a statue of Hatshepsut is on display in the Egyptian Museum in Cairo, the capital of Egypt. Hatshepsut declared herself pharaoh, a position normally reserved for men. To strengthen her claim as pharaoh, she ordered that all statues and paintings depict her as a man, with a fake beard and male clothing.

Egyptian archaeologists announced in 2007 that they had identified the mummy of Hatshepsut, a female pharaoh who ruled Egypt for about 15 years in the 1400's B.C.

Archaeologist Zahi Hawass, secretary general of Egypt's Supreme Council of Antiquities, examines four mummies that were candidates to be Hatshepsut. Hawass and his team used computed tomography scans to discover which mummy's jaw fit a broken tooth known to come from Hatshepsut. Scientists were also conducting DNA tests to match the mummy's genetic profile to those of mummies known to be relatives of Hatshepsut.

The mummy thought to be that of Hatshepsut reveals that she was between 45 and 60 years old and obese at the time of her death and that she may have died from bone cancer. Some historians had previously speculated that Hatshepsut's stepson, Thutmose III, killed her to assume full power for himself. After Hatshepsut's death, Thutmose destroyed many of her monuments.

lighting the importance of Gamal Mubarak succeeding his father.

A government crackdown on the Egyptian press also occurred in 2007. Seven journalists were sentenced to one-year prison terms after being convicted of reporting distorted information about President Mubarak and his family.

Religious freedom in Egypt continued to be one-sided in 2007, favoring the Muslim majority. The Christian minority of Copts, who number 10 million and claim descent from the ancient Egyptians, were systematically discriminated against and prevented from building new churches. On May 11, in the village of Bahma in the Giza region, militant Muslims who were angered by plans to enlarge a Coptic church attacked and burned scores of homes and shops owned by Copt residents. Eleven Copts were injured in the attacks.

The lack of religious freedom was also demonstrated when Mohammed Ahmed Hegazy, a well-known lawyer and political activist, asked the government to change his religion on his official identification papers from Islam to Christianity. In August, after the government rejected his application, Hegazy filed a lawsuit against the Ministry of Interior. Following this development, mounting death threats against Hegazy from militant Muslims forced him into hiding.   ■ Marius Deeb

See also **Iran; Israel; Lebanon; Middle East.**

Elections. United States presidential hopefuls campaigned vigorously in 2007 for party primaries and caucuses scheduled for 2008. Three states held gubernatorial elections in 2007.

Presidential race. The campaign for the 2008 U.S. presidential election was the most wide-open race in decades. Term limits prevented U.S. President George W. Bush from seeking reelection, and Vice President Dick Cheney chose not to run. The 2008 race was, therefore, the first in 80 years that included neither the incumbent president nor the incumbent vice president.

Senator Hillary Rodham Clinton of New York was the leading candidate for the Democratic Party nomination. Clinton, a former U.S. first lady, held double-digit leads over her Democratic opponents in nearly all national polls throughout 2007. The other top contenders, based on polls and media coverage, were Senator Barack Obama of Illinois and former Senator John Edwards of North Carolina. Rounding out the Democratic field were Senator Joe Biden of Delaware, Senator Christopher Dodd of Connecticut, former Senator Mike Gravel of Alaska, Representative Dennis Kucinich of Ohio, Governor Bill Richardson of New Mexico, and former Governor Tom Vilsack of Iowa. Vilsack left the race in February.

In the contest for the Republican Party nomination, the top contenders were former New York City Mayor Rudy Giuliani, former Arkansas Governor Mike Huckabee, Senator John McCain of Arizona, former Governor Mitt Romney of Massachusetts, and former Senator Fred Thompson of Tennessee. Giuliani ran ahead of his opponents in most national polls in 2007. Other Republican candidates were Senator Sam Brownback of Kansas, former Governor Jim Gilmore of Virginia, Representative Duncan Hunter of California, conservative activist Alan Keyes of Maryland, Representative Ron Paul of Texas, Representative Tom Tancredo of Colorado, and former Governor Tommy Thompson of Wisconsin. Brownback, Gilmore, Tancredo, and Tommy Thompson left the race before the end of 2007.

The calendar for the 2008 presidential primaries and caucuses underwent significant upheaval in 2007, creating uncertainty about how the nominating process would play out. In almost all states, primaries or caucuses are the means by which voters select the delegates who in turn choose a party's presidential candidate at the party's national convention. Many states scheduled their delegate selection contests earlier than usual in an effort to gain greater influence on the presidential nomination. More than 20 states—including California, Georgia, Illinois, New Jersey, and New York— scheduled primaries or caucuses for Feb. 5, 2008.

Some states scheduled their contests for earlier than February 5, violating national party organization rules. The Democratic National Committee (DNC) in 2007 voted to bar all Florida and Michigan delegates from being seated at the national convention unless those states reversed their decisions to hold January 2008 primaries. Under DNC rules, only Iowa, Nevada, New Hampshire, and South Carolina were authorized to hold January primaries or caucuses. The Republican National Committee (RNC) in 2007 voted to strip five states—Florida, Michigan, New Hampshire, South Carolina, and Wyoming—of half their delegates to the national convention because they scheduled their primaries for January 2008. The RNC did not penalize Iowa and Nevada for their plans to hold January caucuses, because delegates chosen in the caucuses would technically not be bound to vote for a particular candidate. Despite the DNC and RNC sanctions, many political experts predicted that the revoked delegate slots would ultimately be restored.

Governors. In Louisiana, U.S. Representative Bobby Jindal, a Republican, defeated 11 other candidates in the gubernatorial election on Oct. 20, 2007. Jindal, the son of immigrants from India, became the first Indian American to be elected governor of a U.S. state. At age 36, he also was set to become the country's youngest sitting governor upon taking office in January 2008. The Democratic incumbent, Kathleen

Blanco, chose not to run for reelection. She had been widely criticized for the state's response to Hurricane Katrina in 2005.

In Mississippi, Republican Governor Haley Barbour easily won reelection on Nov. 6, 2007. His Democratic opponent was John Arthur Eaves, Jr., a lawyer. In Kentucky, the Democrat, former Lieutenant Governor Steve Beshear, unseated Republican Governor Ernie Fletcher on November 6.

Ballot issues. On November 6, Utah voters repealed a law that would have offered private school vouchers to all families regardless of their income or the performance of their public schools. In New Jersey, voters rejected proposals to borrow $450 million over 10 years for stem cell research and to dedicate 1 percent of annual sales tax revenue for property tax relief. In Oregon, a proposal to raise the state tobacco tax to pay for children's health insurance was rejected, and a proposal to curb the land-use rights of property developers was approved. Texas voters approved a $3-billion bond measure for a cancer research center. Cycling star Lance Armstrong, a cancer survivor, had backed the measure. ■ Mike Lewis

See also **Chicago; Dallas; Democratic Party; Houston; Internet; People in the news** (Mitt Romney); **Philadelphia; Republican Party; State government; Supreme Court of the U.S.; Television.**

Electric power. See Energy supply.

Electronics. With increased public awareness of and interest in global warming and pollution in 2007, the makers and consumers of electronics renewed efforts to be more environmentally friendly. These efforts ranged from promoting the widespread adoption of energy-efficient light bulbs to international studies on the environmental impact of electronics manufacturing.

Greenpeace report. Awareness of electronics' environmental impact was raised in March by a report published by Greenpeace, an international environmental group based in the Netherlands. The report evaluated the environmental impact of 14 large electronics manufacturers, weighing such factors as the amount of toxic chemicals in products and whether the companies used recycled materials for packaging.

Responding to their low report scores, many companies announced plans to become more environmentally friendly. In June, the computer producer Dell Inc. of Austin, Texas, pledged to become "the greenest technology company" by expanding its recycling program and phasing out certain known pollutants, such as mercury.

Compact fluorescent light bulbs. In 2007, many companies and consumers reduced their energy consumption by replacing inefficient incandescent light bulbs with high-efficiency compact fluorescent light bulbs. Wal-Mart Stores Inc.

of Bentonville, Arkansas, made headlines by pledging to sell at least 100 million compact fluorescent bulbs through its retail stores.

Wireless power. While wireless Internet continued to grow in popularity in 2007, scientists at the Massachusetts Institute of Technology in Cambridge succeeded in an experiment in wireless electric power. Using magnetic fields, the scientists were able to transfer electric power using invisible magnetic waves instead of cords, plugs, and outlets. In the experiment, the waves proved strong enough to power a 60-watt light bulb from 6.5 feet (2 meters) away.

Consumer electronics diversify. In the first weeks of 2007, Apple Computer, Inc., of Cupertino, California, officially changed its name to Apple Inc. This name change reflected the trend of many electronics companies away from specialization in one kind of consumer electronics.

Digital cameras and camcorders. According to the Consumer Electronics Association, 62 percent of adults in the United States owned a digital camera in 2007, up 5 percent from 2006.

Technology advances continued to blur the distinction between digital still cameras and camcorders. Although each offered limited features of the other, differences in quality and physical format remained. Traditional digital cameras had small batteries, high resolutions, and removable flash memory storage. Traditional camcorders had large batteries, low resolution, and removable tape cassettes. Gradual advances in preexisting technologies undermined these formats: more efficient batteries, increased flash memory capacity, and high-resolution image sensors that used less power than their predecessors.

A number of electronics companies released camera-camcorder hybrids in 2007. These hybrids used small batteries and flash memory, and many could take a high-resolution still image while also recording hours of video. Many such hybrids featured an upright, single-hand design uncommon to both cameras and camcorders. With compact designs, some of these new hybrids worked underwater, a rare feature for camcorders.

Halo 3. After almost three years of development, Bungie Studios of Kirkland, Washington, released the video game Halo 3 on September 27. As the latest installment of the series, Halo 3 was highly anticipated by video gamers as well as business and industry experts. Neither was disappointed, as gamers spent more than $170 million on Halo 3 in the first 24 hours of its release. This total sales figure set a new record among all types of entertainment, beating out traditional media such as films. ■ Drew Huening

See also **Computer; Environmental pollution; Internet; Telecommunications.**

El Salvador.

In May 2007, El Salvador's National Civilian Police and the Los Angeles Police Department agreed to cooperate to control transnational gangs. Their main target was the Mara Salvatrucha, a gang that had originated among Salvadorans in Los Angeles. By 2007, the gang had about 12,000 members in El Salvador alone. The police planned to share information and tactics to combat gang members, many of whom were living illegally in the United States.

In August, Salvadoran President Elías Antonio Saca reduced the number of Salvadoran troops serving with U.S.-led coalition forces in Iraq by more than 20 percent. Many Salvadorans thought their troops should fight crime at home. El Salvador was the only Latin American country that had sent forces to Iraq.

In February, three Salvadoran politicians and a driver were murdered in Guatemala on their way to a meeting of the Central American Parliament. The politicians belonged to El Salvador's ruling party, the Nationalist Republican Alliance. Guatemalan authorities initially arrested four Guatemalan police officers suspected of the killings. While awaiting trial in prison, the officers were themselves assassinated. ■ Nathan A. Haverstock

See also **Latin America.**

Employment. See Labor and employment.
Endangered species. See Conservation.

Energy supply.

World energy use increased in 2007, and the higher cost of fuels reflected this rise in demand. Petroleum prices surged to a record level for the third straight year as worldwide consumption grew.

Oil and gasoline prices. Speculation of possible supply disruptions also helped to drive oil prices higher. By late November, the price of crude oil was pennies away from the much-watched $100-a-barrel benchmark. (A barrel contains 42 gallons [159 liters].) At the pump, gasoline costs advanced beyond $3 a gallon, and families who heated their homes with oil faced record high fuel bills over the 2007-2008 winter.

Once again, however, long-feared oil-supply disruptions never materialized. Few storms occurred in the Gulf of Mexico, where hurricanes had significantly interrupted output of both oil and natural gas in prior years. Oil continued to flow from the prolific producing regions of the Middle East despite the geopolitical tensions in that area.

Coal prices. The production of coal was relatively flat in 2007. Coal consumption was up slightly, but the increase was met by withdrawals from inventories, according to the Paris-based International Energy Agency (IEA), the energy watchdog for the industrial nations. Coal still generated one-half of the electric power used in the United States, and the IEA estimated demand

for electric power was up 2.1 percent in 2007.

Worldwide petroleum demand increased in 2007, according to the IEA, which reported that world oil demand averaged 85.7 million barrels a day, up 1.2 percent from 2006. In its November 2007 report, the IEA projected that 2008 oil demand would rise a further 2.3 percent to an average of 87.7 million barrels a day. Much of this increase was attributed to climbing energy use in China and India, where industrial operations and domestic economies supported by large populations were rapidly expanding.

United States petroleum demand. Despite a slowdown in demand growth, the United States remained the world's largest consumer of petroleum in 2007, using nearly one-fourth of the global total. The statistical arm of the U.S. Department of Energy reported in late 2007 that the nation's oil use averaged 20.8 million barrels a day, up less than 1 percent from the 2006 level. The 2008 projected domestic oil use was about 1 percent more than in 2007.

The U.S. impact on petroleum prices remained high despite a U.S. slowdown in demand growth. One reason for this influence was continued reliance on imported petroleum. In 2007, the United States imported nearly 60 percent of all the petroleum it consumed. To obtain that much oil, the United States competed against many other nations that also had to shop for petroleum outside their borders.

The United States also held a prominent position in another area affecting world energy. In 2007, petroleum was generally priced and paid for in U.S. dollars around the world. A further decline in the value of the U.S. currency in 2007 cushioned consumers in many nations with stronger currencies from oil's rising dollar costs. It also kept the oil-producing nations' wealth from increasing as much as their higher petroleum revenues, in U.S. dollars, would suggest.

Politics and world oil markets. On the supply side, the war in Iraq and resulting oil export restrictions remained a lingering problem. Furthermore, friction continued to grow between Western industrial nations and Iran over Iran's nuclear ambitions. Both Iraq and Iran are founding members of the Organization of the Petroleum Exporting Countries, or OPEC, and the loss of their exports would severely disrupt world markets.

Indeed, 12 of the 13 members of OPEC were pressed to capacity to meet oil demands in 2007. OPEC produced nearly 40 percent of the world's daily oil supply and held the bulk of the world's oil reserves. Of the 13 member nations, only Saudi Arabia had enough spare capacity to effectively limit the petroleum price escalation.

The increased production of Saudi Arabia was countered by other political developments.

Venezuela was another founding member of OPEC and a leading supplier of crude oil to the United States. Although the United States was his country's main oil customer, Venezuela's President Hugo Chávez grew more belligerent toward the United States throughout 2007.

Other petroleum producers took advantage of the indicated tightness of oil supplies. Russia became more aggressive in international politics because of its growing oil power. Although Russia was not a member of OPEC, it was rapidly moving toward regaining its former role as the world's biggest oil producer.

Alternative energy sources. The leap in oil prices resulted in a greater emphasis on alternate energy in 2007. Possible additions to the nuclear power system were widely discussed, but the spotlight remained focused on solar and wind power and biofuels. Each of these grew in importance in 2007, but their contributions to the energy mix remained small. By year's end, the boom in the use of ethanol as a fuel appeared to be near collapse as the popularity of corn-based energy began to fade.   ■ James Tanner

See also **China; Economics, United States; Economics, World; India; International trade; Iran; Iraq; Latin America; Middle East; Transportation.**

Engineering. See **Building and construction.**

England. See **United Kingdom.**

Environmental pollution.
In November 2007, two oil spills—one in San Francisco Bay and another in the Black Sea—caused much environmental damage. A third spill occurred off the coast of South Korea in December and was called the worst oil spill in that country's history.

The first spill resulted when a cargo ship bumped into the San Francisco-Oakland Bay Bridge. About 58,000 gallons (220,000 liters) of oil leaked from the ship. Officials closed five beaches because of the oil, which washed up as far as 40 miles (64 kilometers) north of San Francisco and threatened wildlife in the region.

Almost 1.3 million gallons (5 million liters) of oil spilled when a Russian tanker ran aground during a storm on the Black Sea. About 30,000 birds became coated in oil and died, and many more fish were believed to have perished as well. Much of the oil spilled into the narrow Strait of Kerch, which is a vital resting ground for a number of migrating birds.

The South Korean oil spill was considerably worse—a barge hit an oil tanker, spilling 2.7 million gallons (10 million liters) of oil across a 12-mile (18-kilometer) area of scenic coastline, including a national park. The spill devastated the ecology of the beaches and threatened the local economy. The affected areas contained wetlands that were important resting sites of

migrating birds, and many South Koreans' livelihoods depended on fishing along the coast.

Pollution in China. In July, a team led by a scientist from the University of North Carolina at Chapel Hill traveled in China to study Lake Taihu, which had turned green from an algal bloom. Algal blooms are often caused by runoff from agricultural fertilizers. When the nutrients from fertilizers enter bodies of water, they provide food for cyanobacteria, also called blue-green algae, which then rapidly multiply and choke out the other organisms in the lake that ordinarily eat them. The government in the nearby city of Wuxi struggled to control the bloom in Lake Taihu, a source of drinking water for more than 2 million people.

Wuxi's efforts reflected a nationwide struggle to control pollution in China's rapidly developing industrial economy. Nearly 500 million Chinese lacked access to safe drinking water in 2007. According to a World Health Organization report in July, 95,600 Chinese people die annually because of polluted drinking water. The same report claimed that China had the world's highest rate of deaths from air pollution, estimating that 656,000 Chinese people die prematurely each year from diseases associated with bad air.

China's pollution in 2007 did not only affect people in China. A March study, published in the *Proceedings of the National Academy of Sciences,* reported that pollution in China affected the environment worldwide. The study showed that pollution from China and India affected winter storms in the Pacific, which spread the pollutants elsewhere, including the western United States.

Air pollution reports. Three reports detailed the harmful effects of air pollution in 2007. The reports linked air pollution to early deaths, premature births, and increased rates of blood clots.

In August, researchers from Imperial College and the University of Bath, both in the United Kingdom, and the University of Washington (Seattle) in the United States published a report on air quality levels in different parts of the United Kingdom over different time periods. More than 5,000 adults were included in the study. The researchers found that black smoke and sulfur dioxide—even in small amounts—were strongly linked to higher chances of an early death.

Also in August, a study by the School of Public Health at the University of California, Los Angeles, found that pregnant women who lived in areas polluted with carbon monoxide or fine particles were up to 25 percent more likely to give birth prematurely. This type of pollution is commonly caused by automobile traffic. Researchers studied more than 2,500 women

In 2007, pollution from India's rapidly developing economy casts a yellow tinge over Agra, home to India's greatest tourist attraction, the Taj Mahal. The Indian government announced in May a $230,000 restoration of the white marble tomb's once-gleaming surfaces.

who gave birth in 2003. They used data from personal interviews to separate the risks from air pollution from other risk factors in the women's lives, such as smoking.

In September 2007, a report in the *Journal of Clinical Investigation* found that air pollution can trigger the formation of blood clots. Researchers found that air pollutants inflame the lungs and cause them to secrete an immune system compound called interleukin-6. The chemical makes blood more likely to clot. Blood clots, in turn, may cause heart attacks and strokes. The report helped to explain the correlation between air pollution and early death.

Mercury "hot spots." Two reports in January focused on accumulations of mercury in several regions in the northeastern United States and southern Canada. Mercury is highly toxic and can damage nerve cells.

The reports, by researchers from Syracuse University in New York and Vermont's Department of Environmental Conservation, analyzed mercury build-up in yellow perch and common loons. Mercury is a cumulative poison—it collects in bodies with repeated exposure and

gradually increases to dangerous levels. When animals eat animals and plants that contain mercury, the toxin builds up and becomes concentrated in their bodies.

Researchers warned that certain areas of the country—where mercury is allowed to leak into the environment from power plants, for example—may have high concentrations of mercury in their ecosystems. The report suggested that the ecosystems of certain "hot spot" regions may be more susceptible to mercury concentration than others.

Fighting the "dead zone." A December study in *Environmental Science and Technology* found potential flaws in the U.S. government's efforts to combat the growing "dead zone" in the Gulf of Mexico. The dead zone is an area of the gulf choked by algal blooms.

Researchers from the University of Michigan at Ann Arbor analyzed the effects of reducing nitrogen and phosphorus inputs—both found in fertilizer runoff—on the dead zone. They found that reducing both nitrogen and phosphorus inputs could effectively shrink the dead zone. However, they warned that reducing only phosphorus, without also reducing nitrogen, could allow more nitrogen-rich waters to flow through the dead zone and spread the algal blooms to other areas. The U.S. Environmental Protection Agency (EPA) was set to enact the report's recommendation of reducing both nutrients in its November 2007 draft report.

Deformed frogs. Fertilizer runoff from farming was also responsible for an increasing number of deformed frogs, according to a September 2007 report in the *Proceedings of the National Academy of Sciences*. Although scientists had previously identified the parasite that causes the deformities, they were uncertain as to why the deformities were so common.

The parasites, called trematodes, grow in snails and then move from their host body to infect frog tadpoles. According to the study, fertilizer from farms washes into ponds and lakes, where it fuels the multiplication of algae. The snails then feed on the excess algae, and their population increases as well. This, in turn, leads to an increase in the number of trematodes, which gain more snail host bodies in which to grow. The large number of trematodes then leave their snail bodies and infect frog tadpoles in increasing numbers.

Emissions standards. In December 2007, the U.S. Congress passed legislation setting higher fuel efficiency standards for cars and light trucks. The legislation also promoted the increased production of ethanol. The EPA ruled in December that individual states cannot set their own emissions standards. The agency claimed that the new federal standards made individual state standards unnecessary.

■ Daniel Kenis

See also **China; Conservation.**

Eritrea. See Africa.

Estonia. Prime Minister Andrus Ansip's center-right Reform Party triumphed in March 4, 2007, elections to Estonia's parliament, taking 31 of the 101 seats. The left-leaning Center Party, the Reform Party's coalition partners in the outgoing government, came in second with 29 seats. Voters delivered a stinging rebuke to the conservative Pro Patria and Res Publica Union, which took only 19 seats. The Estonian Social Democratic Party won 10 seats, and the Estonian Greens and the Estonian People's Union held 6 seats each. The election marked the world's first online voting in a national-level parliamentary election. President Toomas Hendrik Ilves invited Ansip to form a new government. A coalition of the Reform Party, Pro

Patria and Res Publica Union, and the Estonian Social Democratic Party assumed office on April 5.

In April, the government removed a controversial World War II (1939-1945) memorial to Russian soldiers in Tallinn, the capital, unearthing the remains of eight Soviet soldiers in the process. The act enraged Russian officials and ethnic Russians in Estonia and led to two days of rioting. To Russians the statue honored the Soviet victory over Nazi Germany; to Estonians it symbolized the more-than-50-year Soviet occupation of their country. The bodies and the memorial were moved to a military cemetery in Tallinn, which seemed to end the conflict.

■ Juliet Johnson

See also **Europe; Finland; Russia.**

Ethiopia. See Africa.

A woman pays her respects to Russian veterans at a World War II memorial in an Estonian cemetery in May 2007. Estonian officials moved the statue from Tallinn, the capital, in April. The move enraged many of Estonia's ethnic Russians who regard it as a monument to Russia's victory over Nazi Germany. To many Estonians, the monument represents the decades-long Soviet occupation of their country.

EUROPE

In March 2007, the European Union (EU) celebrated the 50th anniversary of the Treaty of Rome, which created the European Economic Community, the forerunner of the EU. The continent's main economic and political bloc began as a group of six industrial nations—Belgium, France, Italy, Luxembourg, the Netherlands, and West Germany—with the goal of creating peace and prosperity on a continent devastated by World War II (1939-1945). Half a century later, the EU had enlarged to 27 members, including 10 countries from formerly Communist Eastern Europe. Bulgaria and Romania joined the bloc on Jan. 1, 2007.

In addition to a much broader membership, the EU celebrated its economic achievements, especially the adoption of the euro, the currency that, in 2007, was used by 13 member nations. Political leaders also noted that Europeans could live and work anywhere on the continent and that a passport-free zone was gradually being created.

EU reform treaty. The leaders of the EU's member nations gathered in Lisbon, Portugal, in December to sign a new reform treaty. The event marked the end of a long series of negotiations that followed the failure of a constitutional treaty to pass in referendums in France and the Netherlands in 2005.

With the exception of Ireland, none of the member countries planned to hold referendums for what was considered a toned-down version of the constitutional treaty. The revised version conspicuously left the word *constitution* out of its title, so as not to alarm citizens of countries concerned about losing national *sovereignty* (independence).

European leaders considered the Treaty of Lisbon necessary because the growth of the EU had complicated the organization's decision-making ability. Under the old treaty, a unanimous vote was needed to pass much of the legislation. The treaty listed 50 policy areas—particularly in matters related to justice and home affairs—that could be decided by a majority vote. (Matters related to such issues as foreign policy and taxation continued to require unanimity.)

The treaty was also expected to streamline EU governance by creating the position of European Council president with a term of 2 ½ years, which would allow for greater continuity in policymaking. Under the old treaty, the presidency rotated to a new member nation every six months. In foreign policy, the treaty created the position of head of foreign affairs. Because many countries objected to the term "foreign minister," the title "High Representative of the European Union for Foreign Affairs and Security Policy" was adopted. In addition, an annex to the treaty created a charter of citizens' rights that would be legally binding on all member nations (except Poland and the United Kingdom [U.K.], which opted out).

Controversy surrounded the new treaty when British Prime Minister Gordon Brown did not attend the signing ceremony but signed the document separately, later in the day. Although Brown maintained that he intended no snub to his European colleagues, analysts noted that public opinion in the U.K. was deeply divided on the question of European integration. The U.K. had not adopted the euro, and many British citizens remained suspicious about transferring too much power to the EU, especially in the realm of foreign policy. Brown faced criticism from anti-EU politicians for avoiding a referendum, which most surveys indicated would result in a defeat of the treaty. Observers believed that his absence from the ceremony was designed to disarm the "Eurosceptics" both in the Conservative opposition and within his own Labour Party.

A number of elements of the new treaty remained to be worked out. There appeared to be significant overlap in the responsibilities of the president of the European Council (the supreme governing body made up of the heads of state or government of each member nation); the president of the European Commission (which proposes legislation and consists of a commissioner from each member nation); and the new High Representative of the European Union for Foreign Affairs and Security Policy. Questions also remained about the creation of a new EU diplomatic service. According to the old treaty, the EU was represented abroad by a foreign policy and security chief, who was subordinate to the European Council. However, the EU's embassies (called "delegations") were staffed by employees of the European Commission. Commentators predicted a dispute over whether the member states or the EU's bureaucracy would control the new diplomatic service.

In addition, the revised treaty contained a number of opt-outs for individual members, protocols, and declarations, all designed to ensure that the signatory officials did not face criticism at home. Poland, for example, opted out of the charter of rights because it contained new rights for gays and lesbians, a position to which the powerful Roman Catholic Church in Poland was opposed. Nearly half of the leaders of member nations insisted that a declaration endorsing the

Fireworks light up the night as thousands of revelers gather before the Brandenburg Gate in Berlin on March 25, 2007, to celebrate the 50th anniversary of the signing of the Treaty of Rome. The treaty established the European Economic Community (the forerunner of the European Union), an organization that sought to remove barriers to the movement of goods, services, and people throughout its member nations.

EU symbols—the flag, the anthem, and the motto, "unity in diversity"—be removed. The ratification process was to take place during 2008 and was expected to be completed in 2009.

The EU and Kosovo. In December 2007, the EU approved a crisis-management mission made up of 1,800 civilians to be deployed to Serbia's breakaway region of Kosovo. Significant differences remained, however, over whether the EU would recognize Kosovo's declaration of independence, which was expected in early 2008. Months of failed negotiations among Serbia, Kosovo, and a United Nations- (UN) appointed "troika" consisting of the EU, the United States, and Russia had failed to resolve Kosovo's status. The Serbs and Russians rejected any

move toward independence until the rights of Kosovo's Serb minority and the security of its churches and cultural institutions were guaranteed. Some EU member countries planned to recognize Kosovo; others declared that they would not do so until either the parties to the conflict themselves agreed on partition or Kosovo's independence was declared valid by the United Nations. Russia maintained that the EU's mission to Kosovo would be illegal unless it received UN authorization.

Member nations were also divided on whether to link Serbia's integration into the EU with the arrest of the remaining major war crimes suspects from the Balkan wars of the

FACTS IN BRIEF ON EUROPEAN COUNTRIES

Country	Population	Government	Monetary unit*	Foreign trade (million U.S.$) Exports[†]	Imports[†]
Albania	3,187,000	President Bamir Topi; Prime Minister Sali Berisha	lek (86.78 = $1)	763	2,901
Andorra	79,000	Co-sovereigns bishop of Urgel, Spain, and the president of France; Head of Government Albert Pintat Santolària	euro (0.71 = $1)	149	1,879
Austria	8,221,000	President Heinz Fischer; Chancellor Alfred Gusenbauer	euro (0.71 = $1)	133,300	134,300
Belarus	9,615,000	President Aleksandr Lukashenko; Prime Minister Sergei Sidorsky	ruble (2,149.00 = $1)	19,610	21,120
Belgium	10,490,000	King Albert II; Interim Prime Minister Guy Verhofstadt	euro (0.71 = $1)	335,300	333,500
Bosnia-Herzegovina	3,923,000	Chairman of the Presidency Zeljko Komsic Prime Minister Nikola Spiric	marka (1.38 = $1)	3,500	8,250
Bulgaria	7,549,000	President Georgi Parvanov; Prime Minister Sergei Stanishev	lev (1.38 = $1)	15,500	23,800
Croatia	4,392,000	President Stjepan Mesic; Prime Minister Ivo Sanader	kuna (5.18 = $1)	11,170	21,790
Czech Republic	10,205,000	President Václav Klaus; Prime Minister Mirek Topolánek	koruna (19.55 = $1)	89,340	87,700
Denmark	5,463,000	Queen Margrethe II; Prime Minister Anders Fogh Rasmussen	krone (5.29 = $1)	93,930	89,320
Estonia	1,334,000	President Toomas Hendrik Ilves; Prime Minister Andrus Ansip	kroon (11.10 = $1)	9,680	12,030
Finland	5,285,000	President Tarja Halonen; Prime Minister Matti Taneli Vanhanen	euro (0.71 = $1)	84,720	71,690
France	61,225,000	President Nicolas Sarkozy; Prime Minister François Fillon	euro (0.71 = $1)	490,000	529,100
Germany	82,414,000	President Horst Köhler; Chancellor Angela Merkel	euro (0.71 = $1)	1,133,000	916,400
Greece	11,128,000	President Carolos Papoulias; Prime Minister Kostas Karamanlis	euro (0.71 = $1)	24,420	59,120
Hungary	10,020,000	President László Sólyom; Prime Minister Ferenc Gyurcsány	forint (179.14 = $1)	67,990	69,750
Iceland	300,000	President Ólafur Ragnar Grímsson; Prime Minister Geir H. Haarde	krona (61.40 = $1)	3,587	5,189
Ireland	4,269,000	President Mary McAleese; Prime Minister Bertie Ahern	euro (0.71 = $1)	119,800	87,360
Italy	58,818,000	President Giorgio Napolitano; Prime Minister Romano Prodi	euro (0.71 = $1)	450,100	445,600
Latvia	2,267,000	President Valdis Zatlers; Prime Minister Ivars Godmanis	lat (0.50 = $1)	6,980	10,330
Liechtenstein	36,000	Prince Hans-Adam II; Prime Minister Otmar Hasler	Swiss franc (1.18 = $1)	2,470	917

*Exchange rates as of Oct. 4, 2007. [†]Latest available data. **in Kosovo only

1990's. The Netherlands insisted that Serbia not be allowed to sign a Stabilization and Association Agreement, generally regarded as the first step toward eventual membership in the EU, until Serbian officials cooperated more fully with the UN chief prosecutor. Others, however, insisted that Serbia should be allowed to sign as long as its leaders showed proof that they had attempted to capture the most important suspect, Ratko Mladic.

Turkey and future enlargement. Turkey's membership talks with the EU, which began in 2005, made little progress in 2007. The talks bogged down over the Turkish government's refusal to permit trade with Cyprus (an EU member) because of an ongoing conflict over Turkish Northern Cyprus. (Cyprus had been divided since 1974 into the Republic of Cyprus and the Turkish Republic of Northern Cyprus. The Republic of

Country	Population	Government	Monetary unit*	Foreign trade (million U.S.$) Exports[†]	Imports[†]
Lithuania	3,374,000	President Valdas Adamkus; Prime Minister Gediminas Kirkilas	litas (2.45 = $1)	14,640	18,250
Luxembourg	469,000	Grand Duke Henri; Prime Minister Jean-Claude Juncker	euro (0.71 = $1)	19,550	24,220
Macedonia	2,048,000	President Branko Crvenkovski; Prime Minister Nikola Gruevski	denar (43.27 = $1)	2,341	3,631
Malta	409,000	President Edward Fenech Adami; Prime Minister Lawrence Gonzi	euro (0.71 = $1)	2,425	4,077
Moldova	3,982,000	President Vladimir Voronin; Prime Minister Vasile Tarlev	leu (11.44 = $1)	1,020	2,650
Monaco	34,000	Prince Albert II; Minister of State Jean-Paul Proust	euro (0.71 = $1)	716	916
Montenegro	629,000	President Filip Vujanovic; Prime Minister Zeljko Sturanovic	euro (0.71 = $1)	171	602
Netherlands	16,513,000	Queen Beatrix; Prime Minister Jan Peter Balkenende	euro (0.71 = $1)	413,800	373,800
Norway	4,671,000	King Harald V; Prime Minister Jens Stoltenberg	krone (5.46 = $1)	122,600	59,900
Poland	38,077,000	President Lech Kaczynski; Prime Minister Donald Tusk	zloty (2.67 = $1)	110,700	113,200
Portugal	10,678,000	President Aníbal Cavaco Silva; Prime Minister José Sócrates	euro (0.71 = $1)	46,770	67,740
Romania	21,517,000	President Traian Basescu; Prime Minister Calin Popescu-Tariceanu	new leu (2.39 = $1)	33,000	46,480
Russia	141,358,000	President Vladimir Putin; Prime Minister Viktor Zubkov	ruble (26.89 = $1)	317,600	171,500
San Marino	29,000	2 captains-regent appointed by Grand Council every 6 months	euro (0.71 = $1)	1,291	2,035
Serbia	9,519,000	President Boris Tadic; Prime Minister Vojislav Kostunica	new dinar (55.50 = $1) euro (0.71 = $1)**	6,428	10,580
Slovakia	5,395,000	President Ivan Gasparovic; Prime Minister Robert Fico	koruna (24.28 = $1)	39,640	41,840
Slovenia	2,001,000	President Danilo Türk; Prime Minister Janez Jansa	euro (0.71 = $1)	21,850	23,590
Spain	44,687,000	King Juan Carlos I; Prime Minister José Luis Rodríguez Zapatero	euro (0.71 = $1)	222,100	324,400
Sweden	9,179,000	King Carl XVI Gustaf; Prime Minister Fredrik Reinfeldt	krona (6.53 = $1)	173,900	151,800
Switzerland	7,542,000	President Pascal Couchepin	franc (1.18 = $1)	166,300	162,300
Turkey	74,824,000	President Abdullah Gül; Prime Minister Recep Tayyip Erdogan	new lira (1.20 = $1)	85,210	120,900
Ukraine	46,060,000	President Viktor Yushchenko; Prime Minister Yulia Tymoshenko	hryvnia (5.06 = $1)	38,880	44,110
United Kingdom	60,590,000	Queen Elizabeth II; Prime Minister Gordon Brown	pound (0.49 = $1)	468,800	603,000

Cyprus was controlled by Cypriots of Greek origin. That government was recognized by all countries except Turkey. The Turkish Republic of Northern Cyprus was controlled by Cypriots of Turkish origin. Their government was recognized by Turkey alone.) Turkey also failed to undertake democratic reforms quickly enough to please some member nations.

In addition, further enlargement of the EU remained unpopular among some member nations.

The new French president, Nicolas Sarkozy, in particular made it clear that he opposed Turkish membership. Immediately after his election, Sarkozy suggested that Turkey become a member of a new Mediterranean Union that France proposed for states bordering Europe that had limited prospects for membership in the EU. Under French pressure, EU officials downgraded "accession" negotiations with Turkey and Croatia in November

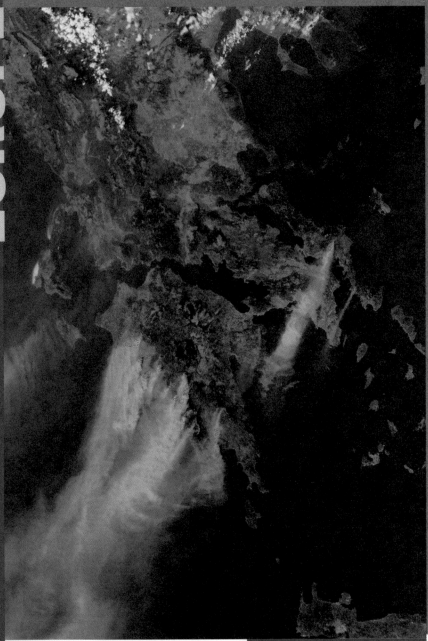

The worst fires in a century—accompanied by several heat waves— swept Greece in the summer of 2007.

Clouds of smoke drift southward from Greece across the Mediterranean Sea in an image captured by the U.S. National Aeronautics and Space Administration's Aqua satellite in August 2007. The fires devastated more than 494,000 acres (200,000 hectares) of forests and farmland and caused the deaths of at least 60 people.

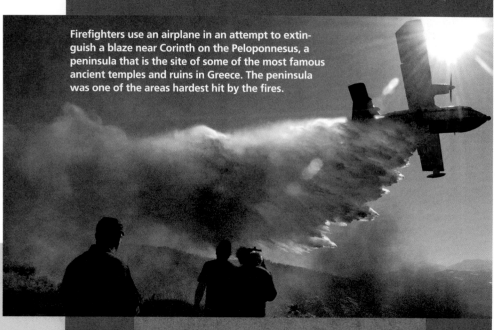

Firefighters use an airplane in an attempt to extinguish a blaze near Corinth on the Peloponnesus, a peninsula that is the site of some of the most famous ancient temples and ruins in Greece. The peninsula was one of the areas hardest hit by the fires.

A winged statue of victory is surrounded by smoke as fires rage around the ancient town of Olympia, the birthplace of the Olympic Games. Firefighters contained the blaze, which threatened to engulf the 2,800-year-old site. Authorities suspected that some of the fires that spread across Greece had been deliberately set by arsonists.

to "intergovernmental conferences." Ultimately, Sarkozy agreed not to block negotiations with Turkey if the EU agreed to set up a "reflection group" on the future of its borders and its relationship with nonmember nations.

Wine reform. In 2007, EU farm ministers negotiated controversial proposals to reform the bloc's wine sector. The blueprint for the reform had been proposed by the European Commission (EC) in July. In a meeting of farm ministers from most of the member nations in December, the members agreed to changes to help EU winemakers survive global competition, especially from such new winemaking nations as Australia and Argentina. Disputes centered on whether to ban the use of sugar in wine, a practice widely used in northern and central Europe, where sunlight is not always sufficient to form natural sugars in the grapes. The ministers agreed to reduce the amount of sugar. A key portion of the reform involved payments to winemakers to cease production of less successful varieties of wine. According to the EC, reducing the amount of wine produced was crucial for preventing a glut on the market.

Climate change. The EU and the United States clashed at a meeting in Bali, Indonesia, in December over measures to prevent dangerous climate change, which most scientists linked to atmospheric emissions of greenhouse gases. The meeting was called to prepare for a new global climate change agreement to replace the Kyoto Protocol, which was scheduled to expire in 2012. The dispute revolved around a proposal supported by the EU but opposed by Canada, Japan, Russia, and the United States to include specific targets for reducing greenhouse gas emissions by 2020.

The United States argued that unless major new industrializing countries (such as China and India) were included in the agreement, any limits on emissions would be unfair. The EU threatened not to attend a U.S.-organized climate meeting in Hawaii in early 2008, which the newly industrializing countries were also to attend. Ultimately, a compromise was reached when all sides agreed to a "Bali roadmap" for a series of negotiations that were slated for completion in 2009.

Border-free travel moves east. On Dec. 21, 2007, nine new countries entered the zone covered by the Schengen Agreement, which permitted internal passport-free travel and eliminated most border posts and markers altogether among signatory nations. The new countries included the Czech Republic, Estonia, Hungary, Latvia, Lithuania, Malta, Poland, Slovakia, and Slovenia. Under the agreement, the other signatory nations—the 15 oldest EU nations with the exception of the U.K. and Ireland and the addition of Norway and Iceland—would stop checking people entering from the east. Concerns were widely expressed that illegal aliens and criminals from farther east would use substandard border controls in new member states such as Hungary, Poland, and Slovakia to make their way west.

Energy and meat. The path to an energy deal between Russia and the EU was finally cleared on December 19, when Poland lifted its objections. Russia had banned imports of Polish meat in 2005 during a series of disputes with Poland's conservative government. A change of government in Warsaw in November 2007 permitted negotiations to resume and the ban to be lifted.

Economy. Europe's primary currency, the euro, rose significantly in value on international markets in 2007, gaining 12 percent against the U.S. dollar, which fell because of a faltering U.S. economy and rising levels of U.S. debt. At first, the rise caused pride among Europeans, but eventually it led to fears that European goods might become too expensive on export markets. President Sarkozy expressed these fears in a speech to the U.S. Congress in November. According to EU economists, the economies of the Eurozone (the countries that use the euro) were slated to grow by 2.6 percent in 2007.   ■ Jeffrey Kopstein

See also **Disasters; Global warming;** various European country articles.

European Union. See Europe.
Farm and farming. See Agriculture.

Fashion presented a split personality of sorts in 2007, with the casual, sometimes untidy, women's clothing seen early in the year giving way to more polished styles later.

This shift occurred in autumn. The summer's bohemian clothing—a short T-shirt layered over a longer T-shirt above a full skirt—was past. Instead, dresses and jackets were often fitted at the waist and shapely. High-waisted, wide-legged pants were also featured. As colder weather approached in 2007, tailored and belted coats appeared, alongside the usual bulky, quilted, and padded styles.

Shoes and bags in 2007 were varied and interesting: Mary Janes with a heel or platform sole and peep-toe or platform pumps. In addition, ballet flats were still in. Boots

On the eve of his retirement, Valentino opens a retrospective in July 2007 featuring hundreds of his designs. The exhibition, celebrating the Italian designer's 45-year career, was staged at Rome's Ara Pacis Museum, which houses the ancient *Ara Pacis* altar honoring Augustus Caesar.

were also popular, including flat, riding-style boots and ankle-high boots with heels. Smaller handbags were shown this year, but it remained to be seen if women could be lured away from large carryalls.

High-end fashion. Accessories continued to be high-ticket items that sold well in 2007. Handbags, in particular, reached stratospheric prices. Lower-priced bags by Prada or Dolce & Gabbana could cost well over $1,000, but prices of $30,000 to $40,000 for specialty purses made in limited quantities were reported in 2007.

Another expensive item, "luxury" jeans, though not as costly as premium handbags, were still surprisingly expensive given their blue-collar roots. Jeans by such makers as 7 for All Mankind or Rock & Republic began at $150 to $200, but many premium jeans sold for $600 or more.

Big business. Once an industry made up primarily of small businesses, fashion had by 2007 largely been taken over by huge corporations. Retailers, manufacturers, and designers were all part of this trend. One example was the September 2007 purchase of Barneys New York, Inc., a chain of department stores with a strong fashion influence. The buyer, Istithmar PJSC, was a Dubai-based holding company for investors. Some feared the continuing corporatization of fashion might begin to inhibit designers from taking artistic risks.

Designers, at least, showed more caution in sales to large corporations. In the past, such well-known designers as Jil Sander and Calvin Klein found themselves no longer able to design under their own name once they ended a relationship with the large company that owned their line. Both Narciso Rodriguez (who was designing under his own name) and Jack McCollough and Lazaro Hernandez (of Proenza Schouler) sold less than controlling interests in their firms in 2007 to avoid the problem.

Seen on the street. Tattoos became ever more popular during the year. Where once a person might have a single tattoo on a shoulder or forearm, now full-body tattoos were frequently seen, especially on young people in big cities. The industry for laser tattoo removal also burgeoned.

American cities, determined to fight another popular fashion, passed new indecency laws to include men sporting sagging pants with underwear showing. The penalty for this style, with its origins in hip-hop fashion, could be a fine, but in some areas jail terms were possible.

An icon retires. In September, Italian designer Valentino Garavani, who had worked under the name Valentino since the 1960's, announced he would retire in 2008. He had celebrated his 45th anniversary in fashion with a three-day extravaganza in Rome in July. Valentino had dressed royalty, socialites, and film stars in glamorous attire.

Deaths. Italian designer Gianfranco Ferré died on June 17, 2007. Ferré had trained as an architect, which heavily influenced his sculptural sense of style. From 1989 to 1997, Ferré was director of the Parisian couture house Christian Dior.

Liz Claiborne, the Belgian-born American designer who pioneered tailored clothing for working women, died on June 26, 2007. In 1986, her company was the first founded by a woman to reach Fortune 500 status. ■ Bernadine Morris

Finland. The governing Center Party under Prime Minister Matti Vanhanen barely defeated a challenge from the National Coalition (Conservative) Party in the March 2007 general election. The Centrists won 51 seats in the 200-member parliament, compared with the Conservatives' 50 seats.

The resultant coalition government, which was formed in April, consisted of both the Center and Conservative parties and two smaller parties—the Greens and the Swedish People's Party. The Greens had won 15 seats, and the Swedish People's Party, 9 seats. The Social Democratic Party, which had participated in every government since 1962, registered its worst performance in half a century. The party lost 8 seats in the parliament, dropping to 45 seats. It was excluded from the governing coalition. The new Cabinet formed in April 2007 had a female majority for the first time in Finland's history. Women held 12 of the 20 positions.

Budget. After budget negotiations in late 2007, the government announced plans to increase energy and alcohol taxes but to implement only modest inheritance, pension, and income tax cuts that had been promised prior to the 2007 election. The small cuts were designed to slow inflationary pressures on the economy. Finland's budget surplus grew in 2007. Government economists expected the surplus to continue to grow until at least 2011, when pension payments for the country's rapidly aging population would require a larger share of funds.

Finland registered the highest growth in *gross domestic product* (GDP) among countries using the euro as their currency in 2006—5.0 percent. (GDP is the total value of goods and services produced in a country in a year.) In 2007, however, European Union economists projected the rate would decline slightly, to 4.3 percent.

Foreign policy. The question of whether Finland should join NATO (North Atlantic Treaty Organization) was renewed in 2007, as Russia adopted a more assertive foreign policy and became especially antagonistic to Estonia, a close ally of Finland. The move was favored by the Conservatives but opposed by 60 percent of Finns, according to a public opinion survey conducted in September. Finland's president, Tarja Halonen, also remained opposed to joining NATO.

School shooting. Finns were shocked in November when an 18-year-old student shot and killed seven students and the principal before killing himself at his school in the town of Tuusula. The teen had apparently posted a video predicting the massacre several hours earlier on YouTube, a video-sharing Internet site. ■ Jeffrey Kopstein

See also **Estonia; Europe; Russia.**

Fire. See Disasters.

Flood. See Disasters.

Food. The safety of the United States food supply came into question in 2007, when various food products from China were found to be contaminated with potentially harmful substances. China was one of the largest exporters of food to the United States. The U.S. Food and Drug Administration (FDA) and the Department of Agriculture (USDA) were responsible for the safety of the U.S. food supply. Because of staff reductions and the volume of imports, however, only 1 percent of the food entering the country was being inspected.

In March, pet owners became alarmed when cats and dogs began to sicken and die after eating pet food that contained wheat flour imported from China. The flour was found to contain melamine, which is often used in making plastics and fertilizer, and cyanuric acid, which is used to maintain swimming pools. The chemicals had been added to the wheat flour to make it appear to contain more protein than it did. At least 17,000 pets became ill, and about 4,000 of them died.

In May, a U.S. producer of broiler chickens reported that feed for the chickens—which included pet food scraps—also contained traces of melamine. More than 2 million tainted chickens, as well as a smaller number of contaminated pigs, had already been sold for human consumption.

In June, the FDA banned several types of seafood from China after tests showed that the prod-

Market vendors in Beijing prepare shrimp for sale in June, when the U.S. Food and Drug Administration banned several types of seafood from China because they contained potentially dangerous substances. The ban was lifted after Chinese officials promised to more closely monitor exports.

ucts contained residue from drugs prohibited in U.S. fish farming. The ban was lifted after Chinese officials promised to closely monitor exports to the United States.

Major recalls. On September 25, the Topps Meat Company of Elizabeth, New Jersey, recalled some 22 million pounds (10 million kilograms) of frozen hamburger patties possibly contaminated with a dangerous strain of *E. coli* bacteria. At least 30 people in eight states had fallen ill after eating the meat. Consumers were particularly concerned to learn that the USDA had known of the possible contamination by September 7 but had failed to act.

On February 14, ConAgra Foods, Inc., of Omaha, Nebraska, recalled all Peter Pan and Great Value peanut butter processed at its Sylvester, Georgia, plant. The peanut butter contained a strain of *Salmonella* bacteria that, by the time it was traced, had sickened nearly 400 people in at least 39 states since August 2006. Public health officials at the Centers for Disease Control and Prevention in Atlanta noted that the incident was the first known case of *Salmonella* infection linked to peanut butter in the United States.

Advertising to children. Twelve major food and beverage companies pledged in 2007 to stop advertising their products to children under age 12 unless those products met certain nutritional standards. The plan, proposed by the Council of Better Business Bureaus, was based upon the 2005 U.S.

Dietary Guidelines and varied according to the products manufactured by each company. The changes included limits on calories, sugar, fat, and sodium in products marketed to children; the elimination of licensed characters such as Shrek unless the product met nutrition guidelines; and increased promotion of healthy foods to children.

Food additives. Some food additives increase hyperactivity and decrease attention span in children, according to a report by British researchers at the University of Southampton in the United Kingdom. The research, published in September 2007, provided the first scientific confirmation that additives can cause such symptoms.

The researchers studied nearly 300 children aged 3 and 8 to 9 for six weeks. Some of the children were given a drink that contained food colorings and a food preservative, while others drank a similar-tasting beverage with no additives. The children's parents and teachers rated their level of hyperactivity and attention problems after they drank the beverages. The children also took a computerized attention test. The researchers found that children who drank the beverage with additives showed an increase in hyperactivity and attention problems. ■ Kristina Vaicikonis

See also **Public health; Safety.**

Football. In one of the most turbulent and unpredictable college football seasons in memory, the Louisiana State University (LSU) Tigers won their first national championship since sharing the title in 2004, topping the Ohio State Buckeyes 38-24 on Jan. 7, 2008, in New Orleans. The Buckeyes lost the Bowl Championship Series (BCS) title game in January 2007 as well.

Ohio State and LSU occupied the top two slots in the rankings in early November, but both were upset by unranked opponents and appeared out of the championship picture. Losses by the top two teams (Missouri and West Virginia) on the final Saturday of the season, however, coupled with LSU's win in the Southeastern Conference championship game in December, set the match-up. Over the course of the 2007 season, 12 BCS teams ranked among the top five were upset by unranked opponents.

In the National Football League (NFL), the Indianapolis Colts won their first Super Bowl in 36 years, toppling the Chicago Bears 29-17 on Feb. 4, 2007, in Miami. Colts quarterback Peyton Manning completed 25 of 38 passes for 1 touchdown and was named the Most Valuable Player.

The 2007-2008 NFL season. The New England Patriots became the first team in NFL history to finish a season 16-0. The Patriots steamrolled over their first eight opponents—winning by at least 17 points in each game and not scoring less than 34 points—and beat the 7-0 Colts in Indianapolis in Week 9 to go to 9-0. The meeting was the latest ever of unbeaten teams in the NFL. New England quarterback Tom Brady set a NFL record with 50 touchdown passes, surpassing the previous record of 49 set by Peyton Manning of the Indianapolis Colts in 2004. New England receiver Randy Moss established a new record for touchdown catches with 23, breaking the previous record of 22 set by Jerry Rice of the San Francisco 49ers in 1987.

Among the other surprises in the season, the Green Bay Packers, riding aging quarterback Brett Favre's arm and a young defense, started the season 10-1. The Dallas Cowboys also started 10-1—the best start in franchise history. Both teams won their divisions. Favre became the all-time leader in touchdown passes and total passing yards, topping the marks set by former Miami Dolphins quarterback Dan Marino.

In another record-setting performance during the 2007 season, Tennessee Titans place kicker Rob Bironas set a new mark with eight field goals in a single game on Oct. 21,

THE 2007 COLLEGE FOOTBALL

NATIONAL CHAMPIONS

NCAA BCS	Louisiana State	38	Ohio State	24
NCAA FCS	Appalachian State	49	Delaware	21
NCAA Div. II	Valdosta State	25	N.W. Missouri State	20
NCAA Div. III	Wisc.-Whitewater	31	Mount Union	21
NAIA	Carroll College	17	Sioux Falls (S.D.)	9

BOWL CHAMPIONSHIP SERIES (BCS) GAMES

BOWL	RESULT			
Rose	Southern California	49	Illinois	17
Orange	Kansas	24	Virginia Tech	21
Fiesta	West Virginia	48	Oklahoma	28
Sugar	Georgia	41	Hawaii	10

OTHER BOWL GAMES

BOWL	RESULT			
Alamo	Penn State	24	Texas A&M	17
Armed Forces	California	42	Air Force	36
Capital One	Michigan	41	Florida	35
Car Care	Wake Forest	24	Connecticut	10
Champs Sports	Boston College	24	Michigan State	21
Chick-fil-A	Auburn	23	Clemson	20
Cotton	Missouri	38	Arkansas	7
Emerald	Oregon State	21	Maryland	14
GMAC	Tulsa	63	Bowling Green	7
Gator	Texas Tech	31	Virginia	28
Hawaii	East Carolina	41	Boise State	38
Holiday	Texas	52	Arizona State	34
Humanitarian	Fresno State	40	Georgia Tech	28
Independence	Alabama	30	Colorado	24
Insight	Oklahoma State	49	Indiana	33
International	Rutgers	52	Ball State	30
Las Vegas	Brigham Young	17	UCLA	16
Liberty	Mississippi State	10	Central Florida	3
Motor City	Purdue	51	Central Michigan	48
Music City	Kentucky	35	Florida State	28
New Mexico	New Mexico	23	Nevada	0
New Orleans	Florida Atlantic	44	Memphis	27
Outback	Tennessee	21	Wisconsin	17
Papa Johns.com	Cincinnati	31	Southern Mississippi	21
Poinsettia	Utah	35	Navy	32
Sun	Oregon	56	South Florida	21
Texas	TCU	20	Houston	13

2007. Minnesota Vikings rookie running back Adrian Peterson rushed for a single-game-record 296 yards on November 4 in a 35-17 victory over the San Diego Chargers. In that same game, the Chargers' Antonio Cromartie returned a missed field goal 109 yards to score in the longest play in NFL history.

Crackdown. NFL commissioner Roger Goodell instituted a major crackdown on objectionable off-the-field behavior. In perhaps the highest profile case, Goodell suspended Atlanta Falcons quarterback Michael Vick indefinitely after he was charged for his role in an illegal dogfighting ring in Virginia. Vick pleaded guilty to a host of charges and was sentenced on December 10 to 23 months in federal prison.

Goodell also punished the New England Patriots and their coach, Bill Belichick, after the team was found using a cameraman to film opposing coaches

CONFERENCE CHAMPIONS

NCAA FOOTBALL BOWL SUBDIVISION (FBS)

CONFERENCE	SCHOOL
Atlantic Coast	Virginia Tech
Big 12	Oklahoma
Big East	West Virginia
Big Ten	Ohio State
Conference USA	Central Florida
Independents	Navy
Mid-American	Central Michigan
Mountain West	Brigham Young
Pacific 10	Arizona State and USC (tie)
Southeastern	Louisiana State
Sun Belt	Troy
Western Athletic	Hawaii

NCAA FOOTBALL CHAMPIONSHIP SUBDIVISION (FCS)

CONFERENCE	SCHOOL
Big Sky	Montana
Big South	Liberty
Colonial	Richmond
Gateway	Northern Iowa
Great West	South Dakota State
Ivy League	Harvard
Metro Atlantic	Iona
Mid-Eastern	Delaware State
Northeast	Albany
Ohio Valley	Eastern Kentucky
Patriot	Fordham
Pioneer	Dayton
Southern	Appalachian State
Southland	McNeese State
Southwestern	Grambling State

ALL-AMERICAN TEAM (FBS)

(as chosen by the Associated Press)

OFFENSE
Quarterback—Tim Tebow, Florida
Running backs—Darren McFadden, Arkansas; Kevin Smith, Central Florida
Wide receivers—Michael Crabtree, Texas Tech; Jordy Nelson, Kansas State
Tight end—Martin Rucker, Missouri
Center—Steve Justice, Wake Forest
Other linemen—Jake Long, Michigan; Anthony Collins, Kansas; Duke Robinson, Oklahoma; Martin O'Donnell, Illinois
Place-kicker—Thomas Weber, Arizona State
All-purpose player—Jeremy Maclin, Missouri

DEFENSE
Linemen—Chris Long, Virginia; George Selvie, South Florida; Glenn Dorsey, LSU; Sedrick Ellis, USC
Linebackers—Dan Connor, Penn State; James Laurinaitis, Ohio State; Jordon Dizon, Colorado
Backs—Aqib Talib, Kansas; Antoine Carson, Arizona; Craig Steltz, LSU; Jamie Silva, Boston College
Punter—Kevin Huber, Cincinnati

PLAYER AWARDS
Heisman Trophy (best player)—Tim Tebow, Florida
Bednarik Trophy (best defensive player)—Dan Connor, Penn State

University of Florida quarterback Tim Tebow shows off the 2007 Heisman Trophy, which is awarded annually to the best player in college football. Tebow is the first sophomore to win the Heisman in the 73-year history of the award. He finished with a school-record 3,970 yards of total offense and accounted for a phenomenal 51 touchdowns during the season.

in the season-opening game against the New York Jets. Goodell fined Belichick $500,000, fined the team $250,000, and forced the Patriots to give up their 2008 first-round draft pick.

Super Bowl XLI. On Feb. 4, 2007, the Indianapolis Colts dominated both in time of possession and yardage but did not pull away from the Chicago Bears until Kelvin Hayden intercepted a pass and returned it 56 yards for a touchdown in the fourth quarter for a 29-17 lead. The Bears' Devin Hester had returned the opening kickoff 92 yards for a score, the first time a Super Bowl began with a touchdown. Playing in a driving rain, the teams committed a combined four turnovers in the first quarter.

2007 NATIONAL FOOTBALL LEAGUE FINAL STANDINGS

AMERICAN CONFERENCE

North Division	W.	L.	T.	Pct.
Pittsburgh Steelers*	10	6	0	.625
Cleveland Browns	10	6	0	.625
Cincinnati Bengals	7	9	0	.438
Baltimore Ravens	5	11	0	.313

East Division	W.	L.	T.	Pct.
New England Patriots*	16	0	0	1.000
Buffalo Bills	7	9	0	.438
N.Y. Jets	4	12	0	.250
Miami Dolphins	1	15	0	.063

South Division	W.	L.	T.	Pct.
Indianapolis Colts*	13	3	0	.813
Jacksonville Jaguars*	11	5	0	.688
Tennessee Titans*	10	6	0	.625
Houston Texans	8	8	0	.500

West Division	W.	L.	T.	Pct.
San Diego Chargers*	11	5	0	.688
Denver Broncos	7	9	0	.438
Oakland Raiders	4	12	0	.250
Kansas City Chiefs	4	12	0	.250

*Made play-offs

NATIONAL CONFERENCE

North Division	W.	L.	T.	Pct.
Green Bay Packers*	13	3	0	.813
Minnesota Vikings	8	8	0	.500
Detroit Lions	7	9	0	.438
Chicago Bears	7	9	0	.438

East Division	W.	L.	T.	Pct.
Dallas Cowboys*	13	3	0	.813
New York Giants*	10	6	0	.625
Washington Redskins*	9	7	0	.563
Philadelphia Eagles	8	8	0	.500

South Division	W.	L.	T.	Pct.
Tampa Bay Buccaneers*	9	7	0	.563
Carolina Panthers	7	9	0	.438
New Orleans Saints	7	9	0	.438
Atlanta Falcons	4	12	0	.250

West Division	W.	L.	T.	Pct.
Seattle Seahawks*	10	6	0	.625
Arizona Cardinals	8	8	0	.500
San Francisco 49ers	5	11	0	.313
St. Louis Rams	3	13	0	.188

*Made play-offs

TEAM STATISTICS

Leading offenses	Plays	Yards per game
New England	1,037	411.3
Indianapolis	987	358.7
Jacksonville	991	357.4
Cleveland	985	351.3
Cincinnati	964	348.0

Leading defenses	Avg. points against	Yards per game
Pittsburgh	16.8	266.4
Indianapolis	16.4	279.7
New England	17.1	288.3
Tennessee	18.6	291.6
Baltimore	24.0	301.6

TEAM STATISTICS

Leading offenses	Plays	Yards per game
Green Bay	940	370.7
Dallas	923	365.7
New Orleans	987	361.3
Philadelphia	957	358.1
Seattle	973	348.9

Leading defenses	Avg. points against	Yards per game
Tampa Bay	16.9	278.4
New York	21.9	305.0
Washington	19.4	305.3
Dallas	20.3	307.6
Philadelphia	18.8	311.4

INDIVIDUAL STATISTICS

Leading scorers, touchdowns	TD's	Rush	Rec.	Ret.
Randy Moss, New England	23	0	23	0
LaDainian Tomlinson, San Diego	18	15	3	0
Braylon Edwards, Cleveland	16	0	16	0
Joseph Addai, Indianapolis	15	12	3	0

Leading kickers	PAT made/att.	FG made/att.	Longest FG	Pts.
S. Gostkowski, New England	74/74	21/24	45	137
Rob Bironas, Tennessee	27/27	32/36	56	123
Shayne Graham, Cincinnati	32/32	30/33	48	122
Adam Vinatieri, Indianapolis	48/50	22/28	39	114

Leading quarterbacks	Att.	Comp.	Yds.	TD's	Ints.
Tom Brady, New England	578	398	4,806	50	8
Ben Roethlisberger, Pittsburgh	404	264	3,154	32	11
David Garrard, Jacksonville	325	208	2,509	18	3
Peyton Manning, Indianapolis	515	337	4,040	31	14
Jay Cutler, Denver	467	297	3,497	20	14

Leading receivers	Passes caught	Rec. yards	Avg. gain	TD's
Reggie Wayne, Indianapolis	104	1,510	14.5	10
Randy Moss, New England	98	1,493	15.2	23
Chad Johnson, Cincinnati	93	1,440	15.5	8
Brandon Marshall, Denver	102	1,325	13.0	7

Leading rushers	Rushes	Yards	Avg.	TD's
LaDainian Tomlinson, San Diego	315	1,474	4.7	15
Willie Parker, Pittsburgh	321	1,316	4.1	2
Jamal Lewis, Cleveland	298	1,304	4.4	9
Willis McGahee, Baltimore	294	1,207	4.1	7

Leading punters	Punts	Yards	Avg.	Longest
Shane Lechler, Oakland	69	3,385	49.1	70
Todd Sauerbrun, Denver	47	2,200	46.8	65
Mike Scifres, San Diego	74	3,430	46.4	70
Dustin Colquitt, Kansas City	85	3,880	45.6	81

INDIVIDUAL STATISTICS

Leading scorers, touchdowns	TD's	Rush	Rec.	Ret.
Terrell Owens, Dallas	15	0	15	0
Adrian Peterson, Minnesota	13	12	1	0
Plaxico Burress, New York	12	0	12	0
Brian Westbrook, Philadelphia	12	7	5	0

Leading kickers	PAT made/att.	FG made/att.	Longest FG	Pts.
Mason Crosby, Green Bay	48/48	31/39	53	141
Nick Folk, Dallas	53/53	26/31	53	131
Josh Brown, Seattle	43/43	28/34	54	127
Robbie Gould, Chicago	33/33	31/36	49	126

Leading quarterbacks	Att.	Comp.	Yds.	TD's	Ints.
Tony Romo, Dallas	520	335	4,211	36	19
Brett Favre, Green Bay	535	356	4,155	28	15
Jeff Garcia, Tampa Bay	327	209	2,440	13	4
Matt Hasselbeck, Seattle	562	352	3,966	28	12
Donovan McNabb, Philadelphia	473	291	3,324	19	7

Leading receivers	Passes caught	Rec. yards	Avg. gain	TD's
Larry Fitzgerald, Arizona	100	1,409	14.1	10
Terrell Owens, Dallas	81	1,355	16.7	15
Roddy White, Atlanta	83	1,202	12.3	6
Marques Colston, New Orleans	98	1,202	12.3	11

Leading rushers	Rushes	Yards	Avg.	TD's
Adrian Peterson, Minnesota	238	1,341	5.6	12
Brian Westbrook, Philadelphia	278	1,333	4.8	7
Clinton Portis, Washington	325	1,262	3.9	11
Edgerrin James, Arizona	324	1,222	3.8	7

Leading punters	Punts	Yards	Avg.	Longest
Andy Lee, San Francisco	105	4,968	47.3	74
Donnie Jones, St. Louis	78	3,684	47.2	80
Mat McBriar, Dallas	63	2,970	47.1	64
Chris Kluwe, Minnesota	81	3,621	44.7	70

2006-2007 NFL play-offs. In the American Football Conference (AFC) wild-card play-offs, the New England Patriots ripped the visiting New York Jets 37-16 on Jan. 7, 2007, in Foxborough, Massachusetts, while the Indianapolis Colts at home beat the Kansas City Chiefs 23-8 on January 6. The Patriots then upset the top-seeded San Diego Chargers on a last-minute, 31-yard field goal on January 14 in San Diego. The Colts defeated the Baltimore Ravens 15-6 in Baltimore on January 13 in a game that featured seven field goals. In the AFC championship game on January 21, the Colts rallied from a 21-3 first-half deficit to stun the Patriots 38-34 in Indianapolis.

In the National Football Conference (NFC) wild-card play-offs, the Philadelphia Eagles defeated the visiting New York Giants 23-20 on January 7, on a field goal as time expired, and the Seattle Seahawks held off the visiting Dallas Cowboys 21-20 on January 6. The following week, the Chicago Bears defeated Seattle 27-24 on a 49-yard field goal in overtime in Chicago, and the New Orleans Saints defeated the visiting Eagles 27-24. In the NFC championship game on January 21, the Bears crushed the Saints 39-14 in cold, wet conditions at Soldier Field in Chicago.

Colleges. The Louisiana State University (LSU) Tigers routed the Ohio State Buckeyes 38-24 to win the Bowl Championship Series (BCS) title in New Orleans on Jan. 7, 2008. Ohio State jumped to an early 10-0 lead before LSU scored 31 consecutive points. Three Ohio State turnovers and several costly penalties helped seal the LSU victory. LSU became the first team to win two BCS championships since college football switched to the BCS national champion selection system in 1998.

An upsetting season. College football underwent more turnover at the top of the polls than at any time in recent years, as seven teams ranked number one or number two suffered upset losses from September to November 2007.

On September 1, Appalachian State stunned Michigan, the number-five ranked team in the country, 34-32 at home in Ann Arbor. The Mountaineers, members of the Football Championship Subdivision (formerly Division I-AA), led 28-14 at one point but had to rally to retake the lead with one minute to play. They then blocked a potential game-winning field goal by Michigan in the final seconds. No Division I-AA team had beaten a team ranked in the Associated Press poll since 1989.

On Oct. 6, 2007, Stanford, a 41-point underdog, scored a touchdown in the final minute for a 24-23 win over the number-two ranked Southern California Trojans. On November 10, Illinois beat a number-one ranked team for the first time since 1956, stunning Ohio State in Columbus 28-21.

Heisman Trophy. On Dec. 9, 2007, University of Florida quarterback Tim Tebow became the first sophomore in the 72-year history of the Heisman Trophy to capture the award. He edged out University of Arkansas running back Darren McFadden. Tebow was the first college player to run for at least 20 touchdowns and throw at least 20 touchdown passes in the same season.

Notable deaths. Bill Walsh, a master innovator as a head coach, whose West Coast offense transformed the San Francisco 49ers into a powerhouse in the 1980's, died at the age of 75 on July 30, 2007. Max McGee, who scored the first touchdown in Super Bowl history as a receiver for the Green Bay Packers, died on October 20 at age 75. Darryl Stingley, the New England Patriot who was paralyzed in a devastating tackle during a game in 1978, died on April 5, 2007, at the age of 55. Famed Grambling State University coach Eddie Robinson, who won more than 400 games, died on April 3 at the age of 88. Sean Taylor, a fourth-year defensive back for the Washington Redskins, died on November 27 at the age of 24 from a gunshot wound he suffered a day earlier in an attempted robbery at his suburban Miami home.

Canadian Football League. The Saskatchewan Roughriders beat the Winnipeg Blue Bombers 23-19 on November 25 in Canada's Grey Cup game in Toronto. With the victory, the Roughriders won their first title in 18 years.

■ Michael Kates

France. On May 16, 2007, Nicolas Sarkozy was sworn in as president of France. Sarkozy succeeded Jacques Chirac, of whom, after 12 years in office, the public had grown tired. Sarkozy's victory, therefore, was remarkable because he had served as an interior minister in Chirac's government and as head of Chirac's ruling party, the Union for a Popular Movement (UMP).

The campaign involved a hard-fought three-way race between Sarkozy on the right; Socialist Ségolène Royal on the left; and François Bayrou, a third-party centrist candidate. Because France's voting system requires that the winner receive a majority of votes, the final election went to a second round with Sarkozy squaring off against Royal, who would have become the first female president of France had she won. Sarkozy won 53 percent of the vote, and Royal took 47 percent. Critics maintained that Royal had provided no clear vision for moving France into the future.

During the campaign, Sarkozy ran against the very government he had served. He called for a "rupture" with its economic policies, which restricted the workweek for many employees to 35 hours and required high taxes and government spending. He also captured as many centrist voters as his competitor while tacking to the right on questions of crime and immigration to win back votes that had gone to the far-right candi-

date Jean-Marie Le Pen in previous elections.

Cabinet and parliament. To head off criticism of his policies, Sarkozy filled his Cabinet with ministers that included members of the opposition party, women, and minority populations. Socialist Bernard Kouchner, cofounder of the not-for-profit organization Doctors Without Borders, became foreign minister. Seven of the 15 Cabinet positions were filled by women, and several ministers were of Muslim or African background.

Parliamentary elections, which took place in June, allowed Sarkozy to follow through on his campaign promises by giving the UMP a decisive majority. The UMP took 314 seats in the 577-seat National Assembly. The Socialists took 185 seats, and the centrists, 3.

Reforms. Sarkozy earned the nickname of "hyperpresident" when he quickly began a series of reforms intended to curb unemployment and improve the economy. In July, the parliament passed a law to cut taxes on overtime pay, dealing a blow to the 35-hour workweek—one of the shortest in Europe. Such a move, Sarkozy maintained, was needed to restore a "culture of work" that he claimed

had deteriorated over the past 25 years. Also in July, parliament granted greater autonomy to the country's complex state-run university system. Legislators stopped short, however, of allowing the underfunded institutions to charge tuition fees.

Finally, Sarkozy attempted to end public sector pension privileges under which 1.6 million government employees were allowed to retire as young as age 50 with full pensions. The measure led to massive strikes among public transportation workers in October and November, shutting down buses and trains, as well as among civil service workers and those in the energy sector. According to analysts, the fact that Sarkozy did not back down but also did not break the striking unions significantly raised his esteem with the public.

Foreign policy. After assuming office, Sarkozy lost no time in portraying himself as a friend and admirer of the United States. He vacationed in New Hampshire and Maine, where he visited United States President George W. Bush at the Bush family retreat and attempted to heal the transatlantic divide caused by the disagreement between Bush and Chirac over the war in Iraq. Sarkozy also sup-

The 220-foot- (67-meter-) long Hall of Mirrors in the Palace of Versailles outside Paris gleams upon its reopening in June 2007 after a complete restoration and cleaning. Despite wars and revolutions, most of the hall's ornamentation, including the 357 mirrors, is the original material installed in 1684 during the reign of Louis XIV.

ported the United States in its dispute with Iran over Iran's nuclear program and began supporting Israel in public statements. Sarkozy's predecessors had typically maintained better relations with Arab and other Muslim nations than with the United States and Israel.

European Union (EU). In May, Sarkozy announced his intention to revive talks on a new EU treaty. French voters had turned down an EU constitution in a 2005 referendum. In October 2007, EU leaders agreed on a treaty during a summit in Lisbon, Portugal. The new treaty, which was signed in December, created the positions of European Council president and EU head of foreign affairs and reformed the rules by which the member nations vote for new legislation.

Sarkozy strongly opposed the enlargement of the EU to include Turkey, which began negotiations for full membership in 2005. He proposed the creation of a Mediterranean Union, which would include those Middle Eastern and North African countries that did not qualify for EU membership.

Economy. The French economy grew by 1.9 percent in 2007, lagging behind other large economies in Europe. This led to a larger-than-expected budget deficit, which forced Prime Minister François Fillon to announce in July that the nation would be unable to meet the EU's budget targets before 2012. Unemployment declined to 8.6 percent from 9.5 percent in 2006. ■ Jeffrey Kopstein

See also **Europe; Middle East; People in the news** (Nicolas Sarkozy); **Turkey: A Special Report.**

Gabon. See Africa.

Gambia. See Africa.

Gas and gasoline. See Energy supply.

Genetic engineering. See Biology; Medicine.

Geology. The global diversification of mammals—that is, the increase in mammal species around the world—has traditionally been linked to the extinction of the dinosaurs approximately 65 million years ago. The dinosaur extinctions would have opened up many land habitats for the spread of new mammal species. In March 2007, however, a study led by evolutionary biologist Olaf R. P. Bininda-Emonds of the Technical University of Munich in Germany proposed that mammal diversification began roughly 93 million years ago, though mammals did not begin to flourish until some 10 million to 15 million years after the dinosaur extinctions.

The scientists concluded that there were two bursts of mammal *speciation* (creation of species). They reached this conclusion by combining an analysis of genetic material from modern mammals with information on extinct mammals from the fossil record. The genetic analysis allowed the researchers to examine evolutionary changes between related groups of mammals, and the fossils helped the researchers estimate the time elapsing between the appearances of these different groups. Together, this information led to the development of a mammalian "supertree," a model showing the diversification of species over time.

The supertree suggested to the scientists that the flourishing of mammal species coincided with a global temperature increase of about 11 °F (6 °C) approximately 55 million years ago. The temperature increase, known as the Paleocene-Eocene Thermal Maximum, would have led to the development of new habitats and new mammal species, according to Bininda-Emonds's team. Some scientists, however, questioned the accuracy of the time estimates used in Bininda-Emonds's supertree model.

Extraterrestrial explosion? In the so-called Younger Dryas (YD) event, global climate abruptly cooled from 13,000 to 11,500 years ago. The origin of the YD event had long been linked to changes in ocean circulation, though the cause of these changes had been in dispute. In May, a group of geologists led by James Kennett of the University of California at Santa Barbara suggested that ocean circulation and climate changed because of the explosion of a huge asteroid or comet, about 3 miles (5 kilometers) wide, over North America.

The researchers based their reasoning on an examination of 12,900-year-old sediment at more than 20 sites across North America. These sites yielded high concentrations of the rare chemical element iridium, as well as tiny spheres of glass and carbon called nanodiamonds. Kennett's team explained that the iridium—because it is so rare on Earth—likely originated in an asteroid or comet; the nanodiamonds could have been formed by the intense heat and pressure created when the asteroid or comet exploded over the ground. The scientists also discovered a thin layer of charcoal, which they attributed to wildfires.

According to the investigators, the heat from the explosion and fires would have melted the Laurentide Ice Sheet, which covered much of North America at the time. Massive amounts of water from this melting would have entered the Atlantic Ocean, disrupting the flow of currents. As warm currents were diverted away from the North Atlantic Ocean, the atmosphere over North America and Europe would have cooled.

Kennett's team speculated that the cooling resulting from this explosion may have been responsible for the extinction of mammoths and other large mammals. The scientists also noted that the cooling could have led to the disappearance of the Clovis culture, one of the earliest cultures of North America.

Powerful Peru earthquake. On August 15, a magnitude-8.0 earthquake jolted the coast of Peru southeast of the capital, Lima, killing more than 500 people and injuring some 1,500 others. The quake occurred at a depth of about 25 miles (40 kilometers) along the boundary of two converging tectonic plates, rigid slabs that make up Earth's outer shell. The quake was followed by several aftershocks. The tremor was the strongest to strike the region since an 8.4-magnitude earthquake off the coast of Peru in 2001.

Who owns the North Pole? The possibility of billions of tons of undiscovered oil and natural gas beneath the sea floor of the Arctic Ocean—coupled with thinning sea ice in the Arctic—encouraged Russia to send an icebreaker and a research ship to the North Pole in August 2007. Researchers in two submarines launched from the research ship traveled more than 13,200 feet (4,023 meters) to the bottom of the Arctic and planted a titanium Russian flag on the sea floor, symbolically claiming *sovereignty* (ownership rights) to all natural resources lying beneath the sea floor. This was a contentious claim because Canada, Denmark, and the United States also claimed mineral rights beneath the Arctic Ocean.

These different claims were based on differing views of the geological origin of the Lomonosov Ridge, a chain of undersea mountains that bisects the Arctic sea floor. Russia maintained that the Lomonosov Ridge is a natural extension of its continental shelf, as did Canada. Denmark maintained that the ridge originated by *rifting* (spreading of sea floor and building-up of ocean crust) from Greenland, a Danish territory. The United States, by contrast, asserted that the ridge is oceanic in origin and, therefore, belongs to no single country.   ■ Henry T. Mullins

See also **Biology; Canada; Disasters; Peru.**

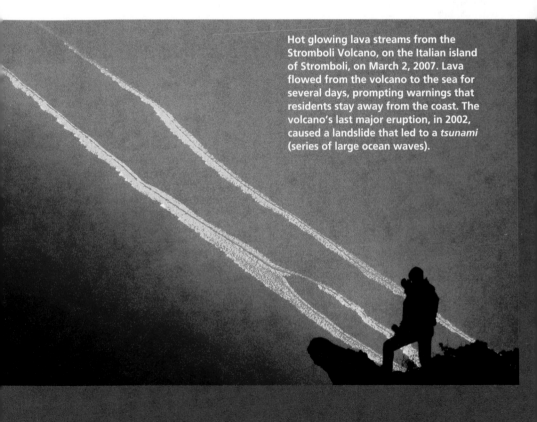

Hot glowing lava streams from the Stromboli Volcano, on the Italian island of Stromboli, on March 2, 2007. Lava flowed from the volcano to the sea for several days, prompting warnings that residents stay away from the coast. The volcano's last major eruption, in 2002, caused a landslide that led to a *tsunami* (series of large ocean waves).

Georgia. An estimated 50,000 antigovernment demonstrators jammed the Georgian capital of Tbilisi in early November 2007 to protest the rule of President Mikheil Saakashvili. Saakashvili, who came to power after the November 2003 "Rose Revolution" that unseated President Eduard Shevardnadze, had grown increasingly unpopular in recent months. Opposition leaders accused him of corruption and human rights violations.

The rally was organized by the National Council, an umbrella group of opposition parties formed after the Sept. 27, 2007, arrest of former Defense Minister Irakli Okruashvili. The government charged Okruashvili with extortion, money laundering, and abuse of office.

On November 7, Georgian police forcefully dispersed the protesters, and Saakashvili declared a state of emergency. The next day, Saakashvili announced that Georgia would hold early presidential elections on Jan. 5, 2008. On Nov. 16, 2007, Saakashvili lifted the state of emergency, sacked Prime Minister Zurab Nogaideli, and nominated Bank of Georgia head Lado Gurgenidze to replace him. Saakashvili resigned as president on November 25. Parliament speaker Nino Burdzhanadze became acting president. Under Georgian law, the serving president cannot campaign. ■ Juliet Johnson

See also **Asia.**

Germany. Angela Merkel continued in 2007 to lead Germany as the country's first female chancellor and head of a so-called "grand coalition" of her own Christian Democratic Union (CDU) and the Social Democratic Party (SPD). However, relations between the coalition members were frequently tense. Merkel resisted attempts by SPD leaders to introduce legislation on a national minimum wage. The parties also disagreed on the privatization of the federal railways, pension reform, and the financing of health care. In October, Vice Chancellor Franz Müntefering of the SPD resigned from office, citing the need to care for his wife, who was ill. Müntefering was widely credited with helping to hold the shaky coalition together, and analysts speculated that without his influence, the coalition may not last until elections scheduled for 2009. The SPD chose Foreign Minister Frank-Walter Steinmeier to succeed Müntefering.

Merkel remained personally popular, but her party grew less so through 2007. The CDU would need to win at least 40 percent of the votes in an election to form a government without the SPD, a development that did not appear likely. Similarly, the SPD, because it had been in government since 1998 (it ruled in coalition with the proenvironment Green Party until 2005), slipped in popularity among its traditional supporters, workers and the poor. It lost both party members and votes to the Left Party, an amalgamation of a radical West German trade union and the Party of Democratic Socialism, a party dominated by former Communists from East Germany. Barring a surge in popularity, a new election could lead to the exclusion of the SPD from government.

Foreign policy. Merkel enjoyed success in foreign policy in 2007. During the year, Germany held the presidency of the Group of Eight (G-8— an informal organization of eight major industrialized nations) and that of the European Union (EU) from January to June.

At the G-8 summit in Heiligendamm in June, Merkel persuaded United States President George W. Bush and other leaders to accept the scientific evidence for global warming. The G-8 also issued a blueprint for proceeding with negotiations for limiting carbon emissions, which scientists believe to be the primary cause of global warming.

As EU president, Germany devoted itself to reviving the initiative for an EU Constitution, which had been put on hold after having been defeated in referendums in France and the Netherlands in 2005. The document outlined reforms to the bloc's inefficient institutions and created the new posts of EU foreign minister and president. Merkel followed the lead of other European leaders in referring to the revised document as a "treaty," rather than a "constitutional treaty," hoping to convince voters that the changes proposed were reasonable and modest. The final text of the revised treaty was approved at a conference in Brussels, Belgium, in June 2007 and was to be put before the parliaments and public of member nations in 2008 for approval.

Merkel faced increasing opposition over Germany's deployment of 3,000 troops to Afghanistan as part of the NATO (North Atlantic Treaty Organization) mission in that country. According to an opinion poll published in October 2007, more than 50 percent of Germans favored an immediate pullout of the troops. Nevertheless, members of the Bundestag (Germany's parliament) voted in October to supply German troops for another year, after Merkel promised that German soldiers would continue to be stationed primarily in the more peaceful northern part of the country. Germany's position irked other NATO members, such as Canada and the Netherlands, whose soldiers were stationed in southern and eastern Afghanistan, where fighting against insurgents was fierce.

Terrorism. On Sept. 4, 2007, German police foiled an attempt by Muslim extremists to set off bombs at the airport in Frankfurt, which is Germany's largest, and at an American air base. Two of those arrested were German nationals who had converted to Islam. A third suspect was a Turkish immigrant. One month earlier, Interior Minister Wolfgang Schäuble proposed legislation permit-

In June 2007, members of Pro Cologne, an extreme right-wing political party, protest plans for the building of a large Islamic mosque in Cologne. The controversy over the mosque re-energized a debate over the role of Islamic immigrants in Germany—most of whom are of Turkish descent—and the limited progress made in integrating them into German society.

ting the government to plant spyware in a suspect's computer to track networks of terrorists. However, the legislation proved highly controversial because of Germany's strict rules restricting police powers. The incident also fed into a general concern about the integration of immigrants from Turkey into mainstream German society. More than 3 million Muslims lived in Germany in 2007, and 70 percent of them were of Turkish origin.

East Germany. The German film *The Lives of Others,* which won the 2007 Academy Award for best foreign film, depicted the grim everyday life of the former Communist state. Although East and West Germany unified in 1990, the economic and social legacies of Communism remained clear in 2007. Eastern Germany's unemployment rate was generally double that of western Germany, wages were significantly lower, and the radical Left Party and the extremist right-wing National Democratic Party enjoyed more popularity than in the west.

Economy. Germany's economy continued solid growth in 2007, with unemployment dropping to 8.1 percent, its lowest level in 14 years. Overall growth, according to EU economists, was expected to reach 2.5 percent, slightly down from 2.9 percent in 2006.   ■ Jeffrey Kopstein

See also **Afghanistan; Europe; Terrorism.**

Ghana. See **Africa.**

Global warming. The IPCC Fourth Assessment Report, a set of reports by the Intergovernmental Panel on Climate Change (IPCC), in 2007 provided new evidence of global warming. In February, the United Nations (UN) panel of scientists and governmental officials from more than 100 nations declared in its first report that the warming of the climate was "unequivocal" and that human activity was "very likely" responsible for most of the increase since the 1950's. The IPCC reported that the primary source of human-caused warming was the addition of heat-trapping greenhouse gases to the atmosphere, mainly by the burning of fossil fuels and land use changes. In November 2007, the IPCC's final report urged governments to stabilize greenhouse gas emissions to prevent dangerous climate change.

The IPCC estimated that the warming from 1906 to 2005 was about 1.33 °F (0.74 °C). The IPCC did not offer a specific prediction for future increases. Instead, a variety of computer climate models were fed with differing greenhouse gas emissions scenarios. The computer projections of warming at 2090-2099 compared with 1980-1999 ranged from 2.0 to 11.5 °F (1.1 to 6.4 °C).

As the climate warms, sea levels rise. The IPCC reported that, during the 1900's, sea level rose from about 5 to 9 inches (12 to 22 centimeters). The IPCC's estimates of sea level rise at 2090-2099 compared with 1980-1999 ranged from about 7 to 23 inches (18 to 59 centimeters).

Climate conference. At the UN Climate Change Conference, held in Bali, Indonesia, in December 2007, delegates agreed on an agenda for negotiations aimed at producing a new climate change treaty to reduce greenhouse gas emissions. The current treaty, the Kyoto Protocol, was set to expire in 2012. The agenda included establishing ways to save tropical rain forests and help the countries most vulnerable to global warming adapt to environmental changes.

The Bali Roadmap, as the agenda was called, passed after the European Union (EU) met United States demands to eliminate specific targets for greenhouse gas emissions. The EU had suggested that developed nations cut their emissions by 25 to 40 percent below 1990 levels by 2020. However, the United States had argued that such restrictions should be voluntary. The United States also had demanded that developing countries, particularly China and India, must also limit emissions. The roadmap called on negotiators to consider ways to encourage developing countries to voluntarily curb the growth in their emissions. The United States reversed its opposition to demands for technological assistance to developing countries in the face of severe criticism from conference delegates.

Heat and fire. Much of Europe experienced exceptional warmth in January 2007. The Netherlands recorded its highest average January temperature since record keeping began in 1706. Austria, Hungary, and Germany also announced record or record-tying averages for January 2007.

Recurrent episodes of searing summer heat in southeastern Europe in 2007 contributed to wildfires in Greece. The European Space Agency reported in August that in that month Greece suffered more wildfires than in all other European countries over the period from 1996 to 2007.

The Met Office, the national weather service of the United Kingdom, revealed in June that the average global temperature from January to April was nearly 0.9 °F (0.5 °C) higher than the long-term average, close to the 0.94 °F (0.52 °C) record-setting value of 1998. However, final data were likely to show that the average global temperature for all of 2007 would be below that of 1998.

In August 2007, the U.S. National Aeronautics and Space Administration (NASA) fixed an error that had placed 1998 as the warmest year on record in the United States. NASA found that 1934 was 0.04 °F (0.02 °C) warmer than 1998. NASA noted that 1998 and 2005 were still tied as the warmest years for the entire globe.

Polar ice. Arctic sea ice dropped in 2007 to its lowest level since satellite measurements started in 1979. The average sea ice extent in September 2007 was 1.65 million square miles (4.28 million square kilometers). That area measured 23 percent lower than the previous record, set in 2005. One factor contributing to the rapid loss was that, in spring 2007, as the Arctic entered its melting season, the region had below-normal ice cover and thinner ice than usual. Another important factor in the year's decline was an unusual wind pattern over the Arctic that forced ice from the eastern Siberian coast to the north and west.

Ice in the Arctic shrank so much that, for the first time on record, the Northwest Passage was completely open, in principle, to ocean vessels for part of 2007. The passage is a sailing path through the straits north of the Canadian mainland that is a short cut between Asia and Europe. However, because of the unusual wind pattern causing ice to drift, the Northern Sea Route near the Eurasian coast, which is frequently partially open, was completely blocked by ice during the summer of 2007.

Although Arctic ice hit a record low in 2007, ice in the Southern Hemisphere reached its greatest extent since record keeping began. According to the University of Illinois at Urbana-Champaign Polar Research Group, Southern Hemisphere ice area reached 6.28 million square miles (16.26 million square kilometers) in September. Antarctic sea ice had shown only a small trend toward decreasing extent. ■ Fred Gadomski

See also **Canada; Weather.**

Golf. Tiger Woods saved his best for last in 2007, capturing his 13th major championship in the last major of the year, the PGA (Professional Golfers' Association) Championship. He posted a record-tying 63 in the second round and cruised to a two-shot victory. The other three men's majors were won by first-timers. Woods also won the PGA TOUR's FedEx Cup, a four-tournament play-off at the end of the season. He collected a $10-million annuity.

In the Ladies Professional Golf Association (LPGA), Morgan Pressel, 18, became the youngest woman to capture a major with her victory in the Kraft Nabisco Championship in April.

Men's professional golf. Zach Johnson, a relatively unknown player, fended off Woods, Retief Goosen, and Rory Sabbatini to capture the Masters on April 8 in Augusta, Georgia. Woods led early in the final round but lost it for the first time ever on a closing round, as Johnson sank three big birdies to close with a 3-under 69 and win by two shots with a 1-over, tied for the worst score by a winner (Sam Snead, 1954, and Jack Burke, 1956).

Angel Cabrera became the first man from Argentina in 40 years to win a major, holding off Woods and Jim Furyk at the United States Open in Oakmont, Pennsylvania, on June 17, 2007. Cabrera shot a 1-under 69 on the final day to finish at 5-over on the tournament. Woods shot

72 on the final day to finish tied with Furyk, one shot back.

Pádraig Harrington became the first Irishman since 1947 to win the British Open, taking advantage of Sergio García's final round collapse at Carnoustie, Scotland, on July 22, 2007. Harrington made up six shots on the final day, shooting a 4-under 67 to García's 2-over 73. Both finished at 7-under. Harrington then beat the Spaniard by a shot in a 4-hole play-off.

Woods's second-round 63 (7-under) on August 10 tied him with four other tournament winners for lowest round in a major and gave him control of the PGA Championship in Tulsa, Oklahoma. Woods built a huge lead and then held off Woody Austin on August 12 to win by two shots with an 8-under 272.

LPGA. Pressel was 18 years, 10 months, and 9 days old when she captured the Kraft Nabisco Championship on April 1 in Rancho Mirage, California. The previous youngest winner was just over 20 years old. Pressel shot a final round of 69 to finish at 3-under 288 to win by a stroke over Brittany Lincicome, Catriona Matthew, and Suzann Pettersen. Pettersen had a four-shot lead with four holes to go but bogeyed three of them.

Pettersen made amends for her disastrous finish by capturing the McDonald's LPGA Championship on June 10 in Havre de Grace, Maryland. Pettersen's final round 5-under 67 left her at -14.

Cristie Kerr made just two bogeys over her final 45 holes to capture the U.S. Women's Open on July 1 in Southern Pines, North Carolina. Kerr's 5-under 279 was good enough for a 2-shot victory.

Lorena Ochoa of Mexico captured the final major of the year on August 5, winning the Women's British Open by four shots. She finished at 5-under on the Old Course at St. Andrews, Scotland.

Champions Tour. On the tour for men at least 50 years old, Denis Watson captured the first major, in the Senior PGA Championship on May 27 in Kiawah Island, South Carolina, shooting a 4-under 68 in the final round to finish at 9-under.

Brad Bryant scored the second biggest final-round comeback in the U.S. Senior Open on July 8, firing a 4-under 68 in Haven, Wisconsin, to rally from 5 shots down entering the final day to overtake Tom Watson and win with a 6-under 282.

Watson won his third Senior British Open in five years on July 29, topping Mark O'Meara and Australia's Stewart Ginn by one stroke at Gullane, Scotland. His 2-over 73 left him at even. Mark McNulty finished with a 16-under 272 to win The Tradition, on August 19 in Sunriver, Oregon, by five strokes. Loren Roberts won the final major of the year, the Senior Players Championship, in Baltimore on October 7.   ■ Michael Kates

See also **Sports.**

Great Britain. See **United Kingdom.**

Lorena Ochoa of Mexico wins the Women's British Open at St. Andrews, Scotland, on August 5, 2007, by four shots. With her victory, Ochoa became the first Mexican player to win a major LPGA championship.

Greece. In parliamentary elections called six months ahead of schedule and held in September 2007, the center-right New Democracy Party of Prime Minister Kostas Karamanlis won a second term in office. New Democracy captured 42 percent of the vote, beating its chief rival, the Panhellenic Socialist Movement (PASOK), which until 2004 had governed the country for most of the past 20 years. PASOK won 38 percent of the vote.

Although New Democracy gained more votes than PASOK, a new system of proportional representation for translating votes into seats reduced New Democracy's parliamentary majority from 30 seats to 4. Political analysts predicted that such a slim margin would likely force New Democracy to cooperate on legislation with the far-right Popular Orthodox Rally (La.O.S.). La.O.S. won slightly more than 3 percent of the vote, the minimum required for a party to hold seats in parliament. Karamanlis called an early election because he sought a new mandate to reform the country's pension system, tackle corruption, and change the constitution to permit nonprofit private universities to operate as an alternative to Greece's state-run institutions. Strikes against pension reform began in late November and continued in December.

Forest fires. Greece experienced its worst wildfires in more than a century in 2007. Dozens of fires broke out in June and July, but the greatest damage occurred in August. Two heat waves with temperatures as high as 115 °F (46 °C) contributed to extremely dry conditions. About 494,000 acres (200,000 hectares) of forests and farmland burned, and more than 60 people died. Critics charged that the government's slow response and outdated firefighting equipment did little to slow the spread of the fires.

The Greek government blamed arsonists for some of the fires. Eyewitnesses reported that fires were set by property developers who hoped to build expensive houses on the cleared forest areas. The government promised that all burnt forests would be restored and that development would be forbidden. However, several months later, such efforts had not yet begun.

Economy. Greece's economy in 2007 continued to be plagued by high youth unemployment. At 25 percent, the unemployment rate among the young was the highest in the European Union (EU). EU economists forecast that the total unemployment rate in 2007 would fall to 8.4 percent, from 8.9 percent in 2006. Economic growth in Greece was expected to decline in 2007, to 4.1 percent from 4.3 percent in 2006, still well above the 2.6 average for the Eurozone as a whole (the group of countries that share the common currency, the euro). ■ Jeffrey Kopstein

See also **Europe; Weather.**

Grenada. See Latin America; West Indies.

Guatemala. Álvaro Colom Caballeros, 56, of the center-left National Unity of Hope coalition won a presidential runoff election on Nov. 4, 2007. Crime figured as the central issue during the most violent political campaign in Guatemalan history. More than 50 candidates and campaign workers were killed in the year leading up to the balloting.

Amid rampant lawlessness, residents of urban slums created and armed vigilante groups to defend themselves against well-organized gangs and drug cartels. The cartels were fighting for control of a main route used to transport illicit narcotics to the United States. In September 2007, the U.S. government agreed to provide Guatemala with $2.3 million to fight drug trafficking, gangs, and organized crime. Some of this aid was earmarked for the prosecution of drug cases.

In late August, the U.S. Coast Guard seized 1,210 pounds (549 kilograms) of cocaine, worth $350 million, from a homemade submarine off Guatemala's coast. Authorities detained four men, floating in the water, who *scuttled* (cut holes in) the craft, sending it and the rest of its cargo to the ocean floor. ■ Nathan A. Haverstock

See also **Latin America.**

Guinea. See Africa.

Guinea-Bissau. See Africa.

Guyana. See Latin America.

Haiti. In early 2007, United Nations (UN) peacekeepers touched off a fierce firefight when they launched an offensive against heavily armed gangs that controlled Cité Soleil, a huge, notorious slum in the Haitian capital of Port-au-Prince. UN forces stepped up arrests of gang members, more than 500 of whom were in custody by July.

In August, UN Secretary-General Ban Ki-moon visited Haiti and called for a one-year extension of the UN mission, which accounted for 85 percent of Haiti's security forces.

Venezuelan aid to Haiti totaled more than $200 million during 2007. Most of this was earmarked for infrastructure projects, including the construction of a small oil refinery and an electric power plant, and airport modernization. Much of the balance paid for health care and garbage collection in Haiti's burgeoning slums.

Tragedies at sea left dozens of Haitians dead in 2007. The United States Coast Guard reported a surge in the number of Haitians arrested while trying to reach the United States in unfit, overloaded boats. In March, about 50 people died or were lost at sea when their boat caught fire off Cap-Haïtien. In May, another vessel capsized near the Turks and Caicos Islands, leaving at least 60 people dead or missing. ■ Nathan A. Haverstock

See also **Latin America; West Indies.**

Harness racing. See Horse racing.

Health care issues. The key health policy debate in the United States Congress in 2007 concerned the State Children's Health Insurance Program (SCHIP), which was originally passed in 1997 and was up for renewal in 2007. SCHIP, which is funded jointly by federal and state dollars and administered by the states, targets children whose families earn too much to qualify for Medicaid but not enough to afford private health insurance.

The administration of U.S. President George W. Bush was willing to spend an additional $5 billion on SCHIP over the five years that began with fiscal year 2008 (Oct. 1, 2007-Sept. 30, 2008). The Democratic-controlled Congress, however, wanted a bill that would broaden SCHIP to cover about 10 million people, mainly children, up from 6.6 million covered in 2007. The bill would have raised SCHIP spending over the next five years from $25 billion to $60 billion.

President Bush vetoed the bill on October 3, saying that it was too expensive, among other concerns. Congress passed a slightly revised version, which the president again vetoed on December 12. A bill to maintain SCHIP's current coverage level until 2009 was passed in late 2007.

State insurance programs. While Congress and the Bush administration fought over expansion of SCHIP, several states reworked health care programs. Maine's effort to broaden insurance coverage continued in 2007, though it faced problems with cost and affordability. Vermont launched Green Mountain Care, a family of low-cost and free health coverage programs for uninsured residents. The California legislature passed a bill providing universal coverage, which Governor Arnold Schwarzenegger vetoed as too costly. The governor and legislators then negotiated a compromise bill that passed the Assembly on December 17. It would require most residents to have coverage but provides financial help for those with lower incomes. Funding, which would involve taxes on employers, hospitals, and tobacco sales, would be put to the voters in the November 2008 election. The state Senate had not voted on the bill at the end of the year.

In September, Indiana received federal permission to expand health coverage under the Medicaid program. Low-income adults in Indiana were asked to contribute to health savings accounts to gain access to as much as $300,000 in coverage. Indiana raised cigarette taxes to pay for the expansion, which was expected to assist 130,000 uninsured families and childless adults.

In 2007, the first year of a Massachusetts program to provide health insurance to all residents, nearly 160,000 low-income people enrolled, far more than anticipated. State officials estimated that the cost of the program could be as much as $147 million over budget for the fiscal year. In December, a state panel approved program changes for 2008, including cutting payments to physicians and hospitals, limiting patient choice, and possibly increasing patient costs.

The uninsured. In August 2007, the U.S. Census Bureau announced that 47 million Americans lacked health insurance in 2006. Texas led with 24.1 percent of the population uninsured; Minnesota had the lowest rate, 8.6 percent.

Food and Drug Administration. The U.S. Food and Drug Administration (FDA), which oversees the safety of drugs, food, and other products, was sharply criticized by Congress and by consumer groups in 2007 for what critics called "lax" approval and inspection procedures. The FDA faced broad public concern over the safety of some drugs, including heartburn and anemia medicines; drug ingredients manufactured in China; and a widely prescribed diabetes drug, Avandia, which some scientists concluded caused heart problems. Critics also faulted the agency for failing to inspect imported foodstuffs, particularly from China; and for the FDA response to outbreaks of *E. coli* bacteria and *Salmonella* bacteria in food.

On September 27, President Bush signed the Food and Drug Administration Amendments Act of 2007, which gave the FDA the authority to determine if approved drugs or medical devices pose health risks. The act provided greater resources and authority to monitor medications and medical devices already on the market.

Walter Reed Army Medical Center in Washington, D.C., a historic site of care for wounded service personnel, was found in 2007 to be providing substandard treatment. In the wake of the scandal, the hospital commandant, Major General George Weightman, was relieved of duty on March 1, and Army Secretary Francis J. Harvey resigned the following day. A panel appointed by Defense Secretary Robert Gates to investigate the situation issued a stinging report in April, citing poor leadership, inadequate facilities, and staff shortages.

The surgeon general. In May, President Bush nominated Kentucky physician James Holsinger, Jr., for U.S. surgeon general. Two days before Holsinger's confirmation hearings, the former surgeon general Richard Carmona announced that he had been "muzzled" by the Bush administration, which did not allow him to speak out or release reports on sensitive issues. Holsinger faced difficult questions during the hearings, based largely on suspicions that he might be subject to political pressure from the Bush administration. Holsinger had yet to be confirmed at the end of 2007.   ■ Emily Friedman

See also **Drugs; Food; Medicine; Public health.**

NATIONAL HOCKEY LEAGUE STANDINGS

WESTERN CONFERENCE

Central Division	W.	L.	OTW.[†]	OTL.[††]	Pts.
Detroit Red Wings*	50	19	5	13	113
Nashville Predators*	51	23	9	8	110
St. Louis Blues	34	35	10	13	81
Columbus Blue Jackets	33	42	9	7	73
Chicago Blackhawks	31	42	9	9	71
Northwest Division					
Vancouver Canucks*	49	26	17	7	105
Minnesota Wild*	48	26	17	8	104
Calgary Flames*	43	29	5	10	96
Colorado Avalanche	44	31	8	7	95
Edmonton Oilers	32	43	4	7	71
Pacific Division					
Anaheim Ducks*	48	20	9	14	110
San Jose Sharks*	51	26	3	5	107
Dallas Stars*	50	25	15	7	107
Los Angeles Kings	27	41	6	14	68
Phoenix Coyotes	31	46	7	5	67

EASTERN CONFERENCE

Northeast Division	W.	L.	OTW.	OTL.	Pts.
Buffalo Sabres*	53	22	15	7	113
Ottawa Senators*	48	25	4	9	105
Toronto Maple Leafs	40	31	8	11	91
Montreal Canadiens	42	34	8	6	90
Boston Bruins	35	41	13	6	76
Atlantic Division					
New Jersey Devils*	49	24	13	9	107
Pittsburgh Penguins*	47	24	16	11	105
New York Rangers*	42	30	12	10	94
New York Islanders*	40	30	10	12	92
Philadelphia Flyers	22	48	4	12	56
Southeast Division					
Atlanta Thrashers*	43	28	14	11	97
Tampa Bay Lightning*	44	33	15	5	93
Carolina Hurricanes	40	34	6	8	88
Florida Panthers	36	31	5	16	86
Washington Capitals	28	40	5	14	70

*Made play-offs   [†]Overtime wins   [††]Overtime losses

STANLEY CUP CHAMPIONS—Anaheim Ducks
(defeated Ottawa Senators, 4 games to 1)

LEADING SCORERS	Games	Goals	Assists	Pts.
Sidney Crosby, Pittsburgh	79	36	84	120
Joe Thornton, San Jose	82	22	92	114
Vincent Lecavalier, Tampa Bay	82	52	56	108
Dany Heatley, Ottawa	82	50	55	105
Martin St. Louis, Tampa Bay	82	43	59	102

LEADING GOALIES (26 or more games)	Games	Goals against	Avg.
Niklas Backstrom, Minnesota	41	73	1.97
Dominik Hasek, Detroit	56	114	2.05
Martin Brodeur, New Jersey	78	171	2.18
Marty Turco, Dallas	67	140	2.23
J.-S. Giguere, Anaheim	56	122	2.26

AWARDS

Adams Award (coach of the year)—Alain Vigneault, Vancouver

Calder Trophy (best rookie)—Evgeni Malkin, Pittsburgh

Clancy Trophy (leadership)—Saku Koivu, Montreal

Hart Trophy (most valuable player)—Sidney Crosby, Pittsburgh

Jennings Trophy (goalkeeper[s] for team with fewest goals against)—Niklas Backstrom and Manny Fernandez, Minnesota

Lady Byng Trophy (sportsmanship)—Pavel Datsyuk, Detroit

Masterton Trophy (perseverance, dedication to hockey)—Phil Kessel, Boston

Norris Trophy (best defenseman)—Nicklas Lidstrom, Detroit

Pearson Award (best player as voted by NHL players)—Sidney Crosby, Pittsburgh

Ross Trophy (leading scorer)—Sidney Crosby, Pittsburgh

Selke Trophy (best defensive forward)—Rod Brind'Amour, Carolina

Smythe Trophy (most valuable player in Stanley Cup)—Scott Niedermayer, Anaheim

Vezina Trophy (best goalkeeper)—Martin Brodeur, New Jersey

Hockey. In the National Hockey League (NHL) in 2007, the Anaheim Ducks won their first Stanley Cup in the franchise's 14-year history, defeating the Ottawa Senators 6-2 on June 6 in Anaheim to become the first team from California to win the title. Ducks captain Scott Niedermayer won the Conn Smythe Trophy as the most valuable player in the play-offs.

Pittsburgh's Sidney Crosby, 19, became both the youngest player in league history to post consecutive 100-point seasons and the youngest scoring champion, with 120 points (36 goals, 84 assists). Crosby won the Hart Trophy as the league's Most Valuable Player.

Play-offs. Anaheim had advanced to its second Stanley Cup finals by eliminating the Detroit Red Wings 4 games to 2. Ottawa gained its first Finals since it joined the league in 1992 (an earlier team also went by the name Ottawa Senators and won multiple Cups) by eliminating the Buffalo Sabres 4 games to 1.

In the Stanley Cup Finals, Anaheim captured the first two games at home but lost Game 3 in Ottawa. Ducks defenseman Chris Pronger was suspended for Game 4 because of an elbow to Senator Dean McAmmond's head in Game 3. It was Pronger's second one-game suspension of the play-offs. Anaheim captured Game 4 and closed out the series back home for a 4-games-to-1 triumph.

Regular season. In the Eastern Conference, Buffalo finished with a league-best 53 wins and 113 points to win the Northeast Division. New Jersey posted 49 wins and 107 points to take the Atlantic, and Atlanta's 43 wins and 97 points were enough to win the Southeast.

In the Western Conference, Detroit won 50 games and finished with 113 points to capture the Central. Anaheim won 48 games to take a closely contested Pacific Division with 110 points, and Vancouver acquired the Northwest title with 49 wins and 105 points.

World championships. Canada won its 24th men's world title with a 4-2 triumph over Finland in the finals on May 13 in Moscow. The Canadians topped the United States 5-1 on April 10 in Winnipeg, Canada, for the women's championship.

Colleges. Michigan State University (East Lansing) won its third men's National Collegiate

Athletic Association (NCAA) championship in school history with a 3-1 victory over Boston College on April 7 in St. Louis. The University of Wisconsin (Madison) women earned their second consecutive championship, beating the University of Minnesota-Duluth 4-1 on March 18 in Lake Placid, New York.   ■ Michael Kates

Honduras. See Latin America.

Horse racing. Three different horses won Triple Crown races in 2007—including the first filly to capture the Belmont Stakes in more than a century—as the racing world was denied a Triple Crown winner for the 29th straight year.

Barbaro, the 2006 Kentucky Derby winner who broke down at that year's Preakness Stakes, was euthanized on Jan. 29, 2007, after an eight-month battle to save his life.

Three-year-olds. On May 5, favorite Street Sense rallied from second-to-last in the 20-horse field to power to a 2 ¼-length victory over Hard Spun in the 133rd Kentucky Derby before 156,635 people, the third largest crowd in Derby history. Jockey Calvin Borel won in his fifth try at the Derby, and it was trainer Carl Nafzger's second victory at Louisville. Street Sense became the first winner of

the Breeders' Cup Juvenile as a 2-year-old to win the Derby the following year, making him the first 2-year-old champion to win the Derby since Spectacular Bid in 1979.

In the Preakness Stakes on May 19, 2007, at Baltimore's Pimlico Race Course, Curlin mustered a late charge and passed Street Sense on his final stride to win at the wire. Two weeks later, filly Rags to Riches outran Curlin down the back stretch to win the Belmont Stakes on June 9 in Elmont, New York—the first female horse to capture that race since Tanya won in 1905. The last filly to win any Triple Crown race was Winning Colors in 1988.

International racing. Invasor captured the $6-million World Cup on March 31, 2007, in Dubai, United Arab Emirates (UAE), beating Premium Tap by 1 ¾ lengths in the world's richest race. Discreet Cat, the only horse to ever beat Invasor, finished last. Invasor had won 11 of its 12 races. Asiatic Boy easily won the $2-million UAE Derby by nearly 10 lengths.

In European racing, Authorized won the Epsom Derby on June 2 by five lengths, ridden by jockey Frankie Dettori. Soldier of Fortune cruised to a nine-length victory in the Irish Derby on July 1. Dylan Thomas, with jockey Kiernan Fallon aboard, won the Prix de l'Arc de Triomphe on October 7 in Paris. Later in 2007, Fallon went on trial in the United Kingdom on race-fixing charges.

Harness. Donato Hanover captured the first and third jewels of the trotting triple crown, the $1.5-million Hambletonian on August 4 and the

Rags to Riches, ridden by John R. Velazquez, wins the 139th running of the Belmont Stakes on June 9, 2007. Rags to Riches was the first filly to take the Belmont since Tanya captured the famous race in 1905.

MAJOR HORSE RACES OF 2007

THOROUGHBRED RACING

Race	Winner	Value to Winner
Belmont Stakes	Rags to Riches	$600,000
Blue Grass Stakes	Dominican	$450,000
Breeders' Cup Classic	Curlin	$2,700,000
Breeders' Cup Dirt Mile	Corinthian	$520,000
Breeders' Cup Distaff	Ginger Punch	$1,220,400
Breeders' Cup Mile	Kip Deville	$1,420,000
Breeders' Cup Sprint	Midnight Lute	$1,080,000
Breeders' Cup Turf	English Channel	$1,620,000
Breeders' Cup Filly & Mare Sprint	Maryfield	$607,500
Breeders' Cup Filly & Mare Turf	Lahudood	$1,150,200
Breeders' Cup Juvenile	War Pass	$1,080,000
Breeders' Cup Juvenile Fillies	Indian Blessing	$1,080,000
Breeders' Cup Juvenile Turf	Nownownow	$540,000
Canadian International Stakes	Cloudy's Knight	$1,242,480
Epsom Derby (United Kingdom)	Authorized	£709,750
Dubai World Cup (United Arab Emirates)	Invasor	$3,600,000
Haskell Invitational Stakes	Any Given Saturday	$600,000
Hollywood Gold Cup Stakes	Lava Man	$450,000
Irish Derby (Ireland)	Soldier of Fortune	€847,500
Jockey Club Gold Cup	Curlin	$450,000
Kentucky Derby	Street Sense	$1,450,000
Kentucky Oaks	Rags to Riches	$300,000
King George VI and Queen Elizabeth Diamond Stakes (United Kingdom)	Dylan Thomas	£425,850
Lane's End Stakes	Hard Spun	$300,000
Oaklawn Handicap	Lawyer Room	$300,000
Pacific Classic Stakes	Student Council	$600,000
Preakness Stakes	Curlin	$600,000
Prix de l'Arc de Triomphe (France)	Dylan Thomas	€1,142,800
Santa Anita Derby	Tiago	$450,000
Santa Anita Handicap	Lava Man	$600,000
Stephen Foster Handicap	Flashy Bull	$498,863
Travers Stakes	Street Sense	$600,000
Woodbine Mile (Canada)	Shakespeare	$600,000

HARNESS RACING

Race	Winner	Value to Winner
Cane Pace	Always a Virgin	$150,000
Hambletonian	Donato Hanover	$750,000
Kentucky Futurity	Donato Hanover	$348,740
Little Brown Jug	Tell All	$240,000
Meadowlands Pace	Southwind Lynx	$500,000
Messenger Stakes	Always a Virgin	$362,740
Woodrow Wilson	Dali	$207,500
Yonkers Trot	Green Day	$322,356

€ = euro (European Union dollar)

$742,000 Kentucky Futurity on October 6. Green Day won the second leg on August 25 in the Yonkers Trot. In the pacing triple crown, Always a Virgin captured two-thirds of the triple crown, winning the Cane Pace on September 3 and the Messenger Stakes on October 27. Tell All won the Little Brown Jug on September 20. ■ Michael Kates

Hospital. See Health care issues.

Housing. See Building and construction.

Houston continued to grapple with both crime and the perception of high crime in 2007. Statistics released by the United States Federal Bureau of Investigation (FBI) in June showed that Houston's homicide rate had reached 18.2 per 100,000 residents during 2006. According to the FBI report, Houston's murder rate ranked second only to Philadelphia's among the 10 largest U.S. cities.

Houston officials blamed much of the homicide increase on evacuees from 2005's Hurricane Katrina, which devastated New Orleans and much of the Gulf Coast. More than 100,000 people relocated from New Orleans to Houston. Police officials reacted by increasing patrols in "hot spots"—areas that experienced spikes in crime. Police credited the strategy for decreasing Houston's homicide rate by 13 percent during the first nine months of 2007, compared with the same period in 2006.

The public remained concerned about the spike in violent crime, however. According to the annual Houston Area Survey, compiled by sociologist Stephen Klineberg of Rice University in Houston, crime topped traffic and the economy as the city's "biggest problem" for the first time in years.

Because crime steadily fell during the 1990's, and as a result of tight budgets, fewer police officers patrolled Houston streets in the 2000's. City officials scrambled to attract new police recruits. The city had 4,800 officers in 2007, compared with a high of 5,400 in the late 1990's.

University scandal. In October 2007, jurors deadlocked after an eight-week trial of ousted Texas Southern University President Priscilla Slade, resulting in a mistrial. Prosecutors said Slade spent more than $500,000 of the Houston-based university's money to support a lavish lifestyle, including $100,000 in bar tabs. Slade was fired in May 2006 after an internal audit found she had failed to follow university procedures and state laws in spending at least $260,000. Immediately after the mistrial, prosecutors said they would retry the case. Although a new trial was scheduled for March 2008, it was unclear at year's end whether prosecutors would follow through.

The initial scandal followed revelations of Slade's spending, and the subsequent trial raised further questions among state officials about the future of an already troubled university with declining enrollment and low graduation rates. In November 2007, the university released a 167-page plan to address the concerns of state lawmakers, including the adoption of new policies that allow regents much tighter control over spending. The policies also beefed up academic counseling and support for students.

Philanthropy. Two Houston hospitals benefited from millions of dollars in donations from members of the city's business community. In September, Robert McNair, the owner of the Houston Texans football team, gave $100 million to Baylor College of Medicine for cancer and neuroscience research. In October, energy magnate Dan Duncan and his wife, Jan, gave $50 million to Texas Children's Hospital for pediatric research.

Light rail expansion. In October 2007, the Metropolitan Transit Authority (Metro) board voted to add five new lines to its existing, 7.5-mile (12-kilometer) starter line, vastly expanding the city's rail transit footprint. The board opted for the more expensive light rail lines over bus rapid transit, which had proved less popular with riders. Officials expected construction on the new lines to begin in April 2008. The planned $1.3-billion expansion—half of which was to be funded by federal dollars—would increase the total length of the Metro system to 40 miles (64 kilometers). Critics had blasted the transit agency for spending too much on a light rail system that served a relatively small segment of the population. Metro's proposed routes were also criticized because some would cut through existing neighborhoods.

Mayor reelected. In November 2007, Houston voters elected Democratic Mayor Bill White to a third and final term with more than 85 percent of the vote. Term limits bar Houston mayors from seeking a fourth term. ■ Eric Berger

See also **City**.

Human rights. See Civil rights; Disability.

Hungary. The center-left governing coalition led by Ferenc Gyurcsány of the Hungarian Socialist Party struggled in 2007 to implement a far-reaching economic reform program, despite sinking approval ratings. Gyurcsány was already politically wounded by revelations in a tape recording released in September 2006 in which he admitted he had made campaign pledges in the country's April parliamentary elections that he had never intended to honor. During 2007, Hungary's economy stagnated, adding to the governing coalition's political burdens.

In a public opinion poll released in November 2007, Prime Minister Gyurcsány registered approval from only 26 percent of respondents. By comparision, Viktor Orbán, the leader of the chief opposition party, scored a 50-percent approval rating. The poll also indicated that if an election was held at that time, Orbán's party would outpoll Gyurcsány's by better than two-to-one.

Economic reform program. In July, the governing coalition proposed a reform program. It was designed to boost the country's sagging economy—which posted a 1.2-percent growth rate in the second quarter of 2007, down sharply from the 3.9-percent growth rate of 2006—and to reduce Hungary's ballooning budget deficit. In 2007, the deficit amounted to more than 9 percent of Hungary's *gross domestic product* (GDP)—the value of

Security guards use umbrellas to shield Budapest Mayor Gábor Demszky from eggs thrown by antigovernment protesters during a ceremony on Hungary's national day, March 15. Many Hungarian officials in 2007 shared in public displeasure at a declining economy and the revelation that President Ferenc Gyurcsány had no intention of keeping campaign promises.

all the goods and services produced in a country in a year. The deficit was of particular concern to European Union (EU) officials and to Hungarian leaders favoring Hungary's entry into the Eurozone, the group of EU nations that use the euro as their common currency. EU rules require that countries admitted to the Eurozone have a current budget deficit no greater than 3 percent of GDP. Hungary joined the EU—but not the Eurozone—in 2004.

The government's 2007 economic reforms included tax and fee hikes and cuts in government energy subsidies to households. In September, parliament approved a massive overhaul of Hungary's health care system, which, when implemented in 2008, would bring private insurers into the system for the first time. In late 2007, some analysts projected that Hungary could become eligible to adopt the euro sometime between 2011 and 2014.

Protest. On Oct. 23, 2007, tens of thousands of Hungarians filled the streets of Budapest, the capital, to protest the Gyurcsány government's economic austerity and reform policies. The demonstration coincided with the 51st anniversary of Hungary's ill-fated 1956 uprising against Soviet domination. Opposition leaders called for a referendum on the government's economic policies, a proposal that the Gyurcsány government rejected.
■ Sharon L. Wolchik

See also **Europe.**

Ice skating. Brian Joubert became the first Frenchman in 42 years to capture a world championship, and Japanese women grabbed the top two spots, leading a sweep of the women's medals by Asian women at the world ice skating championships in Tokyo in 2007. Kimmie Meissner became the first American woman since 1991 to capture a national title after winning a world championship, which she did in 2006.

World championships. In Tokyo, Joubert built up a big lead in the short program and then held on for the title on March 22, 2007, finishing third in the free skate behind Japan's Daisuke Takahashi and the two-time defending champion Stéphane Lambiel of Switzerland. Takahashi's dynamic performance earned him a silver, the highest finish ever by a Japanese man. Lambiel took the bronze.

In the women's competition, South Korea's Yu-Na Kim scored a record 71.95 in the short program but fell on two triple Lutzes in the free skate and dropped down to third on March 24. Miki Ando captured her first world title, despite finishing second in the free skate behind Mao Asada. Asada finished second.

China's Shen Xue and Zhao Hongbo won their third pairs title on March 21, and Bulgaria's Albena Denkova and Maxim Staviski captured their second ice dancing title on March 23.

China's Zhao Hongbo tosses his spinning partner, Shen Xue, during the exhibition portion of the World Figure Skating Championships in Tokyo on March 25, 2007. The two had won the pairs gold medal at the world championships competition on March 21.

The U.S. Championships were held in Spokane, Washington, in late January. Meissner took her first national title despite finishing third in the final free skate, moving ahead of Emily Hughes, who tumbled on a jump and into second place. Evan Lysacek won the men's title with a brilliant free skate, beating Ryan Bradley by almost 30 points. Three-time champion Johnny Weir won the bronze medal.

Brooke Castile and Ben Okolski earned their first American pairs title, moving up from third in the short program. Tanith Belbin and Ben Agosto won their fourth straight dance title.

The European championships were held in Warsaw, Poland, in late January. Joubert captured his second European title, rallying from second in the free skate to top Tomás Verner of the Czech Republic. In the women's competition, Carolina Kostner, in her first competition since tearing a ligament in her left ankle, beat Sarah Meier of Switzerland with a personal best 114.33 in the free skate to become the first Italian woman to win the title.

In pairs competition, Russians failed to win for the first time since 1995. Aliona Savchenko and Robin Szolkowy of Germany took the title. Isabelle Delobel and Olivier Schoenfelder of France won the ice dancing title.　■ Michael Kates

Iceland. See Europe.

Immigration continued to be a hot-button political issue in the United States in 2007. One out of every eight U.S. residents that year was an immigrant—the highest rate since the 1920's.

Congress. A failed vote to discontinue debate in the U.S. Senate on June 28, 2007, effectively ended an attempt to overhaul U.S. immigration laws. The bill had bipartisan support, including that of U.S. President George W. Bush, but also faced bipartisan opposition. The bill would have created a means by which many of the country's 12 million illegal immigrants could have gained legal status and eventual citizenship. The bill also would have set up a temporary guest worker program and allocated billions of dollars for border security. Many conservatives opposed the bill's immigrant legalization scheme, calling it amnesty for breaking the law. A number of liberals opposed provisions that would have made it harder for extended family members to join relatives in the United States.

State laws. In November, the National Conference of State Legislatures reported that the legislatures of 46 states had enacted 244 pieces of immigration legislation in 2007—nearly triple the number of enactments (84) in 2006. The 2007 laws ranged from punitive to protective. Arizona enacted a law to revoke the operating license of any business that is twice caught knowingly employing undocumented workers. Oklahoma made

it a felony to transport or harbor illegal immigrants and ended several forms of government aid for such immigrants. Many states passed bills requiring verification of legal status before issuance of a professional or driver's license or before payment of public benefits. However, California extended many of the state's public benefits to migrant workers. On September 21, New York Governor Eliot Spitzer announced a plan to allow illegal immigrants to apply for driver's licenses, but public opposition to the plan prompted him to abandon it on November 14.

The Bush administration on August 10 announced a package of initiatives to tighten border security and pressure employers to fire illegal immigrants. The package included new guidelines for employers who receive "no-match" letters informing them that several of their employees have Social Security numbers that do not match government records. Under the guidelines, if an employee could not resolve the no-match problem within 90 days, the employer would have to discharge the employee or face fines or prosecution. But on October 10, a federal judge ordered an indefinite delay on implementation of the guidelines. He said that the guidelines, though intended to target illegal immigrants, would also harm innocent workers and employers.　■ Mike Lewis

See also **Chicago; City; Latin America; Mexico.**

India. An agreement between India and the United States for cooperation on peaceful nuclear programs developed in 2007 into a controversy that shook the government of Prime Minister Manmohan Singh. The agreement was concluded on July 27 after two years of negotiations. United States President George W. Bush called it an important step in "deepening our strategic partnership with India, a vital world leader." A key Indian national security official said it transformed India's relationship with the United States.

The agreement provided for the United States to sell civilian nuclear technology and fuel to India, which had conducted nuclear tests in 1974 and 1998. Critics in the U.S. Congress and in other countries claimed the agreement violated international efforts to restrict nuclear weapons. They argued that U.S. help would enable India to divert some of its nuclear resources from peaceful power production to weapons. The agreement included U.S. help for India to build a nuclear fuel repository and find other sources of nuclear fuel if further U.S. help were cut off. Under U.S. law, nuclear cooperation would be stopped with any country that tested nuclear weapons.

United States congressional approval of the final agreement remained uncertain in late 2007, and arguments over it erupted in India. Although most technical observers said the United States

Elephants were banned from the traffic-choked streets of India's commercial capital, Mumbai, in July, after animal-rights activists convinced city officials that the animals were not properly fed and that walking on hot roads caused skin and foot problems.

had made key concessions to India, opponents of Singh's government contended that the agreement had compromised Indian sovereignty. Leftist members of Singh's coalition government attacked the agreement. The Hindu nationalist Bharatiya Janata Party (BJP) also joined in the attacks, which disrupted Parliament on August 13. Communists in Singh's coalition joined BJP members in protests that interrupted his presentation of the agreement. The head of the coalition's largest element, Congress Party chairwoman Sonia Gandhi, denounced the Communist opposition as "sloganeering."

On January 25, Russia agreed to help India build four nuclear power plants, in addition to two already under construction with Russian assistance. Russia also planned to expand its help with India's military aircraft industry, which the Soviet Union had begun aiding in the 1960's.

National politics. India's first woman president took office on July 25, 2007. Pratibha Patil was elected by national and state assembly members to the largely ceremonial position. Her election had been strongly opposed amid accusations of scandals during a mediocre political career in the Congress Party. Political experts considered Patil's selection to be an official recognition of the importance of women, who suffered strong discrimination in India.

Gandhi's son, Rahul, was named to a leading role in the Congress Party on September 24. Rahul Gandhi was descended from three generations of Indian prime ministers, and some observers saw his appointment as the first step toward his possible future as a national leader.

The Congress Party lost control of state assemblies in the states of Punjab and Uttarakhand in February elections. Congress and the BJP lost seats in India's most populous state, Uttar Pradesh; a local party won elections in April and May.

Violence continued to wrack India in 2007. The separatist United Liberation Front of Assam, which sought independence and opposed immigrant workers in Assam state, was blamed for attacks in January and February that killed some 90 migrant workers and several government officials. The group was also suspected of involvement in a series of attacks in August that left more than 30 people dead. Maoist guerrillas who operated in scattered rural areas of eastern India in 2007 attacked a police camp at Bijapur in Chhattisgarh state on March 15, killing 55 people.

Other violence was blamed on militant Islamic groups that officials claimed were based in Bangladesh or Pakistan. On February 19, two bombs exploded in north India on the "Friendship Express," a recently opened train service between India and Pakistan, killing 68 people.

International relations. India's relations with neighboring Pakistan remained stable in 2007 despite such events. On February 21, the two nations signed an agreement to reduce the risk of an accidental nuclear war. They also held talks on resolving several border disputes. However, Pakistan expressed displeasure over India's nuclear agreement with the United States.

India and China had long disputed their border along the Himalaya, a situation that escalated to violence in 1962. Negotiations in 2007 on the continuing dispute failed to resolve conflicting claims to remote mountain areas. On April 12, India tested a missile that experts believed capable of carrying nuclear warheads to China's major cities.

India's economy continued to grow strongly in 2007. Nearly 30 percent of its people still lived below the official poverty line, however, and almost half of all children under 3 were malnourished. Speaking on August 15, the 60th anniversary of Indian independence, Singh warned against large areas remaining untouched by economic development amid islands of high growth, whose benefits reached only a small part of the population. ■ Henry S. Bradsher

See also **Asia; Disasters; People in the news** (Pratibha Patil); **Terrorism.**

Indian, American. In April 2007, a new federal judge appointed to preside over the largest class-action lawsuit ever brought against the United States government set a trial date to determine a key element of the case. United States District Judge James Robertson replaced District Judge Royce L. Lamberth, who, according to a federal appeals panel determination in 2006, had lost his objectivity in the case.

The lawsuit was brought in 1996 by Blackfeet tribe member Elouise Cobell on behalf of nearly 500,000 Native Americans. The suit charged that

the U.S. Interior Department had mismanaged more than $100 billion in trust funds that the department had administered for the Indians since 1887. The money was generated by royalties from oil, gas, timber, and mining on Indian lands. The Interior Department acknowledged the mismanagement but claimed the losses involved only hundreds of millions of dollars. The department also began a costly, time-consuming attempt to provide an accounting for the funds, though it admitted that a great number of vital trust records were missing or had been destroyed.

In December 2006, the plaintiffs asked Judge Robertson to determine whether the Interior Department's efforts were adequate or had "unreasonably delayed the completion of the required accounting." Judge Robertson set a trial date of Oct. 10, 2007.

In March 2007, the government offered $7 billion to settle all current and future lawsuits related to the trust lands. The plaintiffs, who had offered in 2005 to accept $27.5 billion to settle the suits, rejected the government's counteroffer.

A Hualapai tribe member participates in the March 2007 dedication of Skywalk, a glass-bottomed observation platform attached to the rim of the Grand Canyon. The U-shaped structure, anchored 4,000 feet (1,200 meters) above the canyon floor, was designed to be the centerpiece of a 9,000-acre (3,600-hectare) tourism site on the Arizona reservation.

In October 2007, Associate Deputy Interior Secretary James Cason argued that the department was doing all it could to account for the funds. In addition, Interior Department officials claimed that the funds needed only be accounted for back to 1994—the year the American Indian Trust Fund Management Reform Act was passed—and not back to the inception of the funds in the 1800's. By the end of 2007, Judge Robertson had not ruled in the matter.

Sand Creek Massacre memorial. Members of the Northern Cheyenne, Southern Cheyenne, and Arapaho tribes gathered on April 28 to dedicate a new national historic site in memory of the victims of the Sand Creek Massacre. The massacre took place along the Sand Creek River on Nov. 29, 1864, in what was then the southeastern section of the Colorado Territory.

On that day, some 700 volunteers of the Colorado Territory militia attacked a peaceful encampment of Cheyenne and Arapaho, even though the group's chief, Black Kettle, raised both an American flag and a white flag of peace. The soldiers killed more than 150 Indians—many of them women, children, and the elderly—following the orders of their commander, who directed them to "kill and scalp all, big and little; nits make lice."

Former Senator Ben Nighthorse Campbell of Colorado, a Northern Cheyenne chief, stated during the dedication ceremony, "… if there were any savages that day, it was not the Indians." Campbell had worked for years to establish U.S. government recognition of the site. The site, called the Sand Creek Massacre National Historic Site, is in Kiowa County, Colorado, about 160 miles (258 kilometers) southeast of Denver. It covers 12,500 acres (5,000 hectares).

Walkway to the sky. The Hualapai (*WAHL uh py*) tribe, whose reservation lies at the western edge of the Grand Canyon in Arizona, opened a massive glass-bottomed walkway in March 2007 as a tourist attraction. The walkway —named Skywalk—extends 70 feet (20 meters) from the rim of the Grand Canyon, about 4,000 feet (1,200 meters) above the canyon floor.

The decision to construct Skywalk was controversial. Environmentalists were concerned about commercialization of a natural landmark, and some tribe members noted that construction might disturb burial sites nearby. However, tribal leaders determined that commercial development was necessary, as one-third of the tribe's 2,200 members lived in poverty. The tribal government planned to add helicopter tours, river rafting, and replicas of a cowboy town and an Indian village to the 9,000 acres (3,600 hectares) of the reservation set aside for tourism.

■ Kristina Vaicikonis

Indonesia. Security forces in Indonesia captured two leaders of the Islamic terrorist group Jemaah Islamiyah (JI) in June 2007. The group is a Southeast Asian affiliate of the al-Qa`ida international terrorist network.

Jemaah Islamiyah was linked to the 2002 bombings on the island of Bali that killed 202 people, including 88 Australians. JI was also accused of involvement in a number of subsequent attacks. In response to increased militant activity, Indonesian authorities created new police units, one to gather intelligence on terrorists and another to make arrests and gather forensic evidence. American and Australian specialists trained and funded the units, which were credited with the 2007 captures.

In March, police raids picked up detailed plans of JI's new command structure. This action led them to the discovery of hideouts on Java. The police captured Abu Dujana, whom they described as the nation's most-wanted fugitive, on June 9 in central Java. Officials believe he was trained in Afghanistan and had headed JI's military arm. Hours later, a police force captured the acting leader of the JI network, Zarkasih. Officials believed he controlled all JI operations in Indonesia.

Corruption. President Susilo Bambang Yudhoyono fired five Cabinet members on May 7 in an effort to reinvigorate his war on corruption. During his 2004 campaign in Indonesia's first direct presidential election, he had promised to fight corruption, but his spokesperson admitted that results had been disappointing. Two of the dismissed ministers were implicated in a case involving Hutomo Mandala Putra, known as Tommy. Tommy is the youngest son of Suharto, who ruled Indonesia from 1966 to 1998. Tommy was found guilty of corruption in 2000 and was then convicted of ordering the murder of one of the judges who convicted him. Tommy spent only five years in jail. On July 19, 2007, he was named as the suspect in a new criminal corruption investigation.

The investigation of Tommy followed the beginning of government efforts to collect $1.5 billion from Suharto, who was accused of siphoning money from charities to companies run by his friends and family. The government had dropped criminal charges against him in 2006 because of his ill health, but a civil suit begun on July 9, 2007, sought to recover some money he was accused of stealing. As Suharto enjoyed his birthday party and attended weddings in 2007, some critics suspected that his supposed ill health was just an excuse to avoid trial.

International relations. Indonesia signed an agreement on April 27 with neighboring Singapore permitting extradition of people accused of corruption and other crimes dating back 15 years. Many Indonesian business people had fled to Singapore when Suharto lost power in 1998. In return for this agreement, Indonesia promised to let Singapore use its air and sea space for military training. Facing controversy at home, however, Indonesia postponed ratifying the two deals.

On Sept. 6, 2007, Yudhoyono and visiting Russian President Vladimir Putin signed an agreement for Indonesia to buy $1.2 billion worth of Russian military equipment, including aircraft, tanks, and submarines. The two made further agreements for nearly $5 billion in long-term trade.

Accidents and disasters. Yudhoyono in 2007 ordered an independent review of Indonesia's transportation system after several plane crashes. On January 1, an Indonesian airliner went down off the coast of the island of Sulawesi, killing all 102 people on board. On March 7, a plane crashed while landing in Yogyakarta, killing 21 people.

Indonesia's islands were shaken by several earthquakes in 2007. A 6.3-magnitude quake on March 6 on western Sumatra killed 70 people. On September 12, an 8.4-magnitude quake, which was followed by a series of aftershocks, left 25 people dead on Sumatra. In late July, days of heavy rain on the island of Sulawesi caused landslides and flooding that left more than 70 people dead and forced more than 16,000 people to evacuate. ■ Henry S. Bradsher

See also **Asia; Disasters; Singapore.**

International trade. The pace of buying and selling of goods and services between nations, a major force behind global economic growth for years, eased in 2007 as consumers in industrial nations tightened their belts and as exporting nations braked their economies to cool surging costs for energy and other commodities. In the second half of the year, a rapidly spreading financial market crisis threatened to further slow world economic growth and trade.

Trade patterns shifted, marked by rising exports from the United States as its imports slowed. The shift reflected both a weakened domestic U.S. economy and a months-long decline in the value of the U.S. dollar against currencies of such major trading partners as Canada and Europe.

The dollar's slide made U.S. goods less expensive abroad and, therefore, more desirable, while raising the cost of imports. Secretary of Commerce Carlos Gutierrez reported on October 11 that U.S. export volume was setting new records and narrowing the U.S. trade deficit. Exports for January through August rose 11.6 percent from 2006 to $1.054 trillion, as imports grew 4.3 percent to $1.526 trillion. In the first eight months of 2007, the U.S. trade deficit fell 8.8 percent, to $472 billion from $517 billion for the same period of 2006.

The U.S. trade deficit with Canada, the largest U.S. trading partner, shrank in mid-2007, as did its

deficits with Japan and the European Union. However, U.S. trade deficits with China and Mexico continued to climb.

The United States was the world's richest import market, making it an engine for global growth. A slowdown in its import demand therefore acted as a brake on world trade and economic growth. Data released in late 2007 suggested that such a slowdown was in progress, with global trade volume forecast to grow by only 6.6 percent in 2007, down from 9.2 percent in 2006. The estimates were made by the International Monetary Fund (IMF), a United Nations affiliate that offers credit and economic advice to countries.

Trade tensions. No major trade wars ensued in 2007, nor did the year bring any breakthroughs in multilateral negotiations on new global trading rules. However, trade tensions flared at times. During the year, a succession of alarms sounded in the United States over various goods imported from China that were found to contain materials harmful to consumers—from toothpaste with dangerous chemicals to children's toys decorated with toxic, lead-based paints.

Trade pacts. The administration of U.S. President George W. Bush continued a policy of seeking bilateral trade deals. The president urged the U.S. Congress to approve regional free trade agreements that the administration negotiated with Peru, Panama, and Colombia. Congress approved the Peru agreement but did not take up the others during 2007.

Trade in mortgage loans. While trade is often understood as moving goods across national borders, international commerce also includes moving loans through the world's credit markets. That system encountered a sharp setback in 2007, threatening to disrupt global credit that bankrolled trade and economic growth.

During the early 2000's, the United States experienced a housing boom, partly fueled by high-risk mortgage loans that U.S. lending banks often resold to foreign financial institutions. A sharp decline in the U.S. housing market in 2007 caused many holders of such mortgages to default, in turn tightening world credit markets. By the third quarter, major U.S. and European banks were reporting huge losses from write-offs of bad mortgage securities.

Central banks of some of the world's major economies—including the European Central Bank and the U.S. Federal Reserve (the Fed)—responded by injecting new money into their banking systems to stabilize credit markets. In the United States, the Fed also began cutting interest rates to ease credit, joined later by authorities in Canada and the United Kingdom.

International mergers. Until the midyear credit squeeze, major corporations continued a strong run of international mergers or acquisitions. Cerberus Capital Management of New York City bought U.S.-based automaker Chrysler from Daimler in Germany. Mexican cement maker Cemex bought the Australian building materials firm Rinker. London-based Rio Tinto acquired Canadian aluminum producer Alcan.

Trade in fuels. Supplies and pricing of crude oil, as well as attempts to displace its use with other fuels, had an impact on trade in 2007. In early 2007, oil was priced under about $50 per barrel. By November, oil was trading at double that price.

Consumers around the world pressed in 2007 for cleaner alternatives to oil as scientific studies continued to show linkage between global warming and carbon buildup in the atmosphere caused by the burning of fuels. Many countries expanded their use of plant-based motor fuels. Brazil in 2007 produced enough ethanol to meet its own needs and to export large quantities of the biofuel. Officials of the Organization of the Petroleum Exporting Countries, however, warned that concentration on biofuels could divert resources away from investments such as oil exploration and construction of refineries, and thus lead to future energy shortages.   ■ John Boyd

See also **Bank; Economics, United States; Economics, World; Energy supply.**

Internet. The number of residents of the United States who used the Internet at home dipped from 150 million in November 2006 to 149 million in November 2007, according to Nielsen//NetRatings, a New York City-based Internet market research firm. In June, the firm reported that over 80 percent of the country's home Internet users had broadband connections.

Cyberattacks on Estonia. Since gaining its independence from the Soviet Union, the small Baltic country of Estonia had become one of the most Internet-capable countries in Europe, if not the world. In 2007, government-funded free hotspots were abundant, and Estonia had one of the only fully functional Internet voting systems.

Beginning on April 27, 2007, the Internet infrastructure of Estonia was slowly crippled by a series of sophisticated attacks launched from outside the country. Military and telecommunications experts suspected it was the largest cyberattack in history.

The attacks coincided with a diplomatic disagreement between Estonia and its former Soviet Union ruler, Russia. According to some security experts, the source, timing, and sophistication of the attacks suggested that Russian citizens or even Russian companies played a supporting role in the attacks.

Growth of Web 2.0. Throughout 2007, so-

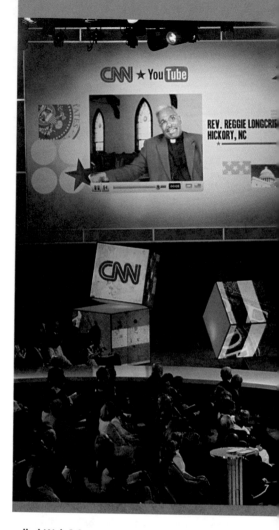

called *Web 2.0* programs and services grew in popularity and commercial promise. Web 2.0 refers to Web sites and Web services that store and organize user-submitted content. Blogs, video-sharing sites, social networking sites, and publicly edited reference sites, such as Wikipedia, are all Web 2.0 sites.

In May, the popular social networking Web site Facebook opened up to outside programmers. These outside programmers wrote a number of new miniapplications that used Facebook data and worked inside the Facebook Web site. This change contributed to Facebook's continued growth while signaling the next phase of Web 2.0 customization and flexibility.

The success of the Web 2.0 model led to many smaller-scale imitations. In 2007, the U.S. government launched A-Space, a MySpace-like network for military and security analysts. A-Space joined Intellipedia, a resource designed to share information used to combat terrorism.

Internet in daily life. According to

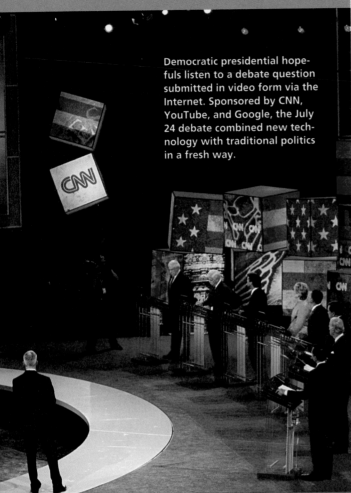

Democratic presidential hopefuls listen to a debate question submitted in video form via the Internet. Sponsored by CNN, YouTube, and Google, the July 24 debate combined new technology with traditional politics in a fresh way.

nects a standard television to the Internet and the contents of a home computer. The popular DVD rental company Netflix of Los Gatos, California, began offering a "Watch It Now" service that sent feature-length films over a broadband connection in minutes rather than through the mail in days. Similar services were released by a number of smaller companies.

"Cloud" computing increased in use and interest in 2007. As high-speed Internet connections became more common, some information storage and processing tasks could be done more efficiently and conveniently by large, centralized servers rather than small personal computers. Information residing on servers can be accessed from anywhere, by any device with an Internet connection. In this way, the information is said to exist "in a cloud." Throughout 2007, cloud services and applications were released by a number of major companies, which also made substantial nontraditional business investments in 2007. These investments included server warehouses in remote locations and transocean fiber-optic cables.

researchers, Internet users passed two important milestones in 2007. For the first time in the history of e-commerce, Internet shoppers spent more money on clothing and shoes than on technology or electronics, according to estimates based on 2006 data. This milestone was especially significant because many experts had predicted that clothing would be difficult to sell online due to such concerns as proper fit and feel of the fabric.

Perhaps even more significant were the results of a 2007 IBM survey of Internet users in the United States. According to that survey, the average American now spent more time using the Internet than watching TV. Experts predicted that this trend was likely to accelerate as more TV and movie content became available through computers and the Internet.

A number of new technologies and Internet services were developed in 2007 aimed at the delivery of video, TV, and feature-length movies. In March, Apple Inc. of Cupertino, California, released AppleTV, a multi-purpose box that con-

Voice over Internet Protocol (VoIP) delivers voice communication through Internet connections instead of traditional phone lines. In July 2007, the German telecom company T-Mobile released a mobile phone system that combined cellular and VoIP services. The integration of the two systems solved a number of problems specific to each. Unlike other VoIP services, users needed no additional equipment, as the mobile phone connects wirelessly to Internet hotspots. Furthermore, an Internet hotspot can provide reliable phone service in homes and locations without reliable cellular reception. Unlike any previous cellular or VoIP system, the T-Mobile phone can transition from one network to the other mid-call with no interruption of service.

Shortly after the T-Mobile release, another mobile VoIP service debuted. This third-party system connected Apple Inc.'s iPhone to the popular Skype network.   ■ Drew Huening

See also **Computer; Electronics; People in the news** (Mark Zuckerberg); **Telecommunications.**

Iran. United States Secretary of State Condoleezza Rice and Secretary of the Treasury Henry Paulson announced economic sanctions against Iran, including the freezing of Iranian assets in the United States, in October 2007. The sanctions stemmed from the State Department's designation of Iran's Islamic Revolutionary Guard Corps (IRGC) and Ministry of Defense as terrorist organizations. According to the Treasury Department, Iran's Quds Force (the foreign operations arm of the IRGC) provided weapons to terrorist organizations, including Islamic insurgents in Iraq and Taliban fighters in Afghanistan. Secretaries Rice and Paulson announced that nine Iranian companies affiliated with the IRGC and three large banks owned by Iran's government were also subject to the economic sanctions.

Filling Iraq's "power vacuum." Iran's President Mahmoud Ahmadinejad claimed in August that the political power of the United States was collapsing in Iraq. President Ahmadinejad added that Iran was prepared to fill the imminent "power vacuum" in the war-torn country.

Hassan Kazemi Qomi, Iran's ambassador to Iraq, met with Ryan Crocker, the U.S. ambassador to Iraq, in May, July, and August to discuss the security situation in Iraq. In the meetings, Ambassador Crocker warned his Iranian counterpart that Iran's support for militia groups in the Iraqi insurgency was undermining the Iraqi government and that attacks by these groups on U.S. troops needed to be halted. Despite Crocker's

warning, many analysts of Middle East affairs noted that it was highly unlikely that Iran would stop supporting the Shi`ah anticoalition insurgents in Iraq. Shi`ah is the dominant branch of Islam in Iran, and—according to the leading Iranian opposition group, the National Council of Resistance of Iran—Ambassador Qomi was a senior officer in the IRGC.

Atomic energy reports. The United Nations' (UN) International Atomic Energy Agency (IAEA) concluded in a November report that Iran's cooperation with the UN nuclear watchdog agency had been "reactive rather than proactive." The IAEA report noted that Iran had put 3,000 centrifuges into operation, giving the country the capability to produce enough enriched uranium fuel to construct a nuclear weapon within 18 months. Iranian officials, however, claimed that Iran's nuclear technology was only for civilian energy production.

The authors of a new U.S. intelligence estimate, released on December 3, concluded that Iran had halted its nuclear weapons program in 2003. In response to the estimate, U.S. President George W. Bush asserted that the assessment, in his opinion, only underscored the need to intensify international efforts to prevent Iran from acquiring a nuclear weapon. ■ Marius Deeb

See also **Iraq; Middle East; United Nations.**

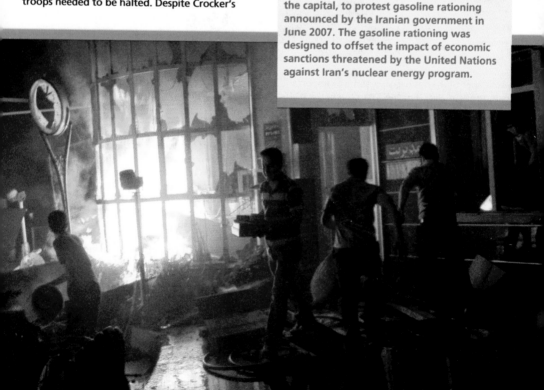

Young Iranians torch a gas station in Tehran, the capital, to protest gasoline rationing announced by the Iranian government in June 2007. The gasoline rationing was designed to offset the impact of economic sanctions threatened by the United Nations against Iran's nuclear energy program.

Iraq. United States President George W. Bush announced in January 2007 that continuing high levels of violence in Iraq made it necessary to adopt a new U.S. strategy for stabilizing the war-torn country. The new strategy, said the president, would include a substantial increase in the number of U.S. troops to assist Iraqi forces in providing security. President Bush ordered the U.S. armed forces to dispatch 30,000 additional troops to Iraq during the first half of 2007, bringing the total number of U.S. military forces in Iraq to approximately 160,000 as of mid-June.

Report by General Petraeus. In September, General David H. Petraeus, commander of the Multinational Force in Iraq, appeared before the U.S. Congress to report on the conflict in Iraq. Appearing with General Petraeus was Ryan C. Crocker, U.S. ambassador to Iraq.

General Petraeus reported that coalition forces and Iraqi security forces had achieved significant progress since January in improving the overall security situation in Iraq. He said that the number of car bombings and suicide attacks by insurgents had declined steadily from a high of 175 per day in March to approximately 90 per day in August. According to General Petraeus, coalition and Iraqi forces had dealt a severe blow to al-Qa'ida forces operating in Iraq. (Al-Qa'ida is a global Islamic terrorist organization.) The general noted that the reduction in insurgency attacks also reflected a reduction in violence related to Iraq's ethnic and religious divisions. General Petraeus maintained that the number of civilian deaths resulting from the conflict in Iraq had declined since December 2006 by 45 percent throughout the country—and by 70 percent in Baghdad, the capital.

General Petraeus also pointed out that Iraqi tribal leaders were increasingly cooperating with coalition and Iraqi forces in Al Anbar province, site of some of the most persistent fighting in the war, to rid themselves of elements of al-Qa'ida. He added that tribal leaders in other areas in Iraq were following the Anbar example.

In his testimony before Congress, General Petraeus claimed that coalition and Iraqi forces used conventional fighting, targeted raids, and surveillance and reconnaissance operations to destroy many safe havens used by al-Qa'ida forces in 2007. Furthermore, the general noted that coalition troops captured the senior leader of al-Qa'ida in Iraq in July and that 100 other key leaders and 2,500 rank-and-file fighters of the insurgency were either apprehended or killed in raids in 2007.

The coalition forces, according to General Petraeus, also targeted Shi'ah militia forces who were responsible for assassinating and kidnapping Iraqi government leaders and attacking Iraqi civilians and U.S. troops. Those militias, said the general, were funded, trained, and—in some cases—directed by the Quds Force (an Iranian special operations unit) and the Lebanon-based Hezbollah (an Islamic militant group backed by Iran and Syria). General Petraeus maintained that the Quds Force was fighting a proxy war for Iran against the Iraqi state and coalition forces.

Report by Accountability Office. The Government Accountability Office (GAO) issued a report in September that included statistics on attacks against coalition forces and Iraqi civilians that differed somewhat from the statistics reported by General Petraeus. According to the GAO report, the security situation in Iraq had not improved as dramatically as described by Petraeus. The GAO noted that the average number of daily attacks by insurgents had decreased only slightly, from approximately 170 in January to about 160 in March. Attacks then increased again by June to about 180, which was similar to the number of attacks in October 2006. The GAO and the Petraeus reports concurred that the average number of daily attacks in August 2007 reached the lowest level since June 2006.

Blackwater shootings. Employees of the private security firm Blackwater USA, of Moyock, North Carolina, were responsible for nearly 200 shooting incidents in Iraq since 2005—in most cases firing their weapons from moving vehicles without even stopping to count the dead or assist the wounded. That was the conclusion of a report issued in October 2007 by the U.S. House of Representatives Committee on Oversight and Government Reform. In one reported incident, an intoxicated Blackwater employee killed a bodyguard of one of the Iraqi government's vice presidents on Christmas Eve in 2006.

In September 2007, Blackwater employees were involved in a shooting in Baghdad that left at least 17 Iraqi civilians dead. The U.S. Department of State initiated three separate investigations of the September shooting, and the Federal Bureau of Investigation dispatched a team to Baghdad to compile evidence for possible criminal prosecution of Blackwater personnel.

Iraqi refugees. More than 4 million Iraqis had been displaced since the war began in 2003, and an additional 2,000 Iraqis fled their homes daily in 2007, according to an August report from the United Nations (UN) High Commissioner for Refugees. Of the 4.2 million refugees, more than half left Iraq, with an estimated 1.4 million fleeing to Syria and between 500,000 and 750,000 fleeing to Jordan. The UN report noted that Egypt also accepted a small number of Iraqi refugees.

Applications by Iraqis for *asylum* (protection against political persecution) soared to record levels in the first six months of 2007, when 19,800

The insurgency and sectarian violence in Iraq escalated in 2007 until an additional 30,000 troops were deployed in midyear.

A convoy of British army vehicles pulls out of Basra, in southeastern Iraq, in September 2007. The withdrawal of the 500 British troops from their base at the Basra Palace left Iraq's second-largest city without foreign military units for the first time since forces led by the United States invaded Iraq in March 2003.

An Iraqi man splashes cooling water on an overheating neighborhood electrical generator in Baghdad, capital of Iraq, in May. Such community generators served as the only source of electric power for many residents of Baghdad in 2007—four years after the war disrupted power supplies in Iraq.

United States Marines on security patrol walk through a field near Fallujah in western Iraq in May. The Fallujah area, which had previously been the site of some of the most intense fighting of the war in Iraq, was relatively peaceful in 2007.

Relatives care for an Iraqi man who was one of at least 27 people wounded by guards from the U.S. security firm Blackwater USA of Moyock, North Carolina, in a shooting incident in Baghdad in September 2007. Seventeen people were killed in the incident, which an Iraqi investigation concluded was unjustified. Officials from Blackwater, which was hired by the U.S. State Department to protect American diplomats in Iraq, contended that its guards opened fire in response to an attack on a convoy they were protecting. The State Department and the Federal Bureau of Investigation both opened investigations into the shootings.

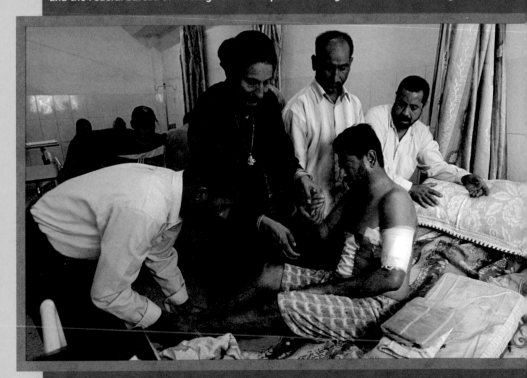

Iraqis applied to be resettled in 36 Western countries. Almost half of these asylum seekers applied to go to Sweden, which had a large Iraqi resident community. As of late September, according to the U.S. Department of State, only 1,135 Iraqis had resettled in the United States since 2003.

In May 2007, an international conference was convened in Sharm ash Shaykh, Egypt, to address the growing problem of Iraqi refugees. However, neither this conference nor a follow-up meeting in July in Amman, the capital of Jordan, were successful in developing long-term, concrete proposals for the refugee problem in Iraq.

Arab League envoy resigns. Mokhtar Lamani, the Arab League's envoy to Baghdad, resigned in early 2007. The Arab League is an association of 22 Arab-speaking nations in the Middle East and Africa. Lamani, a Moroccan who had been appointed in March 2006, was the only Arab diplomat still working in Baghdad. All other Arab embassies moved to Amman after they were repeatedly attacked by armed groups following the outbreak of fighting in 2003. Lamani reportedly resigned because he was disappointed with the lack of Arab initiatives to mediate the conflict in Iraq and with his own inability to achieve positive results in the situation. ■ Mary-Jane Deeb

See also **Armed forces; Iran; Middle East; United Nations; Year in brief.**

Ireland. Prime Minister Bertie Ahern's Fianna Fáil-dominated government won reelection for a third term in 2007. During the election campaign, Ahern, who had served as prime minister since 1997, promised new clinics and schools. His profile as one of the architects of the peace agreement in Northern Ireland worked to his advantage. Nevertheless, he was dogged by charges that he had accepted bribes as a minister in the mid-1990's.

In the May 2007 election, Fianna Fáil won 78 seats, the largest number in the 166-seat Dáil (lower house of the legislature). Fianna Fáil's governing coalition partner, the free market Progressive Democrats, won only 2 seats. The opposition center-right party Fine Gael secured 51 seats. Fine Gael's ally, the Labour Party, won 20 seats; the Green Party won 6; and Sinn Féin, the party that sought to bring Northern Ireland into the Irish Republic, won 4 seats.

Because Fianna Fáil lacked a majority and its former coalition partner failed to win sufficient seats, Ahern had to form a new coalition. Fianna Fáil formed a governing coalition in June with the Progressive Democrats, four Independents, and the Green Party, which served in the government for the first time. Ahern announced that the new term would be his last and that he expected to be succeeded by the deputy leader of Fianna Fáil, Brian Cowen, the finance minister. Cowen added the role of *tánaiste* (deputy prime minister) to his responsibilities.

After the election, Labour Party leader Pat Rabbitte was replaced by Eamon Gilmore. Progressive Democrat leader Michael McDowell lost his seat and was replaced by former party leader Mary Harney.

Mahon tribunal. Ahern was called in September to appear before a tribunal chaired by Judge Alan Mahon. A businessman named Tom Gilmartin charged that Ahern had been bribed by Cork property developer Owen O'Callaghan. Ahern told the tribunal that he had received money from a group of businessmen when he was finance minister in 1993 and 1994 to assist him with an expensive marital separation settlement. He denied that he had done anything wrong, that he had received money from O'Callaghan, or that he had performed favors for the businessmen who had loaned him the money. The tribunal planned to complete its investigation in 2008. At the end of September 2007, Ahern narrowly survived a vote of no confidence in the Dáil.

Economy. The Irish economy remained strong in 2007. In November, Bank of Ireland economists projected that the economy would grow by 5.3 percent in 2007, though growth would probably slow in 2008. ■ Rohan McWilliam

See also **Europe; Northern Ireland.**

Islam. After several years of turmoil, 2007 was a relatively stable year for the religion of Islam, though some trends continued. In Europe, anxieties about the assimilation of Muslims and home-grown terrorism were fanned in June by attempted car bombings in London and at the Glasgow Airport in Scotland. The bombings were plotted by three physicians and an engineer—one British-born Iraqi, one Jordanian, and two of Indian origin. Although the attacks were ineffective—the only resulting death was of one of the attackers—they raised questions once more about Islamism in communities with Muslim immigrants.

In November, a group of moderate Muslim leaders in the United Kingdom proposed a 10-point "code of conduct" for mosques in that country. The parties planned to agree upon a final version by March 2008. The code called for closer scrutiny of mosque leaders, more open and democratic mosque management, and the establishment of women's committees. The charter also called for the condemnation of domestic violence, help in matrimonial conflict, and participation in interfaith activities. The code was well received in government and press circles, but its reception was somewhat mixed among Muslim groups.

The Vatican. In March 2007, Pope Benedict XVI reversed his 2006 decision to diminish the role of the Pontifical Council for Interreligious

Dialogue. Some observers believed the action, which reestablished the council as a separate office, resulted from the controversy that ensued after a speech by the Pope in 2006 strained the Vatican's relations with Muslims.

Turkey. Despite efforts by Turkey's *secular* (nonreligious) establishment to raise the prospect of an Islamist threat to Turkish secularism, the Islamic-rooted Justice and Development Party (AKP) won a substantial victory in the July 22, 2007, parliamentary elections. After winning the elections, the AKP began planning a series of constitutional amendments, including an end to mandatory religion lessons, allowing women to wear Muslim headscarves at universities, and a provision for the direct election of the president. Turkey's president had been elected by parliament since the office was established in 1923.

Iraq. Sectarian violence between Shi`ites and Sunnis, which included some foreign fighters, continued in Iraq in 2007. However, observers noted some reduction in the killing in the second half of the year. Analysts suggested that the decline could be due, in part, to the completion of ethnic cleansing campaigns in various areas.

In January, an attack on Shi`ah Muslims observing the annual Ashura memorial rituals in Najaf was planned by a Shi`ah apocalyptic cult called the Soldiers of Heaven. The group believed that their leader was either an "ambassador" of the Mahdi, a savior-figure in Islam who returns to right the world's wrongs before the end of time, or the Mahdi himself. More than 250 of the group's followers were killed in a battle with Iraqi security forces and U.S. soldiers near Najaf before they could mount their attack.

Pakistan confronted Islamic radicals in July when troops ended a stand-off at the Red Mosque (Lal Masjid) in the capital, Islamabad, by storming the mosque and killing one of its leaders, Abdul Rashid Ghazi. His brother, Abdul Aziz, was arrested in an earlier escape attempt. The government of President Pervez Musharraf had at times confronted Islamic radicals and at times worked with them; in 2005 and 2006, the government settled peace agreements with Waziristan tribes that in fact empowered Islamic militants. Islamists linked to bases in Waziristan were closely tied to the Lal Masjid. Such radicals continued through 2007 to protest the take-over of the mosque with demonstrations and even suicide bombings.

United States. The controversial leader of the Nation of Islam, Louis Farrakhan, in February gave what was regarded as his last major speech, due to ill health. In the speech, Farrakhan directed his followers toward a more conventional understanding of Islam, a direction in which the organization had moved in recent years. Farrakhan did not identify a successor, an issue that raised questions about the long-term viability of his organization after he passes from the scene.

Adam Gadahn, a native-born American, emerged in 2007 as a media spokesman for the terrorist network al-Qa`ida. Gadahn had been drawn to Islam in California in the 1990's and joined al-Qa`ida. He was believed to be in Pakistan.

The first Muslim member of Congress, Keith Ellison (D., Minnesota), was sworn into office in January. Ellison took his oath on a translation of the Qur'an, the Islamic holy book, that had belonged to Thomas Jefferson. Virginia Republican Congressman Virgil Goode, in a December 2006 letter to his constituents, referred to Ellison as "the Muslim Representative from Minnesota" and deplored his election.

Muslim media stars continued to emerge in 2007 as a notable feature of Islamic culture. Televangelists, such as Moez Masoud and Amr Khaled, and religious singers, such as British-Azeri artist Sami Yusuf, became stars throughout Islamdom thanks in part to satellite television. They routinely filled large venues, offering a consumer-friendly, relevant, and nontraditional version of Islam that attracted young Muslims. Some observers suggested that their popularity signaled important changes in Muslims' self-understanding and self-presentation.   ∎ A. Kevin Reinhart

See also **Iraq; Pakistan; Terrorism; Turkey.**

Israel. In January 2007, legislator Ghaleb Majadele of the Labor Party became the first Muslim Arab to become an Israeli government minister when he joined the Cabinet of Prime Minister Ehud Olmert, of the Kadima Party, as minister without portfolio. Labor Party leader Amir Peretz hailed Majadele's appointment as "a significant, historic step toward equality and peace in the region." Muslim Arabs make up approximately one-fifth of the Israeli population.

In June, former Prime Minister Ehud Barak, the newly elected leader of the Labor Party, joined the Cabinet as minister of defense. Also in June, the Knesset (Israeli parliament) elected elder statesman and former Prime Minister Shimon Peres, of Kadima, to the ceremonial post of president. Peres replaced Moshe Katsav, who had resigned the presidency after pleading guilty to several charges of sexual assaults against women who had worked for him.

Winograd Commission report. In September, the Winograd Commission, which was established in 2006, submitted its report on the political and security dimensions of the 34-day war in July and August 2006 between Israel and Hezbollah, a militant Muslim group based in southern Lebanon and backed by Syria and Iran. The conflict left at least 140 Israeli soldiers and civilians dead and more than 1,000 others wounded. The commission concluded that the decision by Prime Minister Olmert and his advisers to retaliate against Hezbollah for its kidnapping of two Israeli soldiers was not based on a thorough military plan or a comprehensive study of military conditions in southern Lebanon. The report maintained that a proper study of these conditions would have revealed that the intensive Israeli military response was bound to lead to the firing of missiles by Hezbollah against northern Israel—attacks that, in fact, resulted in many Israeli casualties.

Israel-Hezbollah exchange. In October 2007, Israeli authorities released a Hezbollah prisoner who was mentally ill and the bodies of two Hezbollah fighters. In exchange, Hezbollah gave Israel the body of a drowned Israeli civilian found on the Lebanese coast. Hezbollah also provided Israel with documents written by Ron Arad, an Israeli Air Force navigator whom militants shot down over Lebanon in 1986.

Gaza declared "hostile territory." The militant Palestinian organization Hamas seized control of the Gaza Strip from the moderate Fatah-led Palestinian government in June 2007. Over the next several months, the Hamas fighters launched hundreds of rocket and mortar attacks against southern Israel from their bases in Gaza, wounding more than 70 Israelis and forcing many others to flee. In response, Israeli forces carried out several air strikes and ground operations against militant sites in Gaza, resulting in the deaths of more than 80 Palestinians and the wounding of more than 150 others.

In September, the Israeli government declared the Gaza Strip to be a "hostile territory" and reduced supplies of electric power to the Palestinian territory. After 10 human rights groups petitioned the Israeli Supreme Court to stop the cutting of Gaza power supplies, Israeli Attorney General Menachem Mazuz ruled in October that the cuts in electric power were illegal actions taken by the Israeli government. Despite this ruling, Minister of Defense Barak maintained that Israel would continue to limit power to Gaza.

Reviving the peace process. After the Hamas take-over of Gaza, the administration of United States President George W. Bush urged Israeli Prime Minister Olmert and Palestinian President Mahmoud Abbas to revive the peace process in anticipation of a U.S.-sponsored Middle East peace conference scheduled for November in Annapolis, Maryland. The Israeli and Palestinian leaders began meeting regularly in June. In a meeting in Jerusalem in October, Prime Minister Olmert and President Abbas emphasized their "joint commitment to a two-state solution" to the Israeli-Palestinian conflict.

The Israeli government also took a number of

In September, an Israeli archaeologist explores a newly found drainage channel beneath the Old City of Jerusalem that dates from Biblical times. A team of archaeologists led by Ronny Reich of the University of Haifa (in Israel) said the channel was used by Jews as a hiding place during the Roman conquest of Jerusalem in A.D. 70.

other steps to support the moderate Palestinian president and his Cabinet. In July, the Israeli government began transferring withheld tax and customs revenues worth approximately $500 million to the Palestinian Authority. In July and October, Israeli authorities released about 350 Palestinian prisoners in two batches. In August, the Israeli government offered *amnesty* (pardon) to some 170 wanted Fatah militants, provided that the militants renounce violence. Israeli officials also removed some roadblocks and checkpoints in the West Bank to ease the movement of Palestinians, and they promoted several internationally backed economic projects in Palestinian areas. These projects included an industrial zone in Tarqumieh supported by Turkey and a "Corridor of Peace and Prosperity" in Jericho sponsored by Japan.

Attack on suspected nuclear site. According to widely circulated reports, Israeli fighter jets on September 6 launched a strike on a partly constructed nuclear reactor being built in northeastern Syria with assistance from North Korea. Israeli officials reportedly suspected that, when completed, the reactor would be used to produce nuclear fuel that could be reprocessed into bomb-grade plutonium. Plutonium is used to make nuclear weapons.   ■ Marius Deeb

See also **Judaism; Lebanon; Middle East; Syria.**

Italy. Prime Minister Romano Prodi's left-of-center government, a coalition of nine parties, remained unstable and fragile throughout 2007. After losing a key parliamentary vote in February when several senators from parties that had previously supported Prodi voted against a piece of foreign policy legislation, Prodi offered his resignation. He quickly managed to reconstitute a governing majority. Prodi remained unpopular for much of the year because of his efforts to rein in tax evasion, which some analysts estimated at about a quarter of Italy's *gross domestic product* (GDP—the value of all goods and services produced in a country in a year). However, many Italians considered the alternative on the center-right, media tycoon Silvio Berlusconi, who had served five scandal-ridden years as prime minister from 2001 to 2006, to be an unacceptable alternative.

Electoral reform. Italy's political party leaders in 2007 discussed ways to reform the country's system of proportional representation in an effort to stabilize the government. Italy had changed governments 61 times since World War II (1939-1945), in part because the large number of small parties allowed them to prevent parliamentary majorities from forming. Reformers hoped to encourage smaller parties with similar platforms to merge and to make it more difficult for parties that receive few votes to enter parliament.

In October 2007, Walter Veltroni, the mayor of Rome, was elected leader of the new Democratic Party. The party was formed by a merger of the two largest parties of the center-left coalition, the Left Democrats and the Democracy and Freedom Party. Veltroni was regarded by some as a leader who could unify Italy's fractious left, though others considered him to be strong on image but unable to handle the serious problems of Italy's capital city.

On the center-right, Berlusconi moved in November to create his own new party, called the Freedom People party. The new party absorbed Berlusconi's Forza Italia, Italy's largest political party. Most elements of the right, however, resisted inclusion in a new, Berlusconi-dominated umbrella organization.

Foreign policy. The crisis that temporarily brought down Prodi in February was ignited by a disagreement within the ruling coalition over Italy's continued presence in Afghanistan as part of the North Atlantic Treaty Organization- (NATO) led mission in that country. Having withdrawn Italy's troops from Iraq in 2006, Prodi's government maintained that the troop presence in Afghanistan was legitimate, as it was part of a United Nations-mandated mission. Nevertheless, the NATO connection caused anti-American legislators to vote against further funding for the mission. In addition, some legislators objected to a plan for expanding a United States Air Force base in Italy. Prodi eventually found support for continuing the mission.

In March 2007, however, debate broke out again over Italy's role in Afghanistan when Italian journalist Daniele Mastrogiacomo was kidnapped. The journalist was freed but only after Italy pressured the Afghan government to release five Taliban prisoners.

Immigration. A wave of violent crimes attributed to Romanian Roma (Gypsies) in October set off an outcry about the estimated 560,000 Romanians who had immigrated to Italy over the past five years. (Former Prime Minister Berlusconi waived visa restrictions for Romanians in 2002, before Romania joined the European Union [EU].) After a particularly brutal murder committed by an immigrant, the Italian Cabinet gave the Interior Ministry the power to expel citizens of other EU nations as long as the ministry did so backed by a court order. Despite some controversy over the decree at EU headquarters in Brussels, Belgium, the EU accepted it as an emergency measure. In November 2007, the prime ministers of Italy and Romania agreed on further measures to address the problem.

Mafia. In November, Italian police arrested Salvatore Lo Piccolo near Palermo. Lo Piccolo was the highest-ranking Sicilian Mafia boss still at large and had avoided capture for 24 years. He was taken into custody along with his son and two other members of Italy's "30 most wanted." After the arrest in 2006 of Bernardo Provenzano, the last of Italy's "boss of bosses," and several other high-ranking mobsters, Italians speculated that the Mafia may be in long-term decline.

Economy. After initially optimistic forecasts, EU economists reduced their projected growth rate for Italy in 2007 to 1.9 percent, the same growth rate that the country experienced in 2006. Nevertheless, Italy's deficit, which had risen for four years above the 3-percent-of-GDP EU-imposed limit for countries that use the euro, fell to 2.3 percent in 2007.

Pavarotti. On September 6, opera singer Luciano Pavarotti died at age 71. Known for his soaring voice, his charisma, and his flamboyant style, the Italian tenor became famous for attracting audiences who ordinarily would not attend opera. In 1990, he sang in concert with Plácido Domingo and José Carreras. Thereafter, the "Three Tenors" performed together for over a decade. Pavarotti was criticized by opera insiders for being undisciplined and commercial, but he generally shrugged off such criticisms by pointing to the size of his audiences and loyalty of his fans.   ■ Jeffrey Kopstein

See also Classical music; Europe.

Ivory Coast. See Côte d'Ivoire in Africa.

Jamaica. See Latin America; West Indies.

Japan. Yasuo Fukuda became prime minister of Japan on Sept. 25, 2007. He succeeded Shinzo Abe, who resigned on September 12 after only a year as head of the government and leader of the Liberal Democratic Party (LDP).

When the LDP elected Fukuda as its new leader, he promised to try to revitalize the party. He said he would pursue economic and social reforms introduced by Junichiro Koizumi, the prime minister who preceded Abe. Some LDP leaders worried, however, that those reforms had reduced the party's ability to win elections by directing public works projects and other benefits to voters. Many parts of the country felt left behind economically. With public debt at an unusually high 150 percent of Japan's *gross domestic product* (GDP)—the value of all goods and services produced in country in a given year—there was little to spend to benefit local areas to win elections.

The LDP turned to the 71-year-old Fukuda as a symbol of experience and stability after tumult under Abe, who at 52 was Japan's youngest prime minister since World War II (1939-1945). Fukuda was the son of Takeo Fukuda, an LDP member who was prime minister from 1976 to 1978. Yasuo Fukuda was noted for working to achieve consensus on issues. He was considered conservative on financial issues, moderate on social problems, and an advocate of improving relations with neighboring countries.

A woman and her child maneuver past mounds of garbage in Naples, Italy, in May 2007. The city suffered a garbage crisis when local dumps, filled to capacity, could take no more. The crisis eased in July when the government ordered new dumps to be opened, despite protests by local residents.

Fukuda had served as chief Cabinet secretary longer than anyone else until resigning in May 2004. In that job, he worked with Koizumi on free-market reforms. Koizumi was noted for charismatic flare, while Fukuda was seen as a dull, even dour, policy specialist. Some Japanese political analysts suggested that he might be a short-term caretaker prime minister.

Koizumi had shaken up LDP tradition by reaching outside the LDP leadership for well-qualified Cabinet ministers. Fukuda reverted to naming heads of the LDP's many factions to key ministerial positions. The head of the largest faction, former foreign minister Nobutaka Machimura, became chief Cabinet secretary.

Fukuda was elected prime minister by the LDP majority in the lower house of parliament, despite a vote against him in the upper house. The LDP had lost control of the upper house in elections on July 29, 2007. Abe, plagued by bureaucratic and Cabinet scandals, quit rather than face possible defeat in that house for some of his policies.

Abe's reign. When Abe was elected prime minister on Sept. 20, 2006, he sought to emphasize patriotism in Japanese education. A strong nationalist, he also wanted to change the Constitution, written during the American occupation after World War II, that restricted the use of armed forces. The defense agency was upgraded to ministry status on Jan. 9, 2007, but Abe failed to get the Constitution changed.

Abe's premiership was marked by public embarrassments. In May, the government was forced to disclose that Japan's Social Insurance Agency had for years mishandled some 50 million pension records, so people were not receiving the full payments to which they were entitled. Retirement money of another 14 million people had never been entered in official records. A bureaucratic blunder rather than Abe's responsibility, it nevertheless hurt him politically because of what was seen as his failure to take adequate corrective steps.

Residents of Kashiwazaki, Japan, survey damage caused by a July 16 earthquake. The 6.8-magnitude quake killed at least 10 people and damaged the world's largest nuclear power plant.

Several of Abe's ministers came under intense public scrutiny in 2007. In January, the health minister described women as "breeding machines," causing a public outcry. The defense minister later made statements that seemed to justify the United States' dropping atomic bombs on Hiroshima and Nagasaki during World War II. On May 28, the agriculture minister committed suicide before he was scheduled to face a parliamentary inquiry into financial dealings. Two subsequent agriculture ministers resigned in the following months amid similar accusations of corruption.

Election. Abe's troubles led to what commentators called the LDP's worst election defeat in 52 years of almost uninterrupted rule. In the July voting for half of the 242 seats in the upper house of parliament, the Democratic Party of Japan (DPJ) won control of the house in a landslide victory. Although less important than the lower house, the upper house can block legislation.

Defying convention, Abe refused to resign after the defeat. Instead, he reshuffled his Cabinet on August 27 in an attempt to win new support. Two weeks later, however, he abruptly resigned and entered a hospital with stress-related stomach problems. He later apologized for leaving the political vacuum that Fukuda finally filled two weeks after the resignation.

Foreign relations. In April, China's prime minister, Wen Jiabao, met with Abe in Tokyo. On April 11, the two issued a vaguely worded pledge of cooperation on defense, environmental matters, and other subjects. Wen said friendship would prevail between the two nations. Three months later, a Japanese government paper expressed concern over China's improving military capabilities. Although Japanese officials continued to deny that they considered China a threat, the paper issued on July 6 pointed with apprehension at China's increasing military power.

Nuclear accident. On July 16, a magnitude-6.8 earthquake on Japan's northwest coast killed at least 10 people and damaged the world's largest nuclear power plant. It was later revealed that the plant had been built directly over an undetected seismic fault. The quake greatly exceeded the plant's design limits. No injuries were reported at the plant, but the release of 317 gallons (1,200 liters) of radioactive water into the Sea of Japan caused great national concern over the unexpected vulnerability in a nuclear industry that produced much of Japan's electricity. International experts said it could take up to a year to restart the Kashiwazaki plant.

Economy. Japan bounced through economic ups and downs in 2007 that failed to bring a long-sought return to rising prosperity after nearly 20 years of stagnation. Despite a midyear drop of the unemployment rate to a nine-year low, companies cut investments and prices fell. Cautious consumer spending reflected public concern over economic prospects.

Crime. On April 17, Itcho Ito, the popular mayor of Nagasaki, was murdered on the street by a prominent member of the *yakuza,* organized criminal groups that police said had at least 85,000 members. Once considered close to LDP governments, the yakuza had fallen in public repute in recent years. The mayor's murder caused a public outcry over continued underworld operations.

■ Henry S. Bradsher

See also **Asia; China; People in the news** (Yasuo Fukuda).

Jordan. The Jordanian government introduced new immigration regulations in February 2007 designed to limit the number of Iraqis entering Jordan as refugees from the war in Iraq. Almost 1 million Iraqi refugees lived in Jordan in 2007. In August, the United Nations praised Jordan for allowing tens of thousands of children of Iraqi refugees to enroll in Jordan's public and private schools.

A Jordanian military court in March sentenced four terrorists belonging to the terrorist organization al-Qa'ida to death for attacking Jordanian truck drivers in Iraq.

To stem the growing influence of Islamic militants in Jordan's government prior to municipal elections held in July, Jordanian authorities lowered the age of eligible voters from 19 to 18 and allowed, for the first time, members of the armed forces to vote. The new law also required that 20 percent of mayoral positions and seats on municipal councils be allocated to women.

Parliamentary elections in November resulted in a considerable decline in political power for Islamic militants, represented by candidates with the Islamic Action Front, which won only 6 seats in the 110-seat parliament. Independent candidates won 98 seats. Six parliamentary seats were won by women candidates. ■ Marius Deeb

See also **Iraq; Middle East.**

Judaism. Some of the leading Jewish events of 2007 revolved around educational institutions, a sign of their importance in Jewish life. In March, Arnold Eisen, the newly elected chancellor of the Jewish Theological Seminary in New York City, announced that qualified gay and lesbian students would be admitted into the seminary's rabbinical and cantorial programs. The issue formed part of a broader conversation within Judaism's Conservative movement about its mission and core values.

In January, former United States President Jimmy Carter made a controversial visit to Brandeis University in Waltham, Massachusetts, to discuss his book *Palestine: Peace Not Apartheid* (2006). Many Jews felt that the account of the Israeli-Palestinian peace process from Carter's presidency (1977-1981) to the present placed too much blame on Israel for the conflict. That month, 14 members of the Carter Center's Board of Councilors resigned in protest over the book. Observers noted that the book raised concerns among some Jews that U.S. support for the State of Israel was eroding.

Israel also figured in a dispute between the American Armenian and Jewish communities in 2007 over a proposed congressional resolution that condemned the mass killings of Armenians in Turkey during World War I (1914-1918) and soon after as an act of genocide. The Anti-Defamation League (ADL), based in New York City, had refused to support the resolution, fearing that it would adversely affect Turkish-Israeli relations and the safety of Turkish Jews. In response, the town council of Watertown, Massachusetts, voted in August 2007 to remove the ADL's "No Place for Hate" program from its community, which has a large Armenian American population. The New England ADL board and regional director dissented from the national ADL stance. That and other criticism led the ADL to change its position.

The Ben Gamla Charter School, the first U.S. Hebrew charter school, opened in Hollywood, Florida, in August. Hebrew lessons were stopped briefly out of concerns over a possible constitutional violation of the separation of church and state, but lessons resumed after the Broward County School Board approved the curriculum.

World. Iran's nuclear program and the anti-Israel and anti-Jewish statements of its president, Mahmoud Ahmadinejad, continued to raise concerns in 2007 throughout the Jewish world. Many Jews were disturbed following a December 2006 conference, hosted by Iran, whose participants questioned the extent of or denied the Holocaust.

The June 2007 groundbreaking of the Museum of the History of Polish Jews, in Warsaw, marked new interest in recovering the history of pre-World War II (1939-1945) Jewry. The museum, to stand in an area where Jewish life thrived before the war but which the Nazis turned into the Warsaw Ghetto, was to chronicle the history of Polish Jews from the Middle Ages to the present.

Israel. Prospects for peace with the Palestinian group Fatah in the West Bank seemed to brighten after the radical Islamic group Hamas seized the Gaza Strip in June 2007. Palestinian Authority President Mahmoud Abbas, of Fatah, dissolved the Hamas-led government and installed an independent administration. Israel and the United States continued to reject Hamas, raising concerns about conditions in Gaza, and resumed financial support to Abbas's West Bank-based government.

A regional conference to advance Middle East peace was held on Nov. 27, 2007, in Annapolis, Maryland. At the urging of U.S. President George W. Bush, Israeli Prime Minister Ehud Olmert and Abbas agreed in writing to begin negotiations toward a peace treaty and to work to conclude it before the end of 2008. Other Arab parties in attendance included Saudi Arabia, Lebanon, and Syria, which chose to attend only after the United States agreed that Syria could raise the status of the Golan Heights in the deliberations. Some observers linked this demand to a September 2007 Israeli air strike on what Western analysts described as a partly built Syrian nuclear facility.

◼ Jonathan D. Sarna and Jonathan J. Golden
See also **Israel; Middle East.**

Kampuchea. See Cambodia.

Kazakhstan. President Nursultan Nazarbayev approved a set of controversial constitutional amendments on May 22, 2007, that removed term limits for him and reduced the presidential term to five years from seven beginning in 2012. The amendments also increased the size of the lower house of parliament (Mazhilis) from 77 seats to 107 and the upper house (Senate) from 39 seats to 47. Of the 107 lower-house deputies, 98 would be elected by party list and 9 would be nominated by the Assembly of the Peoples of Kazakhstan, an unelected body representing Kazakh ethnic and cultural groups.

On June 20, 2007, Nazarbayev dissolved the Mazhilis and called elections for August 18. Opposition party leaders slammed the decision as a way to prevent them from adequately organizing campaigns. Nazarbayev assumed the leadership of the ruling Nur-Otan party on July 4, replacing his daughter, Darigha Nazarbayev. Nur-Otan took 88 percent of the vote in the August 18 elections, winning all 98 contested seats. None of the six participating opposition parties cleared the 7-percent threshold necessary for representation. International observers noted that, though the elections were an improvement on previous polling, they still did not meet international standards.   ◼ Juliet Johnson
See also **Asia.**

Kenya. Presidential and parliamentary elections dominated Kenyan politics in 2007. By September, 144 political parties had registered to contest the elections.

In past elections, Kenya's political parties formed coalitions to improve their chances. President Mwai Kibaki's election victory in 2002 was made possible by the National Rainbow Coalition (NARC). NARC's victory ended 39 years of rule by the Kenya African National Union (KANU). However, NARC disintegrated in 2005 due to disagreements over the constitutional referendum that year.

Presidential candidates. In September 2007, Kibaki assembled a new alliance named the Party of National Unity (PNU). The PNU consisted of several parties that had participated in the former NARC. Surprisingly, former rival party KANU, led by Uhuru Kenyatta, also joined the PNU coalition. Kibaki may have wanted to attract the votes of the Kikuyu, the country's largest ethnic group, as he and Kenyatta were prominent Kikuyu leaders. Kenyan voters tended to vote according to their ethnic affiliations. Analysts suggested Kenyatta might be rewarded for his support with a Cabinet post. Kibaki ran on the country's promising economic growth during his term and the rise in school attendance since his introduction of free primary education in 2003.

Raila Odinga, leader of the Orange Democratic Movement (ODM), was Kibaki's main challenger in the 2007 elections. The ODM was formed in 2005 to oppose Kibaki's constitutional proposals. Odinga was a member of the Luo, the country's second largest ethnic group. In November 2007, Odinga led Kibaki in polls. Kalonzo Musyoko, a former Cabinet minister, was a third contender.

Election results. On December 27, Kenyans voted for president. On December 30, Kibaki was declared the winner with 47 percent of the vote and was immediately sworn into office. Odinga received 44 percent of the vote, and Musyoko received 9 percent. According to Western observers, Kenya's election commission ignored clear evidence of vote fraud to keep Kibaki in power. Odinga accused Kibaki of election fraud and demanded a recount. Kibaki's clouded victory and Odinga's accusations triggered a wave of violence that left hundreds of people dead in what was described as "tribal warfare."

Economy. In 2007, Kenya's *gross domestic product* (GDP)—the total value of goods and services produced within a country in a year—grew by about 6 percent. The growth was mostly due to investment in infrastructure, expansion of tourism, and good harvests. ■ Pieter Esterhuysen

See also **Africa**.

Korea, North. After years of negotiations and agreements, which the United States accused North Korea of breaking, United Nations (UN) inspectors confirmed in July 2007 that North Korea had shut down its main nuclear reactor. In return, the impoverished Communist nation began receiving fuel oil and economic aid. After talks with China, Japan, Russia, South Korea, and the United States, the North agreed on October 3 to disable its main reactor and provide complete details of its nuclear program in return for further aid.

Denuclearization. In 1994, North Korea had agreed with the five countries to freeze nuclear weapon development. The country then received some aid, but this was halted when it became known that nuclear work continued. In 2003, the North reactivated its nuclear facilities. On Oct. 9, 2006, the North tested a small nuclear device.

On Feb. 13, 2007, after international talks resumed, North Korea agreed with the five nations to close its nuclear plants within 60 days in return for aid and security pledges. This agreement was stalled by problems in returning $25 million to the North from a bank in Macao, China. United States officials had frozen the money in Macao on charges that the North had gained the money through illegal means, but the issue was resolved by June. Further talks by the six nations led to the October 3 agreement. The question of whether

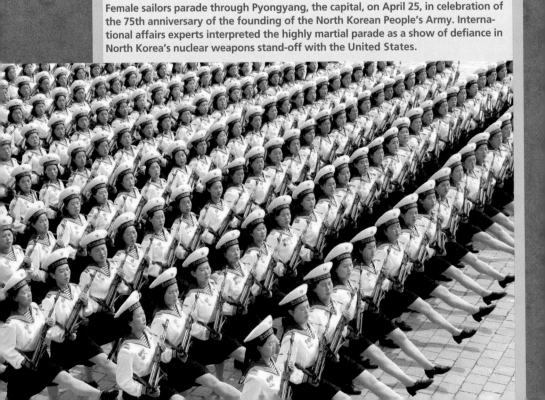

Female sailors parade through Pyongyang, the capital, on April 25, in celebration of the 75th anniversary of the founding of the North Korean People's Army. International affairs experts interpreted the highly martial parade as a show of defiance in North Korea's nuclear weapons stand-off with the United States.

Shim Jin-pyo (center) mourns over the coffin of his son, Shim Sung-min, who was one of 23 South Korean Christian missionaries captured by Taliban militants in Afghanistan on July 19, 2007. Shim Sung-min and another male captive were murdered. The 21 others were eventually released.

North Korea would suspend its nuclear weapons program remained open at the end of 2007.

The agreement stipulated that the United States would begin a process of taking North Korea off its list of state sponsors of terrorism, with the process moving in parallel with solving remaining nuclear issues. American and Japanese economic sanctions limiting trade and other contacts with the North were also contingent upon progress. The United States held off on North Korea's desire to sign a peace treaty replacing the armistice that had halted the Korean War (1950-1953) and to establish normal diplomatic relations.

Meeting with the South. From October 2 to 4, 2007, North Korea's leader, Kim Jong-il, met with South Korean President Roh Moo-hyun in the North's capital, Pyongyang. The leaders agreed to seek a permanent end to the Korean War and made plans for further economic cooperation. On December 11, regular freight train service began between the two nations for the first time since the 1950's.

Disasters continued to plague North Korea in 2007. After a week of heavy rains in August, North Korean officials reported that flooding had left at least 450 people dead and much of the nation's farmland and infrastructure destroyed or badly damaged. ■ Henry S. Bradsher

See also **Asia; Disasters; Korea, South.**

Korea, South. Voters in South Korea elected Lee Myung-bak to a five-year term as president on Dec. 19, 2007. He was scheduled to take office in February 2008.

Elections. In August 2007, the Uri Party of President Roh Moo-hyun disbanded as its members sought to distance themselves from the increasingly unpopular president. Uri members merged with the United New Democratic Party and selected Chung Dong-young as that party's candidate. The opposition Grand National Party chose former Seoul Mayor Lee Myung-bak as its candidate. Lee had headed several parts of the Hyundai Corporation before being elected mayor of the South Korean capital.

Summit. Roh met in Pyongyang, the capital of North Korea, with North Korea's Communist leader, Kim Jong-il, for three days beginning on October 2. Roh sought to improve relations between their heavily armed, mutually hostile countries. The meeting was only the second between the two countries since the end of the Korean War (1950-1953). South Korea's President Kim Dae-jung visited Pyongyang in 2000.

Roh's 2007 trip was seen by some as an attempt to end his much-criticized administration by claiming to have improved relations on the Korean peninsula. It was also seen as a political ploy to influence the presidential election.

Roh and Kim Jong-il agreed to seek a permanent end to the Korean War, replacing the 1953 armistice. The leaders planned further economic cooperation, focusing on investment and developing the North's natural resources. They also planned a cooperative economic zone in southwestern North Korea and a joint fishing area in disputed waters of the Yellow Sea. On December 11, regular freight train service began between the two nations for the first time since the 1950's.

Oil spill. On Dec. 7, 2007, a barge collided with an oil tanker off the western coast of South Korea, causing the tanker to spill some 2.8 million gallons (10.6 million liters) of crude oil into the sea. The government declared a state of disaster.

Hostages. Public attention in late July and August 2007 focused on the July 19 kidnapping by the Taliban in Afghanistan of 23 Christian volunteers from South Korea. The Taliban—Islamic extremists who once controlled much of Afghanistan—killed two of the hostages. After lengthy negotiations, the 21 others were released amid strong criticism for traveling to Afghanistan despite warnings that it was unsafe for foreigners. The South Korean government denied the kidnappers' claim that it had paid a ransom of $20 million.   ■ Henry S. Bradsher

See also **Afghanistan; Asia; Korea, North.**

Kuwait. See Middle East.

Kyrgyzstan. President Kurmanbek Bakiev of Kyrgyzstan signed into law on Jan. 15, 2007, a new Constitution increasing presidential powers. Prime Minister Felix Kulov and his Cabinet had resigned on Dec. 19, 2006, sparking a brief constitutional crisis. Azim Isabekov served as prime minister from Jan. 29, 2007, to March 29, when he resigned after clashing with Bakiev. Parliament approved Bakiev's new choice for prime minister, opposition leader Almaz Atambaev, on March 30.

On September 14, the Constitutional Court overturned the new Constitution. Parliament held an emergency session on September 18 and voted no confidence in the Constitutional Court. Bakiev then called a constitutional referendum for October 21. Voters approved the new Constitution as well as amendments changing the electoral system to proportional party list representation and increasing seats in parliament from 75 to 90. After the vote, Bakiev dissolved parliament and called new parliamentary elections for December 16.

Atambaev resigned as prime minister on November 28 as a condition of the new Constitution. Bakiev's Ak Zhol party won nearly all 90 parliamentary seats in the December elections, which were denounced by international observers. Former energy minister Igor Chudinov became the new prime minister.   ■ Juliet Johnson

See also **Asia.**

Labor and employment. The expansion of the United States economy that began in 2004 slowed in 2007, with 1.5 million jobs created in 2007 and an unemployment rate of 4.6 percent. Economic expansion in the three-year period created 7.2 million jobs compared with the 16 million created over a similar period of recovery from the 1991-1992 recession. Some labor analysts speculated that the less-than-robust 2004-2007 recovery reflected the impact of industry deregulation and globalization of labor. Others cited such one-of-a-kind events as the 2001 terrorist attacks on the United States and the wars in Afghanistan and Iraq.

In late 2007, the jobless rate for men stood at 4.1 percent and at 3.9 percent for women. The jobless rate for teen-age workers was 15.4 percent. By race and ethnicity, unemployment rates were 4.1 percent among white workers, 8.2 percent among African American workers, and 5.6 percent among Hispanic workers.

Compensation (wages, salaries, and benefits) rose 3.3 percent in the 12 months ending in September 2007, according to the Employment Cost Index of the U.S. Bureau of Labor Statistics (BLS). Wages and salaries alone rose 3.3 percent, and benefits rose about the same—3.2 percent.

Airline industry. Collective bargaining in the airline industry in 2007 occurred in the continuing context of fallout from the 2001 terrorist attacks and economic problems in the industry, including bankruptcies of several major airlines. Price competition resulting from deregulation, huge unfunded pension liabilities, and steadily rising fuel costs kept most airlines struggling financially in 2007.

Bargaining between airlines in or emerging from bankruptcy and unions—the Air Line Pilots, the Association of Flight Attendants-CWA (AOFA), the machinists, and others—was overseen by bankruptcy court judges. These negotiations occurred in the absence of previous contractual arrangements because terms of the bankruptcies abrogated such agreements. Both US Airways of Tempe, Arizona, and United Airlines of Elk Grove Village, Illinois, declared bankruptcy in 2002; Northwest Airlines of Eagan, Minnesota, and Delta Airlines of Atlanta declared bankruptcy in 2005.

Bargaining at Northwest Airlines, which emerged from bankruptcy in 2007, typified the new situation. In 2006, a bankruptcy court gave the airline permission to unilaterally impose pay and other reductions upon the AOFA after union members refused to agree to the terms. In April 2007, a bankruptcy court rebuffed the AOFA petition to "ease" the imposed cuts. Later that month, the airline and the union reached agreement on a swap—$195 million in cuts affecting union workers in return for a $187-million creditor claim due the company after it emerged from bankruptcy. The creditor claim resulted in a distribution of cash to union workers and funds to their retirement accounts later in 2007.

Automobile manufacturing. Union representatives conducted bargaining with U.S. automobile firms in a climate of factory closings and steady job loss. The BLS reported that from 2000 to 2005, U.S. automobile employment declined by more than 16 percent, but the fall-off among the U.S. "Big Three"—General Motors (GM) Corporation of Detroit; Ford Motor Company of Dearborn, Michigan; and Chrysler LLC of Auburn Hills, Michigan—was especially steep.

Officials of the United Automobile Workers (UAW) announced in early 2007 that, in negotiations with the Big Three, they would focus on job security, protection of pensions, and limiting use of temporary workers. However, in an agreement concluded with financially troubled Ford Motor Company in April, the union accepted terms requested by the automaker to "improve efficiency" at Ford plants in Ohio and Kentucky. The terms involved working four 10-hour days a week, permitting the outsourcing of some jobs, and changes in job classifications. In exchange, Ford promised to invest millions in U.S. plants to keep them open.

The automakers and the UAW concluded comprehensive, four-year labor contracts for Big Three union employees in the second half of 2007. The contracts—with GM in September, Chrysler in October, and Ford in November—included signing bonuses and lump-sum payments instead of general wage increases and reduced starting wages for new hires by 50 percent. In return, the companies agreed to invest in U.S. plants to protect domestic jobs. The most significant provision of the contracts, judged industry and labor experts, was an agreement to transfer responsibility for health care of retired workers to a fund to be managed by the UAW. The companies would transfer billions of dollars to the fund. In return, they ultimately would divest themselves of liability for an expense that was likely to increase dramatically over time.

At Delphi Corporation of Troy, Michigan, a parts manufacturer spun off by GM in 1999, a bankruptcy court in July 2007 approved a UAW-Delphi agreement covering 17,000 workers. The contract called for reduced wages for current employees, lower starting wages for new hires, retirement incentives, and severance and relocation benefits. In August, the International Union of Electrical Workers and the Communication Workers of America ratified separate contracts with Delphi incorporating similar provisions.

Health industry. In January, the Service Employees International Union (SEIU) reached agreement with the League of Voluntary Hospitals and Homes of New York on a contract covering 65,000 workers. The employers agreed to contribute $42 million to the benefits fund and to help reduce a $700-million shortfall in the fund by 2011. The Minnesota Nurses Association concluded a three-year contract in 2007 with 13 Minneapolis-St. Paul area hospitals. The contract, which covered 10,750 members, stipulated annual wage increases of between 3.3 and 4 percent. In April, Stanford University hospitals and clinics in California agreed with the Independent Committee for Recognition of Nursing Achievement on a three-year pact providing annual increases of from 5.5 to 6 percent.

Food industry. During 2007, the United Food and Commercial Workers Union (UFCW) concluded agreements with major grocery chains in California, the New England states, and western Washington state, all of which included wage and salary increases. The contract with supermarkets in Washington included an innovative health care plan emphasizing preventive care.

Entertainment industry. On November 5, the Writers Guild of America struck the Alliance of Motion Picture and Television Producers (AMPTP), a trade association of makers of entertainment media. The dispute concerned sharing revenue from DVD sales, computer downloads, and other new sources of revenue for movies and

CHANGES IN THE UNITED STATES LABOR FORCE

	2006	2007*
Civilian labor force	151,428,000	153,000,000
Total employment	144,427,000	146,017,000
Unemployment	7,001,000	6,983,000
Unemployment rate	4.6%	4.6%
Change in weekly earnings of production and nonsupervisory workers (nonfarm business sector)		
Current dollars	3.9%	3.6%
Constant (1982) dollars	0.7%	1.0%
Change in output per employee hour (nonfarm business sector)	2.1%	2.5%

*All 2007 data are through the third quarter of 2007 (preliminary data).
Source: *World Book* estimates based on data from the U.S. Bureau of Labor Statistics.

television shows. The strike threatened to dry up new productions, resulting in early television reruns, notoriously during the November sweeps. Bargaining between the Writers Guild and the AMPTP resumed in mid-November.

In late 2007, a strike by Local 1 of the International Alliance of Theatrical Stage Employees, representing the striking stagehands, shut down numerous Broadway shows. At the center of the dispute were "work rules in the stagehands' contract that [the League of American Theaters and Producers] considered costly and inefficient." The 19-day strike ended on November 28 with an agreement, ratified on December 9, providing the producers with greater flexibility in the number of hours stagehands work. It also called for the minimum number of stagehands for certain production calls. In return, the union members received raises substantially higher than the 3.5-percent increase initially offered.

In May, six service trades locals approved a 41-month agreement with Disney World, owned by the Walt Disney Company of Burbank, California. The provisions, which affected 21,000 employees of the central Florida complex, included pay increases, health care coverage, and pension enhancements. Officials of the UNITE HERE union ratified agreements in 2007 with Las Vegas-based entertainment companies Harrah's Entertainment, Inc., and MGM Mirage. The agreements, which covered a total of 36,000 workers, provided a $3.47 hourly pay increase.

Postal industry. In January, the American Postal Workers Union reached agreement with the United States Postal Service on a new contract covering 272,000 postal workers. The workers were to receive a pay increase of 1.3 percent retroactive to Nov. 25, 2006, a 1.2-percent increase in 2009, and a one-level classification upgrade. In July 2007, the National Association of Letter Carriers agreed with the United States Postal Service on a five-year pact covering 222,000 workers. The agreement included an 8.65-percent wage increase over five years.

Rubber industry. In April, members of six United Steelworkers locals ratified a three-year contract with Bridgestone Americas Holding, Inc., of Nashville, covering 5,000 workers in several states. The contract preserved pay levels for current employees but reduced pay for new hires by 17 percent. It also required retired employees to pay more for health care. The company agreed to invest $100 million in U.S. plants.

In July, United Steelworkers at four Goodyear Engineered Products plants ratified a five-year pact with the Carlyle Group of Washington, D.C., a private equity firm that purchased the division of Goodyear in March. The agreement provided for profit-sharing plans to be established by Carlyle Group. The plans would distribute 8 percent of profits annually up to maximums specified in the contract.

Union membership in the United States fell from 12.5 percent of the workforce in 2005 to 12 percent in 2006 (reflecting the most recent BLS annual data available). The number of U.S. union members totaled 15.4 million in 2006. The highest percentage of unionized workers in any industry sector was 23.2 percent in transportation and utilities; the lowest proportion—1.4 percent—was in finance and insurance.

In January 2007, the Service Employees International Union (SEIU) announced the creation of a new national health care union for its 1 million members in the health care field. The new union was called SEIU Healthcare and was headed by Dennis Rivera, the leader of United Healthcare Workers East, a New York-based local union of health care workers.

Federal government. In May 2007, the U.S. Congress passed and U.S. President George W. Bush signed legislation to increase the federal minimum wage from $5.15 an hour to $5.85 an hour in 2007; to $6.55 an hour in 2008; and to $7.25 an hour in 2009. The act also included $4.8 billion in tax relief for small businesses.

In Congress, proposals to deal comprehensively with immigration generated debate but no legislation. According to economists, significant sectors of the U.S. economy were highly dependent upon the labor of temporary foreign workers—whether legal or illegal—and the lack of a legal framework in which to use such workers caused dislocations in the economy and headaches for law enforcement agencies. Immigration experts estimated that approximately 12 million illegal immigrants were living and working in the United States in 2007.

International unemployment. In 2007, nations with the lowest unemployment rates included the Netherlands, at 3.1 percent, and South Korea, at 3.2 percent, according to the Organisation for Economic Co-operation and Development (OECD). Many industrialized nations, including the United States, reported unemployment rates in the 4-percent to 4.9-percent range. Among OECD members, Slovakia had the highest unemployment rate, at 11.1 percent, while Poland experienced the greatest improvement, with joblessness declining from 13.8 percent in 2006 to 8.8 percent in 2007.   ■ Robert W. Fisher

See also **Automobile; Aviation; Economics, U.S.; Economics, World; Health care issues; Television; United States, Government of the.**

Labrador. See Canadian provinces.

Laos. See Asia.

LATIN AMERICA

During 2007, incumbent left-of-center administrations consolidated their hold on power in Argentina, Brazil, and Venezuela and welcomed the rise of similarly oriented regimes elsewhere in Latin America. In January, Brazilian President Luiz Inácio Lula da Silva, of the Workers' Party, was inaugurated for a second term. The same month, Venezuelan President Hugo Chávez Frías was sworn in for a third term. He promptly organized the new United Socialist Party of Venezuela to tighten his political control of the nation.

In December, Cristina Fernández de Kirchner, of Argentina's ruling Justicialist (Peronist) Party, succeeded her husband, the popular outgoing President Néstor Kirchner. An experienced politician in her own right, Fernández de Kirchner had served as a senator since 1995.

Two more leftist presidents were inaugurated in January 2007, in accord with the socialist trend sweeping Latin America. In Ecuador, Rafael Vicente Correa Delgado, a former professor and economy minister, immediately embarked upon a nationalistic course of government like that imposed by the Kirchners in Argentina.

In Nicaragua, Daniel Ortega was sworn in for a second term as president following a political comeback that amazed some experts. During his first term as elected president from 1985 to 1990, the government of United States President Ronald Reagan covertly supported an armed rebellion against Ortega, a self-avowed Marxist. Although it did not drive Ortega out of office, the rebellion forced him to hold a presidential election, which he lost.

Elections in 2007. In Guatemala, businessman and engineer Álvaro Colom of the center-left National Unity of Hope coalition won the presidential runoff election on November 4. He was scheduled to take office in January 2008. Following one of the most violent election campaigns in Guatemalan history, Colom pledged to crack down on crime. More than 50 candidates and political supporters had been killed in the year leading up to presidential, parliamentary, and local elections held on Sept. 9, 2007. Candidates attributed the bloodshed to drug traffickers attempting to control the outcomes of individual races.

Patrick Manning, the incumbent prime minister of Trinidad and Tobago, was sworn in for a third term on November 7, two days after voters gave his centrist People's National Movement party a major-

Bolivian children play near a memorial to Ernesto "Che" Guevara in the village of La Higuera. The Argentine-born leftist revolutionary was executed in La Higuera in 1967 while attempting to overthrow Bolivia's government. Forty years after his death, the memory of "Che" inspires mixed opinions from admirers who consider him an idealist and critics who view him as a vicious killer.

FACTS IN BRIEF ON LATIN AMERICA

Country	Population	Government	Monetary unit†	Foreign trade (million U.S.$) Exports††	Imports††
Antigua and Barbuda	84,000	Governor General Louisse Lake-Tack; Prime Minister Baldwin Spencer	XCD dollar (2.69 = $1)	47	378
Argentina	39,746,000	President Cristina Fernández de Kirchner	peso (3.15 = $1)	46,600	31,690
Bahamas	336,000	Governor General Arthur Hanna; Prime Minister Hubert Ingraham	dollar (1.00 = $1)	451	2,160
Barbados	282,000	Governor General Sir Clifford Straughn Husbands; Prime Minister Owen Arthur	dollar (2.00 = $1)	209	1,476
Belize	312,000	Governor General Sir Colville Young, Sr.; Prime Minister Said Wilbert Musa	dollar (1.97 = $1)	360	543
Bolivia	9,764,000	President Evo Morales	boliviano (7.68 = $1)	3,668	2,934
Brazil	193,540,000	President Luiz Inácio Lula da Silva	real (1.84 = $1)	137,500	91,400
Chile	16,763,000	President Michelle Bachelet	peso (506.75 = $1)	58,210	35,370
Colombia	43,127,000	President Álvaro Uribe Vélez	peso (2,022.13 = $1)	24,860	24,330
Costa Rica	4,550,000	President Óscar Arias Sánchez	colón (18.56 = $1)	7,931	10,880
Cuba	11,371,000	President Fidel Castro*	peso (1.00 = $1)	2,956	9,510
Dominica	80,000	President Nicholas Liverpool; Prime Minister Roosevelt Skerrit	XCD dollar (2.69 = $1)	74	234
Dominican Republic	9,290,000	President Leonel Fernández Reyna	peso (33.39 = $1)	6,495	11,390
Ecuador	13,832,000	President Rafael Correa	U.S. dollar	12,560	10,810
El Salvador	7,218,000	President Elías Antonio Saca	colón (8.75 = $1) U.S. dollar	3,686	7,326
Grenada	106,000	Governor General Daniel Williams; Prime Minister Keith Mitchell	XCD dollar (2.69 = $1)	40	276
Guatemala	13,532,000	President Álvaro Colom	quetzal (7.74 = $1)	3,710	9,911
Guyana	753,000	President Bharrat Jagdeo	dollar (204.45 = $1)	622	707
Haiti	9,037,000	President Réne Préval; Prime Minister Jacques-Édouard Alexis	gourde (36.33 = $1)	444	1,721
Honduras	7,691,000	President Manuel Zelaya	lempira (18.90 = $1)	1,947	4,860
Jamaica	2,695,000	Governor General Kenneth Hall; Prime Minister Bruce Golding	dollar (70.75 = $1)	2,087	4,682
Mexico	110,915,000	President Felipe Calderón Hinojosa	peso (10.91 = $1)	248,800	253,100
Nicaragua	5,458,000	President Daniel Ortega	gold cordoba (18.68 = $1)	1,714	3,202
Panama	3,394,000	President Martín Torrijos Espino	balboa (1.00 = $1)	8,087	9,365
Paraguay	6,352,000	President Nicanor Duarte Frutos	guarani (4,995.00 = $1)	1,690	4,500
Peru	29,180,000	President Alan García Pérez	new sol (3.03 = $1)	22,690	15,380
Puerto Rico	3,959,000	Governor Aníbal Acevedo Vilá	U.S. dollar	46,900	29,100
St. Kitts and Nevis	44,000	Governor General Cuthbert Montraville Sebastian; Prime Minister Denzil Douglas	XCD dollar (2.69 = $1)	70	405
St. Lucia	172,000	Governor General Pearlette Louisy; Prime Minister Stephenson King	XCD dollar (2.69 = $1)	82	410
St. Vincent and the Grenadines	121,000	Governor General Sir Frederick Nathaniel Ballantyne; Prime Minister Ralph E. Gonsalves	XCD dollar (2.69 = $1)	37	225
Suriname	458,000	President Runaldo Ronald Venetiaan	dollar (2.75 = $1)	881	750
Trinidad and Tobago	1,316,000	President George Maxwell Richards; Prime Minister Patrick Manning	dollar (6.28 = $1)	12,500	8,798
Uruguay	3,370,000	President Tabaré Ramón Vázquez Rosas	peso (22.78 = $1)	3,993	4,532
Venezuela	28,112,000	President Hugo Chávez Frías	bolívar (2,147.30 = $1)	69,230	28,810

*Since July 2006, Raúl Castro has been acting president.
†Exchange rates as of Oct. 4, 2007.　　　　††Latest available data.

ity of seats in the legislature. Manning said that his government would work to diversify the economy of Trinidad and Tobago and bridge the racial divide in his country between people of African and East Indian ancestry.

Elsewhere in the Caribbean, the center-left Jamaica Labour Party (JLP) narrowly won September 3 parliamentary elections by fewer than 3,000 votes. The victory marked the end of an 18-year stretch during which the JLP had not controlled the government. Party leader Bruce Golding was sworn in as prime minister on September 11. He succeeded Portia Simpson Miller, Jamaica's first female prime minister, of the People's National Party.

Hugo Chávez: Man of the year or tyrant? Venezuelan President Hugo Chávez dominated headlines from Latin America in 2007, a year during which he seized virtual dictatorial powers at home. The legislature and the judiciary, controlled by Chávez supporters, approved without debate most of the president's Socialist reforms. Amid swirling controversy over his methods, Chávez could legitimately claim that his actions were benefiting millions of ordinary people.

Chávez drew upon Venezuela's windfall petroleum revenues to provide more than $8.8 billion in direct assistance and financing for governments and welfare organizations in more than 20 Western Hemisphere countries during the first eight months of the year. Recipients included several nonprofit groups in the Bronx, New York City, such as the North Star Fund, Point Community Development Corporation, Youth Ministries for Peace and Justice, and Rocking the Boat. These groups shared approximately $4 million in grants for environmental restoration and social programs from Citgo, a Houston-based subsidiary of Petróleos de Venezuela, Venezuela's state-run oil company.

Giving to the neediest. In accordance with Chávez's pledge to help the poor, Venezuela provided $2 million for the construction of a homeless shelter in Georgetown, the capital of neighboring Guyana. In 2007, petroleum-rich Venezuela was among the world's most generous donors to the Western Hemisphere's poorest nation, Haiti. Most of Venezuela's $200 million in aid to Haiti was invested in infrastructure projects and reducing the cost of fuel imports. Some of it also paid for new garbage trucks to collect mountains of festering trash in Haiti's urban ghettos and for Cuban medical teams that provided a modicum of health care in the country's burgeoning slums. In March, when Chávez visited the Haitian capital of Port-au-Prince, he received a hero's welcome.

Regional energy initiatives. Chávez shrewdly spent a large share of Venezuelan aid on efforts to centralize Latin America's energy industry in Caracas, the Venezuelan capital. In an attempt to break the stranglehold on petroleum commerce long

enjoyed by a handful of foreign-owned multinational companies, Chávez's government helped finance the construction of new refineries or the modernization of existing ones in Bolivia, Cuba, Ecuador, Haiti, Jamaica, Nicaragua, and Uruguay. The refineries, supplied with crude oil from Venezuela, were large enough to meet each country's consumption requirements.

In August, Chávez pledged to continue his PetroCaribe program, through which Venezuela provided extremely low-interest financing on oil exports to poor, energy-short Caribbean nations. The program, initiated in 2005, had saved its members an estimated total of $450 million per year. By 2007, 15 nations and several metropolitan communities in the United States were participating in the PetroCaribe program.

Also in August, Chávez met with Argentine President Néstor Kirchner and Bolivian President Evo Morales in Tarija, Bolivia. During his visit, Chávez pledged to help finance $600 million in oil exploration through a new joint Venezuelan and Bolivian venture. The meeting also resulted in President Kirchner promising to provide $450 million in loans to build a gas separation plant near the border separating Bolivia and Paraguay. The new plant would help satisfy the urgent, rapidly increasing energy demands of Argentina's industrial sector.

Mining strikes occurred during 2007 in some Andean countries whose mineral resources provided much of their national wealth. During a year when international prices for copper, gold, nickel, tin, zinc, and other minerals were high, Chilean and Peruvian union employees demanded a living wage and improved health benefits. They also called for stricter enforcement of existing labor laws and more frequent government inspections of safety and working conditions at the mines. Environmental militancy accompanied the strikes in mining communities, where mining operations often devastated the land or posed a threat to human health.

Mining strikes also targeted the common practice of *outsourcing* work to nonunion laborers hired by private companies, which were not bound by union contracts. Nonunion employees earned less than half as much as those belonging to unions or employed directly by state-controlled companies.

Former leaders face justice. In January, Argentine courts ordered the arrest of María Estela "Isabel" de Perón, president of Argentina from 1974 to 1976, on charges of human rights abuses committed while in office. Police in Spain, where Perón had been living in exile, detained her. An official request for her *extradition* (handing over) to Argentina, where she would face a trial, was to be settled by Spanish courts.

In December 2007, former Peruvian President

Alberto Fujimori was convicted in Lima, Peru, of having authorized an illegal search while in office. He received a sentence of six years in prison. Fujimori also was on trial for human rights violations committed during his administration, which lasted from 1990 to 2000. The human rights trial was expected to stretch into 2008. In September 2007, Fujimori was extradited to Peru from Chile, where he had been detained in 2005. In handing over Fujimori, Chilean authorities departed from the time-honored practice of granting former Latin American leaders immunity from extradition.

Immigration reform. Despite bipartisan efforts and the support of U.S. President George W. Bush's administration, the U.S. Congress failed to reform immigration laws that affected millions of Latin Americans living illegally in the United States in 2007. Proposed reforms included a guest worker program and provisions for illegals already in the country to obtain legal status and U.S. citizenship.

In a year when the status of illegal immigrants was a major political issue in U.S. presidential election campaigns, the U.S. Congress authorized funding for the construction of barrier walls along the U.S.-Mexico border. United States federal agents conducted numerous raids at scattered locations to enforce existing immigration laws. While netting illegals, the raids often led to the traumatic breakup of families that included legal and illegal residents. Several U.S. states and municipalities rushed to enact laws to discourage illegal immigration. Legal scholars questioned whether some of these laws were consistent with the U.S. Constitution.

Investment in the United States. Latin American multinational companies continued making sizable investments in the United States in 2007. Major players included CEMEX of Monterrey, Mexico, which had about 10,000 employees in the United States, where it was the top supplier of cement and ready-mix concrete. Gerdau Ameristeel, the U.S. subsidiary of the Gerdau Group, based in Pôrto Alegre, Brazil, ranked as North America's fourth-largest producer of steel. In July, JBS S.A. of São Paulo, Brazil, acquired Swift & Company of Greeley, Colorado, for about $1.5 billion. The acquisition resulted in the creation of JBS Swift Group, the world's largest beef-processing company.

Papal visit. In May, Pope Benedict XVI visited Brazil, home of the world's largest Roman Catholic population. The visit was his first to Latin America as pope. During the trip, Benedict criticized Marxism and unrestrained capitalism as "systems that marginalize God." He also spoke out strongly against abortion, artificial contraception, and drug trafficking and urged the Catholic clergy to halt the steady decline of Catholicism in the region, where the Church had lost many members to evangelical Protestant denominations. In addition, Benedict canonized the first Brazilian saint.

Dengue surge. Health authorities blamed global warming, changes in human migration patterns, and faltering mosquito eradication efforts for a dramatic surge of dengue fever in Latin America in 2007. According to the Washington, D.C.-based Pan American Health Organization, more than 700,000 cases had been reported by early November. The countries hit hardest by dengue included Brazil, Colombia, Paraguay, and Venezuela.

Patagonian giant unearthed. In October, Argentine and Brazilian paleontologists announced they had discovered the fossil remains of a dinosaur that roamed an arid region of Patagonia 88 million years ago. The plant-eating creature, thought to belong to a new species, measured 105 feet (32 meters) long and stood four stories high. It was named *Futalognkosaurus dukei* after the Mapuche Indian words for *giant* and *chief,* and for Duke Energy Argentina, which helped finance the excavation.

Ancient seeds found in the Andes. In June, scientists announced that domesticated squash seeds discovered in northern Peru were about 10,000 years old. The age of the seeds indicated that farming began in the Andes region twice as long ago as previously thought. Scientists also found traces of fruits, grain, and manioc, as well as stone hoes, garden plots, and irrigation canals from around the same period.   ■ Nathan A. Haverstock

See also various Latin American country articles.

Latvia. President Vaira Vike-Freiberga in May 2007 called for a national referendum on two controversial amendments to Latvia's security laws passed by the legislature on March 1. She vetoed the bills on March 10, but the legislature overrode her veto. The July 7 referendum failed because only 23 percent—rather than the required 50 percent—of those eligible voted.

On May 31, the legislature chose Valdis Zatlers, ruling coalition candidate and head of the Latvian Orthopedic and Traumatology Hospital, to replace Vike-Freiberga when her term ended on July 8. Zatlers won out over opposition candidate and former Constitutional Court judge Aivars Endzins.

An antigovernment demonstration broke out in Riga, the capital, on October 18, over Prime Minister Aigars Kalvitis's attempt to fire anticorruption chief Aleksejs Loskutovs. Opponents viewed the attempt as politically motivated. Kalvitis survived an October 23 parliamentary no-confidence vote, but the crisis failed to abate. On October 31, the government suspended its decision to dismiss Loskutovs. After continued protests, Kalvitis and his center-right coalition government resigned on December 5. Kalvitas then stayed on in a caretaker capacity. On December 20, parliament selected Ivars Godmanis as prime minister.   ■ Juliet Johnson

See also **Europe.**

Law. See **Civil rights; Courts; Crime.**

Smoke billows over buildings destroyed by a bomb at a Palestinian refugee camp in northern Lebanon in August. Lebanese troops clashed with Syrian-supported Islamic militants using the name "Fatah al-Islam" in this region from May until September, when the Lebanese army finally prevailed.

Lebanon. A general strike called by pro-Syria opposition leaders in Lebanon failed on Jan. 23, 2007, as supporters of Lebanon's anti-Syria "Cedar Revolution" majority prevented opposition efforts to cut off Beirut, the capital, from the rest of the country. Lebanese police and troops opened roads blocked by tires set on fire by opposition forces, and prodemocracy counterprotestors rallied against the strikers. Although the primary objective of the general strike had been to prevent Prime Minister Fouad Siniora from participating in a conference of donors in Paris on January 25, Siniora was able to attend. There, he obtained more than $7 billion in pledges from the international community to help Lebanon continue its reconstruction after years of war and terrorist attacks.

Terrorist war against Lebanon. Under the name of Fatah al-Islam, hundreds of militant Islamic fighters were dispatched, presumably by Syria, to establish a stronghold in northern Lebanon in May. Fierce battles between the Lebanese army and Fatah al-Islam lasted until September, when the army prevailed. The vast majority of Lebanese people hailed the triumph of the army over the terrorist organization as heroic.

Islamic terrorists attacked the United Nations Interim Force in Lebanon (UNIFIL) on June 24 using a remote-controlled car bomb, killing six peace-keeping troops serving with the Spanish army in southern Lebanon. Analysts of Middle East affairs noted that the car bombing was probably the work of Syria and Hezbollah, Syria's proxy group in Lebanon. Syria and Hezbollah opposed the deployment of the expanded UNIFIL forces in the region from the Litani River to the Lebanese-Israeli border—a deployment mandated by a United Nations (UN) Security Council resolution in 2006.

In June and September 2007, Syrian agents were widely suspected of carrying out the assassi-nation of two prominent members of Lebanon's National Assembly who belonged to the Cedar Revolution movement. Walid Eido, a judge who was an outspoken critic of Syria, was assassinated on June 13, and Antoine Ghanem was killed on September 19. Middle East analysts speculated that these assassinations were meant to intimidate the Cedar Revolution majority and decrease its representation in the National Assembly. Syrian agents were also suspected in the December 12 car-bomb murder of Brigadier General François al-Hajj, chief of operations for the Lebanese army.

Birri blocks National Assembly. Nabih Birri, the pro-Syria speaker (or president) of Lebanon's Chamber of Deputies, prevented the convening of regular sessions of parliament in 2007. Analysts noted that Birri had two main reasons for doing so. First, Birri wanted to prevent the anti-Syria parliamentary majority from endorsing the establishment of an international tribunal to prosecute the culprits behind several political assassinations in Lebanon, including that of former Lebanese Prime Minister Rafik Hariri in February 2005. Despite Birri's efforts, the UN Security Council established the international tribunal in May 2007.

The second reason that Birri blocked the convening of the National Assembly was that he hoped to prevent the parliamentary majority from electing a new president of Lebanon to assume power after the term of pro-Syria President Emile Lahoud expired on November 23. Both Birri and Hezbollah, backed by Syria and Iran, threatened that electing the new president from among the ranks of the Cedar Revolution majority would have "dire consequences."

Cedar Revolution leaders, together with the foreign ministers of France, Italy, and Spain, sought in vain to find a compromise presidential candidate that would be acceptable to both pro-Syria and anti-Syria sides. Consequently, President Lahoud left office in November without an elected successor. In December, the parliamentary majority nominated General Michel Suleiman, commander of the army, as a compromise candidate for president. ■ Marius Deeb

See also **Israel; Middle East; Syria.**

Lesotho. See Africa.
Liberia. See Africa.

Library. The libraries along the Gulf Coast that were devastated by hurricanes Katrina and Rita in 2005 continued their struggle to restore services throughout 2007. By October, New Orleans Public Library had reopened nine of its branches, including one branch in the heavily damaged Lower Ninth Ward. Three more branches were expected to open soon, but three others remained closed indefinitely.

Funding highs and lows. Low tax revenue hurt tax-supported libraries on two fronts in 2007. The property-tax revolt that began in California in 1978 continued to spread nationwide. On top of that, many people lost their homes because they could not meet rising mortgage payments. As the number of unsold houses rose and home values fell in 2007, revenue from property taxes decreased.

In June, Florida passed a law that forced communities to lower their property taxes by between 3 and 9 percent, beginning in October. The tax reduction resulted in less money for libraries, schools, police, fire, and other locally funded services. California Governor Arnold Schwarzenegger surprised librarians by cutting $14 million in support that they had counted on to make up for tight funding from their towns. Minneapolis Public Library spent much of 2007 negotiating a merger with the suburban Hennepin County Library system so that they could share expenses. In the fall, New Jersey legislators considered eliminating a rule that requires each town to spend a uniformly set minimum portion of its property-tax dollars on its library.

There was good news in 2007 as well. For the first time in six years, the public libraries in all five boroughs of New York City offered service at least six days a week. In California, the Salinas County Library was able to increase its hours of operation when the city's 2006-2007 budget resumed financing of the library after having cut its funds in 2004. Chicago Mayor Richard M. Daley persuaded the city council in October 2007 to increase taxes so the 78-branch city library system could maintain quality services.

Federal support. In 2007, for the third year in a row, the administration of U.S. President George W. Bush proposed an increase in overall federal funding for libraries. The proposed $226 million was nearly $6 million more than the amount funded for the previous fiscal year.

The suspension of hundreds of millions of dollars in federal support to 39 states that once depended on a now-ailing logging industry caused the Jackson County and Josephine County library systems in Oregon to close in April. In the fall, Congress introduced a bill that would reinstate the funding through 2011. Jackson County began reopening its 15 branches part-time in October 2007, with local funds and a one-year emergency payment from the federal goverment.

Relevance. To keep up with cultural trends, some libraries began in 2007 offering reference service through instant messaging. Others joined such social networking Web sites as Facebook, MySpace, and Second Life, and an increasing number hosted events for video-game fans. The activities expanded traditional services, which continued to grow. According to a report released by the American Library Association in April, public libraries handled almost 1.8 billion visits in 2004, a 61-percent jump since 1994. Borrowing increased 28 percent over that same period.

Privacy. In August 2007, President Bush signed an emergency bill to amend the Foreign Intelligence Surveillance Act, and Congress began working on a more permanent modification before mid-February 2008, when the emergency modification was scheduled to expire. The bill allowed the government to secretly read e-mails—including those sent and received through libraries—between people in the United States and foreign countries. A month later, a court decided that part of the Patriot Act was unconstitutional because it authorized federal agents to demand records of people's buying and reading habits without a judge's approval. ■ Beverly Goldberg

Libya. The United Nations (UN) General Assembly voted in October 2007 to place Libya and four other nations on the 15-member UN Security Council for two years, beginning in 2008. Libya took the place of Qatar as the Arab countries' representative on the Security Council.

United States-Libya relations. In July 2007, United States President George W. Bush appointed Gene Cretz as U.S. ambassador to Libya. Cretz was serving as deputy chief of the U.S. mission in Tel Aviv, the capital of Israel. If confirmed by the U.S. Senate, Cretz would become the first U.S. ambassador to Libya since diplomatic relations between the two countries were severed in the 1970's, becuase of Libyan support of terrorism.

Accord with France. President Nicolas Sarkozy of France announced in July 2007 an agreement between France and Libya for cooperation in nuclear energy. Under the terms of the agreement, France was to build a nuclear-powered *desalination* plant in Libya (to extract salt from seawater, rendering the water drinkable). In exchange, France was to gain access to Libyan supplies of uranium, a fuel for nuclear reactors.

Nurses freed. Five Bulgarian nurses and one Palestinian physician were freed in July after eight years of detention in Libyan jails. Libyan courts had found the medical professionals guilty of purposely infecting more than 400 Libyan children with HIV, the virus that causes AIDS, at a hospital in the coastal city of Benghazi. The courts then sentenced the prisoners to death. The World Health Organization, however, concluded that the HIV infection spread among the children as a result of unhygienic conditions, such as the reuse of syringes, at the hospital.

The nurses and physician were released at the behest of Cecilia Sarkozy, then the wife of the president of France, and Benita Ferrero-Waldner, the European Union's external relations commissioner, who visited Libya in July 2007 to negotiate with Libyan officials. In exchange for the release of the prisoners, the European Union reportedly agreed to pay $400 million in compensation to the families of the Libyan victims, in addition to providing other benefits.

BP. During a visit to Libya in May, outgoing Prime Minister Tony Blair of the United Kingdom announced the signing of a $900-million agreement by BP plc to explore for and develop natural gas in Libya. This agreement marked the return of the company formerly known as British Petroleum to Libya for the first time since its departure in 1974, when Libyan leader Mu'ammar al-Qadhafi allegedly supported terrorism and the subersion of moderate Arab governments. ■ Mary-Jane Deeb

See also **France; Middle East; United Nations.**

Liechtenstein. See **Europe.**

Bulgarian nurses and a Palestinian physician stand behind bars as they listen to court proceedings in Tripoli, the Libyan capital, in February 2007. Libyan courts had convicted the medical professionals of infecting more than 400 children with HIV, the virus that causes AIDS, but scientific confirmation of their innocence and international pressure caused Libya to release the prisoners in July.

Literature. The publishing event of 2007 may have been the release of *Harry Potter and the Deathly Hallows,* the seventh and final installment of J. K. Rowling's "Harry Potter" series. Preorders of the book ran to millions of copies; more than 10 million copies were sold in the first 24 hours after the book's release, at one minute after midnight on July 21. Around the world, readers engaged in marathon sessions to finish the book before anyone had a chance to spoil its ending for them. The book had been leaked on the Internet prior to publication, so readers had some cause for fear.

Deathly Hallows was widely praised by critics. Michiko Kakutani of *The New York Times* called the series a "monumental, spellbinding epic" and praised its last volume as "a somber book that marks Harry's final initiation into the complexities and sadnesses of adulthood." In the *Chicago Tribune,* Julia Keller described *Deathly Hallows* as a "a deeply engaging book, filled with love and loss, with crackling action and almost unbearable heartbreak."

Pulitzer Prize. The 2007 Pulitzer Prize for fiction was awarded to Cormac McCarthy's *The Road,* a bleak fable about a father and son fighting for survival in a post-apocalyptic landscape. The popularity of the critically acclaimed best seller was further boosted by its selection for Oprah's Book Club. The two other finalists in the Pulitzer's fiction category in 2007 were Richard Powers's *The Echo Maker,* which depicts a man's struggle with a rare neurological disorder called Capgras syndrome, and Alice McDermott's *After This,* an intimate portrait of a suburban Irish-Catholic family in the 1960's and 1970's.

On the Road. The year 2007 marked the 50th anniversary of the publication of Jack Kerouac's *On the Road,* the defining work of the Beat movement of the 1950's. The novel, a semi-autobiographical work about a young man's cross-country road trips, was re-released by Viking Press in a special edition in 2007. Viking also published the unedited text of the 120-foot (36.5-meter) "scroll" on which Kerouac typed his first draft of the novel. The greatest tribute to Kerouac's influence on American literature, however, was his inclusion in 2007 in the prestigious Library of America, with a volume entitled *Road Novels 1957–1960.* The collection begins with *On the Road* and also contains *The Dharma Bums* (1958), *The Subterraneans* (1958), *Tristessa* (1960), *Lonesome Traveler* (1960), and a selection of Kerouac's journal entries.

Other Library of America releases. Saul Bellow was honored with a new Library of America volume. Bellow's *Novels 1944–1953,* published by the Library of America in 2003, was followed in 2007 by *Novels 1956–1964,* which included

Seize the Day (1956), *Henderson the Rain King* (1959), and *Herzog* (1964).

A more surprising addition to the Library of America in 2007 was the science-fiction writer Philip K. Dick, who had worked his entire career to achieve mainstream approval. *Four Novels of the 1960s* is a fine survey of Dick's major subjects—paranoia, the nature of perception and reality, and alienation in modern life. The volume includes Hugo Award-winning *The Man in the High Castle* (1962), *The Three Stigmata of Palmer Eldritch* (1965), *Do Androids Dream of Electric Sheep?* (1968)—on which the film *Blade Runner* (1982) was based—and *Ubik* (1969). This belated recognition of Dick's achievement was perhaps less remarkable given the growing acceptance of genre fiction as serious literature.

In 2007, the Library of America also released *Zuckerman Bound: A Trilogy and Epilogue 1979–1985,* the fourth in an eight-volume series of Philip Roth's works, cementing his already staggering reputation. Roth released *Exit Ghost* in 2007, his ninth and, according to the publisher, final novel about the writer Nathan Zuckerman, to a striking number of negative reviews.

PEN/Faulkner Award. Roth won the 2007 PEN/Faulkner Award for Fiction for his 2006 novel *Everyman,* which the jury "admired for its precise physicality and lyrical brilliance." Roth became the only writer to win the prize three times, previously for *Operation Shylock* in 1994 and *The Human Stain* in 2001. Finalists for the 2007 prize included Charles D'Ambrosio's *The Dead Fish Museum,* Deborah Eisenberg's *Twilight of the Superheroes,* Amy Hempel's *Collected Stories,* and Edward P. Jones's *All Aunt Hagar's Children.*

Medal of honor. Pulitzer Prize-winning American author Harper Lee received the highest honor possible for a civilian in the United States in 2007, the Presidential Medal of Freedom. It was awarded by President George W. Bush on November 5. Lee's only novel, *To Kill a Mockingbird,* a semiautobiographical story with thoughtful handling of American racial problems, had been influential on U.S. culture since its publication in 1960.

Other American literature in 2007. The prolific Joyce Carol Oates published her 36th novel, *The Gravedigger's Daughter,* in 2007. The book's title character, Rebecca, is the youngest child of an immigrant family that escaped Nazi Germany to live in upstate New York. The novel follows 40 years of Rebecca's life and her attempt to escape her past. Although the book returns to Oates's familiar themes of violence and victimization, Brian Hall of *The Washington Post* wrote that it "is neither a depressing story nor an uplifting one" because "Oates succeeds ... in making such judgments feel simple-minded." Also published in 2007 was *The Journal of Joyce Carol*

Oates: 1973-1982, which offered insight into Oates's creative process and her relationships with such other writers as Donald Barthelme, John Gardner, Philip Roth, Susan Sontag, and John Updike.

In 2007, Don DeLillo added to a growing number of novels about the terrorist attacks of Sept. 11, 2001, with Falling Man. The title refers both to an actual photograph taken of a man jumping from the burning World Trade Center and to a character in the novel—a performance artist who "re-creates" this photo around New York City. William Gibson's 2007 release, Spook Country, similarly deals with issues of danger and uncertainty in the modern world.

Denis Johnson's Tree of Smoke, his first novel in almost a decade, was hailed as a masterpiece. The Vietnam epic traces the intersecting paths of a number of characters, including a mysterious veteran of the Central Intelligence Agency (CIA), Colonel Francis Xavier Sands, and his nephew, a young and idealistic CIA operative named Skip; Kathy Jones, a widowed nurse; and a pair of Vietnamese brothers working with U.S. intelligence. Many critics noted the book's resonance with the war in Iraq. Tree of Smoke was awarded the 2007 National Book Award for Fiction in November.

Richard Russo's 2007 novel Bridge of Sighs is a look at the denizens of Thomaston, New York, a small industrial town in decline. It was Russo's first novel since his Pulitzer Prize-winning Empire Falls. Jodi Picoult's novel Nineteen Minutes is also set in a small town, though with darker subject matter: A boy who has been bullied brings a bag of guns to school and kills 10 people.

A promising debut in 2007 was Joshua Ferris's Then We Came to the End, a comical and yet deeply affecting story of employees at a failing Chicago advertising agency. The New Yorker maintained that Ferris "brilliantly captures the fishbowl quality of contemporary office life, where nothing much happens and the smallest events take on huge significance."

Hard-boiled and other crime fiction. Pulitzer Prize-winning author Michael Chabon delighted readers and critics in 2007 with his latest novel, The Yiddish Policemen's Union, a hard-boiled detective story set in an alternate universe in which post-World War II (1939-1945) European Jews have settled in Alaska instead of Israel.

The progenitor of the hard-boiled genre, Dashiell Hammett, was recognized in 2007 with a volume in Alfred A. Knopf's distinguished Everyman's Library series. The volume includes The Dain Curse (1929), The Glass Key (1931), and selected stories, with an introduction by the celebrated crime writer James Ellroy.

The crime genre continued to flourish in 2007, with the publication of Michael Connelly's 13th

"Harry Bosch" novel, The Overlook, and James Lee Burke's 16th "Dave Robicheaux" novel, The Tin Roof Blowdown.

Fiction by emigrés. Khaled Hosseini, the Afghan-born American author whose novel in 2003, The Kite Runner, became a best seller, returned in 2007 with A Thousand Splendid Suns. The book takes place in Afghanistan over several decades—depicting both Soviet and Taliban rule—and examines the plight of Afghan women by way of Mariam and Laila, both wedded to the same abusive husband.

The Haitian-born American writer Edwidge Danticat followed up her 2004 novel, The Dew Breaker, with a memoir about her immigrant family, Brother, I'm Dying. The work focuses on her father and his brother; the latter died while being detained by U.S. immigration officials.

Michael Ondaatje, the Sri Lankan-born Canadian novelist, published Divisadero in 2007, a family saga split between 1970's northern California and pre-World War I (1914-1918) rural France. Ondaatje's acclaimed novel The English Patient was published in 1992.

Man Booker prize. The 2007 Man Booker Prize for Fiction, awarded for novels written by authors of the British Commonwealth or Ireland, went to Irish author Anne Enright for The Gathering. The story follows an Irish family, meeting in Dublin after the suicide of one of its members. British author Nicola Barker's novel Darkmans, about a dysfunctional family in Kent, was short-listed for the Booker.

British writer Ian McEwan's short-listed novella On Chesil Beach got glowing reviews for its depiction of a young couple's awkward wedding night on the cusp of the sexual revolution of the 1960's. Another Man Booker nod went to New Zealander Lloyd Jones for Mr. Pip, a coming-of-age story featuring a girl caught up in a civil war on a South Pacific island and her fascination with Charles Dickens's Great Expectations (1861, in book form). Also nominated was Animal's People, by Indra Sinha, an Indian-born British author. The book concerns a man with deformities caused by a chemical-plant disaster in India.

Finally, The Reluctant Fundamentalist, by Pakistani-born British author Mohsin Hamid, was short-listed. The novel relates a conversation between an American and a young Pakistani who was educated at Princeton University and who had worked in finance in New York City. His treatment after the Sept. 11, 2001, terrorist attacks causes the Pakistani to feel anger and disillusionment with the United States and the "American Dream." ■ Stefan Beck

See also **Literature for children; Nobel Prizes; People in the news** (Doris Lessing; J. K. Rowling); **Poetry; Pulitzer Prizes; Theater.**

Kurt Vonnegut
So It Goes

Kurt Vonnegut became one of American literature's darkest and most humorous voices of the period following World War II (1939-1945). Vonnegut's novels and other writings combine elements of science fiction, wry humor, and memoir to explore the suffering of human beings in what the author viewed as an essentially meaningless universe. His most powerful work, *Slaughterhouse-Five* (1969), blends the author's horrific experiences during the war with a fictional narrative involving aliens and time travel. In the novel, Vonnegut introduced the conceit of repeating, "So it goes," each time a person's death is recounted. The phrase echoes the author's conviction that death, like much of human existence, lies beyond our control and so should just be accepted. Vonnegut died on April 11, 2007.

Vonnegut was born on Nov. 11, 1922, in Indianapolis. He took great pride in having grown up in the American Midwest, tracing his intellectual heritage to such great Midwesterners as the author Mark Twain and the socialist politician Eugene V. Debs. Vonnegut admired Debs's boldly populist social values and shared Twain's belief in the power of humor to redeem human folly.

During World War II, Vonnegut served in a U.S. Army unit that was captured by German troops. As a prisoner of war, he witnessed the bombing of Dresden, one of the war's worst massacres. In February 1945, as Vonnegut and his fellow prisoners huddled in the cellar of a slaughterhouse, Allied aircraft rained incendiary bombs down on the largely unprotected city. Tens of thousands of civilians died in the resulting firestorm. Afterward, Vonnegut and the others were forced to assist in the disposal of bodies. Vonnegut later used these experiences as the basis for the central narrative of *Slaughterhouse-Five*.

After the war, Vonnegut found work writing short stories for popular magazines. The most memorable examples used broadly drawn science fiction premises to explore some fundamental aspect of the human condition. His first novel, *Player Piano* (1952), envisioned a postwar United States in which automation made most labor obsolete. Vonnegut saw that in making people's lives easier, technological advances could also rob them of meaning, a recurring theme in his later works.

Other works explored humanity's seemingly endless capacity to inflict suffering upon itself. In the novel *Cat's Cradle* (1963), for example, a curious scientist, oblivious to the potential danger, invents a substance that can freeze all water on Earth. *Cat's Cradle* also introduced Bokononism, a fictional religion that incorporates many of the author's fatalistic beliefs.

Despite his bleak outlook, Vonnegut endeared readers with his playful writing style, sometimes even decorating the text with crude, hand-drawn illustrations. He also tempered his pessimism with a profound reverence for the simple virtues of kindness and mercy. Vonnegut maintained an uneasy relationship with the literary establishment, which he often felt used the label "science fiction" to exclude his work from serious consideration. But he remained a widely read author and beloved literary figure, continuing to write and make public appearances into the early 2000's.

In his last book, *A Man Without a Country* (2005), Vonnegut joked that when human beings had finally wiped out all life on Earth, the planet itself might observe: "It is done. People did not like it here."

■ Jeff De La Rosa

Literature for children.

Quality picture books enjoyed a resurgence in 2007, and interest in realistic, historical, and fantasy fiction remained strong among middle-school and older readers. Some of the outstanding books of 2007 included the following:

Picture books. *A Good Day* by Kevin Henkes (Greenwillow). The tiny changes that turn a disastrous day into a good one—for a bird, a dog, a fox, and a squirrel—are played out in one little girl's backyard, with warm watercolor washes filling in the strongly edged figures. Ages 2 to 5.

Knuffle Bunny Too by Mo Willems (Hyperion). In a sequel to *Knuffle Bunny* (2004), Trixie takes her precious bunny with her on the first day of school, only to find that another little girl has one just like hers. Ages 2 to 5.

Fox by Kate Banks, illustrated by Georg Hallensleben (Farrar, Straus and Giroux). Hallensleben's rich blues, reds, and greens trace the seasons as a young fox learns from its family the skills it needs to become independent. Ages 2 to 6.

When Dinosaurs Came with Everything by Elise Broach, illustrated by David Small (Atheneum). Running errands with Mom is boring, until one day all the shops start giving away dinosaurs. Mom manages to put them all to work. Ages 3 to 6.

Cowboy & Octopus by Jon Scieszka, illustrated by Lane Smith (Viking Juvenile). Scieszka and Smith trace the friendship of a 1950's-style cowboy cut from a paper-doll book and an octopus clipped from a comic strip through seven tiny episodes. Ages 4 to 8.

Olivia Helps with Christmas by Ian Falconer (Atheneum). Olivia can barely wait as she helps her family prepare for Christmas in yet another story by the Caldecott Honor-winning Falconer about the piglet. Ages 4 to 7.

Pictures from Our Vacation by Lynne Rae Perkins (Greenwillow). It's the annual road trip to the family farm, and a little girl tries to capture the moments on film. She finds that the best memories are ones that a camera alone can't preserve. Ages 5 to 8.

Angela and the Baby Jesus by Frank McCourt, illustrated by Raul Colon (Simon & Schuster). As a child, McCourt's mother (whose story was told in *Angela's Ashes*) worried that the Baby Jesus in the parish nativity scene was cold. Her attempts to keep him warm reveal much about family love. Ages 5 to 8.

Great Joy by Kate DiCamillo, illustrated by Bagram Ibatoulline (Candlewick). From the window of their apartment during the wartime 1940's, Frances watches the organ-grinder and his monkey. When snow falls, she worries where they will sleep. In the end, she invites the organ-grinder to her Christmas pageant. Ages 6 to 8.

Poetry. *Miss Crandall's School for Young Ladies & Little Misses of Color* by Elizabeth Alexander and Marilyn Nelson, illustrated by Floyd Cooper (Wordsong). In sonnet form, Alexander and Nelson tell the story of a Connecticut boarding school that, in 1833 and 1834, began accepting young African American women as students. The school was forced to close because of the malicious actions of the townspeople. Ages 10 to 14.

Fiction. *Remembering Mrs. Rossi* by Amy Hest, illustrated by Heather Maione (Candlewick). After her mother, a sixth-grade teacher, dies suddenly, 8-year-old Annie struggles through a year of changes, as her father forgets her favorite cereal and misunderstands a special "snow day" ritual. A memory scrapbook compiled by Mrs. Rossi's last class helps them through. Ages 9 to 12.

The Aurora County All-Stars by Deborah Wiles (Harcourt). Star pitcher House Jackson is ready to play again after a year off nursing a broken elbow. But the team's big game conflicts with the county's 200th anniversary pageant, run by the girl who broke his elbow. The two orchestrate a compromise, in a story peppered with quotations from such famous figures as poet Walt Whitman and baseball great Ted Williams. Ages 9 to 14.

Way Down Deep by Ruth White (Farrar, Straus and Giroux). In a small Appalachian town, Ruby, now 12, wants to know who left her on the courthouse steps as a toddler. When a new family arrives, she finds answers but also faces the question, "What is a family?" Ages 10 to 12.

The Wednesday Wars by Gary D. Schmidt (Clarion). It's 1967, and Holling Hoodhood, a Protestant, is stuck with his seventh-grade teacher for an extra period on Wednesdays, when the Catholic and Jewish kids go off to religious education. Even worse, his teacher makes him read Shakespeare. Schmidt walks a fine line between hilarity and tears as he balances Holling's coming-of-age struggles, the divisions in the United States during the late 1960's, and the timelessness of Shakespeare's plays. Ages 10 to 14.

The Invention of Hugo Cabret, by Brian Selznick (Scholastic). Selznick, an illustrator, tells the story of young Hugo, an orphan in 1930's Paris, in a 550-page work that, as he puts it, "is not exactly a novel, not quite a picture book, and not really a graphic novel." Hugo lives inside the walls of a railway station, where he tends to the clocks, tries to restore an *automaton* (robot) his father had been working on, and discovers his father's true identity. Ages 10 to 14.

Fantasy. *Harry Potter and the Deathly Hallows* by J. K. Rowling (Scholastic). A masterful plot, a rich revisiting of earlier characters, and an ending that's not over till the very end highlight the seventh—and final—volume of Rowling's spellbinding series. Ages 10 and up.

The True Meaning of Smekday by Adam Rex (Hyperion). Twelve-year-old Gratuity—"Tip"—Tucci's mother is abducted by aliens in 2013, when the Boovs conquer Earth. A renegade Boov who calls himself "J Lo" accompanies Tip and her cat on a road trip to find her mother. Ages 10 to 14.

What-the-Dickens by Gregory Maguire (Candlewick). A disaster knocks out the power, and Dinah, Zeke, baby Rebecca, and cousin Gage wait on an isolated homesite for their parents' return. Gage tells a story about a tooth fairy named What-the-Dickens, from his "hatching" through his training. Dickens knows nothing of how tooth fairies, people, or predatory animals operate, but he survives, and so do the children. Ages 11 to 14.

The Darkling Plain by Philip Reeve (Harper Collins). In the last volume of "The Hungry City Chronicles," Tom Natsworthy and his daughter, Wren, try to uncover a secret in the wreckage of London. London was destroyed in an ongoing war between the traction cities—enormous municipalities that move across Earth destroying everything in their path—and the forces of the Green Storm, which seek to preserve Earth. But a third force may well destroy them all. Ages 12 to 15.

Informational books. *The Real Benedict Arnold* by Jim Murphy (Clarion). Through letters and other original sources, Murphy separates the facts of the army officer's life from the distortions that have sprung up over time. Information about family disasters and bureaucratic opposition to his requests for troop supplies during the war make Arnold's actions more understandable but, according to Murphy, still not acceptable. Ages 10 to 14.

Who Was First? Discovering the Americas by Russell Freedman (Clarion). Freedman takes the arrival question beyond 1492, presenting evidence that suggests human beings may have lived in the Americas 50,000 years ago. Ages 10 to 14.

Race by Marc Aronson (Ginee Seo Books). Aronson traces the history of prejudice from ancient times through the atrocities of the modern era, exploring the ways human beings have built theories about difference. Ages 11 to 15.

Awards. The 2007 Newbery Medal was awarded to *The Higher Power of Lucky* by Susan Patron. The award is given by the American Library Association (ALA) for the "most distinguished contribution to American literature for children" published the previous year. The ALA's Caldecott Medal for "the most distinguished American picture book" was awarded to David Wiesner for *Flotsam*. The Michael L. Printz Award, for excellence in literature for young adults, went to Gene Luen Yang for his graphic novel *American Born Chinese*. ■ Mary Harris Russell

See also **Literature; People in the news** (J. K. Rowling).

Lithuania. See **Europe**.

Los Angeles. The population of the city of Los Angeles surpassed the 4-million mark for the first time in 2007, according to a report released in May by the California Department of Finance. In July, the department said that Southern California's population was projected to reach 31.6 million by 2050, up from 19.5 million in 2000. News of the milestones was accompanied by calls for drastic improvements to meet the needs of a rapidly increasing population.

The Southland, the five-county Southern California region that comprises the Los Angeles-Long Beach-Riverside Combined Statistical Area, has the largest Asian population outside Asia and the largest Latino population outside Latin America. Latino growth is expected to continue into midcentury, the department predicted. Local transportation agencies said that the Southland's freeways and mass transit systems needed significant changes to accommodate what state officials projected as a 60-percent increase in the region's population by 2050. Suggested changes included double-decking freeways and adding toll roads and new rail lines.

Mayor Antonio Villaraigosa, midway in his first term as the city's first Latino mayor in 133 years, abandoned efforts to gain direct legal authority over the entire Los Angeles Unified School District. On May 17, an appeals court unanimously nullified a law that would have given the mayor substantial authority over the nation's second-largest school system. On August 29, Villaraigosa announced a five-year plan to oversee two troubled high schools in the system. On April 19, the mayor unveiled a $6.8-billion budget to increase the size of the police force and combat gang violence. The county also presented a $21-billion budget for fiscal 2007-2008 to increase public safety and renovate the aging jail system.

The mayor also faced scandal when his wife of 20 years filed for a legal separation in June 2007. The mayor had confirmed a long-time personal relationship with a television anchorwoman.

Labor. Grocery workers and port clerks in Southern California agreed to new contracts in July, avoiding costly labor stoppages. Members of the United Food and Commercial Workers approved a four-year contract with three large supermarket chains, and clerks with the International Longshore and Warehouse Union voted for a three-year contract with the Los Angeles/Long Beach ports, the largest U.S. containerized shipping ports. Movie and television writers struck in November. The Writers Guild of America disagreed with the Alliance of Motion Picture and Television Producers over writers' compensation for material accessed via the Internet.

The Catholic Archdiocese. In a record out-of-court settlement, Cardinal Roger M. Mahony

Smoke lit by wildfires rises behind the Griffith Park Observatory, north of downtown Los Angeles, in May 2007. The fires, fueled by dry brush and high winds, burned about 20 percent of historic Griffith Park. However, none of the park's landmarks, which include the city's zoo and botanic garden, was damaged.

and the Catholic Archdiocese of Los Angeles agreed in July to pay $660 million to more than 500 alleged victims of sexual abuse. In all, some 247 priests were accused of sexual abuse of young parishioners over a 20-year period.

The Getty. The J. Paul Getty Trust—the world's wealthiest nonprofit arts organization—essentially ended a two-year dispute with Italy in July by returning 40 works of art that the Italians had claimed were stolen. The works included a 2,400-year-old statue of a goddess believed to be Aphrodite. Earlier, the museum had returned four disputed pieces to the Greek government. However, under the return agreement, the museum and the Getty Villa in Malibu can borrow treasures from the countries in the future.

Hospital. Martin Luther King, Jr.-Harbor Hospital downsized to outpatient status in August after the federal government revoked $200 million in annual funding because of the hospital's failure to meet minimum standards for patient care since January 2004. Many African Americans had valued the institution as a symbol of pride and progress after the 1965 Watts riots. County officials said they would seek a private operator to upgrade the facility. Previous searches had failed, however. ■ Margaret A. Kilgore

See also **Art: A Special Report; City.**
Luxembourg. See Europe.

Macedonia. In May 2007, Macedonia's ruling coalition invited a second ethnic Albanian party to join the government. Formed in August 2006 following parliamentary elections, the ruling coalition included the predominantly Slavic Internal Macedonian Revolutionary Organization and the predominantly Albanian Democratic Party of Albanians. The majority of Macedonians are Slavs, with ethnic Albanians accounting for about one-quarter of the population. Macedonia's political arrangements dated from the signing in 2001 of the Ohrid agreement, a peace pact that ended an armed insurgency led by ethnic Albanians. In June 2007, the enlarged coalition government survived a no-confidence vote brought by opposition parties in parliament.

Economists predicted economic growth in Macedonia in 2007 at a rate of 4.6 percent. Unemployment, however, continued to hover above 35 percent. In preparation for negotiations with officials of the European Union on eventual admission to that European body, Macedonia's parliament enacted a 15-percent flat tax on incomes and a 12-percent flat tax on businesses in 2007. Economists predicted that the new tax code would attract foreign investment to Macedonia.

■ Sharon L. Wolchik

See also **Europe.**
Madagascar. See Africa.

Magazine. Unlike newspaper circulation, which continued to drop in the United States, circulation for most magazines held steady in the first half of 2007. Those magazines that saw increases in U.S. circulation for this period were mostly publications that covered popular culture, such as *OK!* and *In Touch.* Most newsmagazines showed neither gains nor losses; one exception was the North American edition of *The Economist,* which greatly increased its circulation.

Luxury launches. Many of the magazines begun in 2007 were geared toward readers who led, or perhaps one day hoped to lead, lavish lifestyles. In what was reported to be Condé Nast's most expensive magazine launch ever, *Portfolio* began publication in April. This business-news magazine also offered lifestyle coverage on fashion, travel, and very expensive goods. Another magazine launched with a focus on luxury and wealth included the new publication by Forbes Inc., *ForbesLife Executive Woman,* in October.

Closings—edgy and old school. *Jane,* geared to women in their 20's, stopped publication after its August 2007 edition. The magazine was started in 1997 by American Jane Pratt, but she left *Jane* in 2005. Pratt was also founding editor of *Sassy,* a teen-girl magazine that had developed a cultlike following in the 1990's.

A very different type of periodical, *American Heritage,* stopped its print publication with the April/May 2007 issue. Founded in 1954, *American Heritage* had, until 1980, published its history articles in a cloth-bound hardback. The publication accepted no ads until 1982, depending solely on circulation for its revenue. The magazine's owner, Forbes, continued online publication of *American Heritage.*

Another venerable magazine, *House & Garden,* founded in 1901, ceased publication, both print and online, with its December 2007 issue.

The missing swimsuit issue. Librarians were used to the annual swimsuit issue published by *Sports Illustrated (SI)* going missing soon after its arrival in the library. In 2007, however, *SI* decided that it would withhold its February swimsuit issue from public institutions (mostly libraries and classrooms). In response to previous complaints from a few libraries about the issue, and with no warning, some 21,000 subscriptions were withheld. Many librarians were displeased. The American Library Association protested, and *SI* announced that such self-censorship would not occur in the future.

Digital archives. Digital editions of the archives of two iconic magazines became available in 2007. All *Playboy* issues from the 1950's and all issues of *Rolling Stone* from 1967 through autumn 2007 went on sale on DVD.   ■ Christine Sullivan

Malawi. See Africa.

Malaysia. Religious questions roiled public life in predominantly Muslim Malaysia during 2007. Although Islam is the official state religion, the Constitution states that "every person has the right to profess and practice his religion." A 1988 amendment denied civil courts any jurisdiction over matters handled by courts of Islamic law.

A Muslim woman who had married a Hindu man in 2004 and renounced Islam said that in 2007 she had been detained and pressured to reverse her renunciation by local Islamic authorities. On May 30, 2007, Malaysia's Federal Court ruled that civil courts could not uphold another woman's conversion from Islam to Christianity because Islamic courts had authority over her status. She had sought to change the religion listed on her government identity card.

These and other cases caused growing tensions between the nation's Muslim majority and its Chinese Buddhist and Indian Hindu minorities. The minorities, as well as moderate Muslims, were concerned over what was termed "creeping Islamization" of society and law.   ■ Henry S. Bradsher

See also **Asia.**

Maldives. See Africa; Asia.

Malta. See Europe.

Manitoba. See Canadian provinces.

Marshall Islands. See Pacific Islands.

Mauritius. See Africa.

Medicine. Two teams of researchers announced in November 2007 that they successfully used ordinary skin cells to create human embryonic stem cells. Stem cells, which can be programmed to develop into a variety of tissues, may enable physicians to replace damaged tissues and to treat such diseases as Parkinson disease and diabetes. One team was led by Shinya Yamanaka of Kyoto University in Japan; the other, by Junying Yu, a researcher in the laboratory of stem-cell pioneer James Thomson of the University of Wisconsin-Madison. Researchers not involved in the new work cautioned that it is still uncertain whether stem cells created in this way would be as effective in treatment as stem cells obtained from embryos.

Being able to use a patient's own skin cells to create stem cells would eliminate the possibility of the patient's body rejecting the new organs. The technique could also calm the debate about the use of human embryos to obtain stem cells. Currently, human stem cells are harvested from human embryos, a process that has aroused opposition by some people because the embryos are destroyed.

MRSA. Officials in Virginia temporarily shut down 21 schools for cleaning after a high school student died of an antibiotic-resistant staph infection. The 17-year-old senior died on October 15 from complications resulting from infection with methicillin-resistant *Staphylococcus aureus* (MRSA). The strain of staph bacterium quickly spread across the United States, including many schools, causing more annual deaths than AIDS, according to the Centers for Disease Control and Prevention (CDC) in Atlanta. The CDC calculated that MRSA was responsible for more than 94,000 infections and nearly 19,000 deaths annually.

HPV. More than one-quarter of women aged 14 to 59 years in the United States are infected with human papillomavirus (HPV), the primary cause of cancer of the cervix, according to a February report by the CDC. The report, based on clinical tests of almost 2,000 women, found that women aged 14 to 24 had the highest rates of HPV infection. The authors of the study noted that these results underscored the need for young women to get vaccinated against HPV infection and have routine Pap tests, a procedure for detecting cancer cells in the female genital tract. The report estimated that 7.5 million U.S. women aged 14 to 24 were infected with HPV—substantially more than previously estimated.

MRI's for breast cancer. Women at high risk for breast cancer should be screened regularly with magnetic resonance imaging (MRI), in addition to mammography, according to new guidelines released in March by the Atlanta-based American Cancer Society (ACS). Magnetic resonance imaging can detect abnormal blood flow in the breast, an early sign of cancer not visible on the X-ray images produced with mammography. Women who would benefit the most from MRI screening, according to the ACS, include those found to have genetic *mutations* (changes in genes) in the BRCA1 or BRCA2 genes and those with Hodgkins disease or a family history of breast cancer.

Progress for heart patients. "Remarkable improvements" have been made since 1999 in the care of people who have had heart attacks, reported an international team of researchers with the Global Registry of Acute Coronary Events in May. The researchers attributed the progress to the increased use of medications that reduce cholesterol levels or thin the blood and to such treatments as *angioplasty* (a technique for opening arteries that are blocked by deposits of cholesterol, calcium, and other substances).

The investigators examined the care of more than 44,000 heart-attack patients in 14 countries. They reported that 8.4 percent of the patients died in the hospital in 1999, compared with 4.6 percent in 2005. *Heart failure* (failure of the heart to pump blood with normal efficiency) happened in 20 percent of patients in 1999, versus 11 percent in 2005.   ■ Alfred J. Smuskiewicz

See also **AIDS; Drugs; Health care issues; Mental health; Public health.**

Mental health. United States troops serving in Iraq faced unprecedented levels of continual fighting and worsening risks of mental stress, noted a study by U.S. Army psychologists released in May 2007. The study, led by Army colonel and research psychologist Carl Castro, found that U.S. forces in Iraq spent more time in conflict without a break than those who fought in the Vietnam War (1957-1975) or World War II (1939-1945). The study also found that 30 percent of U.S. troops who experienced high levels of combat in Iraq suffered from anxiety, depression, or stress, which were aggravated by multiple tours of duty.

In August 2007, an Army report revealed that 99 U.S. soldiers committed suicide in 2006, most of them in Iraq. The deaths amounted to the highest suicide rate for U.S. soldiers in 26 years.

Post-traumatic stress. An increasing number of U.S. troops returning from the conflicts in Iraq and Afghanistan had post-traumatic stress disorder (PTSD) that often went undiagnosed by their primary care physicians. That was the conclusion of a report published in May 2007 in *JAOA—The Journal of the American Osteopathic Association* by osteopathic physician Roy R. Reeves of the G.V. (Sonny) Montgomery VA Medical Center in Jackson, Mississippi.

Individuals with PTSD suffer from high levels of stress and anxiety from reexperiencing trauma through recollections, dreams, or flashbacks. Reeves noted that the risk of this trauma is increased as a result of such stressful experiences of modern warfare as seeing large numbers of refugees, dead civilians, and destroyed villages, and being concerned about exposure to biological and chemical weapons. More than half of all cases of PTSD in veterans may go undiagnosed, according to Reeves.

Antidepressants benefit children. The benefits of antidepressant medications for children and teen-agers outweigh the risks of increasing suicidal thoughts and behaviors in these patients, according to a study published in April. The researchers, led by Jeffrey A. Bridge, assistant professor of pediatrics at Ohio State University in Columbus, concluded that for every 100 children treated with antidepressants, 1 additional child has suicidal feelings that he or she would not have had without drug treatment. This risk was substantially lower than the rate identified by the U.S. Food and Drug Administration (FDA) in a warning issued in 2004.

In September 2007, the U.S. Centers for Disease Control and Prevention in Atlanta reported that after the FDA warning prompted physicians to prescribe fewer antidepressants for girls and boys in 2004, the suicide rate for people aged 10 to 24 increased by 8 percent. This rate had decreased by 28.5 percent over the previous 14 years.

Five stages of grief. The traditional idea that bereaved people experience five stages of grief—disbelief, yearning, anger, depression, and acceptance—after the death of a loved one was given scientific support by a study published in the *Journal of the American Medical Association* in February 2007. The study, conducted by a team of psychiatrists led by Paul Maciejewski of Yale University in New Haven, Connecticut, reached this conclusion by following 233 people for 24 months after they had lost a loved one.

According to the study, disbelief reaches a peak one month after the loved one's death, then declines. Yearning steadily increases for four months after the death before declining. Anger peaks at five months after the death, and depression at six months. Acceptance gradually becomes more dominant as time passes. The study showed that survivors were better able to cope with grief if their loved ones were diagnosed with a terminal illness more than six months before death.

The authors found that missing a loved one is a more dominant emotion than depression in bereaved people. The researchers also noted that approximately 15 percent of the people in the study experienced prolonged grief, lasting more than six months.   ■ Alfred J. Smuskiewicz

See also **Drugs; Medicine.**

Mexico. In 2007, during his first full year as president of Mexico, Felipe Calderón Hinojosa mounted what he called "a frontal assault" on drug trafficking and urban crime. Mexicans applauded as Calderón's administration tackled corruption within the nation's law enforcement agencies and state and municipal governments.

In January, Calderón ordered thousands of soldiers and federal police to Tijuana, near the Mexico-United States border. Armed officers used pickup trucks and helicopters to monitor the city's crime-infested neighborhoods. Naval vessels watched the coast of Baja California for illicit drug shipments. Calderón temporarily disarmed Tijuana's entire municipal police force of more than 2,000 officers on the grounds that they had become corrupted by powerful drug cartels.

Police corruption became a target of Calderón's government in June, when Secretary of Public Safety Genaro García Luna removed 284 high-ranking federal police officers from their posts. Federal police chiefs in all 32 Mexican states were demoted and ordered to undergo retraining. García Luna's action followed the worst wave of drug-related violence in Mexican history. During the first half of 2007, more than 1,200 civilians, police officers, and soldiers were killed in the crossfire as drug traffickers fought for control of Mexico's billion-dollar smuggling routes.

Huge stash of money found. Mexican authorities seized more than $200 million in a March raid on a Mexico City mansion belonging to Zhenli Ye Gon, a naturalized Mexican businessman of Chinese descent. Ye Gon was accused of importing chemicals to Mexico to make the illegal drug methamphetamine. When U.S. authorities arrested Ye Gon in July near Washington, D.C., he claimed that members of Mexico's ruling National Action Party had forced him to hold onto illicit campaign funds from the 2006 presidential race.

Mexico-U.S. relations. Given the widespread corruption and violence caused by Mexico's drug trade, President Calderón in 2007 lobbied the U.S. government for massive assistance to fight illicit trafficking. In October, U.S. President George W. Bush asked the U.S. Congress to approve $1.4 billion in funding to help Mexico and Central American countries wage the war against drugs.

During the first six months of 2007, Mexico extradited more than 20 drug traffickers to the United States to be tried on outstanding charges. In November, the Mexican government approved the extradition to the United States of Mario Villanueva Madrid, a former governor of the state of Quintana Roo. Villanueva Madrid had been charged with helping cartels smuggle drugs.

Calderón was disappointed by the failure of the U.S. Congress to enact comprehensive immigration reform or a program that would allow Mexicans to work legally in the United States. He was also highly critical of the walls that the U.S. government was constructing along the nations' common border to stem the illegal flow northward of Mexicans seeking jobs.

Attacks on oil and gas pipelines in July and September interrupted power supplies and cost businesses in Mexico millions of dollars in lost revenue. The People's Revolutionary Army (EPR), a leftist guerrilla group, claimed responsibility for explosions that damaged pipelines in central Mexico and Veracruz state. The EPR alleged that the Mexican government had abducted two of their comrades, whom they wanted released.

Flooding caused by heavy rains in October submerged an estimated 70 percent of Tabasco state, affecting about 1 million people. The flooding, reportedly the worst in 50 years, devastated crops and interrupted oil industry operations.

Aztec tomb discovered. Using radar, Mexican archaeologists found what they believed to be the tomb of Ahuizotl, the Aztec emperor when Christopher Columbus landed in the Western Hemisphere in 1492. It lay below Mexico City's main plaza, the Zócalo.   ■ Nathan A. Haverstock

See also **Latin America; People in the news** (Felipe Calderón Hinojosa).

Micronesia, Federated States of.

See **Pacific Islands.**

MIDDLE EAST

A mix of encouraging and discouraging news regarding various conflicts emerged from the Middle East in 2007. In Iraq, some tribal leaders and former insurgents changed sides and began cooperating with United States forces against Qa`ida terrorists. In Lebanon, the army defeated a group of militant Islamic fighters widely believed to have been sent by Syria to undermine the Lebanese government. The take-over of the Gaza Strip by the militant Palestinian group Hamas jolted the Middle East and became an important factor in reviving Israeli-Palestinian peace negotiations. Relations between Libya and the United States improved.

By contrast, relations between Iran and the West worsened in 2007 as Iran continued its uranium enrichment activities and support of insurgents in Iraq and Afghanistan. In Sudan, peace between the government and rebel groups proved elusive. Turkey's secular (characterized by separation of religion and state) establishment was shaken by the election of a new president with strong religious convictions.

Signs of progress in Iraq. In January, U.S. President George W. Bush announced a "surge" in the number of U.S. troops serving in Iraq, bringing the number to about 160,000 by mid-June. This increased troop presence partly helped to curb insurgent and terrorist violence in Iraq. More important, according to many analysts of Middle East affairs, was a new U.S. policy aimed at increasing cooperation between coalition forces and Iraqi tribal leaders. Because of this cooperation, tribal leaders in Al Anbar province were able to largely rid the province of terrorists affiliated with al-Qa`ida. Similar coalition-tribal alliances were forged in the town of Baqubah and in Diyala province. In Baghdad, the Iraqi capital, former Sunni insurgents joined forces with U.S. troops to greatly reduce the presence of al-Qa`ida in their neighborhoods.

In a September appearance before the U.S. Congress, General David H. Petraeus, commander of the Multinational Force in Iraq, described how coalition forces targeted Shi`ah militias that were responsible for assassinating Iraqi leaders and attacking U.S. forces and Iraqi civilians. According to General Petraeus, those militias were supported by the Quds Force—an Iranian special operations unit—and the Lebanon-based Hezbollah—an Islamic militant group backed by Iran and Syria. The general said that Iran's Islamic Republican Guard Corps (IRGC) was using these groups to fight a proxy war against the Iraqi state.

Syria fails in Lebanon. Hundreds of militant Islamic fighters from various countries, using the name Fatah al-Islam, launched an attack on northern Lebanon in May. Most analysts believed that Syria had dispatched the fighters to undermine the anti-Syria government of Lebanon. In September, after approximately 100 days of battle, the Lebanese army defeated the militants in a victory celebrated by many Lebanese people.

Terrorists targeted the United Nations Interim Force in Lebanon (UNIFIL) in June by killing six peacekeeping troops serving with the Spanish army. Experts in Middle East affairs noted that the attack was most likely the work of Syria and Hezbollah, which opposed the deployment of the expanded UNIFIL forces.

Syrian agents were also suspected in the assassination of two anti-Syria members of Lebanon's National Assembly (parliament) in 2007. Walid Eido was killed on June 13, and Antoine Ghanem, on September 19. These assassinations failed to silence the anti-Syria, prodemocracy "Cedar Revolution" majority in Lebanon.

Parliamentary maneuvers. Nabih Birri, the pro-Syria speaker of Lebanon's Chamber of Deputies in the National Assembly, blocked regular sessions of the National Assembly from convening in 2007. Experts in Lebanese affairs believed that Birri hoped to prevent the Cedar Revolution parliamentary majority from endorsing the establishment of a United Nations (UN) international tribunal. This tribunal was to prosecute Syrian agents implicated by the UN in the assassination of former Lebanese Prime Minister Rafik Hariri in 2005, as well as those responsible for many subsequent political assassinations and acts of terrorism in Lebanon. The UN Security Council established the tribunal in May 2007.

Birri also hoped to prevent the parliamentary majority from electing a new president of Lebanon to take over from pro-Syria President Emile Lahoud, whose term ended in late November. The National Assembly was unable to select a compromise candidate for president —acceptable to both the pro-Syria and anti-Syria sides—until after Lahoud left office. The assassination of General François al-Hajj on December 12 led analysts to speculate that

FACTS IN BRIEF ON MIDDLE EASTERN COUNTRIES

Country	Population	Government	Monetary unit*	Foreign trade (million U.S.$) Exports[†]	Imports[†]
Bahrain	722,000	King Hamad bin Isa Al-Khalifa; Prime Minister Khalifa bin Salman Al-Khalifa	dinar (0.38 = $1)	12,620	9,036
Cyprus	853,000	President Tassos Papadopoulos; (Turkish Republic of Northern Cyprus: President Mehmet Ali Talat)	euro (0.71 = $1)	1,408 (includes Northern Cyprus)	7,000
Egypt	77,243,000	President Mohammed Hosni Mubarak; Prime Minister Ahmed Nazif	pound (5.58 = $1)	24,220	35,860
Iran	72,048,000	Supreme Leader Ayatollah Ali Khamenei; President Mahmoud Ahmadinejad	rial (9,310.00 = $1)	63,180	45,480
Iraq	30,958,000	President Jalal Talabani; Prime Minister Nouri Kamel al-Maliki	dinar (1,232.00 = $1)	32,190	20,760
Israel	7,250,000	President Shimon Peres; Prime Minister Ehud Olmert	shekel (4.01 = $1)	42,860	47,800
Jordan	5,816,000	King Abdullah II; Prime Minister Nadir al-Dahabi	dinar (0.71 = $1)	4,798	10,420
Kuwait	2,895,000	Emir Sabah Jabir al-Ahmad al-Jabir al-Sabah; Prime Minister Nasser Muhammad al-Ahmad al-Sabah	dinar (0.28 = $1)	56,060	19,120
Lebanon	3,894,000	President (vacant); Prime Minister Fouad Siniora	pound (1,512.00 = $1)	1,881	9,340
Oman	2,705,000	Sultan and Prime Minister Qaboos bin Said	rial (0.39 = $1)	24,730	10,290
Qatar	841,000	Emir Hamad bin Khalifa al-Thani; Prime Minister Hamad bin Jassim bin Jabr al-Thani	riyal (3.64 = $1)	33,250	12,360
Saudi Arabia	26,362,000	King and Prime Minister Abdullah ibn Abd al-Aziz Al Saud	riyal (3.74 = $1)	204,500	64,160
Sudan	39,076,000	President Umar Hassan Ahmad al-Bashir	pound (2.05 = $1)	7,505	8,693
Syria	20,423,000	President Bashar al-Assad; Prime Minister Mohammed Naji al-Otari	pound (51.20 = $1)	6,923	6,634
Turkey	74,824,000	President Abdullah Gül; Prime Minister Recep Tayyip Erdogan	new lira (1.20 = $1)	85,210	120,900
United Arab Emirates	4,724,000	President Khalifa bin Zayed al-Nahyan; Prime Minister Mohammad bin Rashid al-Maktum	dirham (0.67 = $1)	137,100	88,890
Yemen	23,054,000	President Ali Abdullah Saleh; Prime Minister Ali Muhammad Mujawwar	rial (198.95 = $1)	8,214	5,042

*Exchange rates as of Oct. 4, 2007.   [†]Latest available data.

the National Assembly would likely elect General Michel Suleiman, commander of the army, as the new president.

Israeli-Palestinian talks. In June, the militant Palestinian organization Hamas seized control of the Gaza Strip from the moderate government of Palestinian President Mahmoud Abbas. After the seizure, the Bush administration urged the Palestinian president and Israeli Prime Minister Ehud Olmert to revive the dormant peace process. At an October meeting in Jerusalem, Israel, the two Mideast leaders emphasized their "joint commitment to a two-state solution" to the Israeli-Palestinian conflict.

The Israeli government took a number of steps in 2007 to support the moderate Palestinian government of President Abbas. In July, Israeli officials began transferring to the Palestinian Authority withheld tax and customs revenues amounting to approximately $500 million. From July to October, the Israeli government released hundreds of Palestinian prisoners and offered others amnesty (pardon) if they renounced violence. Israeli officials also removed roadblocks and checkpoints in the West Bank to ease the movement of Palestinians in and out of Israel.

The warm-up in relations culminated in a Middle East peace conference held in November in Annapolis, Maryland. There, Prime Minister Olmert and President Abbas agreed to accelerate their negotiations with the goal of concluding a final accord regarding the establishment of a Palestinian state by the end of 2008. Formal Israeli-Palestinian negotiations resumed in December 2007 in Jerusalem.

Improved U.S.-Libya relations. President Bush appointed Gene Cretz, deputy chief of the U.S. diplomatic mission in Israel, as U.S. ambassador to Libya in July 2007. If confirmed by the U.S. Senate, Cretz would become the first U.S. ambassador to Libya since 1972—when the U.S. ambassador was withdrawn because Libyan leader Mu'ammar al-Qadhafi's alleged support of terrorism and the subersion of moderate Arab governments. The appointment signified a dramatic improvement in relations between the United States and Libya, made possible when Libyan leader Mu'ammar Muhammad al-Qadhafi renounced the use of weapons of mass destruction in 2003.

Growing concerns about Iran. The U.S. government increased economic sanctions against Iran and designated Iran's IRGC and Ministry of Defense as terrorist organizations in October 2007. According to the U.S. Department of the Treasury, the IRGC's Quds Force provided weapons and explosives to terrorists and militants, including insurgents in Iraq and Taliban fighters in Afghanistan.

The Treasury Department also targeted three banks owned by the Iranian government by freezing their assets in the United States. Iran's Bank Saderat was accused by U.S. officials of transferring hundreds of millions of dollars to terrorist organizations every year. Bank Melli and Bank Mellat were accused of facilitating "the proliferation of illicit technologies," including weapons of mass destruction.

The UN's International Atomic Energy Agency (IAEA) reported in November that Iran had put 3,000 centrifuges into operation, giving that nation the capability to produce enough enriched uranium to build a nuclear weapon within 18 months. The report faulted Iranian officials for not allowing IAEA inspectors to have broad access to Iran's nuclear facilities. Iranian officials countered that their nuclear facilities were only for the peaceful use of nuclear energy. In December, Javier Solana, the foreign policy minister of the European Union

(EU), stated that negotiations between the EU and Iran had reached a deadlock because of Iran's refusal to disclose details about its nuclear plans.

United States intelligence agencies concluded in a National Intelligence Estimate, released in December, that Iran had apparently stopped pursuing a nuclear weapons program in 2003. This conclusion contradicted previous assertions by the Bush administration that Iran was on the verge of developing a nuclear weapon.

Peace hopes unravel in Sudan. Mediators from the UN, EU, and African Union (an organization working to achieve cooperation among African nations) met in Libya in October 2007 to negotiate a peace settlement between the Sudanese government and various rebel groups fighting in the western region of Darfur. Although the Sudanese government participated in the talks, some of the major rebel groups refused to attend the meetings, thereby dooming any hopes of an effective peace settlement.

The Sudan People's Liberation Movement (SPLM), the major organization representing the southern Sudanese in their conflict with Sudanese authorities, withdrew from the national unity government in October. The SPLM accused Sudanese officials of not complying with the 2005 Comprehensive Peace Agreement.

Religion and nationalism in Turkey. The secular establishment in Turkey received a major blow in August 2007, when Abdullah Gül, representing the governing Justice and Development Party, was elected president of Turkey. Many Turks feared that Gül, a government minister known for his strong religious convictions, would not respect the country's traditional separation of religion and state.

In January, Hrant Dink, a prominent Armenian journalist, was assassinated by a young Turkish nationalist. Dink had advocated reconciliation between Turks and Armenians, who have a history of ethnic strife going back to the 1800's. Many analysts of Turkish affairs believed that Dink's assassination was representative of a rising tide of Turkish nationalism.

The Turkish military made frequent incursions into northern Iraq in 2007 to try to root out the Kurdish separatist movement in the region. Turkish officials viewed the Kurdistan Workers Party as a threat to Turkey's unity.   ■ Marius K. Deeb

See also **Africa; Armed forces; Iraq; People in the news** (Abdullah Gül; David Petraeus); **Terrorism; Turkey; United Nations; United States, Government of the;** various Middle East country articles.

Mining. See Energy supply.

Moldova. See Europe.

Monaco. See Europe.

Mongolia. See Asia.

A Palestinian wounded by an Israeli missile strike on Gaza City is rushed to a hospital in May. As Fatah and Hamas clashed over Gaza, Israel launched a series of missile attacks against targets controlled by Hamas, the militant Palestinian faction fighting against the moderate Fatah government of Palestinian President Mahmoud Abbas.

Fatah and Hamas—rival Palestinian factions— battled over control of the Gaza Strip in 2007, highlighting continuing violence and chaos in the Middle East.

Qassam rockets launched by Palestinian militants in northern Gaza head toward the Israeli border town of Sderot in May. Palestinian rocket and mortar attacks against the Israeli city continued for many days—with approximately 15 launches per day—reportedly causing 40 percent of the population of Sderot to flee.

A Hamas gunman stands guard at the headquarters of the Palestinian security services in southern Gaza after Hamas seized control of the security compound in June. Hamas overran several key strongholds of Fatah in June to complete its military takeover of the Gaza Strip.

Montenegro. The parliament of Montenegro in October 2007 adopted the new nation's first Constitution. Montenegro declared independence from the union of Serbia and Montenegro on June 3, 2006, following a popular referendum. Before February 2003, Serbia and Montenegro had comprised the nation of Yugoslavia, the remnant of the greater Balkan nation that had broken apart in the 1990's.

The Montenegrin Constitution ensured equal rights for all citizens, specifically for both genders. It also embraced freedom of religion, recognition of minority languages, control of the military by civilian officials, and recognition of the precedence of international law over Montenegrin law.

Also in October 2007, Montenegro's leaders signed a Stabilization and Association treaty with European Union (EU) representatives. The treaty constituted a first step toward EU membership.

Montenegro's economy grew at an annual rate of approximately 8 percent through 2006 and 2007. The unemployment rate fell in late 2007 to 12 percent, the lowest in 20 years. Analysts noted that the rapidly developing tourist industry in Montenegro's Adriatic coastal region was responsible for much of the job growth.

■ Sharon L. Wolchik

See also **Europe; Serbia.**

Montreal. Crumbling infrastructure—from road overpasses and bridges to the underground city—was cause for major concern in Montreal in 2007. A series of events, including a provincial government investigation, uncovered a host of dangerous situations across the Island of Montreal (Île de Montréal). Tragedy was averted on August 24, when a 1,100-ton (1,000-metric-ton) concrete slab separating the basement of the landmark Bay department store from busy de Maisonneuve Boulevard cracked and forced the evacuation of several commercial buildings. The incident also brought the Métro subway system to a halt. The fault was discovered in a tunnel leading to a Métro station near the Bay, and officials feared it would open and swallow a portion of de Maisonneuve. City officials closed that part of the busy artery indefinitely to allow for necessary repairs.

On July 19, the Quebec Transport Department made public a list of 135 bridges, overpasses, and ramps across the province that it had earmarked for extensive investigation over worries that they, too, could collapse. The list included eight overpasses in Montreal. The move came on the heels of the July 5 decision by former Quebec Premier Pierre Marc Johnson to urge Transport Quebec to examine the safety of 332 ramps, bridges, and overpasses that might also be unsafe. Johnson had earlier led a public inquiry into the Sept. 30, 2006,

collapse of a viaduct in suburban Laval that killed five people. On Aug. 2, 2007, Montreal Mayor Gérald Tremblay promised to demolish a weakened 69-year-old overpass in the north end of the city and rebuild it beginning in 2008. He also vowed to increase city inspections of other spans.

Business. Montreal aluminum giant Alcan Inc. was part of the largest take-over in Canadian business history when it was acquired by Anglo-Australian mining conglomerate Rio Tinto for $38.7 billion (all amounts in Canadian dollars), forming the world's biggest aluminum firm. Renamed Rio Tinto Alcan, it was to have dual headquarters in New York City and Montreal. The Rio Tinto bid trumped the attempted hostile take-over by U.S. aluminum rival Alcoa Inc.

Crime. Vito Rizzuto, reputed to be the most powerful mob boss in Canada, was sentenced to 10 years in jail after pleading guilty in a Brooklyn, New York, court on May 4, 2007, to participating in a 1981 gangland slaying of three Mafia captains linked to the Bonanno crime family of New York City. Rizzuto, 61, faced a maximum penalty of 20 years had he gone to trial and been convicted.

On June 27, 2007, Montreal advertising executive Jean Lafleur, a key figure in the federal sponsorship scandal of the late 1990's, pleaded guilty to 28 counts of fraud. His company, Lafleur Communications Marketing Inc., had received almost $65 million in federal contracts and charged the federal government $36 million more in fees, commissions, and other charges from 1994 to 2000. Lafleur was ordered to spend four years in jail and repay nearly $1.6 million for 76 fraudulent invoices to the sponsorship program. The Liberal Party, which was in power in the 1990's, designed the program to undermine the separatist movement in Quebec. Lafleur was also fined $500 for each fraud count for a total of $14,000.

Justin Trudeau, son of former Prime Minister Pierre Elliott Trudeau, was selected on April 29, 2007, as the federal Liberal candidate for the Montreal *riding* (division) of Papineau. Political experts noted that Trudeau's political image may have been somewhat tarnished by the findings of an admittedly unscientific online survey by *The Beaver,* Canada's leading history magazine. The July 30 survey placed his father atop a list of the 10 most loathed Canadians of all time. Three other Canadian prime ministers also made the list.

Sports. The National Association for Stock Car Auto Racing (NASCAR) made a successful Canadian debut during the summer of 2007 with its elite Busch Series on Montreal's Circuit Gilles Villeneuve track. On August 4, defending champion Kevin Harvick won the inaugural NAPA Auto Parts 200. ■ Mike King

See also **Canada; Canadian provinces.**

Morocco. See Africa.

Motion pictures. As blockbusters dominated theaters in 2007, a growing number of consumers chose to download movies to computers. This trend attracted the attention of motion-picture studios and was a contributing factor in the first Hollywood writers strike in 20 years.

On strike. In November, the Writers Guild of America went on strike after contract talks broke down with the Alliance of Motion Picture and Television Producers. Television and film writers wanted more money when films and TV shows were sold on Internet sites such as Apple Inc.'s iTunes Store.

Later that month, iTunes released the first direct-to-digital film, *Purple Violets*, directed by Ed Burns. The move was seen by industry observers as a sign of Apple's push for a movie download hit.

Tentpoles. Big-budget, high-profile summer releases, known within the film industry as *tentpoles*, won the lion's share of box-office returns in 2007. Most were sequels. Summer releases earned $4 billion and ran 8 percent ahead of 2006 in ticket sales. *Transformers, Spider-Man 3, Shrek the Third, Pirates of the Caribbean: At World's End, Harry Potter and the Order of the Phoenix, The Bourne Ultimatum*, and *Ratatouille* each grossed in excess of $200 million in the United States alone. Of these blockbusters, *The Bourne Ultimatum* received the strongest critical support, with Paul Greengrass's jumpy, edgy direction singled out for praise. Another box-office success was the long-awaited animated feature *The Simpsons Movie*, based on the long-running Fox television series.

Westerns. Two fall releases, *3:10 to Yuma* (a remake of the 1957 film), starring Russell Crowe and Christian Bale, and *The Assassination of Jesse James by the Coward Robert Ford*, starring Brad Pitt and Casey Affleck, rejuvenated interest in the Western genre. Both films reflected the laconic, melancholy style of such early 1970's Westerns as Robert Altman's *McCabe & Mrs. Miller* (1971), rather than reviving traditional shoot-'em-up conventions. While *Yuma* was a hit, *The Assassination of Jesse James* flopped at the box office.

War and politics were the focus of several Hollywood films in 2007. Paul Haggis's acclaimed *In the Valley of Elah* featured an understated performance by Tommy Lee Jones as a Vietnam veteran whose son disappears after returning from his tour of duty in Iraq. The drama also starred Charlize Theron and Susan Sarandon. Brian De Palma won the Best Director Prize at the Venice Film Festival for *Redacted*, a montage of stories about U.S. soldiers fighting in Iraq. Angelina Jolie won praise for her performance in *A Mighty Heart*, in which she portrayed Mariane Pearl, the wife of *Wall Street Journal* reporter Daniel Pearl, who was kidnapped and killed by a militant group in Pakistan. Other political films included *The Kingdom*, starring Jamie Foxx; *Rendition*, starring Reese Witherspoon, Jake

Gyllenhaal, Meryl Streep, and Alan Arkin; *Grace Is Gone*, starring John Cusack; and *Lions for Lambs*, directed by and starring Robert Redford, with Tom Cruise and Streep.

Thrillers and crime dramas. David Cronenberg and Viggo Mortensen, director and star, respectively, of 2005's *A History of Violence*, repeated their success together with 2007's violent *Eastern Promises*. The crime thriller examines the Russian Mafia's infiltration of London. Tony Gilroy's feature debut, *Michael Clayton*, starring George Clooney as a "fixer" for a corrupt law firm, also won praise. *The Brave One*, starring Jodie Foster as a violent-crime victim turned vigilante, was compared to an earlier film featuring Foster, the Martin Scorsese 1976 classic, *Taxi Driver*. The hotly anticipated *American Gangster*, Ridley Scott's crime drama set in the 1970's, starred Russell Crowe as an honest cop who attempts to bring down a drug czar (Denzel Washington).

Michael Caine, 74, won acclaim for his performance in Kenneth Branagh's *Sleuth*, a remake of the 1972 film in which Caine also starred, playing a different role. Jude Law also received strong notices for his work in the film. The 83-year-old director Sidney Lumet won some of the highest praise of his career with *Before the Devil Knows You're Dead*. Philip Seymour Hoffman and Ethan Hawke starred in this mordant crime thriller about two brothers who plot the robbery of their parents' jewelry store.

Literary adaptations. Another veteran director, 76-year-old Mike Nichols, also scored with *Charlie Wilson's War*, a dark political comedy based on the 2003 book by George Crile about a Texas congressman's covert dealings with Afghanistan during the late 1970's. The film starred Tom Hanks, Julia Roberts, and Philip Seymour Hoffman.

Legendary actress Julie Christie gave an outstanding performance as a woman with Alzheimer's disease in *Away from Her*. The film was inspired by "The Bear Came Over the Mountain," a 1999 short story by Canadian author Alice Munro that appeared in *The New Yorker*. The film was compassionately directed by Canadian actress Sarah Polley.

Filmmaking siblings Joel and Ethan Coen enjoyed renewed success with the provocative, violent *No Country for Old Men*, based on the 2005 novel by Cormac McCarthy. The film featured Tommy Lee Jones, in another strong perfomance, as a weather-beaten sheriff. Josh Brolin, Jones's co-star in *In the Valley of Elah*, also delivered a fine performance in the Coen brothers' film, while Javier Bardem's electrifying turn as a professional killer riveted critics and audiences.

Marc Forster's adaptation of Khaled Hosseini's 2003 novel, *The Kite Runner*, won praise for its intelligent streamlining of the best seller's story of friendship, betrayal, and redemption during decades of

Forest Whitaker won the 2007 Academy Award for best actor for his performance as Ugandan dictator Idi Amin in *The Last King of Scotland.*

Portraits of a "king" and a queen reigned over the 2007 Academy Awards for best acting. A legendary American director won his first Oscar.

American director Martin Scorsese discusses a scene with actors Leonardo DiCaprio (center) and Matt Damon (right) on the set of *The Departed,* for which Scorsese won his first Academy Award as best director. He had been nominated for the award six other times. The film—which also won Oscars for best picture, best editing, and best adapted screenplay—is a violent yet funny portrait of Boston gangland warfare.

Helen Mirren received the Academy Award for best actress in 2007 for her portrayal of Queen Elizabeth II in *The Queen*. The film focuses on the monarch's conflicts following the death of her former daughter-in-law, Diana, Princess of Wales.

ACADEMY AWARD WINNERS IN 2007

The following winners of the 2006 Academy Awards were announced in February 2007:

Best Picture, *The Departed*

Best Actor, Forest Whitaker, *The Last King of Scotland*

Best Actress, Helen Mirren, *The Queen*

Best Supporting Actor, Alan Arkin, *Little Miss Sunshine*

Best Supporting Actress, Jennifer Hudson, *Dreamgirls*

Best Director, Martin Scorsese, *The Departed*

Best Original Screenplay, Michael Arndt, *Little Miss Sunshine*

Best Screenplay Adaptation, William Monahan, *The Departed*

Best Animated Feature, George Miller, *Happy Feet*

Best Cinematography, Guillermo Navarro, *Pan's Labyrinth*

Best Film Editing, Thelma Schoonmaker, *The Departed*

Best Original Score, Gustavo Santaolalla, *Babel*

Best Original Song, Melissa Etheridge, "I Need to Wake Up" from *An Inconvenient Truth*

Best Foreign-Language Film, *The Lives of Others* (Germany)

Best Art Direction, Eugenio Caballero and Pilar Revuelta, *Pan's Labyrinth*

Best Costume Design, Milena Canonero, *Marie Antoinette*

Best Sound Mixing, Michael Minkler, Bob Beemer, and Willie D. Burton, *Dreamgirls*

Best Sound Editing, Alan Robert Murray and Bub Asman, *Letters from Iwo Jima*

Best Makeup, David Martí and Montse Ribé, *Pan's Labyrinth*

Best Visual Effects, *Pirates of the Caribbean: Dead Man's Chest*

Best Animated Short Film, *The Danish Poet*

Best Live-Action Short Film, *West Bank Story*

Best Feature Documentary, *An Inconvenient Truth*

Best Short Subject Documentary, *The Blood of Yingzhou District*

turbulence in Afghanistan. Joe Wright's version of Ian McEwan's 2001 romance novel *Atonement* proved to be another of 2007's skillful literary adaptations, starring James McAvoy and Keira Knightley as lovers torn apart by war, duplicity, and family tradition. Emile Hirsch won praise as a suburban teen drawn to the exhilaration and terror of wilderness existence in Sean Penn's adaptation of Jon Krakauer's 1996 best seller, *Into the Wild*. Paul Thomas Anderson's *There Will Be Blood*, based on a 1927 novel by Upton Sinclair, starred Daniel Day-Lewis in an acclaimed performance as a Texas oil driller whose good fortune brings heartbreak.

Musical adaptations. The 2007 remake of the 1988 John Waters movie *Hairspray*, which inspired a hit Broadway musical, starred John Travolta in a well-received performance as Edna Turnblad. One of 2007's most eagerly awaited year-end releases was Tim Burton's film adaptation of Stephen Sondheim's 1979 Broadway musical hit *Sweeney Todd: The Demon Barber of Fleet Street*, which starred frequent Burton collaborator Johnny Depp as the murderous musical barber.

Biographical pictures continued their popularity into 2007. Among the most adventurous was Todd Haynes's freewheeling portrait of Bob Dylan, *I'm Not There*. The film features six actors of both sexes and different races, ranging in ages from 11 to 50, who portray the American musician throughout various stages of his life and career. Among the actors who play Dylan in the film are Christian Bale, Heath Ledger, Richard Gere, and an acclaimed Cate Blanchett in an uncanny impersonation. Blanchett also received notice for her second portrayal of Queen Elizabeth I in *Elizabeth: The Golden Age*. The actress gained international recognition when she played the queen in the 1998 film *Elizabeth*. Critical response for the 2007 film was not as strong as for the first. French actress Marion Cotillard also won plaudits for her portrayal of legendary French singer Edith Piaf in *La Vie en Rose*. Cotillard was noted for her ability to capture the singer's mercurial emotions and tormented genius.

Notable documentaries of 2007 included *Sicko*, Michael Moore's stinging indictment of the U.S. health care industry; *No End in Sight*, Charles Ferguson's probing inspection of the American occupation of Iraq; and *Jimmy Carter: Man from Plains*, Jonathan Demme's portrait of the Nobel Peace Prize laureate and former president. A critically acclaimed but little-seen documentary, *In the Shadow of the Moon*, featured spectacular space footage and commentaries from surviving astronauts of the Apollo missions to the moon.

Foreign films. Among Mexico's many successful features were the ghost story *Km 31* and the two romantic comedies *Niñas Mal* and *Cansada de besar sapos*. Latin American features also flourished in their homelands. Brazil's *Elite Squad* explores the problems of two childhood friends who join the Rio de Janeiro military police department, hoping to bring down local drug lords. Argentina's *The Past*, directed by Héctor Babenco and starring Gael García Bernal, tells the story of a vengeful woman who hounds her ex-husband.

One of Spain's most controversial films of the year, *13 Roses*, dealt with the trial and execution of 13 girls during the Spanish Civil War (1936-1939). The acclaimed thriller *The Orphanage* was Spain's official submission for the best foreign language film category for the 2008 Academy Awards. Spain pioneered simultaneous distribution with its first animated feature, *Going Nuts*, directed by Juanjo Ramírez. Released by Spain's Perro Verde animation studio, the feature made its theatrical and TV debut in Spain and was distributed for worldwide multilanguage Internet and DVD sale in May 2007.

The German film industry enjoyed a renaissance in 2007. Among the country's more popular films were *Grave Decisions*, about an 11-year-old boy who tries to find a new wife for his widowed father; *My Fuhrer: The Truly Truest Truth About Adolf Hitler*, a comedy in which a Jewish professor is released from a concentration camp in 1944 to tutor Hitler in public speaking; *Yella*, about a woman's efforts to flee an abusive husband; and *Four Minutes*, in which an elderly piano teacher trains an inmate at a women's prison. Director Matthias Luthardt's award-winning debut film, *Pingpong*, was compared to the Academy Award-winning *American Beauty* (1999).

Taiwanese-born director Ang Lee's erotic spy thriller *Lust, Caution* was withdrawn as his home country's 2008 Oscar entry for best foreign language film because an insufficient number of Taiwanese participated in the United States/China/Taiwan co-production. One of China's most anticipated films was actor/director Jiang Wen's *The Sun Also Rises* (not related to the Ernest Hemingway 1926 novel of the same name), a group of stories that occur in different time zones and different environments. South Korea's special-effects creature feature *D-War* earned $53 million at home and over $10 million in the United States—a record for a South Korean film. *Kabul Express*, a Bollywood feature about two Indian journalists who cover the 2001 fall of the Taliban regime, was banned in Afghanistan following an outcry from Afghan Hazara tribal leaders.

A notable 2007 offering from South Africa was *Granny's Clever Child*, the first Afrikaans-language film to be released in the country in a decade. Set in 1940, the film tells the story of a mentally challenged white boy who is adopted by a black family. The feature was expected to rejuvenate the South African film industry. ■ Philip Wuntch

Mozambique. See Africa.

Music. See Classical music; Popular music.

Ingmar Bergman
Through a Glass Darkly

One of the indelible images in the history of cinema is that of a medieval knight playing a game of chess with a black-robed figure of Death. Although Ingmar Bergman already had more than a dozen films under his belt, including the critically lauded *Smiles of a Summer Night* (1955), *The Seventh Seal* (1957) heralded his arrival as a major visionary in the world of film. *The Seventh Seal,* an allegorical morality play about a knight trying to justify his life after returning from the Crusades, features two major themes that recur throughout the rest of Bergman's films: faith and human relationships.

Bergman, whose career spanned six decades and included more than 60 films, died on July 30, 2007. Many of his works are considered master-pieces, including *Wild Strawberries* (1957), *Persona* (1966), and *Cries and Whispers* (1972). *The Virgin Spring* (1960) and *Fanny and Alexander* (1982) won best foreign film Academy Awards. A number of Bergman's films also won prizes at the Cannes, Berlin, and Venice international film festivals as well as many others.

Ernst Ingmar Bergman was born in Uppsala, Sweden, on July 14, 1918. In the late 1930's, while attending the University of Stockholm, he became involved in theater. In the early 1940's, he began working for the motion picture company Svensk Filmindustri. His first produced screenplay was *Torment* (1944), and his first directorial effort was *Crisis* (1946). By the mid-1950's, he had hit his stride. He began assembling a stock company of sorts and frequently worked with actresses Bibi Andersson, Ingrid Thulin, and Liv Ullmann; actors Gunnar Björnstrand, Erland Josephson, and Max von Sydow; and cinematographer Sven Nykvist.

His films of the 1950's and 1960's are noted for stark black-and-white photography, a high degree of symbolism, and metaphysical themes. The relationship between humanity and God is a predominant theme in many of Bergman's films. In *The Seventh Seal,* the knight, fresh from the bloodshed and chaos of the Crusades, begins to doubt God's existence. The title of *Through a Glass Darkly* (1961) refers to a biblical passage meaning that the human concep-tion of God is flawed and that true knowledge can only be gained after death. The film cen-ters on the extended family of a woman suffering from schizophrenia. One of the film's characters says that love is the only proof of God that human beings can have and that love makes life bearable by giving us hope. In *Winter Light* (1962), a rural pastor undergoes a crisis of faith when he finds himself unable to console a parishioner who asks for guidance.

Interpersonal relationships, especially dysfunctional ones, form the core of many of Bergman's other major films. In *Persona,* a nurse confesses her deepest secrets to an unspeaking actress in her care, eventually merging the two characters' personalities. *Scenes from a Marriage* (1973), originally a nearly six-hour miniseries for Swedish television, depicts the collapse of a marriage between two people whose only shared characteristic seems to be their mutual dislike for each other. The famed Swedish actress Ingrid Bergman (to whom Ingmar was no relation) made her last motion picture appearance in *Autumn Sonata* (1978), in which a domineering mother attempts to reconcile with her estranged daughter. Ingmar Bergman's last major work, *Fanny and Alexander,* was another six-hour miniseries, this time following the lives of a brother and sister in early 1900's Sweden. His final film was 2003's *Saraband,* in which Ullmann and Josephson reprise their roles from *Scenes from a Marriage* to create a kind of coda to the earlier film.

Bergman died on the Swedish island of Fårö, where he had lived and worked since the early 1960's. His films, which were in part introspective explorations of his own neuroses and fears, will continue to mesmerize viewers for generations to come.   ■ S. Thomas Richardson

Buddhist leaders protest against Myanmar's military government in Yangon, the largest city, on Sept. 23, 2007. Soldiers and police put down the demonstrations by arresting, beating, and killing monks and other protesters.

Myanmar. Members of the army of predominantly Buddhist Myanmar shot Buddhist monks and others in the streets of Yangon, the largest city, in September 2007 to halt protests against the country's *junta* (military government). Officials claimed 15 people were killed, but in December, a United Nations (UN) official reported that the death toll was 31. Thousands of monks and civilians were beaten and detained.

Background. A military junta had ruled Myanmar since 1962, and its total control had caused Myanmar's economy to deteriorate, bringing widespread poverty and malnutrition. The UN World Food Programme reported on Oct. 18, 2007, that 5 million people in Myanmar lacked adequate food.

After the army crushed prodemocracy demonstrations in 1988, killing an estimated 3,000 people, a new junta took power. In 1990, the group ignored the fact that the National League for Democracy (NLD), led by Aung San Suu Kyi, had won a fair election for control of the country. In 2007, she remained under house arrest, as she had been for more than 11 of the past 18 years.

The 2007 protests were touched off when the junta on August 15 unexpectedly raised fuel and gas prices by as much as 500 percent. Military-backed gangs beat and arrested protesters, and soldiers abused protesting monks.

Larger demonstrations began on September 17. Many of the nation's 400,000 monks poured into the streets of Yangon and other towns, prompting thousands to join the protests. On September 26, soldiers and police began beating and shooting monks, other demonstrators, and bystanders. The army raided monasteries, beating and expelling more monks. Midnight arrests of people whom junta officials had identified in the protests continued for weeks.

Under international pressure, the junta began talks with Suu Kyi on October 25. After meeting with NLD leaders on November 9, she expressed optimism at prospects for political change.

New constitution. In 1993, the junta began sporadic meetings of a Constitutional Convention whose delegates ignored the 1990 election results. The NLD boycotted the meetings, which ended on Sept. 3, 2007, with guidelines for a new governmental system of "disciplined democracy" that would keep military control while limiting political parties and human rights guarantees. On October 18, the junta announced the formation of a 54-member commission to write a new constitution. The commission excluded NLD representatives.

■ Henry S. Bradsher

See also **Asia.**

Namibia. See **Africa.**
Nauru. See **Pacific Islands.**

Nepal. Two of the main political parties in Nepal, the Nepali Congress and the Communist Party (Maoist), argued in 2007 over efforts to write a new constitution. They agreed it should end centuries of monarchal rule and establish a republic but could not agree on electing people to write it.

Royal power had been contentious since 1960. In 2005, King Gyanendra Bir Bikram Shah Dev seized absolute power from an elected parliament but in the face violent demonstrations was forced to give up some power in April 2006. Parliament then removed more of the king's powers, including command of the army. An interim constitution written in January 2007 gave the king no role in government, transferring executive power to the prime minister. State money for the monarchy was cut from the nation's budget, which was presented in July. On December 23, Nepal's political parties, intent on bringing the Maoists back into the political process, signed an agreement abolishing the monarchy. According to the pact, the monarchy will cease to exist after a new parliament is elected in April 2008.

The Maoists had entered parliament on Jan. 15, 2007, under the interim constitution. They filled 83 of the 330 seats. After waging a guerrilla war against the government since 1996, which cost some 13,000 lives, the Maoists had agreed to a cease-fire in May 2006. However, in 2007, a Maoist splinter group began operating in the Tarai, the fertile flat land of southern Nepal.

The interim constitution failed to provide for regional or ethnic autonomy, angering people in a nation of great diversity. Some of Nepal's many ethnic groups, Hindu castes, and linguistic minorities had long-standing grievances over domination of the nation by upper-caste Hindus from the lower Himalayan hills.

Clashes. The Madhesis of the southeastern Tarai were specially dissatisfied and demonstrated against the interim constitution, demanding representation. Although some Madhesis had fought alongside the Maoists from 1996 to 2006, violent clashes developed between the two in 2007. In one clash in Gaur in March, 27 people were killed. Most of those killed were Maoists, who were beaten to death by supporters of the Madhesi People's Rights Forum in retaliation for Maoist attacks. Other groups staged strikes that crippled trade and public life. The new ethnic and regional groupings, by voicing public grievances, weakened power that the Maoists had consolidated.

Surprised by the agitation's strength, the interim government's upper-caste Hindu leaders agreed to establish a federal state in which regions would share some powers with the government. The form this would take, however, remained unclear in 2007. ■ Henry S. Bradsher

See also **Asia; Disasters.**

Netherlands. In February 2007, Prime Minister Jan Peter Balkenende formed a new government, after his previous center-right coalition collapsed in 2006. Queen Beatrix appointed Balkenende head of a new coalition that included his own centrist Christian Democratic Appeal, the left-of-center Labor Party, and a small Protestant religious party, the Christian Union.

The new coalition agreed on a program of economic reforms that marked a shift to the center left. The program included plans to increase spending over the next four years in such key areas as health care, child care, education, and the environment. It also called for subsidizing jobs for the long-term unemployed and rejected planned changes that would have made it easier for employers to fire unneeded workers.

European Union (EU) treaty. In October 2007, the leaders of EU member nations agreed on a revised version of an EU Constitution. The Constitution creates the positions of EU president and foreign minister and reforms the rules by which member nations vote on legislation. In its original form, the document was rejected by Dutch voters in a referendum in 2005. Even before the new version of the treaty was finalized, Balkenende's government decided in September 2007 not to hold a new referendum on the treaty. According to the Council of State, a national vote was unnecessary because the new treaty does not violate any elements of the Dutch Constitution. In addition, surveys conducted by the government showed that even the toned-down document was likely to be rejected by voters, who resented any increase in EU power over Dutch affairs. The governing coalition agreed to pass the treaty through parliament by majority vote. Opposition parties planned to actively campaign against the new treaty and to urge that parliament demand a referendum.

Afghanistan. In December, the Dutch parliament voted to extend its military mission in Afghanistan until 2010. The mission was scheduled to be completed in 2008, but continued insurgent attacks by the Taliban and its supporters and the unwillingness of any other European country to take over the dangerous mission forced the government to reconsider withdrawing its troops. After al-Qa`ida leader Osama bin Laden released a tape calling for all Europeans to leave Afghanistan, the Dutch government decided to stay.

Economy. With inflation low and budget surpluses expected, analysts projected the Balkenende government would be able to afford its planned spending increases. EU economists predicted the country's economy would grow by 2.7 percent in 2007, down slightly from its 3-percent growth rate in 2006. ■ Jeffrey Kopstein

See also **Afghanistan; Europe; Iraq.**

New Brunswick. See Canadian provinces.

A plume of steam pours from a Manhattan street near Grand Central Terminal on July 18, 2007, triggering panic about another terrorist attack on the city. The explosion, caused by a simple infrastructure failure, did leave one person dead and several others injured, four of them seriously.

New York City continued to ride the crest of a historic building boom in 2007, six years after the Sept. 11, 2001, terrorist attack on the World Trade Center sent the city's economy into a tailspin. Projects underway in 2007 included a new Yankee Stadium; a new Citi Field for the Mets; a new Second Avenue subway; headquarters for Bank of America and investment banking firm Goldman Sachs; and the 1,776-foot (541-meter) Freedom Tower, the first building to rise on the footprint of the Trade Center site. The New York Building Congress, a coalition of the city's builders and skilled-trade unions, announced in October that construction activity in 2007 would reach a record $26.2 billion.

The owners of the 1,700-room Pennsylvania Hotel announced in January that the hotel had been sold to Vornado Realty Trust, which planned to build an office complex larger in size than the Empire State Building on the site. The hotel, built by the Pennsylvania Railroad in 1919, is considered a pop culture jewel because it has the city's oldest phone number still in use—"Pennsylvania 6-5000." The number, the title of a Glenn Miller song, calls to mind the days when the hotel's Cafe Rouge hosted Miller and other big-band entertainers.

In November 2007, a new headquarters for The New York Times opened on Eighth Avenue. The 52-story glass, steel, and ceramic tower was designed by Italian architect Renzo Piano.

School controversy. The Khalil Gibran International Academy, an Arab-oriented middle and high school in Brooklyn, got off to a difficult start on August 10 when officials forced principal Debbie Almontaser to resign after she failed to condemn T-shirt that read *intifada NYC*. The Arabic term *intifada* commonly refers to two Palestinian uprisings against the Israeli occupation of the West Bank and the Gaza Strip. Almontaser said on October 16 that she would sue to regain her job.

Education decision. The United States Supreme Court stunned officials of the nation's biggest school system on October 10 when, by a 4-to-4 vote, it left standing a lower court ruling that the city must reimburse former Viacom executive Tom Freston for the costs of sending his child, who has special needs, to an expensive private school. The ruling gave more leeway to parents of children with learning disabilities to send their children to private schools, at city expense, if they are dissatisfied with public school programs. Federal appeals courts had earlier ruled the city should pay private school tuition for eligible children even if they had never attended public school.

Officials feared the ruling would cost the city hundreds of millions of dollars. Because the ruling was made by a tie vote, it affected only school districts in New York, Connecticut, and Vermont—states under the jurisdiction of the U.S. Court of Appeals for the Second Circuit, which had made the original ruling in favor of Freston.

Congestion pricing. In an Earth Day speech on April 22, Mayor Michael Bloomberg unveiled a congestion pricing plan, modeled on that of London. Under the plan, cars would be charged a fee of $8 and trucks $21 to enter Manhattan south of 86th Street between 6 a.m. and 6 p.m. on weekdays. The mayor hoped the plan would raise money to fund mass transit while reducing congestion and carbon dioxide emissions in the center of the city. Critics said the plan favored Manhattan residents over residents of the other boroughs and the suburbs. They also worried that the truck fees would be passed along to consumers and that the city's public transit systems could not cope with the expected higher demand from commuters seeking alternatives to driving. In July, the state formed a commission to study the plan. In August, the federal government pledged more than $350 million to the city to implement a congestion pricing plan.

Tree planting. The first of a planned 1 million new street trees was planted on October 9 during a dedication ceremony led by Mayor Bloomberg and entertainer Bette Midler. Midler's New York Restoration Project is helping to raise the $200 million needed for the effort. ■ Owen Moritz

See also Architecture; City; Supreme Court of the United States.

New Zealand. A widely anticipated Cabinet reshuffle by Prime Minister Helen Clark in 2007 to prepare her Labour Party to win a record fourth term in the 2008 general election was overshadowed by controversy. The changes, announced on Oct. 31, 2007, brought three new ministers to the Cabinet and redistributed some *portfolios* (administrative responsibilities), but public interest centered on the fate of senior minister Trevor Mallard. Only a week before the reshuffle, he had punched an opposition member while in the parliamentary lobby. He later apologized but had embarrassed the government, which had announced a major campaign against domestic violence on September 4. In the reshuffle, he was dropped from the nine-member front bench, was relegated from 7th to 10th place in Cabinet ranking, and lost several portfolios.

Cabinet casualties. Mallard was the second minister to incur the wrath of Prime Minister Clark in 2007. On July 26, she accepted the resignation of Environment and Social Development Minister David Benson-Pope following contradictory statements over his involvement in the dismissal of an Environment Ministry staff member whose partner was press secretary to opposition National Party leader John Key. Clark also faced continuing embarrassment over the case of Taito Philip Field, an associate minister who resigned from Labour in February amid allegations of corruption. On October 5, the High Court gave police permission to bring charges, and on November 23, he was charged with 15 counts of bribery and 25 counts of attempting to pervert justice.

Political fortunes. The ruling Labour Party trailed the National Party in political polls throughout 2007. In a May poll, Clark slipped from her position as preferred prime minister for the first time in eight years. The National Party and its leader emerged as potential winners in 2008, though polling revealed a volatile political climate.

Climate. Nature proved equally volatile, with severe storms in the north of the country in February, March, and July 2007. Repeated flooding, which caused an estimated $100 million in damages, led Prime Minister Clark to suggest that some settlements may have to be moved. (All amounts in New Zealand dollars.) Severe weather patterns increased public support for policies related to global warming and the goal of becoming the world's first carbon-neutral nation.

Economy. World prices for dairy products doubled in 12 months, injecting $6.9 billion into the New Zealand economy. Inflation-adjusted growth in the second quarter, at 2.2 percent, was higher than forecast. ■ Gavin Ellis

See also Pacific Islands.

Newfoundland and Labrador. See Canadian provinces.

Selected news from 2007:

Famed New York City stable closes. Claremont Riding Academy, the oldest continuously operated stable in the United States, closed after 115 years on April 29, 2007. The Academy, located only two blocks west of New York City's Central Park, opened in 1892 as a public livery stable. A riding school was founded in 1927. It offered lessons and the renting and boarding of horses for riders on Central Park's bridle paths. The building is listed on the National Register of Historic Places and has been designated as a New York City Landmark, noted owner Paul Novograd, so it cannot be torn down, but the building's future is uncertain.

Running in space. On April 16, 2007, U.S. astronaut Sunita Williams became the first person to run the annual Boston Marathon in space. Williams, who completed the 2006 Houston Marathon to qualify for the 2007 Boston race, ran the marathon on a specially equipped treadmill on the International Space Station. To counteract the effects of weightlessness, she was harnessed to the treadmill. Scientists from the National Aeronautics and Space Administration devised a "vibration isolation system" to keep the pounding of her feet from affecting the orbit of the station.

Williams, who said her goal was "to encourage kids to start making physical fitness part of their daily lives," finished the 26-mile (41.8-kilometer) race in 4 hours, 23 minutes, 46 seconds. The top woman finisher, Lidiya Grigoryeva of Russia, completed the race in 2 hours, 29 minutes, 18 seconds.

When Williams returned to Earth on June 22, she set the new record for the longest unbroken space flight by a woman, at 195 days. The record was previously set in 1996 by Shannon Lucid, who spent 188 days in space.

Thousands of Anne Frank papers donated. On June 25, 2007, during celebrations of the 60th anniversary of the publication of Anne Frank's diary, her cousin, Bernhard "Buddy" Elias, donated a previously private archive to the Anne Frank House in Amsterdam, the Netherlands. The Anne Frank House is a museum incorporating the "secret annex" where the Franks hid from the Nazis from 1942 to 1944. Archivists believe the 25,000 photographs, letters, and other documents will shed additional light on the life of the

CUTTYSARK
Conservation Project

Ned Fiendish the rat catcher is just one of the colorful characters visitors encounter at the newly opened Dickens World theme park in Chatham, Kent, in the United Kingdom. The attraction brings to life the writings of Charles Dickens, which include *A Christmas Carol*, *A Tale of Two Cities*, and *Great Expectations*.

The *Cutty Sark* (below), a famous British clipper ship, caught fire on May 21, 2007 (left), damaging parts of the deck and hold. The ship was in dry dock at the time, undergoing a $50-million restoration. The *Cutty Sark*, which was designed to carry tea from China, was one of the fastest sailing ships ever built.

girl whose diary became one of the most well-known documents of the Holocaust. Although the archive does not contain much information about the time the Frank family spent in hiding, it is believed to contain valuable information about the family's history and cultural background. According to Elias, the letters show that the Franks "were interested in art, in theater. When they went to a concert or a play, they wrote about it." Also in the new archive are postwar letters from Anne's father, Otto, to his mother during the period in which he was compiling Anne's diary for publication.

Invasion of the Mooninites. On Jan. 31, 2007, a guerrilla marketing campaign sparked fears of a terrorist attack in Boston. A subway worker reported a suspicious electronic device, fearing that it might be an explosive. Soon a bus station, a major highway, and parts of the subway were shut down as police searched for additional devices. Eventually, 38 similar devices were located. The situation then evoked a mixture of relief, confusion, and outrage when it became clear that the devices were in fact part of a marketing campaign for an adult-oriented cartoon show called "Aqua Teen Hunger Force." The devices, when turned on, displayed a Mooninite, a character from the show, in LED's (light-emitting diodes). According to the agency responsible for the campaign, the devices had been placed weeks earlier in Boston and nine other cities.

To celebrate the 30th anniversary of the 1977 film *Star Wars*, the United States Postal Service issued stamps featuring characters from the movie. In addition, some 400 mailboxes in 200 U.S. cities were decorated to resemble the robot R2-D2 (right), who appears in *Star Wars* as well as its two sequels and three prequels.

The campaign was part of a trend known as "viral marketing," in which unorthodox or nontraditional methods of advertising are utilized and are intended to generate word-of-mouth. Such campaigns are generally aimed at younger generations, and observers noted that the Boston incident showed a generation gap between younger generations, who "got" the campaign and found it amusing, and older generations, who did not see the humor.

The two men involved in the campaign were charged with disorderly conduct and placing a hoax device, but charges were later dropped after the men performed community service. Turner Broadcasting, which owns Cartoon Network, on which the show is broadcast, paid the city of Boston $2 million in compensation.

Lost Chopin piano found. A Swiss music scholar announced in March 2007 that he had successfully tracked down the piano that Polish-born composer Frederic Chopin took on his last concert tour in 1848. The piano, made by French piano maker Camille Pleyel, was believed lost since Chopin's death in 1849. Jean-Jacques Eigeldinger scoured Pleyel's ledgers for information on the piano. He was able to track it in 2007 to a British collector who bought the instrument at an auction in the 1980's. The piano is now one of four known to have been owned by Chopin, who once called Pleyel's pianos "the last word in perfection."

In September 2007, Moira Cameron (far left) became the first female Yeoman Warder of the Tower of London in the order's 522-year history. In 2007, Alexandra Hai (near left) became Venice's first female gondolier after battling 1,000 years of male-dominated tradition. A Venetian court finally allowed her to pilot one of the city's gondolas, but only in the service of one hotel.

The world's largest photograph, measuring 31.58 by 111 feet (9.62 by 33.83 meters), is displayed inside the world's largest camera. *The Great Picture* shows the control tower, structures, and runways of the Marine Corps Air Station El Toro in California. To capture the image, a hangar at the base was turned into a gigantic pinhole camera. Guinness World Records of London certified the achievements in July 2007.

At auction in 2007: A 1909 Honus Wagner tobacco baseball card sold for a record $2.35 million in February. It then broke its own record, selling for $2.8 million in late August.

A daguerrotype camera, one of the world's oldest cameras, sold for $810,000 in Vienna, Austria, in May. Although the exact age of the camera was unknown, experts said it was made before 1839.

Claude Monet's painting *Nympheas*, which had not been publicly exhibited since 1936, sold for $36.7 million at Sotheby's auction house in London in June 2007. *Nympheas* is considered to be one of Monet's finest water lily paintings. The same week, Monet's *Waterloo Bridge, Temps Couvert*, a painting of the River Thames, sold for $35.5 million at Christie's auction house in London.

Clifford Possum Tjapaltjarri's *Warlugulong* set the record for the highest price paid for Australian Aboriginal art when it sold for more than $2 million in a Melbourne auction in June. It had initially been purchased for $1,000 and had been displayed on a cafeteria wall at a bank training center.

In June, a gold-encrusted sword used in a battle in June 1800 by Napoleon sold in France for $6.5 million, a world record for Napoleon memorabilia. In July 2007, a letter from Napoleon to his future wife, Josephine,

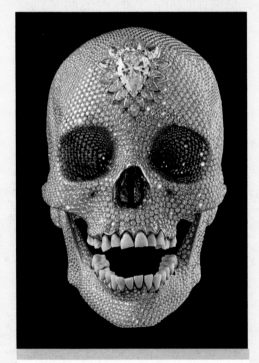

For the Love of God, by controversial British artist Damien Hirst, is a platinum cast of a human skull encrusted with 8,601 diamonds. The work reportedly sold in August 2007 for $100 million, making it the most expensive piece of contemporary art ever. The piece was inspired by a jewel-encrusted Aztec skull on display at the British Museum.

Models of different sizes are exhibited at the U.S.S. *Monitor* Center at the Mariners' Museum in Newport News, Virginia. The center opened on March 9, 2007, the 145th anniversary of the Civil War "battle of the ironclads," which pitted the Union ship *Monitor* against the Confederate ship *Merrimack.*

sold in London for $556,000. In the letter, Napoleon apologizes to Josephine after a fight.

A 1963 Ferrari 250 GT Berlinetta Lusso once owned by actor Steve McQueen sold for $2.3 million in August 2007 at an auction held by Christie's in California. McQueen bought the car in 1963 and drove it frequently until he traded it in 1973.

A flawless 6.04-carat blue diamond sold in October 2007 for $7.98 million, becoming the most expensive gemstone per carat ever auctioned. Sotheby's held the auction in Hong Kong. A Qur'an from 1203 written in gold with margin notes written in silver sold for $2.3 million at Christie's in London in October 2007.

A 1902 Faberge egg made for the Rothschild banking family sold for a record $18.5 million at Christie's in London in November 2007. The gold-and-pink egg, one of only 12 known to be made to imperial standards for private ownership, features a clock face and a diamond-studded rooster that emerges from the egg to crow the hour.

A 5,000-year-old Mesopotamian sculpture known as the Guennol Lioness sold for a record $57.2 million at Sotheby's in New York City in December. The 3 ¼-inch- (8-centimeter-) tall sculpture became the most expensive sculpture ever auctioned.   ■ S. Thomas Richardson

Newspaper. Australian-born media baron Rupert Murdoch acquired *The Wall Street Journal* in 2007. This flagship of the financial publishing firm Dow Jones & Company was highly respected for its journalistic integrity.

In May 2007, Murdoch's company, News Corporation, made an unsolicited bid of $5 billion for New York City-based Dow Jones. The Bancroft family—which had controlled Dow Jones and the *Journal* since the early 1900's—initially declined the offer. They feared Murdoch would diminish the *Journal* in an attempt to increase revenue. Critics also charged that Murdoch had pressured media outlets he owned to downplay stories that would negatively impact his own business deals. Some members of the Bancroft family feared the *Journal's* objectivity might become suspect. Many younger members of the family, however, favored the sale. By August 2007, an agreement was announced. The sale became final in December.

Tribune sale. In April, Chicago-based Tribune Company accepted an offer from billionaire entrepreneur Sam Zell. Tribune Company—which held television stations; newspapers, including the *Chicago Tribune* and the *Los Angeles Times;* and the Chicago Cubs baseball team—was struggling when Zell made the $8.2-billion offer. Shareholders in August approved the purchase, which closed at the end of 2007, leaving the private company around $10 billion in debt.

Online subscriptions ended. *The New York Times,* which had charged online users for access to certain columns and archived articles, announced a change of policy in September. Subscriptions to the online site generated revenues of $10 million per year. Increasing numbers of users sent to the site by search engines, however, caused *Times* executives to believe that advertising to this huge base of readers would be more profitable than charging subscription fees to core readers. In November, Rupert Murdoch followed, announcing that fees to access *The Wall Street Journal's* Web site would be eliminated.

Declining circulation. The number of readers for most print newspapers continued to decline in 2007. Circulation of daily newspapers dropped by 2.1 percent and Sunday papers by 3.1 percent in the three months that ended March 31, 2007. Some of this loss was attributed to readers migrating to online newspapers. Some loss, however, was planned. Advertisers had begun to dismiss the importance of short-term readers garnered through newspaper promotions or given free newspapers by hotels. Because ads are more lucrative than sales of papers to readers, many newspapers had stopped promotions that added numbers to circulation rates only for short periods. ■ Christine Sullivan

Nicaragua. On Jan. 10, 2007, Daniel Ortega, 61, of the center-left Sandinista National Liberation Front, was sworn in for a five-year term as president. Ortega had served as president from 1985 to 1990 and as a member of the military *junta* (group) that ruled Nicaragua from 1979 to 1985.

In 2007, Ortega obtained pledges of foreign help in alleviating worsening power shortages that were hampering business and causing almost daily blackouts in the capital, Managua. Venezuela's government agreed to help finance a new $3.6-billion oil refinery near León, Nicaragua. Venezuela also pledged millions of dollars to build a new cross-country highway, dozens of electric generators, and an electric power plant in Nicaragua. In addition, Venezuela's national bank established a branch in Managua to provide low-interest loans for farmers.

Ortega announced in August that Iran's government would help finance the construction of a $350-million deep-water port on Nicaragua's Caribbean coast and a $120-million hydroelectric power plant. Iran also promised funding to build 10,000 residences to help relieve a growing shortage of low-income housing in Nicaragua.

■ Nathan A. Haverstock

See also **Latin America.**

Niger. See Africa.

Nigeria. In April 2007, Nigeria held parliamentary, presidential, and gubernatorial elections. The polls were to result in the first peaceful transfer of political power from one civilian administration to another in Nigeria's history. Unfortunately, the national electoral authority did not prove up to the task of running the polls smoothly, resulting in numerous irregularities at the polling stations. Opposition parties demanded a rerun of the elections.

Election results. The ruling People's Democratic Party (PDP) improved on its performance at the 2003 elections by winning the governorships in 28 of Nigeria's 36 states as well as obtaining two-thirds majorities in both houses of the National Assembly. Umaru Yar'Adua, the PDP candidate and a former governor, won the presidential race with 70 percent of the vote. Muhammadu Buhari, candidate of the All Nigeria People's Party (ANPP), was Yar'Adua's closest rival with 18 percent. Atiku Abubakar, the former vice president who had fallen out with former President Olusegun Obasanjo prior to the elections and became the Action Congress (AC) candidate, drew only 7 percent of the vote.

Many analysts suggested that Obasanjo, a Christian from southern Nigeria, chose Yar'Adua, a Muslim from the North, as the PDP's presidential candidate to establish the principle that Nigeria's top leadership should alternate between the country's regions to maintain national stability.

After the elections. Yar'Adua inherited many problems from the previous administration. Shortly after his May 29, 2007, inauguration, the country was paralyzed by a general strike called by the labor unions. The matter was resolved with the president yielding to the strikers' major demands. The resumption of rebel activity in the oil-rich Niger Delta region, which continued to disrupt oil production, proved an even bigger problem for the new administration.

Yar'Adua served notice that he was serious about stamping out governmental corruption by arresting several former state governors. He also promised that the government would begin implementing the 15-year Niger Delta development plan, which Obasanjo had announced shortly before the elections.

Yar'Adua announced his Cabinet in June. Like Obasanjo, Yar'Adua did not appoint a minister of energy but kept the post, which included control of the important oil industry, for himself. To calm emotions after the flawed elections, he offered Cabinet posts to the main opposition parties in a government of national unity. The ANPP received two ministerial posts, but the AC rejected the offer.   ■ Pieter Esterhuysen

See also **Africa.**

Nobel Prizes in literature, peace, economics, and the sciences were awarded in October 2007 by the Norwegian Storting (parliament) in Oslo and by the Karolinska Institute, the Royal Swedish Academy of Sciences, and the Swedish Academy of Literature, all in Stockholm. Each prize was worth about $1.5 million.

The 2007 Nobel Prize in literature went to English writer Doris Lessing, whose fiction reflects her cosmopolitan awareness of racial and class inequalities. Most of her works stress the complexity of life and deal with humanity's struggle to understand the world. In awarding the prize, the Swedish Academy described her as "the epicist [epic-writer] of the female experience who with skepticism, fire, and visionary power has subjected a divided civilization to scrutiny."

Lessing made her literary debut with *The Grass Is Singing* (1950). Her most famous novel, the feminist political classic *The Golden Notebook* (1962), describes the anxiety and confusion that a woman encounters in the modern world. Her other works include *The Summer Before the Dark* (1973), an exploration of middle age, and *The Cleft: A Novel* (2007), an alternative history of human origins. Lessing has also written a series of philosophical science-fiction novels called *Canopus in Argos: Archives* (1979-1983) as well as plays, poems, short stories, and two autobiographies.

The 2007 Peace Prize was awarded to former United States Vice President Al Gore and the Intergovernmental Panel on Climate Change (IPCC) for "their efforts to build up and disseminate greater knowledge about man-made climate change, and to lay the foundations for the measures ... to counteract such change." Gore won acclaim and numerous awards for his 2006 film, *An Inconvenient Truth,* a documentary about the causes and effects of global warming. The Nobel committee praised Gore for being "probably the single individual who has done most to create greater worldwide understanding of the measures that need to be adopted." The IPCC is a United Nations committee that provides scientific information to world governments on the impact of human activities on global warming. In 2007, the panel reported that emissions of heat-trapping greenhouse gases from human activities are "very likely" the reason for the "unequivocal warming of [Earth's] climate system" over the past 100 years.

The 2007 Nobel Prize in economics went to three American economists for their work in mechanism design theory, a widely used framework for comparing different types of economic institutions to determine the most efficient way of reaching a particular goal and creating mechanisms for improving outcomes. The winners were Leonid Hurwicz, a Russian-born American at the University of Minnesota in Minneapolis; Eric S. Maskin of Princeton University in New Jersey; and Roger B. Myerson of the University of Chicago. Mechanism design theory has political and social applications as well as economic uses. It can be applied to problems as diverse as auctioning radio frequencies to mobile phone companies, building social welfare systems, negotiating labor disputes, and designing government regulations.

The 2007 Nobel Prize in physiology or medicine was awarded to Mario R. Capecchi, an Italian-born American at the University of Utah in Salt Lake City; Oliver Smithies, a British-born American at the University of North Carolina at Chapel Hill; and Sir Martin J. Evans at Cardiff University in the United Kingdom. The scientists were honored for their contributions to what has become a widely used method of studying the role of specific genes in disease and the function of cells and organs in mammals. They developed methods to produce *knockout mice,* strains of laboratory mice in which a particular gene has been inactivated or "knocked out." Such mice are widely used to study the origin and development of diseases, particularly genetic diseases, as well as the effectiveness of such treatments as gene and drug therapy.

The 2007 Nobel Prize in physics went to Albert Fert of the Paris-Sud 11 University in Orsay, France, and Peter Grünberg of the Institute of Solid State Research at Jülich Research Center in

Germany for their independent discovery in the 1980's of a phenomenon called giant magneto-resistance (GMR). This physical effect has been fundamental to the development of digital music players, laptop computers, and other devices that can be used to retrieve large amounts of information from what have become increasingly smaller hard disks. The two scientists discovered that the electrical resistance of a stack made of layers of magnetic metal and other materials changes significantly as the strength of a magnetic field applied to it increases or decreases.

The 2007 Nobel Prize in chemistry was awarded to Gerhard Ertl of the Fritz Haber Institute of the Max Planck Society in Berlin. Ertl was honored for his pioneering studies of the chemical reactions that occur on the surface of solids. The Nobel committee praised Ertl for being one of the first to see additional applications for processes involved in the production of semiconductors, which are widely used in computer chips, transistors, LED's (light-emitting diodes), and solar cells. One of Ertl's most important achievements was providing a detailed explanation for an economically significant process by which nitrogen can be extracted from air for use in artificial fertilizers.

■ Barbara A. Mayes

See also **Literature; People in the news** (Al Gore; Doris Lessing); **Physics.**

Northern Ireland. An important breakthrough in the Northern Ireland peace process was made in 2007 with the creation of a power-sharing government. The purpose of the new executive body was to heal the divide between the Protestant majority (most of whom wanted Northern Ireland to remain part of the United Kingdom [U.K.]) and the Roman Catholic minority (most of whom wished the province to become part of the Republic of Ireland).

Ireland had been divided in 1921, with the six largely Protestant counties of Ulster remaining part of the United Kingdom. Fighting between Protestant and Catholic groups broke out in 1969, leading to the deployment of British troops to keep the peace. The "Troubles" lasted until the Good Friday Agreement of 1998, which U.K. Prime Minister Tony Blair and Irish Prime Minister Bertie Ahern negotiated between the Protestant Ulster Unionists and the Catholic political group, Sinn Féin.

The agreement resulted in a cease-fire and an Assembly in which both sides were represented. However, the Assembly collapsed in 2002, following allegations that the Irish Republican Army (IRA), the military wing of Sinn Féin, had not abandoned violence, and the province returned to direct rule from London. In the Assembly election of 2003, moderate parties were beaten by more

hard-line parties. Ian Paisley's Democratic Unionist Party (DUP) became the chief Protestant party, taking over from the Ulster Unionist party. Sinn Féin, led by Gerry Adams, won Catholic votes from the more moderate Social Democratic and Labour Party (SDLP). Ian Paisley refused to govern with Sinn Féin. In 2006, the Northern Ireland Assembly reconvened and, following the St. Andrews Agreement, all parties agreed conditionally to the creation of a power-sharing executive body.

Election. In January 2007, a special conference of Sinn Féin delegates agreed to support the Police Service of Northern Ireland. (The previous police force, the Royal Ulster Constabulary, had been hated because it was dominated by Protestants.) This willingness to support the new police service was one of the key terms of the St. Andrews Agreement and allowed new elections to the Northern Ireland Assembly to take place. Blair insisted that the Assembly had to agree to quickly create a power-sharing executive.

In the March 7 election, Paisley's DUP took the most seats—36 in the 108-member Assembly. Sinn Féin was the second most popular party with 28 seats. The Ulster Unionists and the SDLP gained 18 and 16 seats, respectively. The Green Party gained a seat in the Assembly for the first time. And Anna Lo (born in Hong Kong) of the Alliance Party became not only the first member from an ethnic minority to be elected to the Northern Ireland Assembly but also the first ethnic Chinese person to be elected to any legislature in Europe.

The executive body. On March 26, Paisley and Adams announced the creation of a new power-sharing executive body. Paisley became first minister of Northern Ireland, and Martin McGuinness, spokesman for Sinn Féin, became deputy first minister. In April, the parties divided the government jobs between them. The DUP took control of four ministries; Sinn Féin took three; and the Ulster Unionist Party and the SDLP each took two. The British and Irish governments offered a financial package to help the new executive body and further stimulate the peace process. Power was devolved from the United Kingdom to the Assembly on May 8, ending the period of direct rule.

British troops leave Northern Ireland. Another milestone in the peace process was reached in July, when the deployment of British troops in Northern Ireland—the longest military operation in British history—came to an end. A total of 763 soldiers had been killed in the conflict. A "peacetime garrison" of 5,000 soldiers in training for service in other parts of the world remained.

■ Rohan McWilliam

See also **Ireland; United Kingdom.**

Northwest Territories. See **Canadian territories.**

Norway. Prime Minister Jens Stoltenberg's government, a coalition of the Labor Party, the Socialist Left Party, and the Center Party that came to power in 2005, remained stable in 2007. Nevertheless, important differences in several significant areas, including environmental policy, arose throughout the year. Following a disappointing showing in local elections in September, the dominant Labor Party reshuffled the Cabinet to address some of those differences. Former Minister of International Development Erik Solheim took over the department of the environment in addition to heading a reconfigured department of development cooperation.

Salmon dispute. The European Union (EU) and Norway continued in 2007 a dispute concerning the bloc's restrictions on imported Norwegian salmon. The dispute began in 1989, when salmon farmers in Scotland and Ireland—both members of the European Community (EC), the predecessor of the EU—accused Norway of dumping its salmon on the European market at prices below production costs. (Norway did not belong to the EC, nor does it belong to the EU.) The EC imposed restrictions on the minimum price Norwegian exporters could charge for their salmon. The measures were strengthened further in 2004 and again in 2006. In mid-2006, Norway asked the World Trade Organization (WTO), based in Geneva, Switzerland, to mediate the dispute.

The WTO ruled in November 2007 that in applying its "safeguard measures," the EU had acted "inconsistently" with international trade rules in this case. Nevertheless, the WTO did not order the EU to drop its measures. Both sides claimed victory, and the dispute remained unresolved.

The economy of Norway—Europe's largest exporter of crude oil—continued to boom in 2007, because of high oil prices. As in previous years, Norway channeled much of its oil revenue into a fund designed to preserve the nation's wealth for a time when oil supplies dwindle. Although the budget contained both high revenues and surpluses, the government did not cut tax rates appreciably lower than those of other Scandinavian countries.

Government economists forecast that Norway's *gross domestic product* (GDP—the value of all goods and services produced in a country in a year) would grow by 3.1 percent in 2007, up from 2.9 percent in 2006. The unemployment rate fell from 3.4 percent in 2006 to 2.6 percent in 2007. ■ Jeffrey Kopstein

See also **Europe**.

Nova Scotia. See Canadian provinces.
Nuclear energy. See Energy supply.
Nunavut. See Canadian territories.
Nutrition. See Food.

Ocean. Swarms of voracious jumbo squid invaded California coasts in the spring and summer of 2007, clogging fishing nets and eating huge numbers of anchovies, rockfish, sardines, and other fish. Jumbo squid, also known as Humboldt squid, are notoriously aggressive predators equipped with razor-sharp beaks and retractable tentacles covered with hooked suckers. Mexican fishers know the red squid as *diablos rojos* (red devils) for their large size and insatiable appetite. Commercial fishers in California worried that the jumbo squid might eat so many fish that they would reduce their catches, particularly of valuable Pacific hake.

Other people seemed to enjoy the unusual animals. The squid are fierce, intelligent fighters when hooked, and they quickly became a favorite of sports fishers. Some divers went swimming with the squid—a seemingly daring adventure since the squid can grow to more than 6 feet (2 meters) and 100 pounds (45 kilograms) and have been known to attack divers when threatened.

Biologists Louis Zeidberg of Stanford University in Stanford, California, and Bruce Robison of the Monterey Bay Aquarium Research Institute in Monterey, California, suggested in July that the presence of jumbo squid so far north might be related to overfishing of tuna, sharks, and swordfish that normally prey on the squid, keeping their numbers in check. The squid had been observed periodically off California since 1912, but they usually retreated quickly to their historic range in the warmer tropical waters from Mexico south to the equator. By the early 2000's, the red giants had been spotted as far north as Oregon, British Columbia, and Alaska. Biologists believed that jumbo squid were breeding as far north as central California—a sign that they may have expanded their natural range.

Some biologists suggested developing a commercial jumbo squid fishery to control the population. The jumbo squid fishery is Mexico's largest commercial fishery, with about 720,000 tons (800,000 metric tons) caught annually.

Glass sponge reefs. Oceanographers led by Paul Johnson of the University of Washington in Seattle in June 2007 discovered a large reef of glass sponges growing on the sea floor off the coast of Washington. Scientists had thought that reef-building glass sponges, ancient organisms with a skeleton consisting of fine hairs of glass-like material called *silica,* had gone extinct about 100 million years ago. But in 1991, they were discovered in the protected waters of the Georgia and Hecata straits off the west coast of Canada. The 2007 discovery suggested that even more reefs survived elsewhere in the northern Pacific.

The Washington glass sponge reefs cover hundreds of square feet of ocean floor about 650 feet

(200 meters) below the ocean surface. Glass sponges have a unique physiology that allows them to survive in the total darkness of the deep ocean. In turn, the reef supports a thriving ecosystem of fish, crustaceans, and plankton in a region of ocean floor that is otherwise barren.

Call to halt destructive fishing. An international group of fisheries biologists led by Daniel Pauly and Rashid Sumaila, both at the University of British Columbia in Vancouver, in February called for continuing negotiations to end a destructive fishing technique known as bottom trawling. In this practice, huge weighted nets are dragged for miles across the seabed, scraping up fish, mollusks, sponges, coral, rocks, and mud. The damage left behind leaves the sea floor barren. Once trawled, the sea floor communities can take decades to recover their original species diversity.

The scientists argued that continued unregulated bottom trawling might lead to the collapse of valuable fisheries as whole sea floor ecosystems are destroyed. They proposed eliminating fuel subsidies for fishing fleets, which would make bottom trawling economically unviable. Many conservation groups had long supported a ban on bottom trawling to protect fragile sea floor habitats, but the practice continued largely without regulation.　　■ Christina S. Johnson

See also **Biology.**

Olympic Games. The International Olympic Committee (IOC) voted on July 4, 2007, to award the 2014 Winter Olympic Games to the Russian city of Sochi, which edged out Pyongchang, South Korea, in the second and final balloting. Pyongchang led the first round of voting ahead of Sochi and Salzburg, Austria. With Salzburg eliminated, Sochi leapfrogged into the Games on the second ballot.

Critics of Sochi's proposal to be the first Russian host city of a Winter Games cited the lack of roads and railroads to the mountain area and the lack of existing venues at the Black Sea resort. Voters, however, were moved by the Russian government's guarantee of support.

Seven cities applied to host the 2016 Summer Olympics. The winner was to be selected in a vote in 2009. The cities were Baku, Azerbaijan; Chicago; Doha, Qatar; Madrid; Rio de Janeiro; Prague, the Czech Republic; and Tokyo.

In an attempt to make it easier for new sports to be added to the Olympics, the IOC voted in 2007 to change its charter. New events will be added with the vote of a simple majority of members, rather than the two-thirds majority previously needed.　　■ Michael Kates

Oman. See **Middle East.**
Ontario. See **Canadian provinces.**
Opera. See **Classical music.**

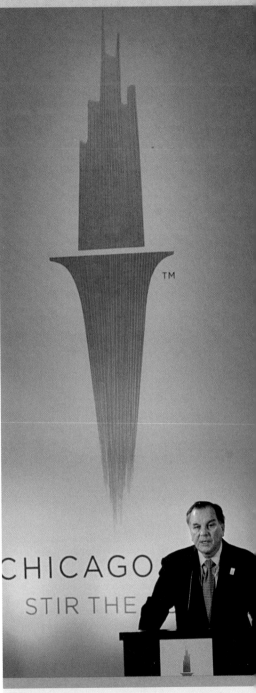

Mayor Richard M. Daley announces in April that Chicago has been chosen as the United States entrant in the international competition to host the 2016 Summer Olympic Games. Chicago was competing against such cities as Madrid, Rio de Janeiro, and Tokyo.

FACTS IN BRIEF ON PACIFIC ISLAND COUNTRIES

Country	Population	Government	Monetary unit*	Foreign trade (million U.S.$)	
				Exports†	Imports†
Fiji	876,000	President Ratu Josefa Iloilovatu Uluivuda; Interim Prime Minister Frank Bainimarama	dollar (1.56 = $1)	720	1,462
Kiribati	106,000	President Anote Tong	Australian dollar (1.13 = $1)	17	62
Marshall Islands	68,000	President Kessai Hesa Note	U.S. dollar	9	54
Micronesia, Federated States of	112,000	President Emanuel Mori	U.S. dollar	14	133
Nauru	15,000	President Marcus Stephens	Australian dollar (1.13 = $1)	0.06	20
New Zealand	4,188,000	Governor General Anand Satyanand; Prime Minister Helen Clark	dollar (1.33 = $1)	23,690	25,230
Palau	21,000	President Tommy Esang Remengesau, Jr.	U.S. dollar	5	107
Papua New Guinea	6,253,000	Governor General Sir Paulius Matane; Prime Minister Sir Michael Somare	kina (2.88 = $1)	4,096	1,686
Samoa	187,000	Head of State Tuiatua Tupua Tamasese Efi; Prime Minister Tuila'epa Sailele Malielegaoi	tala (2.56 = $1)	94	285
Solomon Islands	510,000	Governor General Nathaniel Waena; Prime Minister Derek Sikua	dollar (7.25 = $1)	171	159
Tonga	107,000	King George Tupou V; Prime Minister Feleti Sevele	pa'anga (1.94 = $1)	34	122
Tuvalu	11,000	Governor General Filoimea Telito; Prime Minister Apisai Ielemia	Australian dollar (1.13 = $1)	1	9
Vanuatu	223,000	President Kalkot Mataskelekele; Prime Minister Ham Lini	vatu (98.38 = $1)	34	117

*Exchange rates as of Oct. 4, 2007.   †Latest available data.

Pacific Islands. In 2007, voters in Papua New Guinea and the Federated States of Micronesia voted in parliamentary and congressional elections, respectively. Samoa elected a new head of state after the death of its first leader. Voters in Kiribati overwhelmingly reelected that country's president. The head of Fiji's military retained his grasp on that nation's government. The prime ministers of the Solomon Islands and Nauru were ousted in no-confidence votes.

Papua New Guinea. Nationwide elections were held from June 30 to July 14 to choose the 109-seat National Parliament. Voting was originally scheduled to end on July 10, but delays in transporting ballot boxes to isolated parts of the country forced an extenaion of the process. For the first time, voters used a system in which they numbered in order their three favorite candidates.

The National Alliance Party, led by Michael Somare, PNG's first prime minister, received 27 votes, the largest total by a single party in the multiparty parliamentary system. Somare formed a coalition that once again elected him prime minister.

Federated States of Micronesia. Elections for Micronesia's 14-member Congress were held on March 6. Joseph Urusemal, who was president at the time of the election, was reelected to Congress but not chosen president by his fellow parliamentarians. On May 11, Congress elected Emanuel Mori to succeed Urusemal to become the country's seventh president. In June, Mori formed a task force to deal with budget problems in the states of Chuuk and Kosrae, which faced serious financial shortages.

Samoa. Malietoa Tanumafili II, Samoa's head of state, died on May 11 at the age of 94. He had led the country since it became independent from New Zealand in 1962. Malietoa was the last of his generation of Pacific leaders, which included Ratu Sir Kamisese Mara of Fiji and King Taufa'ahau Tupou IV of Tonga.

On June 16, 2007, Samoa's parliament elected Tuiatua Tupua Tamasese Efi to replace Malietoa. Tupua's election as head of state was the first under the Constitution established in 1962. He was to serve a term of five years.

Kiribati. In parliamentary elections held on Aug. 22, 2007, President Anote Tong was reelected to his parliamentary seat. Parliament then nominated candidates for the October presidential election, but the country's main opposition party threatened a boycott of the elections after neither of its nominees were selected for the ballot. In the election, held on October 17, Tong was reelected by an overwhelming majority.

Fiji. The head of Fiji's military, Frank Bainimarama, who overthrew the elected government in December 2006, addressed the United Nations (UN) General Assembly in New York City on Sept. 28, 2007. Bainimarama restated Fiji's commitment to UN conventions on human rights, rule of law, and democratic governance and attempted to justify the coup. New Zealand's foreign minister, Winston Peters, later addressed the General Assembly and accused Bainimarama of providing a misleading picture of Fiji's status and said his claims were "hollow."

Solomon Islands. On April 2, an 8.1-magnitude earthquake struck the northwestern Solomon Islands. This was followed by a *tsunami* (series of waves) that devastated coastal communities. Some 52 people were killed, hundreds of others suffered injury and illness, and more than 6,000 people were left homeless. Months later, many displaced people were still living in temporary camps established throughout the western islands.

On December 13, the country's Parliament voted no confidence in Prime Minister Manasseh Sogavare. A week later, Parliament selected former Education Minister Derek Sikua to replace him. Sikua had defected from Sogavare's government in November and had pushed for the no-confidence vote

Nauru. The Parliament of Nauru voted no confidence in President Ludwig Scotty and ousted him on December 19. He was replaced by former weightlifter Marcus Stephens.

■ Eugene Ogan

See also **Australia; Disasters; New Zealand.**

Painting. See Art: A Special Report.

Pakistan. In the face of a growing crisis, President Pervez Musharraf suspended Pakistan's Constitution and declared a state of emergency on Nov. 3, 2007. Amid public protests, his government jailed an estimated 5,600 lawyers, human rights activists, and opposition party members. He later promised to hold parliamentary elections in January 2008. On Dec. 27, 2007, former Prime Minister Benazir Bhutto, the head of the opposition Pakistan People's Party (PPP), was assassinated.

Crisis. The months of political turmoil began when Musharraf fired Pakistan's chief justice, Iftikhar Muhammad Chaudhry, on March 9, 2007, over charges of misconduct. Observers suggested that Musharraf considered Chaudhry too independent, and the president wanted to eliminate any challenges to his policies by the Supreme Court.

Lawyers supporting Chaudhry led months of national protests. Two days of gun battles during a May strike called in support of Chaudhry left some 40 people dead. On July 20, the Supreme Court ruled the dismissal illegal, and Chaudhry returned to the court.

Sharif. The court ruled on August 23 that former Prime Minister Nawaz Sharif could return from exile and reenter politics. He had been prime minister from 1990 to 1993 and from 1997 to 1999, when Musharraf seized power. After Sharif was imprisoned on corruption charges in 2000, he agreed to go into exile. When he arrived in Islamabad on Sept. 10, 2007, he was arrested and deported but was allowed to return in November.

Election. The Supreme Court ruled on September 28 that Musharraf could seek election to another term as president while he was still the army commander. Musharraf said he would give up military command if he won the election. On October 6, national and provincial assemblies elected Musharraf to a new term, but many members boycotted the voting, saying it violated Pakistan's Constitution for the head of the army to run for president. The Supreme Court weighed further challenges to Musharraf's eligibility and were believed to be about to rule his victory illegal when Musharraf issued the November 3 emergency decree. Under the decree, Musharraf dismissed the court's judges and replaced most of them with his supporters.

Politics. Amid the trouble, Musharraf agreed to drop corruption charges against Benazir Bhutto, who had served as prime minister from 1988 to 1990 and from 1993 to 1996. During both terms, she was accused of misconduct and dismissed by army-backed presidents. United States officials, concerned about instability in nuclear-armed Pakistan, urged Musharraf to allow her to return from exile so the PPP might compete in elections that could lead to a government with a popular mandate.

A burning car illuminates a campaign poster featuring former Pakistani Prime Minister Benazir Bhutto, who was targeted by suicide bombers on her return to Pakistan on Oct. 18, 2007, after eight years of exile. The assassination attempt in a crowd of hundreds of thousands in Karachi left 140 people dead. On December 27, an assassin succeeded in killing her as well as some 20 other people.

As some 200,000 people lined the streets of Karachi to celebrate Bhutto's return on October 18, suicide bombers attacked, killing 140 people. Bhutto was briefly placed under house arrest to keep her from attending anti-Musharraf rallies.

Bhutto and Musharraf met in November to discuss forming a power-sharing government, but Bhutto quickly withdrew from the talks. In late November, Musharraf resigned as head of the military and was sworn in for a new term as president. He ended the state of emergency and reinstated the Constitution on December 15. Then, on December 27, Bhutto was assassinated in a suicide bomb attack after speaking at a rally in Rawalpindi. On December 30, her son, 19-year-old Bilawal Bhutto Zardari, was chosen to head the PPP, which his father, Asif Ali Zardari, was to run on a day-to-day basis.

Fighting intensified in 2007 along Pakistan's border with Afghanistan. Members of the terrorist group al-Qa`ida had retreated to these mountainous areas after U.S.-led forces drove them and their militant Taliban hosts from Afghanistan in 2001. From these border regions, militants recruited and trained guerrillas and launched attacks into Afghanistan, Pakistan, and elsewhere.

In 2006, President Musharraf had attempted to convince local tribal leaders to work with government troops against the militants. However,

the tribal leaders proved unable or unwilling to stand up to the combined strength of al-Qa`ida and the Taliban. Pakistan's interior ministry warned in June 2007 that militants threatened stability nationwide. Under international pressure, Musharraf sent his army back into the rugged terrain in 2007.

The army, untrained for counterinsurgency warfare and apparently demoralized, fared poorly. Militants captured more than 200 soldiers on August 30 and executed at least 3. On November 4, Musharraf approved the release of 25 captured militants in return for the release of the soldiers. Attacks continued throughout the year.

Red Mosque. For a number of months in 2007, well-armed Islamic extremists based in Islamabad's Red Mosque illegally seized people whom they accused of irreligious and immoral activities. Officials charged several of the militants with involvement in a 2004 attempt to assassinate Prime Minister Shaukat Aziz. After a week of attempted negotiations, Pakistani army commandos stormed the mosque on July 10, 2007, killing nearly 100 people, including Abdul Rashid Ghazi, one of the mosque's leaders.

■ Henry S. Bradsher

See also **Afghanistan; Asia; Disasters; Terrorism; United States, President of the.**

Palau. See Pacific Islands.

Paleontology. A team of American pale-ontologists unveiled a reconstruction of the world's oldest fossil tree in April 2007. The reconstructed fossil of *Wattieza,* a plant that resembled modern palms and tree ferns, provided scientists with their first view of the overall shape and size of early trees and helped explain how forests came to dominate the land beginning in the Middle Devonian Period, about 380 million years ago. The team was headed by William Stein of the State University of New York at Binghamton and Linda VanAller Hernick and Frank Mannolini of the New York State

Museum of Albany. The scientists based the reconstruction on two fossils discovered in 2004 and 2005 near Gilboa in eastern New York state.

Fossil *Wattieza* stumps preserved in their original soils were first discovered in 1870 along Schoharie Creek in Gilboa. However, paleontologists were unable to determine the size of *Wattieza* and the appearance of its foliage until 2004, when a large fossil of the crown foliage was discovered. A fossil tree trunk found nearby in 2005 allowed scientists to estimate *Wattieza's* height at about 28 feet (9 meters). The two fossils together provided paleontologists with a view of a complete tree for the first time.

The scientists believe *Wattieza* was a distant relative of modern *conifers* (cone-bearing trees), and they suggested that the rise of these first forests may have had important effects on the

A woman in a Beijing museum photographs the fossilized skull of *Gigantoraptor,* a giant, birdlike dinosaur found in Mongolia in 2007. A scale model shows how *Gigantoraptor* may have looked in life, complete with feathered forearms.

global ecosystem. The first trees provided shelter or food for smaller plants and small land animals and helped form soils. These early trees also extracted carbon dioxide from the atmosphere and stored it in their tissues. By removing this greenhouse gas from the atmosphere, the trees may have helped cause a period of global cooling, making the climate more similar to present-day conditions.

Oldest bony fishes. An analysis of fragmentary fossil jaws and teeth determined that the 423-million-year-old remains represent the earliest examples of modern fish. The analysis was reported by paleontologist Hector Botella of the University of Valencia in Spain and his colleagues in August 2007. Members of the class Osteichthyes, called bony fish, make up the largest group of *vertebrates* (animals with backbones) in the world. This diverse group includes such familiar spiny-finned forms as salmon and goldfish, as well as the lobe-finned fish, a group that includes lungfish, coelacanths, and the ancestors of land-dwelling *tetrapods* (four-legged, land-dwelling, air-breathing animals). Bony fish are distinguished from more primitive fish, such as sharks and rays, which have skeletons made of a tough, elastic substance called cartilage. For many years, scientists have been uncertain about when Osteichthyes first appeared in the fossil record.

Botella and his colleagues reported that the fossils show typical features of the jaw characteristic of Osteichthyes, but that the teeth are more primitive, suggesting that the fossils represent a very early ancestor of the bony fishes. The scientists believe teeth developed from small knobs, called tubercles, found on the surface of bony plates that make up the jaws. These fossils show that the ancestors of modern bony fishes existed by the Late Silurian Period. Within a few million years, the group spread and diversified into fresh waters, becoming one of the largest and most successful vertebrate groups.

Feathered dinosaurs. A study published in September 2007 by paleontologist Alan H. Turner of the American Museum of Natural History in New York City and his colleagues reported evidence that *Velociraptor,* a large-bodied raptor dinosaur, had feathers. The paleontologists observed structures called quill knobs on the ulna, one of the two bones of the forearm, on *Velociraptor* fossils excavated from the same Late Cretaceous rocks in Mongolia, dating from 70 million to 80 million years ago. Similar knobs of bone, regularly spaced along the ulna, are seen in many species of birds. In modern flying birds, the knobs serve to anchor strands of connective tissue from the *quills* (bases) of large feathers to the bones of the

forearm that make up the wing. Many scientists suspected that *Velociraptor* may have had feathers, but they lacked direct evidence until now. The important fossil also shows that some larger, non-flying dinosaurs retained feathers inherited from smaller ancestors. The paleontologists speculated that the feathers may have been used by these larger dinosaurs in displays to attract mates or possibly to shield their young in nests.

In an earlier article published in June 2007, Xing Xu of the Chinese Academy of Science in Beijing and co-workers reported the discovery of a gigantic birdlike dinosaur from Mongolia. This animal, called *Gigantoraptor,* was more than 25 feet (8 meters) long and stood about 11 feet (3.5 meters) high at the hip. The scientists estimated that it weighed up to 3,000 pounds (1,361 kilograms) in life. *Gigantoraptor* lived in what is now central Asia during the Late Cretaceous Period.

The dinosaur had toothless jaws and looked like the birdlike *Oviraptor,* a small dinosaur that resembled an ostrich. Despite its great size, many features of *Gigantoraptor*'s anatomy were more birdlike, rather than less, as experts would have expected. Most paleontologists assumed that dinosaurs got smaller as they became more birdlike. The scientists believe that long-legged *Gigantoraptor* was a fast runner and had feathers on its forearms like *Velociraptor.*   ■ Carlton E. Brett

Panama. An explosion that reduced a hillside to rubble on Sept. 3, 2007, marked the beginning of a $5.25-billion modernization of the 93-year-old Panama Canal. Plans called for the completion, by 2014, of two new sets of locks and a new shipping lane capable of handling vessels too large to transit the existing canal.

Former United States President Jimmy Carter was present to wish Panamanians well as they embarked upon the revitalization of the historic waterway. At his side was Panamanian President Martín Torrijos Espino, son of the late military leader Omar Torrijos Herrera, with whom the Carter administration had negotiated the 1977 treaty that ceded territorial jurisdiction over the canal zone and operational control of the canal to Panama in 1979 and 1999, respectively.

In preparation for the construction, Panamanian engineers oversaw the reforestation of the entire length of both sides of the canal. By doing so, they created an arboreal buffer zone designed to absorb enough water to replenish the canal's water level and keep its locks full even in dry years. In the past, traffic through the canal occasionally has been interrupted by a shortage of water.   ■ Nathan A. Haverstock

See also **Latin America.**

Papua New Guinea. See **Pacific Islands.**

Paraguay. See **Latin America.**

in 2007 included those listed below, who were from the United States unless otherwise indicated.

Ban Ki-moon (1944-), a South Korean diplomat, became the eighth secretary-general of the United Nations (UN) on Jan. 1, 2007. The UN General Assembly elected Ban in October 2006 to a five-year term to succeed Kofi Annan.

Ban Ki-moon

At the time of his election, Ban was South Korea's minister of foreign affairs and trade. As such, he played a leading role in the six-nation talks aimed at halting North Korea's nuclear weapons program. Participants in the talks, including the United States, China, the two Koreas, Japan, and Russia, have met periodically in Beijing, China, since 2003.

Ban has been associated with the United Nations since 1975. In 1999, he served as chairman of the Preparatory Commission for the Comprehensive Nuclear Test Ban Treaty Organization, a UN organization that seeks international adherence to a treaty banning nuclear testing that the UN General Assembly passed in 1996. In late 2001, Ban played a major role in getting a UN resolution passed condemning the Sept. 11, 2001, terrorist attacks on the United States.

Ban Ki-moon was born on June 13, 1944, in Chungju, Korea (later South Korea). In 1962, when Ban was 18 years old, he met U.S. President John F. Kennedy at the White House in Washington, D.C., as a participant in an American Red Cross program. Ban traces the beginnings of his interest in a diplomatic career to that meeting. Ban earned an undergraduate degree in international relations from Seoul National University in South Korea in 1970 and a master's degree in public administration from Harvard University in Cambridge, Massachusetts, in 1985.

See also **United Nations.**

Bayless, Rick (1953-), an American chef, operated two award-winning Chicago restaurants, Frontera Grill and Topolobampo, and hosted a cooking series on PBS television in 2007, all devoted to the regional cuisine of Mexico. Bayless's Frontera Grill won the Outstanding Restaurant award from the James Beard Foundation in

May. James Beard (1903-1985) wrote a series of cookbooks that revolutionized U.S. cuisine, according to many food experts.

Rick Bayless started Frontera Grill in 1987. In 1989, he opened Topolobampo next door. Frontera Grill was a casual venue, while Topolobampo offered a more formal dining experience. Both restaurants featured authentic Mexican regional cuisine.

Bayless had published six books on Mexican cuisine. Many food critics regarded his first book, *Authentic Mexican: Regional Cooking from the Heart of Mexico* (William Morrow, 1987), as a classic. Bayless's wife, Deann Groen Bayless, collaborated on several of his books and has assisted in running the two Chicago restaurants. Rick Bayless's first television series, "Cooking Mexican," appeared on PBS in 1978. Since 2000, he has hosted the series "Mexico—One Plate at a Time" on PBS.

Rick Bayless was born in Oklahoma City, Oklahoma, in 1953. His family ran a barbecue restaurant in the Oklahoma capital. In college, Bayless studied Latin American studies and linguistics. Rick and Deann Bayless lived in Mexico from 1980 to 1986.

Rick Bayless

Brown, Gordon (1951-), became prime minister of the United Kingdom (U.K.) on June 27, 2007, upon the resignation of Tony Blair. The Labour Party selected Brown to replace Blair as party leader and, by virtue of the party's majority in the House of Commons, prime minister.

Since 1997, Brown had served as chancellor of the exchequer, the chief financial officer of the British government. He was appointed to that position by Tony Blair when Blair became prime minister following Labour's overwhelming electoral victory in May 1997. As chancellor, Brown wielded powers greater than those of many of his predecessors. Among the most far-reaching financial reforms of his 10-year tenure—the longest of any chancellor in more than a century—was the transferal in 1997 of the power to set interest rates from the government to the Bank of England. Financial experts praised the reform and compared the Bank of England's assumed role to that of the United States Federal Reserve.

James Gordon Brown was born on Feb. 20, 1951, in Glasgow, Scotland, the son of a Church of Scotland minister. He grew up in Kirkcaldy, an industrial town near Edinburgh, Scotland. Brown attended Edinburgh University, from which he graduated with honors in 1972. He entered politics as a member of the Scottish Labour Party and in 1983 was elected to the British Parliament from a Scottish *riding* (electoral district). By the early 1990's, Brown had become a close political ally of Tony Blair in the House of Commons.

Gordon Brown and his wife, Sarah, married in 2000. Their first child, Jennifer, was born prematurely in 2002 and died in infancy. As a memorial to her, the couple set up the Jennifer Brown Research Fund to sponsor research into the causes of premature death in children. The Browns have two sons, the youngest of whom has been diagnosed with cystic fibrosis, a life-threatening hereditary disease.

See also **United Kingdom; United Kingdom, Prime Minister of.**

Calderón Hinojosa, Felipe (1962-),

became president of Mexico on Dec. 1, 2006. He had been elected on July 2 in the closest election in Mexican history. Calderón was the candidate of the National Action Party (PAN), the party of outgoing President Vicente Fox Quesada. Calderón pledged to continue Fox's market-oriented policies. The election result remained in doubt until early September, when Mexico's top electoral court declared Calderón the winner. Calderón's chief opponent in the election, Andres Manuel López Obrador of the Democratic Revolution Party, led protests in the capital, Mexico City, and refused to accept the verdict of the electoral court.

On July 2, 2007, the first anniversary of the presidential election, López Obrador and 80,000 of his supporters rallied in Mexico City's main square. Despite the show of support for the defeated candidate, political analysts noted that in polls taken in mid-2007, President Calderón was enjoying approval ratings above 60 percent. Mexicans gave Calderón high marks, the analysts said, for his aggressive law-enforcement campaign against drug traffickers.

Felipe Calderón Hinojosa was born on Aug. 18, 1962, in Morelia, the provincial capital of Michoacan, a state in Mexico's interior to the west of Mexico City. His father was a cofounder of PAN in the 1930's. Rising through the ranks of PAN, Felipe Calderón won election first to the legislative assembly of Mexico's Federal District, then later to the Mexican Congress. From 2000 to 2006, during the administration of President Fox, Calderón served in several Cabinet positions.

See also **Mexico.**

Dudamel, Gustavo (1981-), was

appointed music director of the Los Angeles Philharmonic Orchestra in April 2007, to succeed current director Esa-Pekka Salonen beginning in the 2009-2010 concert season. Dudamel, a native of Venezuela, made his American debut conducting the Los Angeles Philharmonic at the Hollywood Bowl in 2005. A product of Venezuela's widely praised *sistema* (system) of national music education, Dudamel began receiving international notice at age 17 as conductor of the Venezuela-based Simón Bolívar National Youth Orchestra.

Venezuela's National System of Youth and Children's Orchestras—*El Sistema*—is a national, government-funded institution that provides free music education to children in Venezuela and runs 200 youth orchestras. Founded in 1975 by professional economist and musician José Antonio Abreu, *El Sistema* has in recent years garnered international praise for turning out some of the world's most highly acclaimed young musicians.

Gustavo Dudamel was born in 1981 in Barquisimeto, a city in western Venezuela. He started violin lessons at age 4. At age 12, Dudamel began to show an aptitude for conducting, and teachers in the *sistema* guided him into that field of musical performance. Dudamel became conductor of the Simón Bolívar National Youth Orchestra in 1999. In 2004, the young conductor won the first Gustav Mahler Conducting Competition in Bamberg, Germany. In 2006, he was named principal conductor of the Göteburg Symphony in Göteburg, Sweden. In 2007, Dudamel expressed his intention to retain his role as conductor of the Simón Bolívar Orchestra while taking up duties with the Göteburg and Los Angeles orchestras.

See also **Classical music.**

Fukuda, Yasuo (1936-), became prime

minister of Japan in September 2007. Fukuda, of the Liberal Democratic Party (LDP), succeeded Shinzo Abe, also of the LDP, who resigned after one year as prime minister. Political analysts speculated that Fukuda would try to strengthen ties with the leaders of China and South Korea. Japanese relations with these countries had become strained under Abe, a nationalist, who had made several public visits to a Japanese cemetery where members of the military regime that had led invasions of China and other countries in the 1930's and 1940's were buried.

Yasuo Fukuda, son of Takeo Fukuda, prime minister of Japan in 1976 and 1978, was born in 1936 in Gunma Prefecture (province) north of Tokyo but grew up in Tokyo. Educated as an economist at Tokyo's Waseda University, Yasuo Fukuda worked as an executive with a Japanese oil company from the late 1950's to the mid-1970's. He began his political career as his father's secretary during Takeo Fukuda's tenure as prime minister.

Yasuo Fukuda was elected to parliament in 1990. From 2000 to 2004, he served as chief Cabinet secretary to prime ministers Yoshiro Mori and Junichiro Koizumi.

See also **Japan.**

Gates, Robert (1943-),
became United States secretary of defense in December 2006. President George W. Bush appointed Gates to the Cabinet post after Donald H. Rumsfeld resigned and one day after the November 2006 midterm elections, in which the president's party, the Republicans, lost control of both houses of Congress. Political experts blamed the election losses on the unpopularity of the Iraq War, and Rumsfeld was held responsible by many analysts for mistakes in the prosecution of the war.

Robert Michael Gates was born on Sept. 25, 1943, in Wichita, Kansas. He attended the College of William and Mary in Williamsburg, Virginia; Indiana University in Bloomington; and Georgetown University in Washington, D.C., from which he received a doctorate in 1974 in Russian and Soviet history. Gates served in the U.S. Air Force from 1966 to 1968.

From 1966 to 1993, Gates held a variety of positions in the Central Intelligence Agency (CIA) and the National Security Council. He advised Presidents Ronald Reagan (1981-1989) and George H. W. Bush (1989-1993) on Soviet affairs as those presidents dealt with changes in international relations due to the approaching end of the Cold War. Gates also helped develop and implement policies concerning Afghanistan in the 1980's and Iraq in the early 1990's.

From 2002 to 2006, Gates served as president of Texas A&M University in College Station. During 2006, he was a member of the Iraq Study Group, an independent commission that delivered policy recommendations concerning the Iraq War to President George W. Bush in late 2006.

See also **Armed forces; Cabinet, U.S.**

Gibson, Charles (1943-), anchor of "ABC
World News with Charles Gibson," led the ABC nightly news program to first place in ratings among the three traditional U.S. television networks in 2007. ABC had named Gibson as sole anchor of the program after Elizabeth Vargas

Robert Gates

resigned in May 2006 to begin a family and her coanchor, Bob Woodruff, had been severely wounded while on assignment in Iraq.

Charles DeWolf Gibson was born in Evanston, Illinois, on March 9, 1943. His family subsequently moved to Washington, D.C., where Gibson grew up. There he attended high school at Sidwell Friends School, a private college-preparatory academy. Gibson earned a bachelor's degree in 1965 from Princeton University in Princeton, New Jersey; while at Princeton, he was news director for the university radio station. Gibson worked at several broadcasting outlets before joining ABC in 1975. From 1987 to 1998 and again, from 1999 to 2006, he cohosted the ABC morning news show, "Good Morning America."

In his 30-year career with ABC News, Gibson has interviewed seven U.S. presidents and many international celebrities, including Kofi Annan, Tony Blair, Nelson Mandela, and the late Yasir Arafat. In October 2004, during the presidential campaign, he hosted a televised debate between President George W. Bush, the Republican candidate, and Senator John Kerry, the Democratic candidate.

See also **Television.**

Gore, Al (1948-), a former vice president of
the United States, won the Nobel Peace Prize in 2007 for his efforts to raise global awareness of climate change. Gore shared the award with the United Nations Intergovernmental Panel on

Al Gore

Climate Change. In February 2007, *An Inconvenient Truth,* a documentary film in which he appeared and which he narrated, won an Academy Award. The film presents issues concerning global warming, including scientific evidence supporting the assertion that Earth is warming rapidly due to human activities. Since the late 1800's, the global average temperature has increased about 1.0 to 1.8 °F (0.6 to 1.0 °C), and many scientists estimate that it will rise an additional 2.0 to 11.5 °F (1.1 to 6.4 °C) by 2100.

Albert Gore, Jr., was born on March 31, 1948, in Washington, D.C. His father, Al Gore, Sr., served in both the U.S. House of Representatives and the U.S. Senate as a Democrat from Tennessee. The younger Gore attended Harvard University in Cambridge, Massachusetts, graduating in 1969 with a bachelor's degree in government. From 1969 to 1971, Gore served in the U.S. Army, including six months in a non-combat role in Vietnam during the Vietnam War (1957-1975).

In 1970, Al Gore married Mary Elizabeth (Tipper) Aitcheson. During the early 1970's, Gore attended graduate school at Vanderbilt University in Nashville, Tennessee. In 1976, Gore won election to the U.S. House of Representatives from a district in Tennessee, and he won again in the next three elections. He successfully ran for the U.S. Senate from Tennessee in 1984 and won reelection to that body in 1990.

In 1992, the Democratic Party nominated Gore for vice president at the request of the party's presidential nominee, Bill Clinton. Clinton and Gore won the November 1992 presidential election and were inaugurated on January 20, 1993. They were reelected in 1996.

Vice President Gore sought and won the Democratic nomination for president in 2000. In a historically close and contested election, Gore outpolled his Republican opponent, George W. Bush, by more than 500,000 popular votes, but lost to Bush in the electoral college, 271-266.

See also **Global warming; Nobel Prizes.**

Gül, Abdullah (1950-), was elected

president of Turkey by the Turkish parliament on Aug. 28, 2007. Gül, of the ruling Justice and Development Party (APK), became the first president since the founding of the modern Turkish Republic in 1923 to have an Islamist background. (An *Islamist* is a conservative political leader who is closely associated with Islamic clergy and religious practices.) The APK was founded by Gül; Recep Tayyip Erdogan, Turkey's prime minister since 2003; and other Turkish Islamists. Traditionally, Turkish politicians have supported complete separation of

religion and state, but since 2002, the Islamist APK has dominated the Turkish parliament.

Gül served as caretaker prime minister in 2002–2003—a period during which Erdogan was barred from holding office because of his defiance of a law barring public readings of Islamic literature. Afterward, Gül served as the Erdogan government's foreign minister. In that capacity, he worked for closer ties with the European Union (EU) and internal reforms that would advance Turkey's case for admission to that European body.

Abdullah Gül was born on Oct. 10, 1950, in Kayseri, an industrial city some 75 miles (120 kilometers) southeast of Ankara, the capital. He attended Istanbul University, eventually earning a doctorate in economics. Gül, who speaks Turkish, English, and Arabic, conducted some of his graduate studies in the United Kingdom and worked for seven years as an economist at the Islamic Development Bank in Jiddah, Saudi Arabia.

See also **Turkey; Turkey: A Special Report.**

Lessing, Doris (1919-), won the Nobel

Prize in literature in 2007. Lessing, 88 years of age when the prize was announced in October, is a novelist whose works examine human freedom and moral responsibility and humanity's struggle to understand the world.

Doris Lessing's probing exploration of the emotional lives of women has made her an icon of the feminist movement, particularly in her groundbreaking 1962 novel, *The Golden Notebook.* Literary critics have noted the extraordinary range of Lessing's fiction, from depictions of postcolonial society in Africa, to the urban experience in the United Kingdom in the late 1900's, to a mythical galactic setting in her five-novel science fiction series, *Canopus in Argus:*

Doris Lessing

Archives (1979-1983). Lessing collaborated with composer Philip Glass in bringing two novels of this series to the opera stage, with Lessing contributing the libretti and Glass, the musical scores. The operas are *The Making of the Representative for Planet 8* (1986) and *Marriage Between Zones Three, Four, and Five* (1997). Lessing has also written short stories, plays, poems, and memoirs.

Doris Lessing was born Doris Taylor in Kermanshah, Persia (now Bakhtaran, Iran), on Oct. 22, 1919. She grew up in Rhodesia (now Zimbabwe), where she was educated in a convent school. Her formal education ended at the age of 14.

Married and divorced two times in Rhodesia, Doris Lessing left her second husband, Gottfried Lessing, in 1949 and settled in London with her son, Peter Lessing. She published her first novel, *The Grass Is Singing,* in London in 1950. A nearly unbroken chain of published works—most of them remained in print in 2007—link that novel to her most recent novel, *The Cleft,* published in the summer of 2007.

See also **Literature; Nobel Prizes.**

Mirren, Helen (1945-), won the Academy

Award for best actress on Feb. 25, 2007, for her portrayal of Britain's reigning Queen Elizabeth II in *The Queen.* The film was a study of the queen's personal struggle to make a politically acceptable response to the sudden death of Princess Diana, former wife of Prince Charles, in August 1997.

Helen Mirren has performed widely in films, on television, and on the stage. She began her acting career in the mid-1960's with Britain's National Youth Theatre and the Royal Shakespeare Company. She has brought a variety of roles, both classic and modern, to the stage.

Mirren made her motion-picture debut in *Herostratus,* a British film, in 1967. She received critical acclaim for her portrayal of Queen Charlotte, wife of George III, in *The Madness of King George* (1995) and for her performance as a housekeeper in an English manor house in *Gosford Park* (2001). In television, Mirren won international popularity for her portrayal of a tough police inspector in the British television series *Prime Suspect* (1991-2006).

Helen Mirren was born Ilyena Vasilievna Mironov in London on July 26, 1945. Her father was a Russian official who happened to be stationed in England at the time of the 1917 Russian Revolution. Mirren's parents subsequently legalized a change of her name to its English form. In 2003, Helen Mirren was made a Dame Commander of the Order of the British Empire.

See also **Motion pictures.**

Mukasey, Michael (1941-), became

United States attorney general in 2007. President George W. Bush appointed him to the post to replace Attorney General Alberto R. Gonzales, who resigned. Prior to being named attorney general, Mukasey served as a federal judge and as a lawyer in private practice.

Mukasey was born on July 28, 1941, in New York City. He received a bachelor's degree from Columbia University in 1963 and a law degree from Yale Law School in 1967.

After graduation, Mukasey worked as a lawyer for a private firm. He served as an assistant U.S. attorney in New York from 1972 to 1976, before returning to private practice. In 1987, President Ronald Reagan appointed Mukasey to a federal judgeship for the Southern District of New York. Mukasey served in the position from 1988 to 2006. As a judge, he presided over a number of terrorism-related cases, including the trial of a number of defendants accused of plotting to blow up the United Nations and other New York City landmarks in 1993.

Mukasey retired from the federal bench in 2006 and became a partner in a private law firm. Bush nominated him for attorney general in September 2007, and he was confirmed by the U.S. Senate in November.

See also **Cabinet, U.S.**

Patil, Pratibha (1934-), became presi-

dent of India on July 25, 2007, having been elected to the position by India's electoral college on July 21. The electoral college consists of national and state governmental officials. Patil is the first woman ever to serve as president of India. She was nominated for the position by Sonia Gandhi, leader of the ruling Congress Party. Analysts regarded Patil as a close ally of the Gandhi family, a political dynasty in India.

Pratibha Patil was born on Dec. 19, 1934, in a town in Maharashtra state, a large region around Mumbai (Bombay) in western India. She studied at a local college and then obtained a law degree from the Law College, Bombay.

Patil won election to the state legislature of Maharashtra in 1962 and remained a member of that body until 1985, when she was elected to the upper house of the Indian Parliament. In 1991, she won election to the more powerful lower house of Parliament, but she withdrew from national politics in the late 1990's. In 2004, Patil was appointed governor of Rajasthan in northwestern India, becoming that state's first female chief executive. (According to India's Constitution, state governors are appointed by the president.) She held that position until her election in 2007 as president.

See also **India.**

Pelosi, Nancy (1940-), became speaker of the United States House of Representatives in January 2007 and is the first woman to hold that position. Pelosi is also the first woman to head a national political party in either house of the U.S. Congress. In 2003, Pelosi became the leader of the Democratic Party in the House, when the Democrats were in the minority. As a result of their gains in the November 2006 midterm elections, the Democrats took control of the House of Representatives in January 2007 and elected Pelosi speaker. Pelosi has represented a San Francisco congressional district in the House since 1987.

Representative Pelosi and her counterpart in the U.S. Senate, Senator Harry Reid (D., Nevada), pledged themselves in early 2007 to reducing U.S. troop levels in Iraq and eventually bringing an end to the U.S. role in that conflict. However, the Democratic leaders failed to attract enough Republican supporters to get legislation through Congress mandating such policy changes. Pelosi and other Democratic leaders supported such domestic policies as a hike in the federal minimum wage and renewal of federal funding for state-run programs providing health insurance for children. Throughout her congressional tenure, Pelosi has been recognized as an advocate for health research, AIDS funding, and family planning programs.

Nancy Pelosi was born Nancy Patricia D'Alesandro on March 26, 1940, in Baltimore. Her father, Thomas D'Alesandro, Jr., was a Democratic politician who served several terms in the U.S. House of Representatives in the 1940's and as mayor of Baltimore during the late 1940's and 1950's.

Nancy D'Alesandro graduated from Trinity College in Washington, D.C., in 1962. She married Paul F. Pelosi, a San Francisco native, in 1963. The couple have five children and several grandchildren.

See also **Congress of the United States; Democratic Party.**

Petraeus, David (1952-), took command of the allied armed forces in Iraq in February 2007, following nomination by United States President George W. Bush and confirmation by the U.S. Senate. Petraeus became closely associated with "the surge," the policy of boosting U.S. troop levels during 2007 to secure parts of Iraq that had become destabilized because of the activities of *insurgents* (guerrilla fighters). In September 2007, General Petraeus delivered an assessment of the surge policy to the U.S. Congress in which he asserted that the military objectives were being met, despite a level of civilian casualties that was "clearly too high."

David Petraeus

David Howell Petraeus was born on Nov. 7, 1952, and grew up in Cornwall-on-Hudson, New York. His father, Sixtus Petraeus, was a Dutch merchant marine officer who came to New York City after escaping from Holland when the Nazis overran the country in 1940.

David Petraeus graduated from the United States Military Academy at West Point, New York, in 1974 and joined the U.S. Army. In 1987, he earned a doctoral degree in international relations from Princeton University in Princeton, New Jersey. Petraeus served in Bosnia in 2001-2002 as part of the NATO peacekeeping mission there.

In March 2003, Petraeus led the 101st Airborne division during the U.S.-led invasion of Iraq. Subsequently, he commanded forces assigned to Mosul, Iraq's third-largest city, and according to Iraq observers, temporarily restored order to the region. In 2005, Petraeus was transferred to the U.S. Army Combined Arms Center in Fort Leavenworth, Kansas, to assume command of that army training center. He used the opportunity to revise the curriculum to focus on *counterinsurgency techniques*—combat methods designed to effectively fight insurgents while minimizing civilian casualties. Petraeus returned to Iraq in January 2007.

See also **Armed forces; Iraq; United States, Government of the.**

Romney, Mitt (1947-), a former governor of Massachusetts, declared himself a candidate for the 2008 Republican nomination for president of the United States in February 2007. Romney was active in Massachusetts politics from the early 1990's, and he played a key role in organizing the 2002 Winter Olympics in Salt Lake City, Utah.

Mitt Romney served as president of the Salt Lake City Organizing Committee for the 2002 Winter Olympics from 1999 to 2002. Before

Romney accepted leadership of the Olympics, the project was troubled by scandal and financial problems, and he gained national attention for helping make the games a critical and financial success. He went on to win the governorship of Massachusetts as the Republican candidate in November 2002 and served one term (2003-2007). As governor, Romney signed into law a measure to provide health care for uninsured Massachusetts residents.

Mitt Romney

Romney is a son of George Romney, an automobile company executive, governor of Michigan, and himself a candidate for the Republican presidential nomination in 1968. Mitt Romney grew up in a suburb of Detroit. Following a year of college at Stanford University in Stanford, California, he went to France as part of a Mormon missionary team. In June 1968, he was critically injured in an automobile accident but recovered and completed his mission. He completed undergraduate studies at Utah's Brigham Young University in 1971 and subsequently earned a master's degree in business and a law degree from Harvard University in Cambridge, Massachusetts. In the 1970's and 1980's, Romney built a successful career in business and finance. In 1994, he won the Republican nomination for the U.S. Senate from Massachusetts, but he lost to Senator Edward M. Kennedy in the general election.

See also **Republican Party.**

Rowling, J. K.

(1965-), released in 2007 for publication the last in her phenomenally successful Harry Potter series of fantasy novels. *Harry Potter and the Deathly Hallows* hit bookstore shelves on July 21, 2007, 10 years after the first book in the series, *Harry Potter and the Philosopher's Stone,* appeared in 1997. (The

J. K. Rowling

novel was published in 1998 in the United States under the name *Harry Potter and the Sorcerer's Stone.*) The Harry Potter books have been translated into more than 60 languages and have sold from 300 million to 400 million copies worldwide. Five highly successful motion pictures based on the series have been released.

Joanne Kathleen Rowling was born on July 31, 1965, near Bristol in southwestern England. She attended England's Exeter University, where she studied French. Following the untimely death of her mother in December 1991 from multiple sclerosis, a disease of the central nervous system, J. K. Rowling went to Portugal where she made a living teaching English. In 1994, she returned to the United Kingdom, settling in Edinburgh, Scotland. There, while unemployed, she completed the first Harry Potter novel. In August 1996, London-based Bloomsbury Publishing accepted Rowling's manuscript of the novel for publication.

See also **Literature; Literature for children.**

Sarkozy, Nicolas (1955-), became president of France on May 16, 2007. Sarkozy, a member of the Union for a Popular Movement (UMP), the party of his presidential predecessor, Jacques Chirac, defeated the Socialist candidate, Ségolène Royal, in a May 6 runoff presidential election.

Sarkozy made history as the first French president born after World War II (1939-1945) and as the first child of an immigrant to become president of France. Sarkozy's father fled Hungary near the end of World War II as Soviet troops invaded the country. His mother was the grandchild of a Jewish-Greek immigrant to France.

As interior minister in Chirac's administration, Sarkozy led the government's response to widespread rioting in 2005 in French cities by youths mainly of Muslim heritage. Although Sarkozy received credit for bringing an end to the unrest, he also

Nicolas Sarkozy

guage. After serving in the U.S. Army in the early 1960's, Simic attended New York University in New York City, earning a bachelor's degree in 1966. Along with writing English poetry and translating poetry into English from Serbian, Croatian, Macedonian, Slovenian, and French, Simic has taught creative writing and literature at the University of New Hampshire at Durham for more than 30 years. Simic has won many awards and honors for his poetry, including the Edgar Allan Poe Award and the Wallace Stevens Award.

See also **Poetry.**

Whitaker, Forest (1961-), received the Academy Award for best actor on Feb. 25, 2007, for his portrayal of Ugandan dictator Idi Amin Dada in the film *The Last King of Scotland.* Amin ruled Uganda from 1971 to 1979 and was responsible for the deaths of thousands of Ugandans. Critics praised Whitaker's performance as a subtle, nuanced interpretation of the brutal and erratic leader.

Forest Whitaker was born in Longview, Texas, on July 15, 1961, but he grew up in southern California. Whitaker attended the University of Southern California (USC) in Los Angeles, where he studied to be an opera singer. After shifting his career focus to acting, he attended USC's Drama Conservatory, graduating in 1982. Whitaker also made his debut in motion pictures in 1982, playing a high school football star in *Fast Times at Ridgemont High.* He has since played significant roles in such films as *The Color of Money* (1986), *Platoon* (1986), *Good Morning, Vietnam* (1987), *The Crying Game* (1992), *Ready-to-Wear* (1994), and *Ghost Dog: The Way of the Samurai* (1999). In 1988, Whitaker won the Cannes Film Festival award for best actor for his portrayal of jazz great Charlie Parker in the film *Bird*.

Forest Whitaker has made many guest appearances in television series. In 1993, he made his directorial debut in *Strapped,* an HBO movie.

See also **Motion pictures.**

Zoellick, Robert (1953-), was elected president of the World Bank on June 25, 2007, by that body's board of executive directors. United States President George W. Bush nominated Zoellick for the position, according to a long-established custom of allowing the U.S. president to select an individual for the job. The World Bank, based in Washington, D.C., is a United Nations-affiliated agency that loans money to countries for development.

Robert Bruce Zoellick was born on July 25, 1953. He grew up in Naperville, Illinois, near Chicago. Zoellick graduated from Swarthmore College in Swarthmore, Pennsylvania, in 1975. He subsequently earned a law degree and a master's

incurred controversy by referring to the youths as "rabble." In his presidential campaign, Sarkozy endorsed such market-oriented reforms as those implemented in the United Kingdom and the United States since the 1980's. He promised to revive the underperforming French economy by restraining spending, cutting taxes, and curtailing the power of labor unions.

Nicolas Sarkozy was born on Jan. 28, 1955, in Paris. His political career began in 1983 when, at the age of 28, he became mayor of the affluent Paris suburb of Neuilly-sur-Seine. In that role, he gained national notoriety by successfully negotiating the end to a school hostage crisis in 1993.

See also **France.**

Simic, Charles (1938-), was designated poet laureate for the United States by the Librarian of Congress in August 2007. Appointed annually by the Library of Congress's librarian, the poet laureate receives a monetary award and is encouraged to promote the reading and writing of poetry in the United States.

Critics have described the poetry of Charles Simic variously as dreamlike and surrealistic, full of ominous imagery and yet ironic and humorous. He endows ordinary objects with unexpected and often sinister meanings, as in the poem "The Fork," in which he describes the common kitchen utensil as a "bird's foot worn around a cannibal's neck."

Charles Simic was born in Belgrade, Yugoslavia (now Serbia), on May 9, 1938. His family immigrated to the United States in the early 1950's. The Simics settled in Oak Park, Illinois, and Charles, then 15, began to learn the English lan-

degree in public policy from Harvard University in Cambridge, Massachusetts.

In 1985, Zoellick was employed by the U.S. Treasury Department, where his work captured the attention of James A. Baker III, then secretary of the treasury in the administration of President Ronald Reagan. When Baker became secretary of state under President George Herbert Walker Bush in 1989, Baker appointed Zoellick an undersecretary of state. In that role, Zoellick fielded a number of diplomatic assignments, including negotiations that led to the reunification of Germany in 1990. From 2001 to 2006, Zoellick served as U.S. trade representative and as deputy secretary of state in the administration of George W. Bush. Zoellick then accepted an executive position with Goldman Sachs Group, a New York City-based investment banking firm.

Zuckerberg, Mark (1984-), is the creator of Facebook, a Web-based utility that enables users to share information easily while retaining control over their privacy. Web analysts have described Facebook variously as a "social networking site" and a "virtual meeting place." Zuckerberg is also the chief executive officer of the Facebook Corporation.

Mark Zuckerberg was born on May 14, 1984, in Dobbs Ferry, New York. He began writing computer programs as a youngster. While attending Harvard University—which he entered in 2002—Zuckerberg created an online registry of university students with photos from information he had obtained by hacking into university computers. Although the 18-year-old was reprimanded by university officials, he went on to create Thefacebook.com, which he launched in February 2004. Harvard students flocked to join up, and Zuckerberg soon had customers at other major colleges and universities as well.

Heeding a suggestion made by Microsoft founder Bill Gates at a Harvard symposium, Zuckerberg took a leave of absence from Harvard and headed to California's Silicon Valley with two friends in the summer of 2004. There Zuckerberg made contact with venture capitalists who invested in his project, then renamed Facebook. Zuckerberg expanded the Facebook user community beyond the college-student population, achieving 1 million users by the fall of 2004 and 5 million one year later. By mid-2007, cyberexperts estimated the Facebook user population at 35 million, and revenues for the year were predicted to hit $100 million. Several buyout offers were made in 2007, but Zuckerberg expressed his intention to stay with Facebook as it grew and matured.

See also **Internet**.

■ Robert Knight

Peru. During 2007, several debilitating strikes occurred in Peru's mining industry, which provides more than half of the country's export earnings. Miners' demands included higher wages at a time when global prices for Peru's minerals were high; better enforcement of national labor laws; and more frequent government inspections of work and safety conditions in the mines.

A strike called by the National Federation of Mining, Metallurgy and Steel Workers hampered production at more than 40 copper, gold, iron, nickel, silver, and zinc mines in April and May. In October, workers went on strike at a smelter and two copper mines in southern Peru, contributing to a drop in copper production and a rise in international copper prices. Also in 2007, Peruvians concerned about environmental damage protested a proposal by a Chinese company to build a $1.4-billion copper mine in the north.

A powerful earthquake occurred near Peru's Pacific coast on August 15. More than 500 people were killed, about 1,500 injured, and thousands left homeless. The earthquake caused extensive damage in the administrative department of Ica. It leveled the port of Pisco, located about 125 miles (201 kilometers) southeast of Lima, the capital. According to Pisco's mayor, at least 200 people were buried in the rubble of a church where they were attending Mass when the earthquake struck. The town of Ica, southeast of Pisco, was also hit hard.

Following the earthquake, President Alan García rushed to Pisco, where he and his Cabinet took charge of relief efforts. The president deployed 1,000 troops to help local police maintain order and control looting in the affected area. He also directed the transport of hundreds of tons of food, clothing, and other supplies to Pisco. A series of presidential decrees provided for aid to help the survivors rebuild their homes and cover funeral expenses. The decrees also created 8,000 temporary jobs for local residents to help with cleanup and reconstruction efforts. According to polls, the president's approval rating among Peruvians rose markedly following the quake.

Teachers strike. José Antonio Chang, Peru's education minister, persuaded more than 160,000 public school teachers to return to their classrooms on July 20, following a two-week strike that left more than 8 million children out of school. The teachers' main grievance was a recent law that would require them to pass regular competency tests. They believed the law was part of an effort to privatize Peru's educational system. The education workers' union pledged to challenge the law's constitutionality in the courts.

■ Nathan A. Haverstock

See also **Latin America**.

Petroleum and gas. See Energy supply.

Philadelphia. Michael Nutter, a former Democratic city councilman, was elected mayor of Philadelphia by a more than 4-to-1 ratio over his Republican opponent, Al Taubenberger, on Nov. 6, 2007. Nutter, 50, had been expected to win the post after a May 15 primary election victory, in a city whose voters are mainly registered Democrats.

In June 2006, Nutter resigned his City Council position, which he had held since 1992, to run for mayor. In the City Council, he had concentrated his efforts on ethics legislation and safe-streets measures and eventually became an opponent of Mayor John Street on some key issues. Nutter raised about $7.5 million for his campaign. In the primary, he campaigned as a reformer and faced two U.S. representatives in a field of five contenders. The mayor-elect graduated from the University of Pennsylvania's Wharton School of business. He worked as an investment manager specializing in public finance before joining the City Council.

School chief resigns. After five years as the head of Philadelphia's schools, Paul Vallas announced on April 11, 2007, that he would leave to become superintendent of the New Orleans Recovery School District. The Philadelphia School Reform Commission, which oversees the city's public schools, had hired Vallas in 2002. At the time, he was chief of Chicago's public school system.

Vallas, 54, hired more certified teachers, standardized the curriculum, emphasized student discipline, and began new programs. Student scores improved on state tests. But Vallas increasingly met resistance from the school commission over his power to make decisions and control spending. He had balanced the district's $2-billion budget for four years, but the schools faced a $73-million shortfall in 2006. The commission voted to extend Vallas's contract through 2009, but it tightened its control over spending. Vallas then resigned to take the New Orleans position.

New art museum wing. The Philadelphia Museum of Art opened a new wing on September 15 to house its prints, drawings, costumes and textiles, photographs, and other collections, particularly those sensitive to light. The wing is in an Art Deco building across from the main museum. The building had been the headquarters of the now-defunct Fidelity Mutual Life Insurance Company.

The $90-million wing, called the Ruth and Raymond G. Perelman Building, opened after a major redesign and building extension by architect Richard Gluckman. Renovations produced five galleries, along with offices, workshops for conservation and other museum-related endeavors, a library, and storage.

State senator indicted. A federal grand jury handed down a 139-count indictment on February 8 against state Senator Vincent J. Fumo, a Philadelphia Democrat with a wide network of appointees and a reputation as one of the most powerful dealmakers in the state legislature.

Federal prosecutors alleged that Fumo, 64, defrauded the nonprofit Citizens' Alliance for Better Neighborhoods of more than $1 million. Prosecutors also said that Fumo defrauded the city's Independence Seaport Museum, obstructed investigations by the Federal Bureau of Investigation and Internal Revenue Service, and used state Senate employees for personal errands.

Smoking ban. On Jan. 10, 2007, the city began enforcing a smoking ban affecting about 4,000 Philadelphia restaurants and bars. The City Council had passed the measure late in 2006. First-time violations carry a $75 fine for the restaurant or tavern owner; second-time violators are fined $150; and third-time violators, $300, the maximum. The ban exempts hotels, private clubs, and some other establishments.

New theater. A 365-seat theater opened downtown on South Broad Street—an area called the Avenue of the Arts—on Oct. 21, 2007. The $25-million Suzanne Roberts Theatre is home to the Philadelphia Theatre Company, which is known for its presentations of American plays. It became the first new arts venue to open on the street, the site of many live-performance theaters, in six years. ■ Howard S. Shapiro

See also **City.**

Philippines. Some 30 million Filipinos voted for a new Congress and for local offices on May 14, 2007. According to the police, 126 people died in election-related violence, down from 189 deaths during the 2004 elections.

National politics. Supporters of President Gloria Macapagal-Arroyo in 2007 won enough of the 212 contested seats in the House of Representatives to retain control of the House for another three years. However, Macapagal-Arroyo's supporters failed to gain control of the Senate, winning only 2 of the 12 contested seats.

Although Macapagal-Arroyo's support in the House protected her from any repeat of a 2005 attempt to remove her from office, Senate opponents renewed their attack on her. They reopened an investigation into charges that she had improperly influenced vote counting in her narrow presidential election victory in 2004. They also intensified accusations of corruption in her administration. One of their targets was José Miguel Arroyo, Macapagal-Arroyo's husband. He was accused of helping a Chinese telecommunications manufacturer improperly win a $330-million government contract. He denied interfering in any government transactions.

After a six-year trial, former President Joseph Estrada was convicted on Sept. 12, 2007, of embezzling approximately $80 million while in office from 1998 to 2001. He was ousted and replaced by then-Vice President Macapagal-Arroyo. She pardoned Estrada on Oct. 25, 2007.

Coup attempt. On November 29, at least 36 people seized a hotel in Manila, the capital, and attempted to launch a *coup d'etat* (government take-over). The rebels included 14 soldiers fleeing trial for an earlier coup attempt. After a six-hour standoff, the coup leaders surrendered to government troops and were charged with attempting to stage a rebellion.

Strife. A cease-fire between the government and Islamic extremists in the southern Philippines broke down in 2007. Islamic groups had long fought for a separate Muslim state in the south. One faction, Abu Sayyaf, also engaged in bombings, kidnappings, and other crimes. United States officials believed the group was linked to terrorist organization al-Qa`ida.

Abu Sayyaf killed 14 Filipino marines in jungle fighting on July 10 on Basilan Island. In August, the group killed 25 soldiers on nearby Jolo island. The ensuing military counterattack drove nearly 24,000 people from their homes.

Human rights. According to a Filipino human rights group, more than 830 people had been killed by security forces since Macapagal-Arroyo took office in 2001. The army denied allegations that it was behind the killings. Many of those killed were political activists, religious leaders, and journalists. Domestic and foreign criticism intensified in 2007 over unsolved cases. Some of these cases involved people who belonged to legal organizations that security forces suspected were Communist fronts. Others were journalists who investigated political bosses and landowners.

In her July 23 State of the Nation address, Macapagal-Arroyo asked Congress to tighten pertinent laws. She blamed "rogue elements" in the military and police for political assassinations. Macapagal-Arroyo sought special courts to try cases of extrajudicial killings, harsher penalties for convictions, and new measures for the protection of witnesses.

Economic growth was faster in 2007 than the official goal of from 6.1 to 6.7 percent. Second-quarter growth was 7.5 percent higher than in the previous year. Tax increases in 2006 had temporarily reduced budget deficits and permitted increased government spending on public works and social services. A weakening of tax collections in the first half of 2007, however, sent the official deficit back up. Remittances from Filipinos working abroad also helped economic growth. Some 8 million Filipinos worked in foreign countries, most of them in low-skill jobs. They sent home more than $13 billion a year, mostly to support relatives. ■ Henry S. Bradsher

See also **Asia; Disasters.**

Physics. In April 2007, a team of scientists headed by physicist Francis Everitt of Stanford University in California released the first results from the Gravity Probe B experiment. Gravity Probe B (GP-B), a satellite launched into Earth orbit in April 2004, contained four gyroscopes that were designed to collect gravitational data for 50 weeks. The experiment's results provided data to confirm aspects of the general theory of relativity, the explanation of gravity announced in 1915 by German-born scientist Albert Einstein.

According to the general theory of relativity, the directions of gyroscope axes on a satellite should slowly drift from their original directions because of two effects: the geodetic effect and the frame-dragging effect. In the geodetic effect, the gravity of a large mass, such as Earth, distorts *space-time* (the combination of space and time that permeates the universe like a fabric) near the mass. Calculations indicated that this distortion would shift the gyroscope axes by about 2/1,000 of a degree per year. In frame dragging, an additional shift in axes, at right angles to the geodetic effect and 170 times smaller in magnitude, should result from Earth's rotation dragging the distortions of space-time with it, like a spoon stirring a liquid.

Magnetic sensors on GP-B tracked the directions of the gyroscope axes, and these directions were then compared with the position of a reference star viewed by an on-board telescope. This comparison and orientation allowed scientists to determine exactly how far the axes drifted from their original positions.

The results of the analysis confirmed the theorized geodetic shift within an accuracy of 1 percent. The GP-B scientists said that further analysis of the data would be required to verify the more subtle frame-dragging effect.

Heat to sound to electricity. In June 2007, a research team led by physicist Orest Symko of the University of Utah in Salt Lake City demonstrated a small cylindrical device that can capture heat, convert the heat into sound, and then convert the sound into electric power. When heat is applied to the device, a stream of warm air moves through a cylinder, generating sound waves similar to those in a flute. The pressure of the sound waves squeezes a piezoelectric crystal, a device that produces electric voltage in response to pressure.

Symko's team reported that the overall efficiency of the process was low, with only about 15 to 25 percent of the heat energy being converted into electrical energy. Nevertheless, this level of efficiency would be sufficient to use the device for such applications as cooling computer chips and helping to power laptop computers. The researchers noted that if the device could be scaled up and made more efficient, it could be used to capture waste heat from nuclear power plants and boost electric power production at the plants. The device, they added, already compared favorably with solar-power cells in terms of both cost and energy efficiency.

Homestake mine, the former gold mine in South Dakota that had also been a historic laboratory site from the 1960's to the 1980's, was selected in July 2007 by the National Science Foundation (NSF) as the preferred location for the Deep Underground Science and Engineering Laboratory. Should this selection be finalized by subsequent NSF and congressional actions, the Homestake mine would become the largest and deepest (approximately 8,000 feet [2,438 meters] deep) underground laboratory in the world.

Physicists use such facilities to avoid background radiation originating from cosmic rays that constantly bombard Earth's surface from space. This radiation interferes with sensitive detectors designed to look for rare phenomena associated with *dark energy* (a form of energy that makes the universe expand more rapidly), *dark matter* (invisible matter that makes up most of the universe), *neutrinos* (electrically neutral particles that interact feebly with matter), and particle decay.   ■ Robert H. March

See also **Nobel Prizes.**

Poetry. Belgrade-born American poet Charles Simic was chosen in 2007 to succeed Donald Hall as poet laureate of the United States. In announcing the appointment, the librarian of Congress, James H. Billington, commended Simic's poetry for its "stunning and unusual imagery," adding that Simic's poems exhibited "shades of darkness and flashes of ironic humor."

Born in Yugoslavia (now Serbia) on May 9, 1938, Simic arrived in the United States in the early 1950's. He began writing poetry a few years after learning English. In addition to his 18 books of poetry, Simic is an essayist (for *The New York Review of Books* and elsewhere), translator, editor, and professor emeritus of creative writing and literature at the University of New Hampshire at Durham.

W. H. Auden's centenary. The 100th anniversary of the birth of British-born poet Wystan Hugh (W. H.) Auden took place on Feb. 21, 2007. The poet was celebrated for his masterly verse technique, playful wit, and resonant public voice. While widely considered one of the most accomplished poets of the 1900's, Auden became the object of particular attention in recent years, following the terrorist attacks on the United States on Sept. 11, 2001. "September 1, 1939," a poem written by Auden in New York City to mark the invasion of Poland by Nazi Germany, was widely quoted in the press in autumn 2001 to help express widespread feelings of turmoil: "Waves of anger and fear / Circulate over the bright / And darkened lands of the earth, / Obsessing our private lives; / The unmentionable odour of death / Offends the September night."

Auden was born in the United Kingdom and educated at Christ Church College at Oxford University. He moved to the United States in 1939 but divided most of the second half of his life between New York City and Kirchstetten, Austria, near Vienna. He died in Vienna in 1973. Among his most famous poems are "Musée des Beaux Arts" and "Funeral Blues." The latter poem figured prominently in the popular 1994 film *Four Weddings and a Funeral.*

Some of the events memorializing the poet's birth were exhibitions (including one at Oxford's Bodleian Library), recitals, and readings (including readings at Westminster Abbey and the British Library in February), and tributes.

Popular translations. Robert and Jean Hollander completed their landmark translation of Dante Alighieri's *Divine Comedy* with the release of *Paradiso* (Paradise) in 2007. The first canticle, *Inferno* (Hell), appeared in 2000, followed by *Purgatorio* (Purgatory) in 2003. Considered one of the greatest of poems, *The Divine Comedy* was written in Italian in the early 1300's.

The Hollanders were well-suited to the task of this joint translation. Robert was professor emeritus of Princeton University in New Jersey, where he had taught Dante for decades, and Jean was an accomplished poet. As stated in their introduction, the Hollanders' goal in translating Dante's tale of a journey through Hell, up the mountain of Purgatory, and into Paradise, was to establish "a helpful bridge to the untranslatable magnificence of Dante's poem." The easy elegance of their translation provides an excellent introduction for first-time readers, and their ample footnotes achieve a scholarly thoroughness.

In addition to their translations, the Hollanders created an online Dante resource, The Princeton Dante Project. The site began publishing in 1999.

The Hollanders' translations followed on a trend in publishing—translations of classic works of poetry generating both critical acclaim and surprisingly healthy sales. After releasing well-received translations of Homer's *Iliad* (1990) and *Odyssey* (1996), American professor Robert Fagles had another popular translation with Virgil's *Aeneid* in 2006. In 2000, the Irish poet Seamus Heaney's translation of the Anglo-Saxon epic *Beowulf* attained best-seller status. A film based on this epic poem, directed by Robert Zemeckis, was released in November 2007.   ■ David Yezzi

See also **Literature; People in the news: (Charles Simic); Pulitzer Prizes.**

A boy peeks through the eye socket of a colossal head, a sculpture by Polish sculptor Igor Mitoraj, in the market square of Kraków, Poland. A number of works by Mitoraj, an internationally acclaimed sculptor who studied at Kraków's Academy of Fine Arts, were on display in the city's market square and International Cultural Center in 2007.

Poland. Elections in October 2007 ended the two-year, right-wing coalition government led by President Lech Kaczynski and his twin brother, Prime Minister Jaroslaw Kaczynski. Although their Law and Justice Party lost power, Lech Kaczynski retained the largely ceremonial role of president. The liberal Civic Platform Party, led by Donald Tusk, emerged the winner with 209 seats in the 460-seat lower house of parliament. In November, Tusk's party formed a new government in coalition with a small centrist party. Although parliamentary elections had not been scheduled for 2007, President Kaczynski precipitated them by dismissing several coalition ministers in August on allegations of corruption. In the process, he dismantled his brother's Law and Justice-led governing coalition.

On taking office, Tusk pledged to withdraw in 2008 Poland's 900 troops supporting the United States-led coalition in Iraq and to improve relations with Russia. Relations with Poland's eastern neighbor became strained after the Kaczynski brothers endorsed a U.S.-sponsored plan to install components of a missile defense shield (MDS) in Poland. (A MDS is a military strategy and its associated systems designed to shield an entire country from incoming intercontinental ballistic missiles.) Tusk also endorsed the European Union (EU) Charter of Fundamental Rights, which the Kaczynski government had rejected in opposition to the inclusion of gay rights in its declaration of human rights.

Relations with the United States. President George W. Bush paid an official visit to Poland in June 2007, and President Kaczynski reciprocated in July with a visit to Washington, D.C. Analysts interpreted the exchange as a signal that both administrations were cultivating closer relations. At a press conference following his meeting with President Bush in Washington, Kaczynski reported that "the case of the deployment of a U.S. antimissile shield [the MDS] in Poland is practically sealed." The plan drew protests from some Polish politicians and from Russian President Vladimir Putin, who in July suspended Russia's participation in the Conventional Armed Forces in Europe pact, a post-Cold War peace treaty.

Economic trends. Poland's economy continued to grow in 2007. Economists projected that the *gross domestic product*—the value of all goods and services produced in a country in a given year—would expand by 6.5 percent in 2007, compared with 6.1-percent growth in 2006. Inflation remained low at 2.5 percent. However, the rate of unemployment—14.8 percent—was one of the highest in the EU. ■ Sharon L. Wolchik

See also **Europe.**

Pollution. See **Environmental pollution.**

Popular music sales declined dramatically in 2007 even as total sales of Apple Inc.'s iPod digital music players topped the 110-million mark. Accelerating a seven-year trend, sales of music CD's plummeted 20 percent during the first three months of 2007 compared with the same period in 2006. Early in 2007, Nielsen SoundScan, which monitors album sales at point of purchase, recorded the two lowest-selling number-one albums since the system began tracking numbers in 1991. Digital album sales also dropped, while digital singles sales rose. Although CD sales accounted for 85 percent of music sold, the growth in digital sales did not offset the overall decline in music sales. Both artists and executives looked to bold new business models to survive in a struggling industry.

A strike against music piracy. In October 2007, the Recording Industry Association of America (RIAA) scored an important legal victory for record labels and other copyright owners in the first federal jury trial against an individual computer user for music piracy. RIAA won a lawsuit against a Duluth, Minnesota, woman for the illegal sharing of 24 songs using the Kazaa peer-to-peer file-sharing application. The jury imposed a penalty of $222,000, or $9,250 per song.

Giving it away. As music sales sagged and piracy continued to impact the recording industry, some big-name acts elected to give their music away in 2007. In July, Prince had 2.5 million copies of his new CD, *Planet Earth,* released inside a British newspaper to publicize his show at London's O2 Arena in August.

In October, the British band Radiohead offered its seventh album, *In Rainbows,* as a digital, no-label release for whatever price consumers wished to pay. The only charge for the download was a credit card handling fee. In the first weeks after the album's release, more than half of those who downloaded it elected to pay nothing. The album was also released in physical form in December.

In addition to Radiohead, two other established British bands chose to eliminate the middleman with no-label, digital releases in October. Oasis issued its digital track, "Lord Don't Slow Me Down," as a self-released single. The Charlatans made their single "You Cross My Path" available at no charge through the United Kingdom radio station Xfm's Web site, with the rest of their 10th album to follow as a free download via the site.

As records, CD's, and digital downloads became

devalued, some music industry executives came to regard recordings as mere promotional tools to support the sale of concert tickets and fan merchandise. Many of these executives saw free and "pay-what-you-wish" music—especially digital self-releases—as a future business model for the industry.

A bad rap. In the general decline, sales of rap CD's took the biggest hit. Earlier in 2007, Nielsen SoundScan reported that rap sales were down 33 percent from 2006—twice the decline for the industry overall. One factor may have been the marketing emphasis on singles and cell-phone ring tone sales over albums. Some industry observers saw the decline as an indication that music buyers had become disinterested in the "gangsta" attitude associated with many rap artists. Music sales by established rap stars such as Nas, Diddy, Ludacris, and Snoop Dogg were eclipsed in 2007 by such artists as rock guitarist and singer Chris Daughtry and jazz-pop performer Norah Jones.

Nonetheless, in November, rapper Jay-Z tied Elvis Presley's record when his album *American Gangster,* inspired by the year's film of the same name, became his 10th to top the charts. The film was based on the true story of 1970's New York City heroin kingpin Frank Lucas.

Rap rivalry. Rap sales—and the music industry in general—also saw some signs of recovery with the sales of the latest albums by rap rivals Kanye West and 50 Cent. West's *Graduation* was originally scheduled for a later release, but West moved the release date up to September 11 so that the album could compete head to head with 50 Cent's *Curtis,*

Paul McCartney's album *Memory Almost Full* debuts at a Starbucks store in June 2007. The CD was the first release on the chain's new Hear Music label, launched in March.

which was also released on that date. 50 Cent fueled the feud by announcing that he would retire if *Graduation* outsold *Curtis*. According to Nielsen SoundScan, *Graduation* sold 957,000 copies in its first week. The album was number one on *Billboard*'s pop chart and sold nearly 1 million copies in its first six days on sale. *Curtis* followed at number two with 691,000 copies sold. 50 Cent later backed off his promise to retire.

Country KO's rappers. The week after West's and 50 Cent's new releases hit the top slots of the *Billboard* chart, country star Reba McEntire took both rappers down a peg when her new album, *Reba Duets,* debuted at number one. The album, which includes collaborations with Rascal Flatts, Faith Hill, Kenny Chesney, Justin Timberlake, and Kelly Clarkson, was McEntire's first number-one album and her best sales week in Nielsen Sound-Scan history. McEntire's release was surmounted the following week by the country-pop trio Rascal Flatts's third number-one album, *Still Feels Good*.

Oops!...She did it again. Britney Spears remained in the public eye throughout most of 2007—more for her personal problems than for her musical contributions. In September, during an appearance on the MTV Video Music Awards that was billed as her comeback, a languid Spears seemed disoriented and appeared to forget lyrics and dance steps as she lip-synched "Gimme More" from her upcoming album. In October, after almost a yearlong court battle, Spears's former husband Kevin Federline was given temporary custody of their children. Spears's album, *Blackout,* originally scheduled for a November release, was

GRAMMY AWARD WINNERS IN 2007

Record of the Year, "Not Ready to Make Nice," Dixie Chicks
Album of the Year, *Taking the Long Way,* Dixie Chicks
Song of the Year, "Not Ready to Make Nice," Dixie Chicks
New Artist, Carrie Underwood
Pop Vocal Performance, Female, "Ain't No Other Man," Christina Aguilera
Pop Vocal Performance, Male, "Waiting on the World to Change," John Mayer
Pop Performance by a Duo or Group with Vocal, "My Humps," Black Eyed Peas
Traditional Pop Vocal Album, *Duets: An American Classic,* Tony Bennett
Solo Rock Vocal Performance, "Someday Baby," Bob Dylan
Rock Performance by a Duo or Group with Vocal, "Dani California," Red Hot Chili Peppers
Hard Rock Performance, "Woman," Wolfmother
Metal Performance, "Eyes of the Insane," Slayer
Rock Song, "Dani California," Red Hot Chili Peppers
Rock Album, *Stadium Arcadium,* Red Hot Chili Peppers
Alternative Music Album, *St. Elsewhere,* Gnarls Barkley
Rhythm-and-Blues Vocal Performance, Female, "Be Without You," Mary J. Blige
Rhythm-and-Blues Vocal Performance, Male, "Heaven," John Legend
Rhythm-and-Blues Performance by a Duo or Group with Vocal, "Family Affair," John Legend, Joss Stone, and Van Hunt
Rhythm-and-Blues Song, "Be Without You," Johnta Austin, Mary J. Blige, Bryan-Michael Cox, and Jason Perry
Rhythm-and-Blues Album, *The Breakthrough,* Mary J. Blige
Contemporary Rhythm-and-Blues Album, *B'Day,* Beyonce
Rap Solo Performance, "What You Know," T.I.
Rap Performance by a Duo or Group, "Ridin," Chamillionaire
Rap Album, *Release Therapy,* Ludacris
Rap Song, "Money Maker," Christopher Bridges and Pharrell Williams
Contemporary Jazz Album, *The Hidden Land,* Béla Fleck and the Flecktones
Jazz Vocal Album, *Turned to Blue,* Nancy Wilson
Jazz Instrumental, Solo, "Some Skunk Funk," Michael Brecker
Jazz Instrumental Album, Individual or Group, *The Ultimate Adventure,* Chick Corea
Large Jazz Ensemble Album, *Some Skunk Funk,* Randy Brecker, with Michael Brecker, Jim Beard, Will Lee, Peter Erskine, Marcio Doctor, and Vince Mendoza
Country Album, *Taking the Long Way,* Dixie Chicks
Country Song, "Jesus, Take the Wheel," Brett James, Hillary Lindsey, and Gordie Sampson
Country Vocal Performance, Female, "Jesus, Take the Wheel," Carrie Underwood
Country Vocal Performance, Male, "The Reason Why," Vince Gill
Country Performance by a Duo or Group with Vocal, "Not Ready to Make Nice," Dixie Chicks
Country Vocal Collaboration, "Who Says You Can't Go Home," Bon Jovi and Jennifer Nettles
Country Instrumental Performance, "Whiskey Before Breakfast," Bryan Sutton and Doc Watson

moved up to an October release to combat unauthorized Internet leaks.

Paul McCartney released his 21st solo album, *Memory Almost Full,* in June. The album was the first release on the Starbucks Hear Music label. The former Beatle was lured to the new label from his long-time label EMI in March. The album debuted on the iTunes Music Store at number two on its main charts. It received generally favorable reviews, with critics comparing its sound to that of McCartney's former band Wings as well as the Beatles album *Abbey Road* (1969).

High School Musical 2. Following on the success of the 2006 Disney Channel original movie *High School Musical* and its top-selling soundtrack, the soundtrack for *High School Musical 2* debuted in August 2007 at number one on the *Billboard* 200 chart and on the iTunes store. It was the first television movie soundtrack to debut at number one on the *Billboard* chart. The soundtrack sold nearly 2 million copies worldwide in six weeks, while the TV movie was the highest-rated basic-cable broadcast of all time.

Hannah mania. The year's hot concert ticket was "Hannah Montana/Miley Cyrus: Best of Both Worlds Concert Tour," featuring the teen-age Cyrus performing in concert as the character she portrays on the popular Disney Channel TV show. Tickets sold for as much as $4,500 apiece in some cities, with parents often purchasing the tickets for their preteen children.

The biggest "Bang." "A Bigger Bang" world tour, staged by the Rolling Stones, became the highest-grossing music tour in history after wrapping up at O2 Arena in late August. The tour, which began in the fall of 2005, earned over $550 million.

Material girl. Madonna left her long-time label Warner Brothers Records in October 2007 for a $120-million deal with the concert promoter Live Nation. The agreement called for three albums from the singer and the exclusive rights to promote her concerts and market her merchandise.

Led Zeppelin reunites, goes digital. In December, legendary British rock band Led Zeppelin performed together for the first time in nearly 20 years. Guitarist Jimmy Page, singer Robert Plant, bassist John Paul Jones, and drummer Jason Bonham—the son of the band's late drummer, John Bonham—performed at O2 Arena as part of a tribute concert to Atlantic Records cofounder Ahmet Ertegun, who died in 2006. More than 1 million fans entered a drawing for the chance to buy 1 of the 10,000 tickets to the concert, which was to aid the Ahmet Ertegun Education Fund. In November, the group released its back catalog online. Led Zeppelin was one of the last major musical acts to resist digital distribution.

■ Shawn Brennan

Population. For the first time in world history, more than half of the world's population, or nearly 3.5 billion people, were expected to be living in cities and towns by 2008, the United Nations (UN) Population Fund reported in May 2007. The UN's report on the state of the world population, "Unleashing the Potential of Urban Growth," disclosed that by 2030, about 5 billion people would be living in urban areas. The authors noted that the demographic shift toward cities and towns should provide women and girls with increased opportunities in education, jobs, and living conditions. "No country in the industrial age has ever achieved significant economic growth without urbanization," the authors concluded.

Growth in the developing world. According to the report, the largest urban growth would take place in Africa and Asia, where the number of urban residents was expected to double by 2030. The report estimated that Asia's urban population would grow from 1.36 billion in 2000 to 2.64 billion in 2030. During the same period, Africa's urban population would grow from 294 million to 742 million, and Latin America and the Caribbean would experience growth from 394 million to 609 million. By contrast, the developed nations' urban population was expected to grow relatively little, from a total of 870 million people in 2000 to 1.01 billion in 2030.

The report's authors expected births to account for most of the urban growth, with migration from rural to urban areas accounting for the rest. Much of the growth was expected to take place in small towns and cities rather than in megacities.

Poverty. The authors of the UN report noted that poverty was growing faster in urban than in rural areas, particularly in developing countries. Of the 1 billion people living in slums, 90 percent of them were in developing countries. "Cities concentrate poverty, but they also represent the best hope of escaping it," concluded the authors.

The UN called on governments to accept the right of the poor to live in cities and to drop plans to prevent migration from rural to urban areas. It also called on governments to adopt broad and long-term policies for the use of urban space. Such policies include providing land for housing and planning for sustainable land use to minimize the impact of development on the environment.

The young and the old. A June 2007 report by the UN Population Division revealed that 28 percent of the world's population in 2007 was made up of children (people under the age of 15). About 10 percent consisted of what the UN called the aging population (those 60 years of age and older). The population of this group was expected to triple, from 705 million in 2007 to 2 billion by 2050.

■ J. Tuyet Nguyen

See also **Census.**

Portugal. The Socialist Party government of Prime Minister José Sócrates put its credibility on the line in 2007 by strongly supporting a referendum to ease Portugal's strict abortion laws. In early 2007, Portugal was one of only four European Union (EU) nations that restricted abortion. A pregnancy could be terminated only if the mother's life was at risk, if she had been raped, or if there was a strong chance that the child would be born with a birth defect. According to government estimates, these laws resulted in more than 20,000 illegal abortions being performed each year and a significant amount of "abortion tourism." Pregnant women traveled to Spain or to other European countries where abortion is legal to have the procedure performed.

After a heated campaign in which the Roman Catholic Church strongly opposed any change to the existing law, 60 percent of voters supported changes in a February 11 referendum. However, only 44 percent of the country's eligible voters participated in the polling. A participation rate of 50 percent or greater is required by the Constitution for a referendum to be valid. In March, Portugal's parliament passed legislation that legalized abortion in the first 10 weeks of pregnancy. The law went into effect in July.

Economy. Sócrates continued his efforts in 2007 to strengthen the nation's economy. After impressive growth during the 1990's, Portugal's economy had slowed considerably in the early 2000's. In 2005 and 2006, the nation's budget deficit significantly exceeded the benchmark 3 percent of gross domestic product (GDP) allowed for nations that use the euro, the EU's common currency. (GDP is the total amount of goods and services produced in a country in a year.) Through strict budget cuts and increased taxes, Sócrates managed to reduce the deficit to the permitted level in 2007. The prime minister devoted a great deal of his political capital to reforming the public sector by reducing salaries, increasing the minimum retirement age, and cutting sick pay. Health care workers, teachers, and police officers went on strike several times in 2007 to protest the cuts.

EU economists projected that Portugal's GDP would grow by 1.75 percent in 2007, up slightly from 1.3 percent in 2006. The unemployment rate rose from 7.7 percent in 2006 to 8.0 percent in 2007, the highest it had been since Portugal adopted the euro in 1999. With elections scheduled for 2009, political analysts predicted that any new reforms in 2008 would not go beyond those already undertaken. ■ Jeffrey Kopstein

See also **Europe.**

President of the United States.
See **United States, President of the.**

Prince Edward Island. See **Canadian provinces.**

Prisons. Statistics released by the United States Department of Justice (DOJ) in December 2007 revealed that the number of adults in U.S. state or federal prisons, in local jails, or on probation or parole in the United States reached 7.2 million at the end of 2006. This number represented an increase of 159,500 compared with a year earlier. According to DOJ officials, approximately 3.2 percent of the U.S. adult population, or 1 in every 31 adults, was in prison or jail or on probation or parole in December 2006.

The DOJ report also noted that, during 2006, the number of women in state or federal prisons increased by 4.5 percent, to reach 112,498 prisoners. The number of men in prison increased by 2.7 percent during this period.

For the first time, noted DOJ officials, the number of men and women on probation or parole in the United States reached 5 million at the end of 2006. Statistics revealed that among individuals released from prison to parole during 2006, about 16 percent were reincarcerated.

Veterans in prison. There were an estimated 140,000 veterans in state or federal prisons in 2004, amounting to approximately 10 percent of the prison population, according to the DOJ's "Veterans in State and Federal Prison" report issued in April 2007. The percentage of imprisoned veterans had steadily declined since the 1980's. Thirty-six percent of incarcerated veterans in 2004 had served in the Vietnam War (1957-1975); 14 percent in the Persian Gulf War (1991); and 4 percent in one of the ongoing conflicts in Afghanistan or Iraq. Fifty-seven percent of imprisoned veterans in 2004 were serving time for violent offenses, compared with 47 percent of imprisoned nonveterans. Veterans were twice as likely as nonveterans to be imprisoned for sexual assaults.

Death sentences. During 2006, at least 3,861 people were sentenced to death in 55 countries, and at least 1,591 people were executed in 25 countries, according to a 2007 report by Amnesty International, a human rights organization based in London. The vast majority (91 percent) of these executions were carried out in only six countries: China (at least 1,010 executions), Iran (177), Pakistan (82), Iraq (65), Sudan (65), and the United States (53). Amnesty officials noted that statistics on executions in China are a state secret, and as many as 8,000 people may have been executed in that country in 2006. The human rights organization estimated that as many as 24,646 condemned individuals were awaiting execution around the world at the end of 2006. ■ Alfred J. Smuskiewicz

See also **Civil rights; Courts; Crime; State government.**

Prizes. See **Nobel Prizes; Pulitzer Prizes.**

Protestantism. A document issued by the Vatican in June 2007 provoked Protestants by reasserting the Roman Catholic Church's claim that it is the only true church. Although many theologians had thought the Catholic Church was more accepting of other Christian groups since its reforms in the 1960's, the new statement reiterated the view that Protestant churches "suffer from defects." Some Vatican officials, among them Cardinal Walter Kasper, set out to soften the tone. Kasper said that the Vatican's statement meant that Protestant churches "have a different understanding of what the church is." At the same time, numerous Protestant leaders stayed calm and reaffirmed their commitments to positive Catholic-Protestant dialogue and action.

Mainline and evangelical Protestants, seen by many observers as the two flanks of Protestantism in the United States, overlapped in some ways in 2007. For example, within the chiefly mainline Episcopal Church, numerous parishes continued to move to the supervision of conservative evangelical Anglican dioceses in Africa. The parishes made these provocative moves in protest of the Episcopal Church's liberal policies, especially its approval of the ordination of gay clergy.

Evangelical diversity. Many members of the evangelical camp, often seen as conservative and hard-line, ventured into diverse new missions in 2007. Some observers saw the moves as born of frustration, in part a reaction to scandals involving prominent evangelical figures in recent years.

One new mission involved a growing emphasis on environmental issues. Although some evangelicals had seen many environmentalists as Earth-worshippers and enemies of the Christian faith, in 2007 evangelicals increasingly focused on "creation care," theologically motivated care for Earth. Some old-guard evangelicals, such as James Dobson of the conservative group Focus on the Family, responded by going on the defensive. In March, Dobson wrote to the board of the National Association of Evangelicals criticizing its vice president of governmental affairs, Richard Cizik, for his work to raise awareness about global warming. The board responded with support for Cizik and his efforts.

On another evangelical front, Pentecostal churches continued in 2007 to welcome ever-larger numbers of Latinos to membership. Ron Cruz, executive director of the Secretariat for Hispanic Affairs for the U.S. Conference of Catholic Bishops, stated that 85 percent of Latinos in the United States were Catholic only a few decades ago. According to a report by the Religion News Service, studies estimated that the figure in recent years ranged from 60 to 70 percent.

Baptist alliance. In January, two former U.S. presidents, Jimmy Carter and Bill Clinton, who were raised as Southern Baptists, helped promote a conference to mark the formation of the New Baptist Covenant Network, an alliance of Baptist groups from throughout North America, in early 2008. Some observers saw the Democratic former presidents' involvement as an effort to demonstrate more political variety within Baptist circles. The vast Southern Baptist Convention denomination has been firmly and publicly linked to conservative politics since the 1980's.

Iraq War. Growing numbers of Protestants condemned the "troop surge" in Iraq and other features of a war they considered immoral. In January 2007, the National Council of Churches said President George W. Bush's call for more troops was "morally unsupportable." Evangelical activist Jim Wallis of the Christian social justice organization Sojourners/Call for Renewal argued that by fighting the war, "America is losing its soul."

Deaths of prominent Protestants in 2007 included Ruth Graham, 87, wife of evangelist Billy Graham; Bruce Metzger, 93, a main agent in producing the New Revised Standard Version of the Bible; Brevard Childs, 83, an influential Biblical scholar; Robert Webber, 73, an expert on worship who led many into traditional worship practices; and Jerry Falwell, 73, well-known televangelist and political activist. ■ Martin E. Marty

See also **Roman Catholic Church.**

Psychology. See **Mental health.**

Public health. Andrew Speaker, a lawyer from Atlanta who was believed to be infected with the most dangerous form of tuberculosis bacterium, set off an international health scare in May 2007 when he traveled by commercial airplane to several countries, placing his fellow passengers at risk for infection. Speaker had flown from the United States to Europe for his wedding and honeymoon after a medical test indicated that he carried a strain of tuberculosis bacterium that causes extensively drug-resistant tuberculosis (XDR-TB), which is resistant to most drugs.

While in Rome, Speaker was contacted by the U.S. Centers for Disease Control and Prevention (CDC) in Atlanta, which warned him not to do any additional traveling. Despite the warning, Speaker flew with other passengers to the Czech Republic and then to Canada. Next, a border inspector allowed him to enter the United States by automobile. Speaker was finally hospitalized in isolation after a CDC director reached him by telephone in upstate New York.

In June, the World Health Organization (WHO)—a United Nations organization that helps to build better health care systems—strongly criticized the inability of U.S. authorities to prevent Speaker from traveling. In July, the CDC reported that Speaker had a less severe form of tuberculosis than originally believed.

Threats from Chinese imports. Several products imported from China raised public health concerns in the United States in 2007. The U.S. Food and Drug Administration (FDA) announced in late June that it was blocking all shipments of farm-raised shrimp, catfish, eel, basa, and dace from China until tests showed these products to be free of certain drugs. The FDA reported that it had detected residues of antimicrobial and antibiotic drugs in samples of these Chinese imports. At high-enough levels, these drugs could pose a threat to human health.

In early June, the FDA warned consumers not to use toothpaste made in China because it contained diethylene glycol, a poisonous substance normally found in antifreeze. In May, the FDA launched a surveillance program of all facilities in the United States that use wheat gluten and rice protein to manufacture food. The surveillance program was intended to help prevent products contaminated with melamine or other chemicals from entering the human food supply. Melamine, a compound that can trigger kidney failure in animals, as well as another chemical used to maintain swimming pools, had been detected in some pet foods imported from China. The food was manufactured with chemical-tainted wheat flour incorrectly labeled as wheat gluten and rice protein.

Botulism scare. In the first cases of botulism linked to the U.S. commercial canning industry in nearly 40 years, Castleberry's Food Company of Augusta, Georgia, recalled more than 721,000 pounds (327,040 kilograms) of canned meat products in July and August. The recall, prompted by a small number of people becoming ill after consuming the company's products, included such items as canned chili, beans, barbecue pork, and beef hash. Botulism, which can result in respiratory failure and paralysis, is caused by a toxin produced by the bacterium *Clostridium botulinum*. The bacterium grows in improperly canned or preserved food. According to Castleberry's, an equipment malfunction may have led to the problem.

Politics over public health. Richard H. Carmona, surgeon general of the United States from 2002 to 2006, testified before the U.S. Congress in July 2007 that the administration of President George W. Bush had censored his speeches for political reasons and prevented him from discussing scientifically accurate information on public health. Carmona testified that when he was surgeon general, he was repeatedly blocked from speaking out on such politically sensitive issues as the benefits of stem cell research and public-school education about contraceptives. Two other former surgeons general added that political interference with this office had recently grown.   ■ Alfred J. Smuskiewicz

See also **AIDS; Drugs; Food; Medicine; Safety.**

Puerto Rico. In July 2007, Puerto Ricans celebrated the 55th anniversary of their island's unique status as a self-governing commonwealth of the United States. They were deeply divided over the question of whether Puerto Rico should remain a commonwealth or seek to become a U.S. state. A small minority of Puerto Ricans believed that the island should become an independent nation.

Ultimately, Puerto Rico's political status depended upon the actions of the U.S. Congress, where several bills that dealt with the issue languished during 2007. Each bill would provide Puerto Ricans with a voice regarding possible changes in the island's relationship to the United States. Governor Aníbal Acevedo Vilá, of the pro-commonwealth Popular Democratic Party, favored a bill that called for the creation of a constitutional convention to debate Puerto Rico's status. The convention, including representatives from all the island's political parties, would then submit their proposal to Puerto Rican voters in a binding referendum.

A new political party, Puerto Ricans for Puerto Rico, was officially certified in May. Its founder, chemical engineer Rogelio Figueroa, said that Puerto Rico could succeed under any political status. He urged people to focus instead on resolving urgent local problems, including corruption, the mediocrity of politicians, and the destruction of natural resources. The new party emphasized environmental issues, even as Governor Acevedo sought to revive sagging tourism.

Environmental issues. In August, a 10,000-gallon (38,000-liter) oil spill occurred along Puerto Rico's southwest shore, near Guayanilla Bay. The spill posed a threat to coastal wildlife and to an offshore coral reef popular with scuba divers. The source of the spill was unknown. Also in 2007, public health authorities mounted a campaign to clean up Puerto Rico's beaches. Meanwhile, developers laid plans to exploit the tourist potential of government-owned property, including attractive parcels of land on Vieques Island and at the former U.S. Naval Station Roosevelt Roads, in eastern Puerto Rico.

Phony medical licenses. In August, a U.S. federal grand jury in San Juan, the capital, indicted 91 people in a scheme to provide fraudulent medical licenses to physicians. Those charged included physicians and some employees of the Board of Medical Examiners of Puerto Rico. The indictment alleged that in some instances, individuals received false licenses in return for bribes of up to $10,000. One employee of the board was charged with falsifying results on revalidation examinations for physicians.   ■ Nathan A. Haverstock

See also **Latin America.**

Pulitzer Prizes

Pulitzer Prizes in journalism, letters, drama, and music were announced on April 16, 2007, by Columbia University in New York City on the recommendation of the Pulitzer Prize Board.

Journalism. *The Wall Street Journal* won the public service prize for its probe into backdated stock options for business executives. The prize for breaking news reporting went to the staff of *The Oregonian* in Portland for its coverage of a missing family in the Oregon mountains. Brett Blackledge of *The Birmingham* (Alabama) *News* won the investigative reporting award for his exposure of corruption in the state's two-year college system.

The explanatory reporting prize was shared by reporters Kenneth R. Weiss and Usha Lee McFarling and photographer Rick Loomis, all of the *Los Angeles Times,* for their reports on Earth's distressed oceans. Debbie Cenziper of *The Miami Herald* won the local reporting prize for exposing corruption and mismanagement at the Miami-Dade Housing Agency. Charlie Savage of *The Boston Globe* won the national reporting award for his reports on U.S. President George W. Bush's efforts to expand presidential power. The international reporting prize went to the staff of *The Wall Street Journal* for its examination of the adverse effects of growing capitalism in China.

Andrea Elliott of *The New York Times* won the feature writing prize for her report on an immigrant *imam* (spiriual leader) in the United States. Cynthia Tucker of *The Atlanta Journal-Constitution* won the commentary award. The criticism award went to Jonathan Gold of *LA Weekly* for his restaurant reviews. Arthur Browne, Beverly Weintraub, and Heidi Evans of the *Daily News* of New York City were honored for their editorial writing on the health problems of Ground Zero workers. Walt Handelsman of *Newsday* in Long Island, New York, won for editorial cartooning. Oded Balilty of the Associated Press won for breaking news photography. The feature photography prize went to Renée C. Byer of *The Sacramento* (California) *Bee.*

Letters, drama, and music. Cormac McCarthy was awarded the fiction prize for his novel *The Road.* David Lindsay-Abaire won the drama prize for *Rabbit Hole.* Gene Roberts and Hank Klibanoff took the history award for *The Race Beat: The Press, the Civil Rights Struggle, and the Awakening of a Nation.* Debby Applegate won the biography prize for *The Most Famous Man in America: The Biography of Henry Ward Beecher.* Natasha Trethewey's *Native Guard* won for poetry. Lawrence Wright won the nonfiction prize for *The Looming Tower: Al-Qaeda and the Road to 9/11.* Ornette Coleman's *Sound Grammar* won for music.   ■ Shawn Brennan

See also **Literature; Newspaper.**

Qatar. See **Middle East.**

Quebec. See **Canadian provinces.**

Radio. In 2007, talk-radio host Don Imus created controversy with remarks he made on the air about young African American women. CBS Radio had broadcast the show of this long-time radio personality, "Imus in the Morning," from 1971 to 1977 and again beginning in 1979. The show was also syndicated nationwide and simulcast on cable television on MSNBC as of the mid-1990's. Imus's show featured politicians, sports figures, and journalists, but critics long noted vulgar humor and a shock-radio aspect to the broadcast as well.

On April 4, 2007, Imus used a racial slur in referring to the women's basketball team of Rutgers University (New Brunswick, New Jersey). A media-watch group posted a video clip of the remark online, and Imus found himself at the center of a national debate. His broadcast apology did not defuse the situation. Imus was fired from both MSNBC and CBS Radio a little over a week after the remark was made. In August 2007, Imus and CBS agreed to a settlement that compensated him for the remaining time on his contract. Imus was then signed by ABC Radio to host a program that began in December.

Satellite merger. Sirius Satellite Radio of New York City and XM Satellite Radio Holdings of Washington, D.C., announced plans to merge in February 2007. Subscribers to satellite radio had increased every year since 2004, but neither company had yet shown a profit. Large amounts paid for rights to broadcast events and huge salaries paid to media personalities contributed to their losses.

A merger would allow both companies to save billions of dollars in costs. On Nov. 13, 2007, shareholders voted to approve the merger. However, antitrust issues required the merger to be approved by the Federal Communications Commission (FCC). If the FCC determined the satellite radio market to be made up only of Sirius and XM, the merger would likely be seen as creating a monopoly. If, however, the FCC considered the market to include the many music options available to consumers, then such a merger was not as likely to be seen as anticompetitive. The FCC was expected to rule in 2008.

Internet radio. In 2007, the Internet radio industry struggled with a new ruling concerning how royalties on music were assessed. Radio stations transmitting, or *webcasting,* over the Internet had operated since the mid-1990's. Some Internet stations had terrestrial stations and "simulcast" their programs on the Internet. Others were stand-alone Internet stations—some with programs hosted by amateurs for a niche market of fewer than 100 listeners.

In May 2007, a congressionally appointed panel decided upon a rate hike for the music royalties charged to Internet radio stations. There had been no increase to the royalties charged to webcasters for several years, so the increase was retroactive to 2006. The new fees could make most small stations unviable. Web radio organized a national protest on June 26, 2007, called the "Day of Silence." A large number of stations completely stopped their stream of music or transmitted static for the day. By autumn, the group that collected royalties, SoundExchange, was trying to compromise with Internet stations, offering payments with maximums on the amount assessed per year or, for very small stations, royalties assessed on revenue instead of songs played.

Arbitron, the company that provided data about radio listeners to both stations and advertisers, introduced a new way to collect that data. Formerly, selected radio listeners were issued a paper journal in which they entered data on what they listened to each week. The new system, unveiled in Philadelphia and Houston in 2007, featured a pager-sized device, called a Portable People Meter, that was worn by listeners. The device recorded audio codes embedded in radio broadcasts and related this data back to Arbitron. The system was likely to be unveiled soon in other large cities. ■ Christine Sullivan

See also **Telecommunications.**

Religion. See **Eastern Orthodox; Islam; Judaism; Protestantism; Roman Catholic Church.**

Republican Party. In January 2007, the Republican Party—also called the G.O.P. (Grand Old Party)—ceded control of both houses of the United States Congress to the Democrats. Several Republicans in Congress announced in 2007 that they would not seek reelection, souring G.O.P. hopes of regaining control of either house in the 2008 election. The campaign for the 2008 U.S. presidential election got off to a vigorous start in 2007, with 12 candidates seeking the Republican Party nomination and hoping to maintain G.O.P. control of the presidency. Republicans also picked up one governorship and lost another in 2007 elections, keeping the number of G.O.P. governors at 22 compared with the Democrats' 28.

Presidential race. The top contenders for the Republican nomination, based on polls and media coverage, were former New York City Mayor Rudy Giuliani, former Arkansas Governor Mike Huckabee, Senator John McCain of Arizona, former Massachusetts Governor Mitt Romney, and former Senator Fred Thompson of Tennessee. Giuliani ran ahead of his Republican opponents in most national polls in 2007, but many political experts considered the race to be wide open going into 2008. The other candidates were Senator Sam Brownback of Kansas, former Virginia Governor Jim Gilmore, Representative Duncan Hunter of California, conservative activist Alan Keyes of Maryland,

Representative Ron Paul of Texas, Representative Tom Tancredo of Colorado, and former Wisconsin Governor Tommy Thompson. Brownback, Gilmore, Tancredo, and Tommy Thompson left the race before the end of 2007.

The calendar for the 2008 presidential primaries and caucuses underwent significant upheaval in 2007, creating uncertainty about how the nominating process would play out. In almost all states, primaries or caucuses are the means by which voters select the delegates who in turn choose a party's presidential candidate at the party's national convention. Many states scheduled their delegate selection contests earlier than usual in an effort to gain greater influence on the presidential nomination. More than 20 states—including California, Georgia, Illinois, New Jersey, and New York—scheduled primaries or caucuses for Feb. 5, 2008.

Some states scheduled their contests for earlier than February 5, violating national party organization rules. On Nov. 8, 2007, the Republican National Committee voted to strip five states—Florida, Michigan, New Hampshire, South Carolina, and Wyoming—of half their delegates to the national convention because they scheduled their primaries for January 2008. Iowa and Nevada were not penalized for their plans to hold January caucuses, because delegates chosen in the caucuses would not be bound to vote for a particular candidate.

Governors. U.S. Representative Bobby Jindal, a Republican, defeated 11 other candidates in Louisiana's gubernatorial election on Oct. 20, 2007. Jindal, the son of immigrants from India, became the first Indian American to be elected governor of a U.S. state. At age 36, he also was set to become the country's youngest sitting governor upon taking office in January 2008. The Democratic incumbent, Kathleen Blanco, did not run for reelection. She had been widely criticized for the state's response to Hurricane Katrina in 2005.

In Mississippi, Republican Governor Haley Barbour easily won reelection on Nov. 6, 2007. His Democratic opponent was John Arthur Eaves, Jr., a lawyer. But in Kentucky, former Lieutenant Governor Steve Beshear, a Democrat, unseated Republican Governor Ernie Fletcher on November 6. Fletcher had been accused of political discrimination in a hiring scandal during his term.

Retirements. Five Republican U.S. senators—Wayne Allard of Colorado, Larry Craig of Idaho, Pete Domenici of New Mexico, Chuck Hagel of Nebraska, and John Warner of Virginia—announced in 2007 that they would not seek reelection in 2008. Former Majority Leader Trent Lott (R., Mississippi) resigned his Senate seat in late 2007. More than 15 Republicans in the House of Representatives announced that they would not seek reelection. Former Speaker Dennis Hastert (R., Illinois) resigned his House seat in late 2007.

Craig's retirement decision came after news reports revealed in August 2007 that he had been arrested on June 11 in connection with an airport rest room incident and had pleaded guilty on August 8 to disorderly conduct. An undercover police officer alleged that Craig sat in a stall next to him and used hand and foot signals to try to solicit sex. But Craig said that his actions had been misread and that his guilty plea had been a mistake. He asked to withdraw the guilty plea, but a judge denied Craig's request on October 4.

Fund-raising. During the first six months of 2007, Republican Party committees—including the Republican National Committee, the National Republican Senatorial Committee, the National Republican Congressional Committee, and state and local committees—raised $108.8 million and spent $87.1 million, according to the Federal Election Commission. Their Democratic counterparts raised $111.5 million and spent $67.7 million during the same period. The Republicans' fund-raising total was 24 percent lower than their total for the first half of 2005 and 22 percent lower than their total for the first half of 2003.　　　■ Mike Lewis

See also **Cabinet, U.S.; Congress of the United States; Democratic Party; Elections; People in the news** (Mitt Romney); **State government; United States, Government of the; United States, President of the.**

Roman Catholic Church.

The Vatican made numerous attempts in 2007 to reassert traditional notions of Roman Catholic identity. The church's chief doctrine office, the Congregation for the Doctrine of the Faith, issued two key declarations, one permitting traditional worship practices and another claiming that the true church exists "in all its fullness" only in the Roman Catholic Church. The Vatican also continued investigating two major theologians who had authored books that differed with the Vatican's view of Jesus Christ and the role of the Catholic Church. Some observers viewed the acts as efforts by Pope Benedict XVI, long known as a conservative, to move the church in a more traditional direction.

Latin Mass. In July, the Vatican released a document personally approved by the pope that allowed priests to celebrate in Latin, a version of the Mass that was universally used prior to the Second Vatican Council. The council, also known as Vatican II, was a worldwide gathering of bishops that enacted wide reform during the 1960's.

The pope emphasized that celebrating the Mass in the vernacular, or language of a given location, would remain the norm. However, under the new ruling, priests were no longer required to seek permission from their local bishop before using the old ritual.

Traditional view of the church. The Congregation for the Doctrine of the Faith in June 2007 issued a statement reversing a common understanding of how the Vatican views Catholicism and other Christian groups. The statement, which contained five questions and answers about doctrine, discussed a phrase in a Vatican II document that states that the Church of Christ "subsists in" (as opposed to "is") the Catholic Church. The phrase formed the basis of the view, held widely since Vatican II, that the council departed from the belief that the Catholic Church is the only "true church." Many believed that the phrase indicated openness to other Christian groups.

The new document ruled that the phrase "indicates the full identity of the Church of Christ with the Catholic Church." However, the statement reiterated another Vatican II view that "numerous elements of sanctification and of truth" exist in other Christian denominations. Some observers noted that the new document repeated the thinking set out by the office of then-Cardinal Joseph Ratzinger—now Pope Benedict XVI—in the 2000 statement *Dominus Iesus.*

Observers did not know what effect the new statement would have on ecumenical relations—efforts to promote Christian unity. Although some non-Catholics felt angry about the document, a number of Christian groups seemed to take it in stride. "To be surprised" by the recent statement "is surprising," said Reverend Leonid Kishkovsky of the Orthodox Church of America, a participant in ecumenical discussions.

Criticisms. The doctrine office in March 2007 issued a "notification" about the work of Father Jon Sobrino of Central American University in El Salvador. The document criticized Sobrino's books *Jesus the Liberator* (1993) and *Christ the Liberator* (2001), which focus on Jesus Christ as liberator of the oppressed and emphasize the "church of the poor." Although not barred from teaching or publishing, Sobrino was criticized for failing to place sufficient emphasis on the divinity of Jesus Christ.

The Vatican in 2007 also continued its investigation of *Being Religious Interreligiously: Asian Perspectives on Interfaith Dialogue* (2004) by Vietnam-born Father Peter Phan, a professor at Georgetown University in Washington, D.C., and the former president of the Catholic Theological Society of America. Phan came under investigation for his views on religious diversity and, in the Vatican's estimation, for diminishing the role of Jesus Christ as a unique savior and that of the Catholic Church as the one true path to salvation.

Sobrino and Phan were the latest in a string of theologians in recent years whose work in the area of Christology, the theological study of Jesus Christ as both God and human, had come into question by the church.　　　■ Thomas W. Roberts

See also **Protestantism.**

On New Year's Day 2007, Romanian revelers wave EU flags in Bucharest, Romania's capital, to celebrate their country's entry into the European association of 27 nations.

Romania. On Jan. 1, 2007, Romania, and neighboring Bulgaria, joined the European Union (EU). Unlike the other post-Communist eastern European nations admitted in 2004, Romania and Bulgaria were subject to postaccession review to ensure they met EU criteria, such as judicial reform and anticorruption measures.

A feud between Prime Minister Calin Popescu Tariceanu and President Traian Basescu dominated Romanian politics in 2007. In April, Tariceanu dismissed all Cabinet members belonging to Basescu's right-of-center Democratic Party and reconstituted the government with members of his left-of-center National Liberal Party and another coalition party. Days later, parliament voted to impeach Basescu, requiring the president to submit to a referendum. In the May 19 poll, 74 percent of voters approved retaining Basescu as president. Tariceanu's minority government, though weakened, remained in power.

Economic growth in Romania surpassed 6 percent in 2007. Unemployment hovered around 5 percent, and inflation declined to just under 4 percent. However, EU and other economists warned that Romania's government would need to reduce spending to sustain economic growth.

■ Sharon L. Wolchik

See also **Bulgaria; Europe.**

Rowing. See Sports.

Russia. Parliamentary elections gave a strong vote of confidence to President Vladimir Putin in December 2007, as the pro-Kremlin United Russia party swept to an overwhelming victory in the polls. The government continued to centralize its control over Russia's economic resources and take assertive foreign policy stances in 2007, escalating tensions with the United States and Europe.

Economy. According to a November report by the World Bank, a United Nations agency, the Russian economy grew by nearly 8 percent in the first six months of 2007, leading to higher inflation and international reserves. High oil and gas prices, the rising value of the ruble, and the falling value of the U.S. dollar contributed to these trends. As of November 1, Russia held $447 billion in total reserves, up more than $140 billion from the previous year. Russia's reserves remained the third highest in the world, after China's and Japan's. Russia's inflation rate was expected to reach 11 percent for the year. On October 24, in anticipation of the December elections, key food producers and retailers bowed to government requests to freeze prices for essential food items through January 2008.

Russian legislation prohibiting noncitizens from working as salespeople in Russian markets and kiosks came into full force on April 1, 2007. The move came in response to violent conflicts in 2006 involving ethnic Russians and migrant workers from the

Boris Yeltsin
Russia's first president

Boris Yeltsin, who played a major role in the demise of the Soviet Union and then became the first democratically elected president of Russia, died on April 23, 2007. Yeltsin became a hero both in and outside of Russia in August 1991 when he climbed on an army tank in Moscow to rally fellow Russians against right-wing forces attempting to overthrow reformist Soviet leader Mikhail Gorbachev. "You can erect a throne on bayonets," he told the soldiers positioned to attack the headquarters of the Russian parliament, "but you cannot sit on it for long."

Boris Nikolayevich Yeltsin was born on Feb. 1, 1931, in Sverdlovsk (now Yekaterinburg). He and his family lived in a one-room apartment with no running water. They slept on the floor and, in winter, huddled with the family goat for heat. After graduating from Ural Polytechnic Institute in 1955, Yeltsin worked in a variety of construction jobs. In 1961, he joined the Communist Party, rising to party head in Sverdlovsk in 1976.

In 1985, Mikhail Gorbachev, then general secretary of the Communist Party, invited Yeltsin to Moscow as part of his efforts to restructure the Soviet political system and economy. Gorbachev and Yeltsin, however, became bitter rivals, with Gorbachev accusing Yeltsin of advocating radical changes to win popular approval and Yeltsin criticizing Gorbachev for moving too cautiously to implement reforms. In 1987, at a meeting of party leaders, Yeltsin resigned from his posts and attacked Gorbachev, who led a ferocious counterattack that left Yeltsin a political outcast. In 1988, however, Yeltsin made a triumphant comeback in the Soviet Union's first contested elections, crushing the party-backed candidate to win a seat in the newly created Congress of People's Deputies. In spring 1990, Yeltsin was elected to the Russian legislature, which soon declared the republic's *sovereignty* (supremacy) over the Soviet government.

Yeltsin's opposition to the August 1991 attempted coup saved Gorbachev's government, though it proved only a temporary reprieve. In December, Yeltsin and the presidents of Byelorussia (now Belarus) and Ukraine formed the Commonwealth of Independent States and declared that the Soviet Union no longer existed. Other former Soviet republics soon joined. On December 25, Gorbachev resigned.

As Russian leader from December 1991 to December 1999, Yeltsin abolished government censorship of the press and took steps to shift Russia's highly centralized economy to a free-market system. However, his years in office were also marked by skyrocketing prices, social upheaval, massive corruption, and soaring crime rates. One of his greatest failures was his 1994 invasion of Chechnya, an oil-rich republic in southwestern Russia that had declared independence in 1991. Groups across the political spectrum in Russia and abroad opposed the war, which left thousands of Chechen civilians dead and the capital city of Groznyy in ruins.

Blunt, tough, and dedicated, Yeltsin was hobbled by poor health and personal weaknesses. Yet in 1999, he became the first leader in Russian history to give up power voluntarily according to constitutional processes. ■ Barbara A. Mayes

Caucasus and Central Asia. Many market vendors were forced to cut back or close for lack of labor.

State-business relations. A dispute over transit prices led Russia to halt oil supplies to Belarus briefly in January 2007, affecting several European countries that receive oil through the same pipeline. On April 16, President Putin signed a decree merging Russia's oil product pipeline monopoly Transnefteprodukt with its crude oil pipeline monopoly Transneft, further concentrating pipeline operations. On October 22, Russian officials reiterated their refusal to ratify the European Union Energy Charter, which would require Russia to open access to its pipelines.

Rosneft, the state oil company, completed its takeover of the former Yukos oil empire in 2007, becoming Russia's largest oil company. Yukos was declared bankrupt in August 2006. On March 27, 2007, Rosneft repurchased nearly 10 percent of its own stock from Yukos. In May, Rosneft won auctions for Yukos's Tomskneft and Samaraneftegaz oil production units, as well as other assets.

On July 12, the state gas monopoly Gazprom announced a deal with the French oil company Total to participate in development of the Shtokman gas field in the Barents Sea. In September, a Russian newspaper reported that the United States company ConocoPhillips and Norway's Statoil-Hydro would also participate in the development but that Gazprom would retain a majority stake in the venture.

Politics. Prime Minister Mikhail Fradkov and his government resigned on Sept. 12, 2007, to allow President Putin to form a new government before parliamentary elections. Putin chose Federal Financial Monitoring Service head Victor Zubkov to replace Fradkov as prime minister.

Parliamentary elections. The pro-Kremlin United Russia party dominated December 2 elections to the lower house of the Russian parliament (State Duma), winning 64.3 percent of the vote. President Putin ran at the head of the United Russia party list, making the election a referendum on his government's policies and an indicator of how voters may act in the presidential elections scheduled for March 2008. Putin was constitutionally barred from seeking a third consecutive term as president. In December 2007, Putin expressed his support for First Deputy Prime Minister Dmitry Medvedev to succeed him as president. Medvedev then announced that he wanted Putin to be prime minister if he became president, and Putin said he would accept the post.

The Communist Party came in second with 11.6 percent, followed by the nationalist Liberal-Democratic Party (LDPR) with 8.1 percent and center-left

World leaders and dignitaries, including Russian President Vladimir Putin and former U.S. presidents George H. W. Bush and Bill Clinton, attend the funeral of former Russian President Boris Yeltsin on April 25, 2007, in Moscow's Christ the Savior Cathedral. The state funeral was the first in the cathedral since the death of Czar Alexander III in 1894.

A Just Russia with 7.7 percent. None of the other seven participating parties surpassed the new 7-percent threshold necessary for parliamentary representation (the previous threshold was 5 percent).

For the first time, all 450 parliamentary seats were allocated through party list voting. In previous elections, half of the representatives were elected by party list (proportional representation) and half by single-member district (first past the post). United Russia was given 315 seats in the new parliament; the Communist Party, 57; the LDPR, 40; and A Just Russia, 38. The election left the Communists as the lone opposition party in parliament, as United Russia, the LDPR, and A Just Russia all supported the Putin government. International observers criticized the election as unfair, noting strong media bias, harassment of opposition parties, and voting irregularities. United Russia had also refused to participate in campaign debates with other parties. The Russian government rejected the charges.

International affairs. Russian leaders reacted angrily in 2007 to U.S. plans to install a missile defense system in Poland and the Czech Republic, arguing that the move threatened Russia and could lead to a new arms race. The U.S. government in January announced plans to install ground-based missile interceptors in Poland and a radar station in the Czech Republic. In a February 10 speech in Munich, Germany, President Putin denounced the actions of NATO members and their widespread refusal to ratify the 1999 amendments to the 1990 Treaty on Armed Conventional Forces in Europe (CFE). NATO members called on Russia to remove its military bases from Georgia and Moldova before ratification. In June 2007, Putin suggested to U.S. President George W. Bush that the two counties jointly develop a missile radar base in Azerbaijan, but the United States rejected the plan. In July, Putin officially suspended Russia's participation in the CFE treaty.

In May, the British government demanded the extradition of Andrei Lugovoi, a suspect in the November 2006 killing of former Russian spy Alexander Litvinenko in London. Russian officials refused to give up Lugovoi, citing the Russian Constitution's prohibition on extradition of Russian citizens. Both sides expelled diplomats in response. Lugovoi, who denied involvement in the murder, was elected to parliament as a representative of the LDPR in the December elections, giving him immunity from prosecution within Russia.

On August 2, Russian scientists planted a flag on the seabed of the Arctic Ocean under the North Pole. The Russian government claimed that the North Pole lies on Russia's continental shelf. Under international law, Russia, Canada, Norway, the United States, and Denmark (through Greenland) each control a 200-mile (320-kilometer) zone in the ocean extending from their coastline. The Canadian government, which had long asserted sovereignty over the area, rejected the Russian claims. Experts believe the region contains oil and gas reserves.

Winter Olympics. On July 4, the International Olympic Committee awarded the 2014 Winter Games to the resort town of Sochi, Russia. Sochi narrowly defeated Pyongchang, South Korea, by a 51-47 vote on the second ballot. It would be the first time the Winter Olympic games were held in Russia. Moscow hosted the 1980 Summer Olympics.

Disasters. A methane gas explosion on March 19, 2007, at a mine in the city of Novokuznetsk killed 110 miners. It was Russia's worst mining disaster in decades. A methane gas explosion at a nearby mine on May 24 killed at least 39 miners.

A severe storm wrecked at least 11 ships in the Kerch Strait, which connects the Black Sea and the Sea of Azov, on November 11. One sunken tanker released some 360,000 gallons (1,300 metric tons) of oil, creating an environmental disaster for the region.

Deaths. Former Russian President Boris Yeltsin died of heart failure on April 23 in Moscow. Yeltsin served as Russian president from June 1991 until his surprise resignation on Dec. 31, 1999.

■ Juliet Johnson

See also **Canada; Disasters; Estonia; Europe.**

Rwanda. See Africa.

Safety concerns about aging bridges across the United States intensified on Aug. 1, 2007, when a busy 40-year-old bridge on Interstate 35W collapsed into the Mississippi River in Minneapolis. The collapse, which killed 13 people, prompted many state and city governments to increase funding for bridge inspections, repair, and replacement.

Hazards in imported toys. Toy manufacturers and the U.S. Consumer Product Safety Commission (CPSC), an independent agency of the U.S. government that works to protect consumers from unsafe products, issued a series of recalls in 2007 of children's toys and jewelry made in China. The items were recalled because they contained high levels of lead or other hazards.

In one of the largest such recalls, Mattel Inc., headquartered in El Segundo, California, reported in August that 18.2 million recalled dolls and other toys can shed small magnets that could rip through intestines if swallowed. The company also reported that hundreds of thousands of recalled toy cars were made with lead paint. Lead is a toxic substance that, if ingested by young children, can lead to a variety of serious health problems, including brain damage, kidney damage, and behavioral problems.

All-terrain vehicles. Safety standards for all-terrain vehicles (ATV's) need to be mandated by the U.S. Congress, a representative from Japan-based ATV manufacturer Yamaha Motor Corporation testified at a congressional hearing in May. All-terrain vehicles, motorized off-road vehicles typically designed for one driver, caused 767 deaths and 136,700 injuries in 2005, according to a December 2006 report by the CPSC. Many of the injuries involved children.

The Yamaha spokesman expressed concern that ATV's imported from China posed the greatest safety risks, because Chinese manufacturers had not adopted the same voluntary safety standards as had American and Japanese manufacturers. In June 2007, the CPSC warned that children could be injured or killed while riding the Kazuma Meerkat 50, a Chinese ATV, as a result of braking problems and other defects. ■ Alfred J. Smuskiewicz

See also **Disasters; Food; Public health; Toys and games.**

Sailing. See Boating.
Saint Kitts & Nevis. See Latin America; West Indies.
Saint Lucia. See Latin America; West Indies.
Saint Vincent & the Grenadines. See Latin America; West Indies.
Samoa. See Pacific Islands.
San Marino. See Europe.
São Tomé and Príncipe. See Africa.
Saskatchewan. See Canadian provinces.

Saudi Arabia. Saudi officials introduced an Israeli-Palestinian peace plan in March 2007 at a summit of Arab nations convened in Riyadh, capital of Saudi Arabia. At the conclusion of the summit, delegates called for the resumption of the Israeli-Palestinian peace process based on a "land-for-peace" formula.

In February, Angela Merkel, chancellor of Germany, visited Saudi Arabia to meet with King Abdullah and other Saudi officials about revitalizing the Israeli-Palestinian peace process and supporting the Lebanese government in its standoff with the pro-Syria Hezbollah organization. Tony Blair, former prime minister of the United Kingdom, visited Saudi Arabia in September as the new peace envoy for the Quartet, an association of the European Union, Russia, the United Nations, and the United States working to achieve peace between the Israelis and Palestinians.

United States, Iraq, and Iran. United States Vice President Dick Cheney met with King Abdullah in May while on a trip to the Middle East. The purpose of his trip was to rally "moderate" Arab leaders to use their influence to rein in violence between Sunni and Shi`ah Muslims in Iraq. King Abdullah had warned in April that Sunni-Shi`ah strife could spread into Saudi Arabia if it were not quickly diffused in Iraq and Lebanon.

In July, Zalmay Khalilzad, U.S. ambassador to the United Nations, criticized the Saudis for not doing more to prevent Sunni fighters from crossing into Iraq from Saudi Arabia. Despite the criticism, U.S. Secretary of State Condoleezza Rice and Secretary of Defense Robert Gates visited Saudi Arabia in early August to discuss a multibillion-dollar arms deal to nations in the Middle East, the bulk of which would go to Saudi Arabia.

Petroleum. At a September meeting in Vienna, ministers of the Organization of the Petroleum Exporting Countries (OPEC) voted to raise petroleum production levels by only 500,000 barrels per day—a move that caused the price of U.S. crude oil to reach an all-time high of $99.29 a barrel in November. Before the meeting, there had been much anticipation that Saudi Arabia would call for a more substantial increase in production to lower oil prices on world markets.

Mobile phones. In March, Mobile Telecommunications, the largest operator of mobile telephones in Kuwait, won a new Saudi mobile phone license by agreeing to pay $6.1 billion for the license. Until 2007, Saudi Arabia had only two mobile phone operators—the local Saudi Telecom and Etihad Etisalat, a United Arab Emirates consortium. ■ Mary-Jane Deeb

See also **Iran; Iraq; Israel; Middle East.**

School. See Education.
Senegal. See Africa.

Serbia. The status of Kosovo, a nominal Serbian province, dominated politics in Serbia throughout 2007. On December 10, an international deadline to broker a deal between Serbia and the breakaway region of Kosovo passed after more than four months of intermittent negotiations. The negotiations, brokered by the European Union, Russia, and the United States, failed to break a tense stalemate between Kosovo's ethnically Albanian majority and Serbia's national government in Belgrade, the capital. International affairs experts speculated that with no deal in sight, Kosovo would likely declare itself independent, creating a situation that could stir instability in the Balkans and trigger new tensions between Russia and the West.

Kosovo had, since 1999, been administered by United Nations (UN) officials backed by NATO peacekeepers. International oversight of Kosovo was undertaken to end an armed conflict between Kosovo and Serbia under then-President Slobodan Milosevic. Milosevic had moved Serbian troops into the province to crack down on the ethnic Albanian population. The incursion, accompanied by widely reported atrocities and massive displacement of the ethnic Albanians, resulted in a NATO bombing campaign on Serbia and Serbia's eventual withdrawal.

Since 1999, the status of Kosovo remained

controversial, with most ethnic Albanians support-ing independence and the province's Serb minor-ity, backed by Serbia, opposing it. In interna-tionally monitored elections in Kosovo in Novem-ber 2007—largely boycotted by the Serb minor-ity—Hashim Thaçi, an ethnic Albanian and former guerrilla leader, emerged as the likely leader of a sovereign Kosovo government.

Serbia's coalition government. Elections in Serbia in January led to parliamentary deadlock, which was resolved only after four months of intense negotiations. The ultranationalist Serbian Radical Party won 81 seats in the 250-seat parlia-ment; the Democratic Party of pro-Western Presi-dent Boris Tadic took 64; the Serbian Democratic Party of Prime Minister Vojislav Kostunica held only 47; and the reformist G17 Plus Party took 19. In May, the parties of Tadic, Kostunica, and the G17 Plus Party agreed to form a government, with Kostunica as prime minister.

Economic trends. Economists predicted that the Serbian economy would grow by 6.5 percent in 2007, compared with 5.3 percent in 2006. Infla-tion declined from 12.7 percent in 2006 to an esti-mated 5.7 percent in 2007. Despite these positive trends, about 30 percent of the labor force was unemployed in mid-2007. ■ Sharon L. Wolchik
See also **Europe.**

Sierra Leone. See Africa.

Singapore. In 2007, leaders in Singapore viewed with alarm looming population problems of their prosperous island state. Birth rates had fallen in recent years, and many young profession-als have sought better-paying jobs elsewhere.

On February 9, National Development Minister Mah Bow Tan announced the government's goal of increasing the nation's population from about 4.5 million in 2007 to 6.5 million by 2027. The gov-ernment encouraged couples to have more chil-dren and tried to lure skilled foreign workers. Foreigners already made up more than a fourth of Singapore's population and a third of its work force. According to official estimates, some 87 percent of the 670,000 foreigners working in Sin-gapore were in low-paid, low-skilled work. Some citizens complained that high wages for skilled foreigners and low wages for unskilled workers hurt their own opportunities.

The country's economy was the subject of fur-ther debate after officials announced in April 2007 that Cabinet ministers would receive a 60-percent pay increase by 2008. Officials justified the increase by saying that the government needed to remain competitive with private employment. Prime Minister Lee Hsien Loong promised to give his raise to charity. ■ Henry S. Bradsher
See also **Asia; Indonesia.**

Skating. See Hockey; Ice skating; Sports.

Skiing. Anja Paerson of Sweden made a triumphant return to skiing following knee surgery in 2007, capturing her first three races at the Alpine World Championships in Åre, Sweden, in February.

However, on the World Cup circuit, the Aus-trian women reigned, capturing 23 races and all the discipline titles for the first time since the 1998-1999 season. Austria's Nicole Hosp captured the overall lead on the second-to-last race of the season at Lenzerheide, Switzerland, and then secured the championship by winning the final event—the giant slalom—on the final day of the season.

In men's skiing competition, Aksel Lund Svindal of Norway captured the overall World Cup title on the final day as well. Svindal fin-ished 15th in the final slalom, and he also was victorious in the giant slalom and combined disciplines.

Men's World Cup. Svindal barely held off defending overall title holder Benjamin Raich of Austria to grab his title, finishing with 1,268 points. Had Svindal finished 0.08 seconds slower in the final slalom—which Raich won to claim that discipline's title—he would have finished second. Other title winners were Switzerland's Didier Cuche (downhill) and American Bode Miller (super-giant slalom).

Women's World Cup. Hosp took the lead in the overall chase away from teammate Marlies Schild on March 17 by winning the slalom in Lenzerheide. Schild, who won the first seven slalom races of the season and the discipline title, finished second in the overall points with 1,482, which was 90 behind Hosp. Renate Götschl won the downhill and super-giant slalom titles. Schild also won the combined title.

Alpine world championships. After win-ning the super-giant slalom on February 6 in Åre, Paerson captured the combined race on February 9 and the downhill on February 11. Paerson's run ended when she fell in the giant slalom on February 13, which was won by Hosp. Paerson added a fourth medal—a bronze—in the slalom on February 16. Sárka Záhrobská of the Czech Republic won the race.

Svindal was the only male skier to capture more than one title and became the first Nor-wegian to win the downhill gold at a world championship. His victory came on February 11. Svindal won the giant slalom three days later.

Italy's Patrick Staudacher won the super-giant slalom on February 6, Switzerland's Daniel Albrecht won the combined two days later, and Austria's Mario Matt took the slalom on February 17. Austria won the team event on February 18. ■ Michael Kates
See also **Sports.**

Slovakia. In 2007, the ruling coalition led by Prime Minister Robert Fico—comprised of Fico's left-of-center Smer Party, the Movement for a Democratic Slovakia, and the extreme nationalist Slovak National Party—continued to modify the strongly market-oriented policies of his predecessor, Mikulas Dzurinda. The Fico government followed up its 2006 successes of raising the minimum wage and halting major privatization plans with reforms to the country's labor code in July 2007. The reforms strengthened job protection for workers and gave labor unions greater negotiating power with management. Some economists cautioned that such policies might brake Slovakia's dynamic economy, which in recent years attracted substantial foreign investment.

Slovakia's economy grew by an estimated 8 percent in 2007, compared with 8.3-percent growth in 2006. The rate of unemployment fell to 8.3 percent in June 2007 from 9.4 percent in December 2006. The inflation rate, which had been running at above 4 percent in 2006, decreased to 2.4 percent in 2007. Slovakia's success in reducing inflation positioned it to adopt the euro—the currency used in 13 member nations of the European Union (EU)—on schedule in 2009, noted EU observers.

Foreign affairs. Prime Minister Fico honored a 2006 campaign pledge by bringing home the approximately 100 Slovakian soldiers and engineers participating in the United States-led coalition in Iraq. The last Slovaks left Iraq in late 2007.

In May, Fico traveled to Moscow for an official visit with Russian President Vladimir Putin. They discussed Russian oil and gas deliveries to customers in Slovakia and a Russian offer to help Slovakia expand its nuclear power industry. At a press conference on his return to Bratislava, the Slovak capital, Fico criticized EU and U.S. leaders for developing plans to build an antimissile defense system in Europe, with installations planned for the Czech Republic and Poland. Analysts speculated that Fico's remarks might chill Slovak-U.S. relations.

Relations with neighboring Hungary frayed in 2007, in part due to a criminal case that stirred considerable controversy among Slovakia's Hungarian minority. The case involved a Hungarian woman who claimed that she had been beaten by Slovakian youths in Bratislava in August 2006 because she was speaking Hungarian. Local Slovakian police investigating the incident alleged that the woman had fabricated her story. In September 2007, Slovak's general prosecutor turned the case over for further investigation to a five-member panel to be monitored by the country's interior minister.   ■ Sharon L. Wolchik

See also **Europe; Russia.**

Slovenia. See **Europe.**

Soccer in 2007 continued to be the world's most popular team sport. There were almost 400 national leagues as well as major international competitions.

International soccer. With the 2010 World Cup scheduled for South Africa and the 2014 event in Brazil, interest focused on two major continental competitions. European national teams contested the qualifying stages for the 2008 European Championship. England failed to qualify, and Coach Steve McLaren was fired, while Scotland lost its final match to Italy. African squads from 47 nations focused on the preliminary rounds for the Africa Cup of Nations, to be played in Ghana in 2008. International calls leading to the absence of highly paid players from club squads for weeks, and the frequent resulting injuries, caused occasional friction between club and national coaches.

Continental cups. Indonesia, Malaysia, Thailand, and Vietnam co-hosted the Asian Cup from July 7 to 29, 2007. The tournament brought a rare moment of national jubilation to Iraq, whose team triumphed 1-0 over Saudi Arabia in the final. Iraq earned the right to represent the AFC (Asian Football Confederation) in the FIFA Confederation Cup of 2009. FIFA is the Fédération Internationale de Football Association, the governing body for international soccer.

The Copa America, organized by CONMEBOL (Confederación Sudamericana de Fútbol), was staged for the first time in Venezuela in 2007. Twelve nations competed from June 26 to July 15. Brazil beat old rival Argentina 3-0 in the final, with Mexico defeating Uruguay for third spot. Brazilian ace Robinho (Robson de Souza) was the top scorer in the tournament, with six goals. Despite its loss, Argentina topped Brazil in world rankings, with 2006 World Cup winner Italy in the third spot.

CONCACAF (the Confederation of North, Central American and Caribbean Association Football) restricted its 2007 Gold Cup competition to regional teams. The United States triumphed 2-1 against Mexico in the final on June 24 at Soldier Field in Chicago, its fourth success in the Gold Cup. Respected youth coach John Hackworth was appointed assistant to U.S. men's national team head coach Bob Bradley.

International club competitions. The FIFA Club World Championship, played in December 2006 in Japan, was won by South American champions Sport Club Internacional (Brazil), which beat FC Barcelona (Spain) 1-0.

AC Milan of Italy won the UEFA (Union of European Football Associations) European Champions' League on May 23, 2007. AC Milan beat Liverpool (England) 2-1 in the final in Athens, Greece, with two goals from Filippo Inzaghi earning a fifth winner's medal for captain Paolo Maldini. Another AC Milan star, Brazilian striker Kaká, was named world

David Beckham (right), one of the world's most famous soccer players, left Real Madrid in July to join the Los Angeles Galaxy. The Galaxy management hailed the former captain of the England national team as a global marketing boost.

player of 2007 by FIFPro (the Fédération Internationale des Footballeurs Professionels).

In the MTN African Champions League run by the CAF (Confederation of African Football), Etoile du Sahel of Tunisia beat five-time champions Al Ahly of Egypt on November 10 in Cairo, Egypt. Entente Setif (Algeria) won the Arab Champions League on May 17 in Amman, Jordan. Boca Juniors of Argentina won the Copa Libertadores de América, the cup competition of CONMEBOL, on June 20 in Porto Alegre, Brazil. The Nissan Copa Sudamericana, drawing 34 teams, was won by Pachuca of Mexico on Dec. 13, 2006, in Santiago, Chile. The UEFA Cup in Europe produced an all-Spanish final in Glasgow, Scotland, on May 16, 2007. Sevilla beat Espanyol 3-1 on a penalty shootout, after the teams drew 2-2 in extra time. Sevilla was the first team to win this trophy two years running since Real Madrid in 1985 and 1986.

Domestic leagues. Familiar names triumphed in Europe's domestic leagues, in which so many international soccer stars competed. Manchester United won the English Premiership on May 6; Glasgow Celtic, the Scottish Premiership on April 22; PSV Eindhoven, the Dutch league (for the third successive year) on April 29; VFB Stuttgart, the German Bundesliga on May 20; and Inter Milan, Italy's Serie A on October 10. Real Madrid won the Spanish Primera Liga on June 17 for the 30th time, ending a four-year spell without the title.

The final of the FA (Football Association) Cup, the oldest knockout competition in soccer, returned on May 19, 2007, to its traditional venue, London's Wembley Stadium, newly rebuilt. The result was a 1-0 victory for Chelsea over Manchester United. However, success did not prevent the subsequent departure of Coach José Mourinho, who left the London club in September 2007, after a falling-out with Russian owner Roman Abramovich.

Money talks. Although not on the same scale as the 2006 Italian match-fixing scandal, British soccer was troubled in 2007 by police investigations into alleged illegal financial transactions involving players' agents and transfer deals. Some fans were concerned that the swelling number of billionaire owners in the English Premier League might prove a mixed blessing. Chelsea (Roman Abramovich), Manchester United (Malcolm Glazer, United States), and Liverpool (Tom Hicks and George Gillett, United States) were all foreign-owned, arousing suspicion among British fans about the owners' loyalties and long-term motives. New income enabled such clubs to rebuild stadiums and buy top players at inflated transfer fees but widened the gap between the "super-rich" and the rest. Critics also worried about the future strength of the English and Scottish national teams, with league coaches in both nations usually trying to buy success or survival through experienced imports, rather than by developing young players.

Major League Soccer (MLS). In July, the world's most media-exposed soccer star, David Beckham, moved from Europe (Real Madrid) to MLS in North America. Beckham signed with the Los Angeles Galaxy. The former captain of the England national team was hailed by Galaxy management as a global marketing boost. Beckham joined other designated players under the rule implemented for 2007 that allowed each MLS club to sign up to two players normally considered outside its salary cap. Other newcomers included Denilson de Oliveira (FC Dallas), Cuauhtemoc Blanco (Chicago Fire), and Juan Pablo Angel (New York Red Bulls). Debutants Toronto FC made a slow start in the Eastern Conference of the MLS but received enthusiastic crowd support at their BMO Field.

SuperLiga. This new competition featured eight teams in two pools from Mexico and the United States. Pachuca of Mexico beat the L.A. Galaxy 4-3 on penalty kicks after a 1-1 tie on August 29 in Carson, California. MLS Cup champion Houston Dynamo and Supporters Cup winner DC United also made the final round of four, emphasizing the growing strength of the MLS. Another team enjoying success was the New England Revolution, which beat FC Dallas 3-2 to win the Lamar Hunt U.S. Open Cup on October 3 in Frisco, Texas.

Women's soccer. The women's game continued to grow in 2007, with national teams in nearly 150 countries. The highlight of the year was the Women's World Cup, held in China in September, with 16 teams competing. The United States, Brazil, Norway, and Germany made it to the last four. The strong German team, captained by veteran striker Birgit Prinz, demonstrated its intent with an 11-0 trouncing of Argentina in the opening game and won the final 2-0 against Brazil. Brazil's Marta Veira da Silva, an exciting, skillful 21-year-old, was the top scorer with seven goals and the individual star of a tournament that was a tribute to the growing professionalism of the women's game. Fans looked forward to the next World Cup, to be held in Germany in 2011.

The United States took third place in the 2007 World Cup, beating Norway 4-1 in the play-off match. U.S. Soccer president Sunil Gulati announced that women's national team coach Greg Ryan would leave his post at the end of his contract in 2007.

Death. Alan Ball, one of England's 1966 World Cup-winning team members, died on April 25, 2007, at age 61. He played in 975 games from 1962 to 1983 and won 72 caps. ■ Brian Williams

Social Security. In their 2007 report, the Social Security and Medicare trustees projected that, without reforms, the Social Security trust fund would be exhausted by 2041, and the Medicare hospital insurance trust fund would be exhausted by 2019—in each case, one year later than had been projected in 2006. The 2007 report, issued on April 23, also predicted that both funds' payments to beneficiaries would grow rapidly between 2010 and 2030 and that the rapid growth of Medicare payments would continue past 2030. Social Security payments would begin to exceed tax revenues in 2017, the report projected, and Medicare hospital insurance payments were expected to begin exceeding tax revenues in 2007. The rise in payments was expected because of the retirement of *baby boomers*—the 78 million people born from 1946 to 1964—and, in the case of Medicare, because of rising health care costs. The trustees expressed increasing concern about congressional inaction on entitlement reform.

On Oct. 17, 2007, the Social Security Administration announced that monthly Social Security and Supplemental Security Income benefits would increase by 2.3 percent in 2008. This cost-of-living adjustment was smaller than the 3.3-percent increase in 2007. ■ Mike Lewis

See also **Health care issues.**

Solomon Islands. See Pacific Islands.

Somalia. By early 2007, the transitional government of Somalia had regained control of Mogadishu, the country's capital and largest seaport. During December 2006, heavy fighting between Ethiopian-led forces supporting the transitional government and militias fighting for the Union of Islamic Courts (UIC), the Islamist movement that captured Mogadishu in mid-2006, forced the UIC to evacuate the city.

By early January 2007, both the principal government leaders, President Abdullahi Yusuf Ahmed and Prime Minister Ali Mohamed Ghedi, had established themselves in the capital. However, the 275-member National Assembly provisionally remained based west of Mogadishu in Baydhabo.

As many of the Islamist troops fled southward to the port city of Kismaayo and the Kenyan border, they were seen as a threat to Kenya's security. Moreover, United States forces, suspecting al-Qa`ida collaborators to be among the fleeing forces, launched an air strike on suspected terrorist training camps near the Kenyan border on January 7. Ethiopian warplanes also bombed Islamist bases during this offensive. Qa`ida associates thought to be in southern Somalia included men wanted by the United States for masterminding the bombing of the U.S. embassies in Kenya and Tanzania in 1998.

The involvement of Ethiopian forces in Somalia proved to be very unpopular among the Somali clans and prompted clan leaders to declare a *jihad* (holy war) on what they considered invaders. The dilemma for the Somali transitional government was that it relied heavily on military assistance from outside the country to enforce stability. Moreover, many African countries had already made a heavy commitment to contribute troops to the enlarged United Nations-African Union (AU) peacekeeping force in Sudan's Darfur region, which made it difficult for them to provide troops for a Somalian peacekeeping force. Nevertheless, several African countries promised to send troops for the proposed 8,000-member AU peace force to Somalia (known as AMISOM), though only about 1,500 Ugandan soldiers had arrived by the end of the year.

Regional division. The troubles in Somalia also led to a split in the Intergovernmental Authority on Development (IGAD), a regional organization established in 1986 to promote cooperation for development among the countries in northeastern Africa. On the one hand, the countries of Kenya, Ethiopia, and Uganda, which had welcomed the agreement leading to a transitional Somalian government in 2004, continued their support for this government. On the other hand, the country of Eritrea, which had tense relations with Ethiopia after their 1998-2000 war, was accused of assisting Ethiopia's enemies in Somalia. Djibouti, which borders the northern Somaliland region of Somalia, took a more neutral stance. Somaliland regarded itself as having seceded from Somalia in 1991 and had since been striving for international recognition. It therefore had avoided becoming embroiled in Somalian affairs or anything that might jeopardize its internal stability.

In the middle of 2007, the transitional government convened a reconciliation conference with the various clan leaders, but no breakthroughs were made. By the end of the year, Somalia remained one of the most unstable countries in Africa. The numerous instances of violence included bombings, gunfights, and assassination attempts on Prime Minister Ghedi, President Yusuf, and other members of the transitional government. The country increasingly suffered from Iraq-style suicide attacks. By the end of the year, about 1 million people had fled their homes because of the violence.

In October, Ghedi resigned as prime minister. Analysts suggested it was due to several disagreements that arose between Ghedi and Yusuf. In November, Yusuf nominated Nur Hassan Hussein, also known as Nur Adde, as prime minister.

■ Pieter Esterhuysen

See also **Africa; Sudan; United Nations.**

South Africa. Throughout 2007, public debate in South Africa focused on the succession struggle within the African National Congress (ANC), the country's governing party, and on other related matters. In December, the ANC held a national conference to elect six of its top officeholders, including the president. It was the first contested ANC leadership election in 58 years.

ANC presidential race. South African President Thabo Mbeki, who had served as the ANC president since 1997, indicated that he would be available for another term as ANC president, though the country's Constitution precluded him from serving another term as South Africa's president. His term as national president was to end after national elections in 2009. The Constitution allows a president to serve a maximum of two terms.

Mbeki's main rival for the ANC presidency was ANC Deputy President Jacob Zuma. Zuma enjoyed wide support in 2007, including that of the ANC alliance partners, the Congress of South African Trade Unions (COSATU) and the South African Communist Party (SACP). Members of the ANC Youth League were among the deputy president's most ardent supporters.

However, the National Prosecuting Authority (NPA) seemed likely to reinstate corruption charges against Zuma (which had been delayed since 2006). As a result, many analysts initially felt that it would be difficult for Zuma to mount a credible leadership bid at the ANC conference. The business sector also expressed concerns that the ANC's successful market-oriented economic policies would change should Zuma come to power. However, Zuma went out of his way to assure business people, including overseas investors, that he would support the party's current policies.

Because of the ANC party division over Mbeki and Zuma, the names of a few ANC stalwarts, including successful businessmen Cyril Ramaphosa and Tokyo Sexwale, were mentioned as possible compromise candidates. Ramaphosa's name was put forward as an ANC presidential candidate in October 2007, despite warnings that his image as a capitalist was not appealing to ANC left-wingers. Sexwale later withdrew his name from the presidential race to become ANC chairperson.

Political experts noted that the person elected ANC president would have a good chance of becoming South Africa's next president in 2009. The South African president is not elected by popular vote, as is the case in most republics, but by the members of both houses of Parliament in a joint parliamentary session. Therefore, it was a foregone conclusion that the majority party's presidential candidate, which is usually the party president, would be elected as South Africa's president in 2009.

The ANC election. In December, the ANC held its leadership conference and nominated only Mbeki and Zuma for the presidency of the party. After two days of fierce debate, the delegates voted overwhelmingly for Zuma, who won 2,329 votes, compared with Mbeki's 1,505 votes. Zuma supporters were also elected to the other five leadership positions. On December 28, prosecutors charged Zuma with racketeering and tax evasion, throwing into doubt his candidacy as the future president of South Africa.

Economy. In February 2007, Finance Minister Trevor Manuel surprised Parliament by presenting a national budget showing a surplus, the first in South Africa's history. The surplus resulted from higher tax revenue, mostly due to increasingly efficient tax collection. Manuel also conceded that some of the funds in the previous budget could not be spent because of the lack of administrative skills among civil servants.

Nevertheless, the budget reflected several years of economic growth (just under 5 percent on average), mainly the result of sound economic policies and management of the nation's finances. Development indicators issued by the government revealed a number of positive aspects. *Per capita* (per person) growth in the economy, which had been negligible in the 1980's and 1990's, increased substantially in the early 2000's, reaching almost 4 percent in 2006. Furthermore, government debt as a percentage of the *gross domestic product* (GDP)—the total value of goods and services produced by a country in a year—had declined to about 30 percent, and further declines were expected. In 1994, the year that the ANC government first took office, government debt stood at about 45 percent of the GDP.

By 2007, the South African government's policy was to accelerate economic growth by making substantial expenditures on transport infrastructure, power generation, education (including labor skills), and health services. Most economists agreed with the ANC government that the country's high crime rate and the unacceptable unemployment and poverty levels would in the long run be significantly reduced through high economic growth.

Labor strikes. At the end of May, hundreds of thousands of South African civil servants and teachers from across the country demonstrated and marched for higher wages. Represented by their respective unions, the workers demanded a pay raise of 12 percent to help keep up with inflation, which had risen to 5.5 percent. The government initially offered a pay raise of 6 percent. The strike was the largest in South Africa since the end of apartheid, the nation's former policy of racial segregation, in 1994. After four weeks of the strike, which shut down businesses, schools, and hospitals, the government and the unions compromised with a 7.5-percent raise in pay.

Sports. In October 2007, South African rugby fans cheered as the South Africa Springboks beat England's team in the Rugby World Cup. The Springboks last won the Webb Ellis trophy in 1995. The victory was seen by many South Africans as a symbol of unity for the country, even as a debate raged on about the possibility of imposing a racial quota on the team.

Deaths. Adelaide Tambo, a political activist and wife of ANC leader Oliver Tambo, died on Jan. 31, 2007, at the age of 77. Marais Viljoen, the last ceremonial president of South Africa, died on January 4 at age 81. He had served as president from 1979 to 1984. Lucky Dube, a reggae and *mbaqanga* (a highly rhythmic Zulu musical form) singer and musician, was killed by thieves on Oct. 18, 2007, at the age of 43. Percy Sonn, the first African president of the International Cricket Council, died on May 27 at age 57.

■ Pieter Esterhuysen

See also **Africa; Zimbabwe.**

South America. See **Latin America** and the various country articles.

Space exploration. Weather on two planets wreaked havoc for human and robotic space exploration in 2007. On Earth, a sudden hailstorm at Kennedy Space Center in Florida in February pummeled the insulating foam on the space shuttle Atlantis's huge external propellant tank. The hail caused extensive damage shortly before the shuttle's scheduled March 15 launch to continue assembly of the International Space Station (ISS). On Mars, a planetwide dust storm in July and August blanketed the rovers Spirit and Opportunity, cutting off the sunlight that their solar cells turn into electric power to drive their systems.

Both bouts of bad weather delayed scheduled activities. Controllers at the Jet Propulsion Laboratory in Pasadena, California, feared the Mars Exploration Rovers would not survive the dust storm and would fall silent for good as their batteries ran down. But careful power management kept the rovers alive until the atmosphere cleared. In fact, the rovers performed so well as they resumed their missions at opposite ends of Mars that National Aeronautics and Space Administration (NASA) administrators extended their mission—for the fifth time—through 2009.

ISS engineers at NASA and its European and Japanese partners worried that the time needed to repair Atlantis's hail damage would delay installation of the Columbus and Kibo laboratory mod-

Saturn glows blue and gold as its dark rings cast reverse images of themselves onto the planet in an image captured by the Cassini spacecraft in February. One of Saturn's moons, Dione, appears as a tiny speck in the distance (above).

The Cassini spacecraft, launched in 1997, captured stunning images of Saturn and its moons in 2007.

Pock-marked mountains about 6 miles (10 kilometers) high dot an equatorial ridge on Iapetus, another of Saturn's moons. Cassini flew to within 2,400 miles (3,870 kilometers) of the planet's surface during its only close flyby in September to capture this image.

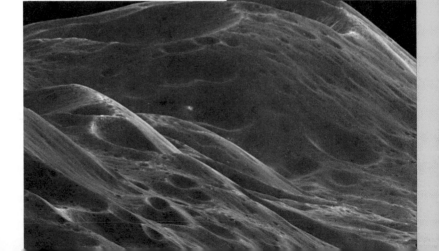

Saturn and its rings appear in their entirety in an unusual full-on view that Cassini captured from above the planet in January. Daylight glows on one side of the planet, nighttime covers the other side in darkness, and a narrow strip of twilight around the middle of the sphere allows scientists a glimpse of Saturn's atmosphere. The planet casts its shadow over its rings on the dark side.

Saturn and many of its main rings are captured in an infrared image taken by Cassini in April, as the space probe flew 900,000 miles (1.4 million kilometers) above the planet's surface. Saturn's rings are reflected in colored bands back onto the planet, and a small storm swirls in the planet's center, just above the uppermost of the two bands.

United States astronaut Barbara Morgan operates a control panel on the space shuttle Endeavour while docked to the International Space Station in August 2007. Morgan was the backup "teacher in space" in 1986 when the shuttle Challenger, carrying teacher Christa McAuliffe, exploded.

ules. Space station construction was on a tight schedule, because the space shuttles were slated to be retired in 2010. However, hard work and good luck allowed NASA to get back on track.

Space shuttle and ISS. After repairs to Atlantis were completed, NASA and its partners made good progress building the orbiting outpost. Atlantis was launched on June 8, 2007, carrying a third set of 240-foot- (73-meter-) long solar arrays. In a series of space walks, astronauts installed the arrays on the *starboard* (right) side of the station's main truss. When the task was completed, the station's appearance was finally symmetrical. The solar arrays rotated like windmills, allowing as much sunlight as possible to reach their electricity-generating solar cells. Atlantis astronauts also finished folding up a solar array—designated P6—in preparation for its move to the port (left) side of the truss. The P6 had been providing power for the station since November 2000.

Work continued in August 2007 with mission STS-118 on the shuttle Endeavour. While engineers on the ground analyzed a small gouge in three of the fragile thermal protection tiles on the orbiter's belly—caused by a piece of insulating foam that fell off the external fuel tank during the August 8 launch—the crew conducted four more spacewalks to continue assembling the ISS. They installed a short "spacer" at the starboard end of

the truss to provide clearance for the fourth and final solar array wing later in the assembly sequence and cleared hardware out of the way so the station's mobile transporter could carry the P6 array wing down the truss rails to the port end.

Spacewalkers also replaced a gyroscope that had been shut down when it began vibrating dangerously and brought the unit home for analysis and repair. The station has four gyroscopes that help keep the solar arrays pointed toward the sun without using precious fuel.

Students on the ground got a long-awaited lesson from space when astronaut Barbara Morgan taught classes on space flight from the ISS. Morgan was the backup "teacher in space" in 1986 when the explosion of the space shuttle Challenger took the lives of New Hampshire teacher Christa McAuliffe and the rest of the crew. It took 21 years to reschedule the activity.

In October 2007, the shuttle Discovery returned to the station for what was to be the most complex mission in the nine-year assembly sequence of the ISS. The STS-120 crew delivered the "Harmony" pressurized node, a capsule to which Europe's Columbus and Japan's Kibo laboratories were to be attached, and helped the ISS crew move the P6 array wing to its final position. When Discovery docked with United States astronaut Pamela Melroy in command, she and her crew were greeted by astronaut Peggy Whitson, the first woman to command the ISS. The meeting also marked the first time that the shuttle and the space station were commanded by women at the same time.

The already complicated mission grew even more so when the P6 array tore as it was being unfurled. Astronaut Scott Parzynski rode an improvised crane to the site to make repairs. His tools were covered in insulating tape to protect him from electric shock, because the arrays cannot be turned off once they are exposed to the sun.

In December, Atlantis was scheduled to carry the Columbus laboratory to the ISS. However, problems with a gauge in the fuel tank forced NASA to postpone the flight until January 2008. Japan's Kibo was to be launched in 2008 as well.

Robotic probes from many nations were launched or continued their missions to the planets, the moon, and other celestial bodies in 2007. In January, NASA launched the New Horizons probe, which swung past Jupiter on its way to Pluto. The probe captured spectacular images of the largest planet, its almost-invisible rings, the volcano Tvashtar on Jupiter's moon Io, and the frozen surface of Jupiter's moon Europa. NASA launched the Phoenix Mars Lander in August, which was expected to reach Mars in May 2008. NASA's Messenger probe, en route to Mercury, made its second pass of Venus in June 2007. Dawn, NASA's probe to the asteroids Vesta and Ceres, was finally launched in September after a series of delays.

In April, the Japan Aerospace Exploration Agency's (JAXA's) Hayabusa probe began its return to Earth from the asteroid Itokawa. Scientists believed it was carrying a sample of the asteroid in a storage canister. On September 14, JAXA launched its Selene probe for the moon. Selene (for *Sele*onological and *En*gineering *Ex*plorer) was nicknamed Kaguya after a moon princess in Japanese folklore. The probe—the largest spacecraft to reach the moon since Apollo 17 in 1972—went into orbit on Oct. 4, 2007, exactly 50 years after the former Soviet Union launched Sputnik I, the first artificial satellite to orbit Earth. Kaguya was to study the moon's gravity and magnetic field and search for water ice.

China launched its first probe to the moon on October 24, from the Xichang Satellite Launch Center in southwestern China. The Chang'e 1 (named after a goddess who flew to the moon in Chinese folklore) was to orbit the moon for a year, analyzing its composition and mapping its surface.

India launched a space capsule in January that successfully orbited Earth for 11 days and splashed down in the Bay of Bengal on January 22.

◼ Frank Morring, Jr.

See also **Astronomy.**

Spain. Prime Minister José Luis Rodríguez Zapatero's Socialist Workers' Party (PSOE) prepared in 2007 to confront the opposition conservative Popular Party in general elections in March 2008. The governing party, which had ruled from a minority position with the toleration of several regional parties since 2004, lagged behind the Popular Party in local elections in May 2007. The Popular Party, which governed from 1996 to 2004, regained popularity in 2007 because of Zapatero's perceived inability to control the Basque separatist group ETA. ETA, whose initials stand for Basque Homeland and Freedom in the Basque language, had been fighting for independence for Spain's northern Basque region since the late 1960's.

ETA. In March 2007, controversy surrounded Zapatero's decision to permit an ETA terrorist to serve the final portion of a three-year sentence under house arrest rather than in prison. The terrorist, Iñaki De Juana, had previously served an 18-year sentence for killing 25 people during ETA attacks. He began a hunger strike to publicize the cause of Basque independence and his second internment, which was for writing articles interpreted as threatening further ETA violence. Pro-government observers claimed that Zapatero's act of leniency was designed to prevent De Juana's being revered as a martyr, should he die in prison from his hunger strike. The majority of Spaniards polled in surveys, however, considered the move an unwise act that would strengthen extremists.

Some 350,000 demonstrators, led by Popular Party leader Mariano Rajoy, marched in Madrid, the capital, on March 10 to protest the prisoner's release. Under pressure from both his own party and the opposition, Zapatero banned ETA's allied political party, Batasuna, from running in the May local elections. In June, ETA announced an end to its self-imposed 15-month cease-fire.

Terror trial. In October, a Madrid court convicted 21 defendants—most of them Islamic radicals—for the bombing of four trains on March 11, 2004, that left 191 people dead and 1,800 others injured. The trial ended persistent rumors that ETA was involved in the bombings. Most of the guilty were North African Muslim immigrants not directly affiliated with al-Qa`ida but clearly inspired by the Islamic terrorist group. The victims' families were angered because only three defendants were convicted of murder; the investigation did not uncover who masterminded the conspiracy; and 18 of the defendants received sentences that the families deemed too lenient.

Economy. Spain continued to experience strong economic growth in 2007. European Union economists projected the economy would grow by 3.8 percent in 2007, down slightly from 3.9 percent in 2006.

◼ Jeffrey Kopstein

See also **Europe.**

Sports. Scandals permeated professional sports in 2007, including criminal behavior by National Football League (NFL) players, gambling allegations against a National Basketball Association (NBA) official, and doping violations that knocked out the Tour de France leader and stained a past champion. State and federal investigations into illegal online distribution of steroids and other performance-enhancing drugs led to a February raid on a Florida pharmacy that ensnared athletes in several sports and threatened to mushroom into a larger scandal as the year ended.

Barry Bonds, the San Francisco Giants slugger, was indicted by a federal grand jury on five charges of perjury and obstruction of justice in November as part of the Bay Area Laboratory Co-operative (BALCO) steroid distribution investigation. On the field, Bonds established a new Major League Baseball record for regular-season home runs, passing Hank Aaron by hitting his 756th homer on August 7 in San Francisco.

On December 13, former U.S. Senator George Mitchell issued a 409-page report on steroid use in professional baseball. The report outlined rampant abuse of steroids and human growth hormone and gave the names of 87 players who allegedly had taken the drugs.

The NFL's new commissioner, Roger Goodell, instituted severe punishments for repeat criminal offenders. In the most noteworthy case, Goodell suspended indefinitely Atlanta Falcons quarterback Michael Vick, one of the league's most popular and marketable players, after Vick pleaded guilty in a federal dogfighting case in Virginia. Vick allegedly bankrolled the operation on his property and was present when dogs were killed. On December 10, a federal judge sentenced Vick to 23 months in prison.

NBA Commissioner David Stern accepted the resignation of official Tim Donaghy, who authorities said fed information on games he was officiating as well as his "picks" to gamblers and bookies. Donaghy also reportedly gambled on games he officiated but was not accused of fixing games.

Titles. In professional team sports, the San Antonio Spurs in June captured their third NBA title in five years; the Anaheim Ducks in June won their first Stanley Cup in the National Hockey League (NHL); the Indianapolis Colts triumphed in the 2007 Super Bowl in the NFL in February; and the Boston Red Sox ran away with Major League Baseball's World Series in October.

In professional golf, Tiger Woods captured one major title and finished second in two others. He also became the fifth golfer to notch 60 PGA TOUR victories. In tennis, Switzerland's Roger Federer for the second straight year won three of the four majors, taking the Australian Open, Wimbledon, and U.S. Open tournaments and losing in the final

of the French Open. American tennis champions Venus and Serena Williams enjoyed rebound years, with each winning a major title.

Tour de France. Alberto Contador, a 24-year-old Spanish rider, captured the Tour de France on July 29, winning the 2,205-mile (3,550-kilometer) race by 23 seconds over Cadel Evans of Australia. However, the race was tainted by massive scandal. In September, Floyd Landis, the 2006 champion, lost his title and faced a two-year suspension for alleged doping violations. In October 2007, he filed an appeal. Kazakh Alexandre Vinokourov, a pre-race favorite, tested positive for a banned blood transfusion after winning a time trial on July 21, 2007, prompting his team to pull out of the Tour on July 24. The next day, leader Michael Rasmussen of Denmark was removed from the race after winning the 16th stage. He was just four stages away from victory and was heavily favored. Rasmussen's team said he was expelled for violating team rules and providing incorrect information about his whereabouts after he missed a random drug test in June. He had also missed a test in May.

Before the race even started, the 1996 champion, Danish cyclist Bjarne Riis, and two teammates admitted taking performance-enhancing drugs. Officials asked Riis to return his yellow jersey. The revelation linked the top three finishers in the 1996 event to doping. Riis's admission came only weeks after noted Italian cyclist Ivan Basso admitted his involvement in a 2006 doping scandal.

Duke lacrosse scandal. All remaining charges against three lacrosse players at Duke University in Durham, North Carolina, were dropped in April 2007. The players, who were falsely accused of rape, received a settlement from Duke and sought $30 million from Durham. In September, Mike Nifong, the district attorney who prosecuted the case, served one day in jail for lying under oath. He was also disbarred for ethics violations.

Award. Russian-born American swimmer Jessica Long of Baltimore in April became the first paralympian to win the AAU James E. Sullivan Award, which is presented to the top amateur athlete in the United States by the Amateur Athletic Union. Long holds 12 paralympian swimming records.

Biathlon. Noway's Ole Einar Bjorndalen captured gold medals in the 12.5-kilometer pursuit and 10-kilometer sprint, and Germany's Magdalena Neuner took gold medals in the 10-kilometer pursuit, 7.5-kilometer sprint, and 4x6-kilometer relay at the World Championships in Antholz, Italy, in early February 2007.

Bobsled and skeleton. Yevgeni Popov of Russia won the men's four-man World Cup title, and American Steve Holcomb captured the two-man title. Sandra Kiriasis of Germany won the women's two-man World Cup title. Zach Lund and Katie Uhlaender of the United States won the season skeleton World Cup titles.

At the world championships in St. Moritz, Switzerland, in February, Kiriasis and fellow German André Lange each captured two-man titles, and Ivo Rüegg piloted Switzerland to the four-man bobsled title. American Noelle Pikus-Pace and Switzerland's Gregor Stähli won the skeleton world championships. Kiriasis and Karl Angerer of Germany took the inaugural bobsled-skeleton combined title.

Cross-country skiing. Tobias Angerer of Germany and Virpi Kuitunen of Finland easily captured World Cup titles in Oslo, Norway, in March.

Equestrian. Beat Mändli of Switzerland won the individual show jumping title at the 2007 World Cup Final in April in Las Vegas. Germany's Isabell Werth took the top prize in dressage.

Gymnastics. Shawn Johnson won the United States gymnastics championships women's all-around title on August 18 in San Jose, a day after David Durante won the men's title. At the world championships in Stuttgart, Germany, the U.S. women won the gold. Defending champion China came in second, with Romania placing third. In the men's team competition, China captured the gold; Japan was second; and Germany was third. Johnson also won the women's all-around title. Chinese gymnast Yang Wei became the first man since 1926 to repeat as all-around champion.

Marathon running. In terrible weather conditions that nearly forced the cancellation of the 111th Boston Marathon, Kenya's Robert Cheruiyot became the eighth man to win at least three races by capturing the 2007 installment on April 16. Russian Lidiya Grigoryeva won the women's race.

Nordic combined. Finland's Hannu Manninen won his fourth straight combined World Cup title as well as the 7.5-kilometer sprint at the world championships in Sapporo, Japan, in March. Norway finished atop the medal standings with 16.

The top male runners set off in terrible weather that nearly forced the cancellation of the Boston Marathon, held on April 16, 2007, in Hopkinton, Massachusetts. Robert Cheruiyot of Kenya won the men's race, and Lidiya Grigoryeva of Russia placed first in the women's race.

Rodeo. Trevor Brazile won his fifth all-around World Champion Cowboy title in the past six years in the Wrangler National Finals Rodeo, held in December in Las Vegas.

Rowing. The Canadian clubs Shawnigan Lake School and Victoria City Rowing Club captured the marquee event, the Grand Challenge Cup, on July 8 at the Henley Royal Regatta in Henley-on-Thames, England, beating a crew from the Australian Institute of Sport by ¼ length. A team from Harvard University in Cambridge, Massachusetts, topped Molesey Boat Club of England and the New York Athletic Club by one length to win the Ladies' Challenge Plate.

At the world championships in Munich, Germany, in September, the United States defended its title in the women's eights race, and Canada collected its first title since 2003 with its win in the men's eights race. New Zealand's Mahe Drysdale (men's singles sculls) and Belarus's Ekaterina Karsten (women's singles sculls) won their third straight gold medals.

Ski jumping. Adam Malysz of Poland won his fourth World Cup title in March 2007, in Planica, Slovenia, with his third consecutive large-hill victory.

Sled dog racing. Lance Mackey of Fairbanks, Alaska, won his state's Iditarod Trail Sled Dog Race on March 13, becoming the first musher to win major long-distance North American sled dog races back to back. He finished the 1,150-mile (1,850-kilometer) Iditarod, which goes from Anchorage to Nome, in 9 days, 5 hours, 8 minutes, and 41 seconds, his first win in six attempts. On February 20, Mackey had won his third straight Yukon Quest International Sled Dog Race, which covers 1,000 miles (1,600 kilometers) from Fairbanks to Whitehorse, Canada.

Soap Box Derby. Kacie Rader of Mechanicsville, Maryland, won the Masters Division of the 70th annual All-American Soap Box Derby on July 23 in Akron, Ohio.

Speed skating. At the World Sprint Championships in Hamar, Norway, on January 21, South Korea's Lee Kyou-hyuk won the men's title, and Anni Friesinger of Germany won the women's title. At the World All-Around Speed Skating Championships in Heerenveen, Netherlands, Sven Kramer of the Netherlands broke his own 10,000-meter world record and won the men's overall title on February 11. Ireen Wüst, also of the Netherlands, won the women's title.

Five world records fell at the World Single Distances Championships in March in Kearns, Utah. South Korea's Lee Kang-seok set a new mark in the 500 meters, Germany's Jenny Wolf broke a six-year-old mark in the women's 500 meters, Sven Kramer set a new mark in the 10,000 meters, Martina Sáblíková of the Czech Republic set a new

mark in the 5,000 meters, and the men's team from the Netherlands set a new record in the team pursuit.

At the World Short Track Championships in Milan, Italy, in March, South Korea's Ahn Hyun-Soo won the men's title, while South Korea's Jin Sun-Yu won the women's title. South Korea dominated the event, winning 18 medals in the 12 categories, including 9 gold medals.

Triathlon. Vanessa Fernandes of Portugal and Daniel Unger of Germany won at the world championships in Hamburg, Germany, in September.

Other champions:

Archery. The International Archery Federation's World Championships in Leipzig, Germany, in July: men's compound, Dietmar Trillus, Canada; women's compound, Eugenia Salvi, Italy; men's recurve, Im Dong-Hyun, Korea; women's recurve, Natalia Valeeva, Italy; men's compound team, United States; women's compound team, Belgium; men's recurve team, Korea; women's recurve team, Korea.

Badminton. The Badminton World Federation's World Championship in Kuala Lumpur, Malaysia, in August: men's singles, China's Lin Dan; men's doubles, Indonesia's Markis Kido and Hendra Setiawan; women's singles, China's Zhu Lin; women's doubles, China's Zhang Jiewen and Yang Wei; mixed doubles, Indonesia's Nova Widianto and Lilyana Natsir.

Curling. Men's world champion, Canada; women's world champion, Canada.

Field hockey. Men's Champions Trophy, Germany, on December 9 in Kuala Lumpur; women's Champions Trophy, the Netherlands, on January 21 in Quilmes, Argentina.

Lacrosse. Men's National Collegiate Athletic Association (NCAA) champion, Johns Hopkins University in Baltimore; women's NCAA champion, Northwestern University in Evanston, Illinois.

Motorcycle racing. FIM Grand Prix MotoGP champion, Casey Stoner, Australia.

Table tennis. World Champions: men, Wang Liqin, China; women, Guo Yue, China; men's doubles, Chen Qi and Ma Lin, China; women's doubles, Wang Nan and Zhang Yining, China; mixed doubles, Wang Liqin and Guo Yue, China.

Water polo. World Cup champions: men, Croatia; women, United States, both on April 1 in Melbourne, Australia.

Weightlifting. Women's 165-pound (75-kilogram) champion, Natalia Zabolotnaya, Russia; men's 231-pound (105-kilogram) champion, Evgeny Chigishev, Russia. ■ Michael Kates

See also **Australian rules football; Baseball; Basketball; Boating; Boxing; Football; Golf; Hockey; Horse racing; Ice skating; Olympic Games; Skiing; Soccer; Swimming; Tennis; Track and field.**

Sri Lanka. A savage internal war that had ravaged Sri Lanka intermittently since 1983 flared with new intensity in 2007, with thousands of people killed and hundreds of thousands of others driven from their homes. The war was between the government backed by the nation's Buddhist Sinhalese majority and a faction of its Hindu Tamil minority, the Liberation Tigers of Tamil Eelam (LTTE). The LTTE sought independence for Tamil areas of northern and eastern Sri Lanka.

More than 64,000 people were killed in fighting and LTTE suicide attacks prior to a 2002 cease-fire. The LTTE ended the cease-fire in 2006 and, by late 2007, an additional 5,000 people had been killed. Sri Lanka's army claimed it had taken control of formerly LTTE-dominated areas in the east by July, but fighting across the Tamil areas of northern Sri Lanka continued.

Progress and setbacks. The LTTE used air power for the first time in 2007. On March 26, two light aircraft smuggled onto the island bombed the Sri Lankan air force's main base, near the capital, Colombo. On October 22, an LTTE attack on an air force base killed more than 30 people and destroyed eight aircraft.

On September 2, Sri Lanka's army claimed to have captured a base used to smuggle weapons onto the island by sea. On October 7, a navy spokesperson announced that the navy had destroyed the last seaworthy LTTE boat, dealing a major blow to the rebels' smuggling operation.

Many cases of mysterious abductions, torture, and murder were reported from Jaffna, a northern city isolated by LTTE forces. An army general suggested security forces and civilian supporters could be trying to eliminate LTTE operatives in extrajudicial ways. United Nations (UN) Human Rights Commissioner Louise Arbour visited Jaffna on a fact-finding mission in October. She expressed concern, but Sri Lanka rejected calls for a visit by a UN human rights monitoring mission.

Citing security reasons, the government expelled nearly 400 ethnic Tamils from Colombo in early June. The city had been the target of LTTE suicide attacks. Sri Lanka's Supreme Court halted the deportations on June 8.

On November 2, S. P. Tamilselvan, the LTTE's political chief, was killed in an air strike. Tamilselvan had helped negotiate the 2002 cease-fire.

Economy. The Sri Lankan economy's growth rate in 2007 was, at about 6 percent, one of the lowest in South Asia. The war hurt development and discouraged tourists, and the cost of fighting the LTTE continued to rise. The military budget increased 40 percent in 2007. Inflation was running at about 17 percent late in the year.

■ Henry S. Bradsher

See also **Asia.**

State government. Some state governments held off-year elections in 2007, and others pushed for new presidential primary dates and struggled to balance budgets. Discontent over federal programs and policies caused some states to take matters generally considered national affairs, such as immigration, into their own hands.

Elections. Three states elected governors in 2007. On November 6, Democrat Steve Beshear, Kentucky's former lieutenant governor, defeated one-term Republican Governor Ernie Fletcher by almost a 20-percent margin. Beshear called for a public vote on legalizing casino gaming, which Fletcher opposed. Fletcher, the state's first Republican governor in more than 30 years, suffered in public opinion after he pardoned administration officials who were accused of illegally rewarding political supporters with state jobs. In Mississippi, Republican incumbent Governor Haley Barbour defeated Democrat John Eaves to win a second term.

In Louisiana's blanket primary election on October 20, Republican United States Representative Bobby Jindal won 54 percent of the vote over 11 challengers, therefore avoiding a runoff. In 2003, Jindal lost to Democratic Governor Kathleen Blanco. Weakened by her performance following Hurricane Katrina in 2005, Blanco did not seek another term. Jindal, whose parents emigrated from India, became the first person of Asian Indian ancestry to be elected governor of a U.S. state. At age 36, he was also set to become the nation's youngest sitting elected governor.

Nationwide, the gubernatorial party split stood at 28 Democrats and 22 Republicans in late 2007. In the November 6 state legislative elections, Democrats won control of the state senates in Mississippi and Virginia and retained control of both chambers in New Jersey.

Revenue. Most states were in good fiscal shape in 2007, according to a survey released in December by the National Governors Association and the National Association of State Budget Officers. At least 20 states faced prospective budget problems in 2008 due to slow sales tax revenues and the slump in the housing market. The report's authors noted that Wisconsin had to cut its 2007 budget mid-year as well as its fiscal 2008 budget by $116.5 billion.

In October 2007, Michigan Governor Jennifer Granholm and the state legislature agreed on a $9.7-billion budget and $1.3 billion in tax hikes. Also that month, Florida legislators finalized agreements on budget cuts to colleges, public schools, hospitals, and nursing homes to plug a $1.1-billion hole in the state's budget. In November, California Governor Arnold Schwarzenegger ordered all state agencies to prepare plans to cut spending by 10 percent across the board in 2008. Also in November 2007, Maryland passed $1.3 billion in tax increases to address a projected $1.7-billion shortfall for 2008

A gay couple celebrates at the state-house in Boston after Massachusetts lawmakers voted on June 14, 2007, to strike down a proposed ban on same-sex marriage in the state. In 2004, Massachusetts became the only state that allows same-sex marriage.

taxed slot machines to help build a $300-million hockey arena for the Pittsburgh Penguins. Alaska lawmakers approved Governor Sarah Palin's plan to seek bids from firms to construct a pipeline to transport natural gas from Alaska's North Slope to the lower 48 states. Officials expected the pipeline to cost $20 billion.

Environment. In December, the administration of U.S. President George W. Bush denied a bid by Governor Schwarzenegger to regulate greenhouse gas emissions from automobiles in California. Federal law required that states receive permission from the Environmental Protection Agency to implement emissions standards. Schwarzenegger vowed to take the decision to court. Hawaii, New Jersey, Minnesota, and Washington moved in 2007 to limit smokestack emissions of gases, and 12 states agreed to cut greenhouse gas emissions from cars. Legislation prohibiting smoking in public places was signed in Illinois, Maryland, Minnesota, New Hampshire, New Mexico, and Oregon. In November, Governors Bob Riley of Alabama, Charlie Crist of Florida, and Sonny Perdue of Georgia met with U.S. Secretary of the Interior Dirk Kempthorne and other Bush administration officials to settle a dispute over division of water resources when a drought caused water problems for Atlanta. In December, Kempthorne signed a water-sharing agreement with Arizona, California, Colorado, Nevada, New Mexico, Utah, and Wyoming to control the impact of drought on states that draw from the Colorado River.

Federal-state concerns. States dramatically changed the 2008 presidential primary calendar as larger states moved up their election dates. Iowa and New Hampshire laws required that they hold their elections before other states. Although Democratic National Committee rules allowed only Iowa, New Hampshire, Nevada, and South Carolina to select candidates before February 5, Florida and Michigan moved their primary contests to January 2008. More than 20 states chose February 5 to vote on presidential contenders. Several other states also scheduled primaries or caucuses for February 2008.

and cut spending by $550 million. The state doubled the cigarette tax to $2 a pack and coupled a one-cent sales tax hike with a middle-income income-tax cut.

The legislatures of Connecticut, Delaware, Indiana, Iowa, Maryland, New Hampshire, Tennessee, and Wisconsin voted in 2007 to raise cigarette taxes. Additionally, cigarette taxes increased in Alaska, Hawaii, Idaho, and Texas due to previous years' legislative or electoral actions. Florida, Indiana, Montana, Nebraska, New York, North Dakota, Ohio, and Vermont moved to ease property taxes. In Tennessee, both houses voted for the state's first reduction in the food tax, which had been the nation's highest. Arkansas, Utah, and West Virginia also reduced sales taxes on groceries, and South Carolina and Wyoming completely removed the tax. Hawaii offered larger food excise tax credits.

Economic development. The Alabama Legislature approved a $400-million incentive package that successfully lured a German steel mill to the state. Mississippi put up nearly $295 million to attract a Toyota auto plant to Tupelo. Pennsylvania

SELECTED STATISTICS ON STATE GOVERNMENTS

State	Resident population*	Governor†	Legislature† House (D)	House (R)	Senate (D)	Senate (R)	State tax revenue‡	Tax revenue per capita‡	Public school expenditure per pupil§
Alabama	4,599,030	Bob Riley (R)	61	43	23	12	$ 8,530,000,000	$1,850	$ 7,670
Alaska	670,053	Sarah Palin (R)	17	23	9	11	2,484,000,000	3,710	10,390
Arizona	6,166,318	Janet Napolitano (D)	27	33	13	17	11,713,000,000	1,900	5,700
Arkansas	2,810,872	Mike Beebe (D)	75	25	27	8	6,959,000,000	2,480	8,910
California	36,457,549	Arnold Schwarzenegger (R)	47	32	25	15	111,347,000,000	3,050	8,830
Colorado	4,753,377	Bill Ritter (D)	39	26	20	15	8,522,000,000	1,790	8,900
Connecticut	3,504,809	M. Jodi Rell (R)	107	44	24	12	12,132,000,000	3,460	13,010
Delaware	853,476	Ruth Ann Minner (D)	19	22	13	8	2,861,000,000	3,350	12,570
Florida	18,089,888	Charlie Crist (R)	42	78	14	26	37,202,000,000	2,060	8,490
Georgia	9,363,941	Sonny Perdue (R)	73	107	22	34	17,034,000,000	1,820	8,800
Hawaii	1,285,498	Linda Lingle (R)	43	8	21	4	4,919,000,000	3,830	10,430
Idaho	1,466,465	C. L. "Butch" Otter (R)	19	51	7	28	3,143,000,000	2,140	7,180
Illinois	12,831,970	Rod Blagojevich (D)	67	51	37	22	28,129,000,000	2,190	10,400
Indiana	6,313,520	Mitch Daniels (R)	51	49	17	33	13,626,000,000	2,160	9,330
Iowa	2,982,085	Chet Culver (D)	53	47	30	20	6,119,000,000	2,050	8,140
Kansas	2,764,075	Kathleen Sebelius (D)	47	78	10	30	6,275,000,000	2,270	8,800
Kentucky	4,206,074	Steve Beshear (D)	63	37	#16	21	9,953,000,000	2,370	8,460
Louisiana	4,287,768	Bobby Jindal (R)	**53	50	24	15	9,651,000,000	2,250	8,660
Maine	1,321,574	John Baldacci (D)	**90	59	18	17	3,590,000,000	2,720	12,060
Maryland	5,615,727	Martin O'Malley (D)	104	37	33	14	14,550,000,000	2,590	10,300
Massachusetts	6,437,193	Deval Patrick (D)	140	19	34	5	19,395,000,000	3,010	13,290
Michigan	10,095,643	Jennifer Granholm (D)	58	52	17	21	23,715,000,000	2,350	10,210
Minnesota	5,167,101	Tim Pawlenty (R)	85	49	44	23	17,331,000,000	3,350	10,140
Mississippi	2,910,540	Haley Barbour (R)	75	47	28	24	5,990,000,000	2,060	6,870
Missouri	5,842,713	Matt Blunt (R)	71	92	14	20	10,180,000,000	1,750	8,170
Montana	944,632	Brian Schweitzer (D)	††49	50	26	24	2,126,000,000	2,250	8,680
Nebraska	1,768,331	Dave Heineman (R)	unicameral (49 nonpartisan)				3,961,000,000	2,240	8,310
Nevada	2,495,529	Jim Gibbons (R)	27	15	10	11	6,153,000,000	2,470	6,960
New Hampshire	1,314,895	John Lynch (D)	#239	158	14	10	2,081,000,000	1,580	10,790
New Jersey	8,724,560	Jon Corzine (D)	48	32	23	17	24,849,000,000	2,850	14,680
New Mexico	1,954,599	Bill Richardson (D)	41	28	24	18	5,111,000,000	2,610	9,040
New York	19,306,183	Eliot Spitzer (D)	108	42	29	33	54,549,000,000	2,830	14,210
North Carolina	8,856,505	Mike Easley (D)	68	52	31	19	20,603,000,000	2,330	8,000
North Dakota	635,867	John Hoeven (R)	33	61	21	26	1,622,000,000	2,550	8,230
Ohio	11,478,006	Ted Strickland (D)	46	53	12	21	24,637,000,000	2,150	10,560
Oklahoma	3,579,212	Brad Henry (D)	44	57	24	24	7,784,000,000	2,170	7,080
Oregon	3,700,758	Ted Kulongoski (D)	31	29	#17	11	7,590,000,000	2,050	8,990
Pennsylvania	12,440,621	Ed Rendell (D)	102	101	21	29	29,051,000,000	2,340	11,300
Rhode Island	1,067,610	Don Carcieri (R)	60	13	33	5	2,742,000,000	2,570	11,500
South Carolina	4,321,249	Mark Sanford (R)	51	73	19	27	7,760,000,000	1,800	9,270
South Dakota	781,919	Mike Rounds (R)	20	50	15	20	1,182,000,000	1,510	8,240
Tennessee	6,038,803	Phil Bredesen (D)	53	46	#16	16	10,650,000,000	1,760	7,260
Texas	23,507,783	Rick Perry (R)	69	80	11	20	36,592,000,000	1,560	8,050
Utah	2,550,063	Jon Huntsman, Jr. (R)	20	55	8	21	5,459,000,000	2,140	5,550
Vermont	623,908	James Douglas (R)	‡‡93	49	23	7	2,407,000,000	3,860	13,390
Virginia	7,642,884	Tim Kaine (D)	**44	54	21	19	17,192,000,000	2,250	9,790
Washington	6,395,798	Christine Gregoire (D)	62	36	32	17	16,411,000,000	2,570	8,730
West Virginia	1,818,470	Joe Manchin III (D)	72	28	23	11	4,558,000,000	2,510	10,070
Wisconsin	5,556,506	Jim Doyle (D)	47	52	18	15	13,795,000,000	2,480	10,430
Wyoming	515,004	Dave Freudenthal (D)	17	43	7	23	2,122,000,000	4,120	13,330

*July 1, 2006, estimates. Source: U.S. Census Bureau.
†As of January 2008. Source: National Governors' Association;
National Conference of State Legislatures; state government officials.
‡2006 figures. Source: U.S. Census Bureau.
§2006-2007 estimates for elementary and secondary students in fall enrollment.
Source: National Education Association.

#One independent.
**Two independents.
††One Constitutional Party.
‡‡Six Progressive Party, two independents.

Both major parties punished states for early primaries. Penalties included depriving states of half or all of their delegate seats at the national conventions. However, many political experts predicted that the revoked delegate slots would ultimately be restored.

Impatient with federal inaction to stem illegal immigration, several states implemented their own responses. Arizona adopted tough laws aimed at employers who hire undocumented workers and activated National Guard troops to patrol its border with Mexico. Oklahoma also passed laws aimed at cutting off public benefits to illegal immigrants.

Eight states voted in 2007 to disobey a 2005 federal law setting new criteria for state driver's licenses. The states maintained that the proposed federal requirements, aimed at keeping out terrorists, were costly and ineffective.

Capital punishment. On Sept. 25, 2007, the U.S. Supreme Court announced that it would hear a Kentucky case challenging lethal injection as cruel and unusual punishment banned by the U.S. Constitution. Court observers expected that a majority of justices would block all executions until the court decided the case in the spring of 2008. In December 2007, New Jersey lawmakers abolished the death penalty in that state.

Health. While Congress and the Bush administration fought over extension and expansion of the State Children's Health Insurance Program providing coverage to poor children, at least 16 states expanded their own versions of the federal program. In September 2007, Indiana received federal permission for an expansion of health coverage under the federal-state Medicaid program. Low-income adults in Indiana were asked to contribute a percentage of their incomes to health savings accounts to gain access to as much as $300,000 in coverage. Indiana raised cigarette taxes to pay for the expansion, which was expected to assist 130,000 uninsured families and childless adults.

While President Bush vetoed expanded federal funds for embryonic stem-cell research for the second year in a row, New York in 2007 became the sixth state to finance such research by approving a $600-million program. In a referendum on November 6, New Jersey voters rejected a plan to borrow $450 million for stem-cell research.

Gay rights. Massachusetts lawmakers in June affirmed the commonwealth's three-year-old court ruling allowing gay marriage. In May, New Hampshire became the fourth state to allow civil unions for gay couples, joining Connecticut, New Jersey, and Vermont. Also, Washington and Oregon joined California, Hawaii, and Maine in allowing same-sex couples to register as domestic partners, allowing spousal privileges.   ■ Elaine McDonald

See also **Courts; Democratic Party; Elections; Global warming; Immigration; Republican Party.**

Stocks and bonds. The United States stock market took investors on a roller-coaster ride in 2007. Unlike the steady gains registered in the second half of 2006, share prices seesawed widely throughout 2007, setting record highs and then sliding to a 10-percent loss. Still, by early December, indexes of large-company stocks were up modestly.

Stock-market volatility reflected a global loss of confidence in the market for debt securities linked to U.S. home mortgages; a slowdown in the pace of U.S. corporate profit growth; a run-up in oil prices to nearly $100 a barrel; and evidence that a six-year expansion of the U.S. economy was running into trouble.

By early December 2007, the Dow Jones Industrial Average, an index of the stock prices of 30 major companies, was up more than 8 percent for the year—to 13,518—compared with a 16 percent increase for the full year 2006. The Dow reached a record high of 14,164 on Oct. 9, 2007.

The Standard & Poor's 500 Index, which reflects the stock prices for a diversified group of 500 major U.S. companies, was up 5 percent in 2007. Shares of small companies fared less well. The Russell 2000 Index of 2,000 small-company stocks was off 2 percent, posting its first annual decline since 2002. The decline was also the first time the index fell below Standard & Poor's since 1998.

The first stock market disruption of 2007 occurred in late February, when a slide in both the Shanghai and the Hong Kong stock markets sparked fears that the economic and stock-market boom in China was reversing. China's stocks, which were mainly emerging-market stocks, had become popular with U.S. investors in recent years. On a single day—Feb. 27, 2007—the Shanghai Stock Market dropped nearly 9 percent and the Hong Kong Stock Market dropped nearly 2 percent. But Chinese stocks rallied and, by early December, China's emerging-markets index was up nearly 35 percent for the year.

The second shock to U.S. investors came in August, also from overseas, when the United States was in the midst of a worsening housing market. Investors throughout the world who had purchased high-yielding securities linked to bundles of U.S. home mortgages lost confidence that they—or anyone else—knew what the securities were worth. The credit turmoil quickly spilled into debt securities unrelated to housing.

The Federal Reserve System (the Fed), the central bank of the United States, took extraordinary action aimed at soothing fears. In August, September, October, and December 2007, the Fed cut its interest rate on the loans it makes to banks. In September, October, and December, the Fed cut the interest rates on overnight loans between banks to 4.25 percent, from the 5.25 percent it had held since June 2003. By taking these steps, the Fed hoped to make money more readily available to the banking system.

The stock market rallied in response to most of these measures. In early October, share prices rose to record highs. But fears reemerged in November, as reports suggested that economic growth in the United States was slowing. By late November, stocks had retreated 10 percent from their October record highs.

Bonds rally. Prices of U.S. Treasury bonds fell in the early part of 2007, reflecting a springtime rebound in the economy. But a deepening slump in the housing market and rising fears of mortgage defaults and foreclosures caused investors to buy U.S. Treasury securities as a safe haven.

By early December 2007, the yield on 10-year U.S. Treasury notes was down to 3.9 percent from a peak of 5.3 percent in June. Yields on debt securities move opposite to their price.

Returns on riskier debt securities, known as high-yield debt, declined in 2007, reflecting credit-market fears. As a result, investors in mutual funds who had focused on high-yield debt earned just 1.6 percent through early December, compared with an 8.5 percent return on long-term government bond funds.

Winners and losers. Energy-company stocks were the big winners in 2007. In futures trading, crude oil traded at nearly $100 a barrel in November, up from $61 at the end of 2006. Shares of oil producer Exxon Mobil Corporation were up 16 percent through early December.

Health care stocks rallied late in 2007, as investors switched to health care and consumer-goods companies that tend to do better at times of economic stress. Drug maker Merck & Co. was the top performer in the Dow Jones Industrial Average, up 35 percent by December.

Technology stocks posted better performance in 2007 than in 2006, reflecting improved profitability and investor preference for stocks unrelated to housing. Intel Corporation, a semiconductor manufacturer, was up 34 percent.

Financial service companies, beset with losses in their mortgage operations, were the worst performers in 2007. Citigroup Inc., a global financial services company, fell 40 percent.

International markets. Continued weakness in the U.S. dollar helped investors in overseas markets, even though major non-U.S. stock markets performed in line with Wall Street.

The biggest disappointment was the Tokyo Stock Exchange, where prices were off nearly 10 percent, despite a strong summer rally.

■ Bill Barnhart

See also **Bank; Economics, United States; Economics, World; International trade.**

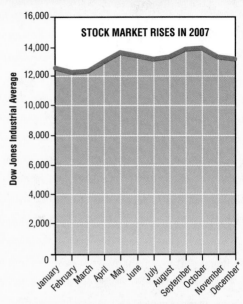

STOCK MARKET RISES IN 2007

Dow Jones Industrial Average

January February March April May June July August September October November December*

Closing month averages for 2007
* December figure is as of the 17th.

Share prices remained relatively stable through the first nine months of 2007 until a credit crisis involving defaulting subprime mortgages drove the Dow from a high of 14,164 on October 9 into a 10-percent slide.

Sudan. The continuing conflict in Darfur, in western Sudan, was the focus of much international attention in 2007. Of at least equal importance, though, was the fact that the fragile peace accord between the Sudanese government and rebel groups in southern Sudan was in jeopardy of dissolving into renewed north-south civil war.

Southern Sudan. In October, the Sudan People's Liberation Movement (SPLM), the largest former rebel group in southern Sudan, withdrew from the national unity government, which had been created as a result of the 2005 Comprehensive Peace Agreement. That accord, between the Sudanese government and the SPLM, granted *autonomy* (limited self-government) to southern Sudan. The SPLM complained that the National Congress Party (NCP), its partner in the unity government, had not lived up to its agreements, including respect for borders of the southern autonomous region, the withdrawal of government troops from southern areas, and the distribution of Sudan's petroleum-generated income.

In November 2007, Clement Juma Mbugoniwia, chairman of the United South Sudan Party, announced that the objective of his party, which was formed in 2005, was to promote peace and democracy. Mbugoniwia maintained, however,

Government-backed Arab militiamen belonging to the Janjaweed ("devils on horseback") patrol the countryside of Darfur near the border with Chad. The Janjaweed continued its attacks on both rebels and civilians in Darfur throughout 2007, terrorizing much of the population.

The conflict between government forces and rebel groups that began in 2003 in the Darfur region of Sudan led to escalating lawlessness and insecurity in 2007.

Soldiers belonging to the Sudan Liberation Movement (SLM), the largest rebel group in Darfur, cruise through a refugee camp in the town of Gereida in March. Strategically located Gereida, in southern Darfur, was a major focal point of fighting between the SLM and Janjaweed in 2007.

Two sisters care for their wounded brother at a hospital in Gereida in March. Bandits attacking a convoy of trucks shot the man in the leg. Villages in Darfur in 2007 were increasingly the targets of roaming bands of criminals and militiamen, who attacked, robbed, and raped the local people.

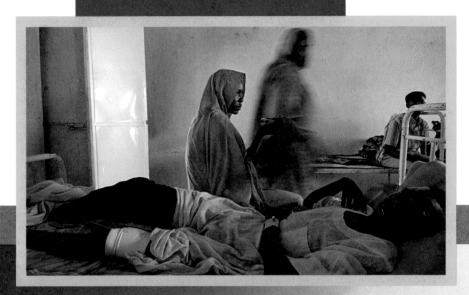

A village in southern Darfur burns after being attacked by Arab nomads backed by government forces. Hundreds of villages have suffered similar fates since the beginning of the conflict in Darfur, resulting in hundreds of thousands of displaced civilians throughout the region.

that although he supported the Comprehensive Peace Agreement, he preferred a fully independent southern Sudan. He called the idea of a united Sudan "unachievable" and "a waste of time, in human life and resources."

Attacks on Darfur peacekeepers. Unidentified gunmen shot and killed five Senegalese peacekeepers from the African Union (AU) in northwestern Darfur in April 2007. The AU is an organization working to achieve cooperation among African nations. In September, a group of rebels attacked an AU peacekeeping base in Darfur, killing 10 peacekeepers and wounding several more people. This attack was the deadliest assault on AU personnel in the three years since the AU peacekeeping mission began in Sudan.

Peace talks in Libya. Mediators from the AU, the European Union, and the United Nations met in Sirte, Libya, in October to negotiate a peace settlement among the various factions involved in the fighting in Darfur. The Sudanese government was represented at the conference, but all of Darfur's rebel movements were not. The Justice and Equality Movement, one of the largest rebel groups in Darfur, boycotted the talks. Abdul Wahid al-Nur, leader of the Darfur-based Sudan Liberation Movement, also refused to attend the meetings, claiming that peace talks should take place only after security was established in Darfur.

Although the outcome of the Sirte talks was inconclusive, the convening of the conference led to the declaration in October of a *unilateral* (one-sided) cease-fire by the Sudanese government.

Block B oil rights. The French petroleum company Total SA assumed operating rights, involving a 32.5-percent stake, to the disputed, potentially oil-rich "Block B" region in southern Sudan in June after reaching agreement with the national unity government. Kuwait-based Kufpec Sudan Ltd. increased its share in Block B to 27.5 percent. Sudapet, the state-owned oil company, and Nilepet, a company operated by the autonomous southern Sudanese government, each maintained their 10-percent shares.

Marathon Oil Corporation, headquartered in Houston, was formerly in partnership with Total SA. However, Marathon was forced to withdraw from the Block B consortium in 2007 because of United States sanctions prohibiting U.S. firms from conducting business in Sudan.

An insult to Islam. British teacher Gillian Gibbons was deported on December 3 after serving 9 days of a 15-day jail sentence for "insulting Islam." Gibbons had allowed her 7-year-old Sudanese students to name a teddy bear "Mohammed," which a Sudanese court found insulting to the Prophet Muhammad. Her sentence of 40 lashes was suspended. ■ Mary-Jane Deeb

See also **Africa; Middle East; United Nations.**

Supreme Court of the United States.

The conservative wing of the Supreme Court flexed its muscle during the court's 2006-2007 term, which lasted from Oct. 2, 2006, to June 28, 2007. Chief Justice John Roberts and Justices Antonin Scalia, Clarence Thomas, Samuel Alito, and Anthony Kennedy—all conservatives—made up the majority in several 5-to-4 rulings on contentious ideological issues, including school integration, abortion, student speech, and campaign finance. The court's tilt to the right was also reflected in probusiness rulings on worker pay and antitrust law. But in a few 5-to-4 decisions, including a ruling on greenhouse gas regulation and the overturning of four Texas death sentences, Kennedy sided with the court's liberal wing—Justices John Paul Stevens, Ruth Bader Ginsburg, Stephen Breyer, and David Souter. In 2007, Kennedy clearly emerged as the court's ideological centrist and, therefore, its pivotal swing voter.

School integration. The court on June 28 struck down two public school district programs that used race as a factor in assigning students to schools. In a 5-to-4 vote, the court ruled that the school placement programs in Seattle and in Louisville, Kentucky, violated the U.S. Constitution's 14th Amendment, which guarantees equal protection. Both programs sought to achieve diversity by setting goals for representation of different racial groups at each school. Both districts were sued by parents of students who had been denied admission to their chosen schools on the basis of race.

In the majority opinion, Roberts wrote that racial classifications may be used only to achieve a compelling government interest. Remedying the effects of past intentional discrimination is a compelling interest, but it was not involved in the Seattle and Louisville cases: Seattle schools had never been legally segregated, and Louisville schools had already been desegregated as much as practicable. In addition, he wrote, the court has previously held that student body diversity is a compelling interest, but it has done so only in the context of higher education and has stressed that diversity programs must consider several factors, not just race alone. Furthermore, he wrote, the Seattle and Louisville districts failed to show that they had considered alternative approaches to achieving their diversity goals.

In a dissenting opinion, Breyer characterized the ruling as a radical departure from settled law. He predicted that the ruling would obstruct efforts to deal with growing resegregation and could lead to a rise in race-related litigation.

Campaign finance. In a 5-to-4 decision on June 25, the court loosened a restriction in the 2002 Bipartisan Campaign Reform Act, also called the McCain-Feingold Act. The court ruled that the act's ban on "electioneering communication" was unconstitutionally broad. Electioneering communication refers to broadcast advertisements, paid for by businesses, unions, or advocacy groups, that mention a candidate for federal office and are aired within 30 days before a primary election or 60 days before a general election. The court held that "issue ads"—that is, ads that deal generally with public issues—can be banned only if they explicitly promote a candidate's election or defeat. Prohibiting any other mention of a candidate, the court ruled, is a violation of the organizations' First Amendment right to free speech.

Abortion. On April 18, 2007, the court issued a 5-to-4 decision upholding the 2003 Partial-Birth Abortion Ban Act, which prohibits a late-term abortion procedure called intact dilation and extraction. The procedure involves removing an intact fetus from the womb via the cervix. In the majority opinion, Kennedy wrote that the ban does not impose an undue burden on a woman's right to an abortion because alternative abortion procedures remain available. He also wrote that there is medical uncertainty over whether the ban subjects women to health risks, and so long as this uncertainty persists, the ban is allowable.

Student speech. On June 25, 2007, the court ruled 5 to 4 that an Alaska high school principal did not violate a student's First Amendment right to free speech when she punished him for displaying a banner reading "Bong Hits 4 Jesus" at a school-sponsored event. After the student refused the principal's demand to take down the banner, the principal suspended the student for 10 days. In the majority opinion, Roberts wrote that schools may censor student expression if it can reasonably be viewed as encouraging illegal drug use.

Greenhouse gas emissions. In a 5-to-4 decision on April 2, the court ruled that, under the Clean Air Act, the Environmental Protection Agency (EPA) has the power to regulate carbon dioxide and other greenhouse gases emitted by new motor vehicles. Furthermore, the court ruled, the EPA cannot refuse to set emissions standards unless it provides a science-based rationale for its refusal. In 2003, the EPA declined to regulate greenhouse gas emissions, saying that it lacked the authority to do so, and that even if it did have the authority, it might choose not to exercise it because of scientific uncertainty about global warming. The court concluded that the EPA failed to provide a reasoned, law-based explanation for its decision not to regulate.

Church and state. On June 25, 2007, the court ruled 5 to 4 that taxpayers could not sue the administration of U.S. President George W. Bush over its use of tax dollars for the White House Office of Faith-Based and Community Initiatives. Bush created the office in 2001 to help religious groups obtain federal grants for social programs. A secular advocacy group sued, alleging that the office violated the First Amendment

clause prohibiting an "establishment of religion" by the state. But the court ruled that taxpayers can make Establishment Clause challenges to federal spending only when the spending results from a specific action or appropriation by Congress.

Worker pay. A 5-to-4 decision on May 29, 2007, made it harder for workers to sue employers for pay discrimination. The court ruled that, under current U.S. law, discrimination suits are allowed only if the worker has filed a complaint with the Equal Employment Opportunity Commission (EEOC) within 180 days after the alleged discriminatory act. The ruling came in a case involving a female supervisor at a Goodyear Tire & Rubber Company plant in Alabama. She alleged that she was being paid less than her male peers because of past sex discrimination. The court ruled that she could not claim damages for pay decisions made years before she filed her EEOC complaint, even if her paychecks issued after the complaint reflected the effects of those decisions.

On June 11, the court ruled 9 to 0 that home health care workers—including those employed by agencies as well as those employed directly by people needing care—are not entitled to minimum wage and overtime pay guarantees under the Fair Labor Standards Act. The ruling upheld a U.S. Labor Department interpretation of the act.

Antitrust law. In a 5-to-4 vote on June 28, the court ruled that manufacturers are not automatically prohibited from setting a minimum price that retailers must charge for the manufacturer's goods. The ruling overturned an antitrust precedent that the court had established in 1911. Under that precedent, the fixing of minimum retail prices was an automatic violation of the Sherman Antitrust Act. But the 2007 court ruled that minimum price agreements could potentially promote competition rather than hinder it and that such agreements should therefore be judged on a case-by-case basis for antitrust purposes.

Sentencing. On December 10, early in its 2007-2008 term, the court issued two 7-to-2 rulings that gave federal judges more leeway in criminal sentencing. The court upheld a crack cocaine sentence that was more lenient than that prescribed by federal sentencing guidelines, which call for tougher sentences for crack than for powder cocaine. Critics have called the guidelines racially unfair, because crack is most often used by blacks, and powder cocaine is most often used by whites. The court also upheld a relatively light sentence involving the drug Ecstasy. In both cases, the court ruled that the sentencing guidelines were advisory and that judges could make reasonable deviations from them.   ■ Mike Lewis

See also **Courts; Disability; New York City.**

Suriname. See Latin America.
Swaziland. See Africa.

Sweden. Prime Minister Fredrik Reinfeldt's right-of-center Moderate Party ruled in a four-party coalition government in 2007. The coalition took over the reins of power in 2006 from the Social Democrats, who had governed for 65 of the past 74 years. Reinfeldt's government quickly found itself embroiled in a series of scandals involving conflict of interest and ministerial resignations. Surveys reported the government's rapidly decreasing popularity and the rising status of the opposition Social Democrats, especially after the party replaced its leader, Göran Persson, with the charismatic Mona Sahlin in March 2007. Sahlin became the first woman to serve as leader of the Social Democratic Party.

The government was determined, however, to avoid the mistakes of previous right-of-center parties, which tended to scare voters by threatening to dismantle Sweden's comprehensive welfare state. Reforms, therefore, although intended to lower taxes and cut unemployment benefits, proceeded slowly in 2007 and only after strong public relations efforts by government leaders.

Foreign policy. Swedes in 2007 expressed concern about Russia's newly assertive stance and began to reconsider the merits of joining the North Atlantic Treaty Organization (NATO). Since the early 1900's, Sweden had remained officially neutral, refusing to join any international military organization. However, in February 2007, Swedish Foreign Minister Carl Bildt remarked that Russia had taken some "steps backwards." In April, Russia supported riots by the minority Russian population of Estonia, Sweden's neighbor across the Baltic Sea. The violence was followed by a "cyber-attack" upon Estonia's computer network that authorities traced to Russian computers. Swedes were especially concerned about a planned Russian-German gas pipeline slated to run along the bottom of the Baltic Sea along Sweden's coast.

Sweden began closer cooperation on surveillance and intelligence with Norway, which belongs to NATO, to monitor Russia more closely. In addition, the Swedish government indicated in April a willingness to join NATO's Response Force, a unit established in 2002 to serve as a rapid-response, antiterror unit. Nevertheless, political analysts maintained that any change in Sweden's security alliance would not occur soon.

Economy. Although Sweden belonged to the European Union (EU), it had not adopted the euro by 2007. After rapid growth in 2006, EU economists predicted Sweden's economy would grow at a still-healthy rate of 3.4 percent in 2007.

Ingmar Bergman. Sweden's highly accomplished film and theater director, died in July at the age of 89. ■ Jeffrey Kopstein

See also **Estonia; Europe; Motion pictures: Ingmar Bergman.**

Swimming. Michael Phelps of the United States became only the second swimmer to win seven gold medals at a major international event with his performance at the 2007 World Championships in Melbourne, Australia. Phelps, who set five world records during the meet, tied fellow American Mark Spitz, who won his seven golds at the 1972 Olympics in Munich, West Germany.

Australian Libby Lenton won five gold medals at the championships (50-meter freestyle, 100-meter freestyle, 100-meter butterfly, 400-meter freestyle relay, and 400-meter medley relay). The 400-meter medley team set a world record. The United States won the most medals at the championships, capturing 36—20 of them gold—and setting 12 of the 15 records in the eight-day event.

In the Pan American Games in July 2007, Brazilian Thiago Pereira broke Spitz's 1967 record of five gold medals during a single Pan Am game when he won the 200-meter backstroke for his sixth gold.

World championships. Phelps dominated, setting four world records in four days. He captured his first gold in the 400-meter freestyle relay on March 25, 2007, and then became the first swimmer to go under 1 minute, 44 seconds in the 200-meter freestyle with a 1-minute, 43.86-second swim on March 27. The next day he broke his own record in the 200-meter butterfly with a swim of 1:52.09, and on March 29 he broke his own mark in the 200-meter individual medley by 0.86 seconds with a swim of 1:54.98.

Phelps teamed up with Ryan Lochte, Klete Keller, and Peter Vanderkaay to win the 800-meter freestyle relay on March 30 in 7:03.24, topping the mark Australia set in 2001 by more than a second. Phelps captured the 100-meter butterfly on March 31, 2007, for his sixth gold, and then took home his final victory by annihilating his own mark in the 400-meter individual medley by more than 2 seconds, cruising home on April 1 with a swim of 4:06.22. He was denied a shot at an eighth gold when the 400-meter medley relay

Michael Phelps of the United States surfaces after winning the men's 100-meter butterfly during the World Championships competition at the Rod Laver Arena in Melbourne, Australia, on March 31, 2007.

team was disqualified during the preliminaries.

Other records in Melbourne. Americans Natalie Coughlin (59.44 seconds) and Aaron Peirsol (52.98 seconds) both improved on their own records in the 100-meter backstroke. The American women's 800-meter freestyle relay team reclaimed the record with a swim of 7:50.09. Leila Vaziri won the 50-meter backstroke in a record 28.16 seconds. Lochte broke Peirsol's mark in the 200-meter backstroke, set in 2006, with a swim of 1:54.32. Katie Hoff won the 400-meter individual medley in 4:32.89, and France's Laure Manaudou set a mark with 1:55.52 in 200-meter freestyle—nearly a second faster than the record set a day earlier in the semifinal by Federica Pellegrini of Italy. ■ Michael Kates

Switzerland. In a parliamentary election held on Oct. 21, 2007, the right-wing Swiss People's Party (SVP) won more votes than any other individual party in the history of the nation, capturing 62 seats in the 200-member National Council (lower house of parliament). The second-largest party, the center-left Social Democrats, won 43 seats. The center-right Radical Democratic Party and Christian Democratic Party earned 31 seats each. The Green Party made its best showing in years, with 20 seats.

According to the Swiss Constitution, the members of the National Council, together with the members of the Council of States (the upper house) elect a Federal Council (Cabinet) made up of seven ministers. The role of president of Switzerland, which is largely ceremonial, rotates among the ministers annually.

After the 2003 national election, the People's Party, the Social Democrats, and the Radical Democrats each held two seats in the Cabinet, and the Christian Democrats held one. After the 2007 election, the parliament in December again elected the same number of members from each of the four parties. However, the members of parliament (MP's) refused to reelect Christoph Blocher, leader of the People's Party, who had served in the previous Cabinet. Instead, the MP's elected a more moderate member of Blocher's party, Eveline Widmer-Schlumpf. In response, the People's Party withdrew from the government, forming the first opposition group in Swiss politics since the 1950's, and vowed not to recognize its two ministers.

The election campaign of 2007 was one of the most heated races in the nation's history. Blocher's Swiss People's Party ran on a platform that was considered by the other parties to be racist. Especially inflammatory was an SVP poster that depicted three white sheep and one black sheep. The white sheep stand on a red field with a white cross—representing the Swiss flag—and one of the white sheep kicks the black sheep off the field. Most Swiss supporting other parties interpreted the poster to mean that foreigners were not welcome in Switzerland. Supporters of the SVP maintained that the black sheep represented only "criminal foreigners." The SVP also called for prohibiting the construction of mosques with minarets, which party members claimed are symbols of Muslim power.

On October 6, radical left-wing opponents of the SVP clashed in demonstrations at an SVP rally in Bern, leading to at least 40 arrests and 20 injuries.

Economy. According to forecasts by economists with the Organisation for Economic Co-operation and Development, the growth of the Swiss economy would slow in 2007, to 2.1 percent from 2.7 percent in 2006. The country's unemployment rate was estimated to fall from 3.8 percent in 2006 to 3.3 percent in 2007.

■ Jeffrey Kopstein
See also **Europe.**

Portraits of Syrian President Bashar al-Assad decorate a government building in Damascus in anticipation of a presidential referendum in May 2007. With no opponent, Assad was "reelected" to a second seven-year term as Syria's leader.

Syria took several actions against the anti-Syria ruling majority in Lebanon in 2007. In May, Syria allegedly dispatched hundreds of Islamic fighters, under the name Fatah al-Islam, to battle the Lebanese army in northern Lebanon. After fierce battles, the Lebanese army defeated the Muslim militants by early September. Syrian agents were widely suspected to be responsible for the assassinations in June and September of two prominent members of Lebanon's National Assembly who belonged to the anti-Syria majority.

Also in 2007, Nabih Birri, the pro-Syrian president of Lebanon's Chamber of Deputies—in collusion with the pro-Syrian and pro-Iranian Islamic organization Hezbollah—worked to prevent Lebanon's National Assembly from meeting to vote on United Nations plans for an international tribunal. The tribunal was to investigate Syrian President Bashar al-Assad for his alleged role in the assassination of former Lebanese Prime Minister Rafik Hariri in 2005.

High-profile visitors. Nancy Pelosi (D., California), speaker of the United States House of Representatives, headed a delegation that visited Syria in April 2007 to meet with President Assad. Isolating Syria diplomatically was the official policy of the administration of U.S. President George W. Bush. The meeting failed to realize Pelosi's objectives of restarting Syrian-Israeli peace negotiations

and driving a wedge between Syria and Iran.

President Mahmoud Ahmadinejad of Iran visited Syria in July. Ahmadinejad declared that Syria and Iran had "excellent and extremely deep relations" and shared common stands on many regional issues.

Syria and Iraq. United States Secretary of State Condoleezza Rice met in Egypt with Syrian Foreign Minister Walid al-Muallem in May to discuss the ongoing conflict in Iraq. The meeting, however, had no impact on Syria's support for insurgent groups fighting U.S.-led forces in Iraq.

Seven major Iraqi insurgent groups convened in Damascus, the capital of Syria, in July to form a coalition dedicated to coordinating and escalating attacks designed to drive U.S. troops out of Iraq. Policy analysts noted that this meeting was an indication that Syria was strengthening its ties to Iraqi Sunni insurgents and to former Iraqi Baathists who had fled to Syria after U.S. forces ousted Iraqi dictator Saddam Hussein in 2003.

Israeli strikes inside Syria. Israeli fighter jets bombed targets in eastern Syria on Sept. 6, 2007. According to one widely circulated theory, the Israelis attacked a nuclear reactor, in the early stages of construction, being built with assistance from North Korea.　　　　■ Marius Deeb

See also **Iran; Iraq; Israel; Lebanon; Middle East.**

Tajikistan. See Asia.

Taiwan. Political struggles between Taiwan's governing Democratic Progressive Party (DPP) and the opposition Kuomintang (KMT) led to fisticuffs in parliament during 2007. The struggles came as the parties prepared for parliamentary elections scheduled for Jan. 12, 2008, to be followed by a presidential election on March 22.

Domestic politics. One legislative brawl went on for four hours in January 2007. Another in May involved lawmakers climbing over each other to try to keep the speaker, Wang Jin-pyng, from presiding. Wang was a member of the KMT, which had held a narrow majority in the old parliament. The DPP accused him of abusing his power to block programs of the DPP-led government. Some political commentators in Taiwan suggested that the brawls were staged to get media attention.

In May, the DPP named Frank Hsieh as its candidate to succeed Chen Shui-bian of the DPP as president. Chen had served two terms and was ineligible for reelection. A former prime minister, Hsieh was selected over Chen's choice, Prime Minister Su Tseng-chang. Su resigned as prime minister and was replaced by Chang Chun-hsiung. The selection process showed disarray within the DPP and many members' unhappiness with Chen's lackluster administration.

The KMT named Ma Ying-jeou, a Harvard University-educated lawyer, as its presidential candidate. When chosen, Ma was charged with embezzling from a special account during his eight years as mayor of Taiwan's capital, Taipei. He was acquitted on August 14.

Relations with China. Ma promised to reinvigorate Taiwan's economy by improving relations with China. China had long claimed Taiwan was a renegade province and had repeatedly threatened to attack if Taiwan declared itself an independent nation. Hsieh was seen as pragmatic on relations with China, despite the DPP's record of wanting Taiwan to become a separate nation.

Proindependence elements in the DPP tried in 2007 to get Hsieh to take a stronger stand. During two terms as president, Chen had shied away from moves that would provoke China. He was under pressure from the United States, which is committed to defending Taiwan but hoped to avoid having to do so.

Chen promoted a referendum on having Taiwan seek membership in the United Nations under the name "Taiwan" instead of its formal name, "Republic of China." He called for the referendum to be put before the public during the March 2008 election. Chinese and U.S. officials opposed this move as being intentionally provocative.   ■ Henry S. Bradsher

See also **Asia; China.**

Tanzania. See **Africa.**

Lawmakers brawl in Taiwan's parliament on May 8, 2007. Observers accused parliamentarians of staging such fights, which were not uncommon, simply to gain media attention.

Taxation. Only a few notable tax bills became law in the United States in 2007. Lawmakers considered other tax changes but did not enact them.

Alternative minimum tax. On December 26, President George W. Bush signed a bill to shield millions of Americans from the alternative minimum tax (AMT) for the 2007 tax year. The original intent of the AMT was to prevent extremely wealthy people from using tax breaks to pay little or no tax. However, because the AMT was never indexed for inflation, many middle-income people were becoming subject to the tax each year. The bill implemented a one-year fix to postpone the expansion of the AMT. Without the fix, the number of people subject to the tax would have risen from about 4 million in 2006 to about 25 million in 2007. Democrats in Congress had hoped to make up the $50-billion cost of the bill by increasing the tax liability of private equity and hedge fund managers, but Republicans refused to back that plan.

Small-business tax breaks were part of an omnibus bill that also raised the federal minimum wage from $5.15 to $7.25 an hour and provided funds for the U.S. wars in Iraq and Afghanistan. President Bush signed the bill into law on May 25. The $4.84 billion in tax breaks was intended to ease the impact of the minimum wage increase on small businesses. Among the tax breaks was an extension and expansion of the Work Opportunity Tax Credit, which is offered to businesses that hire members of certain economically disadvantaged groups, such as high-risk youth, former felons, veterans, or welfare recipients. Other tax breaks included an increase in the maximum deduction for business equipment in the year it is purchased and a simplification of tax rules for married couples who own unincorporated businesses.

To offset the lost revenue from the tax breaks, Congress toughened tax rules for some individual taxpayers. For example, the bill broadened the reach of the "kiddie tax"—that is, the tax on the investment income of children. Under the kiddie tax, income in excess of $1,700 received by children in the form of interest, dividends, or capital gains is taxed at their parents' rates. The new law extended the kiddie tax to all children younger than 19 and all children younger than 24 who are full-time students. Previously, the tax applied only to children younger than 18.

Internet tax ban. On October 31, President Bush signed a bill to extend a moratorium on state and local taxation of Internet access and electronic commerce to 2014. The moratorium, first approved in 1998, had been set to expire in 2007. The bill expanded the moratorium to apply to e-mail and instant messaging. ■ Mike Lewis

Telecommunications. Wireless technologies and networks dominated telecommunications developments in 2007.

The iPhone. Apple Inc., the consumer electronics powerhouse of Cupertino, California, shook the telecommunications industry when it introduced the iPhone in late June. Apple's cell phone featured a touch-screen interface that consumers and product reviewers claimed made the iPhone easier to use than other *smartphones* (cell phones with computer capabilities).

Although the iPhone's initial price of nearly $500 to $600 per handset was well above what customers were accustomed to paying for carrier-subsidized cell phones, Apple sold more than 1 million iPhones within weeks. In September, Apple dropped the price of the iPhone by $200 to boost holiday sales, dismaying customers who had purchased the handset soon after its release. Apple's CEO, Steve Jobs, offered a $100 credit for those who had purchased the iPhone at its original price.

Aside from an early glitch that slowed activation of some phones in the first few days after release, the most common complaint about the iPhone was that it could be used only on AT&T's wireless network. As AT&T's EDGE operating system for transmitting data was deemed less advanced than certain 3G (third-generation) systems offered by other carriers, some consumers felt unduly restricted.

Open access. Concerns about cell phones and wireless devices being tied exclusively to a single network also played out in 2007 on a larger stage, as the Federal Communications Commission (FCC) was determining ground rules for the auction of bandwidth in the 700-megahertz frequency. This bandwidth was to become available in mid-February 2009, when the United States was scheduled to fully convert from analog to digital television.

In July 2007, Eric Schmidt, CEO of Google Inc., of Mountain View, California, announced that his firm would pledge $4.6 billion as a guarantee that Google was a serious bidder for the new spectrum. Schmidt's condition was that the FCC stipulate that the winner of the bid must allow "open access," wherein customers can use any application, device, or service on the network. Google was attempting to end the ability of network operators to control usage as they do on existing wireless networks.

While not agreeing to all of Schmidt's requests, FCC chairman Kevin Martin announced that about one-third of the 700-megahertz bandwidth—which was scheduled to be auctioned in January 2008—would be devoted to open access.

In a further attempt to open the cell phone industry, in November 2007, Google revealed its plan to launch Android—an *open-source* operating system and software platform for cell phones. (Open source means that programs have underlying computer code that is free and public, allowing users and outside software developers to modify the code.) Android, based on open-source Linux software, would allow cell phones to operate more like small, portable computers. Google joined in this venture with more than 30 partners. If Android did well, it could reduce the dominance of major providers of cell phone service and allow for greater ease of displaying ads on phones. Android was intended for release in 2008.

Municipal Wi-Fi systems that were intended to extend wireless (Wi-Fi) connectivity across entire cities failed to gain sufficient customers in places where they were built, causing plans for new Wi-Fi networks elsewhere to stall. One issue that prevented municipal Wi-Fi from thriving was the unanticipated price drop in wired Internet services. Lompoc, California, a city of 40,000, completed its Wi-Fi system in autumn 2006 at a cost of around $2 million. The city estimated it needed 4,000 subscribers to break even but had fewer than 500 a year after the network opened. Several firms, including Clearwire and Earthlink, an Atlanta-based Internet provider, sharply curtailed municipal Wi-Fi operations. ■ Jon Van

See also **Computer; Electronics; Internet.**

Television. Networks in the United States continued to lose audience share in 2007 as they searched for new ways to attract viewers amid enormous changes within the television industry. Consumers increasingly demanded more control over program choices, and the networks responded with new shows, formats, and technological approaches. Hollywood TV writers made demands of their own by going on strike late in the year.

Writers' strike. In November, for the first time in nearly 20 years, Hollywood TV and film writers went on strike. Noisy picketing took place on both coasts with the Writers Guild of America sharply divided in contract talks with the Alliance of Motion Picture and Television Producers over DVD residuals and payments to writers from shows offered on the Internet. The strike forced such late-night talk shows as "The Late Show with David Letterman" and "The Tonight Show with Jay Leno" to air reruns. Production was also halted on at least six prime-time series.

Fox Business Network. In October, Rupert Murdoch's News Corporation launched Fox Business Network (FBN), a new network aimed at American consumers and investors. Industry observers anticipated stiff competition between FBN and the Consumer News and Business Channel.

Changes at NBC. In November, NBC began offering many of its most popular programs as

Apple's iPhone, released on June 29, 2007, features a touch-sensitive screen for navigation. The phone allows users to, among other things, search the Internet, send and receive e-mail, take and store photos, download and listen to music from Apple's iTunes Store, and, of course, make a phone call. By September, Apple had sold more than 1 million iPhones.

downloads for personal computers. Called NBC Direct, the service allowed consumers to download programs immediately after their broadcast for one week at no charge. In the second phase of the service, scheduled for roll-out in mid-2008, consumers would pay a fee for downloads, which they would then own. The service became available several weeks after NBC ended a partnership with Apple Inc.'s iTunes Store because of pricing policy disputes and concerns about privacy protection.

In December 2007, NBC made a unique deal to buy a block of prime-time programming from an outside producer. The network agreed to buy 30 hours of programming from Thom Beers, the producer of the popular adventure dramas "Deadliest Catch" and "Ice Road Truckers," for three new one-hour shows. Each new show could be produced for a fraction of the cost of a scripted network series.

Later that month, NBC cut nearly 20 positions from its news division—including "Today" and "NBC Nightly News with Brian Williams"—and its cable network MSNBC.

No Rosie "View." Rosie O'Donnell, who clashed with copanelists and stirred up controversy —but boosted ratings—during her stormy stint on "The View," resigned from the ABC show in May 2007, several weeks before her two-year contract expired. Actress/comedian Whoopi Goldberg joined the show as moderator in September. Comedian Sherri Shepherd joined the panel later that month.

Although O'Donnell had expressed interest in hosting "The Price is Right" after her friend Bob Barker signed off in June at the end of the CBS game show's 35th season, actor/comedian Drew Carey began hosting the show in September.

Couric in the war zone. In September, on the first anniversary of her well-publicized move from NBC's "Today" to anchor of the "CBS Evening News," Katie Couric traveled to Iraq and Syria to report on the progress of the U.S. war effort in Iraq. The CBS special report, entitled "America in Iraq: The Road Ahead," was intended to signal a new direction for Couric at the network. During the visit, Couric interviewed civilians, American soldiers, President George W. Bush, and General David H. Petraeus, the top American commander in Iraq. Some critics saw Couric's trip to the war zone as a desperate effort to boost ratings for the network's floundering evening newscast, which had been in third place behind ABC's "World News" with Charles Gibson and NBC's "Nightly News with Brian Williams" since Couric took over. The special report tied a record ratings low with just under 5.5 million viewers for the week.

Rather sues CBS. In September 2007, veteran newsman Dan Rather filed a $70-million lawsuit against CBS in relation to his forced retirement as anchor of the "CBS Evening News" in March 2005. The ouster stemmed from Rather's role in an unsubstantiated broadcast report that suggested that President Bush received preferential treatment while serving in the National Guard during the Vietnam War (1957-1975). In November 2007, CBS filed a motion with the New York Supreme Court to dismiss the case.

Ken Burns's *War*. Seventeen years after his 1990 landmark film on the American Civil War (1861-1865), documentary filmmaker Ken Burns returned to the Public Broadcasting Service (PBS) in September 2007 with his epic series "The War." The seven-part series focuses on the ways in which World War II (1939-1945) impacted the lives of American families. When some affiliates voiced concern about the series' strong language, PBS supplied a "clean" version to its 350 member stations. Affiliates could choose which version to air. The series was a ratings success for PBS stations.

Presidential debates go high-tech. In July 2007, CNN (Cable News Network) broke new ground when it aired the first of two CNN-YouTube presidential primary debates. Hosted by CNN's Anderson Cooper, the debates featured videotaped

PRIMETIME EMMY AWARD WINNERS IN 2007

COMEDY

Best Series: "30 Rock"
Lead Actress: America Ferrera, "Ugly Betty"
Lead Actor: Ricky Gervais, "Extras"
Supporting Actress: Jaime Pressly, "My Name Is Earl"
Supporting Actor: Jeremy Piven, "Entourage"

DRAMA

Best Series: "The Sopranos"
Lead Actress: Sally Field, "Brothers & Sisters"
Lead Actor: James Spader, "Boston Legal"
Supporting Actress: Katherine Heigl, "Grey's Anatomy"
Supporting Actor: Terry O'Quinn, "Lost"

OTHER AWARDS

Miniseries: "Broken Trail"
Reality/Competition Series: "The Amazing Race"
Variety, Music, or Comedy Series: "The Daily Show with Jon Stewart"
Made for Television Movie: "Bury My Heart at Wounded Knee"
Lead Actress in a Miniseries or Movie: Helen Mirren, "Prime Suspect: The Final Act"
Lead Actor in a Miniseries or Movie: Robert Duvall, "Broken Trail"
Supporting Actress in a Miniseries or Movie: Judy Davis, "The Starter Wife"
Supporting Actor in a Miniseries or Movie: Thomas Haden Church, "Broken Trail"

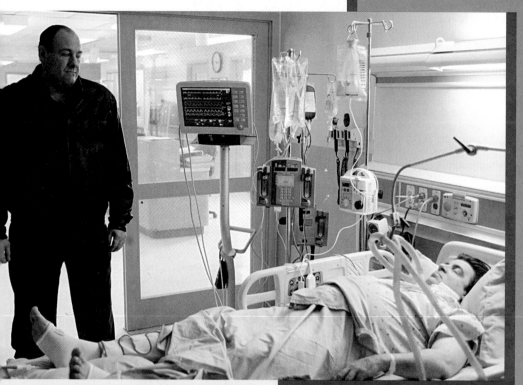

James Gandolfini (left) stars as New Jersey Mafia kingpin Tony Soprano, and Steven Van Zandt stars as Silvio Dante in the series finale of "The Sopranos." The popular, Emmy Award-winning HBO series ended in June 2007 after eight seasons.

TOP-RATED U.S. TELEVISION SERIES

The following were among the most-watched television series for the 2006-2007 regular season, which ran from Sept. 18, 2006, to May 23, 2007.

1. "American Idol" (Wednesday) (FOX)
2. "American Idol" (Tuesday) (FOX)
3. "Dancing with the Stars" (Tuesday) (ABC)
4. "Dancing with the Stars" (Monday) (ABC)
5. "Dancing with the Stars Results" (Wednesday) (ABC)
6. "CSI" (CBS)
7. (tie) "Dancing with the Stars Results" (Tuesday) (ABC)
   "Grey's Anatomy" (Thursday) (ABC)
9. "House" (FOX)
10. "NBC Sunday Night Football" (NBC)
11. "CSI: Miami" (CBS)
12. "Desperate Housewives" (ABC)
13. (tie) "Deal or No Deal" (Monday) (NBC)
    "Without a Trace" (CBS)
15. (tie) "Survivor: Cook Islands" (CBS)
    "Two and a Half Men" (CBS)
17. (tie) "CBS NFL National Post Game" (CBS)
    "NCIS" (CBS)
19. "CSI: New York" (CBS)
20. (tie) "Cold Case" (CBS)
    "Criminal Minds" (CBS)

questions for U.S. presidential candidates submitted by users of the popular video-sharing Web site YouTube. The Democratic debate, which aired on July 23 from Charleston, South Carolina, attracted 2.6 million viewers, the highest Nielsen ratings of any debate broadcast on a cable news network among adults ages 18 to 34. The CNN-YouTube Republican presidential debate, which aired on November 28, from St. Petersburg, Florida, was watched by 4 million viewers, breaking all records for any primary debate in cable history.

Back to *High School.* Following on the huge success of its 2006 original movie *High School Musical,* the Disney Channel in August 2007 aired *High School Musical 2.* The sequel attracted 17.2 million viewers on its premiere night, making it the highest-rated basic-cable broadcast of all time. *High School Musical 3* was scheduled to air on the Disney Channel in 2008.

"The Sopranos" gets whacked. After running eight years and racking up 21 Emmy Awards, HBO's popular Mafia drama "The Sopranos" presented its series finale in June 2007. The series' unexpectedly uneventful closing scene generated controversy as fans pondered its significance.

AMC executives hoped to lure pining "Sopranos" fans with the July debut of its new series "Mad Men," created by "The Sopranos" writer and executive producer Matthew Weiner. Set in the early 1960's, the 13-part series revolves around a cutthroat New York City advertising executive. "Mad Men" was compared to "The Sopranos" for its characters' sexual exploits, substance abuse, and ruthless behavior. Viewership for the premiere was higher than for any other AMC original series. The series also received high critical ratings.

Other series finales. Several other notable TV series ended in 2007. CBS's "The King of Queens," one of TV's longest-running situation comedies, was canceled after 9 seasons. NBC's "Crossing Jordan" and ABC's "George Lopez" were both canceled after 6 seasons. On the CW, "7th Heaven" was canceled after 11 seasons; "Gilmore Girls" after 7; "Reba" after 6; and "Veronica Mars" after 3. Fox's "The O.C." was canceled after 4 seasons. HBO's "Deadwood" was canceled after 3 seasons and "Rome" after 2 seasons.

Reality bytes. The CBS reality series "Kid Nation" premiered in September amid questions of whether it violated child safety and labor laws. On the series, 40 children between the ages of 8 and 15 were placed in an abandoned New Mexico desert town for 40 days, with the goal of creating a functioning society. The children had to fend for themselves with little or no contact with their parents. The American Federation of Television and Radio Actors (AFTRA) launched a probe of the series to determine whether it violated the terms of its contract. The Screen Actors Guild condemned the show's working conditions and stated that it would work with AFTRA to ensure that children on reality shows were covered by union contracts.

Other notable new shows. HBO's "Tell Me You Love Me," which gained early publicity for its graphic sex scenes, premiered in September to strong reviews. The drama follows a therapist as she guides three couples through intimacy issues while dealing with her own relationship problems. Among ABC's fall premieres were the drama "Dirty Sexy Money," starring Donald Sutherland, about a wealthy New York City family and their lawyer; the fantasy "Pushing Daisies," which follows the adventures of a young man who has the power to bring dead people back to life; and "Private Practice," a spin-off of the medical drama "Grey's Anatomy." NBC's fall premieres included "Chuck," about a computer geek who becomes a government operative, and a reimagining of the popular 1970's series "The Bionic Woman." One of Fox's fall offerings was the comedy "Back to You," starring Kelsey Grammer, about a bickering pair of local TV news anchors who are former lovers. ■ Shawn Brennan

See also **Elections; Internet; Labor and employment; People in the news** (Charles Gibson).

Tennis. Switzerland's Roger Federer and Spain's Rafael Nadal engaged in a brilliant and riveting rivalry in men's tennis in 2007, with Federer capturing three grand slam titles and losing the fourth, the French Open, to Nadal, who was the runner-up at Wimbledon.

With 12 grand slam titles, Federer tied with Roy Emerson for second on the all-time list, two behind Pete Sampras. Federer also tied a mark set by Jack Crawford in 1934 by appearing in a seventh straight grand slam final in the Australian Open. Federer then appeared in the remaining three grand slam finals to push the streak to 10.

In women's tennis, Belgium's Justine Henin captured a pair of majors, and the Williams sisters from the United States each captured improbable titles, with Serena becoming just the second unseeded woman in the Open era to win the Australian Open and Venus becoming the lowest-ranked woman to ever win Wimbledon.

Australian Open. Federer became the first man since 1980 to capture a major without dropping a set when he rolled to the title on Jan. 28, 2007, shredding Chile's Fernando González 7-6 (2), 6-4, 6-4 in the final in Melbourne. Serena Williams captured her eighth grand slam title on January 27 by whipping top seed Maria Sharapova of Russia 6-1, 6-2, her first title since winning in Australia in 2005. American twins Bob and Mike Bryan won the men's doubles title; Zimbabwe's Cara Black and South Africa's Liezel Huber took the women's doubles title; and Canada's Daniel Nestor and Russia's Elena Likhovtseva captured the mixed doubles.

French Open. Nadal won his third straight title in Paris with a 6-3, 4-6, 6-3, 6-4 victory in the final over Federer on June 10, 2007. Henin also won her third straight French title—and fourth overall—dismantling Ana Ivanovic 6-1, 6-2 on June 9. Ivanovic, from Serbia, was playing in her first grand slam final.

Nestor and Mark Knowles of the Bahamas won the men's doubles title; Australia's Alicia Molik and Italy's Mara Santangelo took the women's doubles title; and France's Nathalie Dechy and Israel's Andy Ram captured mixed doubles.

Wimbledon. Federer equaled Björn Borg's mark of five straight Wimbledon crowns with a nail-biting five-set victory over Nadal on July 8. In one of the greatest matches in Wimbledon history, No. 1 Federer outslugged No. 2 Nadal 7-6 (7), 4-6, 7-6 (3), 2-6, 6-2.

Venus Williams won her fourth Wimbledon and sixth overall grand slam title with a 6-4, 6-1 rout of France's Marion Bartoli on July 7. Williams, ranked 31st, became the fourth woman since the Open era began in 1968 to win four or more Wimbledon titles.

France's Arnaud Clément and Michaël Llodra won the men's doubles title, Black and Huber secured the women's doubles title, and England's Jamie Murray and Serbia's Jelena Jankovic took the mixed doubles title.

U.S. Open. Despite not playing his best tennis, Federer beat Novak Djokovic of Serbia on Sept. 9, 2007, to become the first man since Bill Tilden (1920-1926) to win four straight U.S. Opens. Federer broke Djokovic's serve late in the first two sets to force tiebreaks as the Serb failed to convert on seven set points. The Swiss star rolled to a 7-6 (4), 7-6 (2), 6-4 victory in New York City.

Top-seeded Henin captured the most one-sided women's final in more than three decades, routing Russian Svetlana Kuznetsova, the fourth seed, 6-1, 6-3, on September 8. Henin cruised through the two weeks without losing a set and by beating both Williams sisters along the way.

Simon Aspelin of Sweden and Julian Knowle of Austria gained the men's doubles title, Dechy and Russia's Dinara Safina took women's doubles, and Belarus's Victoria Azarenka and Max Mirnyi won mixed doubles.

Davis Cup. The United States won the Davis Cup for the first time since 1995, defeating Russia, 4-1, in Portland, Oregon. Andy Roddick and James Blake won their singles matches on Nov. 30, 2007, and the doubles team of Bob and Mike Bryan won their match on December 1 to clinch the victory. ■ Michael Kates

Terrorism. The number of terrorist incidents and the damage caused by them increased in 2007, even though international counterterrorism cooperation improved significantly. Coordination and information sharing among Western nations helped foil a number of terrorist plots.

In June 2007, United States authorities thwarted a home-grown terrorist plot when they uncovered an alleged scheme to destroy the fuel-supply system for the John F. Kennedy International Airport in New York City. In September, German police agents unraveled a plot against U.S. and German targets, arresting two German nationals and one German resident and seizing barrels of bomb-making chemicals.

Despite security improvements, the number of

Venus Williams of the United States hugs her trophy following her victory over Marion Bartoli in the finals of the Wimbledon tennis tournament on July 7, 2007. Williams, who had previously won the Wimbledon title in 2000, 2001, and 2005, defeated her French opponent, 6-4, 6-1.

people killed by terrorist assaults worldwide had more than doubled since 2004, and the risk continued to grow. North America was relatively untouched by terrorist violence in 2007, but other parts of the world continued to experience lethal attacks.

The Middle East. The war in Iraq continued to make that nation the primary source of terrorist activity. Attacks against soldiers and civilians in Iraq increased in 2007, making it the deadliest year in Iraq since the war began there in 2003. In northern Iraq, multiple suicide bombings claimed about 500 lives on a single day, Aug. 14, 2007.

Elsewhere in the region, terrorist activity

declined. In Israel, the deadliest single incident occurred on January 29, when a Palestinian suicide bomber killed three Israelis in Elat. Lebanon suffered from a terrorist attack on June 13, when a car bomb killed 10 people, including Walid Eido, a member of the Lebanese Parliament. Later that month, six members of the United Nations Interim Force in Lebanon were slain near the country's border with Israel.

South Asia. Next to Iraq, Pakistan was the nation most wracked by terrorist violence. In November 2007, the government reported that 667 people had been killed in 157 attacks since January. One of the deadliest bombing incidents took place shortly after former Prime Minister Benazir Bhutto's return to Pakistan after eight years in exile. On October 18, a bomb blast at a rally of her supporters caused about 140 deaths. On December 27, Bhutto was assassinated.

In Afghanistan, as in Iraq, 2007 was the deadliest year since the United States-led military campaign began there in 2001. During the first eight months of 2007, 143 civilians died in suicide attacks. On March 5, Taliban agents kidnapped Italian journalist Daniele Mastrogiacomo and killed both his driver and translator. Mastrogiacomo was released after Italy pressured Afghan President Hamid Karzai to free five Taliban prisoners.

On July 19, Taliban insurgents in Afghanistan took 23 South Korean church workers hostage. Two hostages were executed, and the remaining survivors were released on August 30.

In India, two bombs exploded on a train after it left Delhi on February 18, killing 68 passengers. In May and August, bombings took place in Hyderabad, India, leaving a total of 53 dead.

Africa. Civil strife in Somalia made it highly susceptible to terrorist activities in 2007. The arrival of Ethiopian troops to support Somalia's interim government helped stoke the violence, as insurgents opposed to the troops increased their attacks. On June 3, Prime Minister Ali Mohamed Ghedi survived his third assassination attempt, which killed six guards and wounded 20 others.

Algeria's worst bombing in years took place in Algiers, the capital, on December 11. Two car bombs exploded near government and United Nations buildings, killing about 40 people. A North African branch of al-Qa'ida was suspected.

Europe. On June 30, two Islamic terrorists drove a Jeep loaded with propane canisters into the main terminal of Glasgow International Airport in Scotland and set it on fire. One of the terrorists was the only victim. ■ Richard Rubenstein

See also **Afghanistan; Africa; Algeria; India; Iraq; Korea, South; Middle East; Pakistan; United Kingdom; United States, Government of the.**

Flames rise from a Jeep Cherokee at the main terminal of Glasgow International Airport in Scotland. The suspects, two Islamist terrorists, loaded the vehicle with propane canisters and drove it into the glass doors of the terminal on June 30, 2007. Despite the fire and shattered glass, no one was injured except the driver, who later died.

Thailand. Voters on Aug. 19, 2007, approved a new constitution written under the control of the armed forces, which seized power in September 2006. In parliamentary elections held on Dec. 23, 2007, People's Power Party (PPP), made up of former members of ousted Prime Minister Thaksin Shinawatra's Thai Rak Thai (TRT) party, won a majority of seats and formed a ruling coalition.

Constitution. Observers in Bangkok, the Thai capital, worried that the constitution would weaken the power of elected officials by shifting some authority from voters and politicians to generals and bureaucrats, who had long dominated the nation. The constitution provided for half of the seats in the upper house of parliament and in independent commissions to be appointed by a panel of judges and bureaucrats, and for the judiciary to take some executive powers.

Only about 57 percent of Thailand's 45 million eligible voters voted on the constitution. It was approved by nearly 58 percent of those voting. In the poor rural north and northeast of Thailand, however, 63 percent voted against its ratification. The region had strongly supported Thaksin, whose policies appealed to farmers.

Politics. Thaksin, a telecommunications billionaire, created TRT in 1998 and in 2001 led the party to majority control in parliament. The generals who overthrew Thaksin in 2006 accused him of corruption and other crimes. A military-backed Constitutional Tribunal on May 30, 2007, dissolved TRT on charges of violating electoral laws. The tribunal also banned Thaksin and 110 of his senior colleagues from politics for five years. After TRT was dissolved, more than 200 of its members of parliament joined PPP. In the December elections, PPP won 233 of the 480 seats in the House of Representatives. They joined with less prominent parties to form a governing coalition.

Thaksin. The government in 2007 pursued legal actions against Thaksin and his wife, accusing them of tax evasion and corruption in a 2003 real estate deal. On June 19, 2007, the police ordered the two to return from exile in London to face charges. After they failed to show up, the Supreme Court on August 14 issued a warrant for their arrest. Their trial was later suspended until their return. Thaksin said he had no desire to return to active politics in Thailand.

Separatists. A reign of terror continued in 2007 in the three mostly Muslim southern provinces of Thailand, a predominantly Buddhist country. Since January 2004, a separatist group had been killing Buddhist civilians and soldiers, as well as Muslims suspected of cooperating with the government. Both the army and insurgents were accused of atrocities that had already resulted in the deaths of some 2,500 people by late 2007.

■ Henry S. Bradsher

See also **Asia; Disasters.**

Theater. The Broadway theater season in New York City was interrupted late in 2007 by a labor strike, which caused numerous shows to suspend performances for nearly three weeks in November. The dispute arose between the League of American Theaters and Producers, representing management, and Local 1 of the International Alliance of Theatrical Stage Employees, representing the striking stagehands. The 19-day strike, which ended on November 28, was the longest on Broadway since the 25-day walkout in 1975 by the musicians' union. The stagehand strike was the first in the union's 121-year history.

The strike shuttered 31 Broadway theaters and caused 27 shows to temporarily suspend performances. Ticket sales during the period of the strike dipped to $7.2 million, compared with $42 million generated during the same period the year before. The New York City Comptroller's office estimated that the strike cost the city $2 million a day in revenues, or roughly $40 million total.

According to a November 2007 article by Campbell Robertson in *The New York Times,* at the center of the dispute were "work rules in the stagehands' contract that the producers' league considered costly and inefficient." The agreement, ratified on December 9, provided the producers greater flexibility in the number of hours stagehands work. It also called for the minimum number of stagehands for certain production calls, such as load-in, when sets and other equipment are moved into a theater. In return, the union members received raises substantially higher than the 3.5-percent increase initially offered by the league.

Strike impact. By year's end, it remained uncertain what the full impact of the strike would be on ticket revenues. As reported by the *Daily News* of New York City, some industry insiders predicted a rise in Broadway ticket prices, which had already climbed in the months preceding the strike to $120 a seat for musicals such as *Jersey Boys* (2005) and *Wicked* (2003). While these two shows and other popular musicals quickly returned to sold-out and near-capacity status, a number of previewing dramas—including the newly discovered Mark Twain comedy *Is He Dead?* and *August: Osage County*—lost momentum at the box office, in some cases dipping below 50-percent capacity. The latter play, an explosive dark comedy about a dysfunctional Oklahoma family, premiered at Chicago's Steppenwolf Theatre Company and went on to receive rave reviews on Broadway. Sales for the new play *The Farnsworth Invention* by Aaron Sorkin—about Philo Taylor Farnsworth, the boy genius who invented television—were uncertain after a delayed opening caused by the strike and mixed reviews in the press.

As a gesture to returning theatergoers—many

of whom obtained refunds for closed shows during the strike—the producers' league arranged a special free concert at the Marriott Marquis Hotel in New York City titled "Broadway's Back," featuring performances from a roster of luminaries, including Bernadette Peters and Angela Lansbury.

A touch of the Irish. Another critically acclaimed Broadway play that suffered a dip in sales after the strike was *The Seafarer* (2006), written and directed by the distinguished young Irish playwright Conor McPherson. *New York Times* theater critic Ben Brantley proclaimed McPherson "quite possibly the finest playwright of his generation." An alcohol-soaked story of two brothers on the coast north of Dublin, *The Seafarer* centers on a Christmas Eve poker game in which the Devil—a character named Mr. Lockhart—takes a hand. McPherson's earlier efforts, also praised by critics, included *Shining City* (2004), which played on Broadway in 2006 and featured Martha Plimpton, Oliver Platt, and Brian F. O'Byrne; and *The Weir* (1997), which received the Laurence Olivier Award for Best New Play in London in 1999 and was also seen in New York City that year.

Alliance Theatre. The 2007 Tony Award recognizing excellence in a regional theater went to the Alliance Theatre in Atlanta. Founded in 1968 as the Atlanta Municipal Theatre, it quickly made its mark as a noteworthy regional theater, changing its name to Alliance Theatre Company in 1970. By the end of the decade, it had premiered Tennessee Williams's *Tiger Tail* (1978) and presented performances by such actors as Richard Dreyfuss, Morgan Freeman, and Jane Alexander.

The theater has presented world premieres of many other notable works, including *Elaborate Lives: The Legend of Aida* (1998) by Elton John and Tim Rice, which opened on Broadway in 2000 and received Tony Awards for lighting and scenic design, best actress in a musical, and best original score. The current artistic director of the Alliance, Susan V. Booth, began her tenure in 2001. Under her leadership, the theater has produced several other important world premieres, including stage adaptations of *The Heart Is a Lonely Hunter,* based on the 1940 novel by Carson McCullers, and *The Color Purple*, based on Alice Walker's 1982 Pulitzer Prize-winning novel. *The Color Purple* was produced on Broadway in 2005 and received 11 Tony Award nominations.

Rock and pop music has become a staple of Broadway musicals, including such recent productions as *Jersey Boys,* which tells the story of the pop group the Four Seasons; *Hairspray* (2002), based on the 1988 John Waters film; *Movin' Out* (2002), featuring songs by Billy Joel; and *Mamma Mia!* (1999), with tunes by the Scandinavian pop group ABBA.

Two shows on Broadway at the close of 2007 signaled the ongoing popularity of this exuberant musical style for the theatergoing public. One of the shows, *Spring Awakening,* is a rock musical adaptation of a play written in 1891 by the German playwright Frank Wedekind. Wedekind's original play, which concerns teen-age sexuality among young German students, created a scandal for its frank depiction of sexual acts when it was first staged in 1906. The adaptation, which features music by the pop singer-songwriter Duncan

TONY AWARD WINNERS IN 2007

Best Play, *The Coast of Utopia*

Best Musical, *Spring Awakening*

Best Play Revival, *Journey's End*

Best Musical Revival, *Company*

Best Special Theatrical Event, Jay Johnson, *The Two and Only*

Leading Actor in a Play, Frank Langella, *Frost/Nixon*

Leading Actress in a Play, Julie White, *The Little Dog Laughed*

Leading Actor in a Musical, David Hyde Pierce, *Curtains*

Leading Actress in a Musical, Christine Ebersole, *Grey Gardens*

Featured Actor in a Play, Billy Crudup, *The Coast of Utopia*

Featured Actress in a Play, Jennifer Ehle, *The Coast of Utopia*

Featured Actor in a Musical, John Gallagher, Jr., *Spring Awakening*

Featured Actress in a Musical, Mary Louise Wilson, *Grey Gardens*

Direction of a Play, Jack O'Brien, *The Coast of Utopia*

Direction of a Musical, Michael Mayer, *Spring Awakening*

Book of a Musical, Steven Sater, *Spring Awakening*

Original Musical Score, Duncan Sheik and Steven Sater, *Spring Awakening*

Orchestrations, Duncan Sheik, *Spring Awakening*

Scenic Design of a Play, Bob Crowley and Scott Pask, *The Coast of Utopia*

Scenic Design of a Musical, Bob Crowley, *Mary Poppins*

Costume Design of a Play, Catherine Zuber, *The Coast of Utopia*

Costume Design of a Musical, William Ivey Long, *Grey Gardens*

Lighting Design of a Play, Brian MacDevitt, Kenneth Posner, and Natasha Katz, *The Coast of Utopia*

Lighting Design of a Musical, Kevin Adams, *Spring Awakening*

Choreography, Bill T. Jones, *Spring Awakening*

Regional Theater, Alliance Theatre, Atlanta

Lifetime Achievement, Jerry Herman, composer

Sheik and book and lyrics by Steven Sater, received largely enthusiastic reviews and won the 2007 Tony Award for best musical.

Rock music and politics are the backdrop of renowned British playwright Tom Stoppard's play, *Rock 'n' Roll* (2006), which opened on Broadway in November 2007. The drama's action is divided between Prague in the Czech Republic and Cambridge University in the United Kingdom from 1968 to 1989. It focuses on Jan, a Czech student at Cambridge, whose brother, Max, is a Marxist philosopher who teaches at the university. When Prague is occupied by Soviet tanks in 1968, Jan returns to his native country, where his passion for rock music lands him in trouble. Although not a musical, the play is punctuated by a soundtrack of period rock music from such era-defining groups as the Rolling Stones and Pink Floyd. In the play, the Plastic People of the Universe, a popular Czech band, comes to represent freedom. The governmental suppression of the band suggests the limitations to freedom in Prague at that time. Jan's journey somewhat parallels that of the playwright, who was born in 1937 in Zlin, in what is now the Czech Republic, and moved with his family to the United Kingdom in 1946.

Stoppard's epic three-part drama *The Coast of Utopia* (2002), focusing on Russian intellectuals during the 1800's, closed on Broadway in May 2007. It won the 2007 Tony Award for best play.

Young Frankenstein. One of the year's most anticipated new Broadway musicals, *Young Frankenstein,* was adapted from Mel Brooks's 1974 film of the same name. The musical premiered in November 2007 to disappointing reviews. Most critics felt that the play was not as funny as the film or as entertaining as Brooks's acclaimed Broadway musical *The Producers* (2001).

Frost/Nixon. One of the year's notable Broadway productions, *Frost/Nixon* (2006), was written by British screenwriter and dramatist Peter Morgan, based on a series of 1977 televised interviews between British talk show host David Frost and former President Richard M. Nixon. In August 2007, Ron Howard began directing a film adaptation of the play, starring original cast members Frank Langella in his Tony Award-winning role as Nixon and Michael Sheen as Frost.   ■ David Yezzi

See also **Labor and employment.**

Togo. See **Africa.**

Tonga. See **Pacific Islands.**

Frank Langella gives a Tony Award-winning performance as former President Richard M. Nixon in the 2007 Broadway production of *Frost/Nixon*. The play is based on a series of 1977 televised interviews between British talk show host David Frost and Nixon.

Toronto. In January 2007, Mayor David Miller formally opened the newly restored wrought-iron gates at the entrance to historic Trinity Bellwoods Park, inaugurating what was to become a year of additions to Toronto's cultural facilities. The new gates dramatized the revival of a downtown neighborhood after years of decline.

The Michael Lee-Chin Crystal, an addition to the Royal Ontario Museum, opened on June 2. The Crystal is a $270-million (all amounts are in Canadian dollars) network of girders and glass growing out of the north side of the 95-year-old museum building. It immediately aroused controversy, however. Some complained that the addition, designed by internationally regarded architect Daniel Libeskind, did not suit Toronto. Others pointed out that such innovative structures as Paris's Eiffel Tower, New York City's Rockefeller Center, and Toronto's own clam-shaped City Hall were not initially well received but went on to become iconic symbols for their cities.

On October 8, the Art Gallery of Ontario closed its doors for the final phase of its $254-million renovation. It was scheduled to reopen in 2008. The gallery and the Crystal were but two of the new facilities that city boosters hoped would make Toronto a major cultural center. Others include the recently renovated Gardiner Museum of Ceramic Arts and the Four Seasons Centre for the Performing Arts, home to the Canadian Opera Company and the National Ballet of Canada.

City finances. The city's expansion of artistic life took place against the background of a financial crisis. On April 17, 2007, Treasurer Joe Pennachetti warned the City Council that Toronto faced a $500-million budget shortfall. He said the city could face bankruptcy unless it found new sources of revenue, or unless the provincial government came through with a financial bailout, as it had in other years. After the province declined to rescue Toronto, Mayor Miller proposed two new ways of raising money—a $38-per-year increase in automobile licensing fees and graduated increases in the land transfer tax, a percentage of the purchase price of property.

The proposals faced stiff opposition, however, and the City Council turned down the new taxes in July. Miller responded by announcing service cuts that included closing community centers on Mondays. Many working parents relied on the centers' after-school programs, and protests against the closings led the mayor to back down and allow them to continue to operate.

After an October 10 provincial election produced no new financial commitments to Toronto, the City Council voted on October 22 for the increased land transfer tax and auto licensing fees. The measures were expected to bring in $354 million, but even this amount was not enough to cover Toronto's deficit. The city faced another budget crisis in 2008.

Milestones. Toronto lost three of its most public-spirited citizens in 2007. In April, June Callwood, 82, died of cancer. Callwood began her career as a journalist and became a community activist. Her good works included helping to form the Canadian Civil Liberties Association and establishing Casey House, Toronto's first AIDS hospice.

In June, entrepreneur and arts patron Ed Mirvish, 92, died. He founded Honest Ed's, a discount house that grew to occupy a whole city block. In the early 1960's, he purchased and restored the city's crumbling Royal Alexandra Theatre. He went on to take over Britain's historic Old Vic Theatre for 16 years. Sir Laurence Olivier compared Mirvish to merchant princes of Renaissance Florence, but in Toronto, "Honest Ed" was best loved for staging daylong birthday parties and giving away thousands of free Christmas turkeys.

In August 2007, Richard Bradshaw, 63, the director of the Canadian Opera Company, died suddenly of a heart attack. Bradshaw elevated performance standards and became the driving force behind the creation of Toronto's first opera house, which opened in 2006. More than 1,500 people crowded into St. James Cathedral for Bradshaw's funeral.   ■ David Lewis Stein

See also **Canada; Canadian provinces; City.**

Toys and games. Toy sales started off with a bang in 2007, building on the momentum of strong sales during the 2006 holiday season. Toy sales in the United States in 2006 totaled $22.3 billion. During the first half of 2007, sales rose by almost 3 percent, generating over $8 billion from January to June, compared with $7.8 billion generated during the same period in 2006.

Recalls. The toy industry was plagued in 2007 with recalls of toys that did not adhere to U.S. safety standards. Most of the toys were made in China and were recalled because of high lead content, the presence of hazardous chemicals, or the presence of detachable magnets, which can be deadly if swallowed. In November, the Consumer Product Safety Commission, an independent agency of the U.S. government, estimated that at least 60 toys comprising 25 million product units were recalled in 2007. In response, the Chinese government suspended the export licenses of hundreds of toy manufacturers. In the United States, toy manufacturers retested toys to be sold during the holiday season and implemented procedures to ensure that their suppliers were adhering to safety standards. The U.S. toy industry, along with the American National Standards Institute, began working on a testing accreditation program that the groups hoped to implement in early 2008.

Get it your way. One of the top toy trends

An employee removes toys from a store in August. United States toymakers recalled more than 60 toys in 2007 totaling 25 million units. Most of the toys were manufactured in China and contained dangerous quantities of lead or hazardous chemicals or tiny magnets that could prove fatal if swallowed.

of 2007 involved "personalization." Jewelry kits, craft kits, and MP3 accessories allowed children to make their own accessories, home decorations, and music mixes. Although most children were still trend conscious, the toys encouraged them to combine trends with their own personal style.

Pop culture in play. More than 30 percent of toys sold in a given year are associated with licensed products, including cartoon and movie characters and television, music, and sports celebrities. In 2007, one of the most popular characters was Hannah Montana, the star of a Disney Channel TV show of the same name. From her real-life, common schoolgirl persona to her rock-star, guitar-playing stage persona, favorite Hannah Montana toys included dolls, concert stage playsets, and child-sized role-play sets that allowed girls to pretend they were Hannah Montana.

High School Musical 2 graduated with honors with its August debut. The Disney Channel sequel to its television movie *High School Musical* (2006) set a basic cable telecast record, with 17.2 million viewers. From board games to action figures, tweens and families bought everything *High School Musical* to relive the fun at home.

Summer 2007 became the summer of Spidey with the release of the blockbuster movie *Spider-Man 3*. Kids started the summer months with an array of merchandise, from web blasters to building sets and action figures. The highly anticipated debut of *Transformers*, an adaptation of the 1986 animated film, appealed to a wide audience, from young children to adults looking for a nostalgic fix. Hasbro Inc. of Pawtucket, Rhode Island, delivered, with products from collectible adult-focused action figure sets to the kid-pleasing Transformers Optimus Prime voice changer. *Pirates of the Caribbean 3, Harry Potter and the Order of the Phoenix,* and *Ratatouille* also captured audiences' hearts. Products supporting these crowd-pleasing movies were stocked on toy shelves around the globe.

Electronics as child's play. According to a study released in June 2007 by The NPD Group, a market research firm in Port Washington, New York, the average age at which children begin using electronic devices declined from 8.1 years in 2005 to 6.7 years in 2007. Toymakers were responding to the need for child-friendly cell phones, laptops, digital cameras, MP3 players, and video cameras with products that were durable, sized to fit a child's smaller hand, and lower priced to fit a parent's budget.

■ Adrienne Citrin
See also **Electronics; Public health; Television.**

Track and field. The United States enjoyed many winning performances at the 2007 World Track and Field Championships in Osaka, Japan, in late August and early September.

The Americans captured 14 gold medals and 26 total medals, which matched their record-setting haul in the 1991 world championships. Sprinter Allyson Felix won three gold medals in three days to become just the second woman in history to take three golds. Sprinter Tyson Gay became only the third man to win three gold medals, and distance runner Bernard Lagat became the first man to win both the 1,500-meter and 5,000-meter races. No world records were set at the meet by either the male or female athletes.

Two weeks after a surprisingly poor third-place finish at the world championships, Jamaican sprinter Asafa Powell broke his own world record in the 100 meters by .03 seconds, posting 9.74 seconds at the Rieti Grand Prix in Italy on September 9. Powell eased up in the final few meters, leading some observers to speculate that he could take the record even lower in the coming months.

Ethiopia's Meseret Defar broke the record in the two-mile run that she set earlier in 2007 with a finish of 8 minutes, 58.58 seconds at the Van Damme Memorial in Brussels, Belgium, on September 14. Defar also set world records in the 3,000-meter run indoors on February 3, and the 5,000-meter run outdoors on June 15.

World championships. Gay pulled away in the final meters of the 200 on August 30 to win in 19.76 seconds, breaking the meet record held by fellow American Michael Johnson, set in 1995. The win came four days after he captured the 100-meter sprint in 9.85 seconds. Gay became the third man to sweep the two events in world championship history. With his gold medal as part of the 4x100 relay, he joined Carl Lewis (1983, 1987) and Maurice Greene (1999) as the only men to have won three golds at one championship.

Felix captured the 200 meters on Aug. 31, 2007, in a time of 21.81 seconds, the fastest time by a woman at that distance since 1999. She also ran on the winning 4x100 and 4x400 relay teams, matching the 1983 performance of Marita Koch of the former East Germany as the only triple female winners.

On Aug. 29, 2007, Lagat, born in Kenya and a U.S. citizen since 2004, became the first American runner to win the 1,500 meters, finishing in 3 minutes, 34.77 seconds. He outkicked the field, which had set a slow pace, to win the 5,000 meters on Sept. 2, 2007.

In other notable performances, Jeremy Wariner ran 43.45 seconds, the third-fastest time for the 400-meter dash in history, on August 31 as the Americans took the top three places in the event. Sweden's Carolina Klüft won her third straight heptathlon title on August 26, setting a European record with her total of 7,032 points. Jackie Joyner-Kersee of the United States set the world record in 1988 with 7,291 points.

In one of the closest finishes in world championship history, Jamaican Veronica Campbell edged out Lauryn Williams of the United States to win the 100-meter dash on Aug. 27, 2007. Campbell won in a photo finish with a time of 11.01

WORLD TRACK AND FIELD RECORDS ESTABLISHED IN 2007

Event	Holder	Country	Where set	Date	Record
WOMEN INDOOR					
3,000 meters	Meseret Defar	Ethiopia	Stuttgart, Germany	February 3	8:23.72
5,000 meters	Tirunesh Dibaba	Ethiopia	Boston	January 27	14:27.42
Pole vault	Yelena Isinbayeva	Russia	Donetsk, Ukraine	February 10	4.93m
4X800 meters relay	Moscow Region	Russia	Volgograd, Russia	February 11	8:18.54
MEN OUTDOOR					
100 meters	Asafa Powell	Jamaica	Rieti, Italy	September 9	9.74
20,000 meters	Haile Gebrselassie	Ethiopia	Ostrava, Czech Republic	June 27	56:26.0
Half marathon	Samuel Kamau Wanjiru	Kenya	The Hague, Netherlands	March 17	58:33
Marathon	Haile Gebrselassie	Ethiopia	Berlin, Germany	September 30	2:04:26
1-hour run	Haile Gebrselassie	Ethiopia	Ostrava, Czech Republic	June 27	21,285m
20 kilometers race walk	Vladimir Kanaykin	Russia	Saransk, Russia	September 29	1:17:16
WOMEN OUTDOOR					
5,000 meters	Meseret Defar	Ethiopia	Oslo, Norway	June 15	14:16.63
20 kilometers	Lornah Kiplagat	Netherlands	Udine, Italy	October 14	1:02:57
Half marathon	Lornah Kiplagat	Netherlands	Udine, Italy	October 14	1:06:25
Hammer throw	Tatyana Lysenko	Russia	Sochi, Russia	May 26	*78.61m

m = meters
* = not yet ratified.   Source: International Association of Athletics Federations (IAAF).

seconds. American Carmelita Jeter, the bronze medalist, was just one-tenth of a second behind.

Golden League. Pole vault champion Yelena Isinbayeva of Russia and American 400-meter sprinter Sanya Richards split a $1-million Golden League jackpot for sweeping all six meets in their respective disciplines. Isinbayeva, the world record holder, cleared 4.82 meters (15 feet, 9 3/4 inches) to win the final meet on September 16 in Berlin. Richards captured the 400 meters in the fastest time run in 2007, 49.27 seconds.

Marion Jones. American track star Marion Jones pleaded guilty on October 6 to using illegal performance-enhancing drugs in 1999 and 2000 as well as being involved in money laundering. Jones also returned the three gold medals and two bronze medals she won at the 2000 Olympic Games to the International Olympic Committee.

■ Michael Kates

Transit. See Transportation.

Transportation. The structural failure on Aug. 1, 2007, of a 40-year-old bridge that spanned the Mississippi River in Minneapolis, Minnesota, threw into sharp relief problems with the transportation infrastructure of the United States. During the evening rush hour, the Interstate 35W bridge collapsed. Around 50 vehicles and the people in them plunged some 60 feet (18 meters) into the river, onto its banks, or onto huge slabs of broken concrete below. Thirteen people were killed, and more than 100 others were injured.

The bridge, used by up to 140,000 people per day, had been the most heavily traveled in Minnesota. As early as 1990, engineers had rated it "structurally deficient." Such a designation meant that inspectors had noted cracks and corrosion, but it did not mean that they believed the bridge was imminently unsafe. More than 70,000 bridges—about 12 percent of the bridges in the nation—were classified as structurally deficient as of 2006. Engineers called for a frequent schedule of inspections for the Interstate 35W bridge, believing it would be sound enough to be used until its scheduled replacement date of 2020. After the collapse, the U.S. Department of Transportation called on the 50 states to inspect more than 700 bridges similar in design to the bridge in Minneapolis.

Structures beneath old cities. Another infrastructure problem occurred in 2007 in New York City, where pipes carrying steam used for heating and cooling run beneath some streets. On July 18, one of these pipes, laid more than 80 years ago beneath midtown Manhattan, exploded near Grand Central Station. The blast released a huge geyser that shot steam and

Tyson Gay of the United States expresses jubilation after winning the 100-meter sprint at the world championships in Osaka, Japan, on Aug. 26, 2007. Four days later, Gay won the 200-meter sprint, becoming only the second athlete to sweep both events in world championship history.

debris into the air for hours. One person died, and scores were injured in the incident, which occurred during the evening rush hour. The 20-foot (6-meter) crater left by the explosion disrupted subway service and traffic in a 6-square-block area.

Rail infrastructure. In addition to aging roads, tunnels, and bridges, the passenger rail system in the United States was also in need of major investment in 2007. In July, Amtrak's president, Alex Kummant, told a congressional subcommittee that, of the 21,000 miles (33,796 kilometers) of track Amtrak traveled over, only 626 miles (1,007 kilometers) were owned by Amtrak. The rest were owned by a variety of freight or commuter lines that gave their own trains priority for the track, causing lengthy delays for Amtrak's passengers.

According to Kummant, only a small section of the track Amtrak owned could be considered high-speed. Amtrak's Acela service in the "Northeast Corridor" of the United States had trains that traveled an average speed of 80 miles (130 kilometers) per hour in 2007. By comparison, high-speed trains in Europe traveled at average speeds of about 125 miles (200 kilometers) per hour. In 2007, Amtrak began nonstop trains on the Acela lines between New York City, Philadelphia, and

Washington, D.C., in an attempt to reduce travel times. Kummant reported that travel times could not be further improved without building new, dedicated track line, with an estimated cost of more than $30 billion.

The American Society of Civil Engineers estimated the cost for necessary repair or replacement of infrastructure in the United States could be as high as $1.6 trillion over a five-year period. This did not include such projects as dedicated track for high-speed rail as envisioned by Amtrak.

Transit abroad. Europe's highly successful high-speed train lines were further improved in 2007. In June, the French TGV (train à grande vitesse, or high-speed train) added a new Paris-Stuttgart-Munich route, and Germany's InterCity Express (ICE) began offering service between Frankfurt and Paris.

In November, Eurostar—which offered high-speed trains from such continental cities as Paris and Brussels to the United Kingdom (U.K.)—opened a new link. The Channel Tunnel Rail Link originates at St. Pancras station in London and then runs to the Channel Tunnel. Until this time, lines in the U.K. had not allowed high-speed trains to run the entire distance between London and the tunnel. High-speed trains could now travel the

The first high-speed Eurostar train arrives at London's St. Pancras station from Brussels, Belgium, via the Channel Tunnel in November 2007. The long-abandoned Gothic-revival station and cast-iron-and-glass train shed, completed in the 1800's, reopened for the new service after a $1.6-billion renovation.

entire route from London to destinations in continental Europe.

Gas prices. The price of fuel proved to be another transportation issue in 2007. In July, average gas prices in the United States rose to more than $3 a gallon. Lack of refining capacity was one factor that led to higher prices. Although consumer demand for gasoline had continued to grow, global refining capacity had not. The cost of crude oil, from which gasoline is refined, was another factor. In 2007, crude oil prices reached more than $90 per barrel, up from about $25 per barrel in the early 2000's. Increased demand worldwide also played a part.

The media reported gas prices to be at record highs in 2007, but once inflation was factored in, gas prices were not, for the most part, as high as they had been in the early 1980's. Nevertheless, consumer perception of gas prices and environmental issues shifted demand in the United States from larger cars to smaller, more fuel-efficient vehicles. ■ Christine Sullivan

See also **Aviation; Disasters; Energy supply; New York City.**

Trinidad and Tobago. See Latin America; West Indies.

Tunisia. See Africa.

Turkey. The ruling Justice and Development Party (AKP), a moderate Islamic party, nominated Abdullah Gül, minister of foreign affairs, as its candidate for president of Turkey in April 2007. The nomination of Gül, who held strong religious beliefs, sparked mass protests by people who feared that, if elected, Gül would dismantle Turkey's *secular* political system (characterized by separation of religion and state).

After two earlier rounds of parliamentary voting failed to produce a winner, the Grand National Assembly (Turkey's parliament) elected Gül as president in August, with 339 of 550 votes. Gül assumed office that month as the first president of Turkey with a personal history of involvement in political Islamic movements. On October 21, Turkish voters approved a constitutional amendment to directly elect future presidents.

Parliamentary elections in July resulted in the AKP winning 341 out of 550 seats—a clear parliamentary majority but 10 fewer seats than the party had previously held. The Republican People's Party, Turkey's main secular party, finished second, with about 21 percent of the vote. Another opposition party, the Nationalist Movement Party, finished third, with approximately 14 percent of the vote.

Election analysts noted that various issues appeared to have affected the way people voted, including the war in Iraq, which the majority of Turks opposed, and the lack of progress on the integration of Turkey into the European Union.

Murder of journalist. On January 19, journalist Hrant Dink was shot and killed outside his office in Istanbul, Turkey's largest city. Dink was the editor of the Turkish-Armenian newspaper *Agos* and was best known for advocating reconciliation between Turks and Armenians. Dink had received death threats for several months before his assassination, but the police failed to act on these threats. Dink's assassin, Ogün Samast, a 17-year-old Turkish nationalist, was arrested and taken into custody. A few days after his arrest, photographs obtained by Turkish television showed Samast holding a Turkish flag and surrounded by smiling police officers. The broadcast of the photos led to investigations of the police.

Iraq incursion. In December, Turkey carried out bombing raids on PKK rebels holed up in mountain camps in northern Iraq. Some 300 Turkish soldiers entered Iraq to round up rebels. Demanding an independent Kurdish state that would include southeast Turkey, PKK rebels had regularly crossed into Turkey to attack Turkish troops and civilians. In October, the Turkish Grand National Assembly voted to allow the Iraq incursion to confront the PKK. ■ Mary-Jane Deeb

See also **Europe; Iraq; People in the news (Abdullah Gül). Turkey: A Special Report.**

Modern Turkey: A Delicate Balance

By Berna Turam

Turkey found itself walking a tight rope in 2007. By tradition, Turkey serves as a bridge between West and East, between Europe and the Middle East, and between Christianity and Islam. In July, the pro-Islamic party, *Adalet ve Kalknma Partisi*, or AKP (Justice and Development), retained control of the Grand National Assembly, Turkey's parliament, with 48 percent of the vote in what were judged to be free and fair elections. Subsequently, the AKP and its allies in parliament elected Abdullah Gül, a devout Muslim, the 11th president of Turkey. His nomination had sparked massive protests among the millions of Turkish people who continued to strongly back secular government, that is, separation of religion and the state. Weeks later, Turkish Prime Minister Recep Tayyip Erdogan, supported by Gül, called for the lifting of a ban on women wearing headscarves at state universities. Lifting a ban on the wearing of headscarves would appear to be a minor thing, except in Turkey, the world's only majority Muslim nation with a constitutionally mandated secular government. Head-scarves, which also were banned in public offices, were seen by many as a symbol of fundamentalist Islam.

Later in 2007, Erdogan and Gül became involved in an international crisis triggered by Kurdish rebels who used mountainous redoubts in northern Iraq to launch deadly raids across the border into Turkey. With the strong backing of the parliament, Erdogan demanded in October that Iraq clean out Kurdistan Workers' Party (PKK) strongholds or risk a military incursion into northern Iraq. International affairs experts warned that a Turkish incursion into the Kurdish stronghold in northern Iraq could tip the always-precarious Middle East into open conflict. Erdogan and Gül's pro-Islamic government did indeed find itself at the center of worldwide attention in 2007.

Gül's long road to the presidency

The pro-Islamic AKP initially came to power in 2003, and its retention of parliamentary control in 2007 surprised many in Turkey as well as in the international community. There had been pro-Islamic governments before in Turkey, but they had been short-lived. The establishment of a secular government in Turkey in the 1920's had so relegated Islam from the public and political realm that it seemed impossible that the 80-year tradition could be seriously threatened for long. However, the AKP, unlike previous pro-Islamic parties in Turkey, kept to a moderate path, seeking to maintain friendly relations with other political groups, the military, the United States, and the European Union (EU). Like the majority of Turks, AKP leaders favored joining the EU. However, the controversy surrounding the 2007 presidential election interrupted this process.

Typical of parliamentary systems, Turkey is governed both by the prime minister (the head of the government) and by the president (the head of state and military commander-in-chief). While the prime minister's party is popularly elected, the president is elected not by the people, but by their representatives in parliament. As the AKP occupied the largest number of parliamentary seats, it exerted the greatest influence on who would be elected. Gül's nomination fueled the fears that Turkey was becoming an Islamist country that would fall under the rule of *Shari`ah* (Islamic law).

The first round of voting in April did not reach the necessary mini-mum—367—mandated by the constitution. The failure to reach the minimum sparked a controversy about the necessity of this rule. This prompted the Turkish military, which has a long tradition of inter-vening in the political realm, to issue a *muhtira* (warning) to the AKP, reminding the government of the primacy of secularism. The opposition Republican People's Party brought the controversy before the High Constitutional Court. Following the military's rebuke, the Constitu-tional Court confirmed that 367 votes were necessary to elect a

The author:
Berna Turam is a professor of sociology and Middle East studies at Hampshire College in Amherst, Massachusetts.

president. When Gül failed to receive a sufficient number of votes in the second round in May, he withdrew. Because of a lack of candidates, the presidential electoral process was terminated. This forced parliamentary elections to be scheduled early, for July.

The opposition organizes

The conflict over the presidency stirred a major show of opposition among Turks who supported secularism. Protests were organized in Ankara, the capital; Istanbul, the largest city; and Izmir. An estimated 1 million secularists poured into Ankara's Tandogan Square on April 14. The turnout in Istanbul on April 29 was even larger. In Izmir, some 1.5 million rallied against the pro-Islamic AKP.

Women played a leading role in the protests. Many secularist women had long been active in civil organizations involved in the fight against Islamization in Turkey. Their predominance in the anti-Islamist movement and in the protests grew out of their perception that many Islamic men, including religious leaders in some countries, oppress freedom and human rights for women and oppose their emancipation.

The opposition's major concern was the growing political power of pro-Islamic forces in all three branches of government—the premiership and Cabinet, the parliament, and the presidency. The former president of Turkey, Ahmet Necdet Sezer, had been a hard-core secularist. As long as he was president, he was seen as a guard against further Islamization by the pro-Islamic prime minister. The secular opposition was determined not to compromise the secular quality of the presidency because

Turkey—a physical and cultural bridge between Europe and the Middle East—shares a border on the southeast with Iraq. Kurdish rebels from Turkey have established camps in Iraq's Kurd-dominated northern provinces from which they cross the border to stage terrorist attacks on Turkish military encampments and on the civilian population.

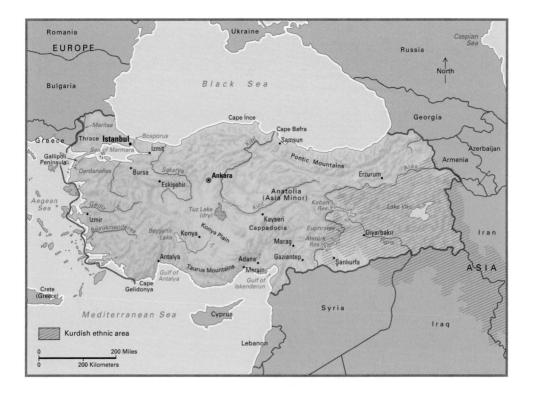

the post was regarded as a nearly sacred position. Turkey's first president and founder, Mustafa Kemal Atatürk, established the government as strictly secular in 1928.

Many of the secularist opponents were also deeply disturbed by the possibility of the president's wife, the nation's first lady, wearing a headscarf. This issue was one reason why so many women participated in the rallies. The use of headscarves had been discouraged by Atatürk himself.

The roots of modern Turkey

When the Ottoman Empire (1299-1922) and its ally Germany lost World War I (1914–1918), the empire's territories were partitioned among the allies—France, Greece, Italy, and the United Kingdom. The Treaty of Sevres, signed on Aug. 10, 1920, left the empire with only northern Asia Minor, parts of eastern Anatolia, and Istanbul, the seat of the last sultan, Vahdettin. Outside the capital, nationalists founded the Grand National Assembly on April 23, 1920, and mobilized the people in a struggle for independence. By September 1922, they had driven out the last of the occupying Greek forces from what is now western Turkey.

After abolishing the sultanate, the Nationalists organized a new nation under the leadership of Ghazi Mustafa Kemal Pasha, a distinguished World War I commander. (Kemal would later be given the surname *Atatürk*, meaning *father of the Turks*.) With the signing of a reorganized peace treaty in 1923, the allies recognized the new Turkish Republic, with borders essentially as they are today.

Turkish Prime Minister Recep Tayyip Erdogan (right), head of the pro-Muslim AKP Party, and Abdullah Gül (left), a devout Muslim who was elected president of Turkey in 2007, greet crowds at a ceremony in Erzurum, Turkey, in May. Many supporters of a secular Turkish government regarded the headscarves worn by Hayrunisa Gül (center left) and Ermine Erdogan (center right)—as a symbol of fundamentalist Islamist ideology.

Atatürk, who founded the Republican People's Party, essentially ruled alone as a benevolent dictator, dismissive of all opposition. Determined to make Turkey a modern Westernized nation, he initiated an all-encompassing series of reforms that modernized and secularized both the government and society. In 1924, he closed traditional religious schools; in 1925, he banned Islamic sects, replaced the Islamic calendar with the Western calendar, and banned men from wearing the *fez* (a flat-topped cap that had been the national headgear of Turkish men). Atatürk's clothing reforms encouraged the adoption of Western dress and discouraged, without forbidding, women from wearing the veil.

In 1926, Atatürk introduced new civil, penal, and commercial laws that were based on European legal systems. Turkey became the world's only predominantly Muslim country with a non-Islamic civil code that covered all matters involving family and marriage. The code outlawed polygamy as permitted by Islam, and marriage became a civil ceremony. A new Turkish alphabet based on Roman letters was introduced in 1928. In 1934, women were given the right to vote and hold elected office.

A woman casts a ballot in Istanbul in 1930 soon after Turkish women were allowed to vote in municipal elections. The right to vote in parliamentary elections was extended to Turkish women in 1934. The status of women in Turkey was also greatly enhanced by the 1926 Civil Code, which abolished polygamy and recognized a woman's right to divorce and inherit property.

Kemalism

The basic framework of Atatürk's reforms is referred to as Kemalism, which became Turkey's official *ideology* (the combined doctrines and intentions of a political movement). Kemalism combined secularism and extreme patriotism with reform and *etatism* (a form of socialism in

which the state uses its power to improve social conditions). Although Atatürk was careful not to dismiss religion in a country of faithful Muslims, he gradually put Islam under the control of the state by adopting from France a system known as laicism. (The French state assumed control over the Roman Catholic Church in France during the Revolution of 1789-1799.) Although Atatürk died on Nov. 10, 1938, the principles of Kemalism remained relatively unchallenged—or rather weakly contested—until after World War II (1939-1945).

Experimenting with democracy

When clamor for the end of one-party rule in Turkey finally grew loud enough, President Ismet Inönü in 1946 allowed the formation of an opposition party, the Democrat Party, or DP, and Turkey peacefully moved from dictatorship to functioning democracy. According to scholars, this smooth transition was unique compared with the rest of the developing world.

Only four years after being formed, the Democrat Party won control of parliament with 55.2 percent of the vote and peacefully took control of the government. In 1954, the party not only retained control but took a record 58.4 percent of the vote. The basis of the DP's popularity was its ability to integrate into the secular system the great majority of the people. At the time, this majority was rural, deeply religious, discon-

College students march in April 2007 through Ankara, the Turkish capital, under a giant banner of Mustafa Kemal Atatürk, the revered founder and first president of the republic. The students demonstrated against the presidential nomination of Abdullah Gül, whose devout Muslim faith was perceived as a threat to the tradition of secular government established by Atatürk in the 1920's.

tented, and often alienated from urban Turks and the government. During DP rule, the government became more inclusive and tolerant of Islamic movements. While the DP remained completely loyal to the Republic, its populist attitudes eventually were seen as a threat to Atatürk's legacy. Non-DP government officials turned against the party, and its relations with the military gradually deteriorated. When the DP responded with less inclusive and less tolerant policies, its popularity declined not only among the rural masses but also with urban intellectuals. In 1960, the DP government was overthrown in a military coup, and some of its leaders, including Prime Minister Adnan Menderes, were executed. Only later did scholars come to realize that Turkey's failed experiment with political pluralism and liberal democracy also opened its secular government to Islamic dissent.

The pro-Islamic party in power in 2007, the AKP, is the most moderate Islamic party in Turkey's history. Its predecessors, parties founded by Necmettin Erbakan (1926-), were far more radical. Erbakan, a professor of mechanical engineering, formed two successive political groups in the 1970's. Both were crushed by Turkey's military. The military eventually returned the government to civilian control, as it had after every coup; and in 1983, Erbakan founded yet another Islamic party, *Refah* (Welfare). In 1996, he managed to form a coalition government and become prime minister. Erbakan challenged the entire

Students from Islamic schools demonstrate against secularization at a protest staged before the Blue Mosque in Istanbul.

tradition of Turkey's secular government by his advocacy of an Islamic state. He also strongly opposed Turkey's efforts to join the EU. In 1998, the Constitutional Court banned Refah, a party that came to power by free and fair elections. Once again, the cost of safeguarding Turkey's secular tradition was the sacrifice of democratic principles. With the suppression of Refah, Erbakan was permanently expelled from politics.

A pro-Islamic party

After breaking ties with Refah and other radical Islamic groups, the AKP promoted itself as "a conservative democrat" party that favored joining the EU. After taking power in 2003, the AKP undertook a series of political and economic reforms in complete concordance with the military and nonparty government leaders. The reforms included implementing restrictions on the military's ability to influence civilian politics. The National Security Council was placed under civilian rather than military control and military security courts were abolished. The AKP greatly revised the penal code. Capital punishment was abolished, and torture was banned. Women gained greater protection against violence and acquired equal rights with men in regard to marriage, divorce, and property. For the first time, women's sexuality was treated as a matter of individual rights, rather than an issue involving the honor of a family. Although discrimination against Turkey's various ethnic

An estimated 1.5 million supporters of secular government demonstrate in Izmir, Turkey, in May 2007 in protest of the prospect of Abdullah Gül becoming president. Gül's candidacy was backed by the pro-Islamic AKP party, which already held the premiership and Cabinet through its control of parliament.

Turkish college students relax in an Istanbul park. The ban on headscarves on university campuses, instituted in the 1920's, remained in effect in 2007, though the pro-Islamic prime minister and president proposed rescinding it.

minorities was not thoroughly resolved, the Kurds and other minorities were permitted to learn and speak their own languages. However, the AKP's progressive attitude toward ethnic issues changed radically as a Kurdish rebel group, the PKK, accelerated its use of terrorist tactics in its effort to carve an independent Kurdish nation out of southeastern Turkey.

Without question, the AKP had made a serious commitment to the principles of democracy by improving and extending basic rights and freedoms. However, in 2006 the party passed antiterror legislation that restricted civil rights and endowed the police with greater power to carry out domestic surveillance—contradictions that brought into question the AKP's commitment to becoming a party of "conservative democratic" principles.

In terms of economics, the AKP made remarkable advances in a relatively short time. Following a program implemented by the International Monetary Fund, a United Nations affiliate, the AKP during the first four years of its tenure reduced inflation to 8.6 percent. The economy grew by 6 percent in 2003, by 9 percent in 2004, by 7 percent in 2005, and by 6 percent in 2006.

Foreign affairs crisis

The AKP enjoyed less success in the field of foreign affairs. Although intent on maintaining good relations with the EU and the United States, associations with both soured in 2007. Turkey's accession into the European Union seemingly was halted, at least temporarily, by Chancellor Angela Merkel of Germany and President Nicolas Sarkozy of France, who revealed that they were united in their opposition. According to international affairs experts, Turkey's chances for EU membership had not been helped by Abdullah Gül's election as president. Islamist terrorist attacks in Europe had also played a part. Massive bombings of public transportation systems in Madrid in 2004 and London in 2005 stirred anti-Muslim feelings across Europe.

Two different situations strained Turkey's relations with the United States in 2007. In October, a U.S. House committee voted to condemn

PKK rebels, who demand that a Kurdish nation be carved out of southeastern Turkey, cross from Iraq into Turkey to stage attacks. In October 2007, Turkey pressed Iraq and the U.S. military to locate the rebels' hidden mountain camps and extradite PKK leaders to Turkey for trial.

the mass killing of Armenians in Turkey during World War I as an act of genocide. This move, designed to satisfy Armenian Americans, triggered a storm of controversy in Turkey, which claimed that mass killings had never taken place. Prime Minister Erdogan responded to the committee vote by recalling the Turkish ambassador from Washington, D.C., for consultations. President Gül then warned that a full congressional vote on the subject would severely damage Turkey's normally friendly relations with the United States. Turkish officials even hinted that a further deterioration in relations could become a major headache for U.S. President George W. Bush. Because of instability in much of Iraq, the U.S. military has moved massive amounts of goods and war material through Turkey and northern Iraq. Dominated by Iraqi Kurds, northern Iraq has remained relatively peaceful, compared with the rest of the country. Losing this supply line would cause grave logistical problems for the U.S. military.

In pursuit of the PKK

Conditions between the two countries continued to deteriorate through the fall of 2007. Days after the congressional committee vote, Turkey's National Assembly voted overwhelmingly to authorize a military incursion into northern Iraq to pursue PKK rebels. Turkey in recent months had moved an estimated 100,000 troops along its border with Iraq in preparation for a cross-border offensive against the rebels.

Intent on carving an autonomous Kurdish nation out of southeastern Turkey, the rebels had for more than two decades carried out cross-border attacks on Turkish troops and civilians from mountain strongholds in Iraq. As many as 30,000 people had been killed in the conflict. The U.S.-led invasion of Iraq in 2003 and the subsequent insurgency allowed the PKK to operate openly in northern Iraq, a situation that infuriated Turkey. Their pleas for a U.S. or Iraqi crackdown on the rebels had been ignored for years.

After a PKK raid on Turkish soldiers deployed along the border left 12 soldiers dead and several others missing on Oct. 20, 2007, Turkey on October 24 launched air attacks on the PKK strongholds and demanded that Iraq extradite all Kurdish fighters. Additional raids were launched in December. The U.S. ambassador to Iraq, Ryan C. Crocker, responded by counseling the Iraqi government to fully cooperate with Turkish demands. He noted, however, that the mountainous region along the border was remote and inaccessible, making an Iraqi military expedition against the PKK rebels "unrealistic."

Erdogan and his Cabinet found the response unsatisfactory, and talks with Iraqi and U.S. diplomats in Ankara were suspended. The United States and Iraqi government officials continued to promise their cooperation and took small steps toward cracking down on the rebels, including shutting down the offices of the Kurdistan Democratic Solution, which was alleged to have close ties with the PKK. Iraqi Prime Minister Nouri Kamel al-Maliki promised to close all PKK offices in Iraq and arrest rebel leaders whenever possible. However, he stopped short of actually sending troops into the Kurdish north. With all available Iraqi forces bogged down with the insurgency in western and

southern Iraq, Maliki had no troops to send, analysts noted. He also was in no position to deploy troops against Kurds in northern Iraq. When the Turkish parliament voted to move against the rebels, the president of the region, Masoud Barzani, responded by declaring that Iraqi Kurds would defend themselves if Turkey's military crossed the border. He rejected Turkey's accusation that his government has aided and abetted the rebels and hinted that Turkey's real goal was to undermine the quasi-autonomous Kurdish state in northern Iraq.

Both Maliki and U.S. officials in Iraq feared than any large military operation in the north would destabilize the country's one relatively peaceful area. International affairs experts warned that open warfare in the north could further destabilize the already war-torn country, which could possibly bring down Maliki's fragile government, producing an even more volatile Iraq—a disaster for the Middle East and for the Bush administration. Alienating the United States would also be disastrous for Turkey, a major recipient of U.S. foreign aid and a major economic partner of the United States.

Despite sporadic clashes between Turkey's Islamists and secularists, the peaceful integration of the AKP into Turkey's secular system indicates at least some degree of success in the democratic transformation of the country. Ultimate success will likely depend on the skill with which AKP leaders engage, negotiate, and cooperate within the confines of secular traditions; and whether they can repair relations with the West without alienating their own Muslim constituency.

A Turkish soldier stands guard at an army post along the Turkey-Iraq border. Turkey deployed tens of thousands of troops in the area in 2007, and the Turkish parliament in October authorized a military incursion into Iraq to clean out PKK rebel encampments.

Turkmenistan in early 2007 was rocked by turmoil because of the Dec. 21, 2006, death of President Saparmurad Niyazov. He had ruled with an iron hand from 1992 until his death.

Deputy Prime Minister Gurbanguly Berdimuhammedov emerged as acting president in December 2006 after a power struggle. According to the Turkmen Constitution, parliament speaker Ovezgeldy Atayev should have succeeded Niyazov. However, Atayev was arrested shortly after Niyazov's death and in February 2007 was sentenced to five years in prison after a closed trial.

Berdimuhammedov won presidential elections held on February 11, taking 89 percent of the vote. No opposition leaders were permitted to run in the election. Foreign observers criticized the elections as a farce. Berdimuhammedov consolidated his power during the year by firing Niyazov-era officials, reshuffling his Cabinet, and taking control of the Democratic Party of Turkmenistan, the country's sole political party.

Berdimuhammedov introduced several reforms in his first months as president, including improvements in pensions, education, and Internet access. He also encouraged greater foreign participation in the development of Turkmenistan's extensive oil and gas resources. ■ Juliet Johnson
See also **Asia**.

Tuvalu. See **Pacific Islands**.

Uganda. Rebel activities in Uganda's border regions with Congo (Kinshasa) and Sudan continued in 2007. The truce signed in 2006 by Uganda and the Lord's Resistance Army (LRA), a rebel group in northern Uganda, did not last, though heavy fighting did not resume.

In early 2007, Mozambique's former President Joaquim Chissano was appointed United Nations envoy to Uganda and renewed attempts to hold peace talks with the LRA in Juba, Sudan. In 2005, the International Criminal Court (ICC) had issued warrants against top LRA leaders for war crimes. The LRA sought the removal of the warrants as a condition for a final peace agreement, hoping instead to face justice in Uganda. In November 2007, the ICC announced that it would not lift the warrants. Peace talks continued, though top LRA leaders remained in hiding.

Energy. A shortage of energy plagued Uganda's growing economy in 2007. In August, construction began on the Bujagali Dam on the Victoria Nile River, near Kampala, the capital. The project, which would provide water for hydroelectric power, was scheduled to be completed in 2011.

In June 2007, oil was discovered in Lake Albert, near the border between Uganda and Congo (Kinshasa). Disputes arose between the two countries over the rights because of their ill-defined border. Violence on and around the lake killed several people. Uganda's President Yoweri Museveni and Congo's President Joseph Kabila met in Arusha, Tanzania, in September. The two leaders agreed to cooperate in improving border security. They also agreed to work together in future development of the oil fields.

Judiciary protest. In March, Ugandan police raided the country's High Court to rearrest captured alleged rebels who had been granted bail. Ugandan judges protested against the infringement on their independence, bringing the courts to a standstill by refusing to hear further cases. Opposition parties supported the judges with protest marches. The judges resumed hearing cases only after Museveni personally apologized for the raid.

Racial tension. In May, a demonstration against deforestation near Kampala turned into a race riot. Ugandans were angry at Kampala's Asian community because an Asian-Ugandan-owned sugar company wanted to remove the forest for sugar-cane cultivation. Asian-owned properties were attacked. The violence led to the death of an Asian man. The racial bias among some Ugandans was a source of concern as many Asians played a key role in the country's economy. ■ Pieter Esterhuysen
See also **Africa**.

Ukraine in 2007 experienced another year of political turmoil as President Viktor Yushchenko, Prime Minister Viktor Yanukovych, and parliamentary opposition leader Yulia Tymoshenko battled for power. The feud culminated in early parliamentary elections held on September 30.

The conflict began in January when President Yushchenko twice vetoed a controversial bill to increase the powers of the Cabinet and parliament at the expense of the president. Parliament overrode the first veto and did not recognize the second, transforming the bill into law on February 2. Parliament then twice rejected Yushchenko's nominee for foreign minister before approving another nominee on March 21. As various conflicts continued, a group of opposition parliamentarians switched allegiance to Prime Minister Yanukovych's ruling *coalition* (partnership).

On April 2, President Yushchenko signed a decree dissolving parliament and calling for new elections on May 27. Governing coalition leaders demanded that the Constitutional Court rule on the decree's legality. On April 26, Yushchenko issued another decree postponing the elections until June 24. Yushchenko then dismissed three Constitutional Court judges for "breach of oath," and the chief judge resigned, citing political pressure. After a brief suspension, the Constitutional Court resumed work on July 11.

On May 27, Yushchenko, Yanukovych, and parliamentary speaker Oleksandr Moroz reached an agreement to hold early elections on September 30. In the elections, Prime Minister Yanukovych's Party of Regions took 34 percent of the vote (175 seats); the Yulia Tymoshenko Bloc took 31 percent (156 seats); President Yushchenko's Our Ukraine–People's Self-Defense (NUNS) bloc took 14 percent (72 seats); the Communist Party took 5 percent (27 seats); and the Lytvyn Bloc took 4 percent (20 seats). Reuniting the 2004 Orange Revolution alliance, Yulia Tymoshenko and NUNS bloc leader Vyacheslav Kyrylenko formed a coalition in which Tymoshenko would become prime minister and NUNS would nominate the speaker of parliament.

On Dec. 6, 2007, Yushchenko officially nominated Tymoshenko for prime minister, but she received only 225 votes in parliament on December 11, losing by 1 vote. One member of parliament claimed that his electronic voting card did not work, so the speaker of parliament called a second round of voting. In the December 18 vote, which the opposition boycotted, Tymoshenko received 226 votes, becoming prime minister.

Disaster. A methane explosion at a coal mine near the eastern city of Donetsk on November 18 left about 100 miners dead. It was the worst mining accident in the country's history.

■ Juliet Johnson

See also **Disasters; Europe.**

Unemployment. See Economics; Labor.

United Arab Emirates. See Middle East.

Opposition leader Yulia Tymoshenko (center) addresses supporters of Prime Minister Viktor Yanukovych in the Ukrainian parliament in March. Tymoshenko, supported by President Viktor Yushchenko, battled Yanukovych for control of Ukraine throughout 2007 and was elected prime minister on December 18.

UNITED KINGDOM

In June 2007, Tony Blair, prime minister of the United Kingdom (U.K.) since 1997 (and head of the Labour Party since 1994), resigned. He was succeeded by Chancellor of the Exchequer (finance minister) Gordon Brown.

"Cash for honours." In early 2007, Blair's government continued to be haunted by allegations that it had promised seats in the House of Lords (the unelected upper house of Parliament) to political donors during the campaign for the 2005 general election. Such use of "cash for honours" became the subject of a police investigation in 2006. Blair was interviewed twice by police as a witness, the first time that a prime minister had been so questioned while in office. In January 2007, the police arrested and questioned Blair's communications director, Ruth Turner, and Labour's chief fund-raiser, Lord Levy. Both denied any wrongdoing. The police submitted a final report in April to the Crown Prosecution Service, which announced in July that there was insufficient evidence in the case and that no charges would be brought.

Iran. On March 23, 15 British sailors serving in Iraq were captured at sea by Iranian forces who claimed the sailors had entered Iranian territorial waters. The sailors were released on April 4. Because of intense international interest in the incident, the British government initially allowed the sailors to sell their stories to the media. The decision was strongly criticized by many groups, including the families of soldiers who had been killed or injured in Iraq. Defence Secretary Des Browne reversed the decision and banned armed forces personnel from accepting payment for interviews in the future. The Conservatives called for Browne's resignation, and Browne was forced to apologize to the House of Commons. He also launched an inquiry into how the sailors came to be seized, which blamed operational problems.

Elections. The Labour Party fared badly in elections on May 3 for the *devolved* (having limited powers to govern) Scottish and Welsh parliaments and in local council elections. Labour lost control of the Scottish parliament. Alex Salmond and the Scottish National Party (SNP) narrowly won the election, gaining one more seat than Labour. Salmond formed a minority administration with the Green Party. The stated goal of the SNP is to withdraw Scotland from the United Kingdom. However, Salmond conceded that creating an effective SNP government should take precedence over gaining independence. Opinion polls showed dissatisfaction with the U.K. Labour government, but only a minority of Scots favored independence. Salmond promised to hold a referendum on independence in 2010 but also demanded that more powers be devolved from the British government in London to the Scottish parliament.

Labour also did badly in the election for the Welsh Assembly, though the party remained the largest in the legislature. Labour's Rhodri Morgan continued as head of a minority administration with Plaid Cymru, the Welsh nationalist party.

The opposition Conservative Party did well in the elections for local councils in England and Scotland, winning 40 percent of the vote. Labour came in second with 27 percent, just ahead of the Liberal Democrats, who won 26 percent. The Conservatives gained 911 council seats throughout the United Kingdom; Labour lost 505. The SNP also won the most seats in Scotland's local council elections. (There were no local government elections in Wales.)

Blair resigns. Blair announced his resignation as prime minister on May 10, a week after the local elections, though not as a consequence of the poor results. (Blair had promised in 2005 that if the Labour Party were elected for another term, he would not serve a full term.) He stated that he would submit his resignation to Queen Elizabeth II on June 27, 2007, giving the Labour Party time to select a new party leader and prime minister.

The top candidate for successor was Gordon Brown, who had served as chancellor of the exchequer since 1997. Two left-wing members of par-

Massive flooding in July turns the medieval town of Tewkesbury, about 110 miles (177 kilometers) northwest of London, into an island. Month-long rains caused the worst flooding in 60 years across many parts of England.

liament (MP's), John McDonnell and Michael Meacher, also ran for the position. However, neither collected enough nominations from fellow MP's to be placed on the ballot. Brown was elected unopposed. At a party conference on June 24, 2007, Harriet Harman, the minister of state for justice, was elected deputy party leader.

Brown becomes prime minister. After accepting Blair's resignation, the queen immediately called on Brown to form a government. Brown moved quickly to restore some of the faith in government that had been lost toward the end of Blair's term. He adopted a low-key approach based on his school motto, "I will do my utmost."

Brown also renewed the Cabinet by bringing in younger ministers and assigning existing members new roles. His long-term ally, Alistair Darling, replaced him as chancellor of the exchequer. Ed Balls, a former adviser to Brown, became secretary of the newly created Department of Children, Schools, and Families. The responsibility for higher education was transferred from the old education ministry to the new Department of Innovation, Universities, and Skills under John Denham. Denham had resigned from Blair's Cabinet in 2003 in protest of British involvement in the Iraq War.

Gordon Brown—prime minister; first lord of the treasury; minister for the civil service

Alistair Darling—chancellor of the exchequer

David Miliband—secretary of state for foreign and Commonwealth affairs

Hilary Benn—secretary of state for environment, food, and rural affairs

Ruth Kelly—secretary of state for transport

Alan Johnson—secretary of state for health

Shaun Woodward—secretary of state for Northern Ireland

Des Browne—secretary of state for defence; secretary of state for Scotland

John Hutton—secretary of state for business, enterprise, and regulatory reform

James Purnell—secretary of state for culture, media, and sport

Ed Miliband—minister for the cabinet office; chancellor of the Duchy of Lancaster

Geoff Hoon—parliamentary secretary to the treasury; chief whip of the House of Commons

Jacqui Smith—secretary of state for the home department

Andy Burnham—chief secretary to the treasury

Harriet Harman—leader of the House of Commons; minister for women

Ed Balls—secretary of state for children, schools, and families

Baroness Ashton of Upholland—leader of the House of Lords; lord president of the council

Jack Straw—secretary of state for justice; lord chancellor

Douglas Alexander—secretary of state for international development

Peter Hain—secretary of state for work and pensions; secretary of state for Wales

John Denham—secretary of state for innovation, universities, and skills

Hazel Blears—secretary of state for communities and local government

*As of Dec. 1, 2007.

HOUSE OF COMMONS

Queen Elizabeth II opened the 2007-2008 session of Parliament on November 6, 2007. As of December 1, the House of Commons was made up of the following:

352	Labour Party
194	Conservative Party
63	Liberal Democrats
9	Democratic Unionist Party
6	Scottish National Party
5	Sinn Féin
3	Plaid Cymru
3	Social Democratic and Labour Party
3	Independent
1	Independent Conservative
1	Independent Labour
1	Respect
1	Ulster Unionist Party

In addition, the unaffiliated speaker and 3 deputies attend sessions but do not vote.

David Miliband was made foreign secretary. The former government whip, Jacqui Smith, became home secretary, the first woman to hold this position. Deputy Leader Harriet Harman was also made leader of the House of Commons.

Mark Malloch Brown, the former United Nations deputy secretary-general who had been a vocal critic of the administration of United States President George W. Bush, became a minister in the Foreign Office and was made a peer so that he could sit in the House of Lords. The appointment, along with that of Denham, suggested that Gordon Brown was adding critics of the Iraq War to his government and shifting British foreign policy in a direction that was more independent of the United States.

Election called off. As Brown rose in the polls over the summer, it was widely expected that he would call a general election in November to earn his own mandate. (The prime minister can set the date of an election as long as it is within five years of the last election.) However, during a Conservative Party conference in October, the shadow chancellor, George Osborne, issued a call to raise the limit at which people must pay an inheritance tax. The Conservatives suddenly pulled ahead in opinion polls. Brown then announced that he needed time to share his vision with the British people and that there would be no election in 2007 nor in 2008. The Conservatives accused Brown of being afraid to call an election that he might lose.

Government crises. Brown's government was rocked in November 2007 when the loss of two discs containing the records of 25 million people claiming child benefits was revealed. The discs had been sent through internal mail—a breach of regulations—by a junior official at a tax agency office. Security experts feared that the discs, which included addresses, birth dates, and insurance and bank account numbers, could fall into the hands of criminals and raised questions about the security of government data.

It was revealed in November that David Abrahams, a property developer, had channeled £600,000 ($1.2 million) to the Labour Party through third parties, which was illegal. Peter Watt, the general secretary of the Labour Party, resigned after admitting that he knew of the donations. Brown called for an investigation.

Economy. In March, Brown delivered his final budget to the House of Commons as chancellor of the exchequer. He cut the basic income tax rate to 20 percent, its lowest level for 75 years (effective April 2008). However, critics noted that the cut was offset by the abolition of the lowest tax rate of 10 percent (which had assisted those with low incomes) and by adjustments to national insurance. Most analysts saw the budget as a political tool to prevent the Conservatives from presenting themselves as the party of low taxes. Brown also reduced corporate taxes, increased duties on heavily polluting vehicles, and raised taxes on alcohol, cigarettes, and fuel. New allowances in the budget eliminated income taxes for many pensioners. Overall, the budget raised as much revenue as it disbursed. The Conservatives criticized Brown for favoring the rich at the expense of the poor. He argued that simplifying the tax system had been his long-term goal.

In April 2007, Brown survived a no-confidence motion introduced by the Conservatives. The Conservatives charged that Brown had ignored advice in 1997 that his move to abolish tax relief on pension fund dividends would damage private pension funds. Brown argued that a decline in the stock market and a large aging population had hurt pensions.

In March 2007, the rate of inflation rose to 3.1 percent, higher than the 2-percent target that the government had set. The increase required the governor of the Bank of England (which sets interest rates) to write a formal letter of explanation to the chancellor for the first time since the new regulations were introduced in 1997.

The government admitted in October 2007 that the pace of the nation's economic growth was slowing. The Bank of England forecast that economic growth would slow from 3.2 percent in 2007 to 2.3 percent in 2008.

Liberal Democratic leader Menzies Campbell resigned in October 2007 after criticism of his leadership. Nick Clegg, the party's home affairs spokesman, was elected party leader in December 2007.

Northern Rock. In September 2007, the Bank of England was forced to rescue the Newcastle-based savings bank Northern Rock (which specialized in mortgage lending). The company had acquired 19 percent of the British mortgage mar-

Former British Prime Minister Margaret Thatcher poses beside a bronze statue dedicated in her honor in the Palace of Westminster, London, after its unveiling in February. Thatcher served as prime minister from 1979 to 1990.

ket but was vulnerable to fluctuations in the international money market on which it relied for funding. Revelations about the poor state of the bank's finances (following the U.S. crisis in sub-prime mortgage lending) led to a run on the bank as customers withdrew their money. The Bank of England temporarily lent Northern Rock £25 billion ($51.6 billion) while the institution searched for a buyer.

Terrorist attacks. In April, five British Muslims were sentenced to life imprisonment for planning terrorist attacks in 2004 that included the bombing of a shopping center in Kent. Three men were sentenced in July 2007 for using the Internet to disseminate propaganda supporting the terrorist group al-Qa`ida.

In another case in July, four men were convicted of an attempt to detonate bombs on London's underground train system on July 21, 2005. Their attempt followed the actual terrorist bombings of London buses and trains on July 7, 2005, in which 52 people were killed. The defendants were sentenced to life imprisonment for involvement in the plot, which was linked to al-Qa`ida. A fifth bomber pleaded guilty in November 2007.

Brown's government was tested by terrorist attacks within days of taking office. On June 29, police defused two car bombs in London. The following day, two men drove a burning car into the entrance of Glasgow International Airport in Scotland. The only person hurt was one of the terrorists (who later died of his burns), and the fire did not spread. Eight people were arrested in connection with the incidents, including three foreign nationals working in the U.K. as physicians. Brown ordered a review of the procedures for recruiting foreign-born doctors.

Natural disasters. Severe rainfall in July led to flooding in western and southern England. At least six people died, and thousands not only had to leave their residences, which were submerged, but also had no access to drinking water because water-processing plants had flooded.

In August, *foot-and-mouth disease* (a contagious disease among cattle) was discovered on a farm in Surrey, about 30 miles (48 kilometers) southwest of London. The government acted swiftly to contain the epidemic, banning the movement of livestock. The European Union briefly banned the export of British live animals.

Litvinenko case. The assassination of former Russian KGB agent Alexander Litvinenko in London in November 2006 continued to cause diplomatic problems in 2007. Russian officials refused to extradite a suspect in the murder, businessman and former KGB agent Andrei Lugovoi. Litvinenko's former associate, businessman Boris Berezovsky (living in exile in the U.K.), held that Russian President Vladimir Putin was responsible

for the killing and claimed that he himself was at risk of being assassinated. In July, the British government expelled four Russian diplomats in protest at the failure to hand over Lugovoi. The Russians, in turn, expelled four British diplomats.

Princess Diana inquest. An inquest into the death of Princess Diana opened in October, just over 10 years after her death in Paris in 1997. The inquest was to examine the causes of the car crash that killed the princess and her friend, Dodi Fayed, as well as the driver.

De Menezes case. The Central Criminal Court in London in November 2007 found the Metropolitan Police guilty of endangering the public in the killing of unarmed Brazilian Jean Charles de Menezes on July 22, 2005. Police had followed de Menezes from his apartment to a London underground station, mistakenly believing him to be one of several men who had attempted to bomb the London underground system the previous day. When de Menezes boarded a train, he was shot by police who thought he might detonate a bomb. It quickly became clear that de Menezes was innocent. The court in November 2007 found the police guilty of "catastrophic" failings in the incident.

■ Rohan McWilliam

See also **Europe; Ireland; Northern Ireland; People in the news** (Gordon Brown); **Russia; Terrorism; United Kingdom, Prime Minister of.**

Tony Blair (right) congratulates Gordon Brown at The Bridgewater Hall in Manchester on June 24, 2007. Brown had just been confirmed as the new Labour Party leader. On June 27, Brown became prime minister when Queen Elizabeth II asked him to form a government.

United Kingdom, Prime Minister of.

Gordon Brown replaced Tony Blair as prime minister in June 2007. Blair had promised before the 2005 general election that if his Labour Party retained control of Parliament, he would not serve a full term in office. Blair also gave up his seat in Parliament and took up a new post as an international envoy to secure peace in the Middle East.

Gordon Brown had been one of the architects of "New Labour" (the attempt to move the former left-wing party to the center). In 1994, he chose not to campaign for the post of prime minister to allow his ally, Blair, to run unopposed. Brown served continuously from Labour's election in 1997 as chancellor of the exchequer (treasury minister) and was credited with masterminding the United Kingdom's relatively strong economic performance.

On becoming prime minister, Brown broke with his predecessor's approach on several issues. He signaled that he would maintain good—but more distant—relations with United States President George W. Bush. He also moved ahead with plans to withdraw British troops from Iraq. Initially, Brown's government rose in the opinion polls and overtook the Conservative Party. However, a decision not to call a November 2007 election because of a sudden Conservative surge in the polls damaged his standing.   ■ Rohan McWilliam

See also **Iraq; Middle East; People in the news** (Gordon Brown); **United Kingdom.**

United Nations.

The United Nations (UN) Security Council agreed in July 2007 to deploy a combined UN-African Union (AU) peacekeeping force to end the ethnic conflict in Sudan's western region of Darfur. The force, called UNAMID, was to consist of about 26,000 troops and was to replace by December 31 the 7,000 AU troops that had been in Darfur since 2005. According to UN reports, more than 250,000 people had died in the conflict in Darfur, and more than 2 million others had become refugees.

The UN-AU mission authorized for Darfur was nearly three times as large as another UN force that has been monitoring a peace agreement in southern Sudan since 2005. That agreement was made by the Muslim-led Sudanese government in Khartoum with former Christian rebel groups.

UN Secretary-General Ban Ki-moon visited Sudan, Chad, and Libya in September 2007 to discuss the political process and deployment of peacekeeping operations. Ban announced a new round of peace talks to begin on October 27 in the Libyan coastal town of Sirte, to work out what he called a "final settlement" of the conflicts in Sudan. The talks proved inconclusive.

Middle East. The European Union, Russia, the UN, and the United States—which formed a diplomatic quartet for peace in the Middle East—attempted in 2007 to end the conflict between the Israelis and the Palestinians. The group and its newly appointed representative, former British Prime Minister Tony Blair, met in New York City on September 23 to reiterate support for the creation of a Palestinian state that would exist in peace with Israel and urged "substantive and serious" talks between Israeli and Palestinian leaders.

On May 30, the UN Security Council passed a resolution to establish a tribunal for the prosecution of those responsible for the 2005 political assassinations of former Lebanese Prime Minister Rafik Hariri and at least 22 other Lebanese politicians and journalists. The activists had opposed Syria's military occupation of their country.

Kosovo. In 2007, UN representatives tried to resolve the dispute over independence between Serbia and its province of Kosovo. Kosovo's ethnic Albanian majority demanded complete independence, but Serbia refused to allow it. On March 26, the UN special envoy for Kosovo, Martti Ahtisaari, a former president of Finland, proposed a plan for Kosovar independence under international supervision. In July, when the plan was presented to the UN Security Council, Russia vetoed the proposal.

The council then delegated responsibility for mediating talks between Kosovo and Serbia to a group of six nations—France, Germany, Italy, Russia, the United Kingdom, and the United States. Ethnic Albanian leaders warned that if no decision was reached, Kosovo would secede from Serbia. The group failed to resolve the matter by the designated deadline of December 10.

Myanmar. The UN also attempted to reduce tensions in Myanmar (formerly known as Burma) after demonstrations in September led by Buddhist monks demanding democracy were met with violence by the ruling *junta* (military regime). UN special envoy Ibrahim Gambari traveled to Yangon, the largest city, in September and November, urging democratic reform and the release of political prisoners and detained demonstrators. Secretary-General Ban demanded the release of Myanmar's opposition leader, Nobel Peace Prize laureate Aung San Suu Kyi, who had been under house arrest for 12 of the past 18 years. In November, Suu Kyi was allowed to meet with members of her National League for Democracy party for the first time in three years, and many of the detained demonstrators were released.

Climate change was the focus of a special UN session on September 24. More than 80 heads of state and government discussed the urgency of combating global warming. Delegates from nearly 190 countries met again on the island of Bali, Indonesia, in mid-December to begin negotiating a replacement for the Kyoto Protocol, a treaty due to expire in 2012 that the U.S. government had refused to sign. At the Bali meeting, the United States and other industrialized nations agreed to help developing nations with technology and financing. In exchange, the developing nations agreed to reduce their greenhouse gas emissions.

On Oct. 12, 2007, the Norwegian Nobel Committee in Oslo awarded the Nobel Peace Prize to the Intergovernmental Panel on Climate Change, a UN-sponsored scientific committee, for studies that created an "informed consensus about the connection between human activities and global warming" and to former U.S. Vice President Al Gore for his contribution to the struggle against climate change.

General Assembly. Former Foreign Minister Srgjan Kerim of the former Yugoslav Republic of Macedonia began his term as president of the 62nd session of the assembly on September 18. Kerim urged the 192-member body to find solutions to such problems as the lack of financing for development in poor countries and the need for UN reform. Special sessions were held to address the continued conflicts in Afghanistan and Iraq.

Security Council. In 2007, five new members—Burkina Faso, Costa Rica, Croatia, Libya, and Vietnam—were added to the council. They joined the five permanent members—China, France, Russia, the United Kingdom, and the United States—and the five returning members—Belgium, Indonesia, Italy, Panama, and South Africa. ◼ J. Tuyet Nguyen

See also **Middle East; Myanmar; Serbia; Sudan.**

United States, Government of the.

Iraq, Afghanistan, and counterterrorism continued to be major areas of focus for the U.S. government in 2007. In addition, the Department of Justice was frequently in the headlines because of a controversy over the firings of federal prosecutors and because of a change in leadership.

Iraq and Afghanistan. In early 2007, U.S. President George W. Bush, a Republican, announced that about 30,000 extra U.S. troops would be sent to Iraq in an attempt to quell high levels of violence in Baghdad and Al Anbar province. This new strategy—dubbed the troop "surge"—ran counter to public opinion. Voters had put Democrats in charge of both houses of Congress in a November 2006 election that many political experts described as a backlash against the president's war policy and as a desire to withdraw U.S. soldiers from Iraq. On Feb. 16, 2007, the House of Representatives passed a resolution opposing the surge. Nevertheless, the extra forces were deployed during the first half of 2007, bringing the total number of U.S. troops in Iraq to about 160,000.

In May, Congress passed a bill that provided about $100 billion for the wars in Iraq and Afghanistan for fiscal year (FY) 2007 (Oct. 1, 2006-Sept. 30, 2007). Enactment of the bill brought the total amount appropriated since September 2001 for Iraq, Afghanistan, and counterterrorism operations to nearly $610 billion. This amount included funds for military operations, base security, reconstruction, foreign aid, embassy operations, and veterans' health care. The Bush administration requested another $195 billion for FY 2008 (Oct. 1, 2007-Sept. 30, 2008). By the end of the 2007 calendar year, Congress had appropriated about $87 billion in war-related funds for FY 2008.

The May 2007 bill established 18 legislative, security, and economic benchmarks for Iraq's government to achieve as a condition for receiving certain U.S. reconstruction aid. The bill required the president and the Government Accountability Office (GAO) to report to Congress on Iraq's benchmark progress. The president's first report, submitted on July 12, claimed satisfactory progress on 8 benchmarks, unsatisfactory progress on 6 others, and mixed progress on 2 others. The GAO report, issued on September 4, was less optimistic. It claimed that Iraq had met only 3 benchmarks, with 4 others partially met and 11 others unmet. The president's second report, submitted on September 14, claimed satisfactory progress on 9 benchmarks, unsatisfactory progress on 3 others, and mixed progress on 4 others. Both of the president's reports gave no progress rating on 2 of the benchmarks, claiming that the conditions needed for progress were not present.

The May bill also required an independent assessment of the readiness of Iraq's military and police forces. A commission of retired U.S. military officers and chiefs of police conducted the assessment. The commission's report, issued on September 6, indicated that Iraq's security forces were improving their performance but would not be able to operate independently within the next 12 to 18 months. The report also recommended that Iraq's National Police force be disbanded and reorganized because of sectarianism in its units.

The May bill also directed Army General David Petraeus, the commander of the multinational coalition force in Iraq, and Ryan Crocker, the U.S. ambassador to Iraq, to give testimony to Congress on military and political progress in Iraq. Their testimony on September 10 and 11 was highly anticipated and received much media coverage. Petraeus told Congress that "the military objectives of the troop surge are, in large measure, being met." Coalition and Iraqi forces have dealt blows to al-Qa`ida in Iraq and to Shi`ite militias, he said, and the number of violent incidents and deaths, while still high, is decreasing. Petraeus said he believed that U.S. forces could be reduced to presurge levels by mid-2008 without jeopardizing

The United States Bureau of Engraving and Printing unveiled a redesigned $5 bill with enhanced security features on Sept. 20, 2007. The new bill was scheduled to begin circulating in early 2008. It features the Great Seal of the United States in purple ink on the front.

these security gains. But he warned that a larger and more rapid withdrawal would likely have devastating consequences. Crocker acknowledged that Iraq's political leaders had made little progress in achieving national accord, but he claimed that the seeds of reconciliation were being planted.

On September 13, President Bush announced that he would accept Petraeus's recommendations and authorize a limited troop withdrawal from Iraq. By the end of 2007, about 5,000 U.S. troops had left Iraq without being replaced.

The U.S. government's use of private security contractors in Iraq came under increased scrutiny in 2007. On September 16, security guards employed by Blackwater USA—a North Carolina-based security firm—shot and killed 17 Iraqis in Baghdad. The guards were escorting vehicles carrying U.S. State Department officials. Blackwater claimed that the guards fired in self-defense after being attacked, but several Iraqi eyewitnesses disputed that account, saying the guards fired without provocation. The incident intensified criticisms about a lack of oversight of private security contractors and a lack of clarity about what laws, if any, applied to them. Shortly after the incident, a joint U.S.-Iraqi commis-

sion began to evaluate the use of private security details and recommend ways to prevent similar incidents. Later in 2007, the Defense and State departments agreed to give the military more control over diplomatic security operations. In November, according to news reports, the Federal Bureau of Investigation found that at least 14 of the 17 Blackwater shooting deaths were unjustified under State Department rules for the use of deadly force by security guards. Later that month, the U.S. government convened a grand jury to investigate multiple shootings involving security contractors in Iraq.

Counterterrorism. In July 2007, a group of 16 U.S. intelligence agencies released a National Intelligence Estimate (NIE) predicting that the country would face "a persistent and evolving terrorist threat over the next three years," especially from the terrorist organization al-Qa`ida. The NIE reported that although counterterrorism efforts had made it harder for al-Qa`ida to attack the U.S. homeland, al-Qa`ida had regained much of its operational capacity, mainly because it had been able to establish a safe haven in northwestern Pakistan.

The Bush administration in 2007 asked Congress for greater authority to conduct surveillance

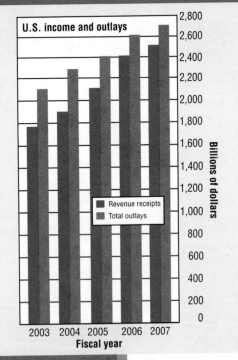

FEDERAL SPENDING   United States budget for fiscal 2007*

	Billions of dollars
National defense	560.1
International affairs	28.5
General science, space, technology	21.0
Energy	-0.9
Natural resources and environment	31.7
Agriculture	19.6
Commerce and housing credit	0.4
Transportation	73.0
Community and regional development	28.6
Education, training, employment, and social services	89.7
Health	266.3
Social security	586.2
Medicare	375.4
Income security	367.4
Veterans' benefits and services	72.8
Administration of justice	37.3
General government	17.8
Interest	237.9
Undistributed offsetting receipts	-82.2
Total budget outlays	**2,730.5**

*Oct. 1, 2006, to Sept. 30, 2007.
  Source: U.S. Department of the Treasury.

U.S. income and outlays

Billions of dollars

Revenue receipts
Total outlays

2003   2004   2005   2006   2007
Fiscal year

SELECTED AGENCIES AND BUREAUS OF THE U.S. GOVERNMENT*

Executive Office of the President
President, George W. Bush
Vice President, Richard B. Cheney
White House Chief of Staff, Joshua B. Bolten
Presidential Press Secretary, Dana M. Perino
Assistant to the President for Domestic Policy,
    Karl Zinsmeister
Assistant to the President for National Security Affairs,
    Stephen J. Hadley
Office of Science and Technology Policy—
    John H. Marburger III, Director
Council of Economic Advisers—Edward P. Lazear, Chairman
Office of Management and Budget—
    James A. Nussle, Director
Office of National Drug Control Policy—
    John P. Walters, Director
U.S. Trade Representative, Susan C. Schwab

Department of Agriculture
Acting Secretary of Agriculture, Chuck Conner

Department of Commerce
Secretary of Commerce, Carlos M. Gutierrez
    Bureau of Economic Analysis—J. Steven Landefeld, Director
    Bureau of the Census—Stephen H. Murdock, Director

Department of Defense
Secretary of Defense, Robert M. Gates
    Secretary of the Air Force, Michael W. Wynne
    Secretary of the Army, Preston M. Geren III
    Secretary of the Navy, Donald C. Winter
    Joint Chiefs of Staff—
        Admiral Michael G. Mullen, Chairman
        General James E. Cartwright, Vice Chairman
        General Teed Michael Moseley, Chief of Staff, Air Force
        General George W. Casey, Jr., Chief of Staff, Army
        Admiral Gary Roughead, Chief of Naval Operations
        General James T. Conway, Commandant, Marine Corps

Department of Education
Secretary of Education, Margaret Spellings

Department of Energy
Secretary of Energy, Samuel Wright Bodman

Department of Health and Human Services
Secretary of Health and Human Services,
    Michael O. Leavitt
    Centers for Disease Control and Prevention—
        Julie Louise Gerberding, Director
    Food and Drug Administration—Andrew C. von Eschenbach,
        Commissioner
    National Institutes of Health—Elias A. Zerhouni, Director
    Acting Surgeon General of the United States,
        Rear Admiral Steven K. Galson

Department of Homeland Security
Secretary of Homeland Security, Michael Chertoff
    U.S. Citizenship and Immigration Services—
        Emilio T. Gonzalez, Director
    U.S. Coast Guard—Admiral Thad W. Allen, Commandant
    U.S. Secret Service—Mark J. Sullivan, Director
    Federal Emergency Management Agency—R. David Paulison,
        Under Secretary

Department of Housing and Urban Development
Secretary of Housing and Urban Development,
    Alphonso R. Jackson

Department of the Interior
Secretary of the Interior, Dirk Kempthorne

Department of Justice
Attorney General, Michael B. Mukasey
    Federal Bureau of Prisons—Harley G. Lappin, Director
    Drug Enforcement Administration—
        Karen P. Tandy, Administrator
    Federal Bureau of Investigation—
        Robert S. Mueller III, Director
    Solicitor General, Paul D. Clement

Department of Labor
Secretary of Labor, Elaine L. Chao

Department of State
Secretary of State, Condoleezza Rice
    U.S. Ambassador to the United Nations,
        Zalmay Khalilzad

Department of Transportation
Secretary of Transportation, Mary E. Peters
    Federal Aviation Administration—
        Robert A. Sturgell, Acting Administrator

Department of the Treasury
Secretary of the Treasury, Henry M. Paulson, Jr.
    Internal Revenue Service—Linda E. Stiff, Acting Commissioner
    Treasurer of the United States, Anna Escobedo Cabral
    Office of Thrift Supervision—John M. Reich, Director

Department of Veterans Affairs
Secretary of Veterans Affairs, Lieutenant General James B. Peake

Supreme Court of the United States
Chief Justice of the United States, John G. Roberts, Jr.
    Associate Justices—

John Paul Stevens	Clarence Thomas
Antonin Scalia	Ruth Bader Ginsburg
Anthony M. Kennedy	Stephen G. Breyer
David Hackett Souter	Samuel Anthony Alito, Jr.

Congressional officials
President of the Senate pro tempore, Robert C. Byrd
Senate Majority Leader, Harry Reid
Senate Minority Leader, Mitch McConnell
Speaker of the House, Nancy Pelosi
House Majority Leader, Steny H. Hoyer
House Minority Leader, John Boehner
Congressional Budget Office—Peter R. Orszag, Director
Government Accountability Office—David M. Walker, Comptroller
    General of the United States
Library of Congress—James H. Billington, Librarian of Congress

Independent agencies
Central Intelligence Agency—General Michael V. Hayden, Director
Commission of Fine Arts—Earl A. Powell III, Chairman
Commission on Civil Rights—Gerald A. Reynolds, Chairman
Consumer Product Safety Commission—
    Nancy A. Nord, Acting Chairwoman
Corporation for National and Community Service—
    David Eisner, CEO
Environmental Protection Agency—Stephen L. Johnson, Administrator
Equal Employment Opportunity Commission—
    Naomi Churchill Earp, Chairwoman
Federal Communications Commission—Kevin J. Martin, Chairman
Federal Deposit Insurance Corporation—
    Sheila C. Bair, Chairwoman
Federal Election Commission—Robert D. Lenhard, Chairman
Federal Reserve System Board of Governors—
    Ben S. Bernanke, Chairman
Federal Trade Commission—Deborah Platt Majoras, Chairwoman
General Services Administration—Lurita Alexis Doan, Administrator
National Aeronautics and Space Administration—Michael D. Griffin,
    Administrator
National Endowment for the Arts—Dana Gioia, Chairman
National Endowment for the Humanities—Bruce M. Cole, Chairman
National Labor Relations Board—Robert J. Battista, Chairman
National Railroad Passenger Corporation (Amtrak)—
    Alexander Kummant, President and CEO
National Science Foundation—Arden L. Bement, Jr., Director
National Transportation Safety Board—
    Mark V. Rosenker, Chairman
Nuclear Regulatory Commission—Dale E. Klein, Chairman
Office of the Director of National Intelligence—
    Mike McConnell, Director
Peace Corps—Ronald A. Tschetter, Director
Securities and Exchange Commission—
    Christopher Cox, Chairman
Selective Service System—William A. Chatfield, Director
Small Business Administration—Steven C. Preston, Administrator
Smithsonian Institution—Cristián Samper, Acting Secretary
Social Security Administration—Michael J. Astrue, Commissioner
U.S. Postal Service—John E. Potter, Postmaster General

*As of Dec. 31, 2007.

for counterterrorism purposes. The administration had come under fire in 2005 and 2006 when it was revealed that the National Security Agency (NSA) had been secretly authorized to monitor phone calls and e-mails between the United States and other countries without a warrant. In January 2007, the administration agreed to seek approval from the Foreign Intelligence Surveillance Court before doing such monitoring. But later in 2007, the administration asked Congress for expanded spying authority, arguing that current law limited intelligence agencies' ability to keep tabs on foreign terrorism suspects. Under pressure from Republicans, Congress in August passed an emergency bill authorizing, until February 2008, warrantless surveillance of any communications involving at least one person outside the United States. Negotiations then began on a more long-lasting overhaul of surveillance law, with Democrats hoping to ensure that the overhaul would not violate privacy rights of U.S. citizens. But Democrats and Republicans failed to reach agreement before the end of 2007.

On July 31, Director of National Intelligence Mike McConnell disclosed that President Bush had authorized the NSA to undertake a number of secret counterterrorism activities under a single executive order in late 2001. The disclosure made clear that the NSA warrantless surveillance program had been only one part of a larger operation.

On July 21, 2007, President Bush issued an executive order setting broad legal boundaries for the interrogation of terrorism suspects by the Central Intelligence Agency (CIA). The order was required by legislation enacted in October 2006. The order allowed the CIA to resume a program of "enhanced" interrogation that had been suspended in 2006 because of criticism that it violated U.S. and international law. Under the order, the CIA program was required to comply with relevant sections of the international treaties known as the Geneva Conventions. But human rights advocates criticized the order because it contained no specifics about which interrogation techniques would be allowed and which would be prohibited.

In December 2007, news reports revealed that the CIA in 2005 had destroyed videotapes of Qa`ida suspects being interrogated in 2002. Many human rights advocates denounced the tape destruction, alleging that the CIA had engaged in torture and was trying to cover it up. CIA Director Michael Hayden said that the tapes were destroyed because they could have exposed CIA officers and their families to retaliation from al-Qa`ida. The Justice Department and CIA launched a joint investigation into the tape destruction. Congressional committees also began inquiries.

Justice Department. In early 2007, the House and Senate judiciary committees started an extensive inquiry into whether nine U.S. attorneys had been fired in 2006 for political reasons. Critics of the prosecutor dismissals, including some of the prosecutors themselves, alleged that they were removed because they had launched investigations of Republican politicians or had failed to launch investigations that would damage Democrats. Congress solicited the testimony of several current and former Bush administration officials. Some of them, including Attorney General Alberto Gonzales, testified that the firings had been routine and based on performance. But other testimony and documents indicated that some attorneys had been targeted for a perceived lack of loyalty to the Bush administration. Gonzales frustrated lawmakers by repeatedly testifying that he could not recall key details related to the firings. The controversy led to the resignations of several Justice Department officials, including Deputy Attorney General Paul McNulty and, eventually, Gonzales himself.

President Bush nominated Michael Mukasey, a retired U.S. judge, to replace Gonzales. On Nov. 8, 2007, the Senate voted 53-40 to confirm Mukasey. Many Democrats voted against Mukasey because during his confirmation hearings, he claimed not to know enough about a harsh interrogation technique called waterboarding to classify it as torture.

Iran. According to a National Intelligence Estimate (NIE) issued in December 2007, Iran halted its efforts to develop nuclear weapons in 2003 but was keeping open the option to develop them in the future. The 2007 NIE was a reversal of previous intelligence assessments, which had judged that Iran was actively working to build nuclear weapons. President Bush asserted that, despite the NIE, Iran remained a danger to international security.

Personnel changes. John Negroponte, director of national intelligence, resigned in February 2007 and became deputy secretary of state. Mike McConnell replaced Negroponte as national intelligence director. Zalmay Khalilzad became U.S. ambassador to the United Nations in April, replacing John Bolton, who had resigned in late 2006.

Several confidantes of President Bush left their jobs in 2007. Karl Rove, a senior Bush adviser who was the "architect" of the president's election wins in 2000 and 2004, resigned in August 2007. Harriet Miers resigned as White House counsel in January. Karen Hughes, a former Bush adviser, stepped down as State Department public diplomacy undersecretary in December.   ■ Mike Lewis

See also **Afghanistan; Agriculture; Armed forces; Cabinet, U.S.; Congress of the U.S.; Courts; Democratic Party; Drugs; Elections; Immigration; Iran; Iraq; Korea, North; People in the news** (Robert Gates; Michael Mukasey; Nancy Pelosi; David Petraeus; Robert Zoellick); **Republican Party; Safety; Social Security; Supreme Court of the U.S.; Taxation; United States, President of the; Welfare.**

An enthusiastic, hands-on crowd greets U.S. President George W. Bush in Fushë-Krujë, Albania, on June 10, 2007. The warm reception in Albania contrasted with the anti-Bush protests that greeted him in Germany, Italy, and other European countries on the same good-will tour.

United States, President of the.

Throughout 2007, President George W. Bush endured low public approval ratings. Most opinion polls indicated that fewer than 40 percent of Americans approved of the president's job performance. A troop "surge" in Iraq was the president's major foreign policy initiative of the year. His main domestic initiatives—immigration reform—failed to win congressional approval.

Iraq troop surge. In early 2007, President Bush announced plans to send about 30,000 additional U.S. troops to Iraq to quell violence. Despite strong opposition from war critics, the extra troops were deployed during the first half of 2007, bringing the total number of U.S. troops in Iraq to about 160,000. By the end of 2007, the surge had helped reduce violence in Baghdad and other areas. However, critics argued that despite the decline in violence, the surge was failing to bring about the hoped-for political reconciliation among competing factions in Iraq.

Immigration. President Bush failed in 2007 to broker the passage in Congress of one of his key domestic priorities: a comprehensive reform of immigration law. The president sought both to curtail the tide of illegal immigrants entering the United States and to resolve the status of illegal immigrants already in the country. He championed a bill that would have created a means for many illegal immigrants to gain legal status and eventual citizenship. The bill also would have set up a temporary guest worker program and allocated billions of dollars for border security. However, a failed vote to end debate in the Senate on June 28 prevented the bill's passage in 2007. Although the bill had bipartisan support, it drew strong bipartisan opposition. Many conservatives opposed the immigrant legalization scheme, calling it amnesty for breaking the law. Several liberals opposed provisions that would have made it harder for extended family members to join their relatives in the United States.

Vetoes. After vetoing only one bill in his first six years in office, President Bush vetoed seven bills in 2007. On May 1, he vetoed a war-spending bill because it would have required the withdrawal of U.S. troops from Iraq according to a specific timetable. The veto forced Congress to pass a revised bill without the troop withdrawal provisions. On June 20, he vetoed a bill that would have loosened restrictions on federally funded embryonic stem cell research. The veto was due to his opposition to the destruction of human embryos. The other vetoes were based on his opinions that the spending levels in the bills were too high. He vetoed two children's health insurance bills, on October 3 and December 12; a water projects bill on November 2; and an appropriations bill for health, education, and labor programs on November 13. Congress overrode the water veto but did not override the others.

Finally, the president, employing the pocket veto, did not sign a defense policy bill passed shortly before Congress adjourned for the year. He objected to a provision that could have exposed Iraq to billions of dollars in legal claims.

Missing e-mails. Two private organizations filed lawsuits in 2007 alleging that as many as 10 million e-mail messages from March 2003 to October 2005 were illegally deleted from White House servers. The 2007 lawsuits were filed by the National Security Archive on September 5 and by Citizens for Responsibility and Ethics in Washington on September 25. According to the two private groups, the missing e-mails may or may not have been preserved on backup tapes. On November 12, a U.S. district judge ordered the Executive Office of the President not to destroy any backup tapes of its e-mail. By the end of 2007, the Bush administration had provided few details about what happened to the e-mails or what steps, if any, were being taken to recover and preserve them. ■ Mike Lewis

See also **Cabinet, U.S.; Congress of the U.S.; Courts; Democratic Party; Elections; Republican Party; United States, Government of the**

Uruguay. See Latin America.

Uzbekistan. President Islam Karimov won a third seven-year term on Dec. 23, 2007, in elections that international monitors denounced. Karimov's nomination for the presidency by the ruling Uzbek Liberal-Democratic Party in November had led opposition leaders to accuse him of foul play. They argued that Karimov was constitutionally prohibited from seeking another term.

Opposition politicians also condemned the timing of the election. Karimov's term technically ended in January 2007, but under the Uzbek Constitution, the election did not have to take place until December. The delay essentially gave Karimov an eighth year in his second term. The Constitution limits presidents to two seven-year terms. Karimov, who had served as president since 1991, extended his own term through national referenda in 1995 and 2002.

In late November 2007, the United Nations Committee against Torture issued a report accusing Karimov's government of routinely using torture to silence the opposition. In November and December, an Uzbek human rights group released details of three torture-related deaths in a prison in the eastern city of Andijon. Karimov denied allegations of systematic torture and human rights violations. ■ Juliet Johnson

See also **Asia**.

Vanuatu. See Pacific Islands.

Venezuela. On Jan. 10, 2007, Hugo Chávez Frías was sworn in for a new six-year term as president of Venezuela. He pledged to speed Venezuela's transition into a socialist state. Soon after his landslide reelection in 2006, Chávez began dissolving his Fifth Republic Movement party and creating the United Socialist Party of Venezuela.

With continued high revenues from petroleum exports and $25 billion in reserves, Chávez in 2007 continued to promote programs that enhanced his status among poorer Venezuelans. He threatened severe penalties against businesses failing to comply with an expanding system of price controls, designed to offset inflation.

Creating "new citizens." Throughout 2007, Chávez expanded the reach of his administration into virtually all aspects of Venezuelan life. In September, he announced that a new socialist curriculum would be phased into both public and private schools. Explaining the change, Chávez said that capitalist ideology had corrupted children's values. State inspectors were to monitor schools' compliance with the new curriculum, designed to educate "the new citizen," according to Adán Chávez, the minister of education and the president's brother. The president said that his government would take over any school that refused to submit to its oversight.

Industry takeovers. During 2007, Chávez nationalized Venezuela's electric power and telephone industries, including the assets of two United States companies—Verizon Communications of New York City and the AES Corporation of Arlington, Virginia. He also threatened other business sectors, including cement and steel producers and banks, with *expropriation* (taking for public use) if they failed to prioritize the needs of Venezuelans above private profit.

On May 1, Chávez imposed government control over the few remaining privately owned oil companies in Venezuela. In late June, four foreign companies—British Petroleum, Chevron of the United States, Total of France, and Statoil of Norway—accepted minority stakes in the development of oil reserves in the Orinoco Belt, estimated at 80 billion barrels or more. Two other U.S. energy giants, ExxonMobil and ConocoPhillips, quit operations in the Orinoco fields.

Land reform begun in 2002 resulted in about 15,000 families being resettled on several million acres of government-confiscated land by mid-May 2007. Venezuelan authorities planned to complete a dozen "communal towns" by the end of the year. Each town would house about 80 families and include such services as free Internet access, radio stations, reading rooms, and schools.

Media censorship. In an effort to silence his political opponents, Chávez did not renew the broadcasting license of Radio Caracas TV (RCTV),

Demonstrators in Caracas, Venezuela, protest the May 2007 shutdown of Radio Caracas TV (RCTV), the nation's oldest broadcaster. President Hugo Chávez refused to renew the network's license, claiming that RCTV had supported a 2002 coup against his government.

the leading opposition media outlet. His decision to replace the privately owned RCTV with a state-sponsored television station in May triggered public protests in Caracas, the capital, and elicited condemnation abroad. In July, RCTV began transmitting its programming via cable and satellite, technologies unavailable to most Venezuelans.

Relations with Colombia and Spain. In November, Chávez severed diplomatic relations with Colombia and Spain following rebukes by the leaders of both countries over his methods and inflammatory statements. Colombian President Álvaro Uribe provoked Chávez's wrath when he dismissed him from his role in negotiating the release of hostages held by leftist rebels. King Juan Carlos of Spain told Chávez to "just shut up" after Chávez called a former Spanish prime minister a fascist at an Ibero-American summit meeting.

Failed referendum. Chávez's increasingly unpredictable behavior helped persuade a majority of Venezuelans to vote "no" in a close December referendum on constitutional reforms. The controversial reforms, proposed by Chávez and approved by the National Assembly, would have allowed the indefinite reelection of the president and ended the autonomy of the central bank, one of the last institutions exercising any degree of independence. ■ Nathan A. Haverstock

See also **Argentina; Bolivia; Cuba; Ecuador; Haiti; Latin America; Nicaragua; West Indies.**

Vietnam. A new National Assembly was elected in Vietnam on May 20, 2007, for a five-year term. The assembly's job was to pass laws, usually without substantive discussion, based on decisions already made by the internally chosen leaders of the Communist Party of Vietnam (CPV).

Of the 493 seats filled in the election, 450 went to CPV members and 42 to candidates approved by the party-controlled Vietnam Fatherland Front. One self-nominated independent candidate also won election.

President Nguyen Minh Triet visited the United States in June. During the visit, the first to Washington, D.C., by a Vietnamese president since the Vietnam War (1957-1975), Triet and U.S. President George W. Bush discussed democracy, trade, and human rights.

Human rights groups in 2007 accused Vietnam of increasing repression of dissidents. They suggested that the Communist regime feared that the country's economic growth might weaken its political control. Prior to Triet's trip to the United States, Vietnam released several prominent critics.

Typhoon Lekima hit Vietnam on October 3, bringing heavy rains and causing floods that left at least 88 people dead. ■ Henry S. Bradsher

See also **Asia; Disasters.**

Vital statistics. See **Census; Population.**

Washington, D.C. Adrian M. Fenty, a native Washingtonian, was sworn into office as the city's mayor on Jan. 2, 2007. A member of the District of Columbia (D.C.) Council, Fenty had won the mayoral election in November 2006 with nearly 90 percent of the vote.

Fenty gave his inaugural address before about 1,000 onlookers at the Washington Convention Center on Jan. 3, 2007. He said his main priorities included improving schools, gaining full representation for the district in Congress, and reducing crime. About 15,000 supporters celebrated his mayoralty at an inaugural ball at the convention center on January 6.

After winning the mayoral primary in September 2006, Fenty began to work on a transition government with outgoing Mayor Anthony A. Williams, also a Democrat. Fenty said he would operate the city as if it were a business.

School reform. The new mayor took control of the city's 55,000-student school system on June 12, 2007, after the D.C. Council approved legislation to transfer power for running the system from the elected school board to his office. Fenty immediately named Michelle A. Rhee, 37, as chancellor of the schools, replacing former superintendent Clifford B. Janey. Rhee founded the nonprofit New Teacher Project, which recruits and trains badly needed teachers for urban schools. Rhee also had served as the group's executive director.

The mayor chose Rhee without following the D.C. Council's requirement that he appoint a group of teachers, parents, and students to review his possible choices. Nevertheless, the council approved Rhee on July 10. Her $275,000 annual salary made her the highest paid chief of schools in metropolitan Washington. The district had 11,500 employees and a budget of about $1 billion. Rhee became the seventh chief of D.C. schools in 10 years.

The mayor and his schools chief faced the challenge of improving Washington schools' student performance, which was among the worst in the country. On October 3, Fenty and Rhee announced a plan to give the schools an additional $81 million from increased D.C. tax collections. Rhee worked to restructure the district's central office as part of an effort to reform the schools.

Voting rights. In September, the United States Senate voted not to consider a bill that would have given Washington residents representation in the U.S. House of Representatives. The motion fell 3 votes short of the 60 needed. The bill had been sent to the Senate after the House passed it in April. Residents had not had full House representation since their city became the home of the federal government in 1800.

The Republican leadership and the administration of President George W. Bush came out strongly against the proposal to give Washingtonians the House vote. The city was overwhelmingly registered Democratic, and observers said a new seat probably would have gone to a Democrat. Senate minority leader Mitch McConnell (R., Kentucky) said that the opposition was based on constitutionality and not on politics. The Republicans argued that the U.S. Constitution states that House members must be chosen by residents of the states, and Washington is not part of a state.

The House bill had been written as a compromise to add two seats to the House. One would have gone to the district, and the other would have gone to Utah, a state with heavy Republican voter registration.

Gun law overturned. On March 9, 2007, the U.S. Court of Appeals for the D.C. Circuit ruled in a 2-to-1 decision that a Washington ban on handguns in homes was unconstitutional. The court cited the Constitution's Second Amendment as its reasoning for overturning the local law. The court's opinion said the district could register arms, but not ban them in homes. In November, the U.S. Supreme Court agreed to review the appeals court's decision in 2008. The law banning the ownership of handguns was passed by the city in 1976. ■ Howard S. Shapiro

See also **City.**

Weather. Exceptionally warm weather across the eastern half of the United States ushered in 2007. More than 100 daily record-high temperatures were set during the first two weeks of January. In the Northeast, the warmth peaked on January 6, when Hartford, Connecticut, and New York City each reached 72 °F (22 °C), their highest January temperatures on record.

In contrast, record chill gripped the West in January. Hundreds of daily record lows were set from the West Coast to the southern Plains. Phoenix had its first subfreezing temperatures since 1990. Freezes in California's agricultural areas caused losses of more than $1 billion.

Farther east, a storm carrying ice and wind-driven snow struck the Plains in mid-January, dumping as much as 3 feet (0.9 meters) of snow in some areas. The storm isolated several towns in the western Plains and caused more than 60 deaths. Over 300,000 residents lost electric power.

In the Midwest and Northeast, the warmth of early winter yielded to colder and snowier conditions from late January through February. Heavy snow, sleet, and ice swept from the mid-Mississippi Valley to the Northeast and into southeastern Canada on February 14 and 15. More than 3 feet of snow fell in the interior Northeast. The storm caused 300,000 people to lose power and claimed more than 30 lives. Hundreds of motorists were stranded on highways in Pennsylvania, and the National Guard was called in to ferry supplies. The flow of frigid air across the Great Lakes generated heavy lake-effect snow. From February 2 to 12, 141 inches (358 centimeters) fell in Redfield, New York.

Winter in Europe. A storm brought torrential rain and damaging winds to parts of western and central Europe from January 17 to 19. Winds gusted to 105 miles (169 kilometers) per hour in the United Kingdom, the strongest recorded there since 1990. Winter 2007 was unusually warm in Europe, with several countries experiencing their warmest January on record. The winter in De Bilt, Netherlands, was the warmest since 1706. On a global scale, the average temperature from December 2006 to February 2007 was the warmest since record keeping began in 1880.

Spring came early across the contiguous United States, bringing the second warmest March on record and an unusually active start to the severe weather season. Several rounds of twisters raked the Plains, Midwest, and South in March. On March 1, more than 60 tornadoes tore through several southern states, killing 19 people in Alabama and Georgia. More than 125 tornadoes touched down from March 23 to 31, including 80 twisters that swept across the western Plains on March 28, killing four people in Kansas, Texas, and Oklahoma.

A late winter chill gripped Alaska, leading to the coldest mid-February to mid-March period in Fairbanks since record keeping began in 1904. In early April 2007, the cold air mass over Alaska streamed into the lower 48 states. Over 1,200 daily record lows were tied or broken from April 4 to 10. Record-low temperatures for April were measured at Jacksonville, Florida (31 °F [-1 °C]), and Charlotte, North Carolina (21 °F [-6 °C]).

In the South, freezing temperatures damaged fruit crops, which had bloomed early because of the warm March. Over 80 percent of the peach trees in Georgia, North Carolina, and Tennessee were damaged, as was nearly 99 percent of the apple crop in Georgia. Record late-season snow hit Dallas with its first April snowfall since 1938.

A powerful storm delivered torrential rain and heavy snow to the East Coast on April 15 to 17, 2007. Utility lines brought down by strong winds caused over 100,000 residents to lose power. New York City received 7.57 inches (19.2 centimeters) of rain, the city's second rainiest day since 1882.

In the Southeast, average rainfall for the region from March to May 2007 was the lowest since record keeping began in 1895. Parched groundcovers helped spark wildfires, including one along the border between Georgia and Florida. More than 474,000 acres (192,000 hectares) in Georgia burned, making it the state's largest wildfire on record. Florida's Lake Okeechobee dropped to its lowest level on record on May 31, 2007.

Severe weather struck the central Plains on May 4 and 5, causing more than 100 tornadoes, including one that destroyed most of Greensburg, Kansas. It was the most intense tornado observed in the United States since an Oklahoma City twister in 1999.

Summer floods and heat. Heavy rain that began early in 2007 over the southern Plains and Texas continued in May and June. On May 7, five Missouri River levees, strained by runoff from excessive rain burst, submerged the town of Big Lake, Missouri. Thousands of people fled their homes. On June 26 and 27, more than 1.5 feet (0.5 meters) of rain flooded parts of central Texas. In late June, flooding claimed 11 lives in Texas.

Record-setting heat plagued much of the western United States in mid- and late summer. In Missoula, Montana, the temperature reached at least 100 °F (38 °C) on 11 days in July, eclipsing the previous July record of 6 days. By late August, Phoenix had established a new record of 29 days with temperatures of 110 °F (43 °C) or higher.

In the Southeast, summer heat peaked in August, causing more than 50 deaths. Afternoon temperatures near and above 100 °F (38 °C) led to all-time record-high temperatures in 13 cities. On August 11, temperatures in Atlanta rose over 100 °F for the fourth straight day, tying the city's

Firefighters attempt to contain a blaze near Lake Hodges in north-central San Diego on Oct. 23, 2007. The fire was one of more than a dozen that burned across southern California in October, fed by brush that had become excessively dry because of a drought and driven by the Santa Ana winds. As many as 1 million people were forced from their residences in the largest evacuation in state history.

Extreme weather in 2007 fueled huge wildfires on two continents and caused massive flooding in Asia, North America, and England.

Enterprise High School in Alabama lies in ruins after a tornado struck the school on March 1. Eight students were killed and dozens of others were injured as the twister—one of more than 60 that struck several southern states that day—ripped through the town.

A resident of Mexico, New York, east of Lake Ontario, clears the path in front of his home in early February. A flow of frigid air across the Great Lakes dumped some 6 feet (2 meters) of snow over a three-day period.

The waters of the Mississippi River swirl around a 23-foot- (7-meter-) tall statue of explorer William Clark in St. Louis on May 12, 2007. Heavy rain to the west caused the Missouri River to flood, which in turn caused flooding below the confluence of the two rivers.

Floodwaters inundate downtown Gainesville, Texas, on June 18, as heavy rain that began early in the year across the southern Plains states continued to pour in North Texas in May and June. Several towns were submerged and at least 6 people were killed as up to 8 inches (20 centimeters) of rain fell over the area in the course of hours.

record for consecutive days of torrid conditions.

River flooding was widespread in August from Minnesota and Iowa to Ohio as thunderstorms formed repeatedly near the edge of the hot air mass over the Southeast. A deluge in Hokah, Minnesota, brought 15.1 inches (38.4 centimeters) of rain on August 18 and 19, setting a 24-hour-rainfall record for the state. In Wisconsin, a monthly rainfall total of 21.74 inches (55.2 centimeters) set the state record for any month.

Summer in Europe. Searing heat and exceptional dryness gripped southern and eastern Europe in the late spring and summer. Moscow reached 91 °F (32 °C) on May 28, the city's highest May temperature since 1891. Temperatures in parts of Greece soared above 104 °F (40 °C) repeatedly during summer 2007, contributing to more than 3,000 forest fires. The European Space Agency reported that more of Greece was burned in August alone than the rest of Europe combined for the last 10 years. At least 64 people were killed by the fires.

The Atlantic hurricane season brought only three major storms. Hurricane Dean strengthened as it moved from the eastern Atlantic into the Caribbean, bringing heavy rain and wind to Jamaica as it passed south of the island on August 19. The storm became a Category 5, the strongest class of hurricane, as it made landfall on Mexico's Yucatán Peninsula. Dean was the first Category 5 storm to make landfall in the Atlantic Basin since Andrew in 1992. Hurricane Felix swept through the southern Caribbean, reaching Category 5 status before making landfall in Nicaragua on Sept. 4, 2007. On September 13, Hurricane Humberto made landfall near High Island, Texas, with 85-mile- (137-kilometer-) per-hour winds. The storm, which had formed only 16 hours earlier, was one of the most rapidly intensifying tropical disturbances on record.

Fires. The 12-month period from June 2006 to June 2007 was the driest in Los Angeles since record keeping began in 1877. The drought turned the undergrowth into a tinderbox. In October 2007, wildfires burned at least 500,000 acres (202,000 hectares) across the state, forcing about 1 million people to flee their residences in the largest evacuation in the state's history. Fires in November again forced thousands of people to flee.

Winter roars in. Several storms struck large parts of the nation in early to mid-December. A storm that began in the Plains States dropped snow and rain that turned into ice across the Midwest and Northeast. At the same time, a storm brought high winds, rain, and snow to the Northwest. Less than a week later, an ice storm swept across the Plains, cutting power to nearly 1 million people and causing the deaths of more than 30 others. ■ Fred Gadomski and Todd Miner

Welfare. According to the United States Administration for Children and Families (ACF), the country's welfare rolls continued to decline in 2007. In March, the caseload for families receiving cash aid under the Temporary Assistance for Needy Families (TANF) program was 1,711,048, down from 1,808,295 in March 2006. The TANF caseload for individuals in March 2007 stood at 3,997,785, down from 4,224,659 in March 2006. TANF cash aid is provided, for up to five years, to needy families with dependent children, with the requirement that the parents must be working, training for work, or seeking work.

By 2007, the numbers of families and individuals receiving welfare payments had fallen significantly since welfare reforms were enacted in August 1996, according to ACF data. Between August 1996 and March 2007, the family caseload fell from 4,408,508 to 1,711,048—a 61-percent decline. The caseload for individuals fell from 12,242,125 to 3,997,785—a 67-percent decline.

On June 5, 2007, the U.S. Food and Nutrition Service reported that 25 million people participated in the Food Stamp Program in 2005, which was 65 percent of the 38 million people who were eligible. The program provides benefits to low-income people to help them buy food. The 2005 participation rate was up from 61 percent in 2004 and 54 percent in 2001. ■ Mike Lewis

West Indies. Bruce Golding, 60, of the centrist Jamaica Labor Party (JLP) was sworn in as prime minister of Jamaica on Sept. 11, 2007. The ceremony followed a hard-fought election decided by fewer than 3,000 votes. Golding succeeded Portia Simpson Miller, Jamaica's first female leader, of the People's National Party. His election marked the end of 18 years in opposition for the JLP.

Golding pledged to crack down on crime, a widespread problem in poor neighborhoods of the capital, Kingston, where a majority of homicides went unsolved in 2007. Golding also promised to reduce Jamaica's huge national debt and to abolish tuition at government high schools and fees charged to patients at public hospitals.

Patrick Manning, 61, of the centrist People's National Movement was sworn in for a third term as prime minister of Trinidad and Tobago on November 7. At his inauguration, Manning pledged to diversify the country's economy and to bridge the racial divide between people of African and East Indian descent.

Venezuelan aid. During 2007, the government of Venezuela supplied fuel to a number of West Indian nations on preferential financing terms. The South American country also pledged $150 million to Dominica to modernize that tiny island nation's airport, provide low-cost housing, and enable young Dominicans to study abroad. In June, the Venezuelan government purchased a 49-percent stake in Jamaica's sole oil refinery for $63.7 million. As part of the deal, the two governments agreed to spend an additional $500 million over a period of three years to modernize the facility.

Subway controversy. Also in 2007, workers rushed to complete the first 9 miles (14 kilometers) of a subway intended to relieve extreme traffic congestion in Santo Domingo, the capital of the Dominican Republic. Initially, the subway was to have 16 stations and run from the northern part of the city and across the Isabela River to the downtown area near the coast. Additional subway lines were planned for the future.

The construction of the subway clogged roads already jammed with cars, buses, bicycles, and other vehicles. The project's opponents objected to its cost, which had ballooned to more than $700 million from an original estimate of $470 million. Hamlet Hermann, a former minister of transportation, suggested that the money might be better spent on improving education and health care or fighting poverty. ■ Nathan A. Haverstock

See also **Latin America.**

Yemen. See **Middle East.**
Yukon. See **Canadian territories.**
Zambia. See **Africa.**

Zimbabwe. By 2007, Zimbabwe's long political and economic crisis had caused division within the ruling party, the Zimbabwe African National Union-Patriotic Front (ZANU-PF), though President Robert Mugabe remained firmly in power. In March, he was nominated as his party's candidate for the 2008 presidential election.

Mugabe continued in 2007 to repress all opposition to his regime. In March, his police assaulted opposition leaders at a peaceful demonstration, causing an international outcry. Shortly after this incident, a meeting of the Southern African Development Community (SADC) reappointed South African President Thabo Mbeki to mediate between Zimbabwe's government and both factions of the opposition party, the Movement for Democratic Change (MDC). The talks were held to establish conditions in Zimbabwe that would allow free and fair elections to take place in 2008.

Religious leaders in Zimbabwe and abroad strongly criticized Mugabe for his oppressive tactics. Anglican Archbishop Emeritus Desmond Tutu of South Africa called the situation in Zimbabwe "a blight on Africa" and, with John Sentamu, the African-born Anglican bishop of York in the United Kingdom, demanded much stronger international action against the Mugabe regime. German Chancellor Angela Merkel criticized Mugabe

A worker in Zimbabwe holds his take-home pay, literally millions of Zimbabwean dollars ($Z). During 2007, inflation in Zimbabwe hit nearly 8,000 percent and, by September, the currency was officially valued at $Z30,000 to $U.S.1.

at a meeting of European and African leaders in December 2007, saying that his actions were "damaging the image of new Africa."

Constitutional changes. In 2007, ZANU-PF and the MDC agreed on several amendments to the Zimbabwe Constitution. The presidential term was reduced from six to five years. In addition, the parliamentary elections due in 2010 were rescheduled for 2008, to take place concurrently with presidential and local polls.

A provision was also made for Parliament to elect a new president should the incumbent be unable to complete his or her term, which many analysts felt was a precaution given Mugabe's age of 83 years. In November 2007, Mugabe signed an amendment into law that would give the president the power to appoint a successor if he retired before the end of his term.

Further agreements concluded by the negotiators included the abolition of the president's power to select about 30 members of the House of Assembly, though the president would still be able to appoint a number of senators. Assembly membership was to be increased from 150 to 210, and the number of senators was to increase from 66 to 93. In addition, the Delimitation Commission (DC) was to be abolished and its work transferred to the Zimbabwe Electoral Commission. The DC in the past had redrawn the borders of electoral constituencies to the ruling party's advantage.

Economy. By 2007, Zimbabwe had the worst-performing economy in the world. Rising prices reflected the economic plight of the people, 80 percent of whom lived in poverty. By September, the official annual inflation rate had reached almost 8,000 percent, though some economists said it could be as high as 13,000 percent. Continuous downturns in food production and exports as well as shortages of foreign exchange and fuel occurred throughout the year. The prices of water, electric power, transport, and everyday household needs grew at the same astronomical rate.

In a frantic effort to bring down inflation, the government ordered sweeping price cuts of up to 50 percent on all goods, including food and fuel. The police, army, and youth groups set out to enforce the price reductions in major cities. However, shop owners refused to restock and sell at a loss, and soon the shelves were empty. As a result, the shortages continued and prices increased even higher than before.

In September 2007, the government was forced to devalue the Zimbabwean dollar ($Z) once again from $Z250 per United States dollar to $Z30,000 per U.S. dollar. This official rate was only a fraction of the black market rate of about $Z250,000 per U.S. dollar. ∎ Pieter Esterhuysen

See also **Africa.**

Zoology. See Biology; Conservation; Ocean.

Zoos. A number of endangered and spectacular zoo animals in the United States gave birth in 2007. Zoos continued to play a role in conservation, both with large, well-known mammals and with lesser-known amphibians on the brink of extinction.

Mammal births. Rare tigers gave birth to litters in several zoos across the United States. In May, a litter of two Amur tiger cubs was born in Brookfield Zoo in Illinois, and three Amur tiger cubs were born in the Philadelphia Zoo. In June, three Sumatran tiger cubs were born at the Los Angeles Zoo. In July, a Malaysian tiger gave birth to a pair of cubs in the Henry Doorly Zoo in Omaha, Nebraska.

Two baby elephants were born early in 2007. An Asian elephant at the St. Louis Zoo gave birth to a calf in February, and an African elephant calf was born in March at the Louisville Zoo in Kentucky. In August, a giant panda was born at the San Diego Zoo—only the fourth giant panda ever born in the United States.

Two zoos, Lincoln Park Zoo in Chicago and the Minnesota Zoo near Minneapolis, recorded births of takin calves in March. Takins are large, hoofed animals closely related to goats and musk oxen. In April, a Sumatran rhinoceros gave birth to a calf at the Cincinnati Zoo. Another rare hoofed animal—a piglike Malayan tapir—was born in July at Seattle's Woodland Park Zoo.

Turtle births. In addition to rare mammals, some notable turtles were also born in U.S. zoos in 2007. In July, two Galapagos tortoises hatched from their eggs at the Gladys Porter Zoo in Brownsville, Texas. Galapagos tortoises are among the largest of all land turtles.

Two other rare turtles, much smaller than the Galapagos tortoises, were also born in zoos in 2007. In April, an Arakan forest turtle emerged from its egg at the Atlanta Zoo. This turtle is found in the wild only in the Arakan Hills of Myanmar, and the hatchling was one of only a dozen living in United States zoos. In June, a Beal's four-eyed turtle was born at the Tennessee Aquarium in Chattanooga. Native to southern China, the turtle gets its name from two white spots on the back of its head, which look like additional eyes. Only 18 of these turtles are in zoos in the United States and Europe.

Saving amphibians. Almost a third of the world's *amphibians* were approaching extinction in 2007. Amphibians are animals, such as frogs and toads, that live part of their life on land and part in the water. To highlight the danger to amphibians, the Association of Zoos and Aquariums (AZA) declared 2008 as "The Year of the Frog."

The AZA hoped to focus on breeding endangered frogs, and in 2007 the Omaha zoo, a leader in breeding rare amphibians, had two major successes. In June, the zoo released 670 Wyoming toad tadpoles into the wild in the Laramie Basin region of Wyoming. The toad was once common there, but scientists declared it extinct in the wild in 1985. They do not know why the toad's population declined, and the Laramie Basin is the only region where it was known to live.

The Omaha zoo also hatched 600 Puerto Rican crested toad tadpoles and flew them to Puerto Rico in May 2007. There, they were released in a specially created toad habitat. The crested toad became critically endangered partly because of competition with the giant marine toad (also called the cane toad), an invasive species brought to Puerto Rico during the early 1900's. Invasive species are organisms introduced into a new area that spread rapidly there. The crested toad population also dwindled because of pollution and habitat destruction.

Tiger kills zoo patron. A female Siberian tiger escaped from its enclosure at the San Francisco Zoo late on Dec. 25, 2007, and killed one patron. Two other people were mauled before security guards shot and killed the tiger. Zoo officials were unsure how it managed to escape its cage. The 4-year-old tiger also attacked a zoo keeper in 2006. Siberian tigers are critically endangered.

Bear exhibits. Two new exhibits, which opened in 2007, focused on bears and their habitat. The $3.7-million Grizzly Gulch, which opened in June at the San Francisco Zoo, houses a pair of grizzly bears that were found as starving orphaned cubs in Montana in 2004. Their mother had been killed for breaking into barns. The bears were displayed to visitors through thick glass fronting the exhibit, which features a meadow and a large pool.

Oregon Zoo in Portland opened Black Bear Ridge in March 2007. The $2-million habitat for black bears was viewable from a 100-foot- (30-meter-) long suspension bridge raised 14 feet (4 meters) above the animals. The exhibit completed the zoo's $36-million Great Northwest exhibit complex.

Western trails. In March, the Oklahoma City Zoo opened Oklahoma Trails, a $10.3-million exhibit that highlights Oklahoma's 11 ecological regions, such as prairies and cypress swamps. It features 140 species of animals native to Oklahoma. Among them are animals that live there now, such as Mexican free-tailed bats, coyotes, and elk. The exhibit also includes native animals that have been driven out of the state because of human development, such as grizzly bears and wolves.　　　　■ Edward Ricciuti

See also **Conservation.**

A young polar bear named Knut plays with a worker at Germany's Berlin Zoo in April 2007. Knut, who was rejected by his mother after his birth and raised by zoo workers, became an international sensation as the zoo showcased him to the public.

Index

How to use the index

This index covers the contents of the 2006, 2007, and 2008 editions.

Each index entry gives the edition year and the page number or page numbers—for example, **Education, Department of, 08:** 202. This means that information on this topic may be found on the pages indicated in the 2008 edition.

A page number in italic type means that there is an article on this topic on the page or pages indicated. For example, there is an Update article on **Elections** on pages 206-207 of the 2008 edition. The page numbers in roman type indicate additional references to this topic in other articles in the volumes covered.

The "see" and "see also" cross-references refer the reader to other entries in the index. For example, information on employment will be found under **Labor and employment,** while additional information on types of energy will be found under **Energy supply.**

When there are many references to a topic, they are grouped alphabetically by clue words under the main topic. For example, the clue words under **Environmental pollution** group the references to that topic under several subtopics.

The indications (il.) or (ils.) mean that the reference on this page is to an illustration or illustrations only, as in **Erdogan, Recep Tayyip,** in the 2008 edition.

Acknowledgments

The publishers acknowledge the following sources for illustrations. Credits read from top to bottom, left to right, on their respective pages. An asterisk (*) denotes illustrations and photographs created exclusively for this edition. All maps, charts, and diagrams were prepared by the staff unless otherwise noted.

8 © Joe Raedle, Getty
9 AP/Wide World
10 © K.C. Alfred, ZUMA Press
12 © Larry W. Smith, Corbis
15 AP/Wide World
16 © David Furst, Getty
19-28 AP/Wide World
31 © Krista Kennell, ZUMA Press
32-35 AP/Wide World
39 © Getty
43 AP/Wide World
44 Global Crop Diversity Trust
48 © Bryan Busovicki, Shutterstock
49 AP/Wide World
50-51 AP/Wide World; APVA Preservation Virginia; AP/Wide World
52-53 © Getty
55 APVA Preservation Virginia
56 APVA Preservation Virginia; © Ira Block, Getty
57 APVA Preservation Virginia
58-60 © Ira Block, Getty
61 APVA Preservation Virginia
62 © Nelson-Atkins Museum of Art
64 © Juan Mabromata, Getty
66 © John Moore, Getty
68 © Metropolitan Museum of Art
69 Terracotta calyx-krater (ca. 515 B.C.) signed by Euxitheos as potter and painter; The Metropolitan Museum of Art, lent by the Republic of Italy (L.2006.10)
70 AP/Wide World
71 © Louisa Gouliamaki, Getty
72 Table Support in the Shape of Griffins Attacking a Doe (325- 300 B.C.), marble and pigment (© Francis Specker, Landov)
73 Goddess, Probably Aphrodite (425-400 B.C.) limestone, marble, and pigment (AP/Wide World)
74 AP/Wide World
75 Bust of Queen Nefertiti (1350 B.C.) painted limestone from the studio of the sculptor Thutmose; Altes Museum, Berlin (© Sean Gallup, Getty)
76 © Roger Viollet, Getty; Granger
77 Demeter, seated with her daughter Persephone, welcoming a figure, probably Hebe (447-432 B.C.) marble, British Museum (© Getty)
78 AP/Wide World
81 © Tariq Mahmood, Getty
84 AP/Wide World; © Corbis; AP/Wide World
86 NASA
88 © Cameron Spencer, Getty
92 © Chris Hocking, Corbis
93 © Dieter Telemans, Panos
94 NASA; © William West, Getty
95 © Jon Hargest, Rex Features; © Craig Borrow, Newspix
98-99 © Getty; © SuperStock
101 AP/Wide World
104 © Richard Clement, Landov
106 © Hans Deryk, Landov
108 © Gregory Shamus, Getty

112-113 © Steve Bloom Images
114 © Ruoso Cyril from Peter Arnold
115 University of Calgary
116 © Steve Bloom, Alamy
117 AP/Wide World
118-119 © SuperStock
120 Frans de Waal, Yerkes National Primate Research Center
122 © D. Roberts, Photo Researchers
124-131 AP/Wide World
132 © Philippe Huguen, Getty
138-148 AP/Wide World
150 © Getty
155 © Corbis
157 © Reg Wilson, Rex Features
159-161 AP/Wide World
168 U.S. Fish & Wildlife Service
170 © Larry Downing, Landov
173 AP/Wide World
176 © Johan Persson, ArenaPAL
178-180 © Landov
181 © Carolyn Mary Bauman, Landov; AP/Wide World
182 © Getty; AP/Wide World
183 © Getty; © David McNew, Reuters
184 © Getty ; AP/Wide World; © Corbis
185 NASA
186 AP/Wide World
187 © Corbis
188-191 LBJ Library
195 AP/Wide World
197 © Justin Sullivan, Getty
204 © Simon Reddy, Alamy; © Landov
205-210 AP/Wide World
211 © Dimitar Dilkoff, Getty
213 © Carsten Koall, Getty
216 NASA
217 © Vassilis Psomas, Corbis; AP/Wide World
219 © Alberto Pizzoli, Getty
221 © Claro Cortes IV, Landov
223-226 AP/Wide World
228 © Massimo Sestini, Getty
230 © Henning Kaiser, Getty
232-236 AP/Wide World
238 © AFP/Getty
239 © Toru Yamanaka, Getty
241-250 AP/Wide World
251 © Joe Raedle, Getty; © Ceerwan Aziz, Landov
254-256 AP/Wide World
257 © Getty
260-265 AP/Wide World
269 © Omar Ibrahim, Landov
271 © Mahmud Turkia, Getty
274 © Rex Features
277 AP/Wide World
284 © Getty
285 © Amir Meiri, Landov; © Ismael Mohamad, Landov
288-289 ZUMA Press; Picture Desk
291 © Getty
292 AP/Wide World
294 © Brian Alpert, ZUMA Press
296 AP/Wide World
297 © Gareth Fuller, Landov; AP/Wide World

298 © Shaun Curry, Getty; USPS; © Manuel Silvestri, Landov; © Fred Prouser, Landov
299 © Robert Johnson, The Legacy Project
300 The Mariners' Museum, Newport News, VA; © Getty
305 AP/Wide World
308 © Athar Hussain, Reuters
309 © Claro Cortes IV, Landov
311 UN/DPI Photo; AP/Wide World
313 Monica King, U.S. Army; © Ints Kalnins, Reuters
314 © Francesco Guidicini, Rex Features
316 AP/Wide World
317 Abby Brack, Romney for President, Inc.; AP/Wide World
318 © Eric Feferberg, Landov
323 AP/Wide World
324 © Spencer Platt, Getty
333 © Andrei Pungovschi, Getty
334 © Wojtek Druszcz, Getty
335 © Landov
340 © German Alegria, Getty
344-346 NASA
349 © Getty
352 AP/Wide World
356 © Espen Rasmussen, Panos; © Sven Torfinn, Panos
357 © Sven Torfinn, Panos; © Lynsey Addario, Corbis
361 © Vladimir Rys, Getty
362 © Khaled al-Hariri, Landov
363 AP/Wide World
365 Apple, Inc.
367 © Rex Features
369 © Alex Livesey, Getty
370 © Alistair Robertson, Landov
373 © Joan Marcus
375-377 AP/Wide World
378 © Jonathan Short, Landov
380 © Umit Bektas, Landov
383 © Landov
384 AP/Wide World
385 © Lynsey Addario, Corbis
386 AP/Wide World
387 © Landov
388 © Dieter Telemans, Panos
389 © Mustafa Ozer, Getty
391 AP/Wide World
393 © Gleb Garanich, Landov
395 © Stephen Hird, Landov
397 © Johnny Green, Landov
399 © Jeff Mitchell, Getty
401 Department of the Treasury
405 AP/Wide World
407 © Juan Barreto, Getty
410 © K.C. Alfred, ZUMA Press
411 © Dennis Nett, Landov; © Mandel Ngan, Getty
412 © Bill Greenblatt, Landov; AP/Wide World
414 © Robin Hammond, Panos
416 © Barbara Sax, Getty